TRAILBLAZERS

TRaiLBLaZeRS

Black Women Who Helped Make America Great

AMERICAN FIRSTS/AMERICAN ICONS

VOLUME 1
ACTIVISM | DANCE | SPORTS

Gabrielle David

Edited by Carolina Fung Feng

Introduction by Chandra D.L. Waring, PhD
Foreword by Lyah Beth LeFlore

FLORIDA ■ NEW YORK
www.2leafpress.org

P.O. Box 4378
Grand Central Station
New York, New York 10163-4378
editor@2leafpress.org
www.2leafpress.org

2LEAF PRESS INC. is a
nonprofit 501(c)(3) organization that promotes
multicultural literature and literacy.
www.2leafpressinc.org

Copyright © 2021 Gabrielle David
Edited by: Carolina Fung Feng

Book design and layout: Gabrielle David

Library of Congress Control Number: 2018901512
ISBN-13: 978-1-940939-79-7 (Paperback)

10   9   8   7   6   5   4   3   2   1

Published in the United States of America

First Edition | First Printing

This publication of *TRAILBLAZERS Black Women Who Helped Make America Great American Firsts/American Icons, Volume 1* was sponsored in part, by Open Meadows Foundation, The Women's Sports Foundation, The National Sorority of Phi Delta Kappa, Inc. (NSPDK), and Alpha Kappa Alpha Sorority, Incorporated, and The International Association of Blacks in Dance (IABD)

2Leaf Press trade distribution is handled by University of Chicago Press / Chicago Distribution Center (www.press.uchicago.edu) 773.702.7010. Titles are also available for corporate, premium, and special sales. Please direct inquiries to the UCP Sales Department, 773.702.7248.

This volume of TRAILBLAZERS received discretionary grants and sponsorship by the following foundations and organizations:

Open meadows
Foundation

THE
NEW YORK
WOMEN'S
FOUNDATION
Radical generosity.

Women's Sports Foundation

PHI DELTA KAPPA, INC.

THE
INTERNATIONAL
ASSOCIATION OF
BLACKS IN DANCE

For Hattie, Undine, Delores, Rosetta, Yvonne, Dolores, Edith (Poogie) and Shirley.

Poem For A Black Woman

I house the legend of Mutima
The heartbeat of the earth
I am the offspring of the moon and the sun
Thrust from the energy of Africa
I am the Black Woman

I am the symbol of love
The channel of creation
The vibration of peace
The anger of storms
The pain of suffering
I am the Black Woman

I have seen the first rain
And the last fire
I am the seasoner of souls
I have many tales untold

My womb has been stretched
across the mouth of the universe
To create rhythms and nations
My body has borne witness to birth
My spirit the taster of death

I have seen the 13th month
The 32nd day
The year 3000 before the year 03

I have cradled the newborn's cry
Yours and mine
Collected the old man's moan
Made diamonds out of stone
Found gold in my soul

I am the right hand of God
The equal part of Man
The spirit of Life
I am the Black Woman

NATURAL TO THE BONE!

—Shirley Bradley Price LeFlore
St. Louis Poet Laureate Emeritus (1940-2019)

"Poem For A Black Woman," from *Brassbones & Rainbows: The Collected Works of Shirley Bradley LeFlore* (2Leaf Press 2013). Used with permission from The Shirley Bradley Price LeFlore Estate.

SHIRLEY BRADLEY PRICE LEFLORE was an oral poet, performance artist and retired adjunct professor of women's and ethnic literature. She was an original board member of 2Leaf Press, and the author of the poetry collections *Brassbones & Rainbows* (2013) and *Rivers of Women, The Play* (2013).

In memory of Erica Garner (1990-2017)
I wish you had a chance. No justice, no peace.

CONTENTS

DANCE | 211

SPORTS | 407

"Black women have had to develop a larger vision of our society than perhaps any other group. They have had to understand White men, White women, and Black men. And they have had to understand themselves. When Black women win victories, it is a boost for virtually every segment of society."

—Angela Davis (Lanker 1999)

ACKNOWLEDGEMENTS

"There are still many causes worth sacrificing
for, so much history yet to be made.... But don't
ever underestimate the impact you can have,
because history has shown us that courage can be
contagious, and hope can take on a life of its own."

—Michelle Obama
"Remarks by The First Lady during Keynote Address at
Young African Women Leaders Forum," June 22, 2011
(Regina Mundi Church, Soweto, South Africa)

WRITING A BOOK is always difficult; it is even harder when you are also responsible for publishing other people's books. Regardless of the time constraints I faced, working on *TRAILBLAZERS: Black Women Who Helped Make America Great* has become one of the most rewarding experiences I could have ever imagined. However, none of this would have been possible without help and guidance from the following people:

Having an idea and turning it into a book is as hard as it sounds, and can be challenging. I want to thank University of Chicago Press at the Chicago Distribution Center, who prints and distributes 2Leaf Press books, for their ongoing support, and especially Levi Stahl and Molly McFee, who saw the vision early on and inspired me to move forward with this project. Special thanks to our printer, Books International (IBI), and especially Tim Knickerbocker and Karla Gallardo, for helping to set a standard for the *TRAILBLAZERS* series.

TRAILBLAZERS began as one book, but then it quickly developed into a six volume series. Then, the decision to use photographs and the rising need to employ a number of editors turned this into an expensive enterprise. It was my good fortune that we acquired discretionary grants from the Open Meadows Foundation, The New York Women's Foundation, Women's Sports Foundation, and sponsorship from the National Sorority Phi Delta Kappa, Inc., Alpha Kappa Alpha Sorority, Inc., and The International Association of Blacks in Dance. Their financial aide and partnership, which represent this volume's featured sections, Activism,

PHOTO: Former President Barack Obama looks at former First Lady Michelle Obama's newly unveiled portrait. Photo by Mark Wilson/Getty Images (2018).

Dance, and Sports, is responsible for the book you now hold in your hands. I am grateful for their support.

Thanks to the team: Carolina Fung Feng, one of the best copy editors on the planet, who has been with me since the founding of 2Leaf Press. She joined the team as an intern, and has stuck by my side through thick and thin; Dr. Chandra D. L. Waring, a sociologist and Assistant Professor at University of Massachusetts Lowell, at the College of Fine Arts, Humanities, and Social Sciences department, who has provided invaluable insight and feedback, and more importantly, has brought to this project a sociological perspective about the conditions of Black women in this country and our journey to greatness; and Lyah Beth LeFlore, who carries on in the spirit of her beloved mother, Shirley Bradley Price LeFlore, one of the founding members of 2Leaf Press, and helped shepherd this project along in every conceivable way.

Special thanks to Ben Lafferty, who scrutinized the historical text and provided queries and suggestions, and Phyllis Huang for setting the stage for the editing. They both assisted with the editing process very early on. Kathryn Siddell is an editorial godsend, who not only dug into the weeds with the manuscript, but also initiated the editorial style sheet. When a book is near completion and the narrative is set, the final step is to "polish" the work with clear and precise copy editing. I had been afforded two of the best copy editors in the business: Nicole Catarino and Eileen Sholomicky, who are caring, critical, discerning, precise, and detail-oriented. A special shout-out to Vynetta A. Morrow, who did a final read to tie up loose ends in the final manuscript. All of the editors who contributed to this project are all worth their weight in gold, and I am eternally grateful for all of their hard work.

Writing the section introductions was a brainstorm that started out as a few pages and, with the help of over one hundred books, papers, and articles, quickly grew into well over fifty pages for each section. As a result, I felt it required critique from experts in their respective fields to review the work. To that end, I want to thank the following scholars for their input: Dr. Naomi R. Williams, Assistant Professor of Labor Studies and Employment Relations (LSER), and a historian and scholar at Rutgers University, School of Management and Labor Relations, as an expert in U.S. History, working class activism and social movements, reviewed the Activist section; Dr. Veta Goler, a modern dance artist, choreographer, dance historian, and Associate Professor and Division Chair for Arts and Humanities at Spelman College, reviewed the Dance section; and Dr. Leslie Heaphy, Associate Chair and Associate Professor of the History department at Kent State University, who specializes in twentieth century U.S. and sports history—in particular, baseball, and the Negro League reviewed the Sports section. I am forever grateful to them for taking time from their busy schedules to critique, suggest, and push me to dig even deeper. The end result is a concise and comprehensive outline that puts the bios that follow in a historical context.

None of this would have come together if it were not for Alexis August, a brilliant young woman who has worn multiple hats as my assistant, organizer, researcher, editor, fundraiser, and publicist. She is also my confidante and friend. This series has many moving parts and she has handled every aspect of this book magnificently. This book would not *be* what it has become without her involvement in this project.

I had some great interns that worked with me to help promote the book. Special thanks to our 2Leaf Press interns: Taylor Hoffman, Elena Mathews, Derek Nesbitt, Tina Li, and Rotrude Saint Louis for their help in creating and disseminating our social media messages to the public.

Elka Samuels Smith is one of the greatest human beings on the planet: artist, mother, a great agent, and our special events coordinator, good friend, and a true believer in the *TRAILBLAZERS* project. Who could ask for more?

I had the good fortune of having our attorney, Justin A. MacLean of Greenberg Traurig LLP in New York, guide me through the process of photo clearance, consents, and all intellectual property matters as it relate to this series. He did so with good cheer and great enthusiasm for this project. My heartfelt thanks also goes out to Shira Peleg and Claire Arritola, who managed 2Leaf Press' reorganization, making the transition period nearly effortless.

Special thanks to Dr. Sean Frederick Forbes, director of the Creative Writing Program and assistant professor-in-residence in the Department of English at the University of Connecticut, Storrs. He is my colleague, literary adviser, and dear friend who held my hand during this birthing process. He had the excellent foresight to suggest Chandra D. L. Waring, and he was absolutely right, *as usual.*

To Abiodun Oyewole, your constant support, guidance, and friendship means the world to me. Thanks to Jacqueline Edwards for her business acumen and friendship during a tough and trying time to finish this project.

I am grateful to all of the photographers (including estate-holders) who graciously participated in this project at nominal costs, or donated their photographs to help this book come to fruition. Special thanks to Getty Images and AP Photos, who afforded us the ability to tell these stories with some of the powerful imagery seen in this volume.

Additional thanks to the following libraries and institutions for painstakingly researching and tracking down the historical photographs needed and, in some cases, providing permission to use their photographs in this volume:

Chicago Public Library, Woodson Regional Library,
    Vivian G. Harsh Research Collection of Afro-American
    History and Literature
Cornell University, Kheel Center for Labor-Management
    Document and Archives, ILWGU Photographs
Global Ministries of the United Methodist Church, Inc.
The Heinz Foundation
Institute for Policy Studies
The International Brotherhood of Teamsters
National Park Service, Maggie L. Walker National Historic Site
The New York Public Library for the Performing Arts
Schlesinger Library, Radcliffe Institute, Harvard University
Smithsonian Institution, National Portrait Gallery and
    the National Museum of American History
Southern Illinois University Carbondale, Special Collections
    Research Center, Morris Library
Temple University Libraries, John W. Mosley Photograph
    Collection, Charles L. Blockson Afro-American
Tennessee State Library and Archives
U.S. Library of Congress' Prints and Photographs
University of Michigan School for Environment and Sustainability

Special thanks to the board of directors of 2Leaf Press Inc.: Andrew P. Jackson (Sekou Molefi Baako), Robert C. Coburn, Lynn Korsman, Lyah Beth LeFlore, Carolina Fung Feng, Sandra A. Garcia-Betancourt, Tara Betts, Eman Rimawi, Chavisa Woods, and Allicia Waukau-Butler. My heartfelt thanks to Andrew (Sekou), Robert, and Lynn for embarking on this journey with me from the very beginning and supporting this project both emotionally and financially. To the poets and authors of 2Leaf Press, I am greatly appreciative of your ongoing support and belief in 2Leaf Press; *you are 2Leaf Press.*

A special shout-out to my woman warriors: Yvonne Shelton, Patricia Walker, Nina Bonner, Jeryl Cunningham Fleming, Michelle Vanderpool, and Carolyn Baker; your sisterhood has helped me stay strong under the most dire circumstances.

Finally, special thanks to the women in this book; those who have passed on and the ones who continue in their footsteps and blaze the trail. I had the distinct pleasure of interacting with many of the women in this volume, and I appreciate their taking time to fill in the gaps of their bios.

It was a joy and privilege reading, researching, dreaming, and writing about these women. This experience gave me incredible insight about who I am, and has made me a better Black woman in the world. Regardless of sex, race, creed or color, I hope readers will be inspired by their stories as they have inspired me. ❖

—Gabrielle David
New York, New York, 2021

FOREWORD:
Storytelling Is Our Roots and Wings

"My work has allowed me to expose all kinds of people to the kind of history that I thought they needed to know."

—Shirley Bradley Price LeFlore, *St. Louis American*, 2018

I GREW UP IN A FAMILY OF STORYTELLERS. I was always awed by how my late mother, Shirley Bradley Price LeFlore, St. Louis Poet Laureate Emeritus, would glide onto a stage wearing something flowy, accessorized with a vibrant jewel-toned shawl or scarf floating behind her. Depending on her mood, her silver silk-like strands of hair draped her shoulders, or she might rock braids or don an elaborate headwrap if she felt compelled to channel the spirit of Mother Africa. Her ears and neck were adorned with dramatic beads or shells. As she gingerly placed her notebook of poems on the music stand, you could hear the faint clattering of bells from the stacked bangles tapping together on her wrists. Shirley was home wherever she was. It didn't matter if she was performing for a small crowd crammed in a smoky, backroom speakeasy, or for hundreds gathered in Carnegie Hall; her presence was commanding, captivating.

When Shirley leaned into a mic, she suddenly transformed from her warm, sometimes coy, whimsical lady-woman-girl-self into a masterful, fantastical and colorful, larger-than-life, warrior woman spirit. All right before my eyes, in front of all those eager-to-be-fed souls in the audience. She started off, as many people did, talking very plain, even a little salty. Her cadence would start to pick up speed, then crescendo from a whisper to a holler. My father, Floyd LeFlore, was a jazz composer and trumpeter, and he told me as a little girl that musicians call that *riffing*.

Shirley's style was undeniable, and she was able to effortlessly take vignettes from everyday life, ordinary observations and weave stories into her poetry, transcending space and time. Like most Southerners, Shirley was a griot, but she was also a psychologist, so she extrapolated and studied people's lives and then lovingly wrote about them.

Most of Shirley's poems focused on women. History and lineage had always been important to my mother because she had known so many great women.

PHOTO: Shirley Bradley Price LeFlore at a reading. Photo by Michael J. Bracey (2014).

For Shirley, poetry more or less became her first language. She often referred to herself as an oral poet. I would later understand she called herself this because she passed on family stories orally, almost poetically, to my two older sisters, Hope and Jacie, and me. My mother had come from a family of women storytellers. It started with my great-great-grandmother, who became a freed slave after her husband purchased her. What she endured gave her the armor to persevere and overcome, and her faith, determination, and strength planted those storytelling seeds that would be passed down in the bloodline.

My great-grandmother was self-educated and would become a leader in her church, a sought-after orator and poet in segregated southern Missouri. She then passed it on to my grandmother, Annette, affectionately called "Dolly." Dolly owned a beauty shop in St. Louis, Missouri. Lady customers in town would flock to hear her tell her own brand of life stories, and she'd even add a dash of Jesus. Dolly's words opened her doors to women from all walks of life—rich, poor, sinner, saved. Their burdens and troubles would be washed away when she put 'em in the bowl. After she pressed, curled, and pinned you up, her storefront philosophies would help you stand up a little taller or help your heart get a little lighter. You felt whole again.

As a young girl, Shirley would soak up those stories, their laughter, and tears. She captured the tone, texture, cadence, and dialect of their voices with her photographic memory. *But it didn't stop there.* Shirley would eavesdrop on the conversations had amongst women riding on the streetcar. Maybe they were headed to church or on their way to do day work for the rich white folk in the suburbs. They fascinated her, and she made up stories about these women—who they were, where they were going, where they had been, where they dreamed of going. She knew some by name, others she may have just met in passing, and could see a story in their eyes, fingernails, hands, or swollen ankles.

During the last few years of her life, she would talk out her stories when she was having problems seeing, and I would write them out. Eventually, I taped them, and at some point, this oral history, along with her poems and stories, will become a book. So, as I was flipping through *TRAILBLAZERS, Black Women Who Helped Make America Great, American Firsts/American Icons,* it reminded me of the women in my family, my childhood, and the hours of Shirley's storytelling. I felt like Gabrielle was sitting across from me at the kitchen table, sipping from a piping hot cup of herbal tea, telling these stories, and I hung onto every word.

This first volume of *TRAILBLAZERS* is part of a six-volume series. As they say in women's basketball, it's the "tip-off" to an epic journey at this crucial time in our society. Each volume reports and analyzes Black women's roles in American society, but unlike any biographical collection, it is also very personal and revealing, in a way that manages to connect Black women to each other.

Throughout this first volume, which features activists, dancers, and athletes, Gabrielle and Chandra's introduction did what we call in the television and film business, "breaking the fourth wall," by sharing some of their personal stories in the text. Breaking the fourth wall is uncharacteristic in a book of this magnitude, but it's subtle when it's done here, which is exactly what makes it so appealing. Gabrielle told me she got tired of constantly referring to Black women as "them." As a Black woman, it made her feel detached, especially when there were moments when it should be "we," "me," and "us." It allowed her to express her inner thoughts through example as she acknowledged her Black womanhood. Her lived experiences complement and validate some of the women's stories featured here without forfeiting the book's historical accuracy.

What is most amazing about TRAILBLAZERS is that I thought I knew about these historical women, but was surprised to find out how little I truly did. I was also reminded of all the strong narratives that have come out of the Black American experience. Storytelling is our roots and wings. For example, Myrlie Evers-Williams, one of the three surviving widows of the civil rights leaders, did what no other widow did: she ran for office, was a corporate executive, remarried, and saved the NAACP, the oldest Black organization in this country, from financial ruin.

I interviewed her in 2015 when I was completing the book Tell The Truth And Shame The Devil: The Life, Legacy, and Love Of My Son Michael Brown, which I co-wrote with his mother, Lezley McSpadden. Her grace was remarkable as she talked about finding purpose after her then-husband, Medgar Evers, was killed. Despite the unimaginable pain she endured alongside her children as she watched her husband gunned down in her front yard, she still found the strength to fight for justice and have hope for America. It took her thirty years to get that justice, but she never gave up. It is astonishing that now, well into her eighties, she is still poised, strong, and focused. Her story and so many others included in TRAILBLAZERS are exactly why this book is so important.

I liken TRAILBLAZERS to the power of music. It's like a history lesson mixtape! From Nancy and Sarah, to Nina, Aretha, and Chaka, on down to Mary J,, Whitney, Jill, MC Lyte, and Queen Latifah; this book is a refreshing remix for the old school and that head-knockin' groove for the new and next generations. TRAILBLAZERS is our "womanifesto," harkening our resilience and fortitude as women. Our fearlessness, fury, and fierceness have fueled us to overcome and fight the ills of slavery, Jim Crow, Michael Brown, and the new face of racism post-Obama that dons a red MAGA hat and spews venomous, divisive tweets into cyberspace. Yes, Black women are trailblazers. We always have been and are still standing in the gap.

As I read the first section, "Activism," I was reminded of a chilly winter night in 1999, when I took my mother to see the late, great Ruby Dee's one-woman show, My One Good Nerve: A Visit With Ruby Dee, at the Kaye Playhouse in New York City. Ruby Dee and her husband, Ossie Davis, dedicated their lives to theater, movies, and being on the front lines of social activism. Perhaps, one of the most profound lines of the night was when Ms. Dee, standing center stage, raised her arms to the high heavens and proclaimed, "Lord, make me do the very thing I fear." I immediately turned to my mother, realizing at that instant that her whole life had embodied that one simple but poignant line, one that I still carry with me today. Women like Shirley and Ruby Dee have always stood fearlessly in the face of the giant, defying the odds, moving to the beat of their own drum.

We met Ms. Dee afterward, and the two of them found an instant connection as artist-activists. Their impromptu, spirited exchange was about everything from the ongoing fight for civil rights in America to Shirley injecting her reflections of working for the Poor People's campaign in the sixties, and Ms. Dee's take on the future of Black theater, and the need for a new breed of Black activists to step up. I found myself once again awestruck standing before these two Black matriarchs. As I fast forward to *TRAILBLAZERS,* that night's epic encounter further proves our greatness and the power that Black women possess. Perhaps, it is even the anecdote to heal the ills that afflict our communities and our country.

I'm especially proud to see Fatima Robinson honored in the "Dance" section of this inaugural volume. There are so many legends who came before her, but she represents the spirit of hip hop, and we are of the same generation. I've known Fatima professionally and personally since the early 1990s. I was a young executive at Uptown Entertainment, and she was a dancer for Mary J. Blige, when Uptown had just released Mary's *What's The 411?* album. However, reading her story in this book was a major revelation for me. I didn't realize how vast her achievements are as a dancer, choreographer, producer, and director. She is phenomenal, beautiful, humble, and unapologetically Black. Fatima reminded me of my mother, who was the same way. I also didn't know how much of Fatima's accomplishments rest on the shoulders of dance greats such as Josephine Baker and Katherine Dunham.

Finally, the "Sports" section was, surprisingly, the most interesting and eye-opening. I admittedly am not a big sports buff. Typically, during the NBA Finals or NFL Superbowl, I jump on the bandwagon and tune in, but primarily for the parties, snacks, and cocktails. Like most Black folk, I always get excited when I see the rare Black or Brown face at the Olympics, like gymnasts Simone Biles or Gabby Douglas; or Simone Manuel winning the gold in swimming and diving; or Debi Thomas winning bronze in figure skating in 1988. I also enthusiastically tune in when Venus or Serena Williams or Sloane Stephens play at Wimbledon or the U.S. Open. However, when I read Gabrielle's profile on WNBA legend Dawn Staley, it took me back to when I met her in 2004. I met Dawn through my close girlfriend, television producer Angela Wells. She brought us together to collaborate on a potential children's book about Dawn's life growing up in Philadelphia and her love for basketball. I was initially interested because I saw it as a project that was less about sports and more about the impact a story could have on young Black girls. However, when I traveled to North Carolina to see Dawn play for the Charlotte Sting, it was a tremendous eye-opener about the WNBA and the importance of sports for girls and women. I attended the season-opening game with Angela, witnessing women's sisterhood and strength firsthand. After the game, we celebrated the Charlotte Sting's win. Women were laughing, crying, and dancing. Basketball was their bond, their passion, their soul.

The WNBA was young at the time, and Dawn, as well as Lisa Leslie and Sheryl Swoopes, were rising stars, along with so many others. Despite the games not having the sold-out arenas, players' pay equity not matching their NBA counterparts, and the women lacking massive multimillion dollar endorsements, Dawn and her baller sisters worked just as hard as their male counterparts. It was a time of great sacrifice, but they were in it for the love of basketball. Laser-focused, they laid the groundwork for future generations of little Black and Brown girls who dreamed of dunking a ball. This changed my whole perspective of women's basketball. So in 2000, when my friend, filmmaker Gina Prince-Bythewood, released *Love and Basketball,* I applauded her for telling such a beautiful and human story in a way that honored female athletes like Dawn, who were part of the trailblazing sisters who refused to wait for the doors in basketball to be opened. They kicked the doors in! Today, having reached iconic status as a WNBA pioneer and as one of women's basketball's leading Black female coaches, Dawn has earned her rightful place in the pages of *TRAILBLAZERS.*

The old Virginia Slims cigarette ad slogan, "You've come a long way, baby," said it all, but we still have so far to go, and the best is yet to come for Black women in sports. Learning about our first sports superstar, Ora Washington, who excelled in tennis and basketball, made me appreciate women like Serena Williams, Jackie Joyner-Kersee, and Cheryl Miller even more. Reading about these generations of women was an affirmation of how essential *TRAILBLAZERS* is to the fabric of American culture. To witness this country elect the first woman, a Black woman, as our new Vice President is proof the tide has turned. Our time is now, and this book is the mirror every young Black girl in America can hold up and see as a reflection of her best self and her tremendous potential.

Gabrielle considers herself a poet and a storyteller rather than a scholar. While she has painstakingly researched and cited her work, the text is poetic and accessible to the average reader. The manner in which it was written draws the reader in as it illuminates the forgotten stories of Black women's greatness. *They are uplifting.* They carry cultural and individual self-knowledge. More importantly, while these stories educate and inform, they help change cultural and political landscapes that can actually disrupt systems of oppression. These stories, including the razor-edged ones of slavery, racism, segregation, discrimination, and disappointment, are the ties that bind us. There is no question that storytelling for Black America is a way of saying, "I am here, and I matter." Without our stories, we are birds without wings.

It should be no surprise that Gabrielle and Shirley had an intensely creative relationship. They both shared an underlying characteristic of creating socially conscious works influenced by feminist activism. They tackled the power and beauty of Black women by defying the stereotypical manner of how we have been historically portrayed. As I read these stories, I am again reminded that this Black womanhood of loving and giving, gathering, doing, and creating, which reaches and stretches beyond generations, is part of who I am as a Black woman in America.

TRAILBLAZERS is a gift to Black women, an intergenerational bridge. *We are badass, bold, and brilliant.* It is for our Black men to revel in our glory, as they better understand why we must be treated, respected, and revered as Queens. It is also a gift to our White, Asian, Latina, and Native American sisters. TRAILBLAZERS gives us our rightful seat at the table, where Black women can raise our diverse voices collectively and be heard.

TRAILBLAZERS is a gift to the world. *We are badass, bold, and brilliant.* And it's time to recognize, once and for all, how we have helped make America great. Like Beyoncé said, "Gimme my check, put some respect on my check…pay me in equity." The women in these six volumes are our sheroes, some unsung, and Gabrielle is shining the light on us, 'cause Black women be about our business. We stand on the shoulders of generations of Black women who embody greatness. These women are our great-grandmothers, our grandmothers, our mothers, aunts, play aunties, and sister-friends. I am who I am because *we* are tomorrow's Harrietts, Fannie Lous, Rosas, Corettas, and so many more. Gabrielle sounds the alarm, serving notice that we are here; we've been here since the beginning of America, and we're just getting started. Breaking barriers and blazing trails is what we do! ❖

—Lyah Beth LeFlore-Ituen
St. Louis, Missouri

PREFACE: Why This Book

"So, I am here today to honor the words of Toni Morrison. 'If there's a book that you want to read but it hasn't been written yet, you must be the one to write it.' I urge everyone here and everyone who hears my voice to join me in telling the stories that aren't told."

—Naomi Wadler, March For Our Lives, 2018

IN 2017, AS I GAZED somewhat dumbfoundedly at the television, listening to incessant news reports about a newly ordained president who was going to "Make America Great Again," and about an emergent #MeToo movement that seemingly ignored the concerns of women of color, I wondered how this would affect the status of African Americans, and especially Black women, in this country. The crushing reality of making America great again is based on a fabricated lie that this country's greatness is contingent solely upon its whiteness. What I find disheartening is that 42.5 percent of America's citizens believe this to be true.[1] It seems that making America great is merely a desire to make America White again—which, by the way, it was never White to begin with since we actually live in Indian country.[2]

It begs the question of why White people long for the 1950s, this "Leave It to Beaver-Ozzie-and-Harriet-Father-Knows-Best-Mayberry" era, when White men ruled, all women were subservient, and people of color had no rights. Yet nearly 60 percent of White people have this idyllic memory (real or imagined) of the 1950s being better than it is today.[3] What has changed since the 1950s—outside of technological innovations—is that White people no longer have an exclusive hold on the best housing, jobs, schools, or the ballot box. From this comes a deep-seated longing for an era when segregation was the norm, and everyone who was non-White was forced to stay in their place while White people got first dibs on everything. The irony here is that even though the playing field has been leveled, White people still fare better than any other group on just about every measure of social or economic well-being, so what gives?

As African Americans continue to advance in this society and gain full citizenship rights, we have been witnessing a wave of "White rage." This rage, which

PHOTO: Naomi Wadler speaking at the anti-gun protest, March For Our Lives, in Washington, D.C. Kevin Mazur/Getty Images (2018).

is being enacted through White nationalists, has been brewing for quite some time within legislative bodies and the judicial sector concerning policies, laws, and rulings that are undercutting our country's advancement. We saw it during Reconstruction and its downfall. We struggled with it during segregation, Jim Crow, and black codes. We dealt with it during the civil rights and Black Power movements. We observed the growing wave after President Obama's election. And today, we are witnessing the full-blown wrath of this rage as it spreads to all people of color, Muslims, Jews, immigrants, women, and the LGBTQ community. *This is not how you make America great.*

Compounding this rage is pure, unadulterated racism. The countless violations of racism have made criminality synonymous with "Black" in the American mind. It is the bigotry that allows poverty to be seen as something that African Americans have beset on the country, rather than the other way around. What is more, through the exceptional forces of racial transference, African Americans have become reasonable game for abuse since they are associated with "blackness"—the ultimate American curse.

None of this is new. It is a message that has resonated since the first slaves landed in America and has been heightened over the years by nativist movements like the Know Nothing Party of the 1850s,[4] or when the Ku Klux Klan pushed for "Americanism" by way of restrictive immigration during the 1920s.[5]

These messages have gained traction every time White Americans encounter societal changes and shifting demographics, even though it goes against America's ideology that it is a country of immigrants. With a Black president, LGBTQ equality, a fast-growing Latino community, and predictions that America will soon become a majority-minority country, these messages have always resonated with a specific segment of the population with great effect. But why now, and to what end?

In the midst of this, the #MeToo movement emerged. In a powerfully persuasive speech at the 2018 Golden Globes, Oprah Winfrey framed the #MeToo movement as the latest episode in a long history of women's resistance to sexual harassment and violence.[6] Her speech was notable for emphasizing the activism of racially and economically marginalized women, including Recy Taylor, who died in 2017 at the age of ninety-eight. Taylor's determination to seek justice for her rape in Jim Crow era Alabama was investigated by a then-unknown NAACP officer, Rosa Parks, who would set the stage for the civil rights movement and, in many ways, today's #MeToo movement. It was fitting that a Black activist, Tarana Burke, followed in Taylor and Parks' footsteps by creating the "Me Too" slogan in 2006. She created it as an initiative to promote "empowerment through empathy" among women of color who have experienced sexual abuse, particularly within underprivileged communities.[7]

Burke may have created the slogan over ten years ago, but when actress Alyssa Milano used the hashtag #MeToo, it went viral, and an entire movement was attributed to her. This reiterated, once again, how women of color are often overlooked and replaced with an overwhelmingly White narrative that ignores the systemic racism that White women will never experience. Several days after her tweet, Milano credited Burke with the movement on Twitter, but the "Me Too" that Burke created and the hashtag that Milano initiated remain on separate tracks.

Unfortunately, the suffrage and women's movements of the nineteenth and twentieth centuries, up to the #MeToo movement of today, have never fully acknowledged active elements of racism, and ignored the needs of women of color who are likely targets of sexual harassment. This has left a bad taste in most Black and Brown women's mouths and has made them suspicious of any feminist initiative. While White feminists have made some inroads to become "intersectional," a term coined by Black feminist scholar Kimberlé Crenshaw,[8] they still have a long way to go. The many middle class White women who have been newly awakened to political fury and protest need to learn the histories of Black and Brown women who have never had a reason *not to be* "woke." Too often, the public narrative about women has focused on White women and their experiences instead of those of Black women and other women of color. Until the contributions of Black and Brown feminists are celebrated and recognizable just as White feminist icons, the #MeToo movement will never be able to call itself a movement by and for all women.

All of this amounts to gendered racism, a term initially coined by sociologist Philomena Essed,[9] which refers to the simultaneous experience of both racism and sexism. So as I witnessed this collision of racism and sexism on my television screen, I thought about the chorus of Black women who, despite the odds, managed to contribute substantially to America's greatness but have been virtually ignored or unacknowledged by the general public. *This is why this book.*

Black women have always struggled with the duality of being Black and female. Amid harsh repression on all fronts, they have managed—sometimes at their peril—to preserve their cultural ancestry and articulate their struggles through resistance, activism, art, and hope. It began when a growing number of Black women emerged during the Civil War and Reconstruction eras and burst into mainstream American culture during the twentieth century to play significant roles in the abolitionist, suffragist, labor, civil rights, and women's movements. They sought economic and social equality while protecting hearth and home. These women were "boots on the ground," the grassroots organizers and strategists who helped build organizational infrastructures through women's clubs, beauty parlors, churches, sororities, and, later, in mainstream organizations, for which the Black liberation, nationalist, civil rights, and Black Power movements flourished. Their army consisted of our grandmothers, mothers, aunts, sisters, and daughters who dealt with the mundanity of everyday life but still contributed their time, money, and resources toward the cause. All of them were "womanists" before the poet and activist Alice Walker devised the term in her 1983 book, *In Search of Our Mothers' Gardens: Womanist Prose*.[10] These women also understood that their fight was not only about racism and sexism; it was also for human rights. America needed to become inclusive. American society required new social structures and political movements free from racism, sexism, classism, misogyny, and homophobia to nourish a vision that would truly make America great. So when they fought and won, they fought and won for all. The idea of making America great was never confined to those who saw it from a racialized perspective; making America great was always about making it great for everyone. *So yes, this is why this book.*

I naïvely led myself to believe I could publish *TRAILBLAZERS, Black Women Who Helped Make America Great, American Firsts/American Icons* in one book. But in time, I found it necessary to develop *TRAILBLAZERS* as a series that now consists of six volumes, with this being the first. Why? Because there are a lot of great Black women out there who have accomplished some incredible things. And while I could not possibly include all of them, I wanted to cover as many of them as possible.

This is not the first book to address this. There have been a number of series that have paid homage to African American women and their accomplishments, many of which I acknowledge in the bibliography. Still, I think it is important to mention upfront these two standouts: *The Notable Black American Women, Books I, II, and III,* edited by Jessie Carney Smith in 1992, 1995, and 2002 respectively, is a phenomenal repository of well over 1,000 women who have contributed to the American landscape. Smith has also published similar books that catalog the achievements of African Americans. Additionally, Darlene Clark Hine's *Black Women in America: An Historical Encyclopedia* celebrates the remarkable achievements of Black women throughout history. It was initially published in 1993 and grew into a third volume in 2005. Both Smith and Hines are exceptional scholars and have produced great reference books that I believe should be included in everyone's library. *TRAILBLAZERS* is a little different. While the aforementioned books are reference books, I wanted to create an affordable and accessible book for both the general public and the classroom.

As the book's title implies, *TRAILBLAZERS* is about Black women as firsts and icons in many areas, from activists to physicians and educators, to artists and actors. In the telling of our history, all African Americans are seen as men, and all women are seen as White. Since history is told through the lens of the slaveholders and conquerors who created a misconception where women and people of color do not exist, historical realities are overlooked, misinterpreted, and often retold to present a false history. Here, it was important to research to provide the most accurate information possible.

Who to put in, who to leave out, and who to feature, laid utmost on my mind. Discovering women I had never heard of, researching women who have been rarely discussed, and revisiting historical figures made the selection process less torturous because I found the process a privilege and a complete joy. I also added women who may not have been firsts but have become icons in their own right and needed to be included in this series.

How did these women qualify as firsts? Any Black woman who wanted to do something and was told she could not, but did it anyway, whether she wanted to be a doctor or lawyer, an artist or actor, a politician, or an athlete, and was willing to fight for it even though there were no Black women before her, is a "first." I read about women who challenged laws, institutions, preconceived notions, stereotypes, societal mores, and anyone or anything that got in their way as they fought ardently against the dual forces of racism and sexism. They did not plan it that way. They did not wake up one morning and say, "I'm gonna be a first" or "I've gotta be an icon." Many of them probably did not think of themselves as "other" until someone went out of their way to tell them that they were, or that they did not have the right to fulfill their ambitions. Blazing a trail and becoming a first was the furthest thing from their minds. I am almost certain that most of them would have preferred the freedom to do whatever they wanted to do, whether it was sitting anywhere on a bus, eating at a lunch counter, going to any school or hospital, retaining work in the field of their choice, becoming a pilot or a ballerina, creating great art, getting a job for equal and fair pay, or simply sipping water from any water fountain without all the fuss. As hurtful as their brushes with racism and sexism were, they did not allow it to define them nor hold them back.

And not all of these women were inclined to march, campaign, or crusade. For some, their significance comes from being a high-achieving, abundantly talented woman who inspires by example and helps others along the way. In the face of these insurmountable circumstances, this chorus of Black women contributed substantially to America's greatness, but has been virtually ignored or unacknowledged by the general public.[11]

Some of the entries in *TRAILBLAZERS* are brief, while some are much longer. Some women made noteworthy contributions, but could not go further because the obstacles they faced were far too great, so they went on to do other things, quietly living out their lives. Some women's lives were shortened due to disease or tragedy, but their contributions still created a path for others to follow. The "Legacy" section appears on some, but not all of the bios of women who have passed on. Some stories are so thorough that a Legacy section was not necessary. I only mention this because people like to look at length and space, then equate it with importance, but in this case, it is quality, not quantity, that counts.

By instinct and forced obligation, Black women have showcased the possibility of pushing through anything and creating greatness out of nothing, while also being responsible for their families and communities' well-being. Through hard work, educational aspirations, entrepreneurship, caregiving, political participation, and more, Black women have created and continue to create opportunities for themselves, and in the process, contribute to America economically as well as culturally. One would think after what we have been through and all that we have achieved, the next generation of Black women would have it much easier, but they do not. While there have been some improvements, we still have to fight stereotypes and perceptions of who we are as Black women.

So besides determining which women blazed the trail with incredible resilience and perseverance as firsts and icons, it was equally important to highlight the young women following their footsteps. Take, for example, eleven-year-old Naomi Wadler at the March for Our Lives rally in Washington, D.C. organized by teenage survivors of the Marjorie Stoneman Douglass High School shooting in Parkland, Florida. Wadler stood before millions of people in 2018 to tell her truth, and spoke on behalf of all the young African American girls killed by gun violence. Her speech was remarkable and moving, but her commitment to change is not all that unique. Black girls and women all over the country are picking up the banner from trailblazers in all aspects of our lives, whether it is activism, the arts and sciences, education, and or even sports.

In 2020, South Carolina high school student Aly Conyers joined her brother to organize Faces of the Future, and led a 2-mile protest march from Howard University to the White House in Washington, D.C., in the wake of George Floyd's death. It was a peaceful march that drew hundreds of people. Conyers is also a standout as a 400-meter runner and hopes to continue sports and activism in college. Another high school student, Thandiwe Abdullah, began attending Black Lives Matter meetings and marches with her mother and her siblings at a young age, but they were often the only children in attendance. So Abdullah decided to help create an offshoot of the organization focused on children, and the BLM Youth Vanguard was born. Since then, the Youth Vanguard and other youth groups across the Los Angeles area have been fighting to protect students. They successfully removed random searches from the Los Angeles Unified School District (LAUSD), and they are now working on removing school police from the campuses entirely. She has also helped launch the Black Lives Matter in Schools campaign, which has been adopted by the National Education Association (NEA) and participated in the March for Our Lives movement. Abdullah was named as one of *Time* magazine's 25 Most Influential Teens of 2018.

Other teen advocates include Amariyanna "Mari" Copeny, also known as "Little Miss Flint," a clean water activist from Michigan, and Kheris Rogers, an anti-bullying activist and fashion designer from Los Angeles who focuses on the bullying of dark-skinned individuals. They have the courage, curiosity, and wisdom to recognize that, at this moment in history, systemic disparities are being cracked open by the #BlackLivesMatter, #SayHerName, and #TimesUp movements that are challenging racism, sexism, and poverty. We have all come to understand that blazing a trail is only sustainable when others pick up the mantle to further the cause. This is unquestionably just the beginning for these young girl's lives, and of course, I cannot wait to see what they do next.

Categorizing these women was equally challenging. For example, Debbie Allen is a whole lot of things: a dancer, actor, producer, and director. Where should she go? I placed her in a future volume as a producer and director because while Allen has had a remarkable career in all these areas, she is at the top of her game and should be acknowledged accordingly. However, I mention Allen prominently in the "Dance" section because it is how she got her start in show business, and in recent years, she has returned to dance by opening a dance school. This is just one example of how difficult it is to categorize Black women who often have to multitask in multiple spheres and wear several hats as they pursue their ambitions. Black women are not flat, one-dimensional beings; we are multifaceted and complex.

What I found most challenging was writing an introduction for each section of the book. My initial thought was to provide a brief historical timeline of the biographical features that followed and mention the women I could not fully feature. Instead, it evolved into something more. I stumbled upon some of the most fascinating and most obscure information during my research, which I pieced together into a historical context strictly from a Black woman's perspective. I found the process arduous yet illuminating.

For example, writing about activism and dance was easier for me due to my personal connection to those areas, but writing about Black women in sports was a huge challenge. Surprisingly, the treatment of Black women's bodies within popular culture came into play, time and again, in both the dance and sports introductions, which I felt required much-needed attention.[12] Throughout the book, I found myself mapping this progress alongside White women and the suffrage/women's liberation/#MeToo movements. My overall objective was to provide information in a way that was informative and relatively easy to digest. I also provided an extensive bibliography, which I hope readers will use to further investigate some of the many great books written primarily by African American scholars. Finally, while I did not plan to write an Afterword, I was compelled to do so after Ayanna Pressley revealed her bald head while announcing she suffered from alopecia. I felt her experience embodied Black womanhood and how we deal with our hair, so I wrote "Ayanna Pressley Reminds Us of Who We Are."

It is worth mentioning that while we celebrate these women in *TRAILBLAZERS*, we should also recognize the great sacrifices they have made on behalf of their communities. In the case of Rosa Parks, the catalyst of the Montgomery Bus Boycott and the mother of the civil rights movement, both she and her husband lost their jobs early on during the boycott, developed health problems, and never found steady work in Montgomery again. In 1957, they were forced to move due to death threats and joined Parks' brother and extended family in Detroit. For a time, Parks' health worsened, landing her in the hospital. She would not work steadily until 1965 (ten years after the boycott began) when she worked for Congressman John Conyers.

Fast forward to over sixty years later when activist Erica Garner, who I dedicated this book to, died after suffering brain damage following a second heart attack at age twenty-seven.[13] Garner was thrust into the national spotlight after her father, Eric Garner, was killed in 2014 while being placed under arrest. She succeeded in igniting public outrage that helped spark the Black Lives Matter movement and eventually achieved justice for her father. For that reason, I felt it was important to acknowledge her sacrifice. Parks and Garner are not the only women who suffered the effects of creating a trail following one that others had blazed. One of the things I hope readers take away from this series is the sacrifices these women have made. *Yes. Sometimes there is a price to pay for being a first or an icon.*

More often than not, Black history is treated separately from "American" history. As a result, many people, especially White people, are unaware of Black achievements, making it easier for them to believe that Black folks have not contributed much of anything to this country. As a matter of fact, most of our contributions were accomplished under the most diabolical circumstances of slavery, segregation, and racism, as we helped shape America. The purpose of *TRAILBLAZERS* is to dispel this notion, including the stereotypes and popular imagery that have reduced Black women to angry, hypersexual, or superhumanly "strong" beings, by exposing our power, reach, and depth.

It is not that Black women have not been acknowledged every now and again, but those celebratory moments have only come when it is convenient or comfortable. Americans appreciate Black women when our voter turnout leads to necessary victories during political campaigns, but when we end up being underrepresented at the local, state, and federal level and complain about it, we are deemed "un-American." They loved Beyoncé until she said, "stop killing us." They loved Debi Thomas when she became the first Black Olympic medal winner in skating, but when she became mentally ill, it was her fault, and she deserved whatever befell her. And they will always love Oprah Winfrey, as long as her messages are not radical or "too Black." There is a great danger in overlooking the roles Black women have played in our society as people pick and choose what they believe is acceptable or not, just because we do not fit neatly into someone else's box, even when we are standing up for ourselves.

It has also become more acceptable in recent years to speak about each other in racist, sexist, or homophobic terms. Anti-immigration rhetoric, as well as sexist behavior, has mainstreamed into daily media, and has become socially acceptable. People no longer attempt to disguise their disgraceful racist and sexist outbursts; now they claim their right to behave in this manner. There is no greatness to be found in this behavior.

This "greatness" I keep bringing up, which has been coined to represent the sociopolitical environment we are currently living in, does not embody all of the terrible things it has recently been associated with. But if America's greatness is measured by how one looks at history, then frankly, there has never been a time in our country when Black folks could say unhesitatingly and unequivocally that America has been great. While our relationship with patriotism has always been fraught with tension due to this nation's history, we continue to live, grow, and thrive as proud Americans eager to achieve the same dreams that White people are so easily able to obtain. The key to America's greatness is that despite the odds, Americans have managed to recognize our pitfalls and drawbacks, make a course correction, and try to learn from them, even if in some cases it has taken us over a hundred years to do so.

One of the main challenges has been the dissembling of White America's tendency to accept discrimination and inequality as the norm, or alternatively, espouse the belief that since slavery and segregation are a relic of the past, there is no need to discuss either of them since we now live in a post-racial society. Any mention of racism is either imaginary or tantamount to "anti-White racism." In other words, White people do not want to feel complicit in a legal and social system of racial separation, even though they are complicit in a de facto system. Killing the post-racial myth and dealing with racism and discrimination head-on was always a step toward greatness that, up until this point, had never been taken seriously.

Preaching the gospel of greatness in order to return to a time when White power went unchallenged and Black people sat in the back of the bus has been losing its appeal. Fractious policies on healthcare, immigration, climate change, tax breaks for the rich, and the disenfranchisement of voting rights were created to pander to a base of haters and appeal to a privileged class of millionaires and billionaires. As we experienced a mismanaged pandemic that killed hundreds of thousands and left our economy in tatters, we also witnessed a public uprising ignited by the police murder of George Floyd. A multicultural coalition emerged with people clamoring to topple police brutality and systemic racism.

At that moment, Breonna Taylor's murder reminded us about Black women's invisible struggle against police violence. It has forced us to ask why the same level of global outrage over the killing of Black men by law enforcement does not easily exist for Black women. It also illuminates why the African American Policy Forum (AAPF), headed by legal scholar Kimberlé Crenshaw, created the #SayHerName campaign. Supporting the #SayHerName campaign means remaining steadfast in the struggle to upend how systemic racism and sexism intersect to disproportionately affect Black women.

In the end, protests are good, but legislation and codified federal laws are even better. Real change, though, will take more than protests, and voting—it will take a national movement that remains committed for the long-run until change takes root.

There is nothing wrong with striving for greatness, but "greatness" requires an unwavering commitment. We need to create a new social contract worthy of our recommitment to a constitutional democracy. We need to be mindful of how we treat one another, and how we live up to our responsibilities in the larger global community. The bedrock on which our country was built is the interrelated unity of our nation's most precious resource: our diverse people. That in itself is the greatness of America. In our quest for greatness, there is an unending story that continuously seeks goodness. It is why the times we live in exemplify a quote that has been improperly attributed to Alexis de Tocqueville, but I will repeat it here: "America is great because America is good, and if America ever ceases to be good, America will cease to be great."[14]

TRAILBLAZERS, Black Women Who Helped Make America Great, American Firsts/American Icons is a starting point, a distillation of research and personal reflection that honors our past. It is but a small example of what Black women have achieved and what is possible. These women have sought and continue to seek goodness, which is why they have helped make America great. More importantly, TRAILBLAZERS embraces the complexities of American history as it transcends our limited views and relationships with each other. I hope people ask questions and dig further for more information; there remain buried treasures that have yet to be discovered. I am grateful and honored to be a member of this tribe.❖

—Gabrielle David
New York, New York

NOTES AND WORKS CITED

1. Jamelle Bouie, "Will America Make Trump Great Again?" The New York Times, June 22, 2019, https://www.nytimes.com/2019/06/22/opinion/trump-2020-win.html. See also Marissa Melton, "Is 'Make America Great Again' Racist?" Voice of America, August 31, 2017, https://www.voanews.com/usa/make-america-great-again-racist.

2. The term "Indian Country" is leveraged broadly as a general description of Native spaces and places within the U.S. It is inclusive of the hundreds of tribal nations that occupy these spaces. It is a term used with positive sentiment within and outside the Native community.

3. Janell Ross, "White Americans long for the 1950s, when they didn't face so much discrimination," The Washington Post, November 17, 2015, https://www.washingtonpost.com/news/the-fix/wp/2015/11/17/White-americans-long-for-the-1950s-when-they-werent-such-victims-of-reverse-discrimination.

4. The Native American Party, renamed the American Party in 1855, was commonly known as the Know Nothing movement (because its members replied,"I know nothing," to outsiders) was an American nativist party that was primarily anti-Catholic, xenophobic, and hostile to immigration. It dissolved in 1861.

5. The Ku Klux Klan has a long history of advocating White supremacy, White nationalism, anti-immigration, anti-Semitism, and the "purification" of American society. Although the Klan's popularity rapidly declined in the latter half of the 1920s, the movement saw a boost in its membership at the beginning in 2017.

6. Giovanni Russonello, "Read Oprah Winfrey's Golden Globes Speech," The New York Times, January 7, 2018, https://www.nytimes.com/2018/01/07/movies/oprah-win-

frey-golden-globes-speech-transcript.html. Transcript of Oprah Winfrey's Golden Globes speech upon accepting the Cecil B. DeMille Award for lifetime achievement.

7. Sandra E. Garcia, "The Woman Who Created #MeToo Long Before Hashtags," *The New York Times,* October 20, 2017, https://www.nytimes.com/2017/10/20/us/me-too-movement-tarana-burke.html.

8. Kimberlé Crenshaw is a civil rights advocate and a leading scholar of critical race theory. She is known for the introduction and development of intersectional theory, the study of how overlapping or intersecting social identities, particularly minority identities, relate to systems and structures of oppression, domination, or discrimination. Crenshaw's scholarship was essential in the development of "intersectional feminism."

9. Philomena Essed is a highly regarded critical race, gender and leadership studies professor at Antioch University's Graduate School of Leadership and Change and an affiliated researcher for Utrecht University's Graduate Gender program. She is known for introducing the concepts of everyday racism and gendered racism in the Netherlands and internationally. Her publications span decades, including the classic book, *Everyday Racism: Reports from Women of Two Cultures* (Thousand Oaks, CA: SAGE Publishing, 1991).

10. Alice Walker, *In Search of Our Mothers' Gardens: Womanist Prose* (New York: Harcourt Brace Jovanovich, 2004). Since women of color have historically had issues about the feminist label, Walker devised the term to define her love of Black womanhood and a commitment to improve lives for all people oppressed due to race or class. Walker proposes a state of Black woman-centered living that is not steeped in the European framework.

11. See viewpoints about feminism from a Black and White perspective. Lindsay H. Hoffman, "Black Woman, White Movement: Why Black Women are Leaving the Feminist Movement," *Huffington Post,* November 12, 2015 https://www.huffpost.com/entry/Black-woman-White-movemen_b_8569540; Tamela J. Gordon, "ENOUGH IS ENOUGH, Why I'm giving up on intersectional feminism," *Quartzy,* April 30, 2018, https://qz.com/quartzy/1265902/why-im-giving-up-on-intersectional-feminism; Britni de la Cretaz, "To White Feminists Who Don't Want to Discuss Racism: Here Are 7 Things You Need to Know," *Everyday Feminism,* October 12, 2015, https://everydayfeminism.com/2015/10/White-feminists-dont-talk-race; and Nyar Afrika, "White Feminism's concept of "unity" is a joke. Shoot me," *AFROPUNK,* January 12, 2018, https://afropunk.com/2018/01/White-feminisms-concept-unity-joke-shoot

12. See Shirley Ann Tate, *Black Women's Bodies and The Nation, Race, Gender and Culture* (U.K.: Palgrave Macmillan) 2015; Michael Bennett, *Recovering the Black Female Body: Self-Representation by African American Women* (New Jersey: Rutgers University Press) 2000; and Brenda Dixon Gottschild, *The Black Dancing Body: A Geography From Coon to Cool* (New York: Palgrave Macmillan) 2005.

13. Vivian Wang, "Erica Garner, Activist and Daughter of Eric Garner, Dies at 27," *The New York Times,* December 30, 2017. https://www.nytimes.com/2017/12/30/nyregion/erica-garner-dead.html.

14. For many years this quote has been attributed to the French diplomat Alexis de Tocqueville's *Democracy in America* (1835), except he never wrote it. *See* John Pitney, "The Tocqueville Fraud,"November 12, 1995, *The Weekly Standard,* https://www.weeklystandard.com/john-j-pitney/the-tocqueville-fraud.

INTRODUCTION:
"You Make Me Proud"

"YOU MAKE ME PROUD TO SPELL MY NAME W-O-M-A-N." These are the strong, supportive words of Dr. Maya Angelou, perhaps one of the most well-known Black women in American history. No other words can better capture the essence of this book. The only crucial caveat that I want—no, need—to add at this historical juncture is B-L-A-C-K. The Black women featured in this series *TRAILBLAZERS, Black Women Who Helped Make America Great, American Firsts/American Icons* altered the course of American history by being authentic, brilliant, creative, dynamic, unstoppable, and ultimately, iconic.

I am, proudly, a sociologist, and what struck me the most about this book is the number of women who challenged the status quo. Every single woman profiled in this book did just that. Of course, to become a trailblazer, you have to do something new. All of these women are iconic because they have shaken the status quo to its core. Ultimately, that is what it has always meant to be a Black woman in America. It means we fight. We support. We create. We chisel our way into a society that has not willingly made room for us. We transfix ourselves by telling stories that defy society's master narrative, poisoned by racism and sexism. And here is the best part: we do not stop there. We hold each other up as we face the overwhelming tsunami of struggle, and we do what we can to lead others along the path that we have found to be painful, yet bearable and necessary. In other words, we "lift as we climb."

The Black women in *TRAILBLAZERS* have "made a way out of no way," a popular expression from the Black community. In the context of this introduction to Volume 1, I use this idiom to explain that Black women cultivated and shared their talents with American society and, in many cases, the world, all while navigating racism and sexism. In most cases, it is classism; in some instances,

PHOTO: Maya Angelou poses for a portrait during an interview in Washington, D.C. Photo by Craig Herndon, The Washington/Getty Images (1974).

heterosexism; and in other situations it may be colorism, but too often it is all of the above. This is what happens in a society that was built on their backs, while repeatedly ignoring, understating, or appropriating their groundbreaking contributions. These fierce Black women make me delighted beyond measure to share their ancestry. By default, I feel as though I come from true greatness, and consequently, I am possible of greatness.

TRAILBLAZERS celebrates not only what it means to be great but how that greatness is intrinsically tied to struggle, resilience, determination, inspiration, hope, faith, agency, and a connection to one's community, society, and the world. The ripened relevance of these women's significance has been made evident due to the paradoxical sociopolitical moment in which we are embedded. Notably, our 45th president has publicly and unapologetically proclaimed that White supremacists are "very fine people,"[1] and yet simultaneously, we have elected more women of color to Congress than ever before[2] in American history. Furthermore, Black women comprise almost 75 percent of the Black population enrolled in graduate studies,[3] yet in 2018, transgender Black women were murdered at higher rates than any other transgender demographic.[4] Simply put, we have made monumental progress, yet concurrently, we have an enormous amount of work to do in the name of equity and inclusion. Ironically, this is the case in a society that frequently boasts of equality and boundless opportunities if one merely "works hard," despite mounting empirical evidence that directly debunks this declaration.[5] In other words, we need change, and change does not materialize without people who are willing to shatter the status quo, despite the sacrifice and hardship this always entails. It is why we need more trailblazers.

Approximately three decades ago, intersectionality was introduced as a theoretical, epistemological, and methodological framework in critical race studies that would more accurately and comprehensively capture the multiple, coexisting realities of women. A Black woman pioneer in her own right, Kimberlé Crenshaw coined this term in 1989 and would change the way inequality was analyzed, both among academics and, eventually, in mainstream society. Intersectionality presents a sophisticated argument about how oppression functions for groups who endure more than one system of domination (for example, Black women, who experience institutionalized racism and sexism).

Crenshaw's term is markedly different from traditional theoretical frameworks of oppression, which is why it is significant. She maintains that incorporating an intersectional lens is the best way to combat structural inequality because it recognizes intra-group diversity of opinions and lived experiences, which inherently de-centers essentialist notions of what it means to be a woman. Intersectionality helps us to understand what Black women have faced and continue to face in American society, and consequently, how their accomplishments are even more outstanding, considering that they achieved greatness, all the while slaying the twin dragons of racism and sexism. They made being both Black and female mean something that it was never meant to mean in America. As such, we truly embody author Toni Morrison's wise words, "Definitions belong to the definers, not the defined."[6]

I am proud to have these innovative, bold Black women to look up to and share an important identity with them. We need to remind ourselves of the lesser told stories of those who have helped make America great—against epic odds—while enduring multiple forms of oppression in a society that was not designed for our success or inclusion in a meaningful way. It is our hope that this series is a reminder of where we come from and how we not only survive but flourish, create, and contribute as a way to experience joy and connect with others. Most importantly, as Black women, I want us to hold onto what it means to be human even when we are denied our fundamental rights.

This series was developed to implore you to think very intentionally about how you are "tamed" and "trained" by the society and world in which you live. In the words of the poet Nikki Giovanni, "We write because we believe the human spirit cannot be tamed and should not be trained."[7] The legends who are profiled in this volume—and honestly, scores of countless Black women who are not featured herein—have made America great *precisely* because they held their human spirit in such high regard that they resisted the "taming" or "training" that society imposed on them to preclude their genius from germinating.

In this first volume of *TRAILBLAZERS*, which centers around Black women who have bravely and successfully left their mark in activism, dancing, and sports, we meet highly regarded historical figures like Harriet Tubman, Raven Wilkinson, and Ora Washington and contemporary sheroes/heroines such as Michelle Alexander, Misty Copeland, and Serena Williams. By featuring women who blazed the trail and those who have followed, *TRAILBLAZERS* underscores the common thread that these women face across career, time, and space. This book also explains how each woman was received by mainstream White America in ways that are inextricably tied to racism and sexism.

As you flip through these pages, a dominant pattern emerges: many Black women icons have been either rendered invisible and erased from American history, or their stories are inaccurate or incomplete. One quickly realizes that many of these Black women helped make America great without much of the fanfare that many of their White female and Black male counterparts have enjoyed throughout American history. Notably, these women did their work with humility and grace. They trailblazed through American society because it was work that needed to be done and was the morally courageous and noble thing to do. *TRAILBLAZERS* humanizes American history and honors these women by portraying them as real people with whom readers can easily identify and relate to.

For example, take Sojourner Truth, a go-to for Black History Month. Her "Ain't I A Woman?" speech is even more extraordinary when you consider that Dutch was her native tongue; Truth learned to speak English at the age of twenty-nine.

Truth's "Ain't I A Woman?" speech was not the only one she gave, and she occasionally traveled on lecture tours across the country. A Black woman born in 1797 into enslavement became a traveling lecturer in her second language, and one of her speeches is still referenced to this day. If that is not a trailblazer, I do not know what is. As spoken word artist Kyla Jenée Lacey—another incredible Black woman—poignantly proclaims, "We learned your French. We learned your English, your Spanish, your Dutch, your Portuguese, your German. You learned our nothing...you call us stupid."[8]

The women's and civil rights movements are often proudly referenced as examples of how American society has been brought closer to social justice. But the unambiguous truth is that had it not been for the passion, leadership, energy, and organizational skills of Black women, these movements would not have unfolded in the ways that they did. The lack of proper credit given to Black women leaders is why the concept of intersectionality exists. For example, Coretta Scott King, Myrlie Evers-Williams, and Betty Shabazz have become known mostly for being the wives of civil rights warriors. Yet, they were warriors in their own right, despite having their contributions perpetually eclipsed by their husbands' legacies and tragic deaths. Other women were activists in ways that have rarely been woven into the American public's imagination. Rosina Corrothers Tucker was one of the first Black labor organization's key organizers, and Peggy Shepard is one of the first environmental justice activists to focus on communities of color. Pauli Murray, a gender non-conforming feminist, was the first Black woman to earn her Juris Doctorate from Yale University and wrote States' Laws on Race and Color (1951), which became known as the "Bible" among civil rights lawyers. Why do we not hear these names during Black History Month? Perhaps now, with the publication of this volume, we and our children will.

Michelle Alexander was born in 1967, the same year as the landmark U.S. U.S. Supreme Court case that outlawed legal restrictions of interracial marriages. She was born to a White mother and Black father, which we have in common. Alexander impressively penned The New Jim Crow: Mass Incarceration in the Age of Colorblindness in 2010, a New York Times Best Seller for almost 250 weeks. In her work, she argues that mass incarceration—the experience of imprisonment, coupled with the subsequent institutional and interpersonal discrimination upon release—is the newest rendition of the second class citizenship status to which African Americans have been relegated.

I was in graduate school when Alexander's book was published and was first told about it by a British student who wanted to complete an independent study with me based on her book. As we read it, not only did it open this White British student's eyes, even though he was fully cognizant of America's racial inequality, but it compelled me to rethink my own family's experience with the criminal justice system by acknowledging the profound emotional impact an incarcerated family member has on a family system. I was able to see my brother, who had been incarcerated from 2000 to 2002, was killed in 2003, through fresh eyes that helped me better understand his life, my enraged reaction to his life-altering (and later, life-ending) decisions, and ultimately helped me heal. On a national level, Alexander's work sparked a much-needed and overdue conversation in American society about our criminal "justice" system and how it interlocks with racism, classism, and a general disregard for human life. In her work, she warns us, "...history will judge us harshly. A human rights nightmare is occurring on our watch" (Alexander 2010).

Speaking of nightmares, on May 25, 2020, the reprehensible, knee-for-a-noose lynching of George Floyd by police officer Derek Chauvin occurred in public in Minneapolis over the course of 8 minutes and 46 seconds. Three other officers in uniform who are trained and paid to "protect and serve"—according to the words plastered across their vehicles—did nothing of the sort. They let a Black man die, slowly and painfully, gasping for air and screaming for his late mother, at the hands of a White law enforcement officer. A brave seventeen-year-old Black girl filmed the public execution and woke White America up to the fact that "being while black"[9] is, and has always been, deadly. As a result, protests exploded across the U.S. and around the world. This brazen abuse of White institutional power and White privilege is a well-documented, centuries-long pattern in this nation. Alexander offered her expertise in the thick of the movement. She guides and cautions us: "We must face our racial history and our racial present...We must reimagine justice...We must fight for economic justice... If we fail to take these obvious steps, our democracy will remain in peril even though Mr. Trump was defeated in November. Police killings, uprisings, and riots will remain a recurring feature of American life."[10] She outlines the haunting trend of racial progress, brutal backlash, purportedly "improved systems," and ultimately, an unchanged America.

What does Floyd's death have to do with Black women? Two months before Floyd's death, Breonna Taylor, a medical worker, was murdered by Louisville law enforcement officers in a disastrous drug raid. Police in plainclothes forced themselves into her home and murdered her. The police, who claimed they announced themselves, entered the wrong home. Her partner—a lawful gun owner—fired a warning shot and phoned 911, begging for help.[11] Sergeant Mattingly, who was hit in the leg, later admitted to firing "at least six rounds in response."[12] Thirty-two rounds later, according to FBI ballistic data, Taylor was dead. Six bullets ended her life. On September 23, 2020, a grand jury indicted one police officer on three counts of wanton endangerment, but none were charged for Taylor's death.

Perhaps what is more disconcerting is that Taylor's death did not receive the same level of national and international attention as Floyd's until later in the year. Although these police murders are different, the collective American response illuminates a pattern that Kimberlé Crenshaw elucidated in her 2016

TED Talk, "The Urgency of Intersectionality": Black women and girls who have been killed and assaulted by police officers have been eerily absent from the conversation of police brutality, even among academics and women's advocacy groups. It is worth noting that many of the public figures who demanded justice for Taylor's death are also Black women: Oprah Winfrey, Michelle Obama, and Kamala Harris.[13] As you consider what you will do to change America as the unforgettable Black women in this volume have endeavored to, I ask that you #SayHerName and recognize that "Black women and girls as young as nine and as old as ninety-three...have been killed by the police."[14]

I am often asked if I was not an educator and researcher, what would I be? A dancer, I say this without hesitation. This surprises many. As much as I love talking and made a career out of my words—spoken and written—there is something magical about communicating entirely with our bodies, not with our mouths. There is a remarkable level of discipline that dancing requires, including exercise routines, dietary decisions, and mental fortitude. For that reason, I have a reverence for dancers. Black women dancers have mastered bodily movement in monumental ways. Josephine Baker was the first Black artist to perform in front of a racially integrated audience. Katherine Dunham, a trained anthropologist, brilliantly blended ballet with Caribbean folk movement, which is now globally recognized with distinction as the "Katherine Dunham Technique." Fast-forward to the twenty-first century to Michaela Mabinty DePrince, who danced her way to the Dutch National Ballet as a soloist after becoming the youngest dancer in the history of the Dance Theatre of Harlem. She achieved all of this despite being orphaned in war-torn Sierra Leone.

Some dancers outsmarted racist and sexist systems by passing as White or Latina and then trained scores of Black children with the knowledge and techniques they gained clandestinely. Some women refused to perform in segregated venues, which cost them professionally but left their activist values intact. Essentially, they fought for not only themselves but for their community, and in doing so, they made personal sacrifices for the greater good. In a staunchly individualistic society, this is nothing short of exceptional. And *that* is what makes America great: facilitating opportunities for others because we are all members of a thriving ecosystem. These women transformed the way we move and remind us that creativity sees no color or gender. But despite these moving stories, I cannot help but wonder who is missing from the dance world? Which dance prodigies went undiscovered because their talent was not cultivated, and they got caught in the crosshairs of racism and sexism in ways that trapped them indefinitely? How is society valuing different forms of dance, and how is that tied to systems of oppression?

For over a century, African American women have been making their mark on sports. As sport-obsessed as our culture is, how many Americans know that Lusia "Lucy" Harris-Stewart was drafted in 1977 to the National Basketball

Association (NBA), holding the distinction of being the only woman drafted in the history of the NBA? In the 1950s, Toni Stone, considered the first African American woman to play professional baseball, played in the Negro Leagues. Talented, daring, and savvy, Stone lied about her age to improve her opportunities, left a team that did not pay her fairly, and refused to be sexualized by wearing a skirt while playing. A biography in 2010 and an Off-Broadway play produced in 2019 helped assure that Stone is no longer a footnote to history.

Before the astonishing tennis phenoms Venus and Serena Williams, there was Althea Gibson, the first Black player to compete in the United States Tennis Association (USTA). Before Gibson, there was Ora Washington, whose talent inspired President Franklin D. Roosevelt's administration to bring tennis courts to urban America. Before Washington, African Americans were not allowed to participate in the USTA. Rather than giving up on tennis altogether, Black doctors, professors, and businessmen responded to overt racism by creating our own league, the American Tennis Association (ATA), in 1916. Persistence, resilience, and creativity. These are the key ingredients of greatness.

Nicknamed "The Tornado, the fastest woman on earth," Wilma Rudolph was the first woman and African American to earn three gold medals in track and field in a single Olympics. Rudolph was chronically ill as a child, suffering from polio, yet with training, tenacity, and talent, she grew up to break records and barriers alike. Dominique Dawes was the first Black woman to win an individual Olympic medal in artistic gymnastics. I remember watching her on television as a little girl in my leotard in the 1990s, beaming with pride and in absolute awe of her skill and greatness while feeling connected to her, even though I was not a gifted gymnast. Once in foster care, Simone Biles performed her way to become the most decorated American gymnast of all by the tender age of nineteen. Her work ethic and accomplishments are inspiring, and being the torchbearer that she is, I cannot wait to see how she shapes the future of gymnastics.

The women in TRAILBLAZERS are the very definition of spectacular. What is more revolutionary than their success is their inclination to impact and inspire people internationally by using their gifts and success as a platform to invest in others. Let us not forget that Harriet Tubman suffered from seizures, yet she guided multiple expeditions that freed enslaved people. Armed with a gun, an unwavering faith in God, and an unparalleled sense of direction, she sang songs about the journey to freedom. Consequently, Tubman earned the name "Moses" and a bounty on her head, yet she prevailed. The visionaries in this volume enriched the opportunities and quality of life for innumerable individuals, families, communities, and nations, which is particularly noteworthy in a society that highly values individualism and competition, and does not meaningfully reward collaboration or community-based success programs, much to its detriment.

These are trying times, to say the least. We have had a president who has referred to African nations as "sh*thole countries"[15] and has mocked the #MeToo movement, which he seems to be immune to, as his accusers have been referred to as the "forgotten women" of the movement.[16] He has been responsible for perpetuating White supremacy and making light of sexual trauma, which is the opposite of greatness. It is abhorrent, even more so given his powerful yet unearned position. But he also needs to know this, in the clever and empowering words of Jamaican-born spoken word artist Staceyann Chin, "...your cavalry is not nearly as committed as mine...what doesn't kill us will make our resistance stronger."[17]

I rest my case with the 2020 election results. Plenty of Americans decided that Trump's America was not "great" enough for re-election. In fact, the majority of voters chose to vote for the twenty-first century ticket, the first to include a Black and Southeast Asian woman, who more accurately reflects an increasing American reality: bi/multiracial ancestry, immigrant parents, interracial relationships, and a blended family. Vice President Kamala Harris honors her Indian mother's wise words, which are deeply relevant to this book: "You may be the first, but don't be the last."[18] It is our 400-year history, much of which is represented in this series, that laid the groundwork for Harris' ascension as vice president of the U.S.

I want to dedicate my introduction to people who have raised awareness of the terrors of racism and sexism and shown how these systems of inequity jeopardize America's potential and change the international narrative about our nation. And I want to say to the young Black girls who read TRAILBLAZERS: You are part of a formidable sisterhood, you are part of history, and you are our future. I want to thank you in advance for the beautiful and essential contributions that you will make to this country and the world. I already appreciate the inspiration that you will provide and the imaginations that you will cultivate in the years and decades to come.

In conclusion, let's follow the lead of the #SayHerName movement and say these black women's names. Let's take it a step further and rejoice in their resilience by sharing their stories. Finally, let's honor the legacies of the trailblazing Black women who have helped make America great.❖

— Chandra D. L. Waring
Boston, Massachusetts

NOTES AND WORKS CITED

1.   Felicia Sonmez and Ashley Parker, "As Trump stands by Charlottesville remarks, the rise of white-nationalist violence becomes an issue in 2020 presidential race," The Washington Post, April 28, 2019, https://www.washingtonpost.com/politics/as-trump-stands-by-charlottesville-remarks-rise-of-white-nationalist-violence-becomes-an-issue-in-2020-presidential-race/2019/04/28/83aaf1ca-69c0-11e9-a66d-a82d3f3d96d5_story.html.

2.   Drew DeSilver, "A record number of women, will be serving in the new Congress," FAC-TANK, Pew Research Center, December 18, 2018, https://pewrsr.ch/2Lp3XMa.

3.   "Blacks Making Solid Progress in Graduate School Enrollments: Women Are in the Lead," *The Journal of Blacks in Higher Education,* 2009, http://www.jbhe.com/news_views/61_gradschoolenrolls.html.

4.   "Fatal Violence Against the Transgender and Gender Non-Conforming Community in 2020," The Human Rights Campaign. https://www.hrc.org/resources/violence-against-the-trans-and-gender-non-conforming-community-in-2020.

5.   Jonathan J.B. Mijs, "Inequality is getting worse, but fewer people than ever are aware of it," *The Conversation,* May 2, 2017, https://theconversation.com/inequality-is-getting-worse-but-fewer-people-than-ever-are-aware-of-it-76642.

6.   Toni Morrison, *Beloved: A Novel* (New York: Alfred A. Knopf Inc., 1987).

7.   Nikki Giovanni, *Sacred Cows—and Other Edibles* (New York: William Morrow & Co, 1988).

8.   Kyla Jenée Lacey, "White Privilege" @WANPOETRY, Write About Now, YouTube Video, 3:38, August 2, 2017, https://www.youtube.com/watch?v=Qkz5UmXugzk.

9.   Laura J. el-Khoury, "Being while Black: Resistance and the Management of the Self." Social Identities 18, no. 1(2012): 85. https://www.tandfonline.com/doi/abs/10.1080/13504630.2012.629516.

10. Michelle Alexander, "America, This, is Your Chance," *The New York Times,* June 8, 2020, https://www.nytimes.com/2020/06/08/opinion/george-floyd-protests-race.html.

11. Christina Carrega and Sabina Ghebremedhin, "Timeline: Inside the Investigation of Breonna Taylor's Killing and its Aftermath," *ABC News,* November 17, 2020, https://abcnews.go.com/US/timeline-inside-investigation-breonna-taylors-killing-aftermath/story?id=71217247.

12. Richard A. Oppel, Jr., Derrick Bryson Taylor, and Nicholas Bogel-Burroughs, "What to Know about Breonna Taylor's Death," *The New York Times,* October 30, 2020, https://www.nytimes.com/article/breonna-taylor-police.html.

13. "Breonna Taylor: What Happened on the Night of Her Death?" *BBC News Online,* October 8, 2020. https://www.bbc.com/news/world-us-canada-54210448.

14. "#SayHerName Campaign," The African American Policy Forum (AAPF), Accessed on December 5, 2020. https://aapf.org/sayhername.

15. Kendi X. Ibram, "The Day Shithole Entered the Presidential Lexicon," *The Atlantic,* January 14, 2019, https://www.theatlantic.com/politics/archive/2019/01/shithole-countries/580054/.

16. MJ Lee, "Donald Trump's Accusers: The 'Forgotten Women" of the #MeToo Movement," *CNN,* July 19, 2019, https://www.cnn.com/2019/07/19/politics/donald-trump-accusers-me-too-movement/index.html.

17. "StaceyAnn Chin Performs 'Tweet This, You Small-Minded M**********r," Video, *Up Magazine* (Nairobi) Urban Suite Jazz, https://www.urbansuitejazz.com/return-to-categories/13-poets-corner-see-all/1401-up-magazine-staceyann-chin-performs-tweet-this-you-small-minded-m-r-in-nairobi.

18. "US Senator Kamala Harris Speaks at Spelman: Remaining Undaunted by the Fight," Spelman College: *News and Events,* August 26, 2018, https://www.spelman.edu/about-us/news-and-events/kamala-harris.

"It's not about supplication, it's about power. It's not about asking, it's about demanding. It's not about convincing those who are currently in power, it's about changing the very face of power itself."

—Kimberlé Crenshaw
"Women, power, and peace" presented at the Omega Institute, Rhinebeck, NY 2007

activism

Black Women Are the Foot Soldiers of the Civil Rights Movement

"I have learned over the years that when one's mind is made up, this diminishes fear; knowing what must be done does away with fear."

—Rosa Parks (*Quiet Strength*, 2000)

FROM THE MOMENT THAT BLACK WOMEN were enslaved and brought to America's shores, we have played significant roles in the ongoing struggle for freedom, equality, and our rightful share of the American dream. Beginning with the abolitionist movement, Black women have always come together to champion causes that promote equal justice for all. They have organized and led struggles to end slavery, anti-lynching laws, the right to vote, fair housing, equal access to education and healthcare, and to obtain full employment for themselves and their men. (Crawford, Rouse and Woods 1993). We took on activism as a means of survival, whether through individual acts or under the leadership of civil rights activists.

As Black women in America, we learned about race, gender, and class barriers, including the legacy of slavery, very early on. To survive, Black women created a psyche of resistance against racial and gender oppression and other societal forces that exist to this day. However, even after breaking free from bondage, gaining citizenship after the Civil War and civil rights movement during the 1960s, systemic racism has continually prevented us from attaining the right to pursue a life of liberty and happiness.

While Black women have always been at the core of organized African American life, their influence within American culture has often gone unrecognized. Even today, as our lives constantly remain at risk, Black women negotiate their place in an American society that continues to depict them as childlike, aggressive, hypersexual, and violent. We always had to work hard to escape these stereotypes while fighting for justice, equality, and peace, even as we opened doors for everyone else.

Not all Black women activists are famous. Many faceless and nameless women—our mothers, grandmothers, aunts, sisters, and daughters—worked

PHOTO: Rosa Parks booking photo taken at the time of her arrest for refusing to give up her seat on a bus in Montgomery, Alabama. Universal History Archive/Getty Images (1955).

tirelessly to keep their families intact and create a path forward for the next generation, contributing to America's greatness. In fact, an awful lot of civil rights organizing took place while preparing and eating food, or sitting on porches shelling beans and drinking lemonade. Few people had cars, let alone telephones, so messages were sent by word-of-mouth. They were the foot soldiers of the civil rights movement. *Willingly, they always answered the call.*

In time, Black women created and relied upon an extensive grassroots network embedded in local institutions such as women's clubs, churches, beauty parlors, and sororities. They especially tapped into historically Black colleges and universities (HBCUs) because they offered a primary network of Black intellectuals and middle class youth, which would grow into a significant social base for civil rights activists and organizations (Starks 2011). They used their businesses as a safe space for community building and as an incubator for political activism (Gill 2010). By the mid-twentieth century, Black women quickly found themselves on the front lines of boycotts, voter registration drives, demonstrations, sit-ins, and other acts of civil disobedience that often landed them in jail—or worse. *Still, they persisted.*

Yet, even though Black women have been at the forefront of political and social activism, many found themselves on the receiving end of harsh criticism inside and outside of the Black community—particularly from Black men. Navigating racism and restrictive gender codes has always been, and continues to be, perilous terrain for Black women activists.

As historians began to revisit the story of the civil rights movement in the late twentieth century, they recognized that while male leaders were credited with the movement's success, the energy and support supplied by Black women had been hushed in historical texts. Without the women, it is highly unlikely that the civil rights movement would have garnered the same outcome as we know it. In an attempt to right this wrong, an unprecedented number of Black women scholars have emerged, publishing papers and books about many of these unsung sheroes and forgotten souls. They are also introducing us to the many sites of struggle that Black women activists organized around.

In recent years, a nascent movement of African Americans has formed with young people in the vanguard, leading to the unmistakable rise in the power of Black women. Inspired by recent social movements that often require policy changes and political solutions, this new generation of activists, who have easier access to communication and funding resources, are flourishing. Many women are experimenting with new, innovative ways to better align their organizations with their values to create movements within communities where everybody is invested and is playing a role. More importantly, they are unapologetic in their demands for equity, justice, and true liberation for all.

The women activists presented here, like civil rights icons Harriet Tubman, Rosa Parks, and Pauli Murray, connect to these modern-day activists who should be viewed as part of this continuing process. Women like Peggy Shepard, Dorceta E. Taylor, Leah Penniman, Glynda C. Carr, and LaSaia Wade represent environmental, food sovereignty, voting rights, and gender equity issues centered around the civil rights activism of today. They proudly carry on the legacy of the women before them, including some who may not be as well-known, but still helped change the history of their communities and this country.

By doing the work to protect their freedom and their families, as well as bolster our democracy, Black women have always been truth-tellers and justice seekers throughout our history. Without question, Black women are standard-bearers who transcend race and class. What follows is a reminder of our activism, how much power we have, and how strong our voices can be.

◆ ◆ ◆

BLACK WOMEN ACTIVISTS made their first official appearance during the abolitionist movement to end slavery. Abolitionism was a radical movement shaped by the refusal of African Americans to accept enslavement. Many Black women worked closely with White women, and together, they waged an assault against slavery as early as the Constitutional Convention in 1787, which intentionally excluded the fate of slavery and suffrage from the Constitution.[1] The notion of Black and White women working together was regarded as an abomination and created widespread anger and hostility toward the abolitionists. Women were supposed to be quiet, submissive, and apolitical, but these women dared to speak out. In fact, only a small minority of Northerners actually supported the anti-slavery cause, and these women were often met with public disrepute and mob violence (Olson 2002).

As the nineteenth century progressed, abolitionists formed many anti-slavery societies. Although some Quakers were slaveholders, they were among the earliest to protest the African slave trade. Collectively, these groups sent petitions to Congress, held abolition meetings and conferences, boycotted products made with slave labor, printed mountains of literature, and gave innumerable speeches for their cause. Although the abolitionists were unable to bring about racial justice, and White abolitionists were fully unconscious of their own racism, the movement pushed a reluctant nation toward egalitarian goals (Harrold 2014). Black women, however, found themselves struggling in both Black and White spheres. For example, some Black men openly opposed the equal participation of women in the civil rights movement, and did not perceive women's rights as a means to achieve racial solidarity. As Black women grappled to gain acceptance

1.   The Constitutional Convention took place from May 14 to September 17, 1787 in Philadelphia to decide how America was going to be governed. Members of the convention agreed that woman suffrage should not be specifically included in the Constitution, and that a condemnation or prohibition of slavery should not be written into the Constitution. The members believed, for the most part, that the purpose of a new constitution was to forge a political union, not a moral union, and that moral considerations should be left to the individual states, not to the national government.

in the dominant White culture, they had to adopt many of the values of White society—which was symbolized by male dominance and female subordination—in order to meet their goal and to help bring slavery to an end (Yee 1992).

Most early Black women activists were freeborn and had access to education, wealth, or other resources, allowing them to freely organize. The Fortens, led by wealthy sailmaker James Forten and his wife Charlotte Vandine Forten, were among the most prominent black families in Philadelphia. They used their wealth and social standing from the mid-nineteenth to the early twentieth centuries to found and finance at least six abolitionist organizations. The couple had many children. The most notable were Harriet Forten Purvis, Margaretta Forten, and Sarah Louisa Forten Purvis, often referred to as the "Forten Sisters," who continued their families' activist traditions.

Harriet was a conductor on the Underground Railroad and opened her home as a haven for fugitive slaves. In later years, she worked and lectured for the Black suffrage movement. Margaretta worked as a teacher for nearly thirty years and supported the suffrage movement by touring and giving speeches, as well as helping to obtain signatures for petition drives. Sarah, a writer and poet, wrote numerous poems and articles for William Lloyd Garrison's abolitionist newspaper *The Liberator* under the pseudonyms "Magawisca" and "Ada" (Sterling 1997).

Charlotte Forten Grimké, daughter to James and Charlotte Forten's son, Robert Forten, was an abolitionist, educator, poet, translator, and influential activist and leader on civil rights. She was a member of the Salem Female Anti-Slavery Society, where she was involved in coalition building and fundraising. Grimké was a cofounder of the Colored Women's League in Washington, D.C. and assisted in forming the National Association of Colored Women.

Since the American Anti-Slavery Society would not allow women to become members, all of the Forten women and fourteen others cofounded in 1833 the Philadelphia Female Anti-Slavery Society (PFASS), the first American biracial organization of women abolitionists.

Frances Ellen Watkins Harper was a teacher, poet, and writer, as well as the first African American woman to publish a short story, the director of the American Association of Colored Youth, and the superintendent of the Colored Sections of Philadelphia. As an influential abolitionist and suffragist, Harper, committed to the temperance movement, was also a member of the Women's Christian Temperance Union (WCTU), a biracial organization committed to expanding federal power after Reconstruction. When she became disillusioned by the WCTU, Harper joined the newly formed national Black women's organization, the National Association of Colored Women (NACW) (Parker 2012). She assisted in the Underground Railroad and lectured on the abolitionist circuit, committed to training the next generation of activists (Stancliff 2010).

Sarah Parker Redmond was an abolitionist, suffragist, lecturer, and physician. She delivered speeches throughout the East Coast against slavery and raised money for the abolitionist movement. A member of the American Anti-Slavery Society, she traveled to Britain to gain support for the growing abolitionist movement in the U.S. and eventually went to Italy to pursue medical training, where she became a physician. Redmond practiced medicine for nearly twenty years and never returned to the U.S. Maria W. Stewart, recorded as one of the first American woman to address a public audience of women and men, wrote pamphlets and speeches for *The Liberator* until she retired in 1833. She publicly criticized the behavior of Black men and advocated for economic independence and education for all women, regardless of race (Yee 1992).

Sarah Mapps Douglass, the daughter of the distinguished Black abolitionist family, the Bustills in Philadelphia, was a founding member of the PFASS and an active member of the Female Literary Association (FLA), a safe space for intellectual political ideas and the social-well being of African American women (Lindhorst 1998). She also published articles in *The Liberator* and the *Anglo-African Magazine*. Mary Ann Shadd Cary, the first Black woman publisher in North America, was a teacher and lawyer who used her newspaper to promote the abolitionist and suffrage movements.

These women's activities demonstrated a larger trend that began to emerge among politically active Black women, especially after Reconstruction. Determined to hold the government accountable to civil rights, they involved themselves in issues and organizations that helped refocus attention on the possibilities of gaining federal power (Parker 2012).

But it was the formerly enslaved Black women who offered the public eyewitness accounts of the suffering they experienced that bolstered the abolitionist movement. Sojourner Truth and Harriet Tubman, the best-known activists of this period, are credited with creating the groundwork for Black women activists to follow.

As activists, Truth and Tubman held distinctly different viewpoints, but shared some common ground: they were both born into slavery. Neither could read or write, but each impacted this nation with their stories of trial and triumph. Truth worked to abolish slavery, promote equal rights for women, and eradicate the use of alcohol. On the other hand, Tubman dedicated her life to creating safe passage for the enslaved to escape to freedom.

It should be no surprise that, more often than not, these differences usually reflect a conservative or liberal position. For example, W. E. B. Du Bois and Booker T. Washington held different views on how African Americans should achieve racial parity. Du Bois supported a liberal stance, which challenged Blacks to be politically active and push for integration, whereas Washington advocated for a more conservative approach, encouraging education, entrepreneurship, and self-reliance rather than directly challenging segregation. The philosophical difference that existed between Truth and Tubman revolved around how to end slavery.

Truth was a patient and obedient slave. Although she escaped to freedom, she believed slavery could end peacefully by moral persuasion, though conceded it would take time. Deeply religious, Truth became a willing activist and gave speeches around the country at abolition meetings and women's rights conventions to build sentiment against slavery. Before she gave a speech, Truth sang hymns to relax a hostile audience. When she spoke of the emotional and physical suffering she endured as a slave, the audience was moved to tears. In 1864, she met President Lincoln and told him he was doing a good job (Mabee 1995).

In contrast, Tubman was a disobedient slave who fought back when her slave owners beat her. She had no patience with slavery. After escaping, Tubman undertook a personal crusade against slavery by helping her relatives and anyone else willing to travel the Underground Railroad to freedom. Unlike Truth, Tubman used hymns as a code to alert the enslaved when it was time to leave. She also carried a revolver, which she pointed at the head of any runaway slave who wanted to turn back. Tubman believed President Lincoln was dragging his feet over freeing the enslaved and had no desire to meet him (Larson 2004).

When Truth and Tubman finally met in Boston in August of 1864, Truth tried to persuade Tubman that President Lincoln was a real friend to African Americans. Tubman insisted he was not because he allowed Black soldiers to be paid less than White soldiers (Mabee 1995). Years later, Tubman regretted not meeting President Lincoln, because she was impressed by his kindness towards Truth and felt she was perhaps too harsh in her assessment of him (Larson 2004).

It is probably Tubman's radical approach that has made her more popular than Truth and is the reason why she is often cited as one of the greatest Black women activists of her time. Rather than leading herself to freedom and living her life in relative comfort, she fought to end slavery by helping over seventy enslaved people to freedom. Her selfless acts inspired generations of African Americans who struggled for equality, among them the countless Black women who have served and continue to serve their communities for justice and peace.

Truth and Tubman have helped deepen our understanding of the coexistence of different ideologies. Their stories also help deconstruct the false narrative that suggests that all Black women think alike and played subservient roles in movements for liberation and resistance, or were absent altogether.

◆ ◆ ◆

BOTH THE SUFFRAGE AND CIVIL RIGHTS MOVEMENTS had their roots in the abolition organizations of the early 1800s, and they shared many members, goals, and methods. However, despite these early commonalities, by the latter half of the century, the two movements would face each other as adversaries. The White suffragists began to cultivate increasingly divergent goals and tactics in the late 1860s, which challenged their relationship with Black women who desired to fully participate in the democratic process.

The suffrage movement began to gather steam in the 1840s, emerging from the broader movement for women's rights. The first women's rights convention convened in 1848 in Seneca Falls, New York. Organized by Elizabeth Cady Stanton, Lucretia Mott, Mary Ann M'Clintock, Martha Coffin Wright, and Jane Hunt, they laid out a list of rights that women could not enjoy at the time, such as the right to attend college, own property, or enter male-dominated professions like medicine and law. Together, they presented the Declaration of Sentiments, which called upon women to fight for their constitutionally guaranteed right to equality as American citizens. Nearly 300 people were in attendance.

While the Declaration of Sentiments critiqued gender inequality in the U.S., it obscured significant differences in women's lived experiences across racial, class, and regional lines. For example, the Declaration of Sentiments was being written at the same moment Native Americans were being displaced to create space for westward expansion. Ironically, it was matrilineal Native societies that inspired the suffragists, and they were often referenced in their claims that American women deserved greater autonomy. Moreover, while African Americans in New York were but a mere generation removed from slavery, there is no evidence that Black women participated in the convention, making it painfully obvious that they were rendered nearly invisible and would be left to labor in the suffragist vineyard. (Terborg-Penn 1998). Ironically, men were invited to participate in the convention, and Frederick Douglass was one of thirty-two men who signed the Declaration of Sentiments as a pledge to support universal suffrage.

During the antebellum period, Black women had already supported universal suffrage when the power of the vote was exclusively for White men. Black women like Harriet Tubman and Frances Ellen Watkins Harper began to speak on behalf of the suffrage movement (Kent 2016). In 1866, Stanton, Mott and Susan B. Anthony, among others, created the American Equal Rights Association (AERA) to promote political rights for African Americans and women. This sentiment would change during Reconstruction.

After the Civil War, some states passed black codes, which had their roots in the slave codes that had formerly been in effect and severely limited African Americans' rights. The codes appeared primarily throughout the South as a legal way to put Black citizens into indentured servitude. They controlled where and how they worked and lived, how and where they traveled, and seized their children for labor purposes. The legal system was further stacked against them, with former Confederate soldiers working as police officers and judges. This made it difficult for African Americans to win court cases and ensured that they were subjected to black codes. The Reconstruction Act of 1867 weakened the black codes' effect by requiring all states to uphold equal protection under the Fourteenth Amendment, particularly by enabling Black men to vote.

In the meantime, divisions among the suffragists over strategy erupted over the Thirteenth, Fourteenth and Fifteenth Amendments. These three amendments passed after the Civil War transformed the suffrage movement. The Thirteenth Amendment, passed in 1865, made slavery illegal. Enslaved Black women were freed and gained new rights to control their labor, bodies, and time. In 1868, the Fourteenth Amendment affirmed the new rights of freedwomen and men, stating that everyone born in the U.S., including former slaves, was an American citizen. No state could pass a law that took away their rights to "life, liberty, or property." However, the Fourteenth Amendment explicitly mentioned gender—the first reference to it anywhere in the Constitution—when declaring that all male citizens over twenty-one years old can vote. In 1870, the Fifteenth Amendment affirmed that the right to vote "shall not be denied...on account of race."

The insertion of the word *male* into the Constitution and the enfranchisement of African American men presented new challenges for the suffragists because it extended political power to Black men but not to women—that is, White women. The emphasis on *male* was no accident; it was added *because* of the suffrage movement (Roberts 2017).

White women activists bitterly fought about whether to support or oppose the Fifteenth Amendment. Stanton and Anthony objected to the new law. They wanted women to be included with Black men. Others—like Lucy Stone—supported the amendment as it was. She believed women would win the vote soon. These developments led White women activists to turn the focus on woman's suffrage to a new constitutional amendment enfranchising women (Roberts 2017). From this disagreement, two rival national suffrage organizations emerged. In 1869, Anthony, Stanton and others formed the National Woman Suffrage Association (NWSA), and Stone and Harper led the formation of the American Woman Suffrage Association (AWSA). The hostile rivalry between these two organizations created such a partisan atmosphere that it endured for decades, affecting even professional historians who study the women's movement (DuBois 1978).

It should be noted that in 1869, Douglass, who never wavered in his support of the suffragists, publicly disagreed with Stanton and Anthony's opposition to the Fifteenth Amendment just because it precluded voting rights to White women. On the other hand, some suffragists further argued that White women were more qualified to vote than Black men and allied with opponents of Black suffrage (Dudden 2014). While earlier suffragists believed African American rights and suffrage could be linked, the passage of the Fourteenth and Fifteenth Amendments forced a division between Black and White women. Seeking a political vote for themselves, White women turned their backs on Black allies who had fought with them for women's rights and to end slavery (Olson 2002).

However, it was the Compromise of 1877, an unwritten deal that was informally arranged by Congress, that disrupted Reconstruction efforts. Under the Compromise, the intensely disputed 1876 presidential election of Republican Rutherford B. Hayes would be resolved by the Electoral Commission with one vote. In return, Hayes would appoint at least one Southern Democrat to his cabinet and back the construction of a transcontinental railroad in the South. More importantly, Hayes would remove the federal troops whose support was essential for the survival of Republican state governments in South Carolina, Florida, and Louisiana. This meant that the Civil War amendments would not be enforced, and African Americans would not be protected.

What followed was the removal of Black men from political office and the expansion of Jim Crow, representing a formal, codified system of racial apartheid that would dominate the American South for three-quarters of a century. In the depression-racked 1890s, racism appealed to Whites who feared losing their jobs to Blacks. Politicians abused these fears to win the votes of poor Whites. Newspapers fed this bias to White readers by frequently making up Black on White crimes. When the U.S. Supreme Court laid out its "separate but equal" legal doctrine of facilities for African Americans in *Plessy v. Ferguson* in 1896, Reconstruction's tragic end was sealed. Jim Crow was upheld, and segregation became a way of life and the law of the land. These laws affected every aspect of public life, mandating segregation of schools, parks, libraries, drinking fountains, restrooms, buses, trains, and restaurants. "Whites Only" and "Colored" signs were constant reminders of the enforced racial order.

This could not be clearer than during the Woman Suffrage Parade in 1913. This first suffragist march in Washington, D.C. was organized by Alice Paul and Lucy Burns for the National American Woman Suffrage Association (NAWSA) to support a constitutional amendment guaranteeing women the right to vote. Black women were discouraged from participating with the rationale that it could cause a rift with delegations from Southern states and offend White supporters (Roberts 2017). So, even though the right to vote was no less important to Black women, they were told they should stay away. *Do not come. We do not want you here.* Only after telegrams and protests poured in from dissenters were Black women allowed to march, but with unexpected ultimatums: they would not be included in the official program, and they were encouraged to march at the back of the parade.

The request was a deeply political and sadly strategic one. While over 5,000 women marched, only a few African American women participated, including women from Delaware, Illinois, Michigan, New York, and Washington D.C. Some Black women did manage to march with their state delegations or their respective professions, though. Distinguished civil rights leaders like Mary Church Terrell participated in the march. Members of the Alpha Kappa Alpha Sorority marched, but did not do so as a group, unlike the Delta Sigma Theta Sorority, who marched together. The outspoken journalist and anti-lynching crusader Ida B. Wells-Barnett, cofounder and leader of the Alpha Suffrage Club of Chicago (believed to be the first Black women's suffrage association in the U.S.), objected strongly to a segregated parade. Wells-Barnett waited until the parade gallantly emerged from the crowd and took her place with the Illinois delegation.

Minutes after the parade began, the crowd, many of them men, spat at the marchers, grabbed their clothing, hurled insults and lit cigarettes, snatched banners, and tried to climb their floats. The police did little to keep order. Over one hundred marchers were taken to the emergency room by the end of the day, and a troop of cavalry from nearby Fort Myer was dispatched to control the crowd.

In its aftermath, the parade signaled the final round in the long fight for the vote. It energized a new generation of activists and sowed the seeds for more visible, aggressive tactics over the next seven years. That being said, it also drew a line in the sand between Black and White suffragists and exacerbated the patriarchal strain between Black women and Black men.

Black men had always argued that because they were responsible for protecting their families, a Black woman's priority should be to support them, especially when it came to fighting against racial discrimination. *This is a historically complex issue.* Looking at this from a Black male perspective, White men succeeded in doing everything they could to oppress Black men during slavery: they raped their women, separated their families, and prevented them from defending their families. After slavery legally ended, the criminalization of Black men began in earnest in American society, perpetuated by myths, stereotypes, socially sanctioned lynchings, and racist ideologies, all hammered down by segregation and Jim Crow. While Black women suffered as well, these discriminatory practices were primarily targeted at Black men. The key to the segregationists' success was to make it difficult for Black men to economically provide for their families, which was not only an attack on their manhood, but also mangled the female and male relationship in Black families. As a result, in the midst of this psychological warfare, the family-building role was thrust primarily onto Black women. Today, this demonization continues to unfold before our very eyes as we witness White police officers use the chokehold, an enforcement mechanism developed to keep Black men in their place and murder them without repudiation. For this reason, some Black men, in reimagining their male identity, adopted sexist attitudes and behavior to make up for being emasculated by White society. *Black women have always understood this.*

To further complicate matters, White women, particularly from the South, feared violating one of society's rigid taboos: working together with Blacks. After the Civil War, White women in the South were actually more ardent than their men when it came to blatant racism. They bemoaned equality for Blacks and promoted the idea of The Lost Cause—the transmutation of the South's defeat into a romantic, heroic crusade (Olson 2002). They instilled beliefs in racial hierarchies in their children, built national networks, promoted White supremacist politics, built monuments glorifying the Confederacy, and played a pivotal role in the rise of post-World War II conservatism, which shaped the rise of the New Right. This went on for decades and reverberates to this day (McRae 2020).

Black women, who held dual oppressive positions in society as Black and female, often felt they had to choose. Between the civil rights and suffrage movements, where did Black women fit in? They had always been the backbone of the civil rights movement, but their contributions were de-emphasized by the movement's leaders. Black men adopted a patriarchal ideology that prevented Black women from assuming public leadership roles, but when Black women flocked towards any of the feminist movements, White women would ignore the unique challenges African American women faced.

Since they believed that race was a more pressing matter, Black women focused their efforts on the civil rights struggle despite experiencing marginalization and sexism in their communities (Standley 1993). Staunch suffragists like Anna Julia Cooper underscored to Black women that their vote would counter the belief that Black men's experiences and needs were more important than theirs (May 2012). In the meantime, White women and Black men sought power for themselves within the rules of this existing patriarchy, rather than uniting across race and gender to challenge White male dominance. *Black women were left out in the cold.*

Unwelcomed in the mainstream suffrage movement, Black women organized at the national level to accomplish their goals for change, and toward the end of the nineteenth century, they began to create local women's clubs. These organizations were central to their support of the suffrage movement. For example, influential educator and activist Mary Church Terrell founded with fellow activists the National Association of Colored Women (NACW) in 1896. The NACW became the largest organization of local Black women's clubs in the country. Terrell served as NACW's first president and used that position to advance social and educational reforms. Club members circulated petitions calling for women's suffrage and worked in political campaigns to obtain the ballot. In 1916, the NACW passed a resolution supporting the women's suffrage amendment and created the Equal Suffrage League, which mobilized the women's clubs nationwide to support the movement (Fradin 2003).

Terrell and Wells-Barnett, who used her skills as a journalist to shed light on the conditions of African Americans throughout the South, became more deeply and publicly engaged by the early 1900s. Their participation in the civil rights movement, like many others, was encouraged by the newly legislated Amendments. While the Fourteenth Amendment dismissed the U.S. Supreme Court's 1857 *Dred Scott v. Sandford* decision—which stated that a Black man, even if born free, could not claim rights of citizenship under the federal constitution—it was undermined in 1896. The Court ruled in *Plessy v. Ferguson* that racially segregated public facilities, if equal, did not violate the equal protection clause of the Fourteenth Amendment. The irony here is that *separate was never equal.*

It was the *Plessy* ruling that became the impetus for civil rights activism. Besides joining clubs, many women became active in the National Association for the Advancement of Colored People (NAACP), founded in 1909, whose founding members included Terrell and Wells-Barnett. They also filed lawsuits, participated in boycotts, wrote articles, published books, and traveled on lecture tours. Because of their outspoken and divergent viewpoints regarding the civil rights and suffrage movements, these Black women activists faced public disapproval, even from Black men. But despite these sentiments, new leading voices committed to social change and economic justice continued to emerge.

Women gained equal voting rights in the U.S. when the Nineteenth Amendment was ratified in 1920. Black men, who had been given the vote in 1870, had already been disenfranchised by state-sanctioned voter discrimination laws and paramilitary violence. As White supremacy reigned victorious particularly throughout the South, the White suffragists had little appetite to fight discrimination on behalf of Black women. As this debate ensued, the marker of superiority switched from Christian to "White." The American public began to equate whiteness with goodness, beauty, and freedom, while consigning blackness to evilness, ugliness and slavery. After abolition, race did not diminish in importance; instead, it increased during the struggle for a new social order (Painter 2011). It would take nearly fifty years and a civil rights movement consisting of Black women in supporting roles before the Black community would become fully enfranchised through the Civil Rights Act of 1964 and the Voting Rights Act of 1965.

Meanwhile, Black organizations flourished. Civil rights activist Mary McLeod Bethune founded the National Council of Negro Women (NCNW) in 1935 to improve the quality of life for African American women and their families (Robertson 2015). Today, the NCNW exists as a nonprofit organization that performs outreach through advocacy, research, and social services in the U.S. and Africa. In 1946, after the Montgomery League of Women Voters barred Black membership, Mary Fair Burks founded the Women's Political Council (WPC) in Alabama. The WPC became famously known for supporting Rosa Parks and initiating the Montgomery Bus Boycott (Robinson and Garrow 1987). Black women were persistent in their attempts to meaningfully engage with the women's and civil rights movements because they felt it was essential to fight for their rights both as women and African Americans. If they could not work alongside White women, they formed their own organizations and did it themselves.

◆ ◆ ◆

ACTIVISTS LIKE ELLA BAKER represent yet another path to activism. Baker was a strong and principled woman who worked as a field organizer for the NAACP in the 1940s. By the end of World War II, her efforts helped the NAACP significantly grow its membership in the South. In 1957, when Martin Luther King Jr. founded the Southern Christian Leadership Conference (SCLC), Baker joined and became its first "temporary" executive director. During her tenure, she often bumped heads with the men in the organization, especially with

King, who balked at the notion that a woman may have ideas beyond his own. When sit-ins, mainly led by college students, swept the South, Baker signed on with the recently formed Student Nonviolent Coordinating Committee (SNCC), where she served as a mentor to a new generation of student activists (Ransby 2005).

During the 1930s and 1940s, activists like Baker and Pauli Murray were also linked to the nonaligned Black left, which consisted of Black women writers, journalists, artists, and activists. This included women like Grace P. Campbell, Esther Cooper Jackson, Louise Thompson Patterson, Marvel Cooke, Claudia Jones, Shirley Graham Du Bois, Alice Childress, Lorraine Hansberry, and Charlotta Bass, who were among a group of radicals often referred to as "Black left feminists" (McDuffie 2011). None of them fully embraced the term "feminist," but most of them adopted a world perspective that connected the fight for racial justice to liberation struggles in Third World nations (Blain and Gill 2019). To push through an equal rights agenda, they joined left and labor organizations, including the Southern Negro Youth Congress, the Communist Party USA (CPUSA), the National Negro Congress, the Civil Rights Congress, and the National Negro Labor Council. These groups were mainly active in the North until anti-communism and Cold War repression during the 1950s decimated their numbers.

Throughout the South, Black women mobilized, energized, protested, and served as bridge leaders for the rest of the community. Bridge leaders foster ties between the movement, the community, and its political strategies, often working behind the scenes to effect changes the movement sought to achieve (Robnett 1997). For example, Daisy Bates, a publisher and activist, created an NAACP youth chapter in Little Rock, Arkansas, and later provided support to the "Little Rock Nine," who desegregated the high school in 1957.

Septima Poinsette Clark used her association with the Highlander Folk School to spread the concept of citizenship education throughout the South. Clark led Highlander's Citizenship Education Schools, which trained over 25,000 people to read so they could pass literacy tests and register to vote. The program was eventually transferred to the SCLC because the state of Tennessee threatened to, and successfully did, close the schools (Clark 1990). When Fannie Lou Hamer was denied the right to register to vote in Ruleville, Mississippi, she became a field secretary for SNCC. Later on, she was the driving force behind the Mississippi Freedom Democratic Party (MFDP), which challenged the all-White state delegation at the 1964 Democratic National Convention in Atlantic City (Lee 1999). Diane Nash was instrumental in organizing and leading the Nashville sit-ins while studying at Fisk University, and became active in SNCC. Black women led and inspired. They were responsible for bridging their community to civil rights leadership and the greater cause (Olson 2002).

Rosa Parks' popular image as the tired seamstress who refused to give up her bus seat to a White person is far from the neophyte that many believe her to be. She attended workshops at the Highlander Folk School during the 1930s and had been active in her local NAACP for years (Hanson 2011). Parks' act of refusal struck a chord with millions of Black women who were tired of being verbally abused and physically assaulted. If the boycott had been merely a protest about segregation, it probably would have shattered, but Parks' action struck at the very heart of Black womanhood. As a result, women became pivotal in initiating this movement and sustaining it into a yearlong boycott.

This iconography extends to all women of the civil rights movement. Leaders like Baker were overlooked until work by African American women scholars introduced them. Even though they achieved far more than their husbands, Coretta Scott King, Myrlie Evers-Williams, and Betty Shabazz, are frequently seen as dutiful widows dedicated to preserving their husbands' legacies. It is not surprising that Pauli Murray, the gender non-conforming activist and legal scholar who coined the term "Jane Crow," is rarely mentioned despite being highly instrumental during the civil rights movement. Murray worked alongside King but was critical of the lack of female leadership within his organization and the movement. Her book, *States' Laws on Race and Color* (1951), has often been referred to as the "bible" of *Brown v. Board of Education*, the U.S. Supreme Court ruling that declared "separate but equal" unconstitutional. Murray's maneuvering through circles of law, politics, and religion illustrate how Black women, even as they were on the precipice of gaining political rights, continued to develop a power that kept them nimble, and in the end, made them more effective (Jones 2020).

For many years, Angela Davis, who became a major figure when she was charged with kidnapping and murder and later became a fugitive, seemed frozen in time as a 1960s brand of so-called "radical chic." Since then, Davis has been recognized for the extensive scholarship she has created on economic, racial and gender issues, and social justice. In recent years, her ideas which were once deemed too radical for mainstream political thinking have bubbled to the surface, transforming a new generation of activists.

The 1960s would become the bellwether of the civil rights movement. Activists were met with the Kennedy administration's grudging attitude, the South's hostility, beatings, lynchings, jailings, the Ku Klux Klan, the White Citizens Council, and a series of assassinations (Olson 2002). It would bring together Blacks, Whites, Native Americans, Latinos, Asians, Northerners, Southerners, and the young and old. Although Black men dominated positions of leadership, their success was always contingent upon the organizational skills and leadership of Black women.

◆ ◆ ◆

THROUGHOUT THE COURSE OF HISTORY, African Americans, both individually and collectively, have challenged racial discrimination in the workplace and fought for better-paying jobs, though with varying degrees of success. Certainly, Black women saw the labor movement as a means for economic justice and freedom.

African Americans have been involved in labor organizations from the very beginning. They have been workers since they first arrived on the shores of the North American continent. At first, they labored as slaves and indentured servants, which helped the country experience economic growth. By the time African Americans were allowed to join the workforce, racism and discrimination prevented them from gaining equal pay and benefits.

In 1850, Frederick Douglass helped organize one of the country's first Black labor unions, the short-lived American League of Colored Laborers (ALCL), in response to Black workers' difficulty in joining White-led unions. A collective for skilled free artisans, the ALCL was undermined by the rise of craft unions, which tended to exclude Black workers.

Even when the National Labor Union (NLU)—the nation's first national labor federation, founded in 1866—declared that it would admit members regardless of race, affiliate unions continued to exclude Black workers and limit competition for jobs. Owing to the failure of integration, African Americans were urged to form separate unions. In 1869, the first national Black labor union, the Colored National Labor Union (CNLU), was established. When Frederick Douglass was elected president in 1871, the CNLU became more political and less engaged in trade union activity. They ceased operation in 1872 (Moreno 2008).

Founded in 1869, the Knights of Labor (officially Noble and Holy Order of the Knights of Labor) was the first mass organization of the working class. Although the Knights accepted African American women and employees as members after 1878, the organization tolerated segregation of the South. Nevertheless, African Americans supported the Knights because it organized workers by industry rather than craft, which meant unskilled workers could join (Berry and Blassingame 1982). In 1887, the Knights ceased operation due to employer backlash. The inheritor of the Knights was an interracial union, the Industrial Workers of the World (IWW). From its formation in 1905 until its destruction in the 1920s, the IWW made their principle of racial equality more explicit by recruiting African Americans, but raised the fear of socialism and violence at the same time. While African Americans liked the fact that the IWW took clear stands against segregation, they also shared the bourgeois aspirations of their White counterparts, so the union's appeals of socialism fell on deaf ears (Moreno 2008).

Simply put, unions believed Black workers would take jobs away from White people. This ideology haunted the labor movement for generations, and for years employers capitalized on racial division by recruiting Black workers as strikebreakers. Most unions virtually ignored the problems of racism and segregation until the mid-1930s, when labor activist A. Philip Randolph, and President Franklin D. Roosevelt, locked horns over discrimination in the workplace (Berry and Blassingame 1982).

The American Federation of Labor-Congress of Industrial Organizations (AFL-CIO) is the largest leading confederation of U.S. trade unions. Founded in 1886, the AFL-CIO was first known as the AFL. Then it splintered into two separate unions due to organizational disputes, which resulted in the creation of the CIO in 1935. Although the AFL preached a policy of egalitarianism regarding African Americans and women, it never really adopted a strict inclusion policy. On the other hand, the CIO leadership undertook serious efforts to suppress hate strikes, educate their members, and support the Franklin D. Roosevelt administration's tentative efforts to remedy racial discrimination in war industries with the Fair Employment Practices Committee (FEPC). The CIO membership's relatively bold attack on segregation directly contrasted to the timidity and racism of the AFL, which is why most African Americans and women in the labor force signed with the CIO whenever possible (Zieger 2000).

What is not widely known is that Black women have always played an enormous role in the labor movement, going as far back as 1866 with the founding of Mississippi's first trade union and the Washerwomen Strikes of Jackson. These efforts were repeated in Atlanta in 1881 when twenty women organized the Washing Society Trade Union. When they went on strike, 3,000 women joined them and it ended up being an unlikely success. Lucy Parsons, the anarchist firebrand, cofounded three influential radical unions, including the IWW, to challenge the AFL. The IWW advocated for "industrial unionization," whereby all workers in a given workplace could join the same union. They also promoted the overthrow of capitalism, and the formation of all workers' allegiance, regardless of race or sex (Renshaw 1999).

The greatest battle for a Black labor union was during the Great Depression, when the climate was not favorable towards unionized labor nor African Americans. Founded in 1925, the Brotherhood of Sleeping Car Porters (BSCP) was the country's first African American-led labor organization. It represented passenger railway workers known as "Pullman porters," who worked for the Pullman Company. The company had a virtual monopoly on railroad sleeper cars, which they manufactured, owned, and operated from the mid-nineteenth to mid-twentieth centuries.

During the 1920s, the Pullman Company was the nation's largest single employer of Black men, many of them formerly enslaved. Its financial success was due, in part, to a profit margin that barely paid its employees. When the porters decided to make another effort to organize, they hired A. Phillip Randolph, a labor organizer not employed by Pullman Company and, thus, beyond retaliation from the company. Over the next twelve years, the BSCP fought a three-front battle against the Pullman Company, the AFL, and the anti-union, pro-Pullman sentiments of the Black community. A major development happened in 1928, when the AFL decided to grant federal charters only to individual BSCP locals. They refused to give an all-Black union a full-fledged international charter. Although

BSCP officials wanted an international charter, they realized that they needed the AFL's support and took what they could get. The AFL finally granted BSCP the international charter it had initially desired in 1935. In 1937, BSCP won its first contract. Dissatisfied with the AFL's racial policies, the BSCP joined the CIO in 1938. In time, BSCP represented a significant breakthrough for African Americans in their quest for equal employment opportunities.

Most people, however, do not realize that the BSCP was a predominantly male trade union that was run by women. In the late nineteenth century, most of the larger unions created a ladies' auxiliary, whose members consisted of union members' wives, daughters, sisters, and mothers. They helped build and sustain the union by playing a central role in organizing labor issues and disseminating them to the broader public. They fed thousands on the picket lines, initiated letter-writing campaigns to improve worker safety, and collectivized around social issues such as health care. These women were usually unpaid but became a viable and powerful force in the early twentieth century's labor movement. Ultimately, the ladies' auxiliaries' activities helped empower working class families and resulted in a higher standard of living, which led to the formation of the middle class (Chateauvert 1998).

In the case of the BSCP, its Ladies' Auxiliary was established in 1925, six weeks after the union became official. Its founding merely formalized what Rosina Corrothers Tucker, a lifelong civil rights activist and the wife of a Pullman porter, had been doing all along: organizing for the porters' union. The porters worked long hours and had little time for union activities. Many also feared that they would lose their jobs if their employer learned of their union involvement. On behalf of the union, Tucker visited some 300 porters at their homes in the Washington, D.C. area to distribute literature, recruit members, and collect dues. As a founding member of the Ladies' Auxiliary, Tucker created a full calendar of social and educational programs for the porters' wives and families. The Ladies' Auxiliary educated other women and children about the labor movement, staged consumer protests, and organized local and national civil rights campaigns ranging from the 1941 March on Washington to school integration to the Montgomery Bus Boycott. They also formed chapters across the U.S., Mexico, and Canada (Chateauvert 1998).

Interestingly, BSCP's male leadership regarded the Ladies' Auxiliary as nothing more than a body of wives, when, in fact, they were a collective voice in the labor movement and national politics, creating the groundwork for the civil rights movement. While the Pullman maids and other female union members claimed the union, they were told to join the Ladies' Auxiliary. Denied fair representation with too few women members to win elective offices in the union, BSCP officials often treated their concerns casually. Surprisingly, the Ladies' Auxiliary also ignored them. The women shared the belief of the times that when men earned good wages, women did not have to work. BSCP duplicated the gender conventions of the day by confining women's participation as workers and wives of union men to the Ladies' Auxiliary (Chateauvert 1998).

Randolph's plans for a March on Washington, D.C. in 1941 successfully pressured President Franklin D. Roosevelt to issue Executive Order 8802, which banned discrimination in companies under contract with federal agencies in the defense industry. Over time, competition from the CIO forced the AFL to moderate its stance on racial equality. After the AFL and the CIO finally resolved their differences, they merged in 1955 to become the AFL-CIO. A Civil Rights Department was created within the federal government to build upon the committee's work to abolish racial discrimination.

In the ensuing years, the Ladies' Auxiliary would adjust to shifting definitions of womanhood in order to maintain a place in the union. The porters' wives wanted to vote in the BSCP elections. The Pullman maids and other female union members appealed for better working conditions and equal pay. Eventually, by 1957, BSCP dissolved the Ladies' Auxiliary. Its demise resulted in several consequences, namely the indifference and hostility of BSCP officers to women's activism (Chateauvert 1998). But the women of the Ladies' Auxiliary achieved a political voice that did not exist in the pre-*Brown* era. Now free of the limitations imposed on them by BSCP, many of the women joined new organizations to continue their work (Chateauvert 1998). In the meantime, Randolph was made a vice president and member of the combined organization's executive council. He remained president of BSCP until 1968.

Even outside the ladies' auxiliaries, Black women had long defended their rights as American workers, even when they had to do it alone. Sylvia Woods, a laundry worker, life-long member of the Communist Party USA (CPUSA), and union activist, participated in one of the first sit-down strikes of the Great Depression. In 1934, Dora Lee Jones helped establish the Domestic Workers Union (DWU) in Harlem. During the 1930s and 1940s, Velma Hopkins helped mobilize 10,000 workers into the streets of Winston-Salem, North Carolina, to bring a union to R. J. Reynolds Tobacco Company. The union, called Local 22 of the Food, Tobacco, Agricultural, and Allied Workers of America, was affiliated with the CIO, and was integrated and led primarily by African American women. They pushed the boundaries of economic, racial, and gender equality. In the 1940s, they organized a labor campaign and a strike for better working conditions, pay, and civil rights. While Local 22 faced setbacks from red-baiting and the power of R. J. Reynolds' anti-unionism, it gained national attention. Although it forced the White power struggle in Winston-Salem to relax the rigidities of segregation, Local 22 ultimately failed to slay the giant. While the union would fold after enduring McCarthyism attacks in the late 1940s, it managed to influence a generation of civil rights activists. Interestingly enough, to this day, R. J. Reynolds' employees have voted against union representation (Korstad 2003).

Sue Cowan Williams represented African American teachers in the Little Rock School District as the plaintiff in *Morris v. Williams*, a case that challenged salary rates based solely on skin color. The lawsuit was filed in 1942, following a 1941 petition filed with the Little Rock School Board demanding equal pay between Black and White teachers. Williams won the case on appeal in 1943. Years later, Dorothy Lee Bolden, who started working as a domestic at the age of nine, founded the National Domestic Worker's Union (NDWU) in 1968, which, at its height, represented 30,000 members. Unfortunately, these women were the exception rather than the rule, and for the most part, Black women were largely excluded from meaningful participation in most unions.

The enactment of segregation, and the rise of the Ku Klux Klan and White Citizens Council, harmed African Americans economically. By the 1940s and 1950s, Black women began to openly organize and challenge this racist system in the U.S. by taking part in what would later be considered the start of the modern civil rights movement. There were consequences for such actions that came in the form of economic reprisals and unemployment, public beatings, and even murder. Nevertheless, the freedom to go anywhere they wanted, attend certain schools, live in certain neighborhoods, vote, and receive equal pay had been denied for far too long.

At some point, the unions began to realize that their segregated policies were self-defeating. By refusing to admit African Americans, employers could turn to them as nonunion laborers to bring down wages or work as labor scabs during strikes to pressure the union. In the mid-twentieth century, union leaders began to look beyond their prejudices and saw that solidarity across racial lines made sense. Organized labor also began backing the civil rights movement by providing financial resources, legal support, publicity, and lobbying efforts in Congress. The convergence of the manufacturing boom, the civil rights movement, the CIO's organizational efforts, and the success of Randolph and the BSCP provided a platform for Black women leadership.

Although segregation kept Black workers out of some of the most powerful labor unions in the U.S., African American women like Maida Springer Kemp, Clara Day, Addie L. Wyatt, and Hattie Canty emerged to lead the struggle in the labor movement. Kemp, who was born in Panama and moved to Harlem as a child, was heavily involved in the International Ladies Garment Workers Union (ILGWU). She was eventually named the AFL-CIO's representative to Africa in 1959, making her the first African American woman to represent U.S. labor abroad (Richards 2000). Day, who served in multiple capacities for the International Brotherhood of Teamsters, including executive vice president, took her vision for community service and civil and women's rights and made them the union's vision (Copeland 2015). Wyatt, known for being the first African American woman elected as international vice president of a major union—the Amalgamated Meat Cutters Union, which later merged into the United Food and

Commercial Workers (UFCW)—worked hard to develop a union more inclusive of women and people of color (Walker-McWilliams 2016). Canty is known as the greatest strike leader in union history. She rose through the ranks of the Las Vegas Culinary Workers Union Local 226 and became its president. Canty led the longest strike in U.S. history—it took six and a half years and emerged victorious. Her leadership helped knit together a labor union made up of members from eighty-four nations (Felder 2020).

Even though they worked for White, male-led organizations, Black women took on leadership roles as local union organizers. They fought long and hard so that all working people could realize not just fundamental workplace rights, but a life of dignity and respect. Their efforts attracted thousands of women and people of color to join unions, and laid the groundwork to support the civil rights movement at its peak. They worked closely with organizations such as The Urban League, SCLC, CORE, and the NAACP to support legal challenges that would eventually produce victories like *Brown v. Board of Education,* the Civil Rights Act of 1964, and the Voting Rights Act of 1965. Black women translated these and many other public victories into concrete local results and initiatives. Their legacies have continued through modern union leaders like Arlene Holt Baker and Pierrette Talley of the AFL-CIO, Luella Toni Lewis of Service Employees International Union (SEIU), and organizers like Sanchioni Butler of United Auto Workers (UAW); Clayola Brown, union leader and president of the A. Philip Randolph Institute; Sandra Joyce Bellamy, who helped organize T-Mobile Workers United and the Communications Workers of America (TU-CWA); and Wilna Destin of Union of Needletrades, Industrial and Textile Employees and Hotel Employees and Restaurant Employees (UNITE).

Although White women have a rich history in the labor movement, Black women were perhaps the angriest, most militant, and most courageous of the working class because they felt the lash of exploitation and gender inequity even more than their White counterparts. They also knew what was at stake economically as well as socially. When my maternal grandfather was a Pullman porter and a member of BSCP, the women in my family (my paternal grandmother and maternal great aunt) were members of the International Ladies Garment Workers Union (ILGWU). My mother was a member of District Council 37 American Federation of State, County, and Municipal Employees (DC 37) in New York City. They were not necessarily activists in their unions. Still, they were proud to be union members and grateful for the job security, pay equity, and benefits of which I was a direct beneficiary. I grew up on DC 37 health benefits, and nothing pleased my mother more than taking us to the local HIP Center for our annual checkups without worrying about paying doctor bills. In the end, the union provided peace of mind to my family and others like it, both Black and White. We were part of an emergent middle class and lived the American dream.

The Black middle class was strengthened by the passage of civil rights laws in the 1960s and 1970s, which made employment discrimination illegal. Along with the emergence of affirmative action and anti-poverty programs, the job market finally began to break down racial barriers. However, a stagnated economy in the 1970s and a conservative political backlash in the 1980s and 1990s weakened the enforcement and efficacy of both laws and programs. In a process known as "capital flight," corporations moved hundreds of thousands of high-wage factory jobs from America's urban centers to suburban and rural areas in the U.S. and in countries like Mexico, India, and China.

There has been a steep decline in unionization rates among workers of all racial and ethnic groups over the past four decades, occurring in tandem with rising racial wage inequality. For example, in 1983, 31.7 percent of Black workers and 23.3 percent of the entire workforce were unionized.[2] In 2017, those numbers had fallen to 12.6 percent and 10.7 percent,[3] respectively. This is largely due to global competition, deindustrialization, and the passage of right-to-work laws in several states. But people are fighting back, especially Black women. This resulting deindustrialization has devastated the nation's inner cities, drying up employment opportunities that were once available to urban workers, both Black and White. Black women, with the highest rate of union membership among all women in the labor movement, have had the most to lose. *But things are changing.*

Witness the recent Amazon union drive. While we mourn its outcome, it showed us that the future of the U.S. labor movement is no longer the stereotypical image of White men in hard hats. Today's labor movement is part of a larger tide of multiracial labor activism that skews Black, Brown, and female. This new generation of labor activists see workplace struggle as an essential staging ground for racial and gender justice. The turn toward intersectional unionism matters because it is the new face of labor militancy in the U.S., and Black women are entrenched in this movement, every step of the way.

◆ ◆ ◆

WHILE THE DOMINANT MAINSTREAM CULTURE has played a significant role in constraining (and making invisible) African American engagement with environmental concerns, nothing could be further from the truth. In fact, African Americans have both individually and collectively challenged environmental injustice that predate today's modern environmental movement (Finney 2014). When Africans were captured and enslaved, they brought to America a deep connection to their environment. Traditional African thought sees nature as an

2.   Cherrie Bucknor, "Black Workers, Unions, and Inequality," The Center for Economic and Policy Research (CEPR), August 2016, https://cepr.net/report/black-workers-unions-and-inequality

3.   Department of Labor. "Union Members, 2020," U.S. Bureau of Labor Statistics, , January 22, 2021, https://www.bls.gov/news.release/pdf/union2.pdf.

interconnected continuum of humans and all-natural objects in harmony. They brought special skills from the places where they had lived and where they had been stolen from to the plantations, and used their knowledge of the natural landscape to escape the plantation system. Several hundred years later, Black people use their environmental know-how in the inner cities to combat the hazardous conditions they face (Glave 2010).

In the late nineteenth century, conservation, the forerunner to the environmental movement, focused on wilderness preservation, wildlife and habitat protection, and outdoor recreation. President Theodore Roosevelt set aside more federal land for national parks and nature preserves than all his predecessors combined. However, it was the publication of Rachel Carson's *Silent Spring* (1962) that energized the movement in the 1960s and led to the creation of Earth Day in 1970, which enhanced environmental mobilization. The nuclear incidents at Love Canal in Buffalo, New York in 1978 and Three Mile Island in Pennsylvania in 1979 put a spotlight on toxic contamination in local communities. This resulted in the formation of grassroots environmental organizations, which brought unprecedented public attention to environmental issues. By the mid-1970s, communities of color recognized this and organized in full force. For example, the Black Panther Party created programs that confronted inequitable trash distribution in predominantly Black neighborhoods. Similarly, the Young Lords, a Puerto Rican nationalist organization based in Chicago and New York City, protested pollution and toxic waste in their communities through their garbage offensive programs. In doing so, these and other organizations in Black and Brown communities served as a precursor to more pointed movements against what is now referred to as environmental racism.

The term "environmental racism" entered into the national lexicon after Benjamin Chavis, then executive director of the United Church of Christ (UCC) Commission for Racial Justice, used it to discuss the results of "Toxic Wastes and Race in the United States:" a national study of hazardous waste published by the Church in 1987.[4] The report exposed what African Americans have known all along; when White people began leaving industrial zones for safer, cleaner, and less expensive suburban locales, poor people, including a large swath of African Americans, were left behind in communities of depressed real estate value. They were exposed to chemical toxins in landfills and rivers, contaminated water, polluted air, and hazardous waste that compromised their physical and mental well-being. Not only did this create poor economic conditions for residents and reinforce a social formation that reproduced racial inequality, it also welcomed

---

4. "The Toxic Wastes and Race in the United States" report is a landmark study that demonstrates a direct correlation between the placement of toxic waste facilities and communities of poverty and/or color. This first report was the groundbreaking study that coined the term "environmental racism." Today, legislation and court cases refer to this term when addressing environmental issues of race and discrimination. The report was amended in 2007. https://www.ucc.org/what-we-do/justice-local-church-ministries/justice/faithful-action-ministries/environmental-justice/environmental-ministries_toxic-waste-20.

benign neglect. Local governments ignored their needs while hazardous waste facility developers and factories could freely operate in Black communities.

Black women are no strangers to the environment. Even Harriet Tubman, who led the enslaved to freedom during the cover of night, used the forest to nourish, guide, and protect her. I remember stories about my maternal great-grandmother, who was Cherokee and lived in North Carolina, shipping herbal concoctions to my grandmother in New York to care for my mother's childhood illnesses. My paternal grandmother from British Guiana grew tomatoes and other vegetables in her backyard in Jamaica, Queens. I remember how important it was not to litter, and I was frequently sent outside of our house to pick up garbage from the street. I remember the fresh produce boxes my aunts sold to the community to encourage healthy eating habits. My mother always insisted that we drink clean water, either by using water filters or, later on, bottled water. All of this was being done long before it became fashionable. We were taught to respect our environment and rely on the land to make us whole to protect our well-being.

As the primary householders in communities concentrated around toxic hazards, Black women bore a disproportionate responsibility to deal with the environmental burdens they faced. For years they have initiated and worked in community cleanup projects and participated in community gardens. By the mid-1980s, several Black women began to emerge nationally on the scene to provide environmental solutions for a green economy and cleaner energy. Since 1985, Karen Washington—a farmer, activist, and physical therapist—has taught young New Yorkers about gardening and community organizing. She is a cofounder of Black Urban Growers (BUGS), an organization committed to building networks and community support for farmers in urban and rural settings.

In 1988, troubled by the noxious odors emitted by the North River Sewage Treatment Plant in West Harlem, Peggy Shepard helped mobilize the community and became a cofounder of WE ACT. The group filed a lawsuit against New York City over the sewage plant, and four years later, won an unprecedented victory. WE ACT has grown into a nationally acclaimed and professionally-staffed environmental justice organization, with offices in New York and Washington, D.C.

Mildred McClain has been educating communities of color and fighting to protect the environment in Savannah, Georgia, for more than forty years. She cofounded and currently serves as the executive director of the Harambee House/Citizens For Environmental Justice. Founded in 1990, Harambee House serves communities at the local, state, regional, national, and international levels. McClain has created partnerships with the Department of Energy, Centers for Disease Control, Environmental Protection Agency (EPA), Agency for Toxic Substances and Disease Registry, and other community-based organizations to address public health concerns and environmental justice issues. She has also encouraged African Americans in her community to become certified in environmental fields like hazardous waste removal, soil remediation, and air monitoring. Beverly Wright, a professor of sociology, is the founder and executive director of the Deep South Center for Environmental Justice in New Orleans. The Center, founded in 1992, addresses environmental and health inequities along the Louisiana's Mississippi River (also known as Cancer Alley) and the Gulf Coast region. Wright also initiated the HBCU Climate Change Consortium and the HBCU-CBO Gulf Equity Consortium under the Center, where her students research the impact of climate on vulnerable communities.

A younger group of Black women activists have now claimed the front lines to fight to enforce environmental laws and regulations. As the first African American and the fourth woman to head the U.S. Environmental Protection Agency (EPA), Lisa P. Jackson's focus was to ensure the environmental safety of vulnerable groups such as children, the elderly, and those living in low-income housing. Jackson is no stranger to fighting for clean air and water. A graduate of Princeton University and the Captain Planet Foundation's 2012 Protector of the Earth honoree, she began working with the EPA in 1987 as an engineer. After sixteen years with the EPA, Jackson joined the New Jersey Department of Environmental Protection (DEP) as assistant commissioner and was later promoted to commissioner. Throughout her tenure, she headed numerous initiatives and programs, including the Highlands Water Protection and Planning Act, which was created to protect the Highlands located in northwestern New Jersey.

In 2009, President Obama appointed Jackson as the Administrator of U.S. EPA, where she served until 2013. Shortly after, Jackson was hired as the Vice President of Environmental Initiatives at Apple. In her new role, Jackson implemented innovative ideas and programs to reduce the massive tech company's impact on the environment. Jackson was promoted to Apple's Vice President of Environmental, Policy, and Social Initiatives, expanding her role to include education programs and government affairs.

Ife Kilimanjaro, a sociologist, is the senior network engagement director at the U.S. Climate Action Network. She was compelled to work on environmental issues after working as an elementary school principal in Detroit, where she witnessed children getting sick and missing school due to air pollution and no access to clean water. Lindsay Harper made history in 2018 as the first Black woman to become the executive director of Georgia WAND, a women-led advocacy group working to end nuclear proliferation and stem pollution. Harper believes that economic empowerment is the best tool for promoting peace.

There is an environmental crisis brewing in Black communities, a truth substantiated by a growing number of studies. In 2011, scientists discovered that counties with the worst ozone levels had significantly larger African American populations than counties with less pollution.[5] Another study, conducted by

---

5.   Marie Lynn Miranda, Sharon E. Edwards, Martha H. Keating, and Christopher J. Paul, "Making the Environmental Justice Grade: The Relative Burden of Air Pollution Exposure in the United States," *Int J Environ Res Public Health.* 2011 Jun; 8(6): 1755–1771. Published online May 25, 2011, https://www.ncbi.nlm.nih.gov/pmc/articles/PMC3137995.

the University of Minnesota in 2014, found that Black and Brown Americans live in communities laden with more nitrogen dioxide than White Americans.[6]

Despite many environmental organizations having missions that aim to meet these very challenges, they have had neither the inclination nor the commitment to work with Black and Brown communities. Some have come to believe that the poor have no interest in environmental issues. Other environmentalists believe that the Black and Brown population is the pollution problem—an idea that has existed since the beginning of nature conservation in America. Leading activist, eugenicist, and conservationist Madison Grant was one of the many thinkers during the 1920s who promoted this train of thought (Spiro 2008). As a result, nativist and eugenics theories continue to be wrapped into environmentalism and climate change. To this day, there has been a persistent tension between White-led conservationists and communities of color. Moreover, environmentalism's whiteness exists not because the movement is irrelevant to people of color, but because it primarily considers the interests of White and wealthier people to the literal exclusion of people of color. Black women—like geographer Carolyn Finney, environmental historian Dianne D. Glave, and Dorceta E. Taylor, one of the country's preeminent environmental justice scholars—have traced the origins of modern environmentalism to colonialism, the seizing of indigenous land, and the racialized conceptualization of nature as a dominated space.

Leah Penniman is a farmer, educator, author, and food sovereignty activist. She is the cofounder and codirector of Soul Fire Farm, in Grafton, New York, an Afro-Indigenous-centered community farm committed to uprooting racism and seeding sovereignty in the food system. The organization teaches farming skills and distributes life-giving food as a means to end food apartheid.

Even young environmentalists and climate activists are making their mark. Amariyanna "Mari" Copeny, also known as "Little Miss Flint," raised awareness about Flint, Michigan's ongoing water crisis at eight years old when she wrote a letter about it to President Obama. Her letter prompted a visit from the president and brought attention to the water crisis in her hometown. Today, Copeny continues to engage in fundraising efforts to support underprivileged children in her community. Nyaruot Nguany is a climate change activist who believes climate change and food production have a connection. She was a high school student when she founded Changemakers, a youth-led organization that connects diverse Mainers with mentorship and the resources needed to create a healthy environment within their communities. As a high school student, Aniya Butler began working with Youth Vs. Apocalypse, a climate activism group that brings together young people in the Bay Area to stand up for environmental justice. These young activists are committed to speaking out on racial issues related to climate change and environmental issues in the Black community.

---

6. Lara P. Clark, Dylan B. Millet, and Julian D. Marshall, "National Patterns in Environmental Injustice and Inequality: Outdoor NO2 Air Pollution in the United States," *PLOS ONE* 9(4): e94431, April 15, 2014, https://doi.org/10.1371/journal.pone.0094431.

True environmental justice requires tackling racial stereotypes and then moving forward to ensure equal protection for all citizens. Without collective action to create and broaden community partnerships that diversify our voices, we will not be equipped to confront the great environmental problems of our time. Calling out nativism, eugenic theories, and racial and gender discrimination is an essential first step toward real equality to help save both the people and the planet.

For the time being, Black women will continue to do what they have always done: protect the future of our families and communities by making the places we live, work, and play into less toxic and more equitable environments.

◆ ◆ ◆

DESPITE ALL THEY HAD ACHIEVED, and for all their work, Black women made little progress in convincing their male counterparts of their right to exercise full leadership within the civil rights movement. When the 1963 March on Washington was being planned, women were relied upon as organizers, recruited as marchers, and featured as singers; however, they were not granted a speaking voice at the March. Dorothy I. Height and Anna Arnold Hedgeman, both NCNW members, raised concerns regarding women's participation in the March with Bayard Rustin of the SCLC (Doak 2007).

To appease their concerns, A. Philip Randolph planned to say a few words about their contributions to the struggle and then invite a group of women on stage to take a bow. When the women would not relent and fought for recognition, the male leaders allowed Daisy Bates to read a speech written by the NAACP's John Marshall. Indeed, this 142-word speech, which read more like a pledge to support male leadership, were the only words spoken by a woman, at any length, during the March (Dixon and Houck 2009). Rosa Parks got to say eight words. Josephine Baker, who was also on the dais, was not allowed to speak during the official program. Parks and Lena Horne were sent back to their hotel because Horne was trying to get Parks press coverage for being the person behind the civil rights movement, not Martin Luther King Jr.

Clearly, the civil rights leaders, who relied upon and coveted these women and their hard work, had great difficulty moving beyond the belief that women were second class citizens. Not only did they ban the women from speaking, they also directed them to March separately behind the men. In an otherwise magnificently staged event, the "Tribute to Women," which should have been a token gesture of solidarity, turned into a spontaneous display of sexism. After the March, when the leaders made their way to the White House to meet with President Kennedy, the women were left behind (Cole and Guy-Sheftall 2003). *This exclusion created a moment of clarity.*

Quiet as it has been kept, Mary McLeod Bethune scheduled a debriefing with the NCNW the day after the March to discuss and assess the treatment women received both during the March and in the overall movement (Collier-Thomas and Franklin 2001). NCNW held a second meeting in November 1963 where Murray spoke of women's critical roles in civil rights work, only to be rebuffed at the March (Jones 2013). During that moment in history, the larger issue then became apparent that, as Black women dealt with the civil rights struggle, they also needed to simultaneously address sexual discrimination from their men. Up until this point, Black women prioritized fighting racism over sexism (Standley 1993). This moment provided clarity, and the women began to tie their civil rights work into their feminist and working class perspectives.

Johnnie Tillmon, a welfare mother in Los Angeles and an early pioneer of addressing the needs of poor Black women, helped found ANC (Aid to Needy Children) Mothers Anonymous in 1963, one of the first grassroots welfare mothers' organizations in the country. ANC later became part of the National Welfare Rights Organization (NWRO), founded in 1966. Through these organizations, Tillmon addressed equal pay for women, childcare, and voter registration. Francis M. Beal, a member of SNCC, was one of the founders of the Black Women's Liberation Committee (BWLC) in 1968. While working at SNCC, Beal and her female colleagues became increasingly concerned about how women's issues were ignored, which motivated them to create a platform for Black women's liberation. During the early 1970s, the BWLC evolved into the Third World Women's Alliance. As the decade progressed, a younger generation of Black women would create women-based organizations to openly challenge racism and sexism.

By the late 1960s, the civil rights movement shifted gears, and a new generation of Black women came to the foreground to play an essential and influential role in the growing Black Power Movement. After the assassinations of Malcolm X and Martin Luther King Jr., the younger activists no longer saw nonviolent protests as a viable means of combating racism. They believed that desegregation was insufficient, and that only through the deconstruction of White power structures could space be made for Black voices and a collective Black Power. While different strategies and tactics existed between the civil rights and Black Power movements, their fundamental goals often converged. For example, while the civil rights movement owes its standing to *Brown v. Board of Education,* the Montgomery Bus Boycott, and the Civil Rights and Voting Rights Acts, it was Black Power activism that built the Black political machines that actually got African Americans elected into office, in addition to implementing inter-ethnic student and faculty activism at many universities.

This younger generation of women held leadership roles in various Black nationalist and political organizations while fighting against sexism from their male members. Notable leaders included Elaine Brown, the first chairwoman of the Black Panther Party; Angela Davis, leader of the Communist Party USA (CPUSA); Denise Oliver-Velez, Minister of Economic Development of the Young Lords; Kathleen Cleaver, National Communications Secretary of the Black

Panther Party; and Assata Shakur, a member of the Black Liberation Army. The U.S. government targeted all of these women for their activism.

Although Black women encountered sexism before 1966, it was not as blatant and combative as it was during the Black Power Movement. Before 1966, the anti-hierarchical and consensus-based infrastructure of organizations like SNCC provided some access to female leadership. On the other hand, while the Black Panther Party had a stated policy of gender equality from the outset, they initially had an all-male, military-like, hierarchical structure where commands were executed from the top down. In some of these organizations, male members looked down on their women leaders and accused them of emasculating them. They believed that in order to reassert their manhood in American society and for Black liberation to occur, Black women had to be dominated by and subservient to Black men. However, Black women recognized the need for women and men to work together to fight against racism and capitalism, so they worked hard towards coexistence. Against a backdrop of the deradicalization and decline of the movement, Black women succeeded in gaining more prominent roles in some of these organizations while challenging sexism and rigid gender roles (Franklin 2001).

The suffrage movement emerged from the abolition movement just as the women's liberation movement grew out of the civil rights struggle. This second-wave feminism led by Betty Friedan, and later Gloria Steinem, initially had Black women allies like Pauli Murray, Shirley Chisholm, and Aileen Clarke Hernandez, who were founding members of the National Organization for Women (NOW) in 1966. However, by the early 1970s, many Black women felt alienated by the main planks of the movement, which primarily focused on a woman's right to work and the expansion of reproductive rights. Earning the power to work outside the home was not seen as an accomplishment by Black women since they had always had to work to support their families. Nevertheless, what frustrated them the most was that the women's liberation movement continued to do what the suffrage movement did before it: hinder the involvement of Black and Brown women due to racist sentiments, and create a narrow set of goals that favored White middle- and upper middle class women.

When the Black Power Movement went into decline in the mid-1970s, many women continued their fight within a heightened Black feminist movement. Newly-formed organizations such as the Third World Women's Alliance and the National Black Feminist Organization (NBFO) sought to address issues unique to African American women, such as racism, sexism, and classism. The NBFO disbanded in 1977. Founded in 1974, the Combahee River Collective included scholars and writers such as Cheryl Clarke, Akasha Gloria Hull, Audre Lorde, and Barbara Smith. It turned out to be one of the most important Black feminist organizations because it argued that the liberation of Black women would lead to freedom for all people. Perhaps the most notable piece to come out of the

Collective was the Combahee River Collective Statement, which helped Black feminists expand on ideas about identity politics (Taylor 2017).

Even though they were invited to participate in the women's liberation movement, many women of color cautioned against the movement's focus on sexism, finding it an incomplete analysis that ignored race and class. Black women felt true liberation addressed access to education, healthcare, housing, jobs, and social justice. Mobilization efforts on the part of Latinas, and Native and Asian American women also challenged traditional feminist and civil rights organizations to broaden their representation to include a wider diversity of women's voices.

Likewise, Black LGBTQ women have always been involved in movement work and organizing. While lesbian and transgender women saw commonalities with women's liberation through the goal of eponymous liberation from sex-based oppression, many believed that the focus was too narrow to confront some of the specific issues they faced, like homophobia. They also had to rise above invisibility and illegitimacy in a racialized and heterosexual world. Several Black LGBTQ activists rose to prominence during the 1970s and 1980s. Audre Lorde, who described herself as a "Black, lesbian, mother, warrior, poet," understood that gender, race, sexual orientation, class, age, ability, and many other dimensions of identity intersected to shape a person's experience. Lorde delivered a historic address in 1983 on the twentieth anniversary of the March on Washington. She died from breast cancer in 1992 at age fifty-eight.

Barbara Smith is a Black LGBTQ activist, writer, and educator who was also influential in developing Black feminism. She was involved in the civil rights movement and helped established the Combahee River Collective in 1974. She also cofounded Kitchen Table: Women of Color Press with other lesbians of color, including Lorde, June Jordan, and Gloria Anzaldúa. The press promoted works by women of color and remained in operation until 1992. Marsha P. Johnson, a self-identified drag queen, was an outspoken advocate for gay rights in New York City. A prominent figure in the Stonewall Inn uprising in New York in 1969, she worked closely with the gay and transvestite advocacy organization Street Transvestite Action Revolutionaries (STAR) was a founding member of the Gay Liberation Front, and was an AIDS activist with ACT UP. Johnson is lauded by many as a pioneer in the transgender community—though that term did not exist during her lifetime.

Many Black LGBTQ women played significant roles during the earliest milestones of the LGBTQ movement. Besides Stonewall Inn, they already led the riots at Cooper Donuts in Los Angeles in 1959, and the Compton's Cafeteria in San Francisco in 1966. Many outed themselves by participating in legal battles against laws that discriminated against the LGBTQ community (Faderman 2016). Since they were already significantly marginalized, they had nothing to lose when they stepped forward. Some formal organizations like the Salsa Soul Sisters and Third World Wimmin Inc. (established in the 1970s and now known as African Ancestral Lesbians United for Societal Change (AALUSC)), provided mobilization and a way to be "out."

Ernestine Eckstein (also known as Ernestine Delois Eppenger), was one of the few visible Black lesbian activists in the 1960s who helped steer the LGBTQ movement. She was a leader in the New York chapter of Daughters of Bilitis (DOB), and her influence shifted the organization's focus from providing a social alternative to lesbian bars, which were subject to raids and police harassment, to supporting women who were afraid to come out. In the 1970s, Eckstein became involved in the Black Women Organized for Action (BWOA). She was one of the most progressive thinkers of her time within the LGBTQ and Black feminist movements (Baumann 2019).

Miss Major Griffin-Gracy is a Black transgender woman activist who was a participant of the Stonewall riots in New York and has always been at the forefront of LGBTQ rights. In recent years, Griffin-Gracy served as executive director of the San Francisco-based Transgender Variant and Intersex Justice Project (TGI), which advocates for incarcerated transgender women. She currently serves as the executive director of the House of GG in Little Rock, which focuses on nurturing the leadership of transgender women of color living in the South.

The LGBTQ community can be as racist as the heterosexual world, with sexism existing between lesbians and gays just as it exists between heterosexual women and men (Loiacano 1989). Black LGBTQ women found themselves a double minority: they were neither fully accepted nor understood by the White LGBTQ community or the Black community. Therefore, support that spoke to their perspective was limited. As a result, organizations were formed in order to address this. The National Coalition of Black Gays, created in 1978, was the first organization to provide a national advocacy forum for African American lesbians and gays when no other organization existed to express their views. Founded by A. Billy S. Jones, Darlene Garner, and Delores P. Berry, they held the first National Third World Lesbian and Gay Conference in Washington D.C. in 1979, which took place in conjunction with the National March on Washington for Lesbian and Gay Rights. It was renamed the National Coalition of Black Lesbians and Gays in 1984 and remained in operation until 1990. The conference spurred more Black LGBTQ people to organize.

The First Black Lesbian Conference, an outgrowth from the Washington, D.C. conference, was held at The Women's Building in San Francisco in 1980. Although there had been previous conferences supporting both lesbians and gays, the First Black Lesbian Conference was the first in the U.S. to solely support Black lesbians. Notable speakers included Andrea Ruth Canaan, Pat Norman, and Angela Davis. Each keynote speaker addressed topics related to lesbians' struggles with oppression while emerging in the feminist movement. Barnard College in New York City hosted a gathering of LGBTQ and cisgender Black women at Beyond Bold and Brave's 2016 Black Lesbian Conference: "The Evolution of Our Community," which marked the thirtieth anniversary of the first conference.

It would not be until the early 1990s that other national organizations would start to appear on the scene. Black Prides, which started as a casual gathering in 1991, grew into a national network and became a nonprofit entity renamed the Center for Black Equity (CBE) in 2012. The Audre Lorde Project was founded in 1994 to address the multiple issues impacting LGBTQ people in the Black community. The National Black Justice Coalition (NBJC), founded in 2003, is America's leading national Black civil rights organization, focused on federal public policy, racial justice, and LGBTQ equality. These organizations countered bias and stigma against the Black LGBTQ community while also raising visibility and consciousness within the Black community.

The first part of the twenty-first century emphasized transgender activism and the increased usage of terminology that questioned binary gender identification. Internet activism also burgeoned while many public spaces that had once defined LGBTQ activism (bars, bookstores, festivals) began to vanish. The usage of "queer" replaced LGBTQ identification for many younger women activists.

However, despite all the hard work that Black LGBTQ trailblazers in the 1960s and 1970s had provided to the movement, White people failed them. In the 1990s, the LGBTQ community shifted from radical action, anti-capitalism, and anti-racism to focus on assimilation and capturing the approval of the mainstream. The leaders largely became White gay men, and the people of color who started the revolution were left behind. White gay men and lesbians reaped the benefits of gay liberation and have been content to ignore the issues that people of color, the most marginalized members of their community, still face.

Nonetheless, the Black LGBTQ community has made enormous contributions in the ongoing fight for social, racial, and economic justice, even as they continue to be marginalized at all levels of society, especially in the Black community. For lesbian and transgender women, the situation is much more difficult because they live at the intersection of racism, sexism, homophobia, and transphobia. Mainstream LGBTQ organizations continue to focus primarily on White lesbians and gay men rather than transgender people or people of color. On the other hand, African American organizations have not fully embraced the LGBTQ community. They need to become more inclusive of LGBTQ rights and issues because any gains in racial justice should be shared by all.

The current crop of Black LGBTQ women activists is mobilizing more visibly than ever before. This moment is long overdue, and Black LGBTQ advocates are determined not to let it slip away. They are fully aware of this history and are doing everything possible to push for equal rights for all Black people, including gay, lesbian, transgender, and gender non-conforming women. Elle Hearns is the executive director of the Marsha P. Johnson Institute, a California-based organization founded in 2015 that advocates to end violence against all

transgender people through transformative organizing, restoration, civil disobedience, and direct action. LaSaia Wade, an open Afro-Puerto Rican indigenous
transgender woman, is the director of Brave Space Alliance, and a member of
the Chicago Transgender Nonconforming Collective and the Trans Liberation
Collective. Page May is a prison abolitionist who founded Assata's Daughters
in 2015, a Chicago-based organization created to support women, nonbinary,
and femme black activists. Zahara Green is the founder and executive director
of TRANScending Barriers Atlanta, a transgender-led nonprofit organization
whose mission is to empower the transgender and gender non-conforming
community with leadership building, advocacy, and direct services. Monica
Roberts, a pioneering journalist and transgender advocate who passed away
in 2020, chronicled the lives and murders of transgender people through her
blog when mainstream media would not. Raquel Willis, a transgender media
strategist, follows the trail blazed by Roberts by promoting social justice for
all Black women through digital activism, nonprofit media strategy, and public
speaking, using them as tools of resistance and liberation for the LGBTQ community. Simply put, these and other LGBTQ activists believe that Black lives
transcend into pride.

As the national conversation around racial justice and equality for Black
people has grown in volume and scope, many Black LGBTQ people have faced
difficult conversations about race, queer identities, or the intersection of both.
This came to light when legal scholar and social theorist Kimberlé Crenshaw
coined the phrase "intersectionality" in 1989, which argues that the experience
of being a Black woman cannot be understood in terms of being Black or being
a woman. Crenshaw felt that each concept should be considered independently while including how interacting identities frequently compound upon and
reinforce one another. Although the traditional feminist movements strived to
eradicate sexism and class oppression, they did so at the cost of ignoring race
as an inhibitor. Nowadays, activists and community organizations call for participation with different overlapping identities, including those within the LGBTQ
community. Intersectionality may seem theoretical, but it is meant to be utilized.

Crenshaw's concept is not new. Since slavery, Black women have eloquently described the multiple oppressions of race, class, and gender that
they face—referring to this concept as "interlocking oppressions," "simultaneous oppressions," "double jeopardy," "triple jeopardy," and other descriptive
terms. "Intersectionality" has become widely adopted because it manages to
encompass, in a single word, the simultaneous experience of the many oppressions Black women endure.

Just like Black women have been forced to choose between sexism and
racism from Black men and White women, many Black LGBTQ women are often
forced to choose between identifying with their blackness or their sexual orientation. The theologically-driven anti-LGBTQ rhetoric in churches has certainly

played a major role in the Black community's homophobic attitude toward the LGBTQ community. Additionally, hypermasculinity has also played an integral part in why homophobia is still significant in the Black community. To be clear, one thing is certain: racism will always prevail regardless of your sexual or gender preference. As a community, we need to address and tend to the Black LGBTQ community. Our failure to recognize intersectionality in this regard is harmful, and it unfairly rejects an entire sector of people in our communities.

Black women have always struggled with exclusion from feminist movements, and #MeToo is no exception. While Black women are no strangers to dealing with sexual harassment, their experiences are regularly relegated to the sidelines, delegitimized, and dismissed. Although the #MeToo initiative was created by a Black woman a decade earlier, the faces of the cause quickly came to represent affluent White women from the mostly rarefied worlds of Hollywood, politics, and television journalism. Yet, it is the poor and working class Black and Brown women in particular who bear the brunt of sexual harassment and abuse, and they should be able to capitalize on any gains the movement might make.

Unfortunately, many White feminists have incorrectly assumed that women of color are not interested in sexism and gender issues. *Nothing could be further from the truth.* Since White feminists have remained hesitant in recognizing intersectionality and are unwilling to include it in their platform, women of color are not inclined to work with them. However, women of color have always advocated for human rights and social justice, and they are committed to bringing an end to sexism and sexual violence for all women, regardless of their class or race.

◆ ◆ ◆

IN 2017, WHEN TRUMP VENTED about the growing number of African immigrants in the U.S., he complained about Nigerian immigrants who would never "go back to their huts." He wondered out loud why the U.S. allowed immigrants from Haiti, El Salvador, and African countries that he dubbed as "sh*thole countries" to enter the country. Trump even suggested that the U.S. should allow more immigration from majority-white Scandinavian countries like Norway.[7] In January 2020, Trump signed an Executive Order that restricted immigration to the U.S. from certain African countries under the guise of "terrorist" concerns.[8]

From rhetoric to action, the Trump administration fostered and promoted immigration policies rife with the drippings of xenophobia. Trump signed more than one Executive Order to ban Muslims from entering the country and tried

7. Ibram X. Kendi, "The Day Shithole Entered the Presidential Lexicon," *The Atlantic,* January 13, 2019, https://www.theatlantic.com/politics/archive/2019/01/shithole-countries/580054.

8. Maria Sacchetti, Abigail Hauslohner and Danielle Paquette, "Trump expands long-standing immigration ban to include six more countries, most in Africa" January 31, 2020, *The Washington Post,* https://www.washingtonpost.com/immigration/trump-expands-long-standing-immigration-ban-to-include-six-more-countries-most-from-africa/2020/01/31/413e93ec-443e-11ea-aa6a-083d01b3ed18_story.html.

to rescind the Deferred Action for Childhood Arrivals (DACA) program—actions that were disputed up to the U.S. Supreme Court. Interestingly, support for DACA has largely revolved around the popular immigration narrative that Latinos are the only ones at risk of being forced from a country they have always known as home. What seems to have been lost in the mix is that Black immigrants are also at risk of deportation if DACA is terminated.

This brings us to the "invisible" Black immigrant, who rarely comes to mind when Americans think about issues central to the immigration reform debate. In the wake of Trump's comments, it seemed Americans suddenly became aware of America's African immigrant population (Greer 2013). In 2020, more than two million Sub-Saharan African and Caribbean immigrants joined the millions of African descendants who have long resided in the nation. Today's Black population (about 13 percent of the overall population) reflects a centuries-long engagement with Africans in the U.S.[9]

While the African American population has been largely attributed to enslaved people from Africa, it should be noted that a large number of people were imported from Jamaica, Barbados, and Antigua. Even after the outlawing of the slave trade in 1808, the flow of Blacks arriving into the U.S. would continue, and Black immigrants who voluntarily managed to migrate to America's shores were mostly from the Caribbean. Many of them settled prominently among free people of color in northeastern port cities, with New York City being their top destination. Outside of the Northeast, South Florida became a major destination, mainly for immigrants from the Bahamas. While the number of Caribbean immigrants was relatively lower during the early nineteenth century, after the 1898 Spanish-American War, the U.S. emerged as a destination for Black international migrants, and their immigration numbers would continue to grow significantly. As a matter of fact, many African Americans have ancestors who were among the thousands who migrated from the Caribbean during the early decades of the twentieth century, and I am one of them.

While my mother's family comes from the enslaved, slaveholders, and the Cherokee Nation in North Carolina, my widowed paternal great-grandmother was from British Guiana (now known as Guyana). She immigrated to this country through Ellis Island from Georgetown, Demerara in 1924. Her only child, my grandmother, followed her in 1928. She married a Guianese man from Georgetown in 1931, had a daughter and a son, and became a widow five years later. My great-grandmother was a domestic and eventually worked as a cook at Montefiore Hospital in the Bronx. My grandmother became a member of the International Ladies Garment Workers Union (ILGWU) and worked as a finisher in a dress factory until her retirement. Together they raised my aunt and father,

9.   Nemata Blyden and Jeannette Eileen Jones, "Between Africa and America, Recalibrating Black Americans' Relationship to the Diaspora," *Perspectives on History,* August 20, 2020, https://www.historians.org/publications-and-directories/perspectives-on-history/september-2020/between-africa-and-america-recalibrating-black-americans-relationship-to-the-diaspora.

and they eventually bought a home in Jamaica, Queens, which remained in the family for nearly fifty years. Given the postwar preference for female immigrant workers, especially nurses and domestics, Caribbean women frequently found it easier than their male counterparts to obtain American visas. In many instances, this strengthened the hand of Caribbean women because they could sponsor their spouses' and children's immigration. It may also explain why my great-grandmother came first, and my grandmother followed later. Their story is like so many others who left the West Indies and the Caribbean to escape colonial rule and meager salaries. Despite America's racial shortcomings, they aspired to become part of the American dream.

By the 1920s, the enforcement of several national origin quota laws (the Quota Act of 1921 and the Immigration Act of 1924) disproportionately impacted Black immigrants. Although these laws aimed to restrict the immigration of Jews and Catholics from Southern and Eastern Europe, they also targeted people of color and effectively excluded Asian and African immigrants. In fact, Caribbean immigrants had arrived so rapidly in what is often referred to as the "first wave" of Caribbean migration to the U.S. (Marshall 1982) that the rate of growth of the foreign-born Black population vastly outpaced the rate of growth of native-born Black and White populations (Reid 1939). This is what prompted their near-exclusion from the country.

Under these new restrictive immigration laws, immigrants from Africa (excluding Egypt) totaled 1,100 compared to 51,227 from Germany.[10] While the number of African and Caribbean immigrants may appear minuscule compared to the millions of Europeans who arrived in America, they still undoubtedly made a historical, social, and cultural impact on the African American community. Unfortunately, immigration from those regions into the U.S. was eventually, by and large, terminated.

Each generation of Caribbean and Asian immigrants express shock when they first encountered American racism, which frequently led to their radicalization. Most Black immigrants have experienced the brutal legacy of European colonization, and those from Latin American nations have a history of slavery in their countries as well. However, many immigrants believed that in their quest to provide a better life for their families, pushing back and criticizing the nation over racism was not in their best interest. Still, a number of Caribbean immigrants contributed greatly toward the civil rights movement. Perhaps the most famous immigrant of the era was Jamaican-born Marcus Garvey. He launched the largest Black movement in history, the Universal Negro Improvement Association (UNIA), and was dubbed the "negro agitator" by the FBI, prosecuted for fraud, and deported. Certainly, their political and social activism and their fight against racism was another reason why the Immigration Act of 1924 practically prohibited Caribbean immigrants' migration to the U.S.

10. Department of Labor. Commissioner General of Immigration, , 1821-1928.

It should be of no surprise that the civil rights movement was never purely a domestic U.S.-based framework either; it was always part of a global framework with many moving parts (Gaines 2008). As early as the mid-nineteenth century, African Americans began to undertake a rather unprecedented global engagement beyond America's shores. Liberia began as a settlement of the American Colonization Society (ACS), founded by White southerners in the nineteenth-century to encourage and support the migration of free African Americans to the continent of Africa—in other words, exiled for their own good. The country was formally realized and declared its independence in 1847, becoming Africa's first and oldest modern republic (Dennis 2008). Although President Lincoln was an early supporter, the Black community and abolitionist movement were overwhelmingly opposed to the project. The mass exodus of African Americans to Liberia never materialized, and by the end of the Civil War, the movement had declined. But the seeds of internationalism were sowed, and a handful of Blacks began to relocate to Europe, Africa, and Canada to escape racism.

The courageous role Africans have played in the resistance to any form of enslavement or colonialism was appreciated among those of African descent worldwide. African Americans already had an abiding identification with the Haitian Revolution (1791-1804), which is considered the most glorious assertion of self-emancipation by enslaved Africans (Blain and Gill 2019). When Africa was overtaken by European rule, Ethiopia managed to escape their colonial yoke and defeated Italy in 1896 with the most catastrophic loss inflicted on a European power. Eventually, the U.S. would invade Haiti in 1915 and remain in control until 1934, and Ethiopia would come under Fascist Italian rule in 1936 until the end of World War II in 1941.

By the early twentieth century, while some African Americans chose to become expatriates after experiencing the inescapability of American racism, Black women activists like Eslanda Goode Robeson, Vicki Garvin, Shirley Graham Du Bois, Alice Windom, Pauli Murray, and Thyra Edwards helped espouse an Afro-diasporic, global consciousness. They created an activism that promoted universal worldwide emancipation of Black people (Blain and Gill 2019). Considered part of the Black Left, they saw themselves as self-described working class internationalists who agreed with socialist and communist ideals because they were against racism, colonization, and imperialism. Through their travels, migrations, and writings, their goal was to make political and cultural connections in far-flung places such as Europe, the Soviet Union, China, Vietnam, Egypt, Cuba, and African countries such as Ghana, Zambia, and Nigeria as advocates for internationalism. While some of these women worked together, they also worked independently to promote Black women in politics, the arts, activism, and global freedom struggles. In the process, they ended up creating a direct link between Black Power politics, Pan-Africanism, and Third World liberation (Blain and Gill 2019).

Indeed, the U.S. civil rights movement unwittingly created global connections, though they may not have been abundantly noticeable during Africa's liberation during the 1950s and the 1960s. Nevertheless, it had a profound influence on Continental Africa. The attainment of independence by African countries also inaugurated a new spectrum of racial pride among African Americans. The Bandung Conference, a meeting of emergent nations of Asia and Africa held in 1955, would prove to be a pivotal event for Black internationalism, greatly impacting the African American's struggle for liberation (Acharya and Tan 2008).

Unlike their male counterparts, Black women immigrants have not received nearly enough credit or recognition for their activism during this time. Mabel Keaton Staupers, a pioneer in the American nursing profession, immigrated from Barbados, West Indies to Harlem. She became a key advocate for racial equality in the nursing profession. Staupers was instrumental in ending the U.S. Army's policy of excluding African American nurses from its ranks during World War II, and in 1948, she successfully lobbied for full integration of the American Nurses Association. In 1951, Staupers was awarded the prestigious Spingarn Medal from the NAACP (Braukman and Ware 2004). Claudia Jones was a Trinidadian and Tobagonian-born journalist, feminist, and activist who pushed back against U.S. imperialism and forced the consideration of race and gender within critiques of capitalism. After living and working in New York, where she was an active member of the Communist Party USA (CPUSA), Jones was deported in 1955 and subsequently relocated to the United Kingdom (Davies 2008). Panamanian-born Maida Springer Kemp was a labor organizer who worked extensively in the garment industry to create labor standards in Local Union 22. She was also known for her extensive work in Africa for the AFL–CIO (Richards 2000).

A second but much smaller wave of immigration from the Caribbean occurred with the onset of World War II and lasted throughout the 1940s and 1950s. This new migration was spurred by American labor shortages during the war and expanding economic demands in the immediate postwar period. At first, many immigrants worked as farm laborers in Florida and other southeastern states, as well as in northeastern states like Connecticut, but they soon dispersed to other states and sectors of the American economy. Later arrivals were affected by the passage of the McCarran-Walter Immigration and Nationality Act of 1952. It abolished racial restrictions but still determined potential immigrants based on nationality and regional distinctions, with preference given to those from non-Communist countries and northern and western Europe.

The efforts of Black activists helped reverse these racist policies, which also paved the way for U.S. immigration policies to become open to a wider variety of migrants. Like other immigrants, foreign-born Blacks would benefit from the Immigration and Nationality Act of 1965, which emphasized family reunification and skilled immigrant labor, enacted one year after the landmark Civil Rights Act. Moreover, the Refugee Act of 1980 loosened immigration restrictions by allowing more immigrants from conflict areas such as Ethiopia and Somalia to seek asylum in the U.S. Finally, the Immigration Act of 1990 sought to increase the number of immigrants from underrepresented nations. Although the act was initially intended to increase the flow of European immigrants, Africans also benefited from the program (Greer 2013). As a result, immigration from the Caribbean and sub-Saharan Africa to the U.S. increased rapidly in the last four decades, causing a socioeconomic stratification in the African American community among its native-borns and newcomers (Hamilton 2019). Before 1965, Black people of foreign birth residing in the U.S. were nearly invisible. By the beginning of the twenty-first century, more people had come from Africa to live in the U.S. than during the centuries of the slave trade. Today, nearly one in ten Black Americans is an immigrant or the child of an immigrant.[11]

Black women immigrants continued to speak out for social justice and, more often than not, did it through the arts. Miriam Makeba was a South African singer, songwriter, actress, United Nations goodwill ambassador, and civil rights activist. Her music was eventually banned and her citizenship revoked because she spoke out against apartheid. When Makeba was exiled from South Africa, she moved to New York City in 1960 (Ford 2015).

These women also impacted politics and government service, either as immigrants or first-generation Americans. Shirley Chisholm, whose parents came from Barbados and British Guiana, was the first African American congresswoman and the first Black woman to run for president. Constance Baker Motley, the first Black woman appointed to the federal bench, had parents from the Caribbean island, Nevis. The writer, feminist, womanist, librarian, and civil rights activist Audre Lorde, whose parents came from Barbados and Grenada, also comes to mind. Lani Guinier was a civil rights theorist and the first woman of color appointed to a tenured professorship as the Bennett Boskey Professor of Law at Harvard Law School. She was inspired by her father, Panamanian-born Ewart Guinier, a labor activist, political candidate, and the first chair of Harvard University's Afro-American Studies Department. Jennifer Sandra Carroll, a Trinidadian-American Republican and retired naval officer, served as the eighteenth Lieutenant Governor of Florida from 2011 to 2013. Born to Haitian parents, Mia Love served as the U.S. Representative for Utah's 4th Congressional district from 2015 to 2019. She was also the first African American elected to Congress from Utah and the first elected as a Republican. Ilhan Omar is the first Somalian-American, the first naturalized citizen of African birth, and the first woman of color to represent Minnesota in the U.S. Congress. She is also one of the first two Muslim women (along with Rashida Tlaib) to serve in Congress.

---

11. Monica Anderson and Gustavo López. "Key facts about black immigrants in the U.S.," Pew Research Center, January 24, 2018, https://www.pewresearch.org/fact-tank/2018/01/24/key-facts-about-black-immigrants-in-the-u-s.

Today's Black immigrant organizations are pushing for political activism on a diasporic and transnational scale. The Black Alliance for Just Immigration (BAJI) was founded in 2006 by Black activists in the Oakland and San Francisco Bay areas. Their mission is to bring African Americans and Black immigrants from Africa, the Caribbean, and Latin America together to dialogue about myths and stereotypes, as well as the cultural, social, and political issues that divide our communities. The UndocuBlack Network (UBN) is a multigenerational network of current and formerly undocumented Black people that seeks to foster community and facilitate access to resources.

Kolu Zigbi is the president of African Communities Together (ACT), an organization of African immigrants fighting for civil rights and a better life for families here in the U.S. and worldwide. Zigbi's commitment to the African diaspora is inspired by her grandfather, a Liberian rice farmer and traditional town chief. Afua Atta-Mensah is the executive director of Community Voices Heard, a multiracial organization principally comprised of women of color to galvanize support for programs benefiting low-income families in New York State. A daughter of Ghanaian immigrants, she has worked in places from Ghana, West Africa to urban centers across America to improve the quality and quantity of fair and equitable housing and defend racial and social justice initiatives. Micere Githae Mugo is a playwright, author, activist, instructor, and poet from Kenya. She was forced into exile in 1982 for activism during the Daniel Arap Moi dictatorship, relocated to Zimbabwe, and then moved to the U.S. Now a literary critic and professor of literature in the Department of African American Studies at Syracuse University, she continues her activism and writing.

Denea Joseph is an undocumented Black DACA recipient and national immigrant rights activist. She immigrated to the U.S. at the age of seven from Belize, Central America. Joseph served as the vice president for the Black Los Angeles Young Democrats (BLAYD), the California Ambassador for the United States of Women (USOW), and most recently as the communications coordinator for the UndocuBlack Network (UBN), advocating for the representation of undocumented Black immigrants within the mainstream immigrant narrative.

It is no secret that tensions exist between African Americans and African and Caribbean immigrants. While there are real and consequential differences in our lived experiences, including conflicting interests that often make us stand in opposition to each other, we also share a common cause in our struggle for inclusion. As we come together culturally, we are also beginning to join forces politically to fight racism and class oppression. African immigrants typically have not accorded racism with the same social import as U.S.-born Blacks; however, the noticeable rallying of Africans in the U.S. and around the world for Black Lives Matter and the call for justice in response to George Floyd's murder represents a remarkable level of collaboration and cooperation that has been considered by many a significant development.

More than ever, African and Caribbean immigrants recognize that solidarity with African Americans does not require a rejection of their own culture, and that our differences will continue to crumble in the face of undiscriminating racism.

◆ ◆ ◆

IN 2020, OVER 400 PROTESTS sparked by the murder of George Floyd, erupted throughout the U.S. and overseas. It has been a half-century since American cities have seen such a burst of outrage. Looking at 1968 and 2020 as flashpoints in law and order makes it difficult to see what has changed and, more importantly, what has not. But the who, where, and why of 2020 cannot be boiled down to a reprise of 1968, nor can we predict sociopolitical responses by catching a glimpse of the past through our rearview mirrors. Instead, we should think about how we got where we are today, the lessons we hopefully learned, and our role in what the future should bring.

The post-civil rights era concluded when major federal legislation ended legal segregation, created federal oversight and enforcement of voter registration and electoral practices in areas with a history of discriminatory practices, and allegedly ended discrimination in renting or buying housing. At the same time, we witnessed the decline of the civil rights movement and the weakening of the push for African Americans' greater integration into mainstream American society. Several factors contributed to this development.

First, there was the passing of key civil rights leaders from the 1950s and 1960s. Those who tried to replace them lacked the leadership, talent, and charisma needed to sustain a national movement. More importantly, the civil rights movement's success in eliminating de jure discrimination in crucial areas and getting White Americans to see how it violated the nation's basic creed of equality led many to believe that civil rights were now well-settled. As a result, the interest of many African American civil rights groups and activists began to diminish as they gave more attention to the opportunities wrought by the success itself.

Female leadership also waned, either from retirement, old age, death, or changing paths and directions. By the early 1970s, Diane Nash removed herself from the national spotlight. Fannie Lou Hamer died from complications of hypertension and breast cancer at age fifty-nine in 1977. Pauli Murray died of cancer in 1985. Ella Baker worked until her death in 1986 at age eighty-three. Elaine Brown returned to school and then lived in France for most of the 1990s, later returning to the U.S. to focus on prison reform. Once Angela Davis was acquitted from three capital felonies, including conspiracy to murder in 1972, she completed her degrees, focused on scholarship by writing books, worked on social justice and political initiatives, and continued teaching. After Assata Shakur was convicted of the murder of State Trooper Werner Foerster in New Jersey, she escaped from prison in 1979 while serving a life sentence and has lived in exile in Cuba since 1984. These circumstances left a void of key Black women activists that could not easily be filled.

Organizations that led the fight for civil rights and desegregation were floundering as well. By early 1967, SNCC was approaching bankruptcy, as its liberal funders refused to support its overt militancy. It was no longer a viable organization and largely disappeared in the early 1970s. When Martin Luther King Jr. was assassinated in 1968, the SCLC leadership was transferred to Ralph Abernathy, who presided until 1977. After Abernathy stepped down, the organization suffered from leadership woes before reinventing itself as a national and international human rights organization. In the 1990s, when the NAACP ran into debt and faced scandal. Myrlie Evers-Williams stepped in as chairperson and helped rehabilitate the organization in 1995. Roy Innis, who served as National Chairman of CORE until his death in 2017, redirected the organization's mission during the 1970s to support more conservative political positions. The Black Panther Party suffered from government oppression as well as the arrests and subsequent murders of its members, which collided with internal conflict. Its demise occurred around 1982. The National Urban League appears to be one of the few organizations that have managed to transition into the new era, as it continues to promote economic and political empowerment and reduce violence and poverty in urban Black America.

During the 1980s and 1990s, African Americans faced affirmative action backlash, a crack cocaine epidemic, and an HIV/AIDS crisis that had a devastating effect on Black communities. This was compounded by modern forms of social and judicial discrimination, resulting in Blacks having the highest incarceration rates, especially in the South. On the other hand, a Black upper class had evolved at the top of the scale. Families with a median income of $50,000 began to emerge, and by 1990, they accounted for 14 percent of all Black families. However, at the same time, the median income for working class families' income began to erode. The working poor's income declined to a twenty-year low, with Black families making up to 31 percent of the demographic (Billingsley 1993). Even with some of the financial and political strides made in the post-civil rights era, African Americans found themselves facing resistance from White people who saw their advancement as robbing them of their middle class entitlement. This perpetuated a backlash and advanced a conservative movement that has become intent on reversing the entitlements of not only African Americans, but anyone who has gained civil rights—including women, immigrants, and the LGBTQ community.

While national organizations lost their power and movements faded away, Black politicians and community leaders began to support local grassroots initiatives and railed against the crack cocaine epidemic, better manage the HIV/AIDS epidemic (which continues to disproportionately impact Black communities), and combat other social ills like police brutality and housing discrimination. By the turn of the twenty-first century, the field of grassroots advocacy exploded. Previously, grassroots initiatives were defined by a "boots on the ground" strategy that involved knocking on doors to gain support for local and national initiatives, which had worked well for Black women activists in the past. However, with the advent of technology and the development of social media, the incredible value in grassroots advocacy has superseded traditional organizations, with websites, apps, emails, tweets, and their social media shares becoming a key part of their outreach strategy.

This tactic was first introduced by former community organizer Barack Obama, who ran a grassroots campaign that relied heavily on social media to help elect him as the first African American President of the U.S. in 2008. At the time of President Obama's election, African Americans had suffered disproportionate unemployment rates following industrial and corporate restructuring, with a rate of poverty equal to that in the 1960s.[12] Additionally, White America's reliable factory and coal mining jobs were disappearing, as communities became entrenched in an opioid crisis that contributed to a steady decline in the quality of life.

In 2013, a movement sprang forth when three women—Alicia Garza, Patrisse Cullors, and Opal Tometi—created and disseminated #BlackLivesMatter on social media. The hashtag was prompted after George Zimmerman's acquittal in the shooting murder of African American teen Trayvon Martin in 2012. In time, the hashtag developed into a loosely organized coalition of Black activists under the name Black Lives Matter, which became nationally recognized for its street demonstrations following the 2014 murders of Michael Brown in Ferguson, Missouri, and Eric Garner in New York City. Black Lives Matter developed into a decentralized network with an informal hierarchy of African Americans, like-minded White and multiracial activists, and grassroots advocacy groups.

Since Black Lives Matter, participants in the movement have demonstrated against numerous African Americans' murdered by police actions or while in police custody. Black Lives Matter's challenge was to figure out how to move beyond the symbolic coming together of a hashtag in order to tackle policy changes that would impact the Black community. Then, in 2015, the Movement for Black Lives was established as an umbrella organization that consists of a coalition of more than fifty movement organizations to represent the interests of Black communities across the U.S. Members include the Black Lives Matter Network, the National Conference of Black Lawyers, the Ella Baker Center for Human Rights, Color of Change, and Race Forward. Organizations such as the National Council of Asian Pacific Americans, ACLU of Northern California, and the National Council of Jewish Women showed support for the Movement for Black Lives by issuing public statements following the publication of the movement's

---

12. Jason L. Riley, "Why Obama's Presidency Didn't Lead to Black Progress," *New York Post*, June 17, 2017, https://nypost.com/2017/06/17/why-obamas-presidency-didnt-lead-to-black-progress.

controversial platform. Meanwhile, Black Lives Matter became involved in the 2016 U.S. presidential election and expanded their project into a national network. Once they recognized the underlying issues at stake, they created a crucial blueprint that normalized confrontation and direct action. But their greatest success lay in using social media as a tool for political engagement.

Yet, despite these advancements, the Black Lives activists had little support outside the communities they served, and by 2017, the movement itself appeared dormant.[13] This was due to a combination of things. Trump's election, like his campaign, brought a new fervor to efforts to crush black organizing and roll back any gains made during the Obama administration. The Trump administration sent a clear message to Black organizers that dissent would not be tolerated and would be severely punished.[14] The FBI's Counterterrorism Division designated Black Lives Matter as a domestic terrorist group,[15] and state governments pushed to pass laws to obstruct their legal right to protest. It appeared that Black Lives Matter seemingly perished—or at the very least, withered on a vine poisoned by the rise of Trumpism.

In 2020, the revival of street protests became a potent political force in the aftermath of George Floyd's murder. At that moment, ideas once deemed too radical meaningfully entered mainstream discourse. In fact, its popularity surged to the point that it has since become widely supported by Americans of all generations and racial backgrounds, triggering a global movement. The speed at which the protests have spread, and the scale of support Black Lives Matter has received, speak to the foundation it has laid over the past several years. It is also the result of the broader grievances in society, including the feeling among many that Trump represented a threat to democracy. Youth activism in recent years on issues like climate change and gun rights helped to cultivate a broader protest culture. Support from prominent celebrities and athletes has also helped to keep the momentum going. The fact that those "Black Lives Matter" T-shirts, yard signs, and chants continue to be seen and heard everywhere is further proof of the movement's enduring impact despite political blowback.

It is important to note that many of the mothers who lost their sons to police violence, such as Kadiatou Diallo, mother of Amadou Diallo; Gwen Carr, mother of Eric Garner; and Lezley McSpadden, mother of Michael Brown; have become activists who struggle to ensure that their sons' murders were not in vain. For decades, Black women have pioneered innovative strategies to

---

13. Dani McClain, "Can Black Lives Matter Win in the Age of Trump?" *The Nation,* September 19, 2017, https://www.thenation.com/article/archive/can-black-lives-matter-win-in-the-age-of-trump.

14. Brandon Patterson, "How the Black Lives Matter Movement Is Mobilizing Against Trump," *Mother Jones,* February 7, 2017, https://www.motherjones.com/politics/2017/02/black-lives-matter-versus-trump.

15. Sweta Vohra, "Documents show US monitoring of Black Lives Matter," *Al Jazeera,* November 28, 201, https://www.aljazeera.com/news/2017/11/28/documents-show-us-monitoring-of-black-lives-matter.

organize and bring national attention to the systemic problem of police violence. Today, Black women are leading the fight to obtain justice and achieve systemic change, because public outrage and support have not always applied to female victims.

As we uneasily witnessed the videotaped police murder of Floyd as he repeatedly exclaimed, "I can't breathe," it reminded me once again of the forgotten Black little girls and women murdered by the police who are missing from the national conversation about race and policing. I was reminded of Eleanor Bumpers, the sixty-six-year-old woman who suffered from mental illness and was murdered by a New York police officer in 1984 because she was behind on her rent. Her shocking murder made it clear to me then, as a young Black woman, that we too are susceptible to police brutality.

There would be more murders in the ensuing years: Alberta Spruill suffered a heart attack when New York police officers mistakenly executed a "no-knock" warrant on her Harlem apartment. Young girls like Aiyana Stanley-Jones in Detroit and Kathryn Johnston in Atlanta were murdered in their homes due to no-knock warrants. Sandra Bland, the twenty-eight-year-old from Naperville, Illinois, was arrested for allegedly assaulting a police officer during a traffic stop in Waller County, Texas, and was mysteriously found dead in a jail cell three days later. The police murders of Rekia Boyd, Tanisha Anderson, Atatiana Jefferson, Charleena Lyles, Meagan Hockaday, Pamela Turner, Dominique Clayton, and so many more may have been covered by the local press and earned some national headlines, but their names have never become a rallying cry in the same way as Yusef Hawkins, Eric Garner, Tamir Rice, Freddie Gray, and now, George Floyd.

Although historically, Black women have been routinely beaten, raped, and murdered by White men, our stories have never garnered much attention (Jacobs 2017). This is what happened with Breonna Taylor, who we only learned about after Floyd's murder, though she was murdered nearly two months earlier. Taylor, a licensed EMT, was fatally shot by police who barged into her apartment in Louisville, Kentucky, as she lay sleeping on March 13, 2020.

The truth is that African Americans live in fear of the police. We fear law enforcement officials armed with weapons who monitor our every behavior, over-police our neighborhoods, pull us over in our cars, and attack us on the streets and in our homes for the slightest alleged provocation and get away with it. Perhaps it has to do with the fact that modern-day American police departments are descendants of a confluence of violent slave patrols that flourished in the South and watch groups from the northern colonies. After the Civil War, these groups managed the legal enforcement of black codes and Jim Crow laws, often working in conjunction with the Ku Klux Klan for the untold number of beatings, lynchings, and disappearances of Black people who forgot their place. From our current viewpoint, not much has changed. The Klan has been replaced by White supremacist and far-right militia groups who have infiltrated U.S. law enforcement agencies in every region of the country.[16] Police departments' mandates evolved to protect White neighborhoods from African Americans rather than protect all neighborhoods equally with the same policing tactics.

So when the police kill Black men, it feels as though the world is flipped upside down. People get angry, as they should. They organize, hit the pavement to protest, and march, and all of our social media timelines and email correspondence encourage participation. However, this same energy is rarely given to a Black woman when she is murdered. In fact, Black women are 17 percent more likely than their white counterparts to be stopped by police and 1.4 times more likely to be killed,[17] yet their murders are less likely to incite as much outrage as male victims, and their names and stories are quickly forgotten. As our nation grapples with reimagining public safety in the wake of the protests following Floyd's murder, it is time to confront and resolve the persistent problem of explicit racism and sexism in law enforcement towards Black and Brown women.

Critiques of national apathy toward the plight of Black women have been building momentum for some time. It came as no surprise when attorney and civil rights advocate Kimberlé Crenshaw launched the #SayHerName campaign in 2014. An initiative engendered by the African American Policy Forum (AAPF) in conjunction with the Center for Intersectionality and Social Policy Studies (CISPS), the #SayHerName campaign brings awareness to the often invisible names and stories of Black girls and women who have been victimized by racist police violence while providing support to their families. The campaign played a key role in drumming up publicity about Sandra Bland, who, until recently, was the most recognized name #SayHerName helped amplify. It is now doing the same for Breonna Taylor.

Having spent years pushing for advocacy and awareness for Black women murdered by police, Crenshaw was elated when the Women's National Basketball Association (WNBA) partnered with the #SayHerName campaign for their 2020-2021 season by displaying the slogan and highlighting Breonna Taylor and other Black women whose stories never received headlines or spurred nationwide marches. While the hashtag has brought awareness to a global platform, more still needs to be done. Knowing these women's names and lifting up their stories provides a much clearer view of the wide-ranging circumstances that make Black women's bodies disproportionately subject to police violence. More organizations and activists need to join the #SayHerName campaign to help reintegrate Black women into mainstream racial justice narratives and figure out ways to prevent future tragedies.

---

16. Michael German, "Hidden in Plain Sight: Racism, White Supremacy, and Far-Right Militancy in Law Enforcement," Brennan Center for Justice, August 27, 2020, https://www.brennancenter.org/our-work/research-reports/hidden-plain-sight-racism-white-supremacy-and-far-right-militancy-law.

17. "Policing Women: Race and gender disparities in police stops, searches, and use of force," Prison Policy Initiative, May 14, 2019, https://www.prisonpolicy.org/blog/2019/05/14/policingwomen.

Today's grassroots community organizers are multifaceted and represented by upcoming Black social media activists building a twenty-first-century civil rights movement. Phaedra Ellis-Lamkins, a social justice advocate and businesswoman, is a cofounder and CEO of Promise, a California-based company reworking the bail system. Jennifer Epps-Addison, president and co-executive director of the Center for Popular Democracy (CPD), creates partnerships with organizations to promote a pro-worker, pro-immigrant, racial and economic justice agenda. Johnetta Elzie, one of the leading forces of the 2015 protests after Michael Brown's shooting, is a cofounder of Campaign Zero, a data-informed platform that presents policy solutions to end police violence in America.

Michelle Alexander, a civil rights litigator, legal scholar, professor, and author-activist, has shown how one book, *The New Jim Crow: Mass Incarceration in the Age of Colorblindness* (2010), can make a tremendous impact pointing out the failures of the criminal justice system. Tarana Burke, a rape survivor who began working to improve the lives of young girls living in marginalized communities as a teenager, emerged as the true founder of the #MeToo movement. And Lateefah Simon went from being a teenage mother on welfare to a nationally recognized advocate for Black girls and women in the Oakland and Bay Areas. But with all of these great women pushing racial and gender equality, the question then becomes: when and how do Black and White women come together to fight gender issues on equal ground?

◆ ◆ ◆

THE YEAR 2020 MARKED the 100th anniversary of the passage of the Nineteenth Amendment, which guaranteed the protection of women's constitutional right to vote. While this is an unparalleled opportunity to commemorate a milestone of democracy, it is worth remembering why Black women had to fight so hard to gain the right to vote and who was fighting against them. The suffrage centennial reminds us how Black women leaders of 2020—from Stacey Abrams and Ayanna Pressley to Kamala Harris—have emerged from a centuries-long struggle for political power in movements led by Black women themselves.

Following emancipation, Blacks were theoretically equal before the law, including suffrage for Black women. However, in reality, most Black women and men were effectively barred from voting. Likewise, Native Americans were largely excluded from voting before the Indian Citizenship Act of 1924, yet some states and localities still passed laws effectively barring them from voting until the late 1940s. And it was not until the 1940s and 1950s that voting restrictions on all Asian Americans were finally removed (Roberts 2017). The struggle for the vote did not end with the ratification of the Nineteenth Amendment because it did not apply to all women, nor did it address the racial terrorism that prevented people of color from casting their votes freely. Women like Septima Poinsette Clark, Fannie Lou Hamer, Unita Blackwell, Ella Baker, and Diane Nash continued fighting for voting rights for all, culminating in the Voting Rights Act of 1965.

When the U.S. Supreme Court stripped the Voting Rights Act with its decision in *Shelby County v. Holder* in 2013, it opened a Pandora's box of voter suppression. They rolled back the provision that required jurisdictions with a history of racially discriminatory laws to get permission from the federal government before changing their voting laws. As a result, a resurgence of state voter ID laws, the shuttering of certain polling places, felony disenfranchisement, and the purge of voter rolls are depriving women and men of color the right to vote. This was much like 120 years ago, when the poll taxes pushed poor voters of all races out of the electorate through the front door, while grandfather clauses let only poor Whites return through the back (Berman 2015). The history of the Nineteenth Amendment is more than a myth; it is a cautionary tale for our own time.

This is why you cannot explain Stacey Abrams and her organization Fair Fight, which has been working to counteract voter suppression, without considering Susan B. Anthony and Elizabeth Cady Stanton largely ignoring Black suffragists. Black women have always known that the Nineteenth Amendment did not resolve voting rights; it just changed the terms by which they engage in this struggle.

Abrams and her organization are not the only ones effectively leading the charge to preserve the electoral process' integrity and encourage Black people to vote. Melanie Campbell, president and CEO of the National Coalition on Black Civic Participation and convener of the Black Women's Roundtable, has defended civil rights, women's rights, voting rights, and social justice issues for over thirty years,. She has served as an advisor to U.S. presidents, congressional members, corporate, labor, and nonprofit executives, philanthropists, faith leaders, and others on critical issues impacting Black America. In recent years, Glynda C. Carr, who has been at the center of the national movement to grow Black women's political power anywhere from the voting booth to elected office, cofounded Higher Heights in 2011. LaTosha Brown, a cofounder of the Black Voters Matter Fund, has led a nationwide movement to bolster Black voting rights and challenge voter suppression tactics. In 2018, Aimee Allison founded She the People, a national network that elevates the political voice and power of women of color. She recently collaborated with Michelle Obama's When We All Vote, an organization supporting voter education, turnout, and targeted voter suppression for the 2020 Presidential election.

These activists tell us something about our own time and how deeply entrenched voter suppression is in our history. Americans have again arrived at a political and cultural flashpoint in which women are playing a transformative role in society. Yet the fight over what it means for women to have political power, or whether they should truly have it, continues. Unfortunately, today's feminist movement is as fractured as it has ever been, stunted by many of the same forces that complicated the fight for voting rights a century ago. So as we celebrate the centennial of the Nineteenth Amendment, we should remember it as merely a milestone, not an endpoint, and it will remain so until all women, including women of color, can freely and easily vote in America.

Why and who we vote for means different things to different people. When thousands of women visited the gravesite of suffragette Susan B. Anthony in Rochester, New York, on Election Day 2016 and left "I Voted" stickers on her tombstone, it was for the same woman who vehemently opposed the Fifteenth Amendment. Few Black women pilgrimed to Anthony's gravesite. Instead, they showed up at the polls and voted for Hillary Rodham Clinton. Symbolic actions are nice, but are rendered meaningless when people do not understand the historical ramifications of their actions or inactions.

But it makes sense. While 94 percent of Black women voted for Clinton, 53 percent of White women in this country believed progressive policies did not speak to them and, instead, voted for Trump.[18] *There is a disconnect here.* When Trayvon Martin was murdered, White mothers uttered not one word. When Sandra Bland was murdered, the White feminists were silent. Had they brought their marching feet and outdoor voices into the public sphere about these and other killings, a different conversation could have occurred. *Their silence spoke volumes.*

This seems to reflect the increasing number of White women who weaponize their fear and discomfort by calling the police over trivial or nonexistent offenses, knowing that such an escalation puts African Americans at risk. This is just one clear example of the deeply ingrained racism that runs rampant and unchecked in our society. Maybe things are changing due to the recent protests over George Floyd's murder, the subsequent trial, and the guilty verdicts, but the end result remains to be seen.

What it does mean is that Black and White women should figure out a way to become true allies. In fact, *they need to, and they must.* Black women, along with other women of color, continue to argue that the intersectionality of sexism, gender, class oppression, and racism has made their experiences inherently different from White women. Their concerns should be recognized and incorporated into a true feminist movement. I also believe some White women out there have a clear passion for feminism and equal rights, and are willing to reckon with our painful history and the racism in our country. Black and White women lost their allyship due to slavery and segregation. The pitting of White women against Black women has produced suspicion and rivalries that have directly affected the abolitionist, civil rights, women's rights, Black Lives Matter, and #MeToo movements and saddled them with Southern attitudes about "pure White womanhood." Facing and reconciling these truths is the first step toward building bridges that engage both Black and White women into a coalition that encapsulates all women's needs.

---

18. Katie Rogers, "White Women Helped Elect Donald Trump," *The New York Times*, November 9, 2016, https://www.nytimes.com/2016/12/01/us/politics/white-women-helped-elect-donald-trump.html.

There comes a time in history when people are forced to come to the table for different reasons. More often than not, it is a fear for survival that brings them together, not some politically correct initiative. We are living in a moment where Brown children at the border are being captured and caged, women's reproductive rights are being destroyed, the environment is being degraded; and the state of healthcare is deteriorating while a pandemic rages worldwide, forcing all of us to come together. For the first time, Black women's voices are being fully heard. *History is clear.* When Black women win political power, we enact policies that help uplift all people and communities because we have the most to lose when equality and our civil liberties are at stake. *We are just what America needs.*

◆ ◆ ◆

BLACK WOMEN HAVE RESISTED OPPRESSION since they were captured and brought to America's shores in the seventeenth century. They remained steadfast in their attempts to attain liberation from the oppressive structures of race, gender, and class, using different forms of resistance to receive citizenship rights. They used their power as bridge leaders and organizers to utilize their invaluable social networks and make things happen. They wrote articles and books, made speeches, and organized meetings and demonstrations. Our existence radiates with the perseverance of these ancestors, but more work needs to be done.

Seventy years ago, civil rights rhetoric was framed in the language of cultural unity and equal opportunity, but it was marred by sexual and ethnic exclusivity. Unlike past movements, a new generation of Black women activists now openly welcomes inclusivity through multicultural, multiracial, and multigender partnerships. They do so on terms that do not distract from their mission to pursue civil rights advocacy for African Americans, especially women. They focus on police brutality, the criminal justice system, and environmental issues that affect the community at large. Black women are always at the forefront, using the power of our tongues for justice.

The hashtag and phrase #BlackGirlMagic, popularized by CaShawn Thompson in 2013, has been routinely used to acknowledge and celebrate the power of Black womanhood. Does the term really reflect racial pride, or does it have a deeper meaning that perpetuates negativity? Granted, I could be over interpreting things, but in the society we live in today, Black women are the most underrated and underappreciated people on the planet. We know we are not literally magic. But as more of our voices are being heard, and as people are learning the truth about what we have achieved historically and what we can accomplish even under the most challenging circumstances, sometimes it sure seems like it.❖

Sojourner Truth
(c. 1797-1883)
Abolitionist, women's rights activist

Sojourner Truth, an abolitionist, is considered this country's first prominent African American woman civil rights activist.

SOJOURNER TRUTH, was born as Isabella (also known as Belle) to Elizabeth and James, the slaves of Revolutionary War Colonel Johannis Hardenbergh, in Ulster County, New York. Truth's father was known as "Bomefree," and her mother was known as Betsey or Mau Mau ("mama" in Dutch) Bett. Truth was the youngest of ten or twelve children, but as a child, she only knew one sibling. Since her birthdate was not recorded, as was typical of children born into slavery, historians estimate that Truth was likely born around 1797 (Painter 2007).

The Colonel was a wealthy Dutch landowner. Although most Ulster Country households had slaves, the Hardenberghs, wealthier than most families, had several (Mabee 1995). Since the area had once been under Dutch control, Truth's family and the Hardenberghs spoke Dutch. When the Colonel died, his son Charles Hardenbergh inherited his father's estate and continued to enslave people as part of that estate's property.

After the death of Charles, and the auction of the property in 1807, at nine years old, Truth was sold to John Neely, near Kingston, New York, for $100. The Neelys did not speak Dutch and Truth did not speak English, so she was savagely whipped because she could not understand them. About a year later in 1808, Neely sold her for $105 to Martinus Schryver of Port Ewen, a tavern keeper, who sold her in 1810 to John Dumont of West Park, New York for $175. Truth's parents, who were too old to sell, were sent to live with a family who did not own slaves (Painter 2007).

Around 1815, Truth fell in love with a slave named Robert from a neighboring farm. Robert's owner forbade the relationship since any subsequent children produced by the union would be the property of Dumont rather than himself. Robert and Truth never saw each other again. Dumont forced Truth to marry Thomas, an older slave from another plantation. She bore five children, but there was an assumption that her first born, Diana, was fathered by Robert. At least two of her daughters and one son would be sold away from her. Truth was to endure physical and sexual abuse from the Dumont family for nearly sixteen years through puberty and marriage. As was the case for most slaves in the rural North, Truth lived isolated from other African Americans as she suffered at the hands of her masters.

In 1799, New York State began to legislate the abolition of slavery.[1] Dumont promised Truth her freedom a year before the state emancipation, but changed his mind. At first, she was infuriated, but she continued working for him to satisfy her sense of obligation. But then, in late 1826, Truth escaped to freedom with her infant daughter, Sophia. She left her other children behind because they would not be legally freed in the emancipation order until they had served as indentured servants into their twenties.

She found her way to the home of Isaac and Maria Van Wagenen in New Paltz, who took her and her baby in. Isaac offered to buy her services for the remainder of the year (until the state's emancipation took effect), which Dumont accepted for about $25. While living with the Van Wagenens, Truth learned to speak English. It was during this time that Truth helped to found the Kingston Methodist Church in 1827, and became sanctified. She lived with the Van Wagenens until the New York State Emancipation Act was enacted a year later.

Truth learned that her five-year-old son Peter had been sold illegally by Dumont, and suffered multiple sales and removals, ending up in Alabama. With the help of the Ulster County Quakers and prominent Dutch lawyers, Truth took the issue to court. In 1828, after months of legal proceedings, she got back her son, becoming one of the first Black women to go to court against a White man and win (Painter 2007). When Truth was reunited with Peter, he was scarred from head to toe, the evidence of having been beaten badly. His return marked the first step toward Truth's life of activism inspired by her religious faith.

In 1828, Truth and Peter moved to New York City with the Grear family. She attended church and accidentally reunited with her brother Michael and sister Sophia. The rediscovery of family members separated by slavery was often sorrowful rather than celebratory.

Truth became involved with different sects of the Methodist church that pressed for moral reform, including the efforts of Elijah Pierson, a Christian Evangelist who evangelized prostitutes. Truth embraced evangelical religion and abolitionist work and gradually fell under his spell. Eventually, Pierson asked Truth to be his housekeeper. In 1832, when Robert Matthews, also known as "Prophet Matthias," introduced himself to Pierson, they discovered they had a lot in common and soon merged forces, but under Matthews' lead through his Kingdom followers. A number of wealthy merchants, including Benjamin Folger, gave him a great deal of money. Truth became an ardent follower and eventually went to work for Matthews as a housekeeper at the Matthias Kingdom communal colony.

---

1. In 1799, New York passed a Gradual Emancipation Act that freed slave children born after July 4, 1799, but indentured them until they were young adults, In 1817, a new law passed that would free slaves born before 1799, but not until 1827.

The public, however, saw the Kingdom as a cult, and Matthews as a lunatic grifter. He was a bully and would not allow the women to preach, a form of subordination that Truth surprisingly accepted. She also began to distance herself from her children. Meanwhile, Pierson, who had begun to experience seizures, died unexpectedly in 1834. His sudden death raised suspicions, and Matthews and Truth were accused of stealing from Pierson and then poisoning him. Both were acquitted of the murder, though Matthews was charged for assaulting his daughter and for contempt of court, and spent several months in prison. In the meantime, Truth had brought a slander suit against Benjamin and Ann Folgers, members of the Kingdom, for publicly accusing her of poisoning Pierson. Remarkably, it was the second time this illiterate Black woman had taken a case to court and won, and in this case she was awarded $125. Upon his release from prison later in 1835, Matthews traveled West, and Truth never heard from him. From this experience, she never allowed herself to submissively trust any authoritarian individual or group again.

Although she never learned to read or write, Truth acquired a wide knowledge of the Bible and, by the 1840s, began working among the Garrisonian abolitionists to become a travelling evangelist. A popular platform figure, she told stories and sang gospel songs that instructed and entertained. The year of rebirth for Truth was in 1843. First, Truth shed her slave name and became "Sojourner Truth," and then she joined the second Adventist movement known as Millerism.[2]

In 1844, she joined the Northampton Association of Education and Industry (NAEI), an abolitionist community in Northampton, Massachusetts. The organization also supported women's rights and religious tolerance as well as pacifism. They lived on a huge stretch of land, raising livestock and running a sawmill, a gristmill, and a silk factory. While there, Truth met William Lloyd Garrison, and prominent Black members Frederick Douglass and David Ruggles. In 1845, Truth joined the household of George Benson, Garrison's brother-in-law. The Northampton Association provided Truth's opening to the reformers of anti-slavery (Painter 2007).

Truth started dictating her memoirs to her friend Olive Gilbert, and in 1850 Garrison privately published her book, *The Narrative of Sojourner Truth: A Northern Slave*. That same year, she purchased a home in what would become the village of Florence in Northampton for $300, and spoke at the first National Women's Rights Convention in Worcester, Massachusetts. In 1854, with proceeds from her book, and the carte-de-visite[3] entitled "I sell the shadow to

---

2.   The Millerites followed the teachings of William Miller who, in 1831, first shared publicly his belief that the Second Advent of Jesus Christ would occur in roughly the year 1843-1844. Coming during the Second Great Awakening, his beliefs were taken as predictions, spread widely, and believed by many, leading to the Great Disappointment.

3.   Carte-de-visite was originally a calling card, especially one with a photographic portrait mounted on it. It was immensely popular in the mid-nineteenth century.

support the substance," she paid off the mortgage held by her friend from the community, Samuel L. Hill (Mabee 1995).

In 1851, Truth joined George Thompson, an abolitionist and speaker, on a lecture tour through central and western New York State. She attended the Ohio Women's Rights Convention in Akron, where she delivered her famous extemporaneous speech on women's rights, later known as "Ain't I A Woman?"[4]

Truth spoke before hundreds of audiences, taking to the stage with a demanding presence. From 1851 to 1853, Truth worked with Marius Robinson, the editor of the *Ohio Anti-Slavery Bugle,* and traveled around the state on a speaking tour. In 1853, she spoke at a suffragist "mob convention" at the Broadway Tabernacle in New York City. That same year, she met Harriet Beecher Stowe, and in 1856, she traveled to Battle Creek, Michigan to speak to a group called the Friends of Human Progress.

Her trip to Michigan prompted Truth to relocate there, where the anti-slavery movement flourished. Truth joined the Michigan abolitionists and the Progressive Friends, some of whom she met at national conventions, as well as former members of the Millerite Movement who had formed the Seventh-Day Adventist Church. According to the 1860 census, her household in Harmonia included her daughter, Elizabeth Banks, and her grandsons, James Caldwell and Sammy Banks.

During the Civil War, Truth helped recruit Black troops for the Union Army. She was employed by the National Freedman's Relief Association in Washington, D.C., where she worked diligently to improve conditions for Blacks. In October of that year, she met President Lincoln at the White House and immersed herself in relief work for freedpeople. During Reconstruction, Truth lent her unique skills to the women's suffrage movement and initiated a petition drive to obtain land for freedpeople, even suggesting the idea of a "Negro state" in the West. In 1865, while working at the Freedman's Hospital in Washington, Truth rode in the streetcars to help force their desegregation. She preached cleanliness and godliness among the freedpeople and dictated many letters about the land question, which provided rich details about that aspect of Reconstruction.

In 1870, Truth tried to secure land grants from the federal government for former enslaved people, a project she pursued for seven years without success. While in Washington, D.C., she met with President Grant in the White House. In 1872, she returned to Battle Creek and tried to vote in the presidential election, but was turned away at the polling place.

---

4.   The first reports of the speech, originally titled "Ar'n't I A Woman," was published by the *New York Tribune* on June 6, 1851, and by *The Liberator* five days later. Both of these accounts were brief, lacking a full transcript. The first complete transcription was published on June 21 in the *Anti-Slavery Bugle* by Marius Robinson, an abolitionist and newspaper editor who acted as the convention's recording secretary. Twelve years later, in 1863, Frances Dana Barker Gage published a very different transcription. In it, she gave Truth many of the speech characteristics of Southern slaves, and included new material that Robinson had not reported. While Gage's version of the speech would become the historical standard, it is largely fiction.

Truth later developed an infection from sores on her legs and was treated at the famous Battle Creek Sanitarium by Dr. John Harvey Kellog. The treatment did not work, and Sojourner Truth died of old age and ulcerated legs in 1883. Her funeral and burial in Battle Creek was the largest the town had ever seen.❖

The Legacy of Sojourner Truth

SOJOURNER TRUTH is perhaps the most famous African American woman from nineteenth-century America. For over forty years, she traveled the country as a forceful and passionate advocate for the dispossessed, using her quick wit and fearless tongue to fight for human rights.

There has always been a distinction between Isabella the slave, the life of Sojourner Truth, and the symbol of Sojourner Truth. While contemporary historians like Nell Painter have painstakingly explored this distinction, it is not as clear-cut as suggested. The reinterpretation of "Ar'n't I A Woman?" that emerged twelve years later with new material by Frances Dana Barker Gage has been embraced by the public for over 100 years. While we acknowledge the mythology, we still connect to the symbolism. And Truth certainly had a role in her own symbolization in terms of compiling her book and other narratives.

But perhaps Truth's most important legacy is her overall presentation, tone, and substance. Almost six feet tall, Truth was a striking woman with a charismatic presence. When she addressed an audience, her low resonant voice, especially when raised in song, could still the most hostile crowd. Truth often testified to the demeaning nature of slavery and spoke about abolition, women's rights, prison reform, and capital punishment, as well as the redeeming power of faith.

Frederick Douglass praised Truth as "honest, industrious, and amiable" as well as "remarkable" for her "independence and courageous self-assertion."[5] Harriet Beecher Stowe, the author of *Uncle Tom's Cabin* (1852), called Truth a "shrewd" woman with more "personal presence" than anyone she had ever known.[6]

Truth's story is the ultimate American story. It is important to look at Truth beyond symbolism and mythology and consider her real-life struggles as a slave. Truth's bold assertion of her own identity, "I am a women's rights," continues to serve as a timely reminder that the fight for equality has always been, and will continue to be, a constant challenge and an ongoing process in our democratic society. Finally, the symbolic importance of Truth as a seeker of truth is perhaps her greatest legacy and why we continue to remember and honor her.❖

---

5.   Charles Sheffield, ed. *The History of Florence, Massachusetts, Including a Complete Account of the Northampton Association of Education and Industry.* Florence, Mass., 1895.

6.   Harriet Beecher Stowe, "Sojourner Truth, The Libyan Sibyl," *The Atlantic*, April 1863, https://www.theatlantic.com/magazine/archive/1863/04/sojourner-truth-the-libyan-sibyl/308775/. Stowe, a founder of The Atlantic, describes her encounter with the legendary activist.

Harriet Tubman
(c. 1822-1913)
Abolitionist, humanitarian, freedom fighter, armed scout, spy

Harriet Tubman is America's leading freedom fighter. She led enslaved people to freedom along the route of the Underground Railroad. She was also one of the few women to lead men into combat during the Civil War.

ARAMINTA ROSS TUBMAN was born enslaved in Dorchester County, Maryland to Harriet "Rittia" Green, owned by Atthow Pattison, and Ben Ross, owned by Anthony Thompson. Tubman was the youngest of approximately seven siblings (Larson 2004). Her birthdate is unknown, and historians have estimated that she was born between 1820 and 1825. While her father's parentage remains unknown, some scholars have deduced that Tubman's grandparents were taken as children from West Africa's Gold Coast in the region now known as Ghana of the Asante ethnic group. They were highly prized by slaveholders because of their strong physical ability and flexibility in performing different work tasks (Larson 2004). Nicknamed "Minty," Tubman would change her name to Harriet around the time of her marriage, possibly to honor her mother. More importantly, the person we know as "Harriet Tubman" endured decades in bondage before becoming the woman we know today.

Her mother's slave owner, Atthow Pattison, was the wealthy patriarch of a long-established Eastern Shore family in Maryland and owned seven slaves. By the late 1700s, the debate of abolition and freeing the enslaved was a moral question that loomed large among the Quakers and Methodists. The elite slaveholders were concerned about the impact of a growing free Black population and their ability to control their economic and political pursuits. But to appease a troubled conscious and protect their purse strings, they felt delayed manumission was the most effective way to phase out slavery, to some degree. Pattison's granddaughter, Mary Pattison Brodess, would inherit Rit, Tubman's mother. The will indicated that Rit and her children were to remain enslaved until they were forty-five years old (Larson 2004).

Brodess had her only son, Edward Brodess, in 1801. She became a widow in 1802 and in 1803, married Anthony Thompson, a landowner who brought to the marriage several slaves, including Tubman's father Ben Ross, who managed

the timbering operations of Thompson's property. This scenario enabled Tubman's parents to get together and start a family, which grew to five children, Tubman being the youngest.

When Brodess died in 1810, she left her slaves to her minor son Edward Brodess, in the care of her second husband, Thompson. When he became twenty-one, Edward Brodess claimed his inheritance and independence from his stepfather's control. He immediately moved out, taking Tubman's family with him and separating them from Ben Ross. Edward Brodess then married Eliza Ann Keene in 1824, and Tubman's family life was dramatically altered.

During the early 1800s, there was an economic downturn of the predominately tobacco-based economy of the Eastern Shores. Due to the rise of cotton and with it, the demand for slaves, Northern slaveholders began selling slaves to the lower South. Family separation became one of the greatest threats to the enslaved, which sent shock waves though the abolition movement and the Black communities in the Eastern Shore. The screams of women and children dragged away from their families stayed with Tubman for the remainder of her life (Larson 2004).

Tubman's early life was full of hardship. Edward Brodess sold three of her sisters to distant plantations, severing the family. When a trader from Georgia approached Edward Brodess about buying her mother's youngest son, Moses, Rit successfully resisted, setting a powerful example for her young daughter to follow. Merely assets for Brodess' gain, Tubman's family was hired out to temporary masters throughout the region, and they were never confident in the stability of their home life.

When Tubman was hired away from the Brodesses, she did multiple jobs, like setting muskrat traps and working as a nursemaid, house servant, and field hand. She endured beatings, whippings, and general neglect, which caused permanent physical injuries and scars. The most severe injury occurred when an overseer threw a two-pound weight at her head. Tubman endured seizures, severe headaches, and narcoleptic episodes for the rest of her life. Tubman often became unconscious in the middle of a conversation or while doing a task. However, this physical impairment reinforced Tubman's religious beliefs, which were nurtured through strong African cultural traditions and powerful evangelical ideas. She had already acquired a passionate faith in God from the Bible stories her mother taught her. In time, Tubman rejected the teachings of the New Testament that urged slaves to be obedient and found guidance in the Old Testament tales of deliverance. When she began experiencing visions and vivid dreams resulting from her head injury, she interpreted them as revelations from God. This religious perspective would inform her actions for the remainder of her life (Larson 2004).

The line between freedom and slavery was hazy for Tubman and her family. In 1840, Ben Ross, was freed from slavery at forty-five, as stipulated in Thompson's will. Nonetheless, he had few options but to continue working as a timber estimator and foreman for the Thompson estate. Although similar manumission stipulations applied to Rit and her children, it appeared her owners chose not to free them. Ben Ross had little power to challenge their decision despite his free status, nor did he have enough money to buy their freedom.

In 1844, Harriet married John Tubman, a free Black man. At the time, it was not unusual to have both free and enslaved people in a family. Little is known about John Tubman or his marriage to Tubman, but it seems likely that she and her husband hoped they would earn enough money to buy her freedom.

Edward Brodess died in 1849. Tubman hired a lawyer to check the probate records of her mother's first owner, Atthow Pattison, and discovered she should have been manumitted at age forty-five. Rit was now sixty-three years old. The Pattison heirs challenged Edward Brodess' will, demanding that ownership of Rit and her offspring should revert to them. Tubman was infuriated. Spurred by rumors of her impending sale and that her family would be further severed, against her husband's wishes, Tubman decided to escape slavery (Larson 2004). Two of her brothers, Ben and Harry, accompanied her. However, after a notice was published offering a reward for their return, her brothers had second thoughts, and they all returned to the plantation. However, Tubman had no plans to remain in bondage. Once she saw her brothers safely home, she soon set off alone for Pennsylvania.

Tubman made her escape using the Underground Railroad, a network of secret routes and safe houses established in the U.S. during the early to mid-nineteenth century. This route was used by slaves to escape into free states and Canada with the aid of abolitionists and allies who were sympathetic to their plight. Tubman traveled nearly ninety miles and crossed into the free state of Pennsylvania with a feeling of relief and awe.

Rather than remaining in the safety of the North, Tubman made it her mission to rescue her family and others living in slavery. She was embraced by the abolitionists and received financial and spiritual support from that community. When Tubman received a warning that her niece would be sold, along with her two young children, she went to Baltimore and brought them to Philadelphia, the first of many trips by Tubman. Abolitionist William Lloyd Garrison recognized her courageous efforts and named her "Moses," alluding to the prophet in the Book of Exodus who led the Hebrews to freedom from Egypt. Tubman's daring missions remained virtually unknown, and her identity a carefully guarded secret. She would sing a version of "Go Down Moses" to signal her refugees along the path to freedom—she changed the tempo to indicate whether it was safe or too dangerous to proceed.

When the Fugitive Slave Law was passed in 1850, escaped slaves could be captured in the North and returned to slavery. This led to the abduction of both former slaves and free Blacks. Law enforcement officials in the North were forced to aid in capturing slaves, regardless of their principles. In response to the law, Tubman re-routed the Underground Railroad to Canada, which unequivocally prohibited slavery.

Meanwhile, slaveholders never knew that this petite, five foot tall, disabled runaway slave was behind so many slave escapes in their region. By the late 1850s, they suspected a northern White abolitionist was secretly enticing their slaves to run away. They even considered John Brown himself had come to the Eastern Shore to lure slaves away before his ill-fated raid on Harper's Ferry in 1859. But despite the best efforts of the slaveholders, Tubman was never captured, and neither were the fugitives she guided.

Tubman repeatedly returned to Maryland in the next decade, rescuing some seventy slaves in about thirteen expeditions. Tubman's dangerous work required ingenuity. Her journeys placed her at tremendous risk, and she used a variety of subterfuges to avoid detection. Tubman usually worked during the winter months to minimize the likelihood that the group would be seen.

One of Tubman's last missions into Maryland was to retrieve her aging parents and lead them north to St. Catharines, Ontario, a community of former slaves that had been established.

Tubman remained active during the Civil War and worked for the Union Army as a cook and nurse. In time, she quickly became an armed scout and spy. She was the first woman to lead an armed expedition during the war, and she guided the Combahee River Raid, which liberated more than 700 enslaved people in South Carolina. Two things sustained her: the pistol at her side and her faith in God. She would not hesitate to use her pistol in self-defense, but it also served to warn the enslaved that there was no turning back.

After the war, abolitionist Senator William H. Seward sold Tubman a small piece of land on the outskirts of Auburn, New York in early 1859. The land became a haven for Tubman following the war, where she spent her remaining years tending to her family and others who had taken up residence there. One of the people Tubman took in was Nelson Charles Davis, a farmer from North Carolina and a veteran of the 8th U.S. Colored Infantry. He began working in Auburn as a bricklayer, and they soon fell in love. He was twenty-two years younger than her when they married in 1869. They adopted a baby girl in 1874. Nelson died from tuberculosis in 1888.

Despite her years of service in the Union Army, Tubman did not receive a salary and was denied compensation. Her unofficial status caused great difficulty in documenting her service, and the U.S. government was slow in recognizing its debt to her. With the help of White allies, Tubman finally received her Civil War pension and her husband's in 1899. Meanwhile, her constant humanitarian work for her family and the former enslaved kept her in a state of constant poverty.

Throughout this period, Tubman was deeply involved with the AME Zion Church in Auburn (Larson 2004). Her Christian faith, which tied all of her remarkable achievements together, had never wavered. When many Black women of the late nineteenth century sought the church as a spiritual sanctuary, the church's countless acts of faith and resistance, piety and protest, and the idea of freedom helped sustain their parishioners. Black preachers provided leadership, encouraged education and economic growth, and were often the primary link between the Black and White communities. Tubman was actively involved in community work, raising money and clothing for the needy, and helped to sustain the church.

Tubman raised funds to aid freedmen, joined Elizabeth Cady Stanton and Susan B. Anthony in their quest for women's suffrage, and worked with White writer Sarah H. Bradford on her autobiography as a potential source of income. Her most memorable appearance was at the organizing meeting in Washington, D.C. of the National Association of Colored Women (NACW) in 1896. Two generations of Black women came together to celebrate their continued strength and struggle for a life of dignity and respect. Tubman, the oldest member present, was honored at the event.

Tubman's fame and reputation never brought her financial security. Her friends and supporters often raised money, and the proceeds of her biography, *Scenes in the Life of Harriet Tubman,* helped support Tubman and her family. Yet, despite her economic woes, she continued to give freely. In 1903, she donated a parcel of her land to the AME Zion Church in Auburn. The Harriet Tubman Home for the Aged opened on this site in 1908.

As Tubman aged, the head injuries she sustained earlier became more painful and disruptive. Confined to a wheelchair, Tubman was eventually admitted into the rest home named in her honor. Surrounded by friends and family, Harriet Tubman died of pneumonia on March 10, 1913. She was buried with military honors at Fort Hill Cemetery in Auburn.❖

The Legacy of Harriet Tubman

IN THE YEARS FOLLOWING Harriet Tubman's death, the Black community maintained Tubman's memory, mostly in segregated classrooms and literature. In time, as her narrative shortened and simplified, it became part of a usable past for African Americans.

Highly fictionalized accounts of Tubman's life began to appear in schoolbooks for children and young adults during the 1930s and 1940s that sought to catch the wave of renewed interest in the Underground Railroad. Interestingly, while the memory of Tubman's active participation in the suffrage movement remained obscured, by the 1930s, the American communist movement began to use Tubman as a feminist icon in recruitment literature aimed at women and the Black community. The Communist Party reminded its readers that Tubman was one of the most courageous women who ever lived, and while the enslaved struggled for freedom, a labor movement emerged dedicated to the freedom of industrial slavery. Once again, Tubman was appropriated as a malleable icon suitable for consumption by a variety of audiences.

In 1943, Earl Conrad published the biography *Harriet Tubman,* under the leadership of Carter G. Woodson at Associated Publishers because other publishers would not. His book was met with limited success, but it laid the foundation for Tubman's fictionalized young adult biographies that helped secure Tubman's place in the pantheon of American sheroes, first as an African American icon, later as a feminist symbol.

In 1944, the U.S. Maritime Commission named a Liberty Ship in honor of Tubman, the SS Harriet Tubman, the first named for a Black woman, and only one of eleven named for an African American. Although the ship survived the war, she was scrapped in 1972. By the 1960s, Tubman's life brought renewed attention to Black history, and in the 1980s, her life story became a staple of juvenile literature. Still, the gender and racial proscriptions have muted and reconfigured Tubman's place in the collective memory, making her suitable for children's biographies but not as a subject of serious historical inquiry. It would not be until the early 2000s that several scholarly biographies emerged to provide meticulous details of her life.

At the end of the twentieth century, a survey named Tubman as one of the most famous civilians in American history before the Civil War, third only to Betsy Ross and Paul Revere (Larson 2004). Her bravery and bold actions continue to inspire. A century after her death, Tubman has received multiple honors in the naming of schools, a Maryland state byway, a national park, and a state park set on land where she was once enslaved. Despite a 2016 announcement that Tubman would be the new face of the twenty-dollar bill, the rollout of the new bill has not yet happened. Tubman's life story was celebrated when director Kasi Lemmons co-wrote and released the movie *Harriet* (2019), a groundbreaking event.

Why has Tubman become such an icon and an inspiration to a new generation of activists? It is because she did not wait on anyone to free her from slavery. Moreover, her loyalty and love for family, which dominated her life, were the impetus behind freeing herself. She did not wait on a leader to rise up. *She* proclaimed herself free. *She* became the leader. Equipped with a steadfast determination that freedom was a given, and that no human had a right to take it away from her, Tubman teaches us that we must first free ourselves by any means necessary and then fight for freedom for the people around us.

Tubman was a crusader against both racial injustice and the oppression of women when most African Americans were enslaved, and most women were treated as second class citizens. A truly brilliant, shrewd, deeply religious, and passionate woman, Tubman coupled her wit, her intelligence, and her intuition with guideposts from mother nature and from her heart. And here, at this moment, her legacy continues to lead us to continue to pursue our freedom.❖

Mary Church Terrell
(1863-1954)
Educator, civil rights activist, suffragist, writer

Mary Church Terrell, one of the first African American women to earn a college degree, was a civil rights activist, suffragist, and a founding member of the NAACP.

MARY ELIZA CHURCH TERRELL was born in Memphis, Tennessee to parents Louisa Ayers Church and Robert Reed Church, both mixed-race former slaves. They became small business owners and made themselves vital members of Memphis' growing Black population. Her mother owned a hair salon, while her father was considered the first Black millionaire in the South due to his business and real estate dealings. When Terrell's parents divorced, her mother moved her and her brother to New York, and her father remarried.

Both of Terrell's parents stressed education. When she was six years old, her parents sent her to the Antioch College Model School in Yellow Springs, Ohio, for her elementary and secondary education. She remained in Ohio to attend Oberlin Academy and Oberlin College, which accepted all races and genders. However, when she arrived at the school, Oberlin provided segregated housing for students of color, which reflected a loss of commitment to racial equality. Terrell pushed forward anyway, majoring in classics at Oberlin College. She was one of the few African American women among mostly White male students. Her freshman class nominated her as class poet, she was elected to two of the college's literary societies, and served as an editor of *The Oberlin Review*. In 1884, she was one of the first African American women to earn a bachelor's degree. When Terrell and Oberlin classmate Anna Julia Cooper graduated in 1888, they were the first two Black women to earn a master's degree (Quigley 2016).

Although her father disapproved of her working, Terrell became a teacher and taught at Wilberforce College. She eventually relocated to Washington, D.C. in 1887 to join the faculty at Preparatory High School for Negro Youth, one of the nation's first high schools for African Americans.[1] Terrell taught German and Latin, and she met Robert H. Terrell, the first African American to graduate magna cum laude from Harvard University, who chaired the Latin department.

---

1. Preparatory High School for Negro Youth was later known as M Street Colored High School, and then renamed the Dunbar High School.

After teaching for a time, Terrell took a sabbatical to study French, German, and Italian in Europe and figure out what to do next. While abroad, Terrell received a steady stream of correspondence from Robert H. Terrell. She also met a White admirer who proposed marriage, but her father would not give his consent, and she was relieved (Quigley 2016).

When Terrell returned to Preparatory High School, Oberlin College offered her a registrarship position in 1891, making her the first Black woman to obtain such a position. However, she declined and instead quit her teaching position and married Robert H. Terrell, a municipal court judge and the first African American man to graduate magna cum laude from. Terrell would have three children who died in infancy. One daughter survived, and the Terrells later adopted a second daughter, however, Terrell was restless and tired of sitting on the sidelines.

Through her father, Terrell met activist Frederick Douglass and Booker T. Washington, director of the Tuskegee Institute in Alabama. She became especially close to Douglass and worked with him on several civil rights campaigns. In 1892, she was elected as the first woman president of the prominent Washington D.C. Black debate organization, Bethel Literary and Historical Society.

That same year, her childhood friend, a successful owner of a wholesale grocery, was lynched in Memphis. He, like Terrell, represented progress, which many White people felt was a direct threat to their commerce and livelihood. Terrell, along with journalist Ida B. Wells-Barnett, organized anti-lynching campaigns to mobilize advocates and generate awareness. When President Harrison failed to produce a public condemnation of lynchings, she formed the Colored Women's League (CWL) in Washington, D.C. with Anna Julia Cooper to address social problems facing Black communities. Terrell became especially involved in the suffrage movement and focused much of her attention on securing the right to vote, but within the movement, she found there was reluctance to include African American women, and in some cases, were outright excluded from the cause.

In 1896, Terrell and fellow activists founded the National Association of Colored Women (NACW), an organization committed to advocating social and educational reforms and community activism. Serving as its first president, Terrell often marched for women's rights in front of the White House and Capitol Hill and at meetings of the National American Suffrage Association (NAWSA), a group led by suffragist Susan B. Anthony. She encouraged the group to include African American women in their agenda. In 1898, Anthony invited Terrell to address the group on "The Progress and Problems of Colored Women" and stressed that African Americans had to confront sexual and racial barriers, earning a reputation as an effective speaker and activist.

As an enthusiastic member of the Republican Party, Terrell served as president of the Women's Republican League in Washington, D.C. She also served on Washington's Board of Education in an unpaid position from 1895 to 1901 and from 1906 to 1911.

In 1904, Terrell spoke at the International Congress of Women in Berlin. She made the speech in German and French. Besides gaining respect and notoriety for her speech's content and form, she provided the audience insight into a world they had never imagined. In fact, many foreign members did not realize she was a "colored" person until Terrell informed them. She was quickly becoming well-known nationally for her unique ability to accurately and intelligently describe the difficulties that Black women faced (Quigley 2016).

In 1909, Terrell was one of two Black women (Ida B. Wells-Barnett was the other) invited to sign the call and attend the first organizational meeting of the National Association for the Advancement of Colored People (NAACP), becoming a founding member. Even within the NAACP though, she could not escape the sexism. Over the decades, she witnessed women relegated to secondary roles, including membership in auxiliaries that raised money to finance the NAACP's antidiscrimination litigation. Meanwhile, her half-brother, Robert R. Church Jr., who founded the NAACP's Memphis branch, sat on the national board. In 1913, she helped organize the Delta Sigma Theta Sorority. More than a quarter-century later, she helped write its creed, which set up a code of conduct for Black women. The first public act of Delta Sigma was its participation in the Women's Suffrage March in Washington D.C. in 1913.

During World War I, Terrell offered her linguistic services to the federal government and obtained a low-level clerk position despite facing severe discrimination. Terrell did not have the level of influence that she briefly held with Theodore Roosevelt's administration and she eventually resigned due to the racial prejudice she experienced.

She was also involved with the War Camp Community Service, which aided in recreation for—and, later, the demobilization of—Black service members. As the war was winding down, Terrell joined Alice Paul and Lucy Burns of the Congressional Union for Woman Suffrage (CUWS) to picket the White House on issues related to Black service members and the need for jobs. Terrell was a delegate to the International Peace Conference after the end of the war. While in England, she stayed with Mr. and Mrs. H. G. Wells.

Terrell continued to work strenuously for the suffrage movement, which pushed for the enactment of the Nineteenth Amendment to the U.S. Constitution. President Harding's 1920 presidential campaign became the first election in which women were given the right to vote. The Republican Party named Terrell director of Colored Women of the East and organized efforts to encourage women to use their right to vote. However, the Democrat-controlled Southern states had passed voter registration and election laws that effectively disfranchised most African Americans, making it almost impossible for Black women and men to vote. Those laws would not become fully overturned until the congressional passage of the Voting Rights Act of 1965 (Quigley 2016).

Terrell's husband had a series of strokes, and, having suffered from their effects, died in 1925.

In addition to founding and chairing numerous organizations, Terrell also had a prosperous career as a journalist, using her writing to advance her social and political agenda. Using the pen name "Euphemia Kirk," she published scholarly articles, poems, and short stories about race and gender, which appeared in numerous journals and magazines in both the Black and White press. In 1940, she wrote her autobiography, *A Colored Woman in a White World,* which details her battles with gender and race discrimination in the U.S.

After World War II, Terrell aligned with progressives who shared her commitment to racial justice and, from time to time, worked with Communists. She also joined the burgeoning efforts to end legal segregation in Washington, D.C. and started what would become a successful fight to integrate restaurants. In 1949, Terrell and colleagues Clark F. King, Essie Thompson, and Arthur F. Elmer entered the segregated Thompson Restaurant. When refused service, they promptly filed the lawsuit, *District of Columbia v. John R. Thompson Co.,* but the NAACP would not lend its support. Terrell's attorneys, Joseph Forer and David Rein, who worked with her on the *Thompson* case, had ties to the National Lawyers Guild, a coalition of public-interest attorneys that House Un-American Activities Committee (HUAC) had deemed a "Communist front" (Quigley 2016). In the three years pending a decision in the case, Terrell targeted other restaurants.

As a grassroots activist, Terrell did not wait for judges to decide her fate. She picketed outside dime stores and theaters, protested Jim Crow lunch counters, and participated in sit-ins. When Hecht's, a department store, refused to abandon its segregated lunch counter, Terrell and her compatriots launched a boycott and a picket line. By January 1952, the store began serving African Americans.

When the U.S. Supreme Court announced it would hear the case, the NAACP scrambled to get involved by filing a friend-of-the-court brief, which the court denied. Finally, on June 8, 1953, the U.S. Supreme Court ruled that segregated eating places in Washington, D.C. were unconstitutional. This happened one year before the *Brown v. Board of Education* ruling, six years before the Montgomery Bus Boycott, and a decade before sit-ins rocked lunch counters in the South.

During her lifetime, Terrell was recognized and honored. In 1933, she received an award honoring her as one of the Top 100 Outstanding Alumni of Oberlin College, and was awarded an Honorary Doctorate for Letters by Oberlin College in 1948. She also received the Diamond Cross of Malta in 1953.

After the age of eighty, Terrell continued to participate in picket lines and protested against segregation. During her senior years, she also persuaded the local chapter of the American Association of University Women to admit Black members. She lived to see the U.S. Supreme Court's decision in *Brown v. Board of Education,* holding the segregation of schools by race unconstitutional. Mary Church Terrell died of breast cancer in her summer home in Highland Beach, Maryland, on July 24, 1954. She was ninety years old. She was buried at The Headquarters Building of the National Association of Colored Women (NACW).❖

The Legacy of Mary Church Terrell

WHEN MARY CHURCH TERRELL died in 1954, her place in civil rights history seemed secure. She had served as the first president of the National Association of Colored Women (NACW) and was a charter member of the NAACP. Her death led to an outpouring of grief in the capital. She was Rosa Parks before Rosa Parks: a dignified, galvanizing veteran of decades of activism. Unfortunately, this extraordinary African American woman, who dedicated her life to civil rights and helped moved and shaped the political community in Washington, D.C. and beyond, was eclipsed by the struggles that immediately followed her death and has been virtually forgotten.

Terrell, long a student of her own press coverage, would probably be surprised by her relative obscurity, and it is a pretty safe bet that she would not like it. Still, her legacy resonates, especially as a new generation of activists rediscover Terrell as they confront police brutality and challenge gender, social, and racial injustice.

With *Thompson,* the Court sent a signal, but it was not far-reaching. It was not a constitutional challenge to segregation, nor did it require the Court to overrule *Plessy* and reject separate but equal. It only dealt with the viability of Washington D.C.'s anti-discrimination laws, and ruled that the era of Jim Crow was over in the capitol. Terrell's case was not as comprehensive as *Brown,* but it paved the way for the landmark school desegregation decision that would happen a year later (Quigley 2016).

If Terrell were alive today, she would probably approve of the emergence of Black women activists fighting for racial and gender equality and Black women running for office. But as a former teacher, she might also offer some sage advice: protest, litigate, and reform. As Terrell's life and legacy attest, civil rights reform was a key component in her struggle for justice.

In 1975, the Mary Church Terrell House in the LeDroit Park neighborhood of Washington was named a National Historic Landmark. In 2009, Terrell was among twelve civil rights pioneers commemorated in a U.S. Postal Service postage stamp series. In 2020, Terrell was inducted into the National Women's Hall of Fame.

Terrell's life had begun in the year of the Emancipation Proclamation and ended two months after *Brown.* She was a college-educated woman, who was the wife of a judge. She was well-read, well-traveled, spoke four languages, and used her skills as a weapon. Terrell had lived through the aftermath of Reconstruction and the attendant despair of activism. She endured retrenchment, insult, deprivation, indignity, hardship, and loss. With *Thompson,* she had triumphed, achieving vindication and managing to defy Washington, D.C.'s entrenched southern culture. Her example should still resonate in the age of Instagram, Twitter, and Facebook. To sum up her legacy, Terrell was a woman who prevailed (Quigley 2016).❖

Rosina Corrothers Tucker
(1881-1987)
Labor organizer, civil rights activist, educator

Rosina Corrothers Tucker is best known for her help in organizing the Brotherhood of Sleeping Car Porters, the first African American labor union, and developing and leading its Ladies' Auxiliary.

ROSINA BUDD HARVEY CORROTHERS TUCKER was born in Northwest Washington, D.C. to Henrietta Harvey and Lee Roy Harvey, both former slaves from Virginia. Her father, who worked as a shoemaker, taught himself to read and write, and fostered a love of books in his children. He was determined that all of his children have a good education and obtain good jobs. He also bought an organ, which he learned to play, and saw to it his nine children studied music and played the organ as well (Tucker and Ruffin 2011). By the time they entered school, they already had a more than rudimentary musical education and were able to read and write. In fact, while still in her teens, Tucker published a concert waltz entitled, "The Rio Grande Waltz," and her sister Marietta gave Duke Ellington piano lessons.

When Tucker was a child, segregation existed everywhere in the District of Columbia except on the street cars and in public buildings. She attended the old Banneker School Building on Third Street in northwest Washington, D.C., and when she completed the eighth grade, entered the M Street School, the predecessor of Dunbar High School.

In 1897, while still in her junior year of high school, Tucker visited an aunt in Yonkers, New York, where she taught Sunday school at the Colored Baptist Church, and met James D. Corrothers, a guest minister. A graduate of Northwestern University, Corrothers became known as a poet and writer of short stories, particularly his sketches on Black humor and folklore. Tucker became Corrothers' third wife when they married in 1899. The couple had one son, Henry Harvey Corrothers, and Tucker also raised a son from Corrothers' previous marriage.

After marrying, the couple first lived in New York City, then relocated to Corrothers' hometown, South Haven, Michigan, where Tucker taught music to over thirty students. The family moved to Washington, D.C. in 1904 when Corrothers got a job with the National Baptist Convention, while Tucker became

an organist for Liberty Baptist Church in the Foggy Bottom section of the District. Two years later, Corrothers became the pastor of the First Baptist Church in Lexington, Virginia. The couple often appeared in church, with Corrothers telling stories and reading poetry while Tucker played classical pieces.

When Corrothers died in 1917, he was eulogized by W. E. B. Du Bois. After his death, Tucker and her young son returned to her parents' home in Washington, D.C., where she worked as a file clerk with the federal government and became involved in civic activities. Through friends, she met Berthea J. "BJ" Tucker, who had worked as a carpenter's helper before becoming a Pullman porter. They married on the eve of Thanksgiving in 1918, when she was thirty-six years old, and moved into a two-story brick house on Seventh Street northeast near Gallaudet College, where she remained for the rest of her life.

Tucker's husband joined a fledgling porters' union, the Brotherhood of Sleeping Car Porters (BSCP) in 1925 with A. Philip Randolph as its president. The porters worked long hours, and had little time for union activities. Many feared they would lose their jobs if their employer learned of their union involvement. Randolph, who took an immediate liking to Tucker when they first met in Washington, D.C., enlisted her help to organize BSCP activities, which needed to be handled under the radar to prevent retaliation from the Pullman Company. Initially, Tucker would visit households to distribute union literature and collect dues, all by way of her handbag. With Randolph's encouragement, she began to make a dedicated effort to convince the wives of Pullman porters of the importance of the union, so that they would encourage their husbands to join despite the risks involved. It was a politically strategic and necessary move. When the Pullman Company discovered Tucker's role in the BSCP, they fired her husband on the spot. However, after Tucker confronted the company's regional director, he was reinstated, and she began to conduct her business out in the open.

Six weeks after the BSCP became official in 1925, Tucker founded and became president of the local Ladies' Auxiliary, also known as the Women's Economic Council in Washington, D.C., which formalized what Tucker had been doing all along. While some of the women believed that the Ladies' Auxiliary supported the union so the men could "bring home the bacon," Tucker believed it was important for Black women to not only support BSCP, but to do so in a way that was politically and socially grounded. Other women's groups soon organized throughout the U.S., including New York, Philadelphia, Chicago, St. Louis, Omaha, Kansas City, Los Angeles, and in Canada. Their organizing efforts and contributions proved critical to BSCP's survival. The women generated funds, organized education initiatives on labor issues, and sought to build networks of support across political, economic and social networks (Chateauvert 1998).

In 1937, when BSCP signed a contract with the Pullman Company, it was the first Black-led union to sign a contract with a major corporation, establishing Randolph as a national civil rights leader. Up until this point, the Women's

Economic Councils were all local units that operated independently. Randolph pulled the independent councils together and founded the International Ladies' Auxiliary Order to the BSCP as "the first international labor organization of Black women in the world" (Tucker and Ruffin 2011), intentionally designed to be subordinate to the BSCP. In 1938, Tucker attended the national union conference in Chicago, where she chaired the Constitution and Rules committee. Delegates from twenty-seven cities elected Halena Wilson as president, Tucker as secretary-treasurer, and recognized twelve other faithful wives with international offices. Randolph became the international counselor to the auxiliary, maintaining his central advisory role in the women's organization.

Many of the leading prominent African American club women and national leaders supported BSCP. Women like Ida B. Wells-Barnett, Irene McCoy Gaines, Mary Church Terrell, and A'Lelia Walker made public endorsements and donations. Black trade union women, although few in numbers, also publicly supported BSCP, such as Gertude Elise MacDougald Ayers, Maida Springer Kemp, and Floria Pinkney. You can be certain Tucker encouraged their support.

Ultimately, the activities of the International Ladies' Auxiliary, coupled with Tucker's fortitude, resulted in a higher standard of living for the porters and their families and empowered them. She challenged sex segregation by working primarily with the male union officials as BSCP's Washington, D.C. liaison. She guided the International Ladies' Auxiliary to help organize unions for laundry workers, domestic workers, and hotel and restaurant workers, all largely African American women's occupations. And whenever there was an anti-racist or civil rights fight to be picked, they were on the front lines (McKay 2002). In 1941, Tucker took part in the union's first March on Washington, which was called off when President Franklin D. Roosevelt issued Executive Order 8802. She used her position in the International Ladies' Auxiliary to participate in civic work in her community, and later helped organize the March on Washington in 1963

The end of the Railroad Age was marked by the rise of car ownership, interstate highway construction, and better air transportation. This precipitated the decline of the BSCP, with shrinking membership and decreasing revenues. At the annual meeting in 1956, the executive board of the Brotherhood voted to disband the Ladies' Auxiliary because they felt it was no longer viable. Tucker fought against their decision by marching a delegation of women to the floor to protest the dissolution, but to no avail; Randolph's support was lukewarm, at best. Although the executive board gave the Ladies Auxiliary a year's reprieve, it was officially dissolved in 1957 (Chateauvert 1998). Its demise led to several consequences, including the BSCP's indifference and hostility towards women's activism and little to no desire to fund and sustain it. This was perpetuated by a generational gap that had developed between the new porters' wives and the old leadership. Tucker retired, along with other Ladies Auxiliary officials, and they were paid the benefits to which they were entitled.

By the 1960s, BSCP had about 3,000 porters who had regular runs. The Pullman Company ceased operations in 1968. The U.S. Department of Justice's antitrust complaint of 1944, which was slowly winding its way up the courts, combined with the decline of ridership, were the main reasons for its demise. The BSCP merged with the Brotherhood of Railway and Airline Clerks in 1969. In 1978, the BSCP officially dissolved during its last convention and became known as the Transportation Communications International Union (TCU). Then, in 1984, The Sleeping Car Porters Division was combined along with Amtrak Clerical employees into a new Amtrak Division of the Union, who are no longer called porters, and no longer excludes African Americans. It was what Tucker had been fighting for all along, and she lived to see it.

But this was not the end of Tucker, who had an unfaltering devotion to social and civil rights. A prominent church, civic, and community activist in Washington D.C., she was an elder of the 15th Street Presbyterian Church, where she had been the superintendent of Sunday School and the director of the Summer Vacation Bible School. Tucker helped found the Northeast Women's Club, served as the first president of the Public Interest Civic Association and its delegate to the city-wide Federal Civics Association (FCA), and served as a liaison between the Black community and the old D.C. Board of Commissioners. Tucker was also the driving force in a campaign for the expansion and construction of better public schools in Washington, D.C., and an active member of the NAACP.

Over the years, she testified before Senate and House committees on education, day care, labor, and voting rights for the District. For example, she participated in public hearings where, after some debate, Congress eventually approved continuation of a limited public daycare program in Washington, D.C. (Stoltzfus 2003). She lobbied Congress for legislation on labor and education, and continued to help organize unions, particularly on behalf of African American women. She also gave lectures across the country.

Tucker told her story and that of the work of the BSCP and the Auxiliary in the 1981 award-winning, hour-long documentary, *Miles of Smiles, Years of Struggle,* produced and directed by Paul Wagner and Jack Santino, which aired on PBS. In the documentary, she also sang "Marching Together," which she wrote in 1939 in honor of the Pullman porters. The documentary won numerous awards, including four regional Emmys and a CINE Golden Eagle. When she was 102 years old, she testified before a Senate Labor and Human Resources subcommittee about aging. In 1985, Tucker participated in an unsuccessful picket at a Safeway market in Washington, D.C. to stop it from moving out of the Black community.

Tucker is a recipient of the humanitarian award from the Leadership Conference on Civil Rights in 1983, the Candace Award for Leadership from the National Coalition of 100 Black Womens' Clubs in 1983, and the honoree of the Coalition of Labor Union Women in 1985. She also received an award for outstanding service from the NAACP.

Rosina Corrothers Tucker died in 1987, at 106 years old, after a century of struggle. She had been a mourner at the funeral of Frederick Douglass and was present when Martin Luther King Jr. delivered his "I Have a Dream" speech. Her only child, Henry Corrothers, died in 1945 and she left no immediate survivors. After her death, an unfinished autobiography was found and published as *My Life as I Have Lived It: The Autobiography of Rosina Corrothers-Tucker, 1881-1987* in 2011.❖

The Legacy of Rosina Corrothers Tucker

AS FOUNDER AND SECRETARY-TREASURER of the International Ladies' Auxiliary and a force in the establishment of its parent organization, the BSCP, Rosina Corrothers Tucker helped raise the income of a large number of African Americans in the U.S. and Canada, which propelled them into the middle class. She organized porters' wives in activities to support the auxiliary and the union, and their efforts helped to ensure the men received adequate pay, decent working conditions, and benefits. With Tucker's assistance, the BSCP fought racism by participating in civil rights activities, including the organization of the Washington D.C. marches in 1941 and 1963.

Tucker's legacy could easily rest on the enormous role she played with the union's development or the fact that she created a training ground for a new generation of African American women union activists. But perhaps her greatest legacy was the creation and preservation of dignity on the job. The first Pullman porters were ex-slaves that were demeaned and stereotyped as grinning servants, even as they made the Pullman Cars an elegant hotel on wheels. With Tucker's help and insistence, the International Ladies' Auxiliary of the BSCP fueled not only the struggle for equality, but propelled and succeeded in gaining dignity and human decency for its members. Tucker understood that economic gains would elevate the Black community into the middle class, which it did.

The work of the International Ladies' Auxiliary sought to complement rather than compete with the BSCP. Tucker believed that women could and should participate in concerns beyond household domesticity. Tucker also devoted her life to her community, her church, piano instruction, civil rights, education causes, and the labor movement. Her legacy rests as a labor union icon of the Black community, and she will continue to be remembered for her life and the way she lived it.❖

Ella Baker
(1903-1986)
Organizer, civil rights activist

Ella Baker, one of the leading African American women in the civil rights movement, was a cofounder of the Southern Christian Leadership Conference (SCLC) and helped launch the Student Nonviolent Coordinating Committee (SNCC).

ELLA JOSEPHINE BAKER was born in Norfolk, Virginia to Georgiana (Anna) Ross Baker, a schoolteacher, healthcare worker and midwife, and Blake Baker, a waiter on a steamer line. Baker was the middle child of three surviving children; she had an older brother and younger sister who died young (Ransby 2005). When she was eight, her parents moved to her mother's rural hometown of Littleton, North Carolina, to be closer to kinfolk and provide their children a better education and richer cultural environment.

Baker grew up in a female-oriented household, and her grandmother and mother were central to her development. She listened to her grandmother, a former slave, tell stories about slave revolts. Baker's mother, a stern and pious woman who believed in discipline as much as she believed in God, taught her daughters to conform to the conventional standards of female respectability and encouraged them to be exceptional. Baker attended church and preached at missionary meetings with her mother, whose female-centric faith extended to secular activism that included anti-lynching legislation, crusading for temperance, and challenging segregation. Her mother's religious and secular activities, coupled with her grandmother's stories, would create the fortitude and compassion Baker required to meet her future political objectives (Ransby 2005).

Baker attended local schools, and at age fifteen, she became a high school student at Shaw University's boarding school, Shaw Academy and later attended Shaw University. Her school experience opened up new intellectual horizons for Baker, exposing her to new ideas. While in school, she came into her own, writing essays, participating in protests and petitions, and became a rebel that challenged the status quo in a philosophical way (Ransby 2005).

Baker graduated college as class valedictorian in 1927. Though she initially considered becoming a medical missionary, a sociologist, or a social worker, Baker moved to New York instead and became enthralled with Harlem, a place she found politically invigorating even during the Great Depression.

After working as a waitress, Baker helped establish the first Negro History club at the Harlem Branch Library, where she later landed a job. She attended meetings at the 137th Street Young Women's Christian Association (YWCA) and met women like Pauli Murray, Dorothy I. Height, and Anna Arnold Hedgeman (Ransby 2005). She also met George Schuyler, a Black journalist and anarchist, who later became an arch-conservative. He founded the Young Negro Cooperative League (YNCL), which sought to develop Black economic power through collective planning. Schuyler also ran a national Black news bureau for which Baker was a contributing writer. Baker also worked as an editorial staff member for the *American West Indian News,* and was an editorial assistant at the *Negro National News.* In 1931, Schuyler selected Baker as the executive director of the YNCL, which developed educational, mutual defense, medical, and political programs. While the YNCL was a short-lived experiment, it launched Baker's career as a behind-the-scenes strategist who would work for various organizations in many of America's progressive movements of the twentieth century.

The Harlem Renaissance greatly influenced Baker, and she immersed herself in the cultural and political milieu of Harlem during the 1930s. She protested Italy's invasion of Ethiopia and supported the campaign to free the Scottsboro defendants in Alabama. Baker advocated widespread, local action as a means of social change. Her emphasis on a grassroots approach to the struggle for equal rights would greatly influence the success of the modern civil rights movement of the mid-twentieth century.

The effectiveness of Baker's work led to a scholarship from the Cooperative League of America to attend Brookwood Labor College in 1931. There, her studies focused on consumer economics and education. Baker joined the staff of the New York Public Library Adult Education Program at the Harlem Branch in 1934. During her time there, she developed consumer education and literacy programs for young mothers, which were held at the YWCA.

In 1936, Baker worked for the Works Progress Administration (WPA) as a consumer education instructor until 1941, when the program folded. From 1937 to 1940, she was a fundraiser for the National Association of Consumers and was the education and publicity officer for Harlem's Own Cooperative. These positions and the many promotions she received in a brief period helped build Baker's reputation as an effective educator and a talented organizer.

In 1939, Baker married Thomas J. Robinson after a ten-year courtship, which began at Shaw University while they were students.

Baker began her long association with the NAACP in 1941 when she accepted the position of assistant field secretary. During her tenure, Baker encouraged local leadership to engage in grassroots initiatives. She also worked to change the culture and image of the organization by appealing to all classes, especially women. She traveled extensively, especially in the South, recruiting members, raising money, and organizing local chapters. She was named director of branches in 1943, making her the highest-ranking woman in the organization. Baker held egalitarian ideals and pushed the organization to decentralize its leadership structure to aid its membership in activist campaigns at the local level. She believed that the strength of an organization grew from the bottom up and not the top down. Baker especially stressed the importance of having young people and women in the organization.

While traveling throughout the South on behalf of the NAACP, Baker met hundreds of people and established lasting relationships with them. She slept in their homes, ate at their tables, spoke in their churches, and earned their trust, forming a network that would become important in the continued fight for civil rights. Between 1944 and 1946, Baker directed revolutionary leadership conferences in several major cities, such as Chicago and Atlanta. She got top officials to deliver lectures, offer welcoming remarks, and conduct workshops.

In 1946 Baker resigned from the NAACP to lead the fundraising efforts of the New York Urban League. Baker's sister died of cancer in 1947, and she became responsible for the care of her young niece. In response to her loss, Baker joined the New York Cancer Society in the education and outreach office but continued working with and organizing for the NAACP in various capacities. In 1953, Baker ran for the New York City Council on the Liberal Party ticket. She lost to her opponent, Earl Brown, who held both the Democratic and Republican parties' nominations.

As the civil rights movement began to heat up following *Brown v. Board of Education*, Baker, along with Bayard Rustin, A. Phillip Randolph, attorney Stanley Levison, and a host of religious and labor groups, formed the organization In Friendship, a coalition aimed to rally financial support around the struggle for school desegregation and voter rights in the South. In Friendship held fundraisers for the Montgomery Improvement Association (MIA) to support the Montgomery Bus Boycott. The founding of In Friendship led Baker to conceive the idea that the Black church in the South needed to provide organizational structure to the desegregation movement. Her idea, which was well received and supported, led to the formation of the Southern Christian Leadership Conference (SCLC), which was officially launched in 1957 with a two-day meeting in Atlanta, Georgia.

Having accepted the position of executive secretary of SCLC, Baker moved back to Atlanta in 1958 to organize general operations and develop administrative and managerial procedures for the office. She considered this her most significant undertaking since resigning from the NAACP and worked with such intense focus and vision, which placed it on the national radar. One of SCLC's initial projects was focused on educating and mobilizing Blacks about voter registration and rights in the South, but it was met with limited success. Baker believed the projects was never fully realized because of the internal resistance from both the members and leadership of the organization. She also dealt with male chauvinism and was conflicted by their adulterous behavior behind closed doors but was still willing to work with them politically (Ransby 2005).

What turned the tide was, in the closing months of her work with SCLC in 1960, was the student sit-ins throughout the South which exploded onto the national scene. Baker, the visionary, understood the cutting edge of this new youth movement. However, their activities would have to be strategic and organized. Within three months of the initial student sit-ins, Baker convinced SCLC to take the lead by funding and organizing a conference for the youth leaders at Shaw University to lay out their own plan of action. This conference provided the first opportunity for the independent and isolated sit-in actions to be coalesced and structured. SCLC, as well as Congress of Racial Equality (CORE), and the NAACP, appealed to the students to join their ranks, and, after a series of gatherings, the Student Nonviolent Coordinating Committee (SNCC) was launched.

Though Baker never held an official position with SNCC, as one of its founders, she remained a political advisor, role model, fundraiser, and mentor, influencing future leaders like Julian Bond, Diane Nash, Stokely Carmichael, Bob Moses, John Lewis, and Bernice Johnson Reagon. SNCC also expanded its grassroots initiative among Black sharecroppers, tenant farmers, and others throughout the South, becoming the most active organization in the deeply oppressed Mississippi Delta.

During the 1960s, the idea of "participatory democracy" became popular. Baker largely argued against the civil rights movement being structured along the organizational model of the Black church. She questioned the gendered hierarchy of the movement, and it was reported that Baker and Martin Luther King Jr. had differences in opinion and philosophy. After leaving SCLC in 1960, Baker took a position in the southern regional student office of the YWCA. From this vantage point, she proved to be an invaluable financial resource to the veterans of the student movement when they returned to the classroom.

For the next ten years, Baker remained active in various organizations. In 1963, she served as a consultant to the Southern Conference Educational Fund (SCEF), an interracial desegregation and human rights group. Baker helped organize the Mississippi Freedom Democratic Party (MFDP) as an alternative to the all-White Mississippi Democratic Party, and accompanied them to the 1964 National Democratic Party convention in Atlantic City, New Jersey. In 1967, Baker returned to New York City, where she continued to give speeches. She collaborated with Arthur Kinoy and others to form the Mass Party Organizing Committee, a socialist organization.

Despite declining health, Baker continued her activism throughout the 1970s and into the 1980s, and counseled numerous organizations and causes. She served as a board member of the Puerto Rican Solidarity Committee and spoke out against apartheid in South Africa. Baker became a consultant to the Executive Council of the Episcopal Church and launched the "Free Angela" campaign, in an effort to free political activist Angela Davis from prison. Baker also allied with several women's groups like the Third World Women's Alliance and the Women's International League for Peace and Freedom. Her life and accomplishments were chronicled in the 1981 documentary *Fundi: The Story of Ella Baker.* "Fundi" was Baker's nickname, a Swahili word that means a person who passes down a craft to the next generation.

Baker was a private person. Many people close to her did not know she was married for twenty years to her college sweetheart. Their busy lives made marriage difficult, and when they divorced in 1958, they did not have any children. Ella Baker remained actively involved in pursuing social change and civil rights justice right up until her death on December 13, 1986, which happened to be her birthday, at the age of eighty-three.❖

The Legacy of Ella Baker

ELLA BAKER EMPOWERED PEOPLE to stand for something and give voice to the voiceless. She was a powerful intellectual presence that provided a moral and ethical compass for her young protégées, who went from their classrooms at Spelman, Howard, Fisk, and Shaw into Baker's classroom, which was infused with a radical pedagogy, epistemology, and worldview, becoming one of the most influential women of the civil rights movement.

Since Baker was in her element behind the scenes, she did not become as well-known as her contemporaries. She put her skills to work organizing and bringing people together to effect change. She stood up to the patriarchal hierarchy, built bridges from one generation to the next, and helped young people develop their ideas into action. Throughout her life, Baker developed model learning, relationship-building, teaching, and leadership.

Nearly all of Baker's honors have come to her posthumously. In 1984 Baker received a Candace Award from the National Coalition of 100 Black Women and was inducted into the National Women's Hall of Fame in 1994. A nonprofit action center, the Ella Baker Center for Human Rights, was established in Oakland, California, in 1996 by Van Jones, Diana Frappier, and Mike McLorne. A 15-unit cohousing community in Washington, D.C., was founded in 2003 and named The Ella Jo Baker Intentional Community Cooperative. In 2009 Ella Baker was honored on a U.S. postage stamp, and in 2014 the University of California at Santa Barbara established a visiting professorship to honor Baker. Her name also graces a K-8 public school on Manhattan's Upper East Side. Historian Barbara Ransby wrote the acclaimed biography, *Ella Baker and the Black Freedom Movement: A Radical Democratic Vision* (2003), the first deeply researched work that re-introduced Baker to the world.

Baker's selfless commitment serves as an outstanding example of altruism and devotion to something larger than oneself. Hers is a legacy of radical intellectualism and grassroots activism with a people-powered approach that has become the basis of today's young activists.❖

Maida Springer Kemp
(1910-2005)
Labor organizer

Maida Springer Kemp, the first African American and woman to become a business agent and to represent U.S. labor abroad, creating a critical labor link between the U.S. and Africa.

MAIDA STEWART SPRINGER KEMP was born in Panama to Adina Forrest Stewart and Harold Stewart. Her father, a Barbadian who immigrated to Panama after being educated in England, was a foreman on the Panama Canal project. At the age of seven, and after her younger sister died at age three, her family relocated to Harlem. At first they lived with relatives, but soon after, her parents separated and eventually divorced. Her mother worked as a domestic, cook and a beautician, and later opened her own shop. Her mother was politically active as well, and Kemp's home became a gathering place for activists and members of the Universal Negro Improvement Association (UNIA), whose accounts of personal experiences with racism had a lasting influence on Kemp (Richards 2000).

After attending St. Mark's Catholic School in New York City, Kemp attended Bordertown Manual and Industrial School, a Black boarding school in New Jersey, for four years, where she heard speakers like W. E. B. Du Bois and Paul Robeson. When she graduated in 1926, Kemp studied at the Malone Beauty School of Beauty and Culture and became a licensed beautician, but realized that the work was not for her. She then worked as a receptionist at Poro College and Malone School. During this time, she met her first husband, Owen Springer, a native Barbadian who was a clerk and dental mechanic for an international dental firm. The couple married in 1928 and Kemp gave birth to a son in 1929. The marriage would end in divorce.

Because of the devastating economic consequences of the Great Depression, Kemp, who had worked as a pinker while in school, went back to work as a hand server and later as a power machine operator in a non-union garment factory in 1932. She quickly realized just how exploitative the garment industry was. The owners required overtime without pay, denied lunch breaks, and demanded that workers remake garments without receiving compensation. These circumstances spurred her to join the Dressmakers' Union Local 22 of the International Ladies Garment Workers Union (ILGWU). Under the leadership of David Dubinsky, Kemp became a member of the Strike Committee that spearheaded the 1933

strike, setting the standard for garment workers to earn fifteen dollars a week. Union membership rose from 50,000 in 1933 to 200,000 in 1934 (O'Farrell and Kornbluh 1996), and Kemp began her career as a union activist.

Kemp realized the key to improving conditions was worker education, so she took courses offered by the American Federation of Labor (AFL), the Wellesley College Institute for Social Progress, the Rand School of Social Services, and the Hudson Shore Labor School. In time, she became an ILGWU shop representative, and eventually rose to the executive board and education committee. In addition to labor issues, Local 22 took an active part in civil rights activities in the Harlem community.

Over the next few years, Kemp became increasingly active in union activities in New York, serving as captain and business agent for the Women's Health Brigade. Because the war effort had seriously depleted the male work force, the incoming worker pool was mainly comprised of women new to the mass worker environment, including refugees from war torn countries and Black southerners, all of whom were despised by the more experienced workers. Kemp's primary goal was to create a common bond among workers and change attitudes about racial, geographic, and gender stereotypes. She created educational programs to inform, instill change, and create solidarity that helped improve wages, work hours, work conditions, and safety measures.

Kemp had a long association with A. Philip Randolph, and kept abreast of his notable successes in forcing changes in federal laws dealing with discrimination in the workplace. She also cultivated a relationship with Black civic and women's rights advocate Pauli Murray, serving as Murray's campaign manager when she ran for city council in Brooklyn's 10th Senatorial District.

Kemp served as the Education Director of Local 132 for the Plastic Button and Novelty Workers' Union from 1942 to 1945, ran for the New York State Assembly on the American Labor Party ticket in 1942, and was appointed to the War Price and Rationing Board of the Office of Price Administration in 1944. In 1945, she was the first African American woman to represent U.S. labor abroad when she traveled to England as an AFL delegate to study wartime working conditions in Great Britain. While in England, Kemp contacted a group of young African trade unionists, and through them, she learned about the Pan-African movement. Going forward, she would dedicate her life to ending colonialism and creating labor unions in independent African nations (O'Farrell and Kornbluh 1996).

In 1946, Kemp helped stage a mass rally in Madison Square Garden to support establishing a permanent Fair Employment Practices Committee (FEPC) after the war ended. While the rally was a success, the FEPC ceased all operations that same year. From 1948 to 1951, she served as a business agent for Dressmakers' Union Local 22 of the ILGWU, and became the first African American business agent to represent a district.

During the 1950s, Kemp began working for the AFL as an advisor to the newly founded labor unions in Tanzania, Kenya, and Ghana, where she came to be known as "Mama Maida." Sponsored by the American Labor Education Service, she traveled to Sweden and Denmark in 1951 to observe workers' education programs. Kemp then took an eight-month hiatus from ILGWU to study at Ruskin Labor College, Oxford University, on an Urban League Fellowship. In 1955, she attended the first International Confederation of Free Trade Unions (ICFTU) conference in Accra, Ghana, as one of five observers. Out of those five, Kemp was the only woman. When she returned to the U.S. after her year long trip, Kemp and her husband divorced.

In 1956, Kemp organized a program to bring African students to Harvard University, and she went to Tanganyika, Africa to develop the program, facing opposition by both the British and U.S. labor officials. In 1957, she played a key role in the founding of Solidarity House in Nairobi.

When the AFL and CIO merged into one federation in 1955, they consolidated their international activities. Kemp went to work for the AFL-CIO's Department of International Affairs as Africa's representative in 1960, and for the next several years, her home alternated between Dar es Salaam (Tanzania), Nairobi (Kenya), and Brooklyn. She worked for the affiliated African-American Labor Center and the Asian-American Free Labor Institute as well. Kemp founded a trade school in Kenya that expanded opportunities for women, established a post-secondary scholarship for Tanzanian girls, and started the Maida Fund to enable farm workers in East Africa to return to school. During the course of her work, she befriended many of Africa's emerging leaders, including Julius Nyerere of Tanzania and Kwame Nkrumah of Ghana. Between 1957 and 1963, Kemp attended the national independence ceremonies of Ghana, Nigeria, Tanzania, and Kenya. In 1964, Kemp represented the U.S. at the 48th Session of the International Labour Organization conference in Geneva.

There were, however, conflicts between the AFL-CIO and the African labor leaders, and Kemp resigned from her AFL-CIO position in 1966. Eventually, the AFL-CIO's efforts to maintain the African labor organization's affiliation with the ICFTU would end in 1969, in part because of the continued contacts between the ICFTU affiliates and unions from Communist countries, which went against the U.S.' anti-communism policies. Also, there was an ongoing failure to increase and properly oversee aid to developing countries[1] (Richards 2000).

Her marriage to James Kemp—a lawyer and former national president of the NAACP—her recurring illnesses, and the health of her aging family contributed to Kemp's decision to take time off from work. She eventually returned to the ILGWU as a general organizer in the South (Richards 2000), and as

1, After an absence of twelve years, the AFL-CIO rejoined the ICFTU in 1982, but the ICFTU affiliates faced continuous pressure to withdraw from the ICFTU. By 2006, the ICFTU was dissolved and merged with the World Confederation of Labour (WCL) to form the International Trade Union Confederation (ITUC).

vice president of the National Council of Negro Women (NCNW) (O'Farrell and Kornbluh 1996).

By the 1970s, Kemp had established a reputation as an international expert in labor education. She worked as the Midwest Director of the A. Philip Randolph Institute, working in voter registration and education. In conjunction with her work at the institute from 1970 to 1973, when the Sahel Drought in western and central Africa struck in 1970, she began coordinating relief programs for the African American Labor Center (AALC). From 1973 to 1976, Kemp became a staff member of the AFL-CIO affiliated AALC, and was the liaison for the American labor movement in Africa during that period. She worked as a consultant for the Asian-American Free Labor Institute (AAFLI), and worked with trade unions in Turkey, where she helped introduce women into the labor movement by establishing the Women's Bureau of TÜRK-İŞ. Kemp and her husband separated in the early 1970s, but remained friends until Kemp's death.

Kemp also worked in Indonesia to encourage more women to join the labor movement. She attended International Women's Year conferences in Mexico and Nairobi in 1975, and the Pan African Conference on the Role of Trade Union Women in 1977. In 1978, she then served as a consultant to the Nairobi Seminar of Women Workers, a meeting that attracted women from fourteen African countries. Kemp's alliances with African leaders such as Julius Nyerere and Tom Mboya prompted her appointment to the ILGWU International Staff in the 1980s, which led to her being named a consultant for the African Labor History Center.

Initially, her efforts were met with resistance by male union leaders, who wanted women to participate in the organizing work but had little interest in women's concerns such as equal pay, equal opportunity, and child care.

Kemp received many awards over the course of her fifty year career, including the National Council of Negro Women's Woman of the Year Award, a Candace Award from the National Coalition of 100 Black Women, the Bessie Abramowitz Hillman Award from the Coalition of Labor Union Women, the first annual Rosina Tucker Award from the A. Philip Randolph Institute, the Women's Rights Award from the American Federation of Teachers, and an honorary Doctor of Humane Letters degree from Brooklyn College, City University of New York. The Maida Springer Kemp Fund, created in her honor by UNITE and the AFL-CIO, combats child labor in East Africa by sending children to school for technical training, providing financial aid to women to start small businesses, and supporting needlework schools.

She was a member of the National Council of Negro Women, the NAACP, the African American Free Labor Institute, the Asian-American Free Labor Institute, the National Organization for Women, and the Coalition of Labor Union Women.

In the late 1970s, Kemp moved to Pittsburgh near her son, where she lived the remainder of her life. Maida Springer Kemp died after a long illness on March 29, 2005. She was ninety-four years old. ❖

Pauli Murray
(1910-1985)
Civil rights and women's rights activist, priest, lawyer, author

Pauli Murray became the first African American woman to earn a J.S.D. from Yale Law School, is responsible for creating the "bible" of the civil rights movement, is a cofounder of the National Organization for Women (NOW), and is the first Black woman to be ordained an Episcopal priest.

ANNA PAULINE "PAULI" MURRAY was born in Baltimore, Maryland to Agnes Fitzgerald Murray, a nurse, and William Henry Murray, a graduate of Howard University, and a high school teacher and principal. Her father suffered from the long-term effects of typhoid fever and went into bouts of depression. When her mother died of a cerebral hemorrhage in 1914, Murray and her five siblings lived with other family members. One of six children, Murray went to live with her maternal aunt, Pauline Fitzgerald, an elementary schoolteacher, and her grandparents Cornelia and Robert Fitzgerald in Durham, North Carolina. Murray's father was eventually confined to Crownsville State Hospital for the Negro Insane, where he was beaten to death with a baseball bat by a guard in 1923 (Rosenberg 2017).

Murray's maternal grandmother was born in bondage; her mother, who was part-Cherokee, was also a slave. Her grandfather, by contrast, was raised in Pennsylvania, attended anti-slavery meetings with Harriet Tubman and Frederick Douglass, and fought for the Union in the Civil War. Together, they formed part of a large and close-knit family whose members ranged from Episcopalians to Quakers, impoverished to wealthy, fair-skinned and blue-eyed to dark-skinned with curly hair. Her family's background would greatly inform her life as an activist.

Murray taught herself to read by age five and devoured books from then on. When she graduated from Hillside High School with a certificate of distinction in 1926 at age fifteen, she was the editor-in-chief of the school newspaper, the president of the literary society, class secretary, a member of the debate club, the top student, and a forward on the basketball team. Her initial goal was to become a writer.

Early on, Murray struggled with what we would today call a transgender identity crisis; she felt outwardly female, but inwardly male. Since her early childhood, she wore her hair short and wore boys' clothing, and at an early age preferred to be called the gender nonspecific "Paul," later settling on "Pauli," a preference most people honored. Although Murray was extremely guarded about her life, her personal papers openly revealed the anguish she faced concerning her gender identity throughout her entire life. Although she became a pioneering leader in both the civil rights and feminist movements, Murray believed that nontraditional gender identity and sexual orientation was a private matter (Rosenberg 2017).

Since the age of ten, Murray began looking North to escape the South. Coming of age in the South instilled in Murray a hatred of racial discrimination and segregation, evils she would combat for much of her life. Shortly following her graduation from high school, she no longer wanted a segregated education. When the time came to choose a college, she set her sights on Columbia University in New York but quickly learned that Columbia did not accept women; Barnard did, but she could not afford the tuition. She could attend Hunter College for free only if she became a New York City resident but not with her current transcript because Black high schools in North Carolina ended at eleventh grade and did not offer all the classes she needed to matriculate into college. Dismayed but determined, Murray appealed to a cousin in Richmond Hills in Queens, New York, and enrolled in Richmond Hill High School.

When Murray graduated from high school, she was only one of four Black students of 232 women (Rosenberg 2017). She briefly returned to Durham to work and save money for college and went back to New York to attend Hunter College, where she continued to finance her studies with various jobs. Not long after, amid the Harlem Renaissance, Murray moved into a room at the Harlem YWCA. While there, she befriended Langston Hughes, met W. E. B. Du Bois attended lectures by civil rights activist Mary McLeod Bethune and went to the Apollo Theater to hear the likes of Duke Ellington and Cab Calloway. As an eighteen-year-old college student living in New York City with plans to become a writer, Murray lived the life in which she had always dreamed.

In 1930, Murray met a young man named William Wynn, also twenty, impoverished, uprooted, and lonely. After a brief courtship, the two married in secret, then spent an awkward two-day honeymoon at a cheap hotel. Almost immediately, Murray realized she had made a mistake. Emotionally, the marriage did not last the weekend and was eventually annulled. Murray would spend the rest of her life wrestling with her sexuality. In a crisis, she took a leave of absence from Hunter, drifted around the country with a girlfriend doing odd jobs, and led a somewhat impractical and carefree lifestyle. When she returned a year later, Murray graduated in 1933, possibly the worst year in U.S. history to enter the job market. She worked at the Work Projects Administration (WPA), was a teacher in the New York City Remedial Reading Project, and worked at the National Urban League. Living on the edge of poverty, Murray was diagnosed with pleurisy and was in danger of developing tuberculosis. Murray's physician enrolled her at

Camp TERA, a racially integrated camp for women in the Bear Mountain area of Upstate New York to rest and regain her health.

During the Great Depression, thousands of the unemployed headed to the woods to serve in the Civilian Conservation Corps (CCC), a New Deal work relief program that gave millions employment on environmental projects, but those jobs were reserved only for men. First Lady Eleanor Roosevelt, however, wanted an option for the two million women who lost work and were equally impacted by the Wall Street Crash of 1929. Many women were forced to seek dwindling private charity or turned to their families. Others became increasingly desperate, living on the streets, and their economic needs were virtually ignored. Roosevelt forged ahead, encountering resistance from her husband's cabinet. Along with the New Deal's most influential women, she managed to get the government to greenlight an experimental camp for women through the CCC.

One such place was Camp TERA (named after New York's Temporary Emergency Relief Administration), designed to provide unemployed women a clean, safe environment to take vocational classes like typing and filing and liberal arts courses. They spent their downtime hiking, playing baseball, swimming, and socializing. Most camps were segregated, as the majority of camps served a white populace from rural communities and small towns, but an estimated twelve camps were dedicated to unemployed Black women.[1]

Murray's time at Camp TERA was cut short after she clashed with the camp's director, who found a copy of *Das Kapital* among Murray's belongings, and she was ejected her from the camp. The sociopolitical issues of the day, including a woman's place in society, the fear of communism and left-leaning ideals coupled with racism, converged at Camp TERA, which further informed Murray of the complexities of the politics of gender and race, and how it socially affected women. But more importantly, while Murray was at the camp, she met and befriended Roosevelt, who would become a mentor, supporter, intellectual ally, and a close friend until Roosevelt died in 1962. She also became deeply curious about *Das Kapital,* a book she had not yet read, and did not know what it meant (Rosenberg 2017).

In the meantime, Murray pursued her writing. She published articles and poems in various publications, including her novel, *Angel of the Desert,* serialized in the Carolina Times. She learned about the labor movement, participated in her first picket line, joined the Communist Party Opposition (CPO), a faction of the Communist Party USA (CPUSA), and then resigned a year later. Murray considered a career in social work but failed to win a needed scholarship. Meanwhile, her relatives in North Carolina were pressuring her to return home.

In 1938, returned to Dunham. Worried about her health and no job prospects, Murray applied to the Sociology Department at the University of North

1. *New Deal Resident Camps for Unemployed Women, A New Deal Program, c. 1933 1937* is a research initiative of PennPraxis, University of Pennsylvania, 2020, https://storymaps.arcgis. com/stories/02050ee5b4d543cf93821f56382367c2.

Carolina to pursue her growing interest in race relations. After being refused entry because of her race, Murray began a campaign with the support of the NAACP to gain entrance to the university. Her story received national attention, and while some faculty members supported Murray's cause, university policy required the administration to reject her. The NAACP would not bring a lawsuit on her behalf. It would not be until 1951 when Floyd McKissick became the first African American to be accepted by the University of North Carolina.

Murray's unsuccessful effort to challenge the university's decision was the first of three pivotal experiences in her journey towards pursuing a career in law. The second occurred shortly after that, in 1940 when Murray was a member of the Fellowship of Reconciliation (FOR). She and a friend were arrested for violating segregation statutes in Petersburg, Virginia, when they refused to sit at the back of the bus. This time, the NAACP was willing to use her arrest to challenge the constitutionality of segregated interstate travel, but Virginia would not take the bait. The police charged Murray and her friend with disorderly conduct, and since neither could not pay the fine, they both had to serve time in jail.

On the coattails of her arrest and short jail term, Murray began to work for the Workers Defense League (WDL), specifically for the legal defense effort of Odell Waller, an African American sharecropper sentenced to death for the murder of his White landlord. Despite Murray's lecture and fundraising tours, the WDL could not win an appeal on Waller's behalf, and he was executed on July 2, 1942. Her work on this case led her to pursue law, and with the help of Leon A. Ransom, a professor at Howard University, she enrolled at Howard University School of Law in 1941 to become a civil rights lawyer. While race ceased to be an issue, gender abruptly became one. Murray termed this form of degradation as "Jane Crow" and would spend the rest of her life working to end it. The following year, she joined with George Houser, James Farmer, and Bayard Rustin to form the Congress of Racial Equality (CORE).Members of CORE were mainly pacifists who had been deeply influenced by Henry David Thoreau, the teachings of Mahatma Gandhi, and the nonviolent civil disobedience campaign he used successfully against British rule in India. The students were convinced that the same methods could be employed by Blacks to obtain civil rights in America.

Academic training by such brilliant and influential African Americans such as Ransom, William H. Hastie, and Spottswood W. Robinson III provided excellent preparation for Murray's activities with the Howard chapter of the NAACP, especially the students' nonviolent, direct action sit-in campaigns to desegregate downtown Washington, D.C. lunch counters. In 1943, she published "Negroes Are Fed Up in Common Sense," and an article about the Harlem race riot in the socialist newspaper, *New York Call.* During her years in law school, Murray pursued her interests in racial justice and gender discrimination.

After Murray graduated from Howard University in 1944, she wanted to attend Harvard University to continue her law studies. In her application for a

Julius Rosenwald Fund Fellowship, she listed Harvard Law School as her first choice. Although she was awarded the prestigious fellowship, Harvard rejected her because of her gender. Murray went to the University of California Boalt School of Law instead and completed her LLM in 1945. Her master's thesis, "The Right to Equal Opportunity in Employment," foreshadowed much of her work that followed. She passed the California state bar that same year.

Murray coined the term "Jane Crow" in 1947 to signal that the impact of gender oppression differed from that of racial discrimination in name only. Jane Crow prevented Black women's full participation in society, including struggles in public spaces (with lower wages and sexual harassment) and conflicts in their private life (with expectations for their roles as wives and mothers and deference to male authority).

After graduation, Murray worked briefly as the Deputy Attorney General of California before returning to New York. After struggling to find sustainable work as an attorney, she opened her own law practice to support the growing civil rights movement. Finding this difficult to sustain, Murray was hired by the Women's Division of Christian Service of the Board of Missions of the Methodist Church to research laws on segregation. She published *States' Laws on Race and Color* 1951, and Thurgood Marshall, head of the legal department at the NAACP, described it as the "Bible" for civil rights lawyers. In the early 1950s, like many African Americans involved in the civil rights movement, McCarthyism affected Murray. In 1952, she lost a post at Cornell University because the people who had supplied her references—Eleanor Roosevelt, Thurgood Marshall and A. Philip Randolph—were considered too radical.

In 1955, Aunt Pauline died. Murray retreated to explore her past and wrote *Proud Shoes: The Story of an American Family,* a chronicle of her family's journey from slavery to citizenship, published in 1956. She accepted a position at the law offices of Paul, Weiss, Rifkind, Wharton, and Garrison as an associate attorney, where she met her partner, Irene Barlow. She worked there until she accepted a teaching position in Ghana in 1960 to help set up a law school. Unfortunately, Ghana proved disappointing. The country was in political turmoil which, manifested in limits on freedom of speech and had a grossly inadequate budget for the law school. This situation prodded her return to the U.S. After co-authoring the book, *The Constitution and Government of Ghana* in 1964, Murray arrived in New Haven to pursue graduate studies at Yale Law School and earned her J.S.D. in 1965, the first African American to do so. As part of her graduate work, she co-authored "Jane Crow and the Law: Sex discrimination and Title VII," which laid the groundwork for an emergent feminist jurisprudence. In the early 1960s, Murray worked closely with Randolph, Rustin, and Martin Luther King Jr. but was critical of how men dominated the leadership of these civil rights organizations.

Unable to secure a teaching position, Murray was commissioned to write *Human Rights U.S.A.: 1948-1966* for the Women's Division of the Methodist

Church. She gained some national recognition from 1965 to 1973 on the National Board of Directors for the American Civil Liberties Union and as co-counsel in the 1966 *White v. Crook* case, which successfully eliminated the use of sex and race discrimination in jury selection. That same year, Murray joined Betty Friedan and others to cofound the National Organization for Women (NOW), promising it would be the "NAACP for women." She was also invited to join President Kennedy's Commission on the Status of Women's Political and Civil Rights Committee, where she advocated an agenda that recognized Black women's double discrimination. After another difficult search for work, Murray finally secured full-time employment as a professor in the American Studies program at Brandeis University from 1968 to 1973.

While Murray accepted that the civil rights movement had sidelined women, she did not think the women's movement would sideline women of color. To her great satisfaction, she managed to get Black women activists like Dorothy I. Height to share her view that the government should not privilege Black men over Black women. Murray was also growing equally concerned that NOW had moved away from its initial vision to support human rights for all women (Rosenberg 2017).

When elite professional women in the organization diverted attention away from women of color and issues of poverty and justice, and decided to make the passage of the Equal Rights Amendment (ERA), its top priority. Murray was disappointed. She believed true equality was contingent on economic justice, Resigned to NOW's becoming the "NAACP for professional White women," Murray left the organization without an obvious home in the social justice movement (Rosenberg 2017).

By 1973, Murray found herself in crisis. Already missing Aunt Pauline, Murray lost her long-time partner, Irene Barlow, who suddenly died from cancer. Although she was both drawn to and disappointed by the Episcopalian church and its limited roles for women, she resigned from her tenured position at Brandeis to enter the seminary. She partly did this because she believed the civil rights and women's liberation movements had become too militant and were going nowhere; and that an emphasis on reconciliation would bring about better results.

Murray received a Master of Divinity degree from General Theological Seminary in New York in 1976. The struggle for the ordination of women was finally settled that same year, and in 1977, Murray became the first officially ordained African American female Episcopalian priest. Before her retirement in 1984 to work on her autobiography, she served as a priest at the Church of the Atonement in Washington, D.C., and later at the Church of the Holy Nativity in Baltimore.

At age seventy-four, Pauli Murray died of pancreatic cancer in the house she co-owned with lifelong friend Maida Springer Kemp in Pittsburgh on July 1, 1985. Her autobiography, *Song in a Weary Throat: An American Pilgrimage*, was published posthumously in 1987.❖

Dorothy I. Height
(1912-2010)
Civil rights leader, women's rights activist, social worker

Dorothy I. Height was an influential civil rights leader who addressed the rights of both women and African Americans as the president of the National Council of Negro Women and an executive of the YWCA.

DOROTHY I. HEIGHT was born in Richmond, Virginia to Fannie Burroughs Height, a nurse and domestic, and James Height, a building and painting contractor. Both of her parents were twice widowed, and both had children from their previous marriages (Height 2005). Height was the oldest of their two daughters. When she was five years old, the family moved to Rankin, Pennsylvania, a multiracial steel town in the suburbs of Pittsburgh. As a young girl, Height suffered from asthma, which was not helped by the industrial air of Pittsburgh.

Height's early life revolved around the church. Her father was a deacon, superintendent of the Sunday School, and choirmaster of the Emmanuel Baptist Church. When she was twelve years old, Height became a member of the Girls Reserves Club, a YWCA youth program. Ironically, she was denied entry to the Chatham Street YWCA's swimming pool due to segregation, and it struck a painful chord in her that reverberated for years to come (Height 2005).

Her mother was very active in the Pennsylvania Federation of Colored Women's Clubs, and she took Height to all the state and national meetings. When she was thirteen years old, she saw for the first time a Black woman, who was an elected official, speak at one of these events, which had a tremendous impact on her. The family also attended chicken dinners at the Church Missionary Society and participated in the Rankin Christian Center events, where she read Bible stories to White children. Height grew up in a Christian environment that promoted multiculturalism and social justice for all.

Height was an active participant in the town's new school, Rankin High School. She sang, co-wrote the school's new alma mater, and was part of a girls' singing group that performed concerts at local churches. Height played on the girls' basketball team and was a member of the debate team. She earned top grades in school and distinguished herself with her oratory skills. Height would be part of the school's first graduating class.

Height won a four-year college scholarship by participating in an oratorical contest held by the Independent Benevolent and Protective Order of Elks of the World. She was admitted to Barnard College in 1929. However, when she arrived in New York, her admission was revoked because the school had an unwritten policy of admitting only two Black students per year. Height instead enrolled in New York University, earning an undergraduate degree in 1932. During her college years, signs of the deepening depression were everywhere, and there were no jobs. Height tutored students; worked as a proofreader for Marcus Garvey's newspaper, *The Negro World;* worked at a laundry; and held other little jobs to make up the difference between her scholarship and make ends meet. She hung around the small group of Black students that attended the university, enjoying lectures by Langston Hughes, Paul Robeson, and W. E. B. Du Bois (Height 2005).

While a graduate student, Height worked for the Brownsville Community Center in Brooklyn to help provide services for the needy. In 1933, Height completed her master's degree in educational psychology. She also volunteered at the Brooklyn Bureau of Charities and eventually became an investigator at the Home Relief Bureau, which helped people gain employment. Her job allowed her to meet community leaders, high-level city officers, and members of Mayor La Guardia's administration.

In her spare time, Height became involved in many organizations that grappled with a wide range of political, social, and religious issues. Height cofounded the United Christian Youth Movement of North America; served as chair of the Harlem Youth Council, and president of the New York State Christian Youth Council, and an officer of the National Negro Americans; was active in the American Youth Congress, and occasionally attended the Young Communist meetings. Height liked meeting people with new and different ideas about how to make the world a better place (Height 2005).

Height accepted the director's position for the Greater New York Federation of Churches, but instead went to work as assistant director of the YWCA at the West 137th Street branch in Harlem. When Height joined the YWCA in 1937, it was during a critical period in the organization's history as it grappled with race. Around this time, Height had a life-changing encounter, meeting educator and founder of the National Council of Negro Women (NCNW) Mary McLeod Bethune and then First Lady Eleanor Roosevelt when they came to visit the YWCA. Soon after, Height volunteered with the NCNW.

In 1939, Height was asked to become executive director of the Phyllis Wheatley YWCA in Washington D.C. After she accepted the position and relocated, Height was shocked at how completely segregated the city was. In 1944, Height returned to the YWCA in New York to become secretary for interracial education of the national board. During the 1940s, Height challenged the YWCA's discriminatory practices by traveling the country and helping local chapters implement the organization's interracial charter. Heads of local chapters in the South would not meet with her, and she was forced to spend nights with local Black families because hotels would not admit her.

Height had always wanted to join a sorority, but segregation prevented her from joining the sorority on New York University's campus. She was initiated at the Rho Chapter of Delta Sigma Theta Sorority at Columbia University and served as its national president from 1947 to 1956. She remained an active member throughout her life, helping to develop leadership training programs and ecumenical educational programs.

In 1958, Height was named president of the NCNW. It was a volunteer position with unpaid staff, which she did while working for the YMCA (Height 2005). As president, she led the group to expand its mission. Her initiatives included training thousands of women—housewives, teachers, office workers, students—to work as community advocates to push for better housing and schools. It was a way to help women escape what Height called the "triple bind of racism, sexism, and poverty" (Height 2005).

During the civil rights movement, she organized "Wednesdays in Mississippi," which brought together Black and White women from the North and South to create a dialogue of understanding. Height was also a founding member of the Council for United Civil Rights Leadership. In 1963, she was one of the organizers of the famed March on Washington. She stood close to Martin Luther King Jr. when he delivered his "I Have a Dream" speech. Despite her skills as a speaker and a leader, Height was not invited to speak that day. In fact, the only woman allowed to speak was Daisy Bates, with a speech written by the NAACP's John Marshall consisting of 142 words, which read more like a pledge to support male leadership. Although Height often collaborated with the civil rights movement's key leaders—including King, Wilkins, James Farmer, John Lewis, A. Philip Randolph and Whitney Young, a group often referred to as the "Big Six"—Height, was often overlooked due to sexism.

In 1965, Height was named head of the YWCA's newly established Office of Racial Justice, charged with leading the organization's campaign against discrimination. American leaders regularly took her counsel. Height encouraged President Eisenhower to desegregate schools and President Johnson to appoint African American women to positions in government. In the mid-1960s, she wrote a column called "A Woman's Word" for the weekly African American newspaper, the Amsterdam News, in New York.

Height served on many committees, including as a consultant on African affairs to the Secretary of State, the President's Committee on the Employment of the Handicapped, and the President's Committee on the Status of Women. She joined the fight for women's rights and, in 1971, helped found the National Women's Political Caucus with Gloria Steinem, Betty Friedan, and Shirley Chisholm. In 1974, she was named to the National Commission for the

Protection of Human Subjects of Biomedical and Behavioral Research, which published the *Belmont Report,* a response to the "Tuskegee Syphilis Study"[1] that remains an international ethical touchstone for researchers to this day.

In addition to her work in the U.S., Height traveled extensively. She served as a visiting professor at the University of Delhi, India, and the Black Women's Federation of South Africa. She retired from the YWCA in 1977 but continued to lead the NCNW for two more decades. Although she stepped down from the presidency in 1997, she remained the organization's board chair until her death.

In the 1980s, Height led African American Women for Reproductive Rights, a pro-choice group, while working with the NCNW. In 1989, she organized the first Black Family Reunion with the NCNW, a three-day cultural event for Black Americans that still occurs annually today.

Height received many honors for her contributions to society. She received more than twenty honorary degrees, as well as the Franklin Delano Roosevelt Freedom Medal and the Citizens Medal Award. In 1994, President Clinton awarded her the Presidential Medal of Freedom. In 2002, Height turned her ninetieth birthday celebration into a fundraiser for the NCNW; Oprah Winfrey and Don King were among the celebrities who contributed to the event. In 2004, President George W. Bush gave Height the Congressional Gold Medal.

She was finally recognized by Barnard College for her achievements and, as a form of apology was made an honorary alumna in 2004 during the college's commemoration of the fiftieth anniversary of the *Brown v. Board of Education* decision. The musical stage play *If This Hat Could Talk* was based on her memoir, *Open Wide The Freedom Gates* (2003). The work showcased her unique perspective on the civil rights movement and details many of the behind-the-scenes figures and mentors who shaped her life, including Mary McLeod Bethune and Eleanor Roosevelt. She befriended President Obama and was an honored guest at his first inauguration.

Height was admitted to Howard University Hospital in Washington D.C. for unspecified reasons. Dorothy I. Height died six weeks later, on April 20, 2010 at age ninety-eight. Her funeral service at the Washington National Cathedral was attended by President Obama, First Lady Michelle Obama, and many other dignitaries and notable people. She was later buried at Fort Lincoln Cemetery in Colmar Manor, Maryland. Height never married and had no children. ❖

The Legacy of Dorothy I. Height

DOROTHY I. HEIGHT WAS KNOWN as the great unifier. As a social worker who became an activist, she understood early on that the way forward was to stand and advocate together. Even when African American civil rights groups did not

---

1. *The Belmont Report,* from the Office of the Secretary. *Ethical Principles and Guidelines for the Protection of Human Subjects of Research,* by The National Commission for the Protection of Human Subjects of Biomedical and Behavioral Research, April 18, 1979. https://www.hhs.gov/ohrp/regulations-and-policy/belmont-report/read-the-belmont-report/index.html.

necessarily get along with each other, and Black and White women's groups were wary of each other, Height always found a way to bridge both worlds. She helped to mediate and resolve differences with grace and dignity, almost always with undeniably stunning results. Hers was a constant presence during the high point of the civil rights movement.

Height never drew the media attention that conferred celebrity and instant recognition on some of the other civil rights leaders of her time. She was often described as the "glue" that held the Black civil rights leadership together. Often the only woman at strategy meetings with Martin Luther King Jr. and other Black male leaders, Height was a determined voice pressing the importance of issues affecting women and children, such as childcare and education.

While doing much of her work out of the public spotlight, she was widely connected at the highest levels of power and influence in government and business. In Height's heyday, she served on numerous government committees, personally knew presidents and CEOs of Fortune 500 companies, was at the forefront of every major civil rights event, and was an advisor to presidential administrations, from Franklin D. Roosevelt to Barack Obama.

It is said Height's lifetime of achievement can be measured by the liberation of Black America. She embodied the true definition of servant leadership, exemplified by her lifelong commitment to fighting for racial equality and women's rights, but it was not easy. She stood for women's rights at a time when the male leadership of the civil rights movement was not ready or willing to join that fight. She engaged women of all races in the struggle for equality for African Americans, even as some women's groups continued to discriminate. Her multicultural connections were a mainstay in her career, and she worked closely with organizations such as the American Indian Movement and the American Jewish Committee.

Height worked closely with many women leaders. African American leader Mary McLeod Bethune was her hero. First Lady Eleanor Roosevelt brought her in as counsel. She sought out relationships with a wide variety of women from different backgrounds, including Anna Arnold Hedgeman, Pauli Murray, Shirley Chisholm, Rosina Corrothers Tucker, Unita Blackwell, Marion Edelman-Wright and so many others. She was also able to engender greater conversations —dialog, communication—between Black and White women. In her fight for humanity, Height succeeded in taking her Christian, civil rights, feminist, and social justice values and rolled them into a unifying force.

Height was a crusader of quiet confidence and is remembered as an icon to all African American women who understand the importance of the human condition. Even into her nineties, when asked if she planned to retire, Height said she would never retire from working for social justice, and she did not. Her legacy of leadership and activism still resonates in the communities she touched. ❖

Rosa Parks
(1913-2005)
Civil rights activist

Rosa Parks, considered the mother of the civil rights movement, became a nationally recognized symbol of dignity and strength in the struggle to end entrenched racial segregation in the U.S.

ROSA LOUISE MCCAULEY PARKS was born in Tuskegee, Alabama to Leona Edwards McCauley, a teacher, and James McCauley, a carpenter and builder. As a child, Parks suffered poor health with chronic tonsillitis. When her parents separated shortly after her brother's birth, she moved with her mother and younger brother to a farm in Pine Level to live with her maternal grandparents. At six years old, she worked as a field hand and picked cotton (Parks and Haskins 1992). Parks' mother was a teacher who valued education and taught her to read at a young age. She attended a segregated, one-room school in Pine Level that lacked adequate school supplies. While Black students were forced to walk to school, the city provided bus transportation and a new school building for its White students. When the school closed, Parks attended an elementary school in Montgomery and lived with relatives during the week.

By age eleven, Parks had attended Booker T. Washington Junior High School and enrolled in a laboratory school for high school students at the Alabama State Teachers' College for Negroes (now known as Albany State University). She left in the eleventh grade to help care for her dying grandmother in Pine Level. When she returned to Montgomery, she worked in a shirt factory for a while and returned to school, but she dropped out to care for her mother when she took ill. In 1932, at age nineteen, she married Raymond Parks, who was ten years older than her, worked as a barber, and was a long-time member of the NAACP. He supported Parks earning a high school diploma, which she received the following year.

Since few industrial jobs were available in Montgomery, Parks put her sewing skills to good use instead of becoming trapped in a domestic job, and she worked as an assistant tailor in a Black-owned tailor shop at the Montgomery Fair department store (Parks and Haskins 1992). She and her husband became respected members of Montgomery's large African American community. Coexisting with White people in a city governed by Jim Crow laws was fraught with daily frustrations: Blacks could attend only certain schools (which were often inferior), drink only from specified water fountains, borrow books only from "Black" libraries, and sit at the back of movie theaters, among other restrictions. Although her husband had previously discouraged her out of fear for her safety, Parks joined the Montgomery chapter of the NAACP in December 1943 and became chapter secretary.

At the urging of NAACP chapter president E. D. Nixon, a Pullman porter who worked closely with A. Philip Randolph, and Virginia Durr, a White NAACP supporter, Parks attended a two-week workshop on public school integration at the Highlander Folk School in Tennessee in the summer of 1955, regarding the U.S. Supreme Court's decision on *Brown v. Board of Education*. Over the years, Parks would attend future workshops at Highlander (Parks and Haskins 1992).

On December 1, 1955, forty-two-year-old Parks was commuting home from a long day of work at the Montgomery Fair department store by bus. Black residents of Montgomery often avoided municipal buses if possible because they found the Negroes-in-back policy demeaning. Nonetheless, 70 percent or more riders on a typical day were Black, and on this day, Parks was one of them.

Segregation was written into law; the front of a Montgomery bus was reserved for Whites, and the seats behind them for Blacks. However, it was only by custom that bus drivers had the authority to tell a Black person to give up a seat for a White rider. There were contradictory Montgomery laws on the books: one said segregation must be enforced, but another, largely ignored, said no person (White or Black) could be told to give up a seat if there was no other seat available. In this case, a White man had no seat because all the seats in the designated "White" section were taken, so the driver told the riders in the first row of the "Colored" section to stand, in effect adding another row to the "White" section. Three riders obeyed. Parks did not. Eventually, the police were called. They stopped the bus and arrested Parks.

Although Parks used her one phone call to contact her husband, word of her arrest spread quickly, and Nixon was there when Parks was released on bail later that evening. Nixon had hoped for years to find a courageous Black person of unquestionable integrity to become the plaintiff in a test case that could challenge the validity of bus segregation. He convinced Parks, her husband, and her mother that she was that plaintiff.

Most people are unaware that the boycott was initiated by the Women's Political Council (WPC)[1] in the wee hours of the morning after Parks' arrest. Its president, Jo Ann Robinson, a newly-hired English professor at Alabama State University, decided to bypass Parks and instead contacted Nixon to inform him that she and her students were already distributing more than 35,000 flyers throughout the community to call for a one-day bus strike when Parks was scheduled to appear in court (Theoharis 2018).

---

1. In 1943 the Women's Political Council (WPC) was founded in Montgomery to address the racial issues in the city. The WPC was responsible for initiating the boycott, and was instrumental in the boycott's organizational structure, which helped sustain it for more than a year.

In the meantime, when it became clear that the boycott was moving forward, the Black ministers and community leaders quickly formed the Montgomery Improvement Association (MIA) that same day under the leadership of Nixon, Martin Luther King Jr., and Ralph Abernathy. King was elected as the MIA's president because, he was relatively unknown and if things went sideways, he would have end up taking the heat. Instead, his leadership catapulted him into the national spotlight.

Since no one knew what to expect, the empty buses were a complete surprise, and Black participation in the boycott was much larger than anyone anticipated. Meanwhile, Parks was found guilty of violating segregation laws in court, given a suspended sentence, and fined $10 plus $4 in court costs. The success of the boycott, and the excitement at the mass meeting on the evening of that day, removed any doubt for its continuation.

The city of Montgomery refused to negotiate to end the boycott. Instead, opposing White people swelled the ranks of the White Citizens' Council, doubling its membership, and engendered anger and violence from Montgomery's White population. Several boycott leaders, including Abernathy, Nixon and King, had their homes bombed. However, the violence did not deter the boycotters or their leaders, and the drama in Montgomery continued to gain national and international attention.

The boycott proved extremely effective, causing economic distress to the city's transit system. Besides organizing carpools, with car owners volunteering their vehicles or driving people to various destinations, the leadership also set up a cab system, and even some White housewives drove their Black domestic servants to work. When the city pressured local insurance companies to stop insuring cars used in the carpools, the boycott leaders arranged policies at Lloyd's of London. When the boycotters were accosted with verbal abuse and violence, they would not give in and prevailed.

When Parks refused to give up her seat, her true motivation was that she had become weary of Jim Crow buses, tired of living her life as a second class citizen under segregation, and saw the need for collective action from the Black community. Furthermore, while she did not outright plan her dissent, she certainly understood its implications. Unbeknownst to male leadership at the time, Parks had a more extensive and progressive political background than many of the boycott leaders. Besides her decade-long affiliation with the NAACP, including her investigation of the rape of Recy Taylor, and her association with Highlander, she had also developed strong ties to leftist organizations (Theoharis 2018).

However, the MIA's strategy was to obscure Parks' long-standing political activities and paint her as an unwitting seamstress who simply refused to get up from her seat because of her tired feet. Under a gender-biased hue, she was reimagined from an assistant tailor to a seamstress and from a political activist to simply a God-fearing Christian. As a seasoned political activist, Parks understood the implication of presenting an image for public consumption, and foregrounding the roots of this movement into the broader mistreatment of the African American community was far more important to her than anything else. Unfortunately, the seeds of the "simple tired seamstress" narrative would take root and become mythologized for years to come (Theoharis 2018).

It should be noted that a movement initiated by Black women quickly became a male-dominated movement, and Parks would become nothing more than a nonthreatening mother figure and a silent symbol who had little input during the boycott. Parks would always admire King, but in time would quietly disagree with and question some of his tactics and the MIA's motives (Theoharis 2018).

Parks was fully aware that she was not the first person to protest bus segregation and that several Black women—Irene Morgan Kirkaldy, Viola White, Geneva Johnson, Sarah Keys, and Epsie Worth—had established a history of bus resistance and fought back. In some cases, they withstood violence when they refused to give up their seats. For instance, nine months before Parks was arrested, fifteen-year-old Claudette Colvin, a protégé of Parks, staged a similar action, for which Parks helped raise defense funds. Parks knew that other Black women had protested before her and always credited them for laying down the foundation of the civil rights movement (Parks and Haskins 1992).

When Parks and her husband lost their jobs and were unable to find employment, they garnered little to no economic support from the MIA or the NAACP (which distanced itself from the early stages of the boycott). Ironically, Parks' symbolic status was crucial to both organizations. As she traveled around the country, made public appearances on behalf of the boycott, and raised thousands of dollars for the cause, she received little to no compensation from either organization. No one wanted to be responsible for Parks' imperiled situation. The impact of living with racial terror, relentless harassment, and economic insecurity had taken its toll on Parks and her family, affecting them mentally, emotionally, and physically. Although she already had chronic insomnia, Parks also developed painful stomach ulcers, and a heart condition emerged that would plague her for the rest of her life. Her husband, who lost his barbershop, began to drink heavily, and was chain-smoking, also suffered from ulcers, and eventually had a nervous breakdown (Theoharris 2013).

It became increasingly clear that many people had grown jealous of Parks' national stature. Parks became bewildered by the animosity and resentments from the African American community, including the MIA, WPC and the NAACP, who all felt they were not getting enough credit for their role in the boycott.

Once the boycott was in full force, three Black women—Aurelia Browder, Mary Louise Smith and Susie McDonald—availed themselves to become plaintiffs in *Browder v. Gayle*. The appeals and related lawsuits winded their way through the courts and up to the U.S. Supreme Court, which ruled that bus segregation was unconstitutional. This case effectively ended the boycott on

December 20, 1956, one day after the court's written order arrived in Montgomery. The boycott had lasted 382 days. Parks, who had lost her job security and feared for her life, was left in the margins while King and the boycott's success transfixed the country. However, the celebration was short-lived. White backlash against the court victory was quick, brutal, and effective. Snipers fired upon buses, churches were bombed, and retaliation was meted toward the few White Montgomerians who had publicly sided with the boycott.

Parks found herself exiled from her hometown because of her stand against segregation. In 1957 Parks, her husband, and her mother moved to Detroit, where her younger brother, Sylvester, lived. She had accepted a job offer as a hostess at the Holly Tree Inn on the campus of Hampton Institute in Virginia, with the proviso that Hampton would relocate her family. When that arrangement never came to fruition, Parks returned to Detroit in 1958. For almost ten years, her family lived in the wilderness with no jobs, little money, and health issues abound.

It was not until 1965 that John Conyers fundamentally shifted Parks' economic situation. Parks had been a dedicated volunteer of Conyers' long-shot campaign. When he was elected as Detroit's second African American member of the House of Representatives, he hired Parks as an administrator, ending a decade of economic and emotional insecurity and turmoil. Parks now had job security, healthcare, and a pension, which restored her independence and dignity. Conyers knew how invaluable Parks' personal and political skills would be to Detroit and was not threatened by her symbolic status in the African American community. For the next fifty years until her death, Parks would fervently fight against segregation behind the scenes for political mobilization as she had done in Montgomery. Working with Conyers, Parks realized that segregation was not a Southern malady but a national one. A committed activist, she drew public attention to the racial inequities of the liberal North, which had gone largely unnoticed. She also fought for women's rights and against the Vietnam War, advocated for prisoners, and supported the growing Black Power Movement (Theoharis 2018).

Besides dealing directly with constituents, Parks continued to travel around the country, appearing at protests and speaking engagements. She donated most of the money she received to civil rights causes and lived on her staff salary and later her husband's pension.

During the 1970s, she lost her closest family members to cancer. Her husband Raymond Parks died in 1977, and her brother, her only sibling, died of cancer several months later. Her mother died in 1979 at the age of ninety-two from cancer and geriatric dementia. Widowed and without immediate family, the depths of her loss did not dissuade her from her political activities. After a period of mourning, Parks re-entered public life and rededicated herself to her civil rights agenda.

She supported Jesse Jackson's 1984 and 1988 presidential campaigns and participated in the anti-apartheid protests. Parks was also part of the welcoming party for Nelson Mandela when he visited the U.S. In 1987, she cofounded the Rosa and Raymond Parks Institute for Self Development with Elaine Steele to educate and direct youth. She retired from Conyers' office in 1988.

After her retirement, Parks wrote her autobiography, *Rosa Parks: My Story* (1992). In 1994, at age eighty-one, Parks was robbed and assaulted in her home in Detroit. Her assailant demanded money from Parks and attacked her. A neighborhood manhunt led to his capture and reported beating. Parks was treated for facial injuries and swelling on the right side of her face. Her assailant, sentenced to eight to fifteen years, was transferred to a prison in another state for his own safety.

In 1996, President Clinton awarded Parks the Presidential Medal of Freedom. In 1999, she was awarded the Congressional Gold Medal, the highest honor bestowed on a civilian. Parks filmed a cameo appearance for the television series *Touched by an Angel* in 1999. It was her last appearance on film. She continued her commitment to civil rights until her death, willingly serving as a symbol of the civil rights struggle. When she died at age ninety-two on October 24, 2005, Rosa Parks became the first woman in the nation's history to lie in state at the U.S. Capitol. She and her husband never had children, and she outlived her only sibling. Parks was survived by her sister-in-law, thirteen nieces and nephews and their families, and several cousins. ❖

The Legacy of Rosa Parks

IN AN ACT OF CIVIL DISOBEDIENCE over sixty years ago, Rosa Parks' refusal to move to the back of a city bus made her a key symbol in America's civil rights movement. Her singular act of defiance, dignified and determined, planted the psychological seed needed to ignite and propel the movement forward, which is why she is treated with such deference and respect.

Parks received hundreds of awards, citations, commendations, and honorary doctorate degrees too numerous to mention here, some of them long after her death. However, while she appreciated the attention, she remained stalwart in her desire to fight for civil rights and political activism (Parks and Haskins 1992).

As one of the few Black women icons of the civil rights movement, Parks left an impact on the nation and the world. Her action gave America a chance to redeem itself and gave it credibility and authority that resounded worldwide. If America is to maintain its international prestige, gained on the backs of civil rights activists like Parks, it must continue to monitor itself and seek higher ground whenever possible. Long after Rosa Parks' death, she still has the power to inspire. ❖

Fannie Lou Hamer
(1917-1977)
Voting and women's rights activist, community organizer

*Fannie Lou Hamer, a cofounder of the Mississippi Freedom
Democratic Party, was a voting rights activist who helped
African Americans register to vote, and focused on financially
empowering African Americans.*

FANNIE LOU TOWNSEND HAMER was born in Montgomery County, Mississippi
to Lou Ella Townsend, a domestic, and James Lee Townsend, a Baptist preacher
and bootlegger. The couple were also sharecroppers east of the Mississippi
Delta. The twentieth child of fifteen boys and five girls, Hamer moved with her
family near Sunflower, Mississippi to work as sharecroppers at E. W. Brandon's
plantation when she was two years old. Her parents were self-sacrificing and
resourceful, and they did not see a contradiction in her father being a man of the
cloth and a bootlegger. He did what needed to be done to support his family. Her
mother, a deeply religious person, was a fighter in every sense of the word and
a fierce protector of her children. More importantly, her mother taught Hamer to
feel good about being Black and to be her authentic self. Hamer's early childhood
experiences also taught her that there was a direct link between race and access
to resources, and that, in order to gain power, one must speak out (Lee 1999).

Like other sharecroppers, the family dealt with an insurmountable combination of hard work entrenched in brutally virulent racism, poverty, exploitation,
and violence. Their stark reality was part of a postbellum system designed to
replace slavery as a cheap source of labor. While Hamer loved school, economic
pressures forced her to drop out of school at age twelve to work in the fields
and pick hundreds of pounds of cotton a day. She would later attend church
and continue developing her reading skills through Bible study, a road to literacy
not uncommon for slaves and ex-slaves (Lee 1999). In 1939, Hamer's father
had a stroke and died shortly after.

While most of her older siblings had already moved out, Hamer remained at
home until she married Perry Hamer, known as "Pap," in the early 1940s. They
eventually moved on to W. D. Marlow's plantation near Ruleville in Sunflower
County, where her husband worked for twelve years.

Since Hamer could read and write, she was promoted to timekeeper, a less physically demanding and more prestigious job within the sharecropping system. To make ends meet, she also worked as a domestic, ran her late father's juke joint—from which they sold bootleg liquor—and for a time worked as an insurance saleswoman (Lee 1999). Nearly blind and suffering from other ailments, Hamer's mother moved in with her. Not long after her mother's death, Hamer went to the hospital to have a small cyst removed and found out she was given a hysterectomy without her knowledge or consent. It was a procedure so common that Hamer called it the "Mississippi appendectomy,"[1] the involuntary sterilization of Black women. Unable to bear children, the Hamers adopted two girls whose families were unable to care for them.

In the summer of 1962, Hamer made a life-changing decision to attend a protest meeting. She met civil rights activists who were encouraging African Americans to register to vote. Hamer, one of a small group of Blacks in her area, traveled to the county courthouse in Indianola to register and encountered opposition. Hamer was fired from her job and driven from the plantation she had called home for nearly two decades just for trying to register to vote. However, these actions only solidified Hamer's resolve to help other African Americans get the right to vote.

Hamer stayed with friends in Ruleville, but it was clear that there would be reprisals against the people who had gone to Indianola. Her husband drove Hamer and their daughters to Tallahatchie County, where they stayed with relatives for a few days before returning to Sunflower County, ready to take up the fight once again. This episode in Indianola was more than a group of poor, disenfranchised Black Southerners going up against a rigid system of exclusion to express a constitutional right. It also represented a significant psychological transformation: people were beginning to believe they had the power to change what had previously been seen as hopelessly unalterable (Lee 1999).

Local organizers had noticed Hamer's willingness to challenge the county registrar, and Student Nonviolent Coordinating Committee (SNCC) field secretary Bob Moses, who saw her as a potential leader, invited Hamer to a SNCC conference at Fisk University in the fall of 1962. After the conference, Hamer left Nashville eager to take on her new role as a community organizer.

Her husband remained at the Marlow plantation to work through the harvest to pay off the family's sharecropping debt, but in the fall of 1962, he rejoined his wife and daughters. Marlow took possession of their belongings, so they started over in Ruleville. The family's main source of income was Hamer's

1.   Birthed from the eugenics movement, in 1928, Mississippi passed forced-sterilization legislation, targeted towards poor, Black women to maintain a White-supremacist hold in the slowly eroding Jim Crow south. Hamer, who coined the term, "Mississippi Appendectomy," made it a point to publicize what had been done to her to bring to light the reality of what Black women faced for nearly fifty years. Unfortunately, and as recently as 2020, immigrants from Latin and African nations have experienced a similar fate, with abusers and supporters of the procedure using the same language to justify human rights violations (Roberts 1999).

ten-dollar weekly stipend from SNCC. She quickly became one of the more well-known local leaders in the area, and combined grassroots support with the power to be heard nationally (Lee 1999).

Throughout 1962 and 1963, Hamer continued to work for desegregation and voter registration and became involved in relief work, distributing food and clothes to the poorest Delta residents. In 1963, Hamer and several fellow activists were returning from a citizenship training program in Charleston when their bus stopped in Winona, Mississippi. In the act of protest, some members of the group sat at the bus station's Whites-only lunch counter. Soon, the police arrived to remove them from the café, and they arrested six people, including Hamer. In jail, the activists were beaten, and the damage done to Hamer would affect her for the rest of her life.

When the activists did not check in with SNCC, organizers knew they were in trouble, and it took several days before they were found and released. After they left jail, Hamer and her colleagues learned that Medgar Evers had been assassinated in front of his home in Jackson the previous day. As the NAACP field secretary, Evers had been the driving force behind integration, including the admission of the first Black student to the University of Mississippi.

In the following months, Hamer increased her public profile, through both her SNCC work and as one of the cofounders of the Mississippi Freedom Democratic Party (MFDP), which challenged the pro-segregation Democratic Party. In early 1964, Hamer ran against veteran Congressman Jamie Whitten as an MFDP candidate. Although Whitten won with an overwhelming majority, Hamer's run set a precedent that set the stage for the MFDP to have a national presence.

The work of the MFDP was part of the 1964 Mississippi Summer Project,[2] which brought hundreds of college students to the state to work for civil rights. Although some organizers were wary of bringing in Whites from the North, Hamer saw value in an integrated movement and convinced many to abandon their objections.

Hamer traveled to Oxford, Ohio to train the volunteers to teach classes and register voters, and taught them the spirituals and movement songs she was known for. She was also busy with the MFDP, holding its conventions at the precinct, county, and state levels to select a group of people to go to the Democratic National Convention in Atlantic City to persuade the convention's Credentials Committee to seat them as delegates. Hamer was elected vice-chair of the integrated delegation, which consisted of sixty-four Black members and four White members. However, President Johnson, who needed Southern Democrats' support in his bid for election, was determined to block them. When Hamer went on television and testified about her eviction from the Marlow

---

2.   The project was organized by the Council of Federated Organizations (COFO), a coalition of the Mississippi branches of the four major civil rights organizations (SNCC, CORE, NAACP, and SCLC).

plantation and her brutal beating in the Winona jail before the Credentials Committee, President Johnson called a last-minute press conference to force the networks to break with their convention coverage and instead broadcast live coverage from the White House.

Nevertheless, President Johnson's ploy did not work. People heard enough of Hamer's compelling testimony that many evening news programs rebroadcast it, granting it a much larger audience than Johnson had predicted. However, President Johnson and Vice President Humphrey still successfully pressured members of the Credentials Committee to drop their support for the MFDP. Democratic officials offered two at-large seats for MFDP representatives as a conciliatory gesture, though Vice President Humphrey made it clear that President Johnson would not stand for one of those seats going to Hamer. The MFDP rejected the offer.

When the MFDP delegation returned to Mississippi, Hamer found herself in high demand as a speaker, often appearing at fundraising events. She traveled to Guinea in Africa with other SNCC workers and singer-activist Harry Belafonte. She was greatly inspired, being in a country where Black people were in power, running both the government and the major financial institutions, and meeting its president, Sekou Touré. The trip also gave Hamer the courage to keep fighting for Black access to power in the U.S.

Hamer spent the remainder of the 1960s balancing national activism with her work in Mississippi. Voting rights always remained a priority, even after the passage of the Voting Rights Act in 1965. Hamer took the lead in lawsuits that led to the first elections in which large numbers of Black residents of Sunflower County were able to vote in 1967. She also organized plaintiffs for a school desegregation lawsuit, instituted livestock and agricultural co-ops to improve economic prospects in the Delta, and was involved in the introduction of Head Start programs for low-income children of all races. Hamer had mixed success, particularly as her worsening health limited her ability for public speaking, which made fundraising difficult. In 1968, the MFDP was finally seated after the Democratic Party adopted a clause that demanded equality of representation from their states' delegations. In 1972, Hamer was elected as a national party delegate.

In addition to her high-profile struggles in the national political arena, Hamer organized grassroots initiatives in Mississippi. In 1968, with support from the National Council of Negro Women (NCNW), she created the Pig Bank, a livestock cooperative to help poor people get more meat in their diets. The following year, she founded the Freedom Farm Cooperative, a project through which 5,000 people came to grow their own food and collectively own 680 acres of land. At the same time, Hamer continued her anti-poverty work. She testified before the Senate's Subcommittee on Poverty in 1967. When the NCNW started the Fannie Lou Hamer Day Care Center in 1970, Hamer became the chair of the board of directors. In 1971, Hamer helped found the National Women's Political Caucus. She was, however, often politically at odds with White feminists because they did not have a clear understanding of the oppression experienced by women of color. She was often blunt in her criticism of White women yet eloquent about why they should fight for Black liberation.

Hamer received wide recognition in the last decade of her life, including an award from the National Association of Business and Professional Women's Clubs. She received a Doctor of Law from Shaw University and honorary degrees from Columbia College Chicago in 1970 and Howard University in 1972. In 1973, a resolution praising Hamer's political contribution was passed by the Mississippi House of Representatives. She received an award from the Congressional Black Caucus in 1976 and was named a leader for change in Mississippi by the University of Mississippi School of Journalism.

Fannie Lou Hamer died from hypertension and breast cancer on March 14, 1977, at age fifty-nine, in Mound Bayou, Mississippi. She was buried in her hometown of Ruleville, Mississippi, with her famous quote on her tombstone: "I am sick and tired of being sick and tired," an epitaph that would become an epigraph of working class exasperation.❖

The Legacy of Fannie Lou Hamer

FANNIE LOU HAMER WAS AN OUTSPOKEN grassroots leader who represented a necessary left-wing arm within the civil rights movement. She functioned as the quintessential victim of racism and poverty who chose to stand tall and unbroken in the face of ever-present defeat. Nevertheless, this same public persona was partly responsible for keeping her outside of mainstream, middle class civil rights activists, many of whom regarded her plainspoken and abrasive manner as an embarrassment. These roles combined represented a curious status for Hamer, the wife, mother, farmworker, and political activist. She had successfully created a duality of being that, on the one hand, allowed her much leverage and influence, but on the other, often left her feeling angry, unfulfilled, wanting, and isolated.

As events around Hamer continued to change in ways that made her an increasingly difficult fit for the mainstream, there were still the exceptional occasions that carried her onto the national stage: conventions, state elections, school desegregation contests, and a passing but significant alliance with White feminists. More wrenching than some of Hamer's political defeats were her battles with depression, hypertension, diabetes and heart disease, which left her periodically exhausted and immobilized. By 1972, breast cancer would accelerate her decline. Also, the devastating death of her daughter Dorothy, who died of internal hemorrhaging after she was denied admission to the local hospital on account of her race and her mother's activism, was a tragedy that was wholly unnecessary and preventable.

Despite these shortcomings, Hamer managed to teach us that we are not powerless in the face of an uncertain political landscape. With the right strategies, we can shape the direction of the nation's shifting allegiances to make real the promise of a multiracial, egalitarian democracy. Hamer's persistence and diligence in her fight for voting rights were integral to the civil rights movement and the eventual passage of legislation that gave all citizens the right to vote.

Hamer's legacy lies in the powerful, populist narrative she articulated of a multiracial working class. She envisioned an upward trajectory for poor Blacks and Whites that extended beyond equality for Black empowerment and integration of the MFDP. Her lived experience and straight-talking personality made her a trusted voice among poor Blacks and Whites in Mississippi. However, when Hamer took advantage of the crumbling political order to win the enfranchisement of African Americans within the Democratic Party, she became one of the most brilliant strategists of the civil rights movement. A populist insurrection today would do well to further Hamer's concept of a multiracial community of "we the people" against a racist cadre of the ultra-wealthy elite. (Goodrich 2017).

Hamer's persistence and diligence in her fight for voting rights were integral to the civil rights movement and the eventual passage of legislation that protected the right to vote for all citizens. Unfortunately by 2013, there was a major setback when the U.S. Supreme Court struck down the Voting Rights Act's preclearance system in *Shelby County v. Holder,* which required states and municipalities with a history of discrimination to seek federal approval for changes in voting procedures. Dozens of states have ushered in new barriers to voting: gerrymandering, voter suppression through questionable voter ID laws, voter intimidation, and the closing of polling locations that have had a disproportionate impact on people of color, seniors, young people, and low-income communities.

However, people are responding, especially Black women, who have always been instrumental in keeping a check on voting rights in this country. Following Hamer's blueprint of direct action, women like Stacey Abrams and Glynda C. Carr have been organizing to reclaim and protect the right to vote. Hamer taught us that we are not powerless in the face of an uncertain political landscape. With the right strategies, we are already witnessing the reshaping of the nation's shifting allegiances.

If Hamer felt forgotten near the end of her life, nothing could be further from the truth. Two universities—Jackson State University in Mississippi and California State University, Northridge—named academic institutes in her honor, and in 1993 she was inducted into the National Women's Hall of Fame in Seneca Falls, New York. The Ruleville post office carries her name today, as does a community center, a memorial park, a youth activities center, and the street on which she lived. Today, Fannie Lou Hamer is remembered more than ever.❖

Clara Day
(1924-2015)
Labor organizer

Clara Day was the first woman and first African American elected to Local 743's Executive Board, and helped found the Coalition of Labor Union Women (CLUW) in 1974.

CLARA TAYLOR DAY was born in Tuscaloosa, Alabama to Belle Taylor and George Taylor as the middle child of eleven children, including three sets of twins. Day's father, believed to be the son of his slave master, was a sharecropper and inherited land from his father along with his four brothers. As a Black farm family that owned its land, the Taylors were more fortunate than most. The farm consisted of some ninety acres, enough to feed the entire family and provide for cash crops.

Day's mother, who had achieved only a third or fourth-grade education, made education a priority for her children. Although the Taylor children were required to help with farm work, they never missed school. Day and her siblings had to leave home to attend high school in town, which meant boarding with another Tuscaloosa family. Stillman Institute, founded as a school for Black theologians, served as a combination of junior college and high school, filling the higher education gap left in a segregated city with no other Black colleges. At Stillman, Day excelled. One of her teachers recognized her talent in poetry and even had some of Day's poems published (Copeland 2015).

While still in high school, she met Joseph Henry Day, a man eight years her senior. Their long talks developed into a relationship, and soon after, they secretly married when she was seventeen years old. When Day became pregnant and had to drop out of high school, Joseph was inducted into the service, but was discharged for bad hearing. With few economic prospects in Tuscaloosa, Day, her husband, and their baby daughter pulled up stakes and moved to Chicago. Joseph subsequently found work in the Chicago stockyards.

Like her parents, Day believed that getting a good education was vital to get ahead. Now married with a child, both she and her husband enrolled in night school to obtain their high school diplomas.

Day applied to Montgomery Ward, a mail-order and department store retailer that was one of Chicago's largest employers. Impressed by Day's determination and forthrightness, the personnel representative at Montgomery Ward hired her to do clerical work, with the stipulation that she obtain her high school diploma. Day worked at Montgomery Ward from 1947 until 1955.

Montgomery Ward was not only a de facto segregated workplace, but it was also anti-union and had a long history that prevented its employees from organizing. A number of unions tried to unionize Montgomery Ward. When the company's 12,000 workers engaged in a nationwide strike in April 1944, the U.S. Army seized the Chicago offices of Montgomery Ward four months into the strike, because the company's chairman, Sewell Avery, refused to settle the strike as requested by the Franklin D. Roosevelt administration.

Then, in 1953, the Teamsters' Local 743 took a stab. One day, a union organizer gave Day a leaflet complaining about the segregated time clock. With her husband's encouragement, Day joined the Montgomery Ward organizing team. In 1954, the Teamsters won big with a 2,766 to 385 vote (Copeland 2015). While the vote represented a tremendous victory, the battle was not over. The union would have to fight hard for contract recognition.

When Day joined the Warehouse and Mail Order Employees Union Local 743 IBT, she was asked to work on the Teamsters' negotiating committee in conjunction with Local 743's umbrella organization, Joint Council 25, which represented forty different Teamsters locals in and around Chicago and consisted of 140,000 union members. Joint Council 25 pledged its support to Montgomery Ward, and two days following that pledge, after more than a year of fruitless negotiations, union members voted to walk off the job. The three-week strike turned the tide, and Avery returned to the table and signed Montgomery Ward's first contract with the Teamsters.

Around 1956, when the white-collar workers, who were predominately White, learned that union workers were making more money than they were, they decided to join the union too (Copeland 2015).

The union and the new contract made a difference in the everyday lives of Montgomery Ward workers. Union representation forced the company to change its policies, which included increased union members' interaction. It also changed the relationship between Black and White workers, who got to know each other for the first time through union meetings. Promotions and advancements on the job were now opened to scrutiny. The contract also required Montgomery Ward to post jobs, which meant that everyone, Black and White, knew when a better position was available and could apply. Posting led to the best qualified getting the job, which led to the integration of its once segregated departments.

In March 1955, with a signed Montgomery Ward contract, the Local needed more staff to handle its expanding membership. Day became an office clerk for the Warehouse and Mail Order Employees Union Local 743. To better meet the union's needs and advance her career, Day returned to school to improve her clerical and administrative skills and attended Chicago's Crane Junior College (now known as Malcolm X College).

In 1957, when it came time to renegotiate the Montgomery Ward contract, then-General President Jimmy Hoffa and Local 743's Don Peters led the negotiations. Peters served as the head of the union's Montgomery Ward Council, negotiating on behalf of 20,000 employees in sixty facilities nationwide. This time around, Sewell Avery was more cooperative, and the union was successful in gaining wage increases, shorter hours, and arbitration of grievances.

Five years after it opened, the Local closed its branch and moved Day and other workers to its main offices on Chicago's West Side. Day continued there as an office clerk, handling the paperwork of the growing membership. In addition to Montgomery Ward and Speigel's, the Local now covered Alden's, another mail-order house; Seeberg's, a pinball machine manufacturer; and 3M Revere, the camera company.

Day's star was rising. She moved from office clerk to assistant business agent. After five years in that role, she requested a transfer to a position that offered better pay. Peters accommodated her request by appointing her to the somewhat experimental position of Director of Community Services, which meant Day had to attend community events as the face of the union, a role that suited her personality. The union was integral to Chicago life, and there were many community activities in which Local 743 was involved. Day soon found herself serving on boards and commissions as part of her job.

Members called on Day for help with all sorts of problems, like providing referrals to banks for loans and cutting bureaucratic red tape to ensure that striking workers received benefits such as food stamps. It was seldom necessary for Day to exert heavy pressure. Instead, she wielded her union clout with a velvet glove, knowing that a call from the Teamsters went a long way.

Day finally became a business agent, a title that carried more weight with her peers than Director of Community Services. It also extended her authority to work on behalf of the membership. Day could now call a strike with the Local 743 Board and the Joint Council's approval. In the early 1980s, there were quite a few strikes in which Local 743 was involved. Day used this tactic judiciously, and she continued her role as the local's Community Services Director (Copeland 2015).

Local 743 represented a variety of occupations from factory workers, nursing assistants, dieticians, janitorial workers, and warehouse staff to clerical workers and psychologists. It also had the largest percentage of women and Blacks of any Teamster local in the country, which placed them in the forefront of civil rights issues in Chicago. Although it was not her official duty to do so, Day often acted as the conduit between the AFL-CIO and the Teamsters on those issues, bridging years of tension going back to the 1957 expulsion of the Teamsters.[1]

---

1. The Teamsters was expelled from the AFL-CIO in 1957 after their leadership, long beset by charges of corruption, had refused to appear before the federation's ethics committee. After thirty years of estrangement, the Teamsters re-affiliated with AFL-CIO in 1985. The Teamsters disaffiliated from the AFL-CIO in 2005 due to structural issues and created a new coalition, Change to Win Federation (CtW) and the Canadian Labour Congress.

Day led a delegation of her union at the historic March on Washington in 1963 in the company of Martin Luther King Jr., and Governor Kerner later appointed her to the Illinois Commission on Human Rights. In 1964, Day's neighborhood organization, the Greater Lawndale Conservation Commission, presented her with an award for promotion of youth activities in the community, and in 1965, the Chicago Citizens Scholarship Committee named her a Woman of Distinction in the field of Labor, Civil, and Community Activities.

By 1967, Mayor Daley appointed Day to the Chicago Human Relations Commission, which meant she simultaneously served on two human relations commissions, one at the state level and one for the city. Later, in 1968, Day was one of three labor leaders to receive a Civil Rights Award from the Jewish Labor Committee at its fourteenth annual conference on civil rights. Day was also very active in the battle to pass the Equal Rights Amendment for Women and was named a spokesperson.

In 1976, Peters appointed Day to a trustee position on the Executive Board to serve out a retiring Local 743 officer's unexpired term. When that term expired, she ran for the Trustee position and was elected, making her the first woman and African American to be elected to Local 743's Executive Board. In 1992, she ran and became Local 743's Recording Secretary. Although the Local's membership was overwhelmingly female, Day remained the Board's only woman member for many years (Copeland 2015). She was also a founding member of the Teamsters National Black Caucus.

In 1977, she visited Sweden, France, and Israel as part of a fact-finding mission to study childcare and women in trade unions. The trip was sponsored by the U.S. German Marshall Fund. Day was also elected National Vice President of the Coalition of Labor Union Women (CLUW). She already served as a CLUW Regional Vice President, but the group wanted her to serve at the national level.

Through CLUW, Day befriended powerful women from other unions and made important contacts in the civil rights movement. She was on a first-name basis with notables such as Coretta Scott King, Gloria Steinem, Jesse Jackson, and Dorothy I. Height, to name a few.

In 1981, Day's involvement and enthusiasm for Harold Washington's candidacy for mayor inspired Local 743 members to get involved in his campaign. Later, in 1989, Day became the Vice President of the NAACP's Chicago Southside Chapter, and in 1990, they awarded her their James Kemp Award for Labor Leadership. In 1991, the CLUW supported candidate Carol Mosely Braun, who would become the country's first Black woman U.S. Senator. As forward-thinking as Local 743 may have seemed when compared to other Chicago locals of the time, things were still difficult. Day's stance on behalf of women was unpopular. A fighter to her core, she did not back down.

After President Reagan fired the air traffic controllers, he signaled to companies that unions could be busted. By this time, many of the companies that the Teamsters had organized were going out of business as well. By 2000, Montgomery Ward was forced to close all of its stores and laid off 37,000 employees nationwide. Yet, despite these setbacks, and with no age restriction for her position, Day was prepared to keep working as long as she could. Foreign travel through CLUW had added a new dimension to her assignments, and she enjoyed meeting like-minded women around the world who fought for social justice. Day did not seek the limelight for herself; she preferred to focus on raising others up and shedding light on the darkness of injustice instead.

In June 2000, Day was discovered passed out by her husband. When the ambulance came, she was barely breathing. When she arrived at the hospital, doctors determined that she had suffered a brain hemorrhage and was in a coma. The prognosis was not good. After seven months, Day emerged from her coma, defying most doctors who had given her little chance of survival. Unfortunately, her illness forced her to retire. She was honored by the National Black Caucus for her contributions. In 2008, the Teamsters published the book, *Clara Day: A Teamster's Life* by Joy M. Copeland.

Clara Day died at age ninety-one on February 6, 2015. ❖

The Legacy of Clara Day

CLARA DAY was one of the union's most memorable leaders, especially beloved in Chicago. She battled both race and gender stereotypes as she climbed up the ladder to attain a leadership position with Local 743.

When others might have taken the easy route, Day persisted in her advocacy of what she knew to be right. She stood with the dynamic women who emerged from Chicago's labor movement to promote change through sisterhood and collective action. Over the years, she would be the recipient of awards and accolades too numerous to mention. Though described as humble by everyone who knew her, Day was proud of her role in providing leadership for positive change, especially on behalf of women workers. Day was also proud of her family, who, through her example, learned the valuable lessons of responsibility to self and family, social action, and community service.

Day was a model for Teamster women at a time when women leaders in the union were few. Her work continues today through the people she inspired during her forty-five years of service to the Teamsters and her community. Local 743's outreach in Chicago has continued through its Community Service Volunteers, the group that Day organized. Her friends and family carry on the tradition of raising money in her name for the Urban League through its Golden Fellowship Dinner. And most importantly, she remains an inspiration for the Black women labor activists who have chosen to follow in her footsteps, furthering the advancement of labor, civil and women's rights.❖

Addie Wyatt
(1924-2012)
Labor leader, pastor, feminist, civil rights activist

Addie Wyatt was the first African American woman to become a senior officer of an American labor union and the first to hold a high-level leadership position in an international union. She was also one of the first women to become an ordained pastor in the Church of God.

ADDIE L. CAMERON WYATT was born in Brookhaven, Mississippi to Maggie Nolan Cameron, a part-time teacher, and Ambrose Cameron, a tailor, as the second child and oldest daughter of five children. When her father struck his White boss during an altercation, the family fled Mississippi and relocated to Chicago in 1930 when she was six years old. They left behind the instability of Southern life for better job opportunities during the Great Depression.

As the family faced economic hardship, they were forced to move frequently. Through it all, Wyatt's mother instilled a love for God and the Christian faith in Wyatt's childhood, which would become an integral part of her upbringing. They regularly attended church at the Langley Avenue Church of God, part of a dynamic movement of Black Protestant Christians in Chicago, where Wyatt played piano and sang in the choir. By age twelve, she became the chief musician of the youth choir and earned one dollar a week. Wyatt also grew up seeing women in powerful positions in the church, which had an effect on how she engaged with the world. Her deeply personal experiences with racism and poverty, combined with the importance of family and faith in her life, guided Wyatt into the social activist and Christian leader she would later become (Walker-Williams 2016).

When attending DuSable High School, Wyatt was a member of the Beta Club, a group of girls who worked in the school's library, and played clarinet in the school's concert band. In 1938, she met an older student, Claude S. Wyatt Jr., and a courtship ensued that would lead to a marriage that lasted nearly sixty-nine years until his death in 2010 (Walker-Williams 2016).

When Wyatt was sixteen years old, the young couple wed in 1940 with support from their parents. Wyatt's mother wanted her daughter to go to college, but her father was against it, even if the costs were not prohibitive. Wyatt, on the other hand, felt that starting her own family was a better option. Soon after, she became pregnant with her first son and Wyatt dropped out of high school.

In 1941, as Wyatt and her husband struggled to make ends meet, she sought employment as a typist at Armour & Company, a meatpacking company. Although she passed the test, Black women were barred from holding clerical positions in the company, and instead, Wyatt was put to work as a butcher and eventually canned stew for the Army. Initially taken aback when she first accepted the position, Wyatt quickly learned she would earn more money working three days in the plant than what she would earn in a week as a typist, thanks to a contract between the company and the new workers' association, the Packinghouse Workers Organizing Committee (PWOC). The PWOC, founded in 1937 under the Congress of Industrial Workers (CIO), was a left-wing union that offered better working conditions and contracts with the biggest packing companies. They were committed to interracial cooperation and pursued anti-discrimination practices, which boasted a significant and active Black and female membership. Within her first few months of employment, Wyatt signed a union card and joined the PWOC in 1942 (Walker-Williams 2016).

Wyatt's appreciation for the union grew when her first grievance against management was amicably resolved and she found herself eligible for a leave of absence during her second pregnancy without demotion or lost of employment. This incident remained in the forefront of her mind when Wyatt later became involved in maternal and childcare legislation campaigns for working women.

A series of personal crises occupied much of Wyatt's life, including raising two small children and grappling with financial issues that put a strain on her marriage. She strayed from the church along the way, and she and her children lived alternatively between Wyatt's parents and her in-laws. Eventually, a renewal of faith compelled a reconciliation between husband and wife. In 1944, Wyatt's mother suddenly died at the age of thirty-nine. When her father could no longer care for her siblings due to his poor health, Wyatt and her husband took them in. They now had six children to raise, which further complicated their lives financially. After they secured housing in the Altgeld Gardens public housing projects, it served as a site for community organizing, and neighborhood pride. Wyatt and her husband founded the Wyatt Choral Ensemble (WCE), and its formation was a turning point in the development of their faith and leadership abilities. The WCE performed at churches and festivals throughout the Chicago area. It also sparked Wyatt with a greater desire to use her religious faith and spirituality to bring about positive change in the community (Walker-Williams 2016).

Wyatt worked at Armour & Company sporadically from 1942 to 1944 due to seasonal layoffs, and would not secure stable employment until 1947. In the meantime, the PWOC had dissolved in 1943 to become the United Packinghouse Workers of America (UPWA). Since the UPWA inherited the PWOC's mission to support civil rights initiatives and progressive social issues, they encouraged Blacks and women to take on local leadership roles. By the early 1950s, Wyatt was developing into a labor organizer and activist.

Due to her deep involvement in her church and community, Wyatt was reluctant to seek office, but at UPWA's urging, she ran for and was elected as the vice president of Local 56 in 1953, becoming the first Black woman to hold a senior office in an American labor union. As she quickly rose to the forefront as one of the country's few Black women labor leaders, Wyatt took advantage of her union's anti-racist and anti-discrimination rules to fight race- and gender-based inequities. Beginning in 1955, Wyatt worked full-time for the UPWA, representing workers across a five-state region. What began as a personal incentive to break away from poverty became a collective struggle against economic, racial, and gender equality (Walker-Williams 2016).

In the meantime, Wyatt's husband, who had served in the Navy during World War II, and worked as a clerk at the post office, was called into the ministry. He earned a master's degree in theology, and together with Wyatt, they founded the Vernon Park Church of God in 1955. In addition to working for the union, Wyatt worked closely with her husband in multiple capacities at the church. They also became involved in grassroots organizing in their community.

The UPWA was an early supporter of the Montgomery Bus Boycott, raised money for civil rights groups, and participated in national campaigns. By 1956, Wyatt was the Program Coordinator for District One of the UPWA. The Wyatts also began their relationship with Martin Luther King Jr. and became labor advisers to the Southern Christian Leadership Conference (SCLC). Due to Wyatt's role in the union, she served on the Action Committee of the Chicago Freedom Movement and was a member of President Kennedy's Commission on the Status of Women in 1961. The commission ultimately led to the formation of the National Organization for Women (NOW) in 1966, of which she was a member. Wyatt would go on to advise presidents Johnson and Carter.

In 1962, Wyatt and her husband cofounded Operation Breadbasket, and King appointed Reverend Jesse Jackson to head its Chicago chapter. Wyatt and her husband worked closely with Jackson to help distribute food to underprivileged families and became involved with the organization's successor, People United to Save Humanity (PUSH). She also fought for the passage of the Equal Rights Amendment (ERA) and the Equal Pay Act of 1963. Eleanor Roosevelt recognized her leadership abilities and appointed Wyatt to a position on the Labor Legislation Committee of the U.S. Commission on the Status of Women.

By the time the UPWA merged with the more conservative Amalgamated Meat Cutters and Butcher Workman of North America in 1968, there was a growing rift between the rank-and-file trade unionists and union leadership. Wyatt lobbied for and became the Women's Affairs and Human Rights department director of the UPWA. That same year, Wyatt was one of the few women who successfully achieved ordination in the Church of God and became co-pastor of her church. She would combine the traditions of a Black woman activist with faith-based activism as part of her ministry.

In 1972, Wyatt was a founding member of the Coalition of Black Trade Unionists (CBTU), which was formed to ensure that Black workers could share in the power of the labor movement at every level. As the first chair of CBTU's National Women's Committee, Wyatt ensured that AFL-CIO-affiliated unions opened leadership positions to women. Her initiatives helped African Americans and women within the labor force become financially independent and effective contributors to the economy. She continued to participate in the push for the ERA and other legislation that sought to eradicate gender discrimination during the 1970s.

Wyatt cofounded the Coalition of Labor Union Women (CLUW) in 1974 to help create a stronger and more effective voice for women in the labor movement. CLUW was an important step forward for the second-wave feminist movement and the advancement of women of color who felt left out by the dominant, mainstream, White feminists. In 1976, Wyatt became the international vice president of UPWA, the first African American woman to take a high-level leadership position in an international union. In 1979, the UPWA merged with the Retail Clerks International Union (RCIU) to become United Food and Commercial Workers (UFCW). More than ever, Wyatt looked to politics, local community empowerment, and grassroots organizing as crucial tools to win additional gains for working class women (Walker-Williams 2016).

By the 1980s, Black labor leaders such as Wyatt recognized the common foe of Reaganomics as a threat to organized labor, and the gains made during the civil rights and post-civil rights era. During this period, she became even more politically active by supporting the elections of Chicagoans such as Harold Washington and Jesse Jackson. In 1984, Wyatt retired from UFCW as arguably the most visible and one of the most highest-ranked African American women in the organized labor movement. But while her retirement signaled an end to her formal career in the union, she furthered her commitments toward coalition building and women's activism (Walker-Williams 2016).

Wyatt pulled together a vast network of memberships and leadership in prominent women's organizations such as the Chicago Network, the League of Black Women, the National Council of Negro Women (NCNW) and the National Congress of Black Women. She also campaigned for Carol Mosely Braun, the first Black woman elected to the U.S. Senate.

In 1999, Wyatt founded the Wyatt Family Community Center in Chicago, the church's multipurpose community center, which continues to serve the community with its diverse programming for families. She was inducted as a Laureate of The Lincoln Academy of Illinois and awarded the Order of Lincoln (the State's highest honor) by the Governor of Illinois in 2003 for Religion and Labor. In 2005, Wyatt's footprints were added to the Civil Rights Walk of Fame in Atlanta to acknowledge her work as an activist, campaigner, and leader.

Wyatt was named one of *Time* magazine's "Women of the Year" in 1975. The publication recognized her for speaking out against sexual and racial discrimination in hiring, promotion, and pay. Her photograph appeared on the magazine's cover with First Lady Betty Ford, tennis great Billie Jean King, and Representative Barbara Jordan. From 1981 to 1983, she was named one of *Ebony* magazine's 100 most influential Black Americans. In 1987, the CBTU established the Addie L. Wyatt Award. She received honorary doctorates from Anderson College in Indiana and Chicago's Columbia College.

Wyatt retired as co-pastor of the Vernon Park Church of God in 2000. In the early 2000s, she suffered a stroke that, along with her arthritis, confined her to a wheelchair. Nevertheless, she remained active in community affairs and mentored community organizers in a limited capacity, including a young Barack Obama. The Reverend Addie Wyatt had a sixty-nine-year marriage, separated only by the death of her husband in 2010. She died on March 28, 2012 in Chicago at the age of eighty-eight.❖

The Legacy of Addie Wyatt

ADDIE WYATT WAS AN AMAZING WOMAN. She accomplished what few women of her generation were able to do: she was a working wife and mother; a community activist; a labor leader; a cofounder, first lady and pastor of a church; and she did all of it with grace, style, and conviction. What is remarkable is that Wyatt managed to successfully traverse the boundaries of her religiosity and connect her ministry to the women's rights and social justice movements, which was no easy feat.

Every step of the way, Wyatt faced opposition. The labor movement questioned her ability to lead as an African American and a woman. They quibbled over the social justice issues Wyatt long promoted throughout her career, and she was ultimately cast as a militant threat to labor leadership. Those in the church questioned her fitness and leadership as a woman, and the secular movements she embraced. She was especially targeted for her support of pro-woman campaigns such as the ERA, which many believed threatened Christian values. Yet despite the odds, Wyatt masterfully juggled her responsibilities with the union and the church with seemingly relative ease. And no matter where she was in the country, she always managed to attend church every Sunday. Wyatt used her faith, beliefs, and philosophy of quality and diversity to bridge the sacred and secular against racism, sexism, and poverty.

Wyatt provided a leadership that was insightful, forward-thinking, and compassionate. She challenged her union members and her ministry to work harder and smarter to strive and thrive for a better society, while urging them to protect and uplift the weak and the poor. Wyatt's legacy can be credited to her unique life story, which helped create a blueprint that blends religion and social justice issues in a manner that is open and inclusive for all.❖

Coretta Scott King
(1927-2006)
Civil rights leader, social justice activist

Coretta Scott King is regarded as one of the matriarchs of the civil rights movement. She founded the King Center for Non-Violent Social Change, campaigned to establish her husband's birthday as a national holiday, and became a social justice activist in her own right.

CORETTA SCOTT KING was born in Marion, Alabama to Bernice McMurray Scott and Obadiah "Obie" Scott, a former police officer who owned a clothing shop, and later a general store with his wife. The second of three siblings, King's parents were committed to ensuring that their children received the best education possible.

King attended Lincoln High School, a private institution in Marion, Alabama where she developed an interest in music, and took formal vocal lessons, and played several instruments. By the age of fifteen, King had become the choir director and pianist of her church's junior choir. She graduated as the valedictorian in 1945 and, eager to leave the South, enrolled in Antioch College in Yellow Springs, Ohio, with a partial scholarship. King majored in elementary education and studied music with Walter Anderson, the first non-White chair of an academic department in a White college (King and Reynolds 2017).

When King relocated to Ohio, she quickly discovered that racism was very much alive outside of the South. The racism she faced made King more determined than ever. She became politically active in the nascent civil rights movement by joining the Antioch chapter of the NAACP and the college's Race Relations and Civil Liberties Committees.

King's major required a two-year internship, and when it came time to fulfill it, Antioch created problems for her. Although the student body was integrated, the teachers and administrative staff were all White, so the Yellow Springs school board refused to allow King to teach in its school system due to her race. When King appealed to the Antioch administration, they were unwilling or unable to change the situation and instead employed her at the college for a second year. Despite this unfortunate experience, King found her years at Antioch rewarding. It broadened her perspective toward different religions and cultures (King and Reynolds 2017).

When King received her BA in music from Antioch College, she received a fellowship to further her music studies at the New England Conservatory of Music in Boston, where she earned a degree in voice and violin. While there, she met Martin Luther King Jr., who was then studying for his doctorate in systematic theology at Boston University's School of Theology. Despite envisioning a music career, King knew it would not be possible if she married Dr. King. However, since he possessed many of the qualities she liked in a man, she forwent her ambitions to assume a pastor's wife's responsibilities.

They were married in 1953, and in 1954, took up residence in Montgomery, Alabama, where Dr. King pastored at Dexter Avenue Baptist Church. Before long, they found themselves thrust to the forefront of the Montgomery Bus Boycott, with Dr. King as the elected leader of the protest movement. With this responsibility came fame and death threats.

During Dr. King's career, King devoted most of her time to raising their four children. From the very beginning, however, she balanced mothering with movement work. Throughout the marriage, the Kings clashed about her role. King was thoroughly committed to the civil rights movement and wanted a more public leadership role, but Dr. King wanted her to focus solely on raising their children. Despite her husband's wishes, King stood by his side in the struggle for civil rights. She made speeches, gave Freedom Concerts, and worked toward getting the Civil Rights Act passed (King and Reynolds 2017).

In 1957, she and Dr. King journeyed to Ghana to mark its independence. In 1958, they spent a belated honeymoon in Mexico, where they observed firsthand the immense gulf between extreme wealth and extreme poverty. In 1959, the Kings spent nearly a month in India on a pilgrimage to see sites associated with Mahatma Gandhi. In 1964, King accompanied her husband to Oslo, Norway, where he received the Nobel Peace Prize. She functioned as a liaison to justice and peace organizations and as a mediator to public officials.

On April 4, 1968, while standing on a balcony of the Lorraine Motel in Memphis, Tennessee, Dr. King was assassinated by James Earl Ray. Four days later, King led her husband's planned march through Memphis to support striking sanitation workers. In the aftermath of her husband's assassination, King founded the Martin Luther King Jr. Center for Nonviolent Social Change (the King Center) in the basement of her home in 1968, serving as its president and chief executive officer. By 1980, a 23-acre site around King's birthplace was designated for use by the King Center. The following year, a museum complex was dedicated to the site. King provided local, national, and international programs that trained thousands of people on Dr. King's philosophy and methods. King passed the reins over to her son Dexter in 1995 but remained in the public eye.

She then broadened her focus to various other causes. As early as December 1968, she called for women to unite during a Solidarity Day speech. King openly expressed disdain for the Vietnam War, an action that placed her under

FBI surveillance. She began traveling internationally, lecturing about racism and economic issues in the U.S. and abroad. In 1969, King was awarded the Universal Love Award, becoming the first non-Italian to hold the distinction. The same year, she published her memoirs entitled, *My Life with Martin Luther King Jr.* She established an annual Coretta Scott King Award to honor an African American author with an outstanding text for children, and in 1979, a similar award was added to honor an outstanding African American illustrator of children's books.

By 1974, King had been building a broad interracial coalition of over one-hundred religious, labor, business, civil, and women's rights organizations dedicated to a national policy of full employment and equal economic opportunity, and had served as co-chair of both the National Committee for Full Employment and the Full Employment Action Council. She also oversaw the fifteen-year fight for formal recognition of her husband's birthday as a federal holiday. In 1983, Congress instituted the Martin Luther King Jr. Federal Holiday Commission, which King chaired until President Reagan signed the bill into law in 1986. Martin Luther King Jr.'s holiday has come to be celebrated by millions of people worldwide.

King tirelessly carried the message of nonviolence and the dream of the beloved community to almost every corner of the globe. She led goodwill missions to many countries in Europe, Africa, Latin America, and Asia. King spoke at peace and justice rallies and met with heads of state, including prime ministers and presidents. She met with many spiritual leaders, including Bishop Desmond Tutu, Pope John Paul, the Dalai Lama, and Dorothy Day. She witnessed the historic handshake between Prime Minister Yitzhak Rabin and Chairman Yassir Arafat at the Middle East Peace Accords signing, and stood with Nelson Mandela in Johannesburg when he became South Africa's first democratically-elected president. In preparation for the Reagan-Gorbachev talks in 1988, King served as head of the U.S. delegation of Women for a Meaningful Summit in Athens, Greece, and as the USSR was redefining itself, in 1990, King was co-convener of the Soviet-American Women's Summit in Washington, D.C.

The King family and others believe that Dr. King's assassination was the result of a conspiracy involving the U.S. government and the Memphis police, and that James Earl Ray was a scapegoat. In 1997, King called for a retrial of her husband's alleged assassin, but Ray died in prison the following year.

King received honorary doctorates from over sixty colleges and universities, issued books of her husband's writings, wrote a nationally syndicated newspaper column, and served on and helped found dozens of organizations.

In August 2005, King suffered a heart attack and a stroke which paralyzed her right side and left her unable to speak. On January 30, 2006, Coretta Scott King died of respiratory failure due to complications from ovarian cancer while seeking treatment in Playas de Rosarito, Mexico. She was seventy-eight years old. Her funeral was attended by some 10,000 people, including four of five living

U.S. presidents. She was the first African American to lie in the Georgia State Capitol and was temporarily buried on the grounds of the King Center until being interred next to her husband in Atlanta. ❖

The Legacy of Coretta Scott King

CORETTA SCOTT KING has always been praised and principally defined as her husband's helpmate, rather than the peace and social justice activist she was her entire life. The memorialization of her lifelong political commitments continues to miss the wider critique of social injustice that underlay her life's work. As with Rosa Parks and the civil rights widows Betty Shabazz and Myrlie Evers-Williams, King was held up and honored as a self-sacrificing mother figure for a nation that has used her life and death for national redemption.

During her marriage, King had to contend with her husband's contradictory beliefs on women's roles. While Dr. King appreciated his wife's politics and the support she provided him, he believed her public role should have been limited to homemaker. Dr. King's reluctance to let Black women participate as equal partners in his organization, the Southern Christian Leadership Conference (SCLC), and in the civil rights movement at large was shared by his Black male counterparts as well as mainstream American society. Yet, were it not for the Black women who organized and supported these civil rights initiatives, it is highly unlikely it would have succeeded.

Shortly after her husband's assassination, King was not expected to stand up and take charge, but she did. She fulfilled her husband's commitments and created a fitting memorial, the King Center, to perpetuate his legacy and address social issues. Unfortunately, the SCLC board did not see it that way. Although she was invited to join the board, they were not interested in King playing a political role. Instead, they expected her to fulfill the symbolic role of a martyr's widow and raise money for the organization. The men were simply incapable of dealing with a strong woman like King, who insisted on being treated equally.

There has always been a tendency in the civil rights movement's history to marginalize King's work and focus only on her efforts to preserve her husband's legacy. Ignoring King's broader life and activism fits with the public erasures of Black women's participation and leadership. The question people now are beginning to ask is, "Who was Coretta Scott King?" King never had any doubt of who she was and what she stood for: "'I am not a ceremonial symbol,' Scott King once said. 'I am an activist. I didn't just emerge after Martin died—I was always there and involved'" (Theoharis 2018).

When King assumed her husband's burden as the chief symbol of the civil rights movement, she fiercely guarded his legacy—often in ways that drew pointed criticism. Operating in her husband's long shadow was a challenge that tested King for the rest of her life.

King's activism did not simply uphold her husband's legacy; she expanded it with her global vision. During the 1950s, she was active in racial justice politics and the peace movement before she married. In the 1960s, King spoke up earlier and more forcefully against American involvement in Vietnam than her husband did, and her critique of American economics and war-making continued for decades after his death, so much so that the FBI continued to actively surveil her. In the 1980s, she supported anti-apartheid, traveled to South Africa, and subsequently met with President Reagan to urge divestment. In the mid-1980s, she became a vocal advocate of gay rights and a supporter of same-sex marriage, despite criticism from civil rights leaders and even her own children.

When President George W. Bush decided to attend King's funeral, he had little knowledge of who she really was and could only speak in generalities about King's beauty and strength. Meanwhile, longtime King family friend and Bush critic Harry Belafonte, who was scheduled to give a eulogy, was disinvited because King's family believed he would embarrass a sitting president and, more importantly, serve as a potent reminder of their mother's enduring critique of racism and war-making.

Management of the King Center has had its ups and downs. All four King children have held leadership positions at one time or another, but none drew universal praise. Since King's illness and subsequent death, they have accused each other of unethical behavior and profiteering, which was further complicated by the sudden death of Yolanda King in 2007, executrix of their mother's estate. The surviving siblings have quarreled among themselves and with others in lawsuits over the fate of the King Center, the use of its funds and their father's copyrighted works, the ownership of his Bible and Noble Peace Prize, and the stewardship of his legacy. Along the way, they found themselves at odds with some of Dr. King's most famous friends and confidants and have disappointed the public with their conduct. But what has become increasingly clear is that we were witnessing the tragic consequence of emotional damage inflicted from both their father's assassination and the murder of their grandmother, Alberta Williams King. Picking up the mantle of a person who was the most hated man in America at the time of his death, but in time became the most revered as the apostle of nonviolence and peace was an enormous expectation. His is a powerful shadow no one can easily escape (Eichenwald 2014).

One of King's most admirable qualities was her ability to meet the challenge of living within her husband's shadow. She understood the need for community and peace and fought for both until the end of her life. In recent years, the King children have learned to compartmentalize their differences for the greater good. Following in their mother's footsteps, they continue to strive to fight against injustice and inequality. This is the true essence of Coretta Scott King's legacy.❖

Myrlie Evers-Williams
(1933)
Civil rights activist, educator, author

Myrlie Evers-Williams' dedication to civil rights is exemplified by an activism that has linked education, business, governmental and social issues to further human rights and equality. She became the first woman and full-time chairperson of the NAACP.

MYRLIE LOUISE BEASLEY EVERS-WILLIAMS was born in Vicksburg, Mississippi to Mildred Washington Beasley, and James Van Dyke Beasley, a delivery man. Evers-Williams' mother was sixteen years old when she gave birth, and her parents separated when she was a year old. Her mother left Vicksburg shortly after, leaving Evers-Williams to be raised by her paternal grandmother, Annie McCain Beasley, and aunt, Myrlie Beasley Polk, both school teachers (Bell 2018). Growing up in Vicksburg, she took piano lessons, and performed at recitals. She also recited poetry at school, in church, and at local clubs.

In 1950, Evers-Williams graduated from Magnolia High School (Bowman High School). Blocked from attending White Southern schools, she enrolled at Alcorn A&M College in Lorman, Mississippi, where she joined the Delta Sigma Theta Sorority. Evers-Williams intended to major in education with a minor in music, but a chance encounter on her first day on campus altered her plans: she met Medgar Evers, a World War II veteran eight years her senior, with whom she quickly fell in love (Bell 2018). They married on Christmas Eve in 1951, and later moved to Mound Bayou, Mississippi, where they would have three children. Evers-Williams worked as a secretary at the Magnolia Mutual Life Insurance Company.

When Medgar Evers became the Mississippi field secretary for the NAACP in 1954, the family relocated to Jackson. Evers-Williams worked alongside Evers as his secretary, and together they organized voter registration drives and civil rights demonstrations. But as prominent civil rights leaders in Mississippi, the Everses became targets for terror and violence. In 1962, their home was fire-bombed after an organized boycott of downtown Jackson's White merchants.

Medgar Evers was assassinated on June 12, 1963. Evers-Williams and their three small children witnessed the murder at the front door of their home. Although Byron De La Beckwith, a known White supremacist, was arrested and brought to trial, an all-White jury would not reach a verdict. After suffering

through two hung jury trials, and De La Beckwith being released in 1965, Evers-Williams and her children moved to Claremont, California in 1967. She would not see justice for Medgar Evers until thirty-one years later.

Evers-Williams emerged as a civil rights activist in her own right. She earned her BA in sociology from Pomona College and spoke on behalf of the NAACP around the country. In 1967, she co-wrote, *For Us, the Living,* which chronicled her late husband's life and work. From 1968 to 1970, Evers-Williams was the director of planning at the Center for Educational Opportunity for the Claremont Colleges. She worked with underprivileged high school dropouts who wanted to receive their diplomas and enter college. Though she made two unsuccessful bids for U.S. Congress, she eventually became the first Black woman to lead the Southern California Democratic Women's Division.

By the early 1970s, Evers-Williams moved her family to New York to serve as vice president of advertising and publicity at Seligman & Latz, which operated beauty salons and jewelry counters in department and specialty stores. In 1975, she moved to Los Angeles to become the national director for community affairs for the Atlantic Richfield Company (ARCO), managing funding for community projects, outreach programs, public and private partnership programs, and staff development. Later, she was promoted to director of consumer affairs and was responsible for defining and evaluating the corporate role in program implementation as well as presenting policy considerations to management. In 1976, Evers-Williams married Walter Williams, a former longshoreman and labor and civil rights activist. They moved to Bend, Oregon in 1989, and together the couple would champion social justice.

By 1987, Evers-Williams returned to politics, running for a seat on the Los Angeles City Council. Again, she lost, but Los Angeles Mayor Bradley appointed her as the first Black woman to serve as a commissioner for the Board of Public Works, a position she held for eight years. She continued to explore ways to serve her community and work with the NAACP.

Around 1989, *The Clarion-Ledger* in Jackson uncovered that the former State Sovereignty Commission, a publicly financed arm of government, helped De La Beckwith's attorneys screen jurors whose deadlock caused a mistrial in 1964. At Evers-Williams' urging, prosecutors were prompted to search for evidence of jury tampering, which led to a new trial. In 1994, she was present when the guilty verdict and life imprisonment were handed down to De La Beckwith. At last, her persistence and faith in the pursuit of justice for the assassination that changed her and her children's lives had come to fruition. At this time, she also narrated a special HBO production, *Southern Justice, the Murder of Medgar Evers* (1994). In 1996, Rob Reiner released the film *Ghosts of Mississippi,* which explored the 1994 De La Beckwith trial with Evers-Williams portrayed by Whoopi Goldberg.

By the mid-1990s, the NAACP was going through a difficult period marked by scandal and financial problems. Evers-Williams decided that the best way to help the NAACP was to run for chairperson of the Board of Directors. She assumed the position in 1995, right after her second husband's death from prostate cancer. As chairperson of the NAACP, Evers-Williams worked to restore the tarnished image of the organization. She also helped improve its financial status, raising $4 million to retire its debt. After securing the NAACP's finances, Evers-Williams decided to not seek re-election as chairperson in 1998. In that same year, she was awarded the NAACP's Spingarn Medal. Evers-Williams received many honors for her work, including being named Woman of the Year by *Ms. Magazine.*

After leaving her post, Evers-Williams established the Medgar Evers Institute (now known as the Medgar and Myrlie Evers Institute) in Jackson, Mississippi. She also wrote her autobiography, *Watch Me Fly: What I Learned on the Way to Becoming the Woman I Was Meant to Be* (1999), and participated in projects that would help preserve her first husband's memory.

Evers-Williams edited *The Autobiography of Medgar Evers: A Hero's Life and Legacy Revealed Through His Writings, Letters, and Speeches* (2005). In 2009, she received the National Freedom Award from the National Civil Rights Museum in Memphis. In 2012, Evers-Williams was a distinguished scholar-in-residence at Alcorn State University. On January 21, 2013, she was the first woman and the first layperson to deliver the invocation at President Obama's second inauguration. In 2014, the University of Mississippi Medical Center established the Myrlie Evers-Williams Institute for the Elimination of Health Disparities.

In 2017, Medgar and Myrlie Evers-Williams' home in Mississippi was named a National Historic Landmark. Later that year, Evers-Williams spoke at the grand opening ceremony for two museums—the Museum of Mississippi History and the Mississippi Civil Rights Museum—in Jackson. She received honorary doctorates from Pomona College, Medgar Evers College, Howard University, and others.

In 2001, Evers-Williams' oldest son, Darrell Kenyatta, an avant-garde painter and entrepreneur, succumbed to colon cancer. He was forty-five years old and is survived by his wife and son. The Evers-Williams family was hit once again with a cancer death in 2018. Her oldest granddaughter, Cambi Evers-Everette Coe, died from breast cancer. She was thirty-four years old.

In 2018, Evers-Williams formally retired on her eighty-fifth birthday and no longer accepts speaking engagements. Instead, she spends her time curating documents from her and Medgar Evers' lifetime.

Evers-Williams is a phenomenal woman of great strength and courage. Her dedication to civil rights is exemplified by her activist role, linked to her business acumen to further human rights and equality. Of the three civil rights widows, she is the sole survivor. Evers-Williams holds the distinction of being the only widow who openly worked alongside her husband, ran for public office, worked in corporate America, and remarried. Her exemplary leadership and unwavering advocacy for women and civil rights consists of a legacy that evokes leadership in activism, politics, and public service.❖

Betty Shabazz
(1934-1997)
Educator, administrator, nurse, activist

Betty Shabazz, who witnessed her husband's assassination, sought to preserve his memory and teachings in a life that became a symbol of perseverance to African Americans, and In the process, developed a following of her own.

BETTY DEAN SANDERS SHABAZZ was born in Pinehurst, Georgia[1] to Ollie Mae Sanders, a teenaged mother, and Shelman "JuJu" Sandlin. By some accounts, Shabazz was abused, and shortly after her birth was raised by her paternal grandmother until her death when she was six years old, and then returning to her mother's care. When Shabazz was about eleven years old, she was taken in by foster parents Helen and Lorenzo Malloy, a prominent businessman in Detroit. The Malloys, who largely sheltered Shabazz from racism, taught her that education meant security and happiness (Rickford 2003).

While attending Northern High School, Shabazz joined the orchestra, the French Club, and was on the Russell Scholarship Committee. After graduation, Shabazz left her foster parents' home in Detroit to study at Lorenzo Malloy's alma mater, the Tuskegee Institute in Alabama. She intended to earn a degree in education and become a teacher, but nothing had prepared her for Southern racism. She eventually changed her field of study from education to nursing, and transferred to the Tuskegee-affiliated program at the Brooklyn State College School of Nursing in New York City. While the racial climate in New York offered a slight improvement, Shabazz often wondered whether she had merely exchanged Jim Crow racism for a more genteel prejudice (Rickford 2003).

During her second year of nursing school, Shabazz met Malcolm X at a Nation of Islam (NOI) dinner, and began attending his lectures. In time, she would teach a woman's class and do secretarial work for Malcolm at Temple Number Seven in Harlem. He always sought her out to ask her questions, and Shabazz was impressed with Malcolm's leadership and work ethic. In 1956, she converted to the NOI, and changed her surname to "X," which represented the family name of her African ancestors that she would never know. Although they had never discussed the subject, Shabazz suspected that Malcolm was interested in marriage. One day,

---

1.   Shabazz's precise birthplace remains somewhat of a mystery, for neither Georgia nor Michigan has a record of her birth certificate (Rickford 2003).

he called and asked her, and they were married on January 14, 1958 in Lansing, Michigan. By coincidence, Shabazz became a licensed nurse on that same day. The couple would go on to have six daughters.

At first, their relationship followed the NOI's strictures concerning marriage; Malcolm set the rules and Shabazz obediently followed them; but over time, the dynamic of their relationship changed. Shabazz chafed under Malcolm's authority. In their seven-year marriage, they briefly separated several times. But their relationship grew in mutual respect, and Malcolm made small concessions to her demands for more independence. She developed curriculum for the sect's parochial schools, and set up classes for women at mosques.

Malcolm had grown disillusioned with the NOI and its leader, Elijah Muhammad. After a period of travel in Africa and the Middle East, which included completing the Hajj, he also became known as el-Hajj Malik el-Shabazz. In 1964, Malcolm X announced that he was leaving the NOI, and declared that he and his family were now Sunni Muslims. Eight days before the assassination, the family's home in East Elmhurst, Queens in New York was firebombed.

On February 21, 1965, in Manhattan's Audubon Ballroom, Malcolm had begun to speak at a meeting of the Organization of Afro-American Unity (OAU), which he recently founded, when a disturbance broke out in the crowd. As Malcolm and his bodyguards moved to quiet the disturbance, a man rushed forward and shot Malcolm in the chest with a sawed-off shotgun. Two other men charged the stage and fired handguns, hitting Malcolm sixteen times.

Shabazz, who was pregnant with the twins, was in the audience near the stage with her daughters. When she heard the gunfire, she grabbed her daughters and pushed them to the floor beneath the bench, and shielded them with her pregnant body. When the shooting stopped, Shabazz ran toward her husband to perform CPR. Police officers and Malcolm's associates used a stretcher to carry him up the block to Columbia Presbyterian Hospital, where he was pronounced dead. Angry onlookers caught and beat one of the assassins, who was arrested at the scene. Eyewitnesses identified two more suspects. All three men, who were members of the NOI, were convicted and sentenced to life in prison.

In the aftermath of Malcolm's assassination, Shabazz worried about how she would support herself and her family. During this fateful moment, she was left alone—widowed, pregnant, homeless, and penniless. Ruby Dee and Juanita Poitier (wife of Sidney Poitier) established the Committee of Concerned Mothers, which held a series of benefit concerts to raise funds to buy a house in Mount Vernon, New York and pay her expenses. Initially, Shabazz had to rely on her husband's share of the royalties from *The Autobiography of Malcolm X* (1965), which was equivalent to an annual salary. In 1966, she sold the movie rights of the book to filmmaker Marvin Worth. She began to authorize the publication of Malcolm's speeches, which provided another source of income. More importantly. Shabazz set out to raise her daughters to become citizens of the global community. She encouraged them to travel so that they could learn about Africa, the West Indies, and the Middle East.

In 1965, Shabazz made the pilgrimage to Mecca (Hajj), as her husband had the year before. She began accepting some speaking engagements at colleges and universities, and spoke about the Black nationalist philosophy of Malcolm X, and her role as a Muslim wife and mother. Shabazz felt that some of the images by the media misrepresented her husband, which she sought to correct.

In late 1969, Shabazz enrolled at Jersey City State College (renamed New Jersey City University) to complete the degree in education she left behind when she became a nurse. She completed her undergraduate studies in one year, and decided to earn a master's degree in health administration. In 1972, Shabazz enrolled at the University of Massachusetts Amherst to pursue an Ed.D. in higher education administration and curriculum development. Shabazz joined Delta Sigma Theta Sorority in 1974, and in 1975, she defended her dissertation and earned her doctorate. That same year, President Ford invited Shabazz to serve on the American Revolution Bicentennial Council. She served on an advisory committee on family planning for the U.S. Department of Health and Human Services.

Shabazz became the associate professor of health sciences at Medgar Evers College in Brooklyn, New York in 1976. The students at Medgar Evers were 90 percent Black and predominantly working class. Black women made up most of the faculty, and 75 percent of the students were female, two-thirds of them mothers—all qualities that made the college attractive to Shabazz (Rickford 2003).

By 1980, Shabazz was overseeing the health sciences department when she was promoted to an administrative position. A year later, she was given tenure. In 1984, Shabazz was promoted to Director of Institutional Advancement and Public Affairs, a position she held until her death.

As Malcolm's legacy attracted growing interest with a new generation during the 1980s, Shabazz's life began to change. Since her daughters had grown up, she fully re-entered the public arena. In 1983, she started a weekly radio talk show on WBLS-FM in New York. She worked with New York City Mayor Koch to rename Lenox Avenue in Harlem to Malcolm X Boulevard. In 1984, Shabazz hosted the New York convention of the National Council of Negro Women (NCNW), and became active in the NAACP and the National Urban League. When Nelson and Winnie Mandela visited Harlem in 1990, Shabazz was asked to introduce Winnie Mandela.

For many years, Shabazz harbored resentment toward the NOI—and Louis Farrakhan in particular—for what she believed was their role in the assassination of her husband, which Farrakhan seemed to boast of in a 1993 speech. Her resentment reverberated not only among her close-knit inner circle, but among family members as well.

In January 1995, Shabazz's daughter Qubilah was charged with trying to hire an assassin to kill Farrakhan in retaliation for the murder of her father. Farrakhan surprised Shabazz when he defended Qubilah, saying he did not think she was guilty, and that he hoped she would not be convicted. That May, Shabazz and Farrakhan shook hands on the stage of the Apollo Theater during a public event intended to raise money for Qubilah's legal defense. Some heralded the evening as a reconciliation between the two, but others felt Shabazz was doing whatever was necessary to protect her daughter. Regardless, nearly $250,000 was raised that evening. In the aftermath, while Shabazz agreed to speak at his Million Man March that October, she maintained a cool relationship with Farrakhan.

Qubilah accepted a plea agreement and in order to avoid a prison sentence was required to undergo psychological counseling and treatment for drug and alcohol abuse. For the duration of her treatment, Qubilah's ten-year-old son, Malcolm, was sent to live with Shabazz at her apartment in Yonkers, New York.

On June 1, 1997, young Malcolm set a fire in Shabazz's apartment. Shabazz suffered burns over 80 percent of her body, and remained in intensive care for three weeks at Jacobi Medical Center in the Bronx. She underwent five skin-replacement operations as doctors struggled to replace damaged skin and save her life. Betty Shabazz died of her injuries on June 23, 1997. Malcolm was sentenced to eighteen months in juvenile detention for manslaughter and arson. In 2013, he would be found murdered in Mexico City.

More than 2,000 mourners attended a memorial service for Shabazz, at New York's Riverside Church. Many prominent leaders attended, including Coretta Scott King and Myrlie Evers-Williams, New York Governor Pataki, and four New York City mayors—Abraham Beame, Ed Koch, David Dinkins, and Rudy Giuliani. U.S. Secretary of Labor Alexis Herman delivered a tribute from President Clinton.

Shabazz's public viewing was at the Unity Funeral Home in Harlem, the same place where Malcolm's had been thirty-two years earlier, and the funeral was held at the Islamic Cultural Center in New York City. Shabazz was buried next to her husband at Ferncliff Cemetery in Hartsdale, New York.❖

The Legacy of Betty Shabazz

IN THE HARD YEARS FOLLOWING the assassination, Betty Shabazz, the then thirty-one-year-old mother of six daughters, retreated from the spotlight. Unlike the widows Coretta Scott King or Myrlie Evers-Williams, Shabazz was not embraced by a nation sympathetic to her grief; she was the widow of a controversial figure. Malcolm neither coveted nor won the support of White America, nor did he have the full support from civil rights activists tethered to King's nonviolence campaign and the Black community at large. He was perceived on both sides as a hateful separatist. When Malcolm began to readjust his views, he alienated his Black nationalist and separatist supporters, and this antipathy he had created was still alive when he was murdered. Shabazz bore the consequences of this shift. As a result, besides being confined by the expectations of public widowhood, this was also compounded by continued surveillance of her family by the NOI, the FBI and CIA. It is why Shabazz chose to lead a relatively quiet life that focused on raising her six daughters, going back to school to earn her degrees, and working as a college administrator.

She always had an unwavering determination to protect Malcolm's legacy from distortion. Shabazz wanted his legacy to reflect that he was a brilliant human rights strategist who was devoted to the cause of peace, equality, and freedom for all. She worked with Pathfinder Press to ensure publication of reliable volumes that would accurately recount his life, words, and works. By 1991, with "X" caps and Malcolm T-shirts proliferating, Shabazz retained CMG Worldwide of Indianapolis to license Malcolm's name and likeness. The rediscovery of Malcolm X and the commercialization around his name both touched and annoyed her. The "X" caps were okay, but she wanted people to hear and understand his words. She felt that Spike Lee's 1992 movie, *Malcolm X,* of which she served as consultant, succeeded in recasting her husband as a daring visionary.

Shabazz was relentless in her efforts to have Malcolm honored with a U.S. Postage Stamp, which was issued in 1999, two years after her death. She established the Malcolm X Medical scholarship at Columbia University. She also formed a coalition of community, political, and educational leaders to establish the Malcolm X Memorial Center at the Audubon Ballroom because she was determined to transform the place of fatal tragedy into one that would triumphantly honor her husband's legacy. It is this grounding that made Shabazz so appealing. She did what most Black women are so often forced to do: reinvent her life in the face of misfortune. And while Shabazz protected her husband's legacy, she unintentionally created her own.

After Shabazz's death, she was honored in her own right. In late 1997, the Community Healthcare Network renamed one of its Brooklyn clinics the Dr. Betty Shabazz Health Center. In 1998, the Betty Shabazz International Charter School was founded in her honor in Chicago. In 2005, Columbia University announced the opening of the Malcolm X and Dr. Betty Shabazz Memorial and Educational Center, located in the Audubon Ballroom where Malcolm X was assassinated. In March 2012, New York City created Betty Shabazz Way at Broadway and West 165th Street in front of the Audubon Ballroom,

Unfortunately, a great part of Shabazz's legacy will forever be connected to the manner in which she died. That a twelve-year-old boy set fire to his vibrant sixty-three-year-old grandmother's home, creating an inferno that was responsible for her untimely death. A boy named after his grandfather, a legendary Black leader with an uncanny resemblance, would find himself murdered at the age of twenty-eight under questionable circumstances. *Two cruel deaths.* Time has passed, but in the remembering, we continue to wonder about Shabazz's seemingly unfinished work and the violence she endured. That said, we are grateful Shabazz ensured her husband's life and works were recorded in history, and along the way, she created her legacy on her own terms.❖

Diane Nash
(1938)
Civil rights activist, leader, strategist

Diane Nash played a pivotal role in creating the first successful civil rights campaigns of the era, including the integration of lunch counters, Freedom Rides, and the Selma Voting Rights Campaign. She is a cofounder of the Student Nonviolent Coordinating Committee (SNCC).

DIANE JUDITH NASH was born and raised in Chicago, Illinois to Dorothy Bolton Nash, a keypunch operator and Leon Nash, who served in the military as a clerk during World War II. Her parents left Nash in the care of her grandmother, Carrie Bolton, until age seven. After the war, Nash's parents' marriage ended. Her mother married John Baker, who worked as a waiter for the Pullman Company's railroad dining cars, and was a member of the Brotherhood of Sleeping Car Porters (BSCP), the first Black union in the country. Growing up in Chicago, Nash lived in a city free from many of Jim Crow's overt restrictions.

Nash attended public and Catholic schools. In 1956, Nash graduated from Hyde Park High School in Chicago and enrolled in Howard University in Washington, D.C., before transferring to Fisk University in Nashville, Tennessee. Nash, who considered becoming a nun, planned to study English and become a secondary school teacher after graduation.

While a student in Nashville, Nash witnessed southern racial segregation for the first time and searched for a way to challenge it. In 1959, she began attending nonviolent protest workshops led by Reverend James Lawson, a divinity student at Vanderbilt University (who would later be expelled for his civil rights arrests), and was affiliated with the Nashville Christian Leadership Conference. Lawson was also a member of the Fellowship of Reconciliation (FOR), and the Congress of Racial Equality (CORE), which advocated nonviolent resistance. He went to India to study Mahatma Gandhi's nonviolent direct action and passive resistance techniques. At the urging of Martin Luther King Jr., Lawson began conducting nonviolence training workshops for the Southern Christian Leadership Conference (SCLC) in Nashville. His workshops included simulations to prepare the students to handle the verbal and physical harassment they would ultimately face during sit-ins and freedom rides. By the end of her first semester at Fisk, Nash had become one of Lawson's most devoted disciples.

The mass sit-ins that began in Greensboro, North Carolina, had spread to Nashville. In 1960, Nash became a member of the Student Central Committee, which comprised of representatives from the colleges and universities in the Nashville metropolitan area who trained in nonviolence techniques. The committee's purpose was to help organize and provide guidance to sit-ins at restaurants and lunch counters throughout Nashville. Nash was eventually elected chairperson of the committee, which she initially declined. First of all, she did not come to the civil rights movement seeking to become a leader. Nash considered herself a strategist and organizer and avoided the limelight (Jones 2020). But she was also afraid. When she finally accepted the position, she took her leadership role seriously, and her fear became a great motivator to be judicious in her approach and be extremely efficient in her role. Nash understood that she and her members could be injured or, even worse, killed (Bell 2018).

The Nashville sit-ins spread to sixty-nine cities across the South, which ultimately involved hundreds of Black and White area college students. Nashville Mayor West called for the desegregation of Nashville's lunch counters and organized negotiations between Nash and other student leaders and downtown business owners. Because of these negotiations, Nashville became the first southern city to desegregate lunch counters. Nash emerged as a national leader due to her well-spoken, composed manner when engaging with the authorities and the press.

The student sit-ins had caught SCLC executive director Ella Baker's attention. By mid-February, Nash had organized and led many protests, and at Baker's urging, students from across the South assembled in Raleigh, North Carolina. There they founded the Student Nonviolent Coordinating Committee (SNCC) in 1960. After the Nashville sit-ins, Nash helped coordinate and participated in the Freedom Rides across the Deep South. Later that year, Nash dropped out of college to become a full-time organizer and an instructor for the SCLC headed by Martin Luther King Jr. In 1961, Nash married civil rights activist James Bevel and moved to Jackson, Mississippi, where she began organizing voter registration and school desegregation campaigns for the SCLC. Although she was four months pregnant, in 1962, she was arrested and sentenced to two years in prison for teaching nonviolent tactics to children in Jackson. She was sentenced to ten days in jail, and was later released on appeal.

Nash played a major role in the Birmingham desegregation campaign of 1963 and the Selma Voting Rights Campaign of 1964. In 1963, President Kennedy appointed Nash to a national committee to promote civil rights legislation. Eventually, his proposed bill was passed as the Civil Rights Act of 1964. When it came to the Selma marches in 1965, which culminated into Bloody Sunday and the crossing of the Edmund Pettus Bridge, Nash harnessed all the principles that had brought her to this moment. She understood the bargain that would bring federal officials to the table when it came to voting rights. While the principles of nonviolence had left marchers especially vulnerable to violence as they put their bodies on the line, it also won them supporters across the country, especially in Washington, D.C. (Jones 2020).

Arrested dozens of times during the early 1960s, Nash and Bevel received the War Resister's League Peace Award in 1964 and the SCLC's Rosa Parks award from King in 1965. King cited their contributions to the Selma Right-to-Vote movement that eventually led to the Voting Rights Act of 1965. Nash would serve in many roles for the SCLC from 1961 to 1965 while under King but would later cut ties with the SCLC, questioning its male- and clergy-dominated leadership structure. She would also split from SNCC in 1965 when the organization departed from its founding pillar of nonviolence. However, Nash remained involved in political and social justice activities, and in 1966, she joined the Vietnam Peace Movement.

Nash and Bevel divorced in 1968, and Nash returned with her children to her hometown of Chicago. She taught in the public schools and worked in real estate, but continued to speak out for social justice, advocate for fair housing, and women's rights. She has been cited in numerous publications, and was featured in the documentaries *John Lewis: Good Trouble* (2020), PBS American Experience's *Freedom Riders* (2010), the inspirational story of American civil rights activists' peaceful fight against racial segregation on buses and trains in the 1960s, the award-winning PBS series *Eyes on the Prize* (2011), and Spike Lee's *Four Little Girls* (1997). Nash figures prominently in the book *The Children* (1998) by historian David Halberstam, who covered the start of the civil rights movement and sit-ins that galvanized a generation.

In 2013, Nash expressed her support for President Obama while also sharing her reluctance to support U.S. involvement in the Iraq and Afghanistan wars. While encouraged by the positive implications of electing America's first Black president, Nash believed true change would only come from its citizens, not government officials. Although she attended the Selma fiftieth anniversary celebrations in March 2015, Nash was noticeably absent from the re-staging of the 1965 Selma march due to President George W. Bush's attendance, whose ideals were counter to her pursuit of nonviolence. Decades later, while she may not maintain the kind of high profile she had during the 1960s, Nash's moral compass and dedication to civil rights prevails.

Nash is the recipient of the Freedom Award from the National Civil Rights Museum in 2008 and, in 2004, the LBJ Award for Leadership in Civil Rights from the Lyndon Baines Johnson Library and Museum. In 2003, Nash won the Distinguished American Award from the John F. Kennedy Library and Foundation. She has been awarded honorary doctorates from her alma mater, Fisk University, and the University of Notre Dame. With the world around her becoming as challenging as ever, Nash's sense of justice and nonviolence is never far from the surface, and she continues to apply it to every aspect of her lifer.✣

Peggy Shepard
(1946)
Environmental justice activist, journalist, politician

Peggy Shepard, an environmental crusader and champion for ecological equality, is the cofounder and executive director of WE ACT, one of the oldest African American-run environmental justice organizations in the U.S.

PEGGY MORROW SHEPARD was born in Washington, D.C. to Evelyn Shepard, a homemaker, and George Shepard Jr., an obstetrician. The oldest of six children, she grew up in Washington, D.C. and Trenton, Ewing, and Lawrenceville, New Jersey, and attended the Solebury and Newtown Friends schools in Pennsylvania. Such early exposure to rural, scenic, and natural areas increased Shepard's appreciation for nature and the more traditional concept of environmentalism. She also enjoyed reading, starting clubs with her friends, and developing some ideas about becoming a writer.

After earning a bachelor's degree in English from Howard University in 1967, Shepard began her career as a journalist, becoming the first African American beat reporter for the *Indianapolis News.* She moved to New York in 1971 to pursue a publishing career. She was a copy editor for *The San Juan Star* and a researcher for Time-Life Books. Shepard then served as an editor at *Redbook* and *Essence,* and landed a position at *Black Enterprise* magazine with plans in the works to launch the first African American lifestyle magazine. When the publisher decided instead to invest in radio stations, Shepard began a career that launched her into the realm of politics and social activism, and she thrived.

In 1979, Shepard was a speechwriter for the New York State Division of Housing & Community Renewal, and Director of Public Information for Rent Administration, and then served as the Women's Outreach Coordinator for the New York City Comptroller's Office. She was the public relations director for Jesse Jackson's 1984 presidential campaign, and then ran for and was elected as West Harlem's Democratic District Leader, serving from 1985 to 1993.

Shepard soon learned that New York City's largest sewage treatment plant, originally sited in a White, upper middle class neighborhood, was being constructed in her community. She also discovered that New York's Metropolitan Transportation Authority (MTA) was building a diesel bus depot across the street from a school and a large public housing development in West Harlem.

Troubled by the noxious odors being emitted by the North River Sewage Treatment Plant, Shepard helped to organize an act of civil disobedience. On Martin Luther King Jr. Day in 1988, she and six other community organizers—the "sewage seven"—donned gas masks and held up traffic near the plant on the West Side Highway to protest the North River plant. They were promptly arrested, but not before they had made their point. Around this time, the environmental justice movement was getting off the ground in Black and Brown communities. Awareness was building around the country that low-income communities and people of color were being targeted by polluting industries in disproportionate numbers. This began another shift in Shepard's career—this time toward environmental justice advocacy.

During this period, the attention and discontent surrounding the plant's operation and the construction of a second bus depot in West Harlem presented the need for a unified movement to address the unequal impact of environmental hazards. When neighborhood activists recognized that West Harlem bore the brunt of toxic pollution, they mobilized, and in 1988, Shepard, along with Vernice Miller-Travis and Chuck Sutton, founded West Harlem Environmental Action (WE ACT) (which later changed its name to WE ACT for Environmental Justice). WE ACT was New York's first environmental justice organization created to improve environmental health and the quality of life in communities of color. Shepard has served as WE ACT's executive director since 1994.

The group immediately filed a lawsuit against New York City over the sewage plant, created partnerships with several organizations such as Columbia University School of Public Health, and went on to win an unprecedented victory that resulted in a $1.1 million settlement and a $55 million commitment to fix the plant. WE ACT also rallied the support of political leaders and the Transit Workers Union (TWU) to help the city transition from gas-powered to natural gas-powered buses and depots. When they failed to get the MTA to change its policies in favor of cleaner fuel alternatives, WE ACT and several community residents filed a complaint with the U.S. Department of Transportation (USDOT).

In 2004, the USDOT found that the MTA failed to comply with the required federal environmental impact analysis in constructing, rehabilitating, and reconstructing bus depots and other facilities. After further local campaigns, followed by state and local authorities' pressure, the MTA started to replace their diesel fuel buses with alternative, cleaner vehicles. The campaign took eighteen years to complete, and the MTA retired its last diesel-burning buses in 2019.

As a dynamic coalition builder, Shepard has helped turn WE ACT from a small group of committed volunteers into a professionally staffed environmental justice organization that works on a national level, with offices in both New York and Washington, D.C. In 1991, WE ACT joined the first People of Color Environmental Leadership Summit in Washington, D.C. to establish the guiding principles for the movement to combat environmental racism.

Shepard, who faced blackouts at the federal level through the Reagan, Bush, and Trump, administrations, has always remained confident that WE ACT and other environmental organizations will always overcome their hardships through commitment and hard work. She continues scaling up civic engagement with electoral work that holds elected officials responsible for addressing environmental issues and keeping their commitments, and ensures that current laws are being enforced and complied with. As Shepard's team garners wins, they set a precedent that helps pave the way for other African American-run environmental organizations in the nation to follow.

Throughout her career, Shepard has served on numerous academic and governmental advisory boards. She was a member of the National Children's Study Advisory Committee as well as the National Advisory Environmental Health Sciences Council of the National Institutes of Health. Shepard has also served on the Committee on Ethical Issues in Housing-Related Health Hazard Research Involving Children, Youth and Families, a project of the National Research Council which published its report in 2006, and is the former chair of the Environmental Protection Agency's (EPA) National Environmental Justice Advisory Council (NEJAC), serving as the co-chair of its Research and Science Workgroup.

As part of WE ACT's agenda, Shepard has also served on numerous committees that help facilitate the organization's partnerships. Besides serving as the first female chair of the NEJAC to the EPA, she was a co-investigator of the Columbia Children's Environmental Health Center; co-chair of the Northeast Environmental Justice Network; and a board member of the Environmental Defense Fund, Earth Day New York, the New York League of Conservation Voters, New York Audubon, and the News Corporation Diversity Council.

Shepard is the recipient of the Sol Feinstone Environmental Award from the SUNY College of Environmental Science and Forestry, Asian Americans for Equality's annual Dream of Equality Award, the Dean's Distinguished Service Award from the Mailman School of Public Health, the 10th Annual Heinz Award for the Environment, and the Jane Jacobs Lifetime Achievement Award from the Rockefeller Foundation. She received an Honorary Doctor of Science from Smith College at its May 2010 commencement. She has also authored and co-authored articles in several leading publications such as *Environmental Justice, Climate Justice, Journal of Urban Health, National Research Council and Institute of Medicine, Environmental Health Perspectives,* and *Fordham Urban Law Journal.*

Shepard successfully combined grassroots organizing, environmental advocacy, and scientific research to become one of the country's most highly respected environmental activists today. She is a pioneer in advancing the cause of environmental equality in our inner cities, ensuring that the entitlement of clean air, water, and soil extends to all people, regardless of their socioeconomic status.❖

Pierrette "Petee" Talley
(1956)
Union leader

Pierrette Talley was the first African American woman to hold one of the two top offices of the Ohio AFL-CIO, which represents more than 500,000 workers in fields ranging from construction to medicine.

PIERRETTE "PETEE" MCCLAIN TALLEY was born in Toledo, Ohio to Ella E. McClain, a factory worker during the war effort and a housewife, and David McClain, who worked as an autoworker, steelworker, and ultimately retired as a custodian at the University of Toledo. Talley was the fifth of eight children. From the very beginning, the union loomed large in Talley's life.

Although her father had good union jobs, taking care of a family of ten was no small feat. But while the family struggled, they never went hungry. Talley attended three different public schools, attended Scott High School, and graduated from Calvin S. Woodward High School in 1974. Talley did not necessarily excel in school, nor did she pursue a particular occupation, but she did receive decent grades. The one thing that greatly impacted her life was taking typing classes, which allowed her to find work to help take care of her family. She also took a business class that Talley found rewarding because it provided her insight for a potential career.

Right after graduation, Talley worked at the Lucas County Clerk of Courts. After being laid off from a tire service company in 1980, the unemployment office referred Talley to a secretarial position at Sears, and as she stood up to leave, the counselor redirected her to a secretarial position at the American Federation of State, County and Municipal Employees (AFSCME) Ohio Council 8 instead. She was immediately hired and quickly became involved in union activities. She loved organizing and getting people engaged and wanted to do more than just clerical work. Talley volunteered on a number of the union's campaigns, working on phone banks or passing out literature.

In 1983, she was on the organizing team to help pass the Ohio collective bargaining law, ORC 4117 and worked on Marcy Kaptur's first campaign for Congress in 1983, who is currently the longest-serving woman in the House of Representatives. In 1992, Talley was assigned to coordinate the union's

campaign to elect President Clinton, which led to the largest turnout of Black voters in Toledo since the 1940s.

After Talley received her Bachelor of Science and Arts degree from the University of Toledo in 1994, where she majored in political science and communications, she was appointed Political and Legislative Director for AFSCME International in Michigan. She worked closely with local and state public workers to help strengthen the union's political program just as the nation's conservative agenda was taking root across the country.

In 1999, Talley became the Ohio Field Director of Mobilization of the National AFL-CIO, where she worked to build strong union cities across the state. Her work included reestablishing and restructuring Central Labor Federations and State Federations through a New Alliance program in order to prepare them for the challenges of the anti-union policies that serve emerging at the state and national level. Talley's work also involved engaging union affiliates in various political, organizing, and legislative campaigns and activities. She worked on the Affordable Prescription Drug Campaign that made prescription drugs more affordable to its members across the state. She negotiated terms with PHARMA and instituted Ohio's Best Rx Program in 2002. When Talley was first elected to Secretary-Treasurer of the Ohio AFL-CIO in 2002, she became the first African American woman to hold one of the top two offices in the sixty-one-year history of the Ohio AFL-CIO. As a member of AFSCME Local 3616, Talley was re-elected and remained in office until her retirement.

While at AFL-CIO, she led several campaigns, notably establishing the Ohio Voter Protection Coalition in 2004, which led to reforms in Ohio voting procedures. In 2006, Talley worked to break the dominance of one-party rule by helping to elect Ted Strickland as governor and other Ohio Democrats to statewide offices. In 2011, Governor Kasich signed into law Senate Bill 5, which was designed to limit the collective bargaining rights of public employee unions. In a historic repeal referendum, Ohio voters overwhelmingly rejected the law. Talley's work to organize the African American community's support was critical to its success. The victory was especially impressive considering heartbreaking losses for state employees in Wisconsin, where Governor Walker had signed and successfully put into action a similar anti-union law. The political acumen Talley displayed in her work reflected her skill, passion, and knowledge of the importance of building strong alliances between African Americans and unions.

In 2012, the AFL-CIO was successful in its Stand Your Ground Voter Empowerment campaign, registering voters and turning them out to the polls to vote. In 2014, she continued to work with a major voter registration experiment that provided research to the Analyst Institute on the best practices of conducting successful voter registration campaigns.

In addition to her official role at the Ohio AFL-CIO, Talley worked with grassroots organizers across the state of Ohio. She volunteered as Convener of the Ohio Unity Coalition, which focused on non-partisan voter registration, voter education, and supporting Get Out The Vote in African American communities across the state. Talley worked to oppose voter suppression efforts when the Ohio general assembly sought to implement voter ID laws and other unreasonable measures to make it more difficult to count every vote. She worked with a team that collected over 800,000 signatures to overturn HB 194 before the legislature decided to pull the bill off the table.

Talley serves on the boards of the Ohio Employee Ownership Center, Universal Health Care Action Network (UHCAN), Progress Ohio, A. Philip Randolph Institute, Coalition of Black Trade Unionists (CBTU), the National Executive Council as the representative for Region V, the Alliance for Retired Americans, and the Ohio Constitutional Modernization Commission. She has received numerous awards, including the coveted Addie Wyatt award from the United Food and Commercial Workers (UFCW); the Rosina Tucker Award from the A. Philip Randolph Institute; the Rising Star and President's Award from the CBTU; the Drum Major Award from the National AFL-CIO MLK Jr. Observance; and The World Peace Prize of Roving Ambassador for Peace Award, awarded by the Irish National Caucus.

Talley is married to Cornell Talley, her husband of thirty-three years. They have a blended family of four children, eleven grandchildren, and one great-granddaughter. In 2019, having served the union for thirty-eight years, Talley decided to retire. She had missed many family milestones, and with the recent passing of her older sister and younger sister in the same year, she decided to step down to focus on herself and her family. Yet retirement has not slowed her down, and she still remains engaged, though on her own terms.

She continues her involvement in the AFL-CIO constituency group, CBTU, and the A. Philip Randolph Institute. But she mostly finds herself heavily immersed in the Ohio Coalition of Black Civic Participation, her nonprofit organization dedicated to increasing civic engagement and voter participation in Black and underserved communities. When COVID-19 hit, Talley found herself working tirelessly to ensure that voters had all the information they needed to make their voices heard in the November 2020 presidential election.

Talley has spent her entire career working in the labor movement to convince both policymakers and disillusioned Black workers of labor's virtue. In many ways, these realities bear witness to the distance that labor still has to go in finding authentic ways to root out persistent discrimination and inequality, and to build true partnerships. Talley is part of a small yet determined circle of Black women unionists who believe that a better future can only be secured when a collective fight is working toward a greater vision. We have not heard the last from Pierrette "Petee" Talley yet.❖

Dorceta E. Taylor
(1957)
Environmental sociologist, activist, scholar, author

Dorceta E. Taylor, considered to be one of the mothers of the environmental justice movement, was the first African American woman to earn a doctoral degree from the School of Forestry and Environmental Studies at Yale University.

DORCETA E. TAYLOR was born in Frankfield, Jamaica to Dorothy A. Taylor, a nurse's aide, and Seymour C. Taylor, a consultant for an engineering firm. The second of four children, Taylor became interested in the environment as a young girl growing up in rural Jamaica. One of her favorite tasks was to tend the family rose garden, and she became fascinated by the flowers, butterflies, and countless fruit trees in the yard. When she was eight, Taylor's grammar schoolteacher introduced her to the concept of "Environmental Studies," and she was mesmerized.

A chance encounter in one of her high school classes with an African American visiting professor inspired her to become a learned woman. The day she met the American visitor, she went home and added "professor" to her to-do list, and began pursuing a doctorate with intense determination. She was steadfast in her love for nature, and her fascination with the environment only grew stronger after she began studying biology in high school. However, she also contemplated becoming a medical doctor—nothing was off the table.

Taylor moved to live with her grandmother in Jamaica's capital city, Kingston, and in 1968, the same year her mother migrated to live in Illinois. While attending high school in Kingston, Taylor specialized in the natural sciences, passing both the University of Cambridge's ordinary-level and advanced-level exams. She entered a teacher-training college and became a certified high school science teacher in 1977. Because of her prowess in zoology, teachers and professors encouraged her to become a medical doctor.

When Taylor migrated to the U.S. in 1978, she contemplated a medical career. Still, she found herself thinking about the environment and finding jobs that would allow her to blend her interest in science and social issues. Taylor soon realized she was most interested in human-environment interactions and completed her undergraduate studies in biology and environmental studies, graduating with high honors from Northeastern Illinois University in 1983. Taylor was admitted to the Yale School of Forestry and Environmental Studies in 1983, becoming the second black woman admitted to this school. At Yale, she pursued a degree in forest science, and she also took courses on inequality to nurture her burgeoning interest in social dynamics.

After completing her Master's of Forest Science in 1985, she gained admission into that year's doctoral program. By 1991, Taylor obtained two additional master's degrees—one a Master's of Arts and another a Master's of Philosophy—she also got a joint doctorate from Yale's School of Forestry and Environmental Studies and the Department of Sociology. Taylor was the first Black woman to receive a doctorate from the Yale School of Forestry and Environmental Studies.

While a student, Taylor received several national and university-wide fellowships to pursue her doctoral and post-doctoral studies. As a student, she was the recipient of a Patricia Roberts Harris Fellowship, a Yale Dissertation Fellowship, Edward Bouchet Dissertation Fellowship, and a National Academies of Sciences Ford Dissertation Fellowship. Taylor also received Mellon Foundation fellowships to conduct dissertation field research in the U.S. Virgin Islands and study organization theory. After completing her doctoral studies, Taylor received a National Science Foundation post-doctoral fellowship in 1991 to visit the University College of London and examine ethnic minority environmental activism in Britain. She then spent a year in Canada, where she worked in the University of Toronto's Sociology Department.

In 1992, she obtained a Ford Foundation/Rockefeller Foundation Poverty and the Underclass Post-doctoral Fellowship at the University of Michigan. The fellowship, jointly administered by the Ford School of Public Policy and the School of Social Work, allowed Taylor to examine how poverty and the environment were connected. That same year, she was offered and accepted a tenure-track position with a joint appointment at the School of Natural Resources and Environment (now known as the School for Environment and Sustainability) and the Center for Afro-American and African Studies (now known as the Department of Afro-American and African Studies) at the University of Michigan. She spent her first year as a post-doctoral fellow and assumed full-time faculty responsibilities in 1993. Taylor is the only Black woman to have been hired as a faculty member with an environmental specialization to be in the School for Environment and Sustainability. She was also the first faculty member hired in the Department of Afro-American and African Studies.

Taylor began laying the groundwork that would help to develop the environmental justice movement in 1989. She is one of the early scholars and movement activists to conduct research and release publications on diversity, equity, and inclusion (DEI). Taylor also developed diversity pathway programs and organized diversity conferences to support like-minded African Americans and other people of color to mobilize and pursue environmental justice. She authored the article, "Blacks and the Environment: Toward an Explanation of the Concern and Action Gap between Blacks and Whites," in 1989. Since then, she has published numerous papers, articles, and books on institutional diversity, environmental history, environmental justice, discrimination in the environmental workforce, environmental hazards, urban agriculture, the plight of black farmers, food insecurity, and food access.

With funding from the Joyce Foundation, Taylor founded the Multicultural Environmental Leadership Development Initiative (MELDI) in 2003. In 2005, she organized a national conference and, in 2007, an international one to assess the status of diversity in the environmental field and develop plans to enhance diversity in environmental organizations. Several papers presented at the 2007 conference were published in the book, *Environment and Social Justice: An International Perspective* (Emerald Publishing Limited, 2010), a compilation of original research articles that examine domestic and international environmental issues from an environmental justice perspective.

Taylor's book, *The Environment and the People in American Cities* (Duke University Press, 2009), focuses on American cities' environmental challenges in the seventeenth through twentieth centuries, and won the Allan Schnaiberg Outstanding Publication Award. She documented the race, class, and gender dynamics that arose as urban dwellers tried to deal with environmental problems. *Toxic Communities: Environmental Racism, Industrial Pollution, and Residential Mobility* (New York University Press, 2014) chronicles the contamination of minority and low-income communities in the U.S. The book incorporates insights from sociology and the study of urban development ignored in earlier environmental scholarship. In *The Rise of the American Conservation Movement* (Duke University Press, 2016), Taylor examines the emergence and development of the American conservation movement from the mid-1800s to the early-1900s. The book illustrates how deeply race, class, and gender influence conservation affairs, and inspires readers to reshape the way they think about environmental history.

In 2012, Taylor became the principal investigator of a six-year U.S. Department of Agriculture grant to study disparities in food access in Michigan. The Food Access in Michigan (FAIM) project examined the relationship between demographic characteristics and the distribution of food outlets in eighteen large and medium-sized cities with substantial populations of people of color. The study also examined emergency food assistance in the state. During the project, Taylor collaborated with researchers from Grand Valley State University, Michigan State University, the University of Michigan-Flint, Lake Superior State University, and the University of Wisconsin-Madison. The FAIM website contains journal articles such as "Food Availability and the Food Desert Frame in Detroit: An Overview of the City's Food System" (*Environmental Practice*, 2015), "Black Farmers in the U.S. and Michigan: Longevity, Empowerment, and Food Sovereignty" (*Journal of African American Studies,* 2018), and "A Geospatial Analysis of Access to Ethnic Food Retailers in Two Michigan Cities: Investigating the Importance of Outlet Type within Active Travel Neighborhoods" (*International Journal of Environmental Research and Public Health,* 2019).

Taylor chaired the Environment and Technology Section of the American Sociological Association from 2012 to 2013. In 2014, she authored the landmark national report, "The State of Diversity in Environmental Organizations: Mainstream NGOs, Foundations, and Government Agencies." The report found that environmental organizations lacked diversity on their staff, on their boards, and among their leadership, and it stimulated intense interest in the topic. Green 2.0, which commissioned "The State of Diversity," continues to track diversity data for the forty largest environmental organizations today. Taylor also published a second diversity report entitled, "Environmental Organizations in the Great Lakes Region: An Assessment of Institutional Diversity," which focuses on gender, racial, and class diversity in the Great Lakes environmental organizations and the diversity initiatives underway.

Taylor and her colleagues also published "Diversity, Equity, and Inclusion and the Salience of Publicly Disclosing Demographic Data in American Environmental Nonprofits" in 2019. Throughout her career, Taylor has conducted several other institutional diversity studies funded by the Joyce Foundation, the Ford Foundation, the Charles Stewart Mott Foundation, the JPB Foundation, the Nathan Cummings Foundation, the National Science Foundation, and others. Her articles appear in *BioScience, Journal of Environmental Education, Research in Social Problems and Public Policy, Environmental Practice, American Behavioral Scientist, Journal of Environmental Studies and Sciences, Sustainability, Environmental Management, Environmental Justice, Environment and Behavior,* and other sources.

In 2015, Taylor became the James E. Crowfoot Collegiate Professor of Environmental Justice and the Director of Diversity, Equity, and Inclusion at the University of Michigan's School for Environment and Sustainability (SEAS). That same year, she launched the Environmental Fellows Program (EFP) in partnership with the Environmental Grantmakers Association. EFP is a national program that reduces entry barriers for mid-career and senior-level jobs in environmental nonprofits and creates foundations for professionals from underrepresented backgrounds. The program provides internships to graduate students, builds networks, and fosters mentoring relationships. As of 2020, the Yale School for the Environment (renamed in 2020) houses the EFP.

Taylor also developed the University of Michigan's Doris Duke Conservation Scholars Program (DDCSP). The program, funded by the Doris Duke Charitable Foundation, operates on several university campuses. DDCSP is a two-year, undergraduate internship program aimed at diversifying the conservation sector by giving opportunities to students from underrepresented backgrounds who are committed to diversity, equity, and inclusion (DEI). Taylor moved the program to the Yale School of the Environment in 2020.

In 2018, Taylor spearheaded a new endeavor, the New Horizons in Conservation Conference. More than 200 students, faculty, EFP and DDCSP alumni, and conservation professionals gathered in Washington D.C. to celebrate and assess diversity, equity, and inclusion in the environmental sector. The conference—attended mostly by people of color—marked a milestone in conservation history. The annual conference draws attendees from across the nation and worldwide who are in varying career stages, including undergraduate and graduate students, academics, environmental professionals, policy advocates, and elected officials. New Horizons engages participants in hands-on professional development workshops and training, local field trips, and presentations from diverse leaders and visionaries in the field. Roughly 900 people—more than half of them people of color—registered and participated in the 2021 conference.

Taylor was motivated to conduct environmental justice research and became active in the environmental justice movement because the American conservation movement systematically discriminated against people of color. It was not until the 1970s that environmental clubs, long the bastion of wealthy White men, began admitting Black people as members. However, despite opening their memberships and a limited number of jobs to people of color, the environmental organizations were slow to address race, class, or gender issues. The environmental justice movement arose, in part, because of the urgent need to understand these three things related to environmental inequalities. From the beginning, Taylor was all in, doing everything possible to improve the lives of people of color through her research, publications, and creation of conferences and programs. Yet, decades later, Taylor is still pushing for people of color to be recognized as equal partners in environmental affairs. In 2020, she addressed these concerns in an article in *Sierra* entitled, "Environmental Justice Demands Listening."

Some of the world's most prominent environmental organizations celebrate Taylor's work. She was the recipient of the Harold R. Johnson Diversity Service Award from the University of Michigan in 2012. In 2014, San Francisco recognized her as one of twenty-nine Black environmentalists for Black Environmentalists during Black History Month. In 2015, Taylor received the Yale School of Forestry and Environmental Studies Outstanding Alumni Award, the Charles Horton Cooley Award for Distinguished Scholarship from the Michigan Sociological Association, and the Fred Buttel Distinguished Contribution Award from the American Sociological Association. She received the Burton V. Barnes Award for Academic Excellence from the Sierra Club Michigan Chapter in 2017.

In 2018, Taylor received the Women in Conservation Rachel Carson Award from the National Audubon Society; the Freudenburg Lifetime Achievement

Award from the Association of Environmental Science and Studies; the National Science Foundation's Presidential Award for Excellence in Science, Mathematics and Engineering Mentoring (PAESMEM); the University of Michigan Distinguished Faculty Achievement Award; the President's Award from the Detroit Audubon Society; and the EcoWorks Detroit Sustainable Communities Champion Award. In 2019, she was honored by the Smithsonian Institution. In 2020, the American Association of Retired Persons (AARP) identified Taylor as one of the six people continuing Dr. Martin Luther King's legacy through her work. That year, she was also recognized by Green America as one of the 8 Black Leaders Who've Revolutionized the Climate Movement. Taylor received the Wilbur Lucius Cross Medal in 2020, which is awarded by the Yale Graduate School Alumni Association to four alumni of the Yale Graduate School for Outstanding Achievements. She was also recognized by Envision Charlotte with the Women in Sustainability: 2020 Cross Sector Leader award. The Michigan Legislative Black Caucus presented her with the Seal of Michigan during 2020 as well. In 2021, LiveKindly recognized Taylor as one of the 7 Black Environmentalists Shaping the Future.

Taylor married Ian Robinson in 1989 and has identical twin daughters Shaina and Justine. She has worked hard to balance her personal and professional life to thrive in both environments successfully.

Taylor has devoted her career to diversifying the environmental movement. After spending twenty-seven years at the University of Michigan, in 2020, she became a professor at the Yale School for the Environment at Yale University, returning to her alma mater thirty-seven years after her first arrival on campus as a graduate student. She is the first Black faculty to be hired by the 120-year-old school—one of the oldest in the nation.

To date, Taylor's achievements have been exemplary. She has written extensively about how communities of color are affected by environmental degradation and exclusion from environmental organizations. She has educated and mentored hundreds of students, prodding them to pursue careers in the environmental field. Hailed as a standard-bearer for environmental justice, Taylor continues to challenge, teach, and inspire us to immerse ourselves in our histories, so that we can find out more about the environmental experiences of people living in Black and Brown communities across America.❖

Kadiatou Diallo
1959
Activist, author, public speaker

Kadiatou Diallo, an African immigrant, was thrust into the social justice spotlight when four police officers of the New York Police Department shot forty-one bullets into her unarmed son, Amadou Diallo, on February 4, 1999. His death ignited a movement of police reform in New York and other cities.

KADIATOU DIALLO was born in the town of Labé in Guinea, West Africa to Diarye Diallo and Amadou Bailo Diallo, a Muslim family of royal descent. She is the granddaughter of a scholar and Imam, and the fourth sibling in a family of four boys and five girls. When Diallo's sister became pregnant as a teen, her father decided to marry off his next daughter to avoid further shame to the family, and Diallo married Saiko Diallo. Her son, Amadou Diallo, the first of their four children, was born in Liberia, where the family lived until they returned to Guinea in 1980. Diallo helped her husband run a business exporting gemstones from Africa to Asia, and they lived in Togo and Bangkok, Thailand. While in Thailand, Diallo separated from her husband, and after the divorce, she moved her children back to Guinea, where they settled in the capital, Conakry. There, an Australian mining company retained her to represent its interests in opening a gold mine.

Amadou attended French-language private schools in Togo and Thailand, where he studied English and computer engineering and developed an interest in American culture. In September 1996, Amadou left for the U.S. and moved to New York City, where he planned to work and attend college on his own terms without his family's assistance. Diallo would never see her son alive again.

Amadou sold merchandise in front of a store at 14th Street and Second Avenue in Manhattan for a time. By late 1998, he made plans to open a small business selling silver and gold rings and was considering marriage. But on February 4, 1999, in the vestibule of his apartment building in the Soundview section of the Bronx, Diallo's twenty-three-year-old unarmed son was murdered by four New York City plain-clothed officers of the Street Crimes Unit. He was struck nineteen times in a shower of forty-one bullets from semi-automatic weapons. The officers later claimed to have mistaken him for a rape suspect and said that he reached for a gun, a claim that was never confirmed by any objective

evidence. All that was found on his body was a wallet. Diallo's murder erupted into a firestorm of controversy, prompting outrage throughout the country. Issues such as police brutality and racial profiling became central to the discussion.

Five days after her son was killed, a grief-stricken Diallo arrived into this tense environment from Guinea. As she staggered towards Amadou's apartment building, entered the vestibule and saw the bullet holes, she cried out for her son. Diallo also immediately found herself immersed in a political struggle dominated by long-time activist Reverend Al Sharpton and then-New York City Mayor Giuliani, from which she soon emerged as an independent figure. Though Diallo requested that the funeral not become political, an impromptu rally began after Mayor Giuliani arrived at the funeral in New York. He tried to speak to the family, but his request was denied. Diallo and her ex-husband took their son's body back to Guinea and buried him next to his grandfather. Thousands of Guineans attended his funeral. Diallo then returned to New York to seek justice for her son.

In March 1999, a Bronx grand jury indicted the four officers on charges of second-degree murder and reckless endangerment. Although Amadou was killed in the Bronx, the officers' legal defense was able to move the trial to the New York state capital of Albany—more than 150 miles away, with a starkly different racial makeup and a detachment from the New York City Police Department (NYPD) and the city's issues. Diallo said it was painful to hear her son described in court and in many news accounts solely as an immigrant street vendor when he was educated, multilingual, and well-traveled. In February 2000, after two days of deliberation, the Albany jury acquitted the officers of all charges. After reeling from the verdict, Diallo leaned on her Muslim faith to address reporters and asked for calm and prayers because "violence should not cause more violence."[1]

In April 2000, Diallo and her ex-husband filed a $61 million lawsuit against New York City and the officers, charging gross negligence, wrongful death, racial profiling, and other violations of her son's civil rights. Diallo made the controversial move of hiring her own lawyer. She also dropped out of a sixteen-city speaking tour that Sharpton had arranged without her approval. While Diallo agreed that racism was an important factor in her son's death, she also criticized the White and Black emphasis on a patriarchy that hampered her ability to seek justice. Furthermore, she sought a better understanding between all parties, including Africans and African Americans.

A federal investigation from the Department of Justice under then-Attorney General Janet Reno found that the Street Crimes Unit did, in fact, engage in racial profiling, as nearly 90 percent of the people who were stopped and frisked were either Black or Latino. In April 2002, due to the killing of Amadou and several other controversial actions, the Street Crimes Unit was disbanded. In March 2004, the Diallo family accepted a $3 million settlement.

---

1   Hayde Adams FitzPatrick, and Carol Guensburg, "Two Decades After Diallo Killing, Mother Finds Hope in New Protests," *Voice of America,* June 25, 2020 "https://www.voanews.com/usa/race-america/two-decades-after-diallo-killing-mother-finds-hope-new-protests.

Diallo has been widely praised for the poise, grace, serenity, and dignity with which she has borne the loss of her son. She quickly became a symbol of the struggle against police brutality in the U.S. and has used her experience to empower others. Soon after her son's murder, she founded The Amadou Diallo Foundation, Inc., a New York nonprofit promoting racial healing and higher education. It provides scholarships to New York City colleges for immigrants or students of African descent, helps improve relations with the police and the community, and provides a mentoring program for young people. Former New York City Mayor Dinkins had served as the foundation's chairman.

She has worked closely with local politicians to pass a racial profiling law in Albany and with Senator Hillary Rodham Clinton to pass one at the federal level. She also worked with Eric Adams, cofounder of 100 Blacks in Law Enforcement Who Care, to improve relations between the police and the community.

Her book, *My Heart Will Cross This Ocean—My Story, My Son, Amadou* (2003), co-written with Craig Wolff, won a 2004 Christopher Award. Diallo was featured in the public television documentary *Every Mother's Son* (2004), a testimonial of three women of different ethnicities, including Iris Baez and Doris Busch Boskey, to show the world that police brutality is a human rights issue. Another documentary, *Death of Two Sons* (2006), explores the political, personal, and spiritual implications of the lives and deaths of Amadou and Jesse Thyne, an American Peace Corps volunteer who lived with Amadou's family in his home village in Guinea and who died less than a year after Amadou. Diallo recently appeared in the Netflix docuseries *Trial By Media* (2020), which examines how the media may have impacted the verdicts. In 2013, Diallo built the school CADITEC in Labé, Guinea, which provides computer technology training to its students.

In the twenty years since her son's murder, Diallo has become the type of leader many people wanted her to be right after her son's murder, and she has done it in her own time with little to no publicity. She has also mended her relationship with Sharpton.

Diallo continues to push for change in part through the Justice Committee, a grassroots New York organization that opposes police violence and aims to empower people of color. It is part of a coalition whose years-long effort has finally led New York Governor Cuomo to approve a package of police reforms that include banning chokeholds and allowing transparency of disciplinary records in the wake of the George Floyd murder in June 2020. Diallo also lectures throughout the country to raise awareness on issues that are fundamental to a democratic society, donating all of the proceeds to her foundation. She remains a source of comfort and strength to many families who have suffered similar tragedies. While some have hailed her as the precursor to the Black Lives Matter movement, Diallo knows there is much work to be done and continues to make it her life's calling to focus on honoring her son's memory by fighting for change.❖

Michelle Alexander
(1967)
Activist, civil rights lawyer, author, legal scholar

Michelle Alexander is best known for her best-selling award-winning book, "The New Jim Crow: Mass Incarceration in the Age of Colorblindness." Since its publication in 2010, "The New Jim Crow" has spawned a whole generation of criminal justice reform activists and organizations dedicated to dismantling America's racist and oppressive prison system.

MICHELLE ALEXANDER was born in Chicago to Sandra Alexander of Wilmette, Illinois, and John Alexander of Evanston, Illinois. As the offspring of an interracial couple (her mother is White; her now-deceased father was Black), she learned firsthand the challenges of racial integration. Alexander and her younger sister spent part of their childhood in Stelle, Illinois, a 300-person intentional community known as one of the country's first models of sustainable living.

Her father faced difficulties in his work life. IBM transferred him to the San Francisco Bay Area in 1975, but after climbing the corporate ladder proved challenging, he eventually left his job. However, despite having to grapple with eviction from her home, frequent family relocations, and attending three different high schools, Alexander managed to do quite well in school.

As a high school senior living in Ashland, Oregon, Alexander planned to attend the University of Oregon like many of her college-bound classmates. Then one evening, an old friend of her mother convinced her to apply to Vanderbilt University. The offer of admission, complete with a scholarship and financial aid, could not have come at a better time. Alexander's family was struggling financially, so they welcomed this opportunity as the chance of a lifetime. Her time at Vanderbilt University helped to put her on a track dedicated to social justice.

Beginning in 1998, Alexander served for several years as the founding director of the Racial Justice Project at the American Civil Liberties Union (ACLU) in Northern California, which spearheaded a national campaign against racial profiling by law enforcement. During those years at the ACLU, Alexander began to awaken to the reality that the nation's criminal justice system functions more like a caste system than a system of crime prevention or control. While attending Stanford Law School, she was greatly inspired by professor Gerald

López, who cofounded a program called Lawyering for Social Change. Alexander began exposing and challenging racial bias in the criminal justice system, ultimately launching and leading a major campaign against racial profiling by law enforcement known as the "DWB Campaign" or "Driving While Black or Brown Campaign." Her experience at the ACLU planted the seeds for her writing of *The New Jim Crow.*

After Alexander graduated from Vanderbilt University with a BA in 1989, she received a law degree from Stanford Law School in 1992. Following law school, she clerked for Justice Harry A. Blackmum of the U.S. Supreme Court and Chief Judge Abner Mikva on the U.S. Court of Appeals for the D.C. Court.

In 2002, Alexander married Carter Mitchell Stewart, a graduate of Stanford University and Harvard Law School. Stewart at the time was a senior associate at McCutchen, Doyle, Brown & Enersen, a San Francisco law firm, and later became a U.S. Attorney for the Southern District of Ohio. They have three children.

As an associate at Saperstein, Goldstein, Demchak & Baller, she specialized in plaintiff-side class-action suits alleging race and gender discrimination. In 2005, Alexander accepted a joint appointment at the Kirwan Institute for the Study of Race and Ethnicity, and the Moritz College of Law at The Ohio State University. She participated in numerous class action discrimination cases and worked on criminal justice reform issues.

Later that year, Alexander received a 2005 Soros Justice Fellowship from the Open Society Institute, which helped her publish her first book, *The New Jim Crow: Mass Incarceration in the Age of Colorblindness* in 2010. The book, concentrates on the mass incarceration of African American men. In it, Alexander argues that one system of racial oppression had been replaced by another: the nation's jails and prisons, filled disproportionately with Black men that were branded with criminal records they would never be able to erase. It was hardly an immediate best seller, but after a couple of years, it seemed to be at the center of discussion about criminal-justice reform and racism in America becoming a touchstone for a new generation.

Since its publication, *The New Jim Crow* has been featured in national radio and television media outlets, including MSNBC, NPR, *Bill Moyers Journal, Tavis Smiley, Democracy Now, Los Angeles Times,* C-SPAN, *The Colbert Show, Real Time with Bill Maher,* and the *Washington Journal,* among others. The book won the 2011 NAACP Image Award for best nonfiction, the Emerson Award, Constitutional Commentary Award, and Silver medalist of the Independent Publishers Association, and has spent nearly 250 weeks on *The New York Times* Best Seller list.

The New Jim Crow has been compared to the work of W. E. B. Du Bois, cited in legal decisions to end stop-and-frisk and sentencing laws, and quoted passionately on stage at the Academy Awards. In 2015, all freshmen enrolled at

Brown University read *The New Jim Crow* as part of the campus' First Readings Program initiated by the Office of the Dean of the College and voted on by the faculty. The book has been the subject of scholarly debate and criticism. Some prisons have placed a ban on the book, concerned over racial overtures and security threats, although interestingly, *Mein Kampf* is permitted. The book also helped inspire the creation of the Marshall Project and the Art for Justice Fund. Alexander has succeeded in getting the issue out in the open as people argue and debate about this glaring wrong with which we have been living. Alexander has traveled the country consulting and advising advocacy organizations that are waging campaigns to mobilize people to end mass incarceration. She's also written about the topic in op-ed pieces for *The New York Times* and in articles for *The Nation* and *Time*. She has spoken at more than 100 events at venues ranging from universities and legal conferences to prisons and churches.

In 2015, the Ford Foundation appointed Alexander as a Senior Fellow, someone who contributes to the foundation's work on democracy, rights, and justice. In 2016, Alexander received the Heinz Award in the public policy category. She was honored for drawing national attention to mass incarceration of African American youth and men in the U.S. and for igniting a movement that is inspiring organizations and individuals to take constructive action on criminal justice reform. The award came with a $250,000 prize, which she used to launch The MOSAIC Fund for Justice, a fund that supports grassroots organizations building movements to end mass incarceration, police violence and racial injustice. Alexander is also the recipient of The Ohio State University, Office of Diversity and Inclusion's Frank W. Hale Jr. Black Cultural Center's MLK Dreamer Award (2017). She joined *The New York Times* as a columnist in 2018.

Alexander resigned from the Ohio State Law School faculty in 2016 to teach and study at Union Theology Seminary in New York City as a visiting professor and scholar, where she is exploring the moral and spiritual dimensions of mass incarceration. She is also devoting much of her time to freelance writing, public speaking, and consulting for advocacy organizations committed to ending mass incarceration.

Ten years later, *The New Jim Crow* continues to offer a useful and revealing way to understanding the current state of affairs in criminal justice. In 2020, The New Press released a Tenth Anniversary Edition, featuring a new preface where Alexander assesses the book's impact and discusses the criminal justice reform movement's current state. Having returned to *The New York Times* Best Seller list, *The New Jim Crow* remains as important now as ever.

Alexander is currently working on a book that is very different from *The New Jim Crow;* it is about her personal journey from being a liberal civil rights lawyer to someone who now believes that a moral and spiritual revolution is also required of us all.❖

Glynda C. Carr
(1972)
Activist, political strategist

Glynda C. Carr is president, CEO and cofounder of Higher Heights for America, an organization that is at the center of the national movement to grow Black women's political power from the voting booth to elected office.

GLYNDA C. CARR was born and raised in Hartford, Connecticut to Delores Yvonne Morgan-Carr, who worked for a department store and was a community activist, and Keith L. Carr Sr., born in Kingston, Jamaica, who was an activist and organizer in Hartford's Caribbean communities. Carr is the youngest of three, with two brothers. Exposed to the arts at an early age, she spent her Saturdays at the Artists Collective (cofounded by jazz alto saxophonist Jackie McLean) and began playing flute in the fourth grade. When she was a young girl, Carr decided she would one day work in the fashion industry.

Carr recognized the importance of taking action early in her life by observing her parents, who blended their cultural and political activism with a commitment to public service. She also learned the importance of Black women raising their voices even when they did not have the right to vote and lacked career opportunities due to their race and gender. Despite such limitations, Carr knew from her great-grandmother, who owned two businesses, that barriers could be broken. As such, Carr's mother used her political activist skills to ensure that her daughter and sons had access to quality educational opportunities. When Carr turned eighteen, her mother drove her to city hall to register to vote, a simple act that proved pivotal for Carr's future in political activism.

In her senior year of high school, as Carr was preparing to move to New York to work in fashion, her mother's pursuit of a quality education for her children paid off. Carr received a scholarship offer from the University of Hartford. Jackie McLean was chair of the African American music program (now known as the Jackie McLean Institute of Jazz) and established the Bachelor of Music degree in Jazz Studies program. Carr enrolled in the program, but midway through college, she decided to major in jazz studies and arts management as well.

The University of Hartford also stirred Carr's other interests, including activism. She became vice president of Brothers and Sisters United (BSU),

which performs community service projects throughout the greater Hartford community. Carr's focus on Hartford's local community issues expanded when the not-guilty verdict was announced for the Rodney King police brutality case in 1992 in Los Angeles. The police officers' acquittals sparked the 1992 Los Angeles riots and the officers' prosecution in a separate federal civil rights case. This event motivated Carr to become involved in Black advocacy.

After she graduated from the university's Hartt School in 1996, Carr worked in Philadelphia for Big Brothers Big Sisters of America. As the senior manager of social marketing and volunteer recruitment, she traveled throughout the country, recruiting more Big Brothers and Big Sisters of color. Yet, she still set her sights on New York. Three years later, her goal was realized when she was hired as the director of national programs for the Thurgood Marshall College Fund. It is the largest organization in the U.S. that exclusively represents the publicly supported HBCUs and predominantly Black institutions.

Carr's work with the College Fund provided her with further knowledge about the burgeoning talent of young Black scholars and emerging Black leaders. She was inspired when Kevin S. Parker first ran for the New York State Senate in 2002 to represent District 21 in Brooklyn, where Carr lived. She began volunteering for his campaign, and after Parker won the race, she was offered and accepted the position of Chief of Staff. During her tenure, Carr organized the senator's local initiatives, shaped policy concerning youth development and economic development, and managed two successful re-election campaigns.

Around 2008, she was asked to serve as the New York state executive director of Education Voters of New York, an advocacy organization that mobilizes low-income families and communities of color to look at public school reform from a political perspective. As the organization shifted its focus, and the overall political environment began to change in Congress and across the country, Carr had to think long and hard about what she wanted to do next.

In 2011, Carr established and became a principal at Liberty Street Capital, a New York-based public affairs, community relations, and political strategy consulting firm. After conducting a series of deep-dive discussions with her "kitchen cabinet" of women—informal advisors, mentors, friends, and sponsors—Carr found herself having a particularly productive conversation with the political fundraiser and event planner Kimberly Peeler-Allen, then a principal of Peeler-Allen Consulting. The two women began talking about the lack of diversity in political organizations and what a Black women's organization would look like. Together, they founded Higher Heights for America in 2011. They also established a sister organization, the Higher Heights Leadership Fund. By 2014, Higher Heights was a full-fledged organization featuring a roster of advisors, endorsements, and ongoing major initiatives and programming.

Higher Heights addresses the dearth of organizing resources for politically active Black women and the lack of support for those who are considering seeking elected office. Under Carr's leadership, the organization developed innovative programs that have quickly solidified its reputation as the political home and go-to resource for progressive Black women.

Carr is also the co-creator of #BlackWomenLead, a powerful coalition movement that creates an environment for Black women to run, win, and lead, and the Higher Heights-powered #BlackWomenVote, a nonpartisan voter-activism campaign that serves as an independent voice for Black women's political concerns. To date, her work has helped to elect eleven Black women to the U.S. Congress—including one to the Senate—and increased the number of Black women holding statewide executive offices—including the first Black woman to serve as New York State attorney general. In 2017, Higher Heights helped elect Senator Jones (D-AL) into office. Black women did not vote for Jones to save the country; they voted and organized because they understood his election's importance. They helped elect Mayor Lance Bottoms of Atlanta and participated in Stacey Abrams' historic gubernatorial campaign in Georgia. Abrams was the first African American female major-party gubernatorial nominee in the U.S.

In 2020, Higher Heights, along with other Black political organizations, helped make history by supporting Kamala Harris' nomination and election as the first woman, the first African American, and first Asian American vice president of the U.S. In 2021, Carr's focus is to provide Black women the tools they need to advocate for themselves, including workshops, social media, and a weekly livestream show, Their mission is to remind Black women that in order to become empowered and gain access to health, education and equal pay, they must be proactive in the political arena and participate in elections..

Recognized for her innovative leadership style, Carr remains committed to expanding the civic participation of communities of color and advancing public policies that build sustainable communities. As part of her political outreach, Carr is a speaker, spokesperson, trainer, and writer. She has appeared on Fox News Live, Cheddar, MSNBC, and several other media outlets. She has also contributed to CNN, *The Root, Ebony, Huffington Post,* The Brock Report, WalkersLegacy.com, BET, NBCBLK.com, and feminist.com. She has been interviewed and quoted in *The Washington Post, The New York Times, US News, BuzzFeed,* and numerous other outlets. Carr is also a contributor on The *SPIN:* All Women's Media Panel. She was named a "Rising Star" in *The Capitol's* 2009 40 under 40 edition and appeared on *Essence* magazine's 2018 Woke 100 list.

Black women are calling into question many issues as we move toward a new administration that is directly tied to COVID-19 and the continued attack on blackness. As political strategists and activists such as Carr remain focused on addressing these issues, their number one priority is to engage Black women as voters, candidates, and influencers to help build economically stable, safe, and healthy communities. This is Carr's end game.❖

Lezley McSpadden
(1980)
Activist, author

Lezley McSpadden is the mother of Michael Brown, who was fatally shot by a police officer in Ferguson, Missouri. His murder marked a change in how social media contributes to civil rights activism in today's society, and changed the trajectory of her and her family's lives.

LEZLEY LYNETTE BINGO MCSPADDEN HEAD was born in St. Louis, Missouri to Desuirea Ewings Harris, a chef and Leslie McSpadden, a foreman on the railroad. Nicknamed "Netty Pooh," McSpadden and her two siblings were raised by their mother, a single parent. Her family lived in some challenging areas that harbored gang and drug activity, but McSpadden prevailed, growing up in a loving environment surrounded by her grandmother, aunts, uncles, and cousins. From kindergarten, McSpadden attended school in the Ladue School District, an affluent suburb in St. Louis, and participated in the now defunct desegregation program. McSpadden played the clarinet in junior high school, ran track in high school, and had a love for adventure and the outdoors. She often went camping, and fishing, a regular family past-time.

McSpadden became pregnant at fifteen. She eventually moved in with Brown's father, Michael Jermaine Brown and his parents in nearby Pine Lawn. Her first child, Michael Orlandus Derion Brown, was born on May 20, 1996. After returning to school she struggled with adjusting, and made the difficult choice to drop out her junior year. McSpadden worked a series of minimum wage jobs to help support her young son. She eventually received CNA certification, and worked at several nursing homes until her pregnancy with her second child, a daughter, with Brown. McSpadden later had two other children with a different partner. She eventually worked in a deli at gourmet market for twelve years preparing and catering food, a position she held until her son's murder.

Eighteen year old Michael Brown graduated from high school and had made plans to attend technical school. Brown, who was six feet and four inches tall, was an amateur rap musician, with big dreams, and posted his songs on popular music sharing sites under the handle, "Big Mike." He was an avid video game player, and he was deft with technology. He never got into trouble with the law as a juvenile, and he did not have a criminal record as an adult.

On August 9, 2014, Brown, who was visiting his grandmother, and another young man who lived in her apartment complex, were walking in the middle of Canfield Drive, a short, two-lane street in Ferguson, Missouri, a suburb of St. Louis. Police Officer Darren Wilson, a white police officer, ordered the young men to use the sidewalk. The interaction grew heated when they refused, and Wilson pulled out his weapon and fired. The officer later attested that Brown turned around and reached under his waistband as if to remove a weapon, but Brown was unarmed. Some witnesses claimed that Brown had his hands up. In the entire altercation, Wilson fired a total of twelve bullets, and struck six times, with two shots in the head. In the aftermath, the police left Brown's body on the hot asphalt for more than four hours as McSpadden and Brown's stepfather moved through a furious and growing crowd of onlookers, unable to push past police to get close to their son. Television cameras and phones filmed as Brown's body laid uncovered most of that time until a sheet was eventually placed over him.

This event ignited unrest in Ferguson, with many of the protests led by Black Lives Matter activists. The protests, both peaceful and violent, continued for several months in Ferguson; police later established a nightly curfew. The response of area police agencies was strongly criticized by both the media and politicians. Concerns were raised over insensitivity, tactics, and a militarized response. Missouri Governor Nixon ordered local police organizations to cede much of their authority to the Missouri State Highway Patrol. In the midst of this melee, McSpadden buried a son. She wanted to make her son more than a hashtag or a catalyst for a movement. She wanted the public to see him as a beloved boy.

In 2014, a St. Louis County grand jury declined to prosecute Wilson, who resigned that November. In 2015, the U.S. Department of Justice cleared Wilson of civil rights violations in the shooting, and concluded that Wilson shot Brown in self-defense. However, their investigation confirmed racial bias in Ferguson's police and court system. McSpadden was at a loss, and had no outlet and nowhere to turn. She found comfort in meeting other mothers who had lost unarmed sons or daughters at the hands of the police. However, it was a subsequent conversation with Beyoncé's mother, Tina Knowles, reminding her of the powerful 1980s movement in Mothers Against Drunk Drivers (MAAD) that sparked her to create her own movement for mothers like her.

In 2015, McSpadden established The Michael O.D. Brown We Love Our Sons and Daughters Foundation, and serves as its president. The initiative, made in her son's honor, focuses on advocating for justice and advancing education. She went a step further and created the program, Rainbows of Mothers, which provides a support system to mothers who have suffered and sustained the premature loss of a child. To help women with this unforeseen tragic circumstance, Rainbow of Mothers offers counseling, legal advice, access to a support fund, and other helpful information to assist in the restorative process of rebuilding and repurposing life after loss. She also sought mental health therapy for herself, which has become a big component of her work.

McSpadden published *Tell the Truth Shame the Devil: The Life, Legacy, and Love of My Son Michael Brown,* with Lyah Beth LeFlore. The book served as a cathartic exercise, and allowed her to communicate directly about unspeakable loss. While the story is tragic, McSpadden manages to celebrate the memory of her son and make the case for change.

In 2015, McSpadden and Brown's father filed a wrongful death lawsuit. They sued the city, former Police Chief Tom Jackson, and Wilson in 2015, citing a police culture hostile to Black residents and claiming Wilson used excessive force. Although Jackson and Wilson denied the allegations, a federal judge in St. Louis approved the settlement, and in 2017 they were awarded $1.5 million.[1]

McSpadden met with Jennings School District Superintendent Art McCoy in 2016 to discuss how her foundation could collaborate with the district. At that meeting, McCoy encouraged her to return to high school and she agreed. In June 2017, McSpadden graduated with about 160 other Jennings High School students—including her eighteen year old daughter.

For years, Missouri lagged in responding to complaints of police mistreatment of Black people. Frustrated with Ferguson's and St. Louis' nonresponse to the murder of her son, in 2018, McSpadden announced a partnership with the Thurgood Marshall Civil Rights Center at the Howard University School of Law to pass legislation, referred to as the "Mike Brown Bill," which, among other things, would provide mental health services to families and communities affected by police violence.

Over the years, Ferguson residents, especially young people, were having an uneasy time interacting with the police. McSpadden realized that Ferguson's law enforcement practices are shaped by the city's focus on revenue rather than by public safety needs, compromising the institutional character of its police department, which has raised due process concerns that sown deep mistrust in the community. McSpadden's repeated requests for the city to institute reform measures was ignored. So in order to help bring about change, McSpadden moved to Ferguson and announced her candidacy for a seat on the city council.

Her objective was for the city to improve police accountability, reform the city's agencies, better mental health resources, and after-school programs for children. In 2019, McSpadden competed in a three-way race, but she lost, finishing third with roughly 20 percent of the vote. Despite her loss, McSpadden continues to work to bring about change in the Ferguson community.

McSpadden lost a son, and cannot bring him back, yet she is managing to rebuild a life without him. Her quest is to secure the lives of not only her children, but the lives of all children by demanding different and smarter strategies for education, safety, protection, and justice for all. So McSpadden continues moving forward, by organizing and helping to amplify our voices. ❖

---

1. Associated Press, "Ferguson attorney: Michael Brown's family settles with city for $1.5 million," *The Los Angeles Times,* June 23, 2017, https://www.latimes.com/nation/nationnow/la-namichael-brown-ferguson-settlement-20170623-story.html.

Leah Penniman
(1980)
Farmer, food activist, educator, author

Leah Penniman is a farmer and food activist who fights against food apartheid by using Afro-indigenous organic and regenerative farming practices to make the environment better and provide healthy and affordable food to Black and Brown communities.

LEAH PENNIMAN was born in Fitchburg, Massachusetts to Reverend Doctor Adele Smith Penniman, a Haitian American Unitarian minister and longtime activist, and Keith Penniman, a librarian and a lay pastor, who is White. Penniman was raised in the Central Massachusetts town of Ashburnham with three mixed-race siblings as one of the only families of color. After her parents split up, her mother moved to Boston, and Penniman and her siblings grew up with her father in rural Massachusetts. Hers was the only multiracial family in the neighborhood, and she and her siblings were bullied by their White schoolmates. Penniman and her sister found solace playing in the forest among the trees, rocks, and streams.

Her earliest memories of growing food are connected to her grandmother. Both sides of her family were historically dispossessed of the land on which they lived, but when her maternal grandmother moved to the Boston area, she owned a little bit of land where she kept a garden and had a crab apple tree and a little strawberry patch. Penniman picked strawberries and helped her grandmother make jam.

Penniman began farming at age sixteen when she worked with The Food Project in Boston in 1996. She was staying with her mother and needed a job to save money for college. Like many teens, Penniman was confused about her identity and her place in the world. At The Food Project, she grew and sold food in farmers' markets in low-income neighborhoods, worked in homeless shelters, participated in leadership development, and learned about fairness in the food system. She found the work stimulating and discovered that farming could be the intersection of the two things she loved most: social justice and the earth. She found the simplicity of planting seeds, harvesting crops, and making sure it got to the people who needed it compelling.

Penniman graduated high school as the valedictorian and received a full scholarship to attend Clark University in Worcester, Massachusetts, where she worked on a student-designed major in environmental science and international development. For a year, Penniman lived in Dismas House, a Worcester halfway house where college students assist paroled prisoners re-entering society. She wanted to take advantage of every opportunity offered to do authentic, community-based learning, and went after every fellowship and research assistant position she could find.

It was this attitude that led Penniman to Richard Ford, who ran Clark's international development program. Ford directed the Participatory Rural Appraisal program, which brought students to dozens of villages in developing countries to help empower residents to build roads, improve the water supply, and get better access to farm fields. He had recently worked in a small village in Ghana and invited Penniman to research the program's success. For four months, she lived in a simple, one-room earthen structure in the rural village of Oborpah-Djerkiti, learning the Krobo language, teaching children, and meeting with the village women to support their goals of creating a new market and school.

Beginning in 1999, Penniman worked at the Farm School and co-managed Many Hands Organic Farm. These initiatives had one thing in common: a fellow Clark student and geography major named Jonah Vitale-Wolff, who liked doing community service and working on farms. He joined forces with Penniman on many of these community projects.

Much of Penniman's time at Clark and in Worcester after graduation was spent in the Main South neighborhood, where she helped create several programs, some of which still exist today, such as the YouthGROW urban farming program. Another program, Worcester Roots, began as a soil remediation project, where volunteers used plants, such as geraniums, to remove lead from the soil in contaminated yards. The Worcester Global Action Network staged anti-war protests and urged the Clark administration to divest from companies involved in sweatshop labor and military-industrial interests.

Penniman married Vitale-Wolff a few months after they graduated with their undergraduate degrees in 2002, in a ceremony officiated by both Penniman's mother and Vitale-Wolff's uncle, a rabbi. They moved to Collective-a-Go-Go, a land trust and urban commune on the edge of Worcester, where members shared bicycles and tools to grow food on the property's six acres. Penniman received an MA in Science Education from Clark in 2003, the year her daughter was born. She chopped wood with her newborn daughter Neshima in a baby carrier as the house's only heat source was a wood stove. In 2005, her son Emet was born, and they moved to Albany, New York. Penniman started and ran the Harriet Tubman Democratic School, an extension of the Albany Free School, for two years, and then was offered a teaching job as part of the founding faculty of Tech Valley High School. Vitale-Wolff started a construction company.

When she and her husband first moved to Albany's south end, they became involved in community service, working in urban gardens. There was clearly a community need for fresh food delivery and safe rural spaces for people of color.

The federal government classified Albany as a "food desert," which Penniman likens to "food apartheid." Penniman and her family began to respond to what the community asked for, and as a result, they purchased a farm.

In 2006, Penniman and her husband scraped together their modest savings and, with loans from friends and family, purchased seventy-two acres of land in Grafton, New York, located in the Upper Hudson Valley, to found Soul Fire Farm. The name is taken from the song "Soulfire" by Lee "Scratch" Perry. They purchased affordable, marginal land that had no human development on it: no roads, no septic, no electric, and no buildings. It consisted of overgrazed pastures and thin, rocky soil over hardpan clay that was not well-suited for growing food. From 2006 to 2010, they did soil repair, built their house and education center using strawbale and timber frame, and instituted a passive-solar building design.

After five years, the farm had its first full harvest and officially opened in 2011 as a sliding scale community-supported agriculture (CSA) consisting of twenty families. Every season, they box up vegetables, pasture-raised chicken, eggs, herbal medicine, and value-added products and bring them to people's doorsteps each week. In the beginning, Penniman and her husband managed the farm on the weekends and evenings while holding down full-time jobs to help capitalize the project.

Soul Fire Farm was born with a somewhat narrow but important goal: getting healthy and affordable food to the people. The initial vision was to grow food using sustainable, regenerative, Afro-Indigenous methods that restore the land and provide food to communities under food apartheid. Over time the farm, now run by Soul Fire Farm Institute, Inc., a nonprofit organization led by people of color, has grown into a community farm, and its mission has expanded substantially. Penniman, who serves as the Co-Executive Director, is part of a team that facilitates powerful food sovereignty programs. Their doorstep delivery feeds well over 100 families every week during the growing season. Recipients pay what they can, even if it means nothing at all, and can use their Supplemental Nutrition Assistance Program (SNAP) benefits. The Solidarity Shares Program of the CSA provides a free share to anyone who is a refugee or has returned to the community from prison.

The farm's flagship program is the Black Latinx Farmers Immersion, a 50-hour course to train beginner farmers. By 2018, 500 individuals had taken the course. As of 2021, there are 2,291 graduates of the farmer training program. There is also an urban gardening program, Soul Fire in the City, which builds gardens for people living under food apartheid and supports them in training, materials, supplies, and social networks with other gardeners, helping them to become food activists. Penniman published *Farming While Black: Soul Fire Farm's Practical Guide to Liberation on the Land* (2018), which details her experiences as a farmer and activist, how she found "real power and dignity" through food, and how people with no experience in gardening and farming can do the same.

Soul Fire Farm is working on policies and practices regionally and nationally that address the return of land, resources and power to the descendants of those from whom it was stolen. The Northeast Farmers of Color Community Land Trust is a collaboration with over a dozen northeastern Indigenous tribal communities, and Black, Latino, Asian, and Indigenous farmers who are struggling with being either dispossessed from their land or reduced to a very small part of their ancestral territories. The goal is to operate both in the sphere of conservation and cultural heritage easements and in the community land trust sphere of affordable housing. They are also working with the HEAL Food Alliance, and the National Black Food and Justice Alliance on their reparations and policy work as well.

Soul Fire Farm is currently held cooperatively. The title was transferred in 2019 from Penniman's family to becoming a cooperative, and the nonprofit is one of the voting member-owners. It has been only a decade since Soul Fire Farm has transformed from a patch of marginal mountain ground into rich topsoil and a fully functional farm that is deeply involved with the Black and Brown communities in Albany, Troy, and Schenectady. Soul Fire Farm has built alliances with organizations such as the Freedom Food Alliance, the National Black Farmers Conference, and La Via Campesina. In 2014, Penniman won a Fulbright fellowship to study Indigenous farming practices in Oaxaca, Mexico. Penniman's family lived in Mexico for nearly half a year and later adopted some of the thousand-year-old practices they observed for use at Soul Fire Farm.

By 2020, the farm's small size had been impacted by the thousands of visitors it receives every year, and the water and septic systems and Penniman's home have suffered from excessive use. Soul Fire Farm is fundraising to cover renovation costs and is building a space where people can learn and stay.

Until 2017, Penniman was a full-time environmental science and biology teacher, and up to 2019, worked part-time at the Darrow School. She has received numerous awards, including a Presidential Award for Science Teaching in 2015, and the James Beard Foundation Leadership Award for facilitating food sovereignty programs in 2019. Penniman's articles and essays have appeared in *Agriculture and Human Values, Schumacher Center for a New Economics, YES! Magazine, New York Organic News* and *Fortune Magazine.* She has been interviewed in *The Natural Farmer, Clark Now, Food Revolution Network, The Sun, healthyish, Savannah Morning News, Eco Farming Daily, Albany Times Union,* and *Emergence Magazine.* The work of Soul Fire Farm has been recognized by the Soros Racial Justice Fellowship, NYS Health Emerging Innovator Awards, Omega Sustainability Leadership Award, and the Andrew Goodman Foundation. Penniman's forthcoming book, *Black Earth Wisdom,* will be published by HarperCollins in 2022.

Besides growing food, Soul Fire Farm offers a space to dance, sing, and share stories. Penniman, who is also a Manye (Queen Mother) in Vodun, is spiritually, emotionally, and physically tied to the land, and will always remain committed to transforming the community and the souls of the people.❖

LaSaia Wade
(1987)
Transgender rights activist, organizer, policy maker, entrepreneur

LaSaia Wade, the founder and executive director of Brave Space Alliance (BSA), the first Black- and trans-led LGBTQ Center in Chicago, is making waves as a change agent for transgender rights across the nation.

LASAIA WADE was born in Chicago, Illinois to Marea Wade, a health aide, and Richard Foster, who owned a business and is of Puerto Rican descent. Wade is the oldest of four girls. Her family lived there until she was five, and then they moved to Tennessee for a better life. As a child growing up, besides grappling with poverty and family members' drug addiction, she struggled with her gender identity, both at home and in school. At a young age, Wade knew she was different, knew she was not gay, and wanted to wear women's clothing like her mother. Hers was not an easy childhood. She had to deal with being poor and queer while figuring out her place in the world.

Wade came out as transgender when she was sixteen years old after she was raped in church. The church turned its back on Wade because she was not the boy they thought she should be, which affected her faith and sickens her even today. Wade also had a tumultuous relationship with her father, and for a few years, nearly every day, they engaged in physical hand-to-hand combat. There were times she was afraid to go to sleep because she feared for her life. Wade finally found her freedom after she was kicked out of the house at age eighteen and went to college. It was a painful experience for Wade, coming from a tight knit family and then being abandoned, but she was determined to meet that challenge by proving to herself that she could make it on her own. During this period, Wade committed to her authentic self as a woman and began her transition in earnest, but publicly stayed under the radar as a transgender woman because she feared for her safety.

Wade attended Murfreesboro Tennessee State University (now known as Middle Tennessee State University) and decided to major in business not only because she wanted to escape poverty, but also because she wanted to learn the tricks of the trade of capitalism and make something good of her life. After receiving her bachelor's degree in 2010, she continued her studies at

Murfreesboro and graduated in 2012 with a master's of Business Administration degree in Business Management. During her last year in college, Wade was hit with a tremendous loss when her friend, another transgender woman, was found murdered by the side of the road. Mired in loss and a cloud of negativity, her friend's death prompted her to get involved in activism after she graduated.

Several years later, Wade was fired from a communications job when they discovered she was transgender, and finding steady employment would become a struggle in the years that followed. Despite having multiple degrees in business, no one would hire her because she was transgender and involved in activism. Frustrated, she took time off to travel and read about activists such as Malcolm X, Fannie Lou Hamer, and Black transgender pioneers Marsha P. Johnson and Lucy Hicks Anderson. She realized that she would have to push a little harder, and drawing on her experience of living through hardship, "make a way out of no way." Wade started working with Black Lives Matter in Nashville. Her initial experience was difficult at first but in time she was fully accepted as a transgender woman. She worked with them for about three years and then moved around, living in New York, San Francisco, and Florida, doing internships and learning different aspects of activism, like working at the Audre Lorde Project in New York, and the Transgender Law Center in San Francisco.

One of the things Wade gleaned from her travels is that she was no longer the person who once craved invisibility. Many transgender people do not publicly announce their true identity because it paints a target on their backs. But given the fact that other transgender activists were putting themselves on the line, this convinced Wade to be open about her gender identity. In 2013, she returned to Tennessee and founded the Tennessee Transgender Justice Project (TNTJ).

TNTJ was created because there were not enough resources for transgender people, especially people of color in Tennessee. And unlike many LGBTQ organizations, TNTJ was run by transgender and gender non-conforming (GNC) people to help the community find healthcare, jobs, housing, and provide training to other organizations to be more inclusive with the transgender community. Access to employment and healthcare are always the biggest hurdles, especially in Tennessee, which does not provide legal protections for LGBTQ workers. While Wade ran TNTJ on her own for the first year, two years later, the organization expanded, growing from one to six chapters, including more employees and partnerships with other organizations.

But even with these successes, TNTJ did not meet Wade's expectations and she ended it in 2016. She was living in a state where White supremacy reigns with little regard for the LGBTQ community. And of the few white-based LGBTQ organizations that thrived in Tennessee, they had no intention of establishing a true partnership with a Black-led transgender organization. So Wade folded her tent and returned to her hometown, Chicago, which she felt would be more inclusive. One of the first things Wade did was announce the creation of and led the Trans Liberation March in 2017. With more than 3,000 attendees, it was the largest demonstration for transgender people in the Midwest at the time. But even then, Wade faced an uphill battle, when she sought employment at LGBTQ nonprofits. They would not hire her because they felt she was overqualified. So Wade began organizing with groups such as Black Lives Matter in Chicago, Assata's Daughters, the #LetUsBreathe Collective, and BYP100.

It soon dawned on Wade that there was no Black- and trans-led organizing in Chicago. She cofounded the Trans Liberation Collective and the Black Trans GNC (Gender Nonconforming) Collective, which fights for sex workers and pushes back on organizations that do not give a living wage to transgender and GNC people, but she felt more could be done. Wade's partner encouraged her to create a registered nonprofit to combat the organizations that are not trans-led and challenge their politics to become more inclusive.

On that advice, Wade founded Brave Space Alliance (BSA) in 2017, the first and only Black transgender nonconforming-led community center on Chicago's South Side. She hit the ground running with $500 in startup money and with a mission statement in hand, challenging other organizations about services for transgender people. Wade worked to pass state bills with the Transformative Justice Law Project requiring single-occupancy bathrooms be gender-neutral; and the Howard Brown Health Center, requiring Illinois Medicaid to cover gender-affirming services, like surgery.

Wade believed that LGBTQ organizations in the Chicago area ignored the needs of transgender people, especially in Black and Brown communities, even though they receive and rely on funding to do this sort of outreach, including the lack of transgender personnel. Wade saw that gap and felt she could provide those services and get the resources needed to redistribute them directly to a transgender community that was very much in need.

Early on, Wade used much of the same framework she developed with TNTJ. First, she designed BSA as a full-blown mutual aid operation. She felt a collective would have difficulties sustaining a structural power base, so she wanted to create something different. Typically, mutual aid groups are member-led, member-organized, and open to all to participate. Mutual aid network participants work together to figure out strategies and resources to meet the organization's needs and its constituency while organizing themselves against the system that created the shortage in the first place. Inspired by a study on "brave spaces" that Wade participated in during college prompted her to name the new nonprofit Brave Space Alliance. It has been structured as a non-hierarchical, non-bureaucratic organization with members controlling all resources. She also believed that Pan-Africanism should be essential to the organization's structure and that its members must be willing to sacrifice for liberation. As a result, BSA has become egalitarian in nature and is designed to support participatory democracy, equality of status, and consensus-based decision-making.

Almost immediately, Wade began to educate and convince other organizations to hire and pay living wages to transgender employees. Transgender people have a high turnover rate in many organizations and often have to turn to sex work to get by. In time, LGBTQ organizations contacted BSA to participate in its Trans 101 training module, which teaches potential employers how to hire and retain a transgender workforce, including tips on how to treat transgender employees, like identifying them by their preferred name and gender. They also offer Trans 201, which talks about pushing the sociopolitical and cultural envelope by openly discussing a narrative against the binary.[1] BSA does at least five to ten training sessions a month.

Wade also developed an internship program to help potential employees meet the demands of BSA and thrive. This enables her to support the hiring of Black and Brown transgender people that may not have the educational background or the notion of how to do this particular type of work but are at least given a chance at BSA when other organizations would not. Besides training, BSA offers resume-building, resources to housing and Medicaid. They offer basic necessities like food and clothes, and have a program called VAMP, which stands for HIV/AIDS Manifesting Prevention. They encourage transgender people living with HIV to openly discuss topics pertinent to their lifestyle, such as sex work, HIV prevention, and how to develop programs that accommodate these issues.

Since BSA's founding, Wade's vision has grown exponentially. It now includes sixteen full-time staff members, who are transgender or non-binary, with over 600 volunteers. The organization's mandate is that it must be run and operated solely by members of the LGBTQ community. Thanks to generous donations, BSA recently purchased its own space in 2020. While BSA has already set many precedents, it is fervently developing new programs and innovative services while maintaining its sustainability.

In 2020, BSA, among several trans-led organizations nationwide, received a portion of $4.5 million from drugmaker Gilead Sciences. Wade wants to turn BSA into the first $1 million-budget trans-led organization in Chicago. With that money, she wants to offer more jobs to transgender people and push out more programming to serve the transgender population. She foresees BSA opening a clinic and offering HIV testing, purchasing a building to permanently house transgender people, and creating a transgender homeless shelter. Wade is putting her business skills to good use by acquiring as much funding as possible.

After protests erupted in Chicago over the treatment of George Floyd, BSA stepped up once again, offering aid to protesters and operating as a drop-off and pickup point. Protesters who were tasered, shot with rubber bullets or beaten with nightsticks could turn to BSA for first aid, clothing, food, and bottles

---

1. In simple terms, binary is the Western concept that there are only two gender options: female or male. A non-binary person is someone who does not identify as exclusively a man or a woman. Someone who is non-binary might feel like a mix of genders, or like they have no gender at all.

of water. The protesters appreciated the help, which enabled them to get right back on the ground and continue to fight.

When Chicago shut down due to the pandemic, BSA was one of the first organizations that quickly mobilized to help residents, regardless of sexual orientation, who suddenly could not afford their next meal. Since then, Wade estimates they have fed more than 280,000 people in 2020 through its food pickup and delivery services making their food pantry one of BSA's proudest achievements. Wade has found that the Black community at large has been very supportive of BSA, proving once and for all the effectiveness of a Black and Brown trans-run organization that is LGBTQ specific, but works in concert with the entire community. Its success is becoming a shining example throughout the country.

Violence against transgender and gender non-conforming people is on the rise. The Human Rights Campaign recorded forty-four deaths in 2020, more than any year since tracking began in 2013.[2] Black and Brown transgender women are often targets and are murdered because of someone else's ignorance. It is why BSA remains steadfast in its mandate to educate and protect its constituents at all costs.

Wade has been honored by a number of organizations. In 2018 she was recognized at Chicago LGBTQA Black History Recognitions ceremony, and in 2019 was the first transgender woman in Illinois celebrated during Women's History Month. In 2015, Wade was named on The Trans 100, an International organization recognizing excellence in service to community by and for transgender people, received the South Side Help Center Award in 2018, and the Outstanding Social Service Award from the Aides Foundation of Chicago in 2019. Wade was named on *Crain's* 40 under 40, 20 Most Inspiring Chicagoans by *Streetwise* magazine, *The North Star's* 33 Inspiring Women, *Bitch Media's* Bitch 50, Champions of Pride, and is listed in *Marquis'* Who's Who in America. In 2021, Mayor Lightfoot's office honored Wade with the LGBTQ + Leadership Award, while still embroiled in controversy over the city's treatment of activists just like Wade. BSA was an Esteem Awards 2019 Chicago finalist for Outstanding Social Services.

When Wade looks back on her life and where she is today, she remembers that while her mother taught her how to be a woman, it was her gay mother, Valerie Spencer, a therapist, minister and activist, who taught her how to be a happy transgender woman. In recent years, her father has learned to love Wade for who she is. Life for Wade could not be sweeter. She recently had her first child with her partner, who is also transgender. Wade will always remain committed to BSA, which was created to help Black and Brown transgender people fight for their liberation. This will always be her ultimate challenge. ❖

---

2. "Fatal Violence Against the Transgender and Gender Non-Conforming Community in 2020," The Human Rights Campaign. https://www.hrc.org/resources/violence-against-the-trans-and-gender-non-conforming-community-in-2020

Dance

The Black Body Beautiful

"You dance because you have to. Dance is an
essential part of life that has always been with me."

—Katherine Dunham
I Dream A World (1989) by Brian Lanker

WHY DO HUMAN BEINGS DANCE? People dance for all kinds of reasons: to mourn, to celebrate, to heal, to demonstrate physical prowess, to give thanks, to preserve cultural heritage and treasured legends, to assert individuality, to get in touch with their body, to provoke, to entertain, and to tell stories. Because the act of dancing itself is a form of liberation and expression, concert dancing allowed dancers to see themselves as artists who willingly gave years of their lives plus sweat, tears, and sometimes blood to have the honor and pleasure of performing on stage. African. Tap. Jazz. Ballet. Modern Dance. Hip-hop. Fast, punchy jumps. Slow and sensual. Dancers make it look so easy, but in actuality, dance is hard work. And Black people, particularly Black women, have played an insurmountable role in the emergence of dance into the distinctively American art form it has become.

Black women have danced in innovative, idiosyncratic, and self-reflective performances that challenged artistic and cultural assumptions for years, yet many of them remain unremembered (Durkin 2019). They developed choreographies to disrupt myths and images to imagine new aesthetic possibilities, but have always had to deal with a historical impassivity of implicit bias. To fully understand Black women's place in dance, one needs to understand vernacular dance[1] as it relates to Black dance and how it engages with wider cultural forces and structures. It means going back to a beginning that points to Africa.

During the settlement of the colonies in early America, dance was characteristically European by nature and was not always received openly by society as a whole. Certain conservative and religious groups objected to the practice of dance, and delivered harsh criticisms and condemnations of it to prevent recklessness and disorder. Dancing was, to a great degree, relegated to public celebrations, entertainment, and spectacles with theatrical entertainment limited

---

1. Vernacular dances are developed "naturally" as a part of "everyday" culture within a particular community. In contrast to the elite and official culture, vernacular dances are usually learned naturally without formal instruction, alongside other concepts of vernacular culture.

PHOTO: Portrait of Katherine Dunham. Photo by Jack Mitchell/Getty Images (1987).

to displays of folk dancing. These obstacles diminished over time as changing cultural circumstances gave rise to an era in which dance was not only seen as an amusement, but as a powerful social tool and form of entertainment.

In Africa, dancing was a part of daily life activities. While styles varied across tribes and nations, dance was deeply steeped in ritual and history. For Africans, dance represented prayer, emotional communication, rites of passage, and much more. Dancing was polyrhythmic in nature with an emphasis on improvisation. The importance of community in African culture is expressed through individuality that releases the need for privacy or focus on the self. People dance with and for the community. And when a solo dancer is moving, they receive encouragement through words, hand clapping, and singing from the audience (Glass 2012). This is very much in contrast to the stratified European world of dance.

Starting in the 1500s, when Africans were captured and brought to North, Central, and South America, as well as the Caribbean for slave labor, they brought their music and dance with them. During the Middle Passage, their captors began the practice of "dancing the slaves," forcing the enslaved to dance "under the lash" to exercise and maintain their health for economic reasons: they looked better and brought a higher price. (Emery 1989) "Dancing the slaves" continued beyond the slave ships and permeated America's Southern plantation culture when slaves performed at the behest of their slave masters (Kolchin 2003).

During their limited leisure hours, particularly on Sundays and holidays, the enslaved danced for themselves, usually accompanied by musical instruments. When slave masters and overseers discovered that drums could be used as a secret means of communication, they were banned. In 1739, South Carolina went so far as to prohibit drums for fear that their rhythms would be used to incite rebellions like the one that occurred in Stono earlier that year.[2]

The division between the sacred and the secular, so prominent a feature of modern Western culture, did not exist in African culture. For slaves, music and dance held both a secular and spiritual meaning that made many Whites leery of potential subversive activities (Stuckey 2013). But even when some slave owners barred slaves from dancing, they still found ways of getting around these prohibitions. For example, since lifting the feet was considered dancing, many dances included foot shuffling along with hip and torso movement instead. Although hand clapping, "pattin' Juba,"[3] and tapping feet in a highly complex and rhythmic fashion were considered a response to the outlawing of drums by

---

2.   The Stono Rebellion (sometimes called Cato's Conspiracy or Cato's Rebellion) was a slave rebellion that began on September 9, 1739 in the colony of South Carolina. It was the largest slave uprising in the British mainland colonies, with twenty-five colonists and thirty-five to fifty Africans killed. As some of the rebels spoke Portuguese, the uprising was led by native Africans who were likely from the Central African Kingdom of Kongo.

3.   Pattin' Juba (also known as "The Juba dance" or "hambone") is an African American style of dance that involves stomping as well as slapping and patting the arms, legs, chest, and cheeks. "Pattin' Juba" would be used to keep time for other dances during a walkaround.

slaveholders, such practices have also been recognized in various West African traditions. Consequently, as a result of these restrictions, the enslaved created new dance steps.

In the process, the enslaved also crafted a rich musical tradition that had an enormous impact on the development of American music and dance. Dances that were dominant throughout the eighteenth century included the Calenda, Chica, Juba, and the Ring-Shout (or Ring dance)—one of the earliest and most important dances to appear in the Americas. While the blending of traditional African tribal dance practices was shared and reinvented in the New World, their African rhythmic sensibility would not die. Nor could it be suppressed (Emery 1989).

In 1828, Thomas Dartmouth Rice, a White man known as the "Father of Minstrelsy," developed the first popularly known blackface character, "Jim Crow," a term that would define segregation following the failure of Reconstruction. Grown largely out of a public interest in African American culture, the minstrel show quickly became the most widespread form of entertainment in the U.S. and by the 1840s, minstrel shows were being performed regularly on the theater circuit by White performers. They painted their faces black with burnt cork or shoe polish and wore tattered clothing to "mimic" Black people. They used ludicrous dialect, belted out one-liners, slapstick, and riddles, and with the most bizarre behavior, they enacted simplistic characters as happy, frolicking plantation "darkies." They also attempted to perform Juba-infused dance styles: a blending of African and European dance elements tied together by rhythm, called jigging (Emery 1989), which would serve as the foundation of tap dancing.

Rice and others merely cemented stereotypes that already existed before minstrelsy. Their performances characterized Blacks as lazy, ignorant, superstitious, hypersexual, and cowardly, which White people found rather entertaining. As the first theatrical form that was distinctly American, blackface grew into a built-in stereotype that to this day has been difficult to shake.

The popularity of blackface not only led to White actors gaining notoriety, but it also spawned industries of music, makeup, and costumes. William Henry Lane, a freed Black man known as Master Juba, was a dancer who toured with White minstrel groups, and was one of the first to perform for White audiences. Because it was the first large-scale opportunity for African Americans to enter show business, other Black men followed and began to perform on the minstrel stage as early as the late-1840s. They believed they were the most authentic performers of such material and worked hard to subtly alter these stereotypes by poking fun at White society. They performed folk songs, took dances from the plantation and moved them onto the stage, and introduced new dances that White people had not yet appropriated, like stop-time, taps, the sand, and the Virginia essence. More importantly, they advertised their authenticity as a selling point to potential audiences, both Black and White. Since a traditional all-male cast performed minstrel shows, few women participated.

The handful of Black women who performed during this era include Sissieretta Jones, Ida Forsyne, Lillyn Brown, and Belle Davis. Nearly forgotten by history, the Hyers Sisters, Anna Madah and Emma Louise, were the first Black women to succeed nationwide as mainstream, concert artists. They began their careers touring as opera singers in 1871 and moved closer towards breaking racial barriers in opera houses around the world. Then, the sisters changed course to use their art to combat a larger issue: the dismantling of Reconstruction and the explosion of negative stereotypes. At a time when minstrel shows intentionally dehumanized African Americans—operating as the entertainment counterpart to the racial terror imposed on Black people—the Hyers Sisters mounted shows and musical experiences that asserted Black dignity with an integrated cast and no blackface. For twenty years, the Hyers Sisters served as the *anti-minstrel* show. Through their productions, they boldly displayed resilience, talent, and resourcefulness, as well as a commitment to their race (Buckner 2012). After their performance at the Brooklyn Academy of Music in 1893, the Hyers Sisters announced their retirement.

As minstrelsy became less popular, vaudeville emerged in the 1880s as family entertainment with higher production values. Tony Pastor, a White ballad and minstrel singer, is credited for giving the first performance of what came to be known as vaudeville and for making it a respectable art form (Fields 2007). In 1881, he established a theater in New York City. His unexpected success encouraged other theater managers to follow his example. By the 1890s, vaudeville quickly became a national industry controlled by just a few businessmen, with chains of theaters extending across the country. By the end of the nineteenth century, the era of the vaudeville chain, owned and operated by White men and consisting of a group of theater houses controlled by a single manager, was firmly established. One of the largest chains was the Orpheum Circuit, which controlled theaters from Chicago to California.

These shows featured both women and men and often included magicians, acrobats, comedians, trained animals, and jugglers. Singing and dancing were expected in every vaudeville show. While White mainstream vaudeville provided some opportunities for African Americans, there were limitations. They were prohibited from headlining and could not perform at major theaters in southern states. In response, a Black vaudeville circuit was established. The Theatre Owners Booking Association (TOBA), often referred to as the "chitlin' circuit," toured in Black theaters only. Although they paid lower rates than White vaudeville tours, TOBA was the best chance African Americans had at performing below the Mason-Dixon line, even when the injustice they faced often outweighed the opportunity to perform. The Black vaudeville circuit was never quite as popular as the predominately White circuits, and the performers and stagehands were treated poorly and unfairly. It is perhaps the reason why the most prestigious Black theaters in Harlem, Philadelphia, and Washington,

D.C. were not a part of the TOBA circuit, and booked their acts independently. Together, Black and White vaudeville would serve as an incubator for jazz dance.

Concert singer Sissieretta Jones was one of the few Black women who had a successful vaudeville revue that also reveled in vernacular music and dance (Hine 1996). When Jones was barred from a career in opera and the concert stage due to her race, she shaped her musical career within the limited professional options available. She created her own variation on the minstrel show, the Black Patti Troubadours,[4] in 1896. She later renamed it the Black Patti Musical Comedy Company and expanded it into a musical and acrobatic act made up of jugglers, comedians, dancers, and a chorus of trained singers. She performed for two decades and for four consecutive presidents from William Harrison to Theodore Roosevelt, and toured Africa, Australia, and Europe. Jones was the highest-paid African American performer of her time and retired in 1915.

Ida Forsyne was a vaudeville dancer who began dancing at age ten for small sums of money. She worked in a few tab shows[5] before joining the Black Patti Troubadours as a dancer. Later, she toured Europe and enthralled audience and critics with her wild dance numbers. By 1911, Forsyne's success led her to Moscow during what would be the peak of her career, and she remained abroad until 1914, just before World War I. The dance routines she had performed overseas were met with consternation by African American audiences who felt that her performances were stereotypical and over the top. Additionally, light-skinned women were favored over dark-skinned women, which shut-out Forsyne from Harlem's nightclub circuit, because she was dark-skinned. Instead, she worked briefly with TOBA before she quit dancing in the 1930s and worked as a domestic servant and elevator operator (Wintz and Finkelman 2012). Forsyne did appear in a few films, including the Black filmmaker Oscar Micheaux's, *A Daughter of the Congo* (1930), and the films *Birthright* (1939) and *The Green Pastures* (1936).

Belle Davis was a choreographer, dancer, and singer. In 1891, she joined *The Creole Show* run by Sam T. Jack, a White burlesque impresario who was another pioneer of the African American vaudeville industry, and toured on his circuit. Davis performed with The Octoroons in America, and then moved to Britain in 1902. She performed at prestigious venues in England, became an international star, and eventually choreographed routines at the prestigious Casino de Paris. Davis was last heard of in Paris in 1929 and may have died there (Lotz 1997).

Lillyn Brown was a light-skinned singer, vaudeville entertainer, and teacher. She first performed in 1894 as "The Indian Princess" with an all-white female string band, and performed in minstrel shows as a male impersonator. Brown appeared in *Broadway Restus* (1921), toured Europe, and performed at the

4. Sissieretta Jones was dubbed "the Black Patti" after Adelina Patti, an Italian nineteenth-century opera singer. It was a nickname she immensely disliked but used to her advantage for publicity purposes.

5. A tab show was a short, or tabloid version, of various popular musical comedies performed in the U.S. in the early twentieth century.

major nightclubs in Harlem and on the Keith-Albee-Orpheum vaudeville circuit during the 1920s. Brown appeared in the Broadway show, *Sing Out the News* (1938), the opera *Regina* (1949), and *Kiss Me Kate* (1952). She operated an acting and singing school in Manhattan during the 1950s, taught at the Jarahal School of Music in Harlem, and was active in the African American Actors Guild. These were some of the countless Black women who were well-known in their lifetime, but have all but vanished from history.

At the turn of the century, New Orleans played a key role in the development of jazz. New Orleans was a colony founded by a French Canadian in 1718, which passed from French to Spanish rule in 1762. Since its settlement, Africans and the influx of West Indians helped distinguish its cross-cultural and multilingual heritage (Emery 1989). By 1817, city laws restricted gatherings of enslaved people to Sunday afternoons in Congo Square, also known as Place Publique (now known as Louis Armstrong Park). Similar to the talking drums of their home-land, this was a way for African tribes to communicate. The early beginnings of jazz emerged in the plantation fields where the enslaved made-up songs to pass the time and keep the culture and traditions of their African homeland alive amid the city's unique social order of Black, White, and Creole residents.

By the early twentieth century—and within eyesight of Congo Square—the resulting interaction between African, Spanish, French, Creole, and Caribbean cultures transposed into a new musical form led by key Black musical figures, known as the New Orleans jazz style. Cornetist Buddy Bolden is often credited as the earliest jazz musician, along with clarinetist "Big Eye" Louis Nelson Delisle and cornetist Freddie Keppard. Stomp-time[6] musicians like pianist-composer Ferdinand "Jelly Roll" Morton and saxophonist, clarinetist, and composer Sidney Bechet also played a key role in the making of jazz (Dicaire 2010).

At the same time, the racial fluidity that shaped much of the early history of New Orleans had collapsed through a series of legislative, judicial, and violent acts. By the late 1890s—as *Plessy v. Ferguson* (a New Orleans case) made Jim Crow a national institution—the city's Creole community, in particular, was broken down as the "one drop"[7] rule destroyed the distinctive racial patterns that had long-defined New Orleans life. This combination of musical inventive-ness and social upheaval provided early jazz a cultural framework that would soon be disseminated across the nation.

As musicians from New Orleans performed in cities throughout the U.S. and abroad, jazz's popularity exploded. Beyond its borders, musicians like Scott Joplin, the "King of Ragtime"; cornetist and bandleader Joe "King" Oliver;

6.   Stomp-time is a technique used to focus on a singer or an instrumental soloist. An ensemble or pianist repeats in rhythmic unison a simple one- or two-bar pattern consisting of sharp accents and rests while the soloist takes command. Meter and tempo remain intact; only the texture of the accompaniment changes.

7.   The one-drop rule is a social and legal principle of racial classification that was historically prominent in the U.S. in the twentieth century. It asserted that any person with even one ancestor of black ancestry is considered black.

trombonist and bandleader Edward "Kid" Ory; and W. C. Handy, known as the "Father of Blues"; led to a proliferation of jazz styles and variegation within the New Orleans tradition (Dicaire 2010). In time, jazz would multiply into many different and unorthodox forms such as swing, bebop, free jazz, cool, and jazz-rock fusion. No longer regionally defined, jazz was becoming American music. The Americanization of African music had begun, and with it came the Africanization of American music, including the simultaneous birthing of an art form that would perpetuate all forms of American dance.

Jazz dance is the one thread that binds even the most disparate pieces of American dance together. *Think about that.* Tap and hip-hop are direct descendants of jazz dance, with modern dance and ballet companies incorporating jazz techniques in their original works as well. Believe it or not, jazz dance is more than just wielding black hats with gloved hands; it is a dance that evolved from music based on African culture, birthed in New Orleans. So I begin this dance history with jazz dancing, its effect on all various forms of dance, and Black women's place in its development.

◆ ◆ ◆

JAZZ. IT IS THE JUXTAPOSITION OF MUSIC AND MOVEMENT that single-handedly became an American native art form, created by African Americans. Jazz evolved from the fringes of American society into one of the most influential and enduring musical movements of the twentieth century. Its origins came from West African traditions, landed in New Orleans, and in time became a Black cultural property finessed and distilled to a form that eventually wended its way into the White realm (Gottschild 2005).

Jazz, the music, is composed of a profusion of forms. Ragtime, which emerged from the complicated context of minstrelsy and vaudeville, and the blues, a music intricately connected to gospel music and the lives of Black Southerners, anticipated the Jazz Age musically as well as culturally. Other key elements of jazz include a combination of brass band marches, Tin Pan Alley sounds, French quadrilles, and the beguine with a collective polyphonic improvisation, including elements from Spanish-speaking cultures. Its many characteristics include syncopation and swing rhythms, a walking bass (a rising/falling sequence of notes), glissandi (finger slides from one note to another), and instrumental breaks. In addition, the various controversies connected to ragtime and the blues—especially in terms of race and morality—found fresh footing in jazz as a new expression of modernity (DeFrantz 2004).

Jazz, the dance that developed alongside the music, first appeared as traditional Black social dances. Inventive and exuberant, jazz dance was an experimental free form that was as fluid as jazz music. On stage, minstrel show performers developed tap dancing from a combination of jigging, English clog dancing, and African rhythmic stomping in the nineteenth century. The Eagle

Rock and the Slow Drag from the late nineteenth century, and the Charleston and the Jitterbug in the early twentieth century share common elements with certain Caribbean and African dances. The ring-shout, an African dance, influenced the cakewalk and shuffle dances performed in vaudeville acts. Later, they appeared in Broadway revues, modern ballets, and social dancing in the form of the shimmy, Black Bottom, rhumba, and the Lindy Hop (Emery 1989). Jazz radically altered the style of the American stage and social dance.

In fact, by the 1920s, a dance craze was underway that restructured American leisure life and the role dance played in it. One contributing factor was technological—the spread of the phonograph and the radio. The popularity of exhibition dance teams such as Vernon and Irene Castle helped blur the boundaries between formal and rag dances, and informal dancing and professional theater. This helped open new possibilities for the public to enjoy dancing as a form of expression beyond professionally-trained, costumed bodies on stage. This was especially novel for the female body, which could now perform with a new vitality and originality that was rare in older social dances, without becoming a sexualized object. This dance craze also sparked a vast increase in the number of dance venues around the country, including ballrooms, cabarets, and nightclubs. Many hotels and restaurants installed dance floors to cater to the public's desire to dance (Cooke and Horn 2003).

As jazz dancing spread to a larger audience, its transformation from the vernacular to becoming assimilated into musical theater, modern dance, and ballet became complex, sometimes disturbing, and was often fraught with racial politics. In time, deep and troubling questions would arise about what jazz dancing was, who could perform it, and what it represented in leisure and art activities.

Nevertheless, opportunities for Black professional dancers during the jazz age expanded somewhat with the success of Black musicals. *Shuffle Along* (1921), was a Broadway breakthrough that featured the Cakewalk and the Black Bottom. In 1923, America encountered one of its first and greatest nationwide fads: the Charleston, a dance step that some claim is a product of either the Ibo ethnic groups or the Ashanti of Africa, the West Indies, or the American-Gullah dance traditions of South Carolina and the Georgia Sea Islands (Millman and Manning 2004). It was a fad that completely engulfed all segments of American culture: Black, White, rich, poor—anyone who could do the simple stylized step. For example, the dance premiered in the popular all-Black Broadway show *Runnin' Wild* (1923). The song associated with the dance, "The Charleston," was composed by James P. Johnson, an African American who first introduced the stride piano method of playing and was one of the early twentieth century's greatest masters of composition. Once it hit Broadway, the Charleston swept the nation and came to define the jazz age (Jasen and Jones 2013).

As other Black musicals followed, dozens of new dance steps emerged. When White choreographers took these dances and copied, altered, and restaged them, they began to lay a crucial role in its mediation and transformation. Musical theater was doing what it does best: adopting something novel and exciting, and performing it to an audience. But since musical theater and movies were controlled by White producers (even when they featured an all-Black cast), the work never quite reflected Black authenticity (Cooke and Horn 2003). From the very beginning, various groups with different interests declared to represent "authentic" jazz dance.

The popularity of New Orleans–style jazz declined during the Depression of the 1930s. Louis Armstrong, Duke Ellington, Cab Calloway, and Count Basie gave birth to the Swing Era (also known as the Big Band Era), which generated well-known dances such as the Boogie Woogie and the Lindy Hop. The full orchestration of jazz by White bandleaders like Paul Whiteman, along with Benny Goodman, Glenn Miller, Harry James, Tommy Dorsey, and Artie Shaw used formal arrangements to replace the group improvisation that Black musicians followed, creating a format more palpable to White audiences.

But it was the Lindy Hop, a dance created in 1928 during a Harlem dance marathon at the Savoy Ballroom, the only integrated ballroom in New York, that had a profound effect on American dance. George "Shorty" Snowden and Mattie Purnell "accidentally" reinvented the breakaway pattern,[8] which helped initiate a worldwide dance craze. Snowden has been credited with the term "Lindy Hop." It is alleged that Snowden was at the end of a long marathon when a reporter watching asked what this crazy dance was called. His quick-witted answer was that it was the "Lindy Hop," and the name stuck (Stevens and Stevens 2011). The move eventually splintered into many spin-offs such as the Jitterbug, West Coast Swing, Boogie Woogie, and rock and roll. Snowden's dance group, the first Savoy Lindy Hoppers, competed in ballrooms, nightclubs, and appeared in Broadway shows like *Blackbirds* (1930) and *Singing the Blues* (1930). It was a fusion of many dances that preceded it or were popular during its development, but it was mainly based on jazz, tap, and the Charleston.

By the 1930s, the Lindy Hop entered mainstream American culture, gaining popularity in dance clubs, theater, and Hollywood films. Even dance studios like Arthur Murray began teaching it. More importantly, Black dance troupes such as the Hot Chocolates and Big Apple Dancers exhibited the Lindy Hop. The big stand out was Whitey's Lindy Hoppers (also known as the Harlem Congaroos), founded by Herbert White, the head bouncer at the Savoy. He was skilled at bringing together the best dancers from the Savoy to join his dance troupe. Frankie Manning, one of Whitey's key dancers, would become known as the "Ambassador of Lindy Hop." He created the troupe's first ensemble routines and functioned as the group's main choreographer. Manning partnered with Norma Miller, who became known as the "Queen of Swing" (Millman and Manning 2007).

---

8. The breakaway is a time-honored method of eliminating the European custom of dancing in couples, and returning to solo dancing—the universal way of dancing, for example, in Africa.

Whitey arranged performances and competitions all over the country, and got his group into quite a few films, including *A Day at the Races* (1937) and *Hellzapoppin'* (1941), and touched off a global dance sensation. Some of his dancers were featured in magazines such as *Look* and *Life*. Willa Mae Ricker was one of those dancers featured with Leon James in the 1943 *Life* magazine article on the Lindy Hop. She was considered one of the most versatile of all the women of Whitey's dances (Stevens and Stevens 2011). But while variants of the Lindy Hop emerged, the only one that survived in the long run was the Harlem dance. The dance succeeded in reflecting the heart of jazz music itself: the beautiful harmony of individualism and teamwork.

A number of Black women were Lindy Hoppers, but a very unfortunate aspect of the Lindy Hop's history, as with most dance history, is that Black women were not given the credit they deserved for their invention and influence. For example, Frieda Washington is credited for performing the first aerial with Manning. During an era where credit was more likely given to men, the Lindy Hop offered a great deal more freedom for women than other partnered dances.

Other women like Norma Miller, Louise "Pal" Andrews, Millie Cruse, Elnora Dyson, Dorothy "Dot" Johnson, Mildred "Boogie" Pollard, and Ann Johnson represent a handful of the many women who were members of Lindy Hop crews. Norma Miller was one of the best and most charismatic member of Whitey's Lindy Hoppers. When it disbanded in the early forties, she formed her own company in California—Norma Miller's Dance Company—and had her own show at Club Alabam in the Watts section of Los Angeles. In the 1950s, she worked with the Del Rio Trio and formed Norma Miller's Jazz Dancers. She appeared in a number of films such as *A Day at the Races* (1937), *Hellzapoppin'* (1941), and *Malcolm X* (1992), and received an Emmy nomination for choreographing the 1993 CBS television film, *Stompin' at The Savoy* (Stevens and Stevens 2011). As a comedienne, Miller worked in Las Vegas with Redd Foxx for over ten years, and made appearances in his television show, *Sanford and Son*. In the 1970s, she formed another Lindy Hop and jazz performance group, the Savoy Swingers, and did a series of performances in the New York City public school system (Millman and Manning 2007).

Louise "Pal" Andrews taught herself to dance by watching the Apollo dancers and gained a reputation that caught the attention of Whitey's team. At just fifteen, she was the youngest of the crew. She worked at the Roxy and in 1940, went on a road trip to the Midwest with the Hollywood Hotel Revue. In 1943, Andrews went to California to dance with Pepsi Bethel in the show *Born Happy,* starring Bill "Bojangles" Robinson (Stevens and Stevens 2011). Millie Cruse, the winner of the second Harvest Moon Ball, was the smoothest of the original Lindy Hoppers. Cruse danced with the Hopping Maniacs before joining Whitey's Lindy Hoppers, worked the Cotton Club, and toured with big band leaders like Cab Calloway in the U.S. and Teddy Hill in Europe.

Elnora Dyson became a Lindy Hopper at the Savoy Pavilion in the 1939-1940 World's Fair and performed with Ella Fitzgerald in Bayonne, New Jersey. Dorothy "Dot" Johnson partnered with Tiny Bunch and was immortalized by Aaron Siskind's photo, "At the Savoy" (1936) as part of the award-winning collection, *Harlem Document, Photographs 1932-1940,* for the Federal Writers' Project. Mildred "Boogie" Pollard, aka Sandra Gibson, became a member in 1937. After Whitey's Lindy Hoppers disbanded, she went on to become a solo blues dancer.

As a member of Whitey's Lindy Hoppers, Ann Johnson appeared in stage shows including *The Ghost Parade* (1929), *Blosson Time* (1931), and Lew Leslie's *Blackbirds* of 1939, as well as the films *Hellzapoppin'* (1941), *Hot Chocolate* (1941), and *Killer Diller* (1948). But she is perhaps most famous for appearing in photos with Frankie Manning in *Life* magazine. The first photo submitted anonymously by a reader and published in 1940 is of Johnson tossed in mid-air, frozen over Manning's head, and appropriately titled "Over the Head." The second photo, which also captures Johnson mid-air during an aerial step sequence with Manning, was featured in the 1941 photo story by W. Eugene Smith. From 1947 to 1952, Johnson was a member of the Harlem Congaroos dance crew (Stevens and Stevens 2011).

Throughout history, Black women dancers have always been overshadowed in both the Black and White dance communities. When we think of Black dance, we often think of men like Bill "Bojangles" Robinson, Asadata Dafora, Talley Beatty, Donald McKayle, Alvin Ailey, Rod Rodgers, Arthur Mitchell, Chuck Davis, Geoffrey Holder, Bill T. Jones, Gregory Hines, and Ishmael Houston-Jones, but with the exception of Katherine Dunham and Pearl Primus, few Black women make that list. This is because African Americans are rarely credited for their artistry and in most cases, their work was co-opted or even worse, largely ignored and dismissed.

There were, however, a number of Black male choreographers from the 1920s to the 1950s, like Clarence "Buddy" Bradley and Billy Pierce, who coached and developed routines for White performers. While most of their work was uncredited, we can assume this arrangement was made from the onset and the choreographers were compensated. On the other hand, Black women working as domestics were sought to train White stage girls, and the dance techniques were expropriated by their choreographers (Brown 2008). One can only imagine how professional Black women dancers were treated.

Edna Guy was an accomplished dancer who struggled to find dance classes and jobs. When she managed to connect with Ruth St. Denis, Guy was often relegated to the role of a seamstress in the pioneering Denishawn School of Dancing and Related Arts (Foulkes 2002). Elida Webb-Dawson was one of the first African American female choreographers. Trained by Aida Overton Walker, Webb-Dawson worked with Josephine Baker, Florence Mills, Fredi Washington, Lena Horne, and Ruby Keeler (Smith and Bracks 2014). When she choreographed the Broadway show *Runnin' Wild* (1923), James Weldon Johnson publicly credited the show's Black male producers for her choreography instead, which shows that even Black contemporaries were ignorant of Webb-Dawson's craft (Durkin 2019). Webb-Dawson danced and choreographed at the Cotton Club, performed in the musical, *Shuffle Along* (1921), staged and presented numerous club acts for Black theaters and cabarets, and had the longest career of any Black female choreographer of her day. Similar to Webb-Dawson's situation, the choreography for the 1940 musical *Cabin in the Sky* is officially attributed to George Balanchine, but his uncredited co-choreographer was the legendary Katherine Dunham, who played the story's sexpot and whose pioneering dance company prominently featured in the cast. After that, Dunham amassed nine Broadway credits as a choreographer, most of them for concert appearances by her company and other Black entertainers.

These early Black women dancers have been difficult to track due to their robbed credit. Bessie Dudley was regarded as one of the greatest tap and snake dancers of her time. At age thirteen, she ran away from home to join the traveling Chocolate Box Revue but soon discovered that life on the road was not exactly what she expected. After two years, Dudley left the group and married the son of a vaudeville performer with his own revue. She went on to work with Florence Hill in the Duke Ellington film, *A Bundle of Blues* (1933). Although both Dudley and Hill appeared in *Gone Harlem* (1938), not much is known about Hill.

Mabel Hart appeared on Broadway as a dancer in the opera, *Four Saints in Three Acts* (1934), *Carmen Jones* (1943), *Run, Little Chillun* (1943), *Lost in the Stars* (1949), and the films *Over the Wall* (1938) and *Isn't It Romantic?* (1948). Alma Sutton, who danced for Asadata Dafora, appeared in *Show Boat* (1946). Lavinia Williams was a dancer and dance educator who studied under Dunham, and a member of the American Negro Ballet. Having encountered racial discrimination in the ballet world, Williams joined Dunham's company, performed for Agnes de Mille, and appeared in *Shuffle Along* (1921). After spending thirty years teaching in the U.S., she traveled abroad and founded national schools of dance in Haiti, Guyana, and the Bahamas. Beryl McBurnie, a pioneer of Trinidad and Tobago's folk dance scene, also performed under the pseudonym Belle Rosette. She immigrated to the U.S. and studied at Teachers College Columbia University in New York under Martha Graham, Charles Weidman, and Maudelle Weston. She taught Dunham and Pearl Primus and performed alongside dancers Doris Humphrey and Martha Graham (Schwartz and Schwartz 2011). McBurnie returned to Trinidad in the mid-1940s to teach and in 1947, founded the Little Carib Theatre in Woodbrook, Port of Spain, which exists to this day.

Alice Barker was a chorus line dancer in New York City in the 1930s and 1940s, performing at nightclubs such as the Apollo Theater and the Cotton Club. She also performed regularly at the Café Zanzibar in New York City, with shows frequently led by Cab Calloway, and danced in numerous movies, commercials

and television shows. In fact, Barker was one of the first African American dancers to appear on national prime time television, making an appearance dancing
on *The Frank Sinatra Show* during the late 1950s.

Josephine Baker was one of the few dancers that had a more direct connection to jazz. She was the first Black woman to leave her mark on the dance
world and created a legacy synonymous with bravery and uninhibited passion.
By the time she sashayed onto a Paris stage wearing only a banana skirt, Baker
had taken Europe by storm. She performed with a comic yet sensual appeal,
epitomizing the Black body beautiful. On the other hand, Margot Webb, a ballroom dancer who professionally performed with Harold Norton as "Norton and
Margot," was one of the few African American ballroom teams in history that
adopted a White repertoire, on par with Astaire and Rogers. They performed on
the Black vaudeville circuits of nightclubs and theaters in Harlem, and around
the Northeast and the Midwest from 1933 to 1947. As a ballroom team, however, they were prevented from elevating to a national stage (Gottschild 2011).
While Baker fled the U.S. and found success in Europe, thrilling audiences at the
Théâtre des Champs-Elysées and the Folies-Bergère, Webb, who never reached
Broadway or any other major White outlet in America, was forced to abandon her
efforts (DeFrantz 2002). Many of these women sought work overseas in revues,
race films, or shorts produced primarily by Black-owned film studios in the U.S.
and abroad.

During the Harlem Renaissance, Black artists consciously drew on the New
Negro movement's philosophy, which promoted the use of art to advance racial
consciousness and heritage. Dancer and choreographer Hemsley Winfield, who
founded the Bronze Ballet Plastique in New York (later renamed the New Negro
Art Theater Dance Group) is credited with instituting Black concert dance (staged
dance) in the early 1930s. He presented a range of works in what many consider
to be a turning point in the presentation and execution of Black dance (Emery
1989). The program also featured leading female dancers like Ollie Burgoyne,
Drusela Drew, and Midgie Lane, including Edna Guy, who assisted Winfield
with his first concert. Guy, who had developed a lifelong relationship with the
modern dance world and studied at Denishawn, would perform and choreograph
a number of seminal pieces before retiring from dance at a relatively early age.

Although Burgoyne is one of the lesser-known African American figures in
entertainment, she has been credited as one of the most significant and influential Black dancers and choreographers of this era. Unlike Guy, Burgoyne had a
remarkable career that spanned fifty years. She began dancing and singing when
she was sixteen years old and later became an actress and businesswoman
during the Harlem Renaissance. Burgoyne distinguished herself as one of the few
Black women who participated in developing theatrical genres, including minstrel
and vaudeville shows, revues, Black and White musicals, and concert dance.
In the early part of her career, Burgoyne danced internationally in vaudeville

shows and performed with her cousin, Ida Forsyne. For a time, she studied and performed in Russia, and opened a lingerie shop in Saint Petersburg (Perpener 2005). When she returned to the U.S., she performed in many Broadway shows, including *Follow Me* (1923), *Make Me Know It* (1929), *Constant Sinner* (1931), and *Run Little Chillun* (1933). Burgoyne had a small part in the film *Laughter* (1930), and in her later life, taught dance in the movie industry. Burgoyne embarked on a career path that illustrated a microcosm of Black performances that transitioned from social dance to theatrical performances (Perpener 2005).

And then there is Hortense Allen Jordan: producer, director, choreographer, dancer, and the first African American woman to put a chorus line in the Paramount on Broadway. Much of her work as a producer, director, and choreographer went uncredited because most people would not accept a Black woman in such a powerful role, so she was only named as a dancer. She began dancing in the 1930s at the age of fourteen. By the time she was twenty, Jordan was producing shows with a revue and had her own chorus line at the Paramount, The Plantation Club, the largest club in Harlem at the time, and the Apollo Theater. She choreographed hundreds of shows, danced every style of dance, sewed costumes for her lines, traveled in road shows, played all the major houses, and taught hundreds of young women how to dance.

Jordan produced and danced in Larry Steele's shows at the Club Harlem in Atlantic City, but eventually they parted ways after they fought over his banning dark-skinned women from the chorus line. She continued producing shows headlined by Sugar Ray Robinson, Louis Jordan, and James Brown. When other people thought stage shows were dead, Jordan was actively producing them at the Robin Hood Dell in Philadelphia in the 1970s, bringing top-notch entertainers to large crowds. By 1994, Jordan was artistic director for *Stepping in Time,* a musical revue of African American performers produced by the Philadelphia Folklore Project. Although Jordan worked for six decades in dance, and her achievements were known largely through word-of-mouth among her contemporaries, she is seldom acknowledged for her work.

Whitey's Lindy Hoppers disbanded around World War II when many of the male dancers entered armed forces. After Manning served in the U.S. Army, he led along with Ricker, the Harlem Congaroos (renamed the Congaroo Dancers), a small performance troupe. The Lindy Hop became less popular and the group disbanded in 1955 (Millman and Manning 2007).

Early jazz compositions and arrangements were heavily influenced to serve the dancers. However, by the 1940s, the Swing Era was on the decline, accelerated by wartime conditions and royalty conflicts. In 1941, the American Society of Composers and Producers (ASCAP) demanded bigger royalties from broadcasters, and the broadcasters refused. Consequently, ASCAP banned the large repertoire they controlled from airplay, which severely restricted what the radio audience could hear. Another blow fell on the market for dance-oriented swing in

1944 when the federal government levied a 30 percent excise tax on "dancing" nightclubs, undercutting the market for dance music in smaller venues. It would explain, in part, why band performances were being increasingly promoted as concerts. Seated listening was encouraged, and in some cases, dancing was banned entirely (Wells 2019).

During this shift, modern dance began to gain steam in the concert and theater worlds. Modern dance was born in America during the turn of the twentieth century when choreographers and dancers rebelled against the two forms of dance prevalent at the time: ballet and vaudeville. They rejected what they interpreted as the rigid and imperialistic nature of ballet, and they wanted to be taken seriously as artists rather than be seen as entertainers.

But it was two Black women, Katherine Dunham and Pearl Primus, who were responsible for creating a Black modern dance movement inspired by African and Caribbean dance forms, combined with vernacular jazz. Dunham, who had a ballet background, reinforced jazz dance's connection to its African origins with a dominating feminine energy and then incorporated it into ballet, creating a starting point for modern dance to evolve. She was fearless, accessible, and daunting, making a name for herself in Broadway musicals like *Le Jazz Hot* (1938) and *Tropics* (1937), and introducing her ballet *L'ag'ya* (1938) at the Federal Theater in Chicago. She studied and explored dance techniques from Haiti, Jamaica, Trinidad, and Martinique. More importantly though, Dunham gave modern dance a coherent lexicon of African and Caribbean styles of movement—a flexible torso and spine, articulated pelvis and isolation of the limbs, a polyrhythmic strategy of moving—that continues to be taught to this day. As one of the first Black women to form her own dance company, Dunham's dancers were the toast of Europe during the 1940s and 1950s, but she was refused support from the State Department's dance panel (a precursor to the National Endowment for the Arts), and was not invited to teach at the American Dance Festival. Even so, Dunham is considered the most important woman of Black dance because she combined culturally-grounded dance movements with key elements of ballet to make a Black modern dance.

Primus, who was less glamorous than Dunham, is considered America's preeminent modern dancer. She used the art form to express the social and political constraints placed on Black people in America. She worked at the New Dance Group Studios, one of the few studios where Black dancers could train alongside White dancers. In 1948, Primus received a federal grant to study dance. She used the money to travel around Africa and the Caribbean to learn different styles of native dance, which she performed and taught in the U.S. Her most famous dance was the "Fanga," an African dance of welcome. This dance introduced traditional African dance to the stage. She also choreographed dances that contained messages about racism and discrimination. One of her dances, "Strange Fruit," protested the lynching of Blacks. Eventually, Primus formed her own dance troupe, which toured internationally, and opened a dance school in Harlem, the Pearl Primus Dance Language Institute. Primus developed a movement language and created works that parallel that of Graham, Charles Weidman, Agnes de Mille, and others who are considered pioneers of American modern dance.

Dunham and Primus, who both acquired academic credentials as anthropologists, succeeded in using anthropology to construct and convey cultural, social, and political ideas in the furtherance of dance. They raised the profile and value of an African-based aesthetic that would encourage the merging of different dance cultures to create new dance forms. They were both influenced by Asadata Dafora, originally from Sierra Leone, who introduced authentic West African culture into their work. Dafora paved the way for Black male choreographers like Donald McKayle and Talley Beatty, who would be recognized as the first wave of the larger American modern dance world. Dunham was a mentor to Alvin Ailey, who later choreographed enduring works for his own company, infusing gospel, blues, and African American spirituals with modern dance and created his own jazzy riff on traditional modern dance.

Jazz music continued to evolve. The early 1940s ushered in the bebop movement, which became an important event in jazz's history. A departure from the Swing Era, bebop features improvisation and complex, rapid chord changes. Since bebop was not intended for dancing, it enabled musicians to play at faster tempos. The music itself seemed jarringly different to the ears of the public, who were used to the bouncy, organized, danceable compositions of the Swing Era, but to jazz musicians and jazz music lovers, bebop was an exciting and beautiful revolution in the art of jazz.

Jazz dance would go on to influence many Black and White choreographers. Modern dance pioneers like Loie Fuller, Isadora Duncan, Ruth St. Denis, and Ted Shawn experimented with jazz dance. The next wave of modern White choreographers such as George Balanchine, Martha Graham, Doris Humphrey, Hanya Holm, Charles Weidman, Lester Horton, and Agnes de Mille used trained dancers to perform highly precise and difficult dance moves. They helped elevate jazz dance into a modern art form that was different than the vernacular jazz dance of New Orleans music bars.

Unfortunately, vernacular jazz dancing never developed into a professional stage dance, like ballet or modern dance. Instead, it became incorporated into choreographers' ideas of what dancers should do with their ballet and modern training. White male choreographers such as Bob Fosse, Jerome Robbins, Eugene Louis "Luigi" Faccuito, and Gus Giordano blended movements from the vernacular, codified the steps, and put their names to them. The fact that it was not authentic was of little importance, and in time, few people understood what vernacular jazz dance was and where it actually came from. The golden age of vernacular jazz dance officially ended around 1960, when jazz music, completely transformed into what is now known as modern jazz.

Of course, there is an argument as to whether or not jazz dance has completely disappeared, or if it morphed into modern and contemporary modern dance. Some believe the forms are distinct enough to be completely unrelated, while others suggest that neither one would exist in its current form without jazz dance. I contend that no matter how sharp or softened the movements are, or whether the dance employs free form or remains themeless, the polyrhythmic timing that has survived in these current forms still point back to Africa.

Helen Tamiris was a pioneer of American modern dance. She was one of the first White modern choreographers to make use of jazz, African American spirituals, and social-protest themes in her work, bringing social consciousness to the concert hall. As a result, the dance community shunned Tamiris. Her status in the dance world during the 1930s reveals the class dynamics at play in the formation of modern dance as a new art form (Foulkes 2002). Tamiris was also the first choreographer to feature Black and White dancers on stage together, which was seen as controversial at the time. Black dancers like Donald McKayle, Pearl Primus, and Talley Beatty—all of whom became well-known dance choreographers—performed in Tamiris' shows.

By the 1950s, some Black women were able to join White-led modern dance companies when vernacular jazz dance started to fall out of favor with the public. It is worth mentioning that lighter-skinned Blacks had less trouble dancing in White companies due to the fact that passing as White or "foreign" was an easier way to enter White studios and perform. However, once Martha Graham started to work steadily, she was one of the few choreographers who welcomed Black dancers into her classes and company. Graham's work was heavily influenced by Native and African American cultures. Black traditions were frequently co-opted by White choreographers, but they did so without dancing Black bodies. In that regard, Graham was the exception rather than the rule. In 1951, she accepted Mary Hinkson and Matt Turney, both trained and educated at the University of Wisconsin as the first Black women to dance in her company.

In 1968, Blondell Cummings, who studied under Graham, was a founding member of Meredith Monk's company, The House. She is known for her experimental choreography that recycled experience into art, becoming a fixture in the New York and Harlem dance scene for decades (Desmond 1997). Shelley Washington, who also started out with Graham, began dancing for Twyla Tharp in 1975. Their achievements were pathbreaking successes that proved African Americans could master different dance styles (Foulkes 2002). Other dance companies such as Paul Taylor Dance Company and the Limón Dance Company employed Black dancers at the highest levels. For example, Carolyn Adams, who also studied with Graham, joined the Paul Taylor Dance Company in 1965 as the company's only Black member. She was a principal dancer until 1982. Later on, Kristen Foote joined the Limón Dance Company in 2000, where she was a principal dancer until 2017. Modern dance was always a bit more inclusive than ballet and somewhat more open to people of color because they did not require a pristine row of white swans.

During the Black Arts Movement, several Black women followed Dunham and Primus by founding dance companies that incorporated teaching and educational programming. In doing so, they created their own distinct brand of modern dance. Dianne McIntyre studied under Viola Farber and Gus Solomons Jr., among others. She found herself drawn into the connection between dance composition, avant-garde jazz, and free jazz, distinguishing herself as one of the few Black dancers to tie them together, and, in the process, connect their relationship to civil rights struggles (Goldman 2010). She has transformed words from acclaimed writers like Ntozake Shange, James Baldwin, and August Wilson, as well as her mother's aviator stories, into dance. McIntyre founded Sounds in Motion in 1972, the only modern dance studio and company in Harlem. Sixteen years after its founding in 1988, McIntyre closed the company to pursue independent work. Her unique approach to movement and musicality spawned generations of dancers charged to explore the conversations between sound and the dancing body.

In 1968, Jeraldyne Blunden left a permanent mark on contemporary dance by founding the Dayton Contemporary Dance Company in Ohio. In 1970, when there was hardly any dance—let alone Black dance—in the Rocky Mountain region, Cleo Parker Robinson established the Cleo Parker Robinson Dance school and ensemble in Denver as a grassroots initiative. The company has since grown into a first class dance company that has performed all over the world. Deborah Vaughan, Elendar Barnes, and Shirley Brown cofounded Dimensions Dance Theater in Oakland, California in 1973 to explore African and African-derived dance. The Dallas Black Dance Theatre was founded by Ann Williams in 1976. In 1978, Blondell Cummings created her own art collective, Cycle Arts Foundation, which promoted interdisciplinary collaboration and navigated between modern and postmodern dance with charismatic gusto. Her cross-cultural activism led her to host workshops for dancers and non-dancers alike, encouraging participants to dive into issues like menopause, life cycles, family, and food.

Lula Washington and her husband, Erwin Washington, established the Los Angeles Contemporary Dance Theatre in 1980, later renamed Lula Washington Dance Theatre. They also created a dance school that provides low-cost and free dance classes in their community. Jawole Willa Jo Zollar founded Urban Bush Women in 1984 as an all-female dance troupe that utilizes the Black female body to highlight social issues through movement and music. Zollar's company also develops local activities in support of community empowerment (George-Graves 2010). Bebe Miller, professor emerita and an award-winning choreographer, formed Bebe Miller Company in 1985. Her choreography has been performed in venues across the country and internationally in Europe and the African continent. She has been commissioned by Dayton Contemporary

Dance Company, Oregon Ballet Theater, Boston Ballet, PHILADANCO, and the United Kingdom's Phoenix Dance Company, among others.

And then there is Judith Jamison, Alvin Ailey's muse and the star of his company. In 1989, she inherited the Alvin Ailey American Dance Theater due to Ailey's failing health and untimely death. While her claim to fame will always be Ailey's quintessential piece, "Cry," in truth, Jamison became someone she never planned to be: the first Black woman to direct and manage an internationally-acclaimed dance company. By 2011, she transitioned into the role of Artistic Director Emerita. As one of the few remaining links to the late Ailey himself, she witnessed the company's sixtieth anniversary in 2018, which cemented both her and Ailey's legacy.

Black women choreographers like Dunham and McIntyre, who ventured into theater and live stage performances, have made notable inroads. For example, they paved the way for women like Mabel Robinson, who made American theater history as the first African American woman to have concurrently running Broadway shows. In 1976, she starred as Dancing Mary in the original production of *Your Arms Too Short to Box with God,* while also working as the choreographer and assistant director in the Broadway revival of *Porgy and Bess.*

When denied the opportunity to further her ballet career, Debbie Allen became an actress, dancer, and singer. Her claim to fame—literally—is the film *Fame* (1980), and the subsequent television show that aired from 1982 to 1987. She released several albums and acted in, directed, and produced staged productions, films, and television shows, but her love for the stage remained constant. Allen's Broadway appearances include the chorus in *Purlie* (1970), the role of Beneatha in the Tony Award-winning musical *Raisin* (1973), *Truckload* (1975), *Ain't Misbehavin'* (1978), and the role of Anita in the Broadway revival of *West Side Story* (1980) for which she received critical acclaim. Allen has also earned three Emmy Awards for choreography, a Golden Globe in 1982 for her role on the television show *Fame,* five NAACP Image Awards, a Drama Desk, an Astaire Award (for Best Dancer), and the Olivier Award. Although she won three Emmys, Allen has been nominated nineteen times, with eleven nominations for choreography. She is the first Black woman to win an Emmy for choreography; the second being Judith Jamison in 1999 for Outstanding Choreography Dance for the PBS documentary, *Dance in America: A Hymn for Alvin Ailey.*

After many years appearing as a dancer on Broadway, Hope Clarke was frequently called in to choreograph various stage and television shows. She choreographed *Jelly's Last Jam* (1992) and for her work, Clarke was nominated for a Drama Desk Award. In 1993, she became the first Black woman choreographer nominated for a Tony. Clarke made history in 1995 when she became the first African American, as well as the first Black woman, to direct and choreograph a major restaging of the opera-musical *Porgy and Bess.* Marlies Yearby would be the second Black woman to receive a Tony nomination for choreographing

Jonathan Larson's *Rent* (1996). Camille A. Brown, an award-winning choreographer, has developed an impressive portfolio within the past decade. Besides choreographing for her company as well as other dance companies, she has worked extensively in theater, especially on Broadway, including *A Streetcar Named Desire* (2012), *Cabin in the Sky* (2015) and *Once on This Island* (2017). In 2019 she became the third Black woman choreographer, in two decades, to receive a Tony nomination for her work in *Choir Boy*.

One can easily see how a new generation of scholars, researchers, and anthropologists are following in the footsteps of Dunham and Primus. Historian and professor-emerita Brenda Dixon Gottschild, a dancer, choreographer, and award-winning researcher, has published several books on dance. Award-winning choreographer and performance artist Cynthia Oliver is creating dance that reflects her ongoing research and scholarship of the intersection between contemporary dance, feminism, Black popular culture, and the expressive performances of Africans in the diaspora and Anglophone Caribbean. Shireen Dickson, a dancer and arts educator, has been a teaching artist, lecturer, and curriculum developer for over twenty years. Raquel Monroe, who has worked closely with choreographers, is an interdisciplinary performance scholar and artist whose research interests include Black social dance and feminism. Makeda Thomas is a dancer, choreographer, artistic director, writer, and curator who has created several works through cross-disciplinary collaboration with artists worldwide. Takiyah Nur Amin is a dance scholar and educator who focuses on twentieth century American concert dance, African diaspora dance performance and aesthetic, and pedagogical issues in dance studies. Igbo-Nigerian American artist, performer, and choreographer Okwui Okpokwasili, and Zimbabwe American choreographer and performer Nora Chipaumire, have dominated the New York City downtown scene with their tenacity and genius.

This is a small sampling of the many Black women dancers and choreographers who have taken an unflinching look at American society and staked their place in it. The growth of radio, television, videos, films and music recordings, which popularized Black music among a broader audience, helped elevate jazz dance to the point that it has permeated all other aspects of dance. Black women have followed Dunham's footsteps by blending and combining dance techniques while experimenting, hybridizing, and improvising new and exciting works. They continue to push their artistic boundaries with a technical prowess and cultural integrity that captures their audience's imagination, and connects their work, and themselves, to their African roots.

◆ ◆ ◆

TAP DANCE IS WHAT THE EYE HEARS. It is a peculiar form of dance that makes its own sound, similar to other foot-stamping forms like flamenco, Irish step dancing, and most Indian classical dance. Even when there is musical accompaniment, the most important sound at any tap performance is the dancer's feet. This sensory doubleness—sight combined with sound—makes tap dancing a unique form of dance.

Unlike ballet with its codification of formal technique, tap dance was developed by people listening to and watching each other dance in the street, dance halls, or social clubs where the steps were shared, stolen, and reinvented. Tap is also connected to other dance forms based on African culture, such as jazz and hip-hop. It was nurtured in the American South and urban environments like the Five Points District in New York City, where a variety of ethnic groups lived side-by-side under crowded conditions, and would later become an integral part of movies, musicals, and nightclub performances (Seibert 2015).

As an indigenous American dance genre, tap dance has been three hundred years in the making. It began as a fusion of West African sacred and secular step dances like the Juba, a dance comprised of stomping and slapping of the arms and legs. The Juba was originally brought by the Kongo people to Charleston, South Carolina, and was routinely performed on Southern plantations by enslaved people. When slave owners took away traditional African percussion instruments, the enslaved turned to percussive dancing to express themselves and retain their cultural identities (Emery 1989). They combined their African step dances with outside European influences like Scottish, Irish, and English clog dances and jigs to create what would become the foundations of tap dancing.

Among the genres that went into this mix were buck dancing, a percussive, weighted flatfooted dance; the jig, which is rapid footwork that consists of a lot of hopping, kicking, and shuffling of the feet; and wing dancing, made up of the flapping of the body, arms, and legs. Buck-and-wing dancing, a combination of Irish clogging, high kicks, and complex African rhythms and steps such as the shuffle and slide, is the primary influence of the tap we know today. "Jigging" became the general term for this new American percussive hybrid, recognized as a "Black" style of dancing (DeFrantz 2002).

By the mid-1800s, jigging competitions were a common form of entertainment. One of the earliest recorded challenges took place in 1844 between Black dancer Master Juba (William Henry Lane), and Irish dancer John Diamond (Emery 1989). Master Juba, who offered a fast and technically brilliant dance style that blended European and African dance forms, won the competition. From jigging competitions staged by slave masters on the plantation or challenge dances in the walk-around finale of the minstrel show, to showdowns in the street, dancers engaged in a dialog of rhythm, motion, and witty repartee while inviting the audience to respond. No matter the contest, challenge dances require the ability to look, listen, copy, creatively modify, and further perfect whatever has come before.

Minstrel shows soon became a primary showcase for jigging. By the time Black performers gained access to the minstrel stage after the Civil War, jigging was being infused with a variety of new steps, rhythms, and choreographic structures. By 1902, the term "tap" came into wide use. In 1910, dance shoes were being made of leather uppers and wooden soles. Later they pounded hobnails or pennies into the toe and heel, which gave way to metal taps attached to the bottom of shoes. In time, the absorption of early ragtime and jazz rhythms evolved tap dance. This transition to "jazz tap" is attributed to John Bubbles, whose rhythm tapping revolutionized tap dancing.

Before Bubbles, dancers tapped up on their toes, emphasizing flash steps (difficult, acrobatic steps with extended leg and body movements), and danced to a quicker tempo (two beats to a bar). Bubbles cut the tempo in half, extended the rhythm beyond the normal eight beats, dropped his heels, and hit unusual accents and syncopations. When he blended the improvisational style of jazz music with the traditional techniques of tap, Bubbles brought a semblance of respectability to the art form that landed on Broadway and films. He also ingeniously anticipated both the new sound of bebop in the 1940s and the prolonged melodic line of cool jazz in the 1950s (Hill 2014).

There is an irony to all of this. Tap's development from African vernacular dance forms is part of a bigger historical narrative that involves slavery, segregation, racism, misogyny, and bigotry. For example, the enslaved were forbidden to play their native drums, so they used their bodies and feet for the beat. Black men wore blackface to counter the stereotypes of Black identity as laughable, primitive and overly sensual, and developed a self-presentation on stage that balanced racist stereotypes and political commentary. As a consequence of this social context, racial and gender issues created divisions in tap dance. By the early twentieth century, segregated America developed two separate styles and aesthetics. The African American hoofers privileged self-expression, improvisation, and syncopation, while White tap dancers focused on entertainment, choreography, and regular rhythm, creating a Broadway style that became popular in American culture. Besides style, segregation affected how tap dance was passed on to the next generation through either teaching or stealing steps.

Unsurprisingly, tap has always been a male-dominated art. The strange absence of women in early accounts of jigging competitions forces a consideration of gender in the evolution of tap dance as it became a "man's game" for most of the twentieth century. That has now become a somewhat mythologized truth, given the plethora of tap histories that sidelined women, especially Black women. Black women tap dancers whose active careers spanned the 1920s to the 1950s were restricted to few roles, often unnamed and uncredited, and largely remained anonymous both within and outside the entertainment industry. With an awareness of social and cultural contexts, I aim to clarify and reaffirm the relevance of some of these Black female tap dancers, who have been overlooked and omitted in the history of a dance genre that owes much of its recent developments to Black women.

I begin with Aida Overton Walker vaudeville performer, singer, actress, buck-and-wing, and Cakewalk virtuoso who was regarded as one of the first choreographers on the American stage. Also known as "The Queen of the Cakewalk," she was the wife of the vaudevillian star, George Walker. She appeared with her husband and his performing partner Bert Williams touring in groups such as Black Patti Troubadours. She was also a solo dancer and choreographer for vaudeville shows like Bob Cole, Joe Jordan, and J. Rosamond Johnson's *The Red Moon* (1908). Walker is well-known for her 1912 modest rendition of the Salomé dance at Hammerstein's Victoria Theatre.[9]

In her solo work for women and her precise choreography for the chorus line, Walker claimed a female presence on the stage. By negotiating the narrow White definitions of "appropriate" Black performance with her own innovative choreography, Walker established Black cultural integrity, and set a model that other African American performers would use to gain acceptance on the professional concert stage. Walker died suddenly from kidney failure in 1914 at age thirty-four. Her interest in African indigenous material anticipated modern dance pioneers Katherine Dunham and Pearl Primus' choreographic work (Hill 2014).

Many White performers executed simple walking steps in square rhythms, which is considered the lowest common denominator in show dancing. However, the most elite of White Broadway stars worked with African American choreographers like Clarence "Buddy" Bradley, who staged dances during the 1920s including revues for Gilda Gray, Ruby Keeler, Florenz Ziegfeld Jr., George White, Earl Carroll, and Lew Leslie. This new art form further developed during the 1930s and 1940s when Hollywood began producing motion pictures featuring White performers like Fred Astaire, Ginger Rogers, Eleanor Powell, and Shirley Temple. Bradley also worked with George Balanchine, who had become greatly inspired by how Black vernacular dance steps could reshape the body and add a new dynamic to musical theater dance (Morris 2005).

Although Black artists were prevented from starring in mainstream films, many dancers appeared in specialty acts, in feature films, musical short subjects, soundies, and Black films. Since its emergence, tap was dominated by Black men like Bill "Bojangles" Robinson and the Nicholas Brothers, while Black women danced in relative obscurity.

The Whitman Sisters (Mabel, Essie, Alberta, and Alice) managed, booked, directed, and toured one of the largest African American companies to play on both Black and White stages from around 1900 to 1943. Credited as the longest-running and most highly-paid vaudeville troupe, the Whitman Sisters served as an incubator of dancing talent while championing desegregation in

---

9.   The Salomé dance craze marked a critical moment in the theatrical representation of female sexuality. Arriving in the U.S. from Europe around 1907, the dance enticed audiences with its high art pedigree, cooch-like choreography, scantily clad performers, grotesque depiction of sexual desire, and references to "deviant" sexual practices. Reformers argued that the dance would corrupt the young and called on officials to intervene but Salomania would not be stopped.

the theater for the rights of Black patrons and performers (DeFrantz 2002). During the 1920s, Alice Whitman—the youngest sister, known as the "Queen of Taps"—took under her wings female dancers like Jeni LeGon, one of the first African American women to establish a solo career in tap, and the only Black woman to dance with Robinson. Florence Mills, who starred in all Black musicals like Noble Sissle and Eubie Blake's *Shuffle Along* (1921), Lew Leslie's *Plantation Review* (1922) on Broadway, and *Blackbirds* (1926) at Harlem's Alhambra Theatre, inspired the growing popularity of tap. Beloved by audiences, Mills tragically died at age thirty-one post-surgery in 1927.

In the following decades, other women tappers emerged, but to be a Black woman tap dancer was to be inherently glamorous and broke. Cora LaRedd was one of the most noted soloists at the Cotton Club during the 1920s and 1930s. Recognized as a brilliant singer and dancer, LaRedd dazzled audiences as the club's leading song-and-dance diva. She also performed in a number of Broadway shows, including the Black musical, *Messin' Around* (1929) (Hill 2014). Lois Bright Miller was a teen performer with the Whitman Sisters. She married Dan Miller and performed as part of the Miller Brothers. She also appeared in the 1947 movie, *Hi-De-Ho* with Cab Calloway (Hill 2014). Edith "Baby Edwards" Hunt was a child star in the 1940s and partnered with Willie "Span" Joseph to form Spic and Span. She was the first Black dancer to perform on the all-White *Horn and Hardart Children's Hour* radio show and worked at the Apollo Theater alongside Lena Horne and Duke Ellington, among others. Mable Lee, a child prodigy from Georgia who moved to New York City in the 1940s and joined the chorus line at the Apollo Theater in Harlem, would become known as the "Queen of the Soundies." She appeared in over a hundred short musical films of the era (Trenka 2021). Ludie Jones, a member of the Lang Sisters, danced with Louis Armstrong and Fats Waller in the 1930s. After the group disbanded, Jones formed the group The Three Poms, which toured with Calloway's band. As one of the few successful Black female tappers during the 1930s and 1940s, Jones worked twenty years as a telephone operator before appearing in the Off-Broadway production of *Shades of Harlem* (1984) at age sixty-eight.

There were also a few Black female rhythm-tap dance teams, like Candi and Pepper and the Edwards Sisters. Candi and Pepper, consisting of Mildred "Candi" Thorne and Jewel "Pepper" Welch, danced throughout the 1930s. They were known for incorporating swinging rhythmic phrases and elements of flash or acrobatics. When Thorne retired in 1944, Welch teamed up with rhythm tap dancer Edwina "Salt" Evelyn. The pair performed together as Salt and Pepper throughout the country until 1954 (Willis 2016). The Edwards Sisters, Ruth and Louise, toured as an added attraction with big bands and stage revues during the 1930s and 1940s. They performed in the Duke Ellington musical short film, *Symphony in Swing* (1949), dancing to Ellington's composition, "Suddenly It Jumped" (Hill 2014). Unfortunately, these women tappers have rarely been acknowledged.

The 1930s was the era of the chorus girls. Because there was little solo work to be had, most Black women tap dancers could be found on chorus lines in theaters around the country. These women came from all over the country and all walks of life, and many had no formal training. They worked four to six shows a day, rehearsed, and learned new numbers every week. But not all of them were paid equally, and certainly not as much as White women. In 1940, when the Black women at the Apollo Theater requested a small raise and their demands were not met, they went on strike. It was a significant event not only in dance history, but also as the first strike initiated by African American performers. After one day of picketing, the women's demands were successfully met with better working conditions, and they received more money than they initially asked for (Hill 2014). They also became members of the American Guild of Variety Actors (AGVA) for Black and White performers nationwide. Chorus lines like those from the Apollo Theater and the Cotton Club helped elevate Black women tap dancers when they were not taken seriously. Aside from not receiving equal pay, they also had to grit their teeth when Black male tap stars told them that they were weak and lacked the strength to perform the rhythm-driven piston and acrobatic steps in the tap virtuoso's routine.

When the popularity of tap began to decline in the 1950s, it struggled to survive as an art form. Broadway changed its style to modern, and fewer movie musicals were produced. There were opportunities on television variety shows, nightclubs, and places like Las Vegas, but access was limited. By the 1970s, Black and White women began to reignite the genre and resurfaced the Black tap dancers from the past. For example, Brenda Bufalino, who trained under Honi Coles when she was a teenager, reconnected with Coles, and they began working together in the early 1970s. They were cofounders of the American Tap Dance Organization and toured with the Copasetics during the 1980s.

The rejuvenation of tap was also due in large part to the women who formed tap dance ensembles that helped keep tap alive. In an effort to court a younger audience, dance ensembles toured on the college circuit. They also revitalized the dormant careers of dozens of unrecognized older Black women around the country. Some of the very same women who went on strike at the Apollo Theater reunited and started the Silver Belles, a tap dance troupe, in 1986 (Benzing 2012). Meanwhile, a slow resurgence had begun in the late 1970s when successful Broadway shows like *Ain't Misbehavin'* (1978), *Eubie!* (1979), *Sophisticated Ladies* (1981), and *Black and Blue* (1989) prominently featured tap.

Gregory Hines was a major figure in the revitalization of tap dancing in the late twentieth century. Hines heavily influenced Savion Glover, who has been rightfully credited with "re-rhythmatizing" tap to make it more appealing to a new generation. This was reflected in many of his projects, especially *Bring In 'Da Noise, Bring In 'Da Funk* (1995), a Broadway musical that made tap dance history through Glover's incorporation of a rough, raw, hard-hitting style of tap dancing inspired by hip-hop culture. But it was Dianne Walker, often referred to as "America's First Lady of Tap," who was the true pioneer of its resurgence. Walker studied under the legendary Leon Collins. When the 1970s resurgence of tap dancing brought him out of retirement, Walker helped him establish a dance school in Boston. Collins made his professional debut in 1983 at Jacob's Pillow at the age of sixty-one, less than two years before he died. While holding a unique place in the tap community as a mentor, teacher, and confidante, Walker's thirty year career spanned Broadway, television, film, and international dance concerts (Hill 2014). Many tap dance artists consider her a transitional figure between the "forgotten Black mothers of tap"—LeGon, Miller, and Edwards—and a younger generation of dancers, such as award-winning tap dancer and choreographer Dormeshia, Robyn Watson, and Ayodele Casel, followed by a newer generation of tap artists like Frances Bradley, Josette Wiggan-Freund, and Star Dixon.

It was Black women like Walker and her TapDancin' Inc. of Boston, and the Silver Belles that paved the way for award-winning choreographer Chloe Arnold. She is the founder of Syncopated Ladies, who became known for their Prince and Beyoncé tributes. Dancer and director Deborah Mitchell founded the New Jersey Tap Dance Ensemble, which has become one of the greatest incubators of dancing talent. Ayodele Casel, an Afro-Puerto Rican tap dancer and choreographer, became the first woman to join Glover's Not Your Ordinary Tappers (NYOT) group, and performed with them for two years. Casel was named a 2019-2020 fellow at the Radcliffe Institute for Advanced Study at Harvard University, where she worked on *Diary of a Tap Dancer,* a theatrical work that focuses on the legacy of unnamed women in tap within a broader historical context. *Finally, Black women tap dancers are getting their due.*

Tap dance is built on a relationship between tradition and innovation. Born as a street form, passed orally and visually, and developed through the culture of stealing steps and cutting contests, tap continues to evolve from consolidated traditions to unexpected innovations in technique and aesthetic. By the late twentieth century, tap dance evolved into a concertized performance on the musical and concert hall stage. Its absorption of Latin American and Afro-Caribbean rhythms has furthered its rhythmic complexity, and its absorption of hip-hop has attracted a fierce and multiethnic new breed of female and male dancers who continue to challenge the dance form, making tap the most cutting-edge dance expression in America today.

In no small measure could this have happened without the participation of Black women. When they saw that their performances and techniques were not taken seriously, they kept tapping. When tap dance was dying, they helped bring tap into the concert dance world and elevated it into an art form. From the old masters of tap, they learned the techniques and historical pieces and helped codify the dance. They created national tap festivals and conferences with tap exchanges among venerated teachers, performers, and historians, which begot a tap dance community. Had they not felt driven to rebel, tap dancing may have never made a comeback.

Black women tap dancers dazzle. They create rhythm with their feet entwined with emotion, weaving supple movements with an ongoing percussive beat. *They are the true ambassadors of tap.*

◆ ◆ ◆

TRADITIONAL AFRICAN-BASED DANCING has been the bedrock of most African American communities for quite some time. Beginning in the late 1960s, organizations took advantage of funding from President Johnson's Great Society[10] and hosted dozens of cultural programs, including free dance classes and performances in their communities. I was a direct beneficiary of these programs and took dance classes in Corona, New York, at the League For Better Community Life (also known as BCL).

I remember the drummers working in concert with our teacher, Mr. Alexander, while he taught us moves during class with a room full of observers. Eager to dance, we did not know where the African steps came from nor what they represented, and we did not care. We were too busy rocking our afros, cornrows, and dashikis, entranced by the drums and the heat, and we always left the class drenched in sweat, embracing our Black culture. Interestingly, people do not generally think of traditional African dance in the same way they think of modern, ballet or tap, due to the perceptual distortion of African imagery and an underappreciation of African values (Mills 1997). Defining traditional African dance as performed in the U.S. is a daunting task, so what follows below is a mere snapshot of its history highlighting Black women dancers, choreographers, and scholars.

Traditional African dance is defined by its relationship between rhythmic musical sound and purposeful, expressive movement that symbolizes the full range of the human spirit. It communicates to performers and observers alike, either independently or interdependently, in a nonverbal, multi-channeled manner. The genesis of traditional African dance in America is from African everyday life. Although each tribe has distinct cultures and languages, they share cultural traditions through metaphorical statements expressed in music and dance. Beginning with their voyage to America, the Africans were forced to dance in bondage and under the lash. They wore shackles and danced in a ring to the beat of a drum, kettle, or a slab of wood. There was no joy or celebration in the dance; they answered to the lash because slave owners wanted their stock in good condition. When the Africans arrived at plantations, their final

10. Philip Kennicott, "The Great Society at 50: Lyndon B. Johnson's cultural vision mirrored his domestic one." *The Washington Post,* May 20, 2014. https://www.washingtonpost.com/lifestyle/style/50-years-later-assessing-lyndon-b-johnsons-legislative-legacy-and-cultural-vision/2014/05/20/726ee3a2-dd35-11e3-8009-71de85b9c527_story.html.

destination, the concept of Black dance would grow—not only from the need or desire to perform, but also from the natural aspiration to maintain a cultural connection to their home and community.

The drum is the most important form of accompaniment for African dance and the primary method of creating auditory rhythms. Although slave owners banned drumming, it did little to discourage Africans from creating other forms of percussion to support the customs they developed in the New World. As the effects of slavery began to weaken African culture, inter-African cultures emerged from different ethnic groups and began to merge with European dance styles. This macro-sociological dynamic offered a background to contemporary America's most vibrant folk cultural and entertainment forms. In the process, Black people managed to regain, on their terms, the joy of dance (Hazzard-Gordon 1998).

The history of traditional African dance as a concert art began during the early twentieth century, when several African dancers such as Efrom Odok, Momudu Johnson, and Asadata Dafora immigrated to New York, a cultural cross-roads for African immigrants. There, they imported the latest styles of African dance to the American studio and concert halls. While Odok has taken credit as the first to present African concert dance in the U.S., it is Dafora who had a profound effect on the form (Heard and Mussa 2002).

Dafora was a Sierra Leonean multidisciplinary artist who is best remembered as one of the pioneers of African dance in America during the 1930s. He displayed a genius for bringing authentic representations of African art and culture, including the polyrhythmic power of drummers, to the Western proscenium stage.[11] In one of his earliest documented concerts, performed in 1934 at the Little Theater of the Harlem YMCA, Dafora debuted *Kykunkor (The Witch Woman),* a musical drama production using authentic African music and dance. His diasporic concert would elevate dance movement that communicated African culture's rich history, combated negative stereotypes, and presented political and social commentary on the struggles of the African diasporic people.

He also succeeded in introducing audiences to a West African dance that was distinguishable from European culture. The flowing quality of African dance was new to the American public. For example, there is a set way to do a pirouette in ballet (spinning on one foot), but the African dancer is unconcerned with the exact position of her head or arms in a turn. She is more interested in how the movement feels than how it looks, and her audience judges her performance on how profoundly her body reveals the flow of her movements. These movements include a bent-kneed, grounded movement that privileges the body giving in to gravity, the isolated articulation of different body parts—particularly the pelvis and the hips—and the symbiotic percussive interplay between dancers

---

11. Polyrhythmic is two or more conflicting rhythms being played simultaneously. Dancers may synchronize the movements of different body parts to different rhythms or alternate fluidly between rhythms.

and drummers. Dafora's work caught the attention of the Black dance community and offered a new positive Black identity rooted in ancient, pre-colonial traditions, which also connected to the Harlem Renaissance and the Négritude movements of that era. However, while most people think of Black men when it comes to traditional African dance, there were quite a few women who played a pivotal role in developing the art form as well.

One of the earliest African traditionalists was Ismay Andrews, who began her career as a stage actor in New York City and appeared in a couple of films. After Andrews studied dance under Dafora, she began teaching African dance at the Abyssinian Baptist Church in Harlem in 1934, becoming one of the earliest teachers of African dance in the U.S. She also taught at Mother African Methodist Episcopal Zion Church, a primary center of African American culture in New York City. Her students included Chief Bey, Pearl Primus, Coleridge-Taylor Perkinson, Alice Dinizulu, and Alexandreena Dixon. Andrews never traveled to Africa but learned African traditions by researching in public libraries and institutions. In the 1940s, she focused on the dances of East Africa. She founded and directed a dance company known as the Swa-Hili Dancers, and choreographed reconstructed East African dances performed in cabarets, at the Stage Door Canteen, and for the United Service Organizations (USO) during World War II.

By the 1940s, Katherine Dunham and Pearl Primus, who studied under Dafora, began to familiarize Americans with African dance. Many of Dunham's works revolved around African-derived dances of Blacks in other parts of the world, such as the West Indies and South America. Following Dunham's lead, Primus also developed an overarching interest in the cultural connections between dance and the lives of the descendants of the enslaved. She drew upon the cultures of the southern region of the U.S., Africa, and the West Indies. These women pioneered the notion that there could be an African American choreography different from contemporary Euro-American choreographers.

White academics set out to create and teach culturally-appropriate African dance curricula throughout the years, but these courses were devoid of any true awareness of Africa. Instead, many of them had an appetite for dance exoticism and disregarded the basic tenet of the form. As a result, most of the research they conducted was devoted to an analysis based on prevailing attitudes and associated descriptions of African dance tempered by ethnocentric bias and racism (Mills 1997). To obtain a more objective understanding of traditional African dance, a new wave of African American scholars emerged who advocated for detailed fieldwork, anthropological theory, and an appreciation of the wider social context of dance and musical productions and performances. Beginning in the 1950s, African and African American scholars became major contributors to African historiography. This notable shift was exemplified during the Black Power Movement of the 1960s, which became a launching pad for the Black Arts Movement that further fueled the academic study of African diasporic dance. African

American dancers, choreographers and scholars traveled to Africa, the Caribbean, and South America, and established the groundwork necessary to bring African, African American, and Afro-Caribbean traditions into their classrooms and dance companies, and introduced them to the public. In time, African-based dance flourished regionally, nationally, and internationally, with performances at universities and colleges across the U.S. (Diouf, Welsh, and Daniel 2019).

By the 1980s, many Black choreographers created works that combined traditional African dance, African diasporan dances, and African American vernacular movement expressions. Some dancers worked harder than others to retain the authenticity of traditional African dances, making conscious, educated choices about the specific movement styles that promote Black aesthetics and African centeredness. African-based performers, such as Chief Bey, Charles Moore, Obara Wali Rahman, Olukose Wiles, and Ladji Camara, helped bring traditional African movement and music to the forefront of the African American performance scene.

Chuck Davis, a renowned dancer and choreographer followed Dafora by becoming widely regarded as America's foremost master of African dance. In 1978, Davis, in conjunction with the Brooklyn Academy of Music (BAM), held the first DanceAfrica, which included Davis, Arthur Hall, Charles Moore, Dinizulu, and the International Afrikan American Ballet. Now an annual Memorial Day weekend celebration, DanceAfrica includes performances by some of the top traditional African dance companies, including visiting guest companies from Africa, and features educational events and an African Bazaar. These dancers, musicians, and scholars, both as immigrants from Africa and of African descent, created an aesthetic of traditional African dance that is reminiscent of various cultures all over Africa.

A number of U.S. dance companies began to blend traditional African and modern dance in their repertoire. They include PHILADANCO in Philadelphia, Step Afrika! in Washington, D.C., and Forces of Nature Dance Theatre Company in New York, to name a few. They provide a fresh and unique approach that transcends notions of traditional, contemporary, and vernacular dance styles. The work of these and other companies would not have been possible without their deep engagement with several diaspora pioneer percussionists—Kimati Dinizula, Babatunde Olatunji, Olukose Wiles—who helped establish the performative style of traditional African dance.

But while most African dance teachers were men, there were also quite a few women who studied and taught African dance and founded dance companies and organizations that support the art form. Dancer and choreographer Ferne Yangyeitie Caulker, born in Sierra Leone, founded the Ko-Thi Dance Company in 1969. Caulker studied with the National Dance Company of Ghana at the University of Ghana, Legon, then returned to the U.S. She began teaching at the University of Wisconsin-Milwaukee in 1971 and introduced courses in African,

Caribbean and African American dance techniques and history. Caulker also nurtured veteran choreographers, dancers, and musicians who now contribute to the repertoire through her dance company. Over the past thirty years, she has developed a cadre of commissioned works by master dancers and musicians throughout the African Diaspora. In 1995, Caulker received a Fulbright Research Fellowship, which allowed her to study in Tanzania, East Africa, for three months. While doing her research, she also taught at the University of Dar es Salaam, lectured children in the Arusha United African American Cultural Center and assisted a UWASA cultural group. She retired from the university as Professor Emerita in 2016.

Olabamidele (Dele) Hart-Husbands cofounded Forces of Nature in 1981. The company has been critically acclaimed for presenting a visceral, thought-provoking, and creatively brilliant repertoire. Forces of Nature utilizes a unique blend of contemporary modern dance, traditional West African dance, ballet, house, and hip-hop forms, and live and recorded music and martial arts. The company has performed and toured widely throughout the U.S., making annual appearances at Aaron Davis Hall, the Apollo Theater in Harlem, and abroad. Forces of Nature has been presented by the Brooklyn Academy of Music's DanceAfrica Festival, the American Dance Festival, and the International Association of Blacks in Dance (IABD) conference, among many other venues.

Hart-Husbands holds degrees from Hampton University, Bowling Green State University, and the University of Calabar, West Africa. Husbands has taught at The Ailey School, the Ruth Williams Dance Foundation, and the department of African and Caribbean Literature at Hunter College Community Works, among others. Besides performing with the Forces of Nature, Hart-Husbands has performed with companies such as Weusi Kuumba African Dance Ensemble, the African Heritage Dancers and Drummers, Chuck Davis Dance Company, and the University of Calabar Dancers of Nigeria. Hart-Husbands has directed and managed numerous dance and theater companies, including Grambling State University in Louisiana, the Mojo Players Theater Group in Bowling Green, Ohio, and the Department of Performing Arts, University of Calabar, in Nigeria.

In 1993, Karen Love founded Umoja Dance Company, a New Jersey-based multicultural company. "Umoja," the Kiswahili word for unity, performs a fusion of contemporary modern and West African dance and performs extensively in the New York and New Jersey areas. In 2006, Love created the Wofabe African Dance and Drum Festival, which provides African dance and drum classes, presents panel discussions, and an evening dance concert. The festival has been held at Newark Arts High School, Science Park High School, Newark Symphony Hall, and the New Jersey Performing Arts Center (NJPAC).

Love earned her MFA from New York University Tisch School of the Arts and her BFA from Montclair State University, where she was awarded the 1992 Excellence in Choreography Award and the 1993 Senior Award. She has studied

West African dance and culture by traveling to Guinea, West Africa, Mexico, and Bermuda under the tutelage of Bangoura. She also traveled to Morocco, Senegal, and the Gambia, West Africa under the direction of Chuck Davis. Her choreography has been commissioned and presented at several venues, including the University of Illinois Urbana-Champaign, Aaron Davis Hall, Bates Dance Festival, Duke University, and New York University. Love is currently the director of the dance department at Hillside High School and the director of the After School Dance Program for Hillside Public Schools District in New Jersey.

The newer and younger women of this generation are weaving together traditional African dance and drumming by adding more stage flair and showmanship to their repertoire. In 2003, Tiffany Knighten-Buddington founded Nkiruka Drum and Dance Ensemble in New Orleans. "Nkiruka" is an Igbo name derived from the country of Nigeria in West Africa, meaning "the best is yet to come" and "good fortune." The company consists of seasoned dancers from diverse backgrounds and performs traditional and modern styles. Knighten-Buddington has over thirty-six years of experience in dance, acting, and professional performances. She has received formal training in numerous dance forms and studied under master African dance teachers Marie Basse-Wiles, Mouminatou Camara, and Youssouf Koumbassa. Knighten-Buddington has been a principal dancer in many dance companies and teams, notably Khadija's School of Dance, Southern University's Dancing Dolls, the Young African American Dance Ensemble, N'kafu Traditional African Dance Company, and Casa Samba. She has served as an African dance teacher for Young Audiences since 2013, and coaches the dance team at West Jefferson High School in La Jolie Rouge.

Tosha "Ayo" Alston founded Ayodele Drum and Dance in 2009, a performance training organization based in Chicago created for women to affirm their self-confidence and strength. Ayodele's performances are based on traditional African cultures and fused with contemporary dance styles. Alston studied under Youssouf Koumbassa, Mouminatou Camara, Chuck Davis, Jawole Jo Willa Zollar, and Rosangela Silvestre. She is an adjunct professor at Columbia College Chicago and serves on the dance faculty at Chicago High School of the Arts. She also developed drum and dance programs at Jones College Prep and Walter Payton College Prep, where Ayodele has trained dancers to teach and gain professional artistic skills and experience.

Throughout her career, Alston has taught, choreographed, and performed at schools and universities locally and nationally, as well as in African and Brazilian countries. She performs as an independent artist and as a member of other companies and organizations, such as Dance Africa, Drum Cafe West, Le Bagatae Company of Guinea, Les Ballets Africans, and Muntu Dance Theatre.

Besides creating, teaching, and performing traditional African dance, several Black woman scholars and dance specialists have laid a groundwork to formally define characteristics common to African dances and the African diaspora, including Dolores K. Cayou, Brenda Dixon Gottschild, Katrina Hazzard-Donaldson, Jaqui Malone, and Kariamu Welsh Asante. They present traditional African dance in creative ways that also authenticate Black women's bodies. These and many other Black women dancers and choreographers have become dedicated to freeing Black women's bodies from a legacy of physical and mental enslavement, social restrictions, sexism, and gender biases. In doing so, they are educating more audiences on the beauty of the Africanist culture through the eyes of African and African American women in the art of dance.

Dancing is a bridge to humanity. Traditional African dance is an expression of that and more—a physical, psychological, and spiritual state of being that enables people to give meaning and context to their greatest joys, hopes, frustrations, fears, or sorrows, and contribute to a sense of wholeness (Snipe 1998). While traditional African dance may not be as popular as other dance styles, it remains our hide-in-plain sight defense against images that feed negative stereotypes. Through African dance, we can tap into our cultural roots and enjoy the essence of who we are as African Americans.

◆ ◆ ◆

BODY TYPING IN DANCE, a coded language that denotes certain body types as "unfit for dance," has permeated the dance world for much of the twentieth and twenty-first centuries. The trouble began for Black women when they made forays into the ballet world. The attacks did not stop at their dark skin; they also had to deal with their body shape and muscularity, which has been hypersexualized and fetishized for centuries. Perhaps more importantly, many people consider ballet to be an art form that reflects the beauty and purity of whiteness, and white swan symbolism. In other words, *there can only be White swans.*

Those of us outside the world of ballet tend to think of it as an ancient art form. But like so many venerable and beautiful things, ballet has been co-opted from its original art form. In the ballet of the French aristocracy, different body types were assigned to different character types—tall people played nobles, shorter people played comic roles—and the choreography always emphasized the king's superiority over the court.

After the French Revolution, those norms changed, and ballet as we know it today derived from a radical reaction against its original ideals. By the nineteenth century, ballet had spread from France to the world stage and grew as a technique in Europe and Russia. During this time, the "cult of true womanhood" surfaced, an ideology that defined women as pillars of virtue who represented the values of piety, purity, submissiveness, and domesticity. It was a stereotype that collided with the "cult of the ballerina," an ethereal being characterized by rounded arms and a forward tilt in the upper body. This gave the woman a flowery, willowy look. Leg movements became more elaborate due to the new tutu length and rising standards of technical proficiency. The plots of many ballets were dominated by these spirit women—sylphs, wilis, and ghosts—who bewitched the hearts and senses of mortal men and made it impossible for them to live happily in the real world. Marie Taglioni became the prototypical Romantic ballerina who epitomized this cult. However, even as ballet has evolved, the cult of the ballerina has remained steadfast in the minds of both dancers and balletomanes, along with the prevailing imagery of the disempowered woman, and the romanticization of female subjugation as a recurring trope (Kelly 2012).

America's racial segregation has helped to feed into this narrative and prevent people of color from accessing elite ballet training and participating in White ballet institutions (Angyal 2021). This was further compounded by George Balanchine, the artistic director of the New York City Ballet, who projected a prepubescent body image on his dancers: a lily-White physique that is lean, long, small, and thin. He liked hyperextension and strength that was mechanical yet "lithe." White women were willing to give up their health and sanity to meet the unrealistic demands of the art form. This ideology is often blamed for the destructive eating disorders that plague the dance world and further alienated many Black women from ballet.

Since Balanchine's era, ballet companies around the world, admittedly some quicker than others, have begun to heed the call for change. Although there has been some progress regarding information about the health risks of severe dieting, artistic directors having "fat chats" to tell dancers to slim down still remains routine. Fortunately, there have been others who are breaking the mold by declaring themselves more open to different body types, including Black ballerinas.

All of this stems off of the Western beauty standard obsessed with whiteness—a standard that Black women will never be able to attain. This leaves open the troubling reality that a Black dancer's unchangeable "defect" is, in fact, her blackness, no matter her body type. Something is very wrong when someone tells you your body is inappropriate for dance, and your feet are wrong for *en pointe*. It is difficult to express what it is like to be told as a young girl that you will never be the swan in pink tights and a white tutu, but this is a reality many Black girls have faced, even when considering ballet as a profession.

I was that Black girl. I too loved dance. I took dance classes at the neighborhood community center during the 1960s, and like most girls my age, I considered a career in dance. I remember my mother taking us to an open house at the Dance Theatre of Harlem in the early 1970s. I was a tween when the school opened. I remember the open brick walls. I remember squeezing into the space and sitting on folding chairs, electricity and anticipation buzzing in the room, as I watched instructors present their students to the audience. I saw girls wearing brown tights that matched the color of their skin. As a little girl, I loved all things pink, so the idea of brown tights was revolutionary to me.

After the recital, my mother told me that if I wanted to take dance seriously, she would figure out a way for me to commute from Queens to attend classes at the Dance Theatre of Harlem. When my mother took us to dance recitals and performances, I did not see race, income, social hierarchies, cultural differences, and other factors that conspired to exclude people of color from such artistic pursuits. In fact, it was only much later that I realized the "option" my mother offered me was less of an option and more of a necessity because there were few places for little Black girls to learn ballet and be taken seriously.

Back in Queens, my ballet teacher told me I was too tall and too curvy to go *en pointe*. I eventually switched to modern dance and performed in local dance recitals up to my early twenties, but I was crushed. To this day, I still love dance, especially ballet, but the idea that my Black female body was not beautiful enough to meet the strict White standards lingers to this day. Eventually, I realized I lacked the passion to push forward. Giving up was easy to do, which is why the Black women who unrelentingly pursued ballet and became formidable in their own right are so impressive. For them, *giving up was never an option.*

These brave Black women have run up against preconceived notions held by teachers, company directors, competition judges, and choreographers regarding what kind of dance they are best suited for. They are told that they have an abundance of explosive strength, but a dearth of grace and delicacy, thus lacking the elegance the art form demands. Besides being too dark, they are often told they are too muscular to dance the girlish, gamine roles that are the staple of white ballets[12] such as *Giselle, Swan Lake, La Bayadère,* and *La Sylphide,* which exemplify both the beginning and the zenith of the art. Although the white ballets were not designed to exclude Black women, over time, this is what has happened. Other factors contributed to ballet's lack of diversity, including few role models for aspiring dancers to emulate, economic inequality—ballet training is notoriously expensive—and a failure on the part of schools and companies to provide support for young dancers of color as they endure the uphill road to professional success. *The Black female body has not been affirmed as a beautiful expression of art in the world of ballet.*

In the beginning, there were only a handful of Black ballet schools, primarily located in big cities like New York, Atlanta, Philadelphia, and Washington, D.C. Ella Gordon created one of the first African American dance schools that exposed the Black community to ballet. In 1919, she opened Gordon's School in the Lafayette Building of Dance in Harlem and taught ballet and tap. Gordon trained individuals who then continued the tradition of training dancers in ballet and other genres, including students Ruth Williams and Henry LeTang.

---

12. "White ballets" also known as "ballets blanc" are so named not because of race, but because the storyline is populated by ghosts, dryads, naiads, enchanted maidens, fairies, or other supernatural creatures and spirits, wearing ashen costumes illuminated in a pale white glow.

During the 1920s, things began to heat up. Essie Marie Dorsey was a fair-skinned Black woman from Greensboro, North Carolina, who often passed as White or Latina to circumvent racial boundaries. This enabled her to study dance with Ruth St. Denis and Ted Shawn at the Billy Pierce Studio. She took private ballet classes with Michel Fokine and William Dollar and studied Spanish dance with Angel Cansino. When Dorsey was unable to pursue a ballet career, she taught ballet and Spanish dance. In 1926, she opened her first studio in her hometown of Philadelphia and eventually expanded her classes to include tap, ballroom dance, and acrobatics. By doing so, Dorsey created a legacy that would contribute tremendously to the African American ballet world, teaching students such as Sydney Gibson King, Marion Cuyjet, and Joan Myers Brown.

Similarly, Marion Cuyjet's fair-skinned complexion allowed her to enroll at the Philadelphia Ballet Company, which did not admit Black students. She studied and performed there until her identity was exposed. Sydney Gibson King, born in Kingston, Jamaica, grew up in Southwest Philadelphia, where her family moved when she was two years old. She began studying ballet under Dorsey's tutelage from the age of seven until she was twenty-one and danced in innumerable community performances. In 1946, Cuyjet and fellow student King opened The Sydney-Marion School of Dance at Dorsey's former location. By 1948, King and Cuyjet dissolved their partnership due to differences in management styles (Dixon 2011). King renamed the school the Sydney School of Dance, and Cuyjet opened the Judimar School of Dance, named after herself and her daughter Judy, in Philadelphia's City Center. Cuyjet's school focused on ballet. On the other hand, King did not think ballet was a practical goal, so the Sydney School offered a more diversified dance curriculum.

Both schools trained hundreds of Black children, with quite a few receiving national and international recognition. Some of Judimar's former students include Judith Jamison, Donna Lowe Warren, Delores Brown Abelson, Tamara Guillebeaux, and China White. In 1971, due to family obligations and failing health, Cuyjet closed Judimar. For more than six decades, and well into the twenty-first century, the Sydney School remained open. Former students include Joan Myers Brown, Billy Wilson, Betsy Ann Dickerson, Lola Falana, and Arthur Hall.

Mabel Jones Freeman was introduced to ballet by her high school physical education teacher in Columbus, Ohio. She then trained privately under Veronine Vestoff, earning a certificate in ballet, and went to Europe to continue to study with Vestoff's brother, Genrich. While there, she cultivated her choreography and artistic skills. When Freeman's finances were depleted, she returned to Columbus and began teaching ballet and creative modern dance. She achieved overwhelming success, but Freeman sought a broader field to work in and relocated to Washington, D.C. (Akinleye 2021).

Around 1926, Freeman founded the Studio for Classical Dancing to introduce classical ballet to promising young black dancers in the city. Freeman also taught at the D.C. Department of Recreation and at public schools, and gave solo performances at venues like Bennett College and Howard University. Over the years, Freeman produced about seventy productions throughout the city featuring many of her advanced students. By the 1940s, Freeman began an association with the Washington Opera Chorus, a chapter of the National Negro Opera Company, and presented concerts with her students. Freeman died around 1967, but her achievements of introducing classical ballet to the general black populace and dance to the public schools was unequalled (Terry 1982). Her former students include Bernice Hammond, Juanita Jones Goodloe, Therrell C. Smith, and Doris Patterson.

Ruth Williams, born and raised in Harlem, began studying dance at the age of four when she studied tap with Ella Gordon. As a child, she performed in an early rendition of *Porgy and Bess,* and toured with her brother in the U.S. and Europe. Williams studied with Eugene Van Grona and hoped to become part of the American Negro Ballet, but her mother forbade her to join the company. She continued to study dance with noted choreographers Syvilla Fort, Charles Moore, Destine, Ajaibo Walrond, Mona Schurman and Charles Weidman. In 1948, she opened the Ruth Williams Dance School in Harlem. After receiving a degree in science from Hunter College, Williams earned a master's in early childhood education from New York University, and successfully completed post-graduate work at Columbia University in administration and supervision. As she pursued her career at New York's Health Department, she continued to dance and teach hundreds of children in her community. When Williams' school closed its doors in 2015, it had recently celebrated its sixty-sixth anniversary.

During her career, Katherine Dunham created and sustained her own dance schools and companies, never giving up when she faced obstacles. In 1930, Dunham formed the Ballet Nègre in Chicago, one of the first Black ballet companies in America. It debuted in 1931, and while well-received, no engagements followed and the group disbanded. By 1933, Dunham gave up on developing ballet companies altogether and opened her first school, the Negro Dance Group in Chicago, which was later renamed the Katherine Dunham and Dance Company. Over the years, her company would come to be known by various names. Dunham disbanded the company in 1960, but old students would still come together to dance with her for special events.

She opened the Dunham School of Dance and Theatre in New York in 1944, which offered ballet classes. The school was then renamed the Katherine Dunham School of Arts and Research, and added other styles of dance, educational components, and cultural studies to the program. Dance notables such as Todd Bolender, Karel Shook, José Limón, and Marie Bryant taught at the Dunham School, and it continued to operate until 1957. Former students include Arthur Mitchell, James Dean, Peter Gennaro, Marlon Brando, Chita Rivera, Eartha Kitt, and José Ferrer.

Therrell C. Smith, born and raised in Washington, D.C., began ballet studies at age eight with Mabel Jones Freeman. As a teen, she choreographed and danced in school shows and at summer camps. After graduating from Fisk University with a degree in sociology, Smith spent summers at the Ballet Arts School at Carnegie Hall in New York. Later, she studied with Russian prima ballerina Mathilde Kschessinska in Paris. Smith returned to Washington, D.C. in 1948 and opened her School of Dance, where she trained girls from Black middle class families for nearly seventy years. Beginning in the 1970s, she also taught ballet in select D.C. public elementary schools to children who would not otherwise have had access to. Beyond ballet, Smith imparted to her students manners and grace, with the understanding that, while most of them would not become professional dancers, the discipline would serve them well as lawyers, doctors, teachers, and parents. Her former students include Virginia Johnson and Hazel O'Leary.

Unfortunately, many of the early Black dance schools were known to discriminate using the brown paper bag test[13] to discourage dark-skinned students from signing up for classes or fully participating in recitals. Additionally, dance students were primarily made up of middle- to upper middle class families who could afford to pay for classes, leaving many working class families out in the cold. Perhaps this is why many of the dance school owners taught at public schools and gave free lessons at public venues so that all children could be exposed to dance. In some cases, those who were exceptionally talented were allowed to join private studios on a limited basis (Terry 1982).

Having studied with Dorsey and the Sydney School, Joan Myers Brown furthered her studies with Syvilla Fort, Karel Shook at the Katherine Dunham School in New York, and Antony Tudor, who left New York to teach in Philadelphia. He put Brown in a production of *Les Sylphides,* which caused quite a stir. But when Tudor returned to New York, Brown found that she had to turn elsewhere to continue dancing. She toured as a jazz dancer with Cab Calloway, Sammy Davis Jr., and Pearl Bailey, and then was the lead dancer and choreographer with *Smart Affairs,* Larry Steele's Atlantic City revue, for six years. First and foremost a ballet dancer, Brown returned to Philadelphia and, in 1960, founded the Philadelphia School of Dance and Arts. In 1970, she founded the Philadelphia Dance Company (PHILADANCO), and having served as the artistic and executive director since its inception, she retired in 2020 and is now the artistic adviser of the company.

Claire Helen Haywood and Doris Jones founded the Jones-Haywood School of Ballet in 1941. Haywood was born in Atlanta. She earned a BA in English at

13. The brown paper bag test is a term used to describe a colorist discriminatory practice within the African American community, in which an individual's skin tone was compared to the color of a brown paper bag. If an individual's complexion was darker than the paper bag, they were barred access to many African American social institutions such as sororities, fraternities, and churches. While the brown paper bag test itself has faded into history, colorism has persisted in the African American community, albeit in a more subtle and insidious form.

Spelman College in 1934, an MA from Howard University in 1936, and a PhD at Catholic University in 1938. Jones established a ballet school in Boston in 1933. Later, she moved to Washington, D.C. to open a dance school with Haywood. To give their students a chance to perform in their hometown, Jones and Haywood founded the racially integrated Capitol Ballet Company in 1961, which Jones directed until it closed in 1989 due to financial challenges. In 1976, they completed *Artists of the Dance,* an hour-long documentary on their life and work. Haywood died in 1978.

In 1980, Jones formed the Jones-Haywood Youth Dancers to broaden performance opportunities for young dancers. Throughout the years, Jones occasionally directed the D.C. Public Schools Dance Program as well. She died in 2006. The school, now known as the Jones-Haywood School of Dance, is still in operation under the direction of Sandra Fortune-Green, who began her dance training at the school at the age of ten. In 1973, she became the first Black woman to compete in the International Ballet Competition and was Capitol Ballet Company's prima ballerina. Former students include Chita Rivera, Hinton Battle, Renee Robinson, and Hope Clarke.

Debbie Allen, best known as a director, producer, choreographer, actress, singer, and author, initially embarked on her career as a ballerina. Allen began studying dance at age five and eventually studied privately with a former dancer from the Ballets Russes. When Allen's family relocated to Mexico City, she danced with the Ballet Nacional de Mexico. After initially being denied admission because of her race, she reauditioned for the Houston Foundation for Ballet in 1964 and was admitted on a full scholarship, becoming the company's first Black dancer. At sixteen, she auditioned for the North Carolina School of the Arts but was rejected because her body was "unsuited" for ballet. This stinging rebuke changed Allen's trajectory; she attended Howard University and focused on acting, establishing an illustrious career in television and film. Allen opened the Debbie Allen Dance Academy in 2001, following in the footsteps of the Black women before her who, unable to fulfill their dreams, passed on lessons in the form of dance to the next generation instead.

With all these great teachers and professionally trained students, the problem remained: where would a Black ballet dancer perform once trained? By the mid-1940s, ballet was beginning to enjoy a great surge of popularity and stature in the U.S. The prominence of ballet in America was being firmly established by New York City Ballet, Ballet Theatre (renamed American Ballet Theatre), and the Ballet Russe de Monte Carlo in the 1950s. Considered the top companies in the country, all of them were based in New York City. Ballet was no longer seen as stuffy, old-fashioned, and elite; it represented a fresh artistic approach that found its way into Broadway musicals such as *Oklahoma!* (1940), *Fancy Free* (1944), and *On The Town* (1944) (Das 2017).

Meanwhile, now and then, a pattern emerged. An actual ballet company would spring up to offer opportunities for aspiring Black dancers, only to later close because they lacked adequate funding. The American Negro Ballet (also known as the Von Grona Ballet) was formed in 1934 by Eugene Von Grona, a German immigrant. Originally comprised of thirty African American jazz dancers, the company focused on serious modern dance. It debuted in 1937 in Harlem and lasted only six months. Joseph Rickard, a former member of the Ballet Russe de Monte Carlo, established the First Negro Classical Ballet (also known as the Hollywood Negro Ballet) in 1947. Although it was not the first Black ballet company, it may have been the first to have its women dance *en pointe* (DeFrantz 2002). After spending several years training his dancers in classical Russian ballet and performing multiple times for sizable audiences, the company disbanded in 1959. During its ten year run, the company played a crucial role in advancing African Americans in ballet.

The Negro Dance Theatre, an all-male repertory company that mixed ballet with modern and "primitive dance," was founded by Englishman Aubrey Hitchins in New York City in 1953. Audience members were not used to seeing Black men touch and lean into one another on stage. The company had to tackle homophobia and heterosexism, even though it was not a gay company. The company disbanded in the mid-1960s. In 1954, the New York Negro Ballet was founded by Edward Flemyng. Black ballet dancer Thelma Hill served as Flemyng's assistant and later codirector for the company. They toured with great success in the United Kingdom, with soloist Delores Brown Abelson dancing the ultra classical *The Sleeping Beauty* in the pas de deux, "Bluebird," with Bernard Johnson. However, when the company's benefactor, Lucy Thorndike, died, it ceased operation in 1957 (DeFrantz 2002). In 1958, Hill, along with a group of top New York dancers including Alvin Ailey, helped form a fledgling dance troupe that would eventually become the Alvin Ailey American Dance Theater in 1960.

Some Black ballerinas had managed, on a few occasions, to hurdle ballet's seemingly insurmountable barriers and were able to perform as guest artists with White companies. Dating back to the 1930s, a handful of White ballet teachers such as Antony Tudor, William Dollar, and Carmelita Maracci bucked convention and taught African American students in regular classes at their studios, in private classes, or as guest teachers at Black ballet schools. Maria Swoboda taught Raven Wilkinson before she joined the Ballet Russe de Monte Carlo in 1956. In the 1950s, members of the New York Negro Ballet Company studied with the former Bolshoi dancer Maria Navelska.

In the 1940s, The School of American Ballet (SAB) opened its doors to Betty Nichols, one of its first Black students. She was also a member of Ballet Society, a nonprofit educational institution founded in 1946 by Lincoln Kirstein and George Balanchine. Nichols toured with Balanchine in Europe before the company was established as New York City Ballet. During the 1950s, Louis Johnson, Delores Brown Abelson, Sylvester Campbell, John Jones, and Arthur Mitchell studied at SAB, but only Mitchell was invited by Balanchine to join the

New York City Ballet in 1956, becoming the company's first African American male dancer. He danced with them for fifteen years. Balanchine's initial plans for diversity were never realized, partly because societal forces opposed the idea of a fully-integrated ballet company. Since the ballet companies remained largely segregated, some Black dancers left the U.S. to join companies in Europe, where the racial climate was more hospitable.

Meanwhile, the number of Black ballerinas in American companies grew painfully slow. On this very short list, Frances Taylor Davis (Miles Davis' wife) was the first Black dancer to perform with the Paris Opera Ballet in 1948. Janet Collins made history as the first and only Black dancer to be promoted to prima ballerina status at the Metropolitan Opera in 1951. Her cousin, Carmen de Laval-lade, would dance lead roles with the Metropolitan Opera, Alvin Ailey American Dance Theater, and American Ballet Theatre (ABT). In 1955, Raven Wilkinson became the first Black ballerina to join the Ballet Russe de Monte Carlo, but had to pass for White while touring the South. She eventually left the company for the Dutch National Ballet. Donna Lowe Warren joined the Philadelphia Grand Opera in 1958 because she studied under its ballet master, Thomas Cannon, and he offered her a contract. Warren, who was light-skinned enough to pass for White, performed with the Opera until 1971. Sara Yarborough danced with the short-lived Harkness Ballet and the Alvin Ailey American Dance Theater throughout most of the 1970s. Even though their skin color initially disqualified them from what was considered a White art form, they nevertheless pursued their careers.

It was Arthur Mitchell who successfully challenged the myth that Black dancers were unsuited for ballet. In 1968, shortly after Martin Luther King Jr.'s assassination, Mitchell left the New York City Ballet and founded the Dance Theatre of Harlem (DTH) with noted teacher Karel Shook. He believed in the power of education to help Black children develop their potential, and used his company as a training base to help them become whatever they wanted to be through dance. DTH performed to great acclaim all over the world, with a reper-tory that included works by major twentieth-century choreographers, including Michel Fokine, Bronislava Nijinska, Balanchine, and Jerome Robbins. Mitchell also commissioned works, some of which explored the origins of Black dance.

In the meantime, Black ballerinas kept pushing forward. Virginia Johnson, a founding member and soloist of DTH, joined the Oakland Ballet company and rose to soloist and principal dancer. In 2009, Johnson returned to DTH as the company's artistic director. Llanchie Stevenson (Aminah L. Ahmad), a founding member and principal dancer at DTH, was the first Black dancer at Radio City Music Hall Ballet Company and later at the National Ballet of Washington, D.C. as part of the corps de ballet. In 1974, Debra Austin was handpicked by Balanchine as the first Black ballerina in the New York City Ballet, but she never rose above soloist. Austin left the company to become the first African American principal dancer for a major ballet company at the Pennsylvania Ballet from 1982 to 1990.

Dancing principal roles in *Swan Lake, Giselle, Coppélia,* and *La Sylphide* with a White partner was a significant breakthrough in the dance world. She currently serves as the ballet master at Carolina Ballet in Raleigh, North Carolina.

In 1978, Anne Benna Sims became the first African American dancer at ABT and the first African American soloist in its history. Nora Kimball joined ABT in the mid-1980s and is often overlooked as the second African American soloist because she is biracial. In 1990, Lauren Anderson became the second Black woman promoted to principal dancer for a major dance company, as part of the Houston Ballet, another important milestone in American ballet. Francesca Harper became a principal dancer in William Forsythe's Ballet Frankfort from 1994 to 1999. In 2005, she founded the nonprofit dance company, the Francesca Harper Project. In 1996, Aesha Ash broke boundaries by becoming an African American member of the prominent New York City Ballet. In 2013, Olivia Boisson became the fifth Black woman to dance with the New York City Ballet, and the first since the departure of Ash in 2003. Alice Graf Mack was a soloist at DTH and a member of the Alvin Ailey American Dance Theatre. Due to an injury, Mack retired from dancing and attended Webster University in St. Louis, receiving her master's in nonprofit management and remained there to teach dance. In 2018, Mack was named Director of the Dance Division at Julliard School in New York, the first woman of color and the youngest person to hold that position.

If a Black ballerina can actually get into a company, they often do not get coveted principal or soloist roles. Browsing through the corps de ballet roster of renowned ballet companies, one can see that diverse swans are in short supply. And this is not just a problem for women. Male dancers of color also feel the sting of this exclusivity, fighting for even fewer opportunities than their female counterparts. Case in point: in 2004, when DTH closed the company due to financial problems, ballerina Tai Jimenez was the only dancer to land a job with a major American ballet company, Boston Ballet, and be hired as principal dancer, the same rank she held at DTH. Other DTH dancers were hired by prominent companies, but they did not transition as successfully as Jimenez. A whole host of talented ballet dancers with an abundance of melanin were swallowed up by financial misfortune. *Careers cut short.* When DTH reopened its dance company in 2013, it rejoined the slim ranks of ballet companies that train and hire Black ballet dancers.

By the turn of the twenty-first century, more Black women were challenging classical ballet. Courtney Henry created a stir when, at six feet tall, she joined Alonzo King's LINES Ballet in 2011, becoming the tallest professional female ballet dancer in the U.S. Michaela Mabinty DePrince, an orphan from war-torn Sierra Leone, became a ballerina against staggering odds. She performed for a year with DTH as the youngest dancer in the company's history before joining the Dutch National Ballet and becoming a soloist in 2016. DePrince suffers from a skin pigmentation disorder called vitiligo that discolors her complexion, which has inspired young women to embrace their flaws. Michigan native Precious Adams made headlines in 2011 when she moved to Moscow and became one of the first African American ballerinas to graduate from Bolshoi Ballet Academy. She accepted an invitation to dance with the English National Ballet in London and was promoted to First Artist in 2017. In 2018, Adams announced that she would retire her pink tights for brown tights to match her skin tone.

Nardia Boodoo from Maryland, who did not study ballet until her early teens, apprenticed for the Pennsylvania Ballet and The Washington Ballet's Studio Company before becoming a member of The Washington Ballet. Chyrstyn Mariah Fentroy, a former principal dancer at DTH, currently dances as a soloist with the Boston Ballet. Rachael Parini is something special. She is a National Merit Scholar, a former intern with the Department of Homeland Security, and holds a bachelor's degree in International Affairs, with minors in both Political Science and Italian. Parini studied at a number of schools, including the Lilburn School of Ballet and The Rock School for Dance Education. She is currently a member of BalletMet in Ohio. All of these Black ballerinas are chipping away the alabaster mold that has preserved the racist standards of beauty and body types in ballet. While they are extremely conscientious about being role models to young Black girls, they are also using dance as a means of protest. *They dance who they are.*

At last, a major New York ballet company has a Black swan. In 2015, Misty Copeland was promoted to principal dancer at ABT, which put ballet back on popular culture's map and ushered in a conversation about diversity in ballet. *So what now?* Classical ballet is still overwhelmingly White, but over the past few years, diversity, for the moment, has become a priority. Accessibility to classes and training certainly plays a role, but it is even more challenging to defeat the old argument that dancers of color ruin the uniformity of a performance.

Despite Copeland's ascension, the number of Black ballet dancers is still very low, and casting opportunities remain limited. Many Black women worry that the lack of Black ballerinas will continue into another generation. In 2018, three Black board members and a top Black administrator of Atlanta Ballet resigned in protest. They believed leadership was not committed to addressing racial and ethnic diversity in a company that represents a city that is 50 percent Black, but still performs before an overwhelmingly White audience.[14] There are still American ballet companies, especially high profile ones in large and racially diverse cities with big budgets and large feeding schools, that have just one or two Black dancers in their ranks (Angyal 2021).

Indeed, ballet's future is in the hands of the companies' administrators, choreographers, and donors who determine whether to allow diversity into its

---

14. Scott Freeman, "Atlanta Ballet called out on social media for not having black female dancers," *ArtsATL*, June 24, 2020, https://www.artsatl.org/atlanta-ballet-called-out-on-social-media-for-not-having-black-female-dancers.

ranks. But sometimes change is motivated for the simplest reason—in this case, *money.* Racial demographics in the U.S. have changed dramatically in the past three decades, and Whites are expected to no longer make up the majority by 2043.[15] Think of it this way: if ballet companies continue to exclude people of color, the pool of potential patrons and audiences will shrink considerably as older White patrons die out because people will not support an art form that excludes them. In other words, while Copeland's rise to stardom has prompted diversification efforts, it has more to do with dollars than with common sense.

When Copeland made headlines as the first Black female principal dancer in ABT's seventy-five-year history, the African American community's response translated into ticket sales. When she became a celebrity spokesperson with multimillion-dollar contracts, unheard of in the dance world, her value caught the attention of even the staunchest balletomanes, who maintain a false narrative of what ballerinas should and should not look like. While it is disheartening that product endorsement has become the strongest measure of mainstream success, it feels good to see a woman—a Black woman—breaking ground in an art form that has historically excluded her and be idolized in a way commonly associated with sports stars. *Money talks.*

Ballet's overwhelmingly and closely guarded whiteness has once again been publicly challenged. Such a reckoning is not just long overdue, but essential if ballet is to survive (Angyal 2021). Some are doubtful that nothing more than tokenism will be achieved because the ballet world is tendentious when it comes to race. But even for the idealists, the fairy tale princess ballerina is vanishing, and many of today's ballerinas have become avatars of change. Copeland, for example, is considered an unlikely ballerina. She is curvy, muscular, and Black, none of which are "acceptable" attributes in ballet. However, her very late beginning and rapid attainment of virtuosity are arguably unprecedented for a ballerina. Is she an exception? Or are there other Copelands out there? Black or White? Asian or Latina? Native American? Either way, the mold has been shattered. And the more aware we become of what Black ballerinas continually face and overcome, the more we should push back against bias, because the more dancers of color we see in a single elite space, the more our children will believe there is a chance for them to make it to the top. *The future of ballet is at stake.*

◆ ◆ ◆

HIP HOP DANCING ORIGINATED as breakdancing in the predominantly Black and Latino economically depressed South Bronx section of New York City during the mid-1970s. It was a performative but informal dance culture created by a community of people that aggressively asserted male dominance with acrobatic

---

15. Associated Press, "Whites to lose majority status by 2043, the census projects," *Politico,* December 12, 2012, https://www.politico.com/story/2012/12/census-whites-no-longer-a-majority-in-us-by-2043-084971.

and martial arts moves. It was inspired by a new form of music and combined complex rhythms and breaks, which consisted of the vestiges of modern, tap, and swing. More importantly, since the moves echoed African line dancing, as opposed to Europe's partnering style (Glass 2012), one could easily conclude that hip-hop dance comes straight from Africa. This was the birth of breakdancing, and the people who initially created these dance moves became known as b-boys and b-girls.

From a historical perspective, the word "hop" is linked to Black urbanity, creativity, and modernity—at least beginning in the Swing Era of the late 1930s. Dancers like George "Shorty" Snowden, Herbert "Whitey" White, Frankie Manning, Norma Miller, and Dorothy "Dot" Johnson helped popularize the spectacular and often physically demanding Lindy Hop by performing a combination of basic techniques and improvisation (Hancock 2013). Hip-hop dance does just that, showcasing various freestyle movements, such as popping and locking from the West coast. It also features a breakdancing style that includes a repertoire of intricate footwork and occasional airborne moves, like the gravity-defying headspins and backspins from the East coast. These dance movements blended into the genre of hip-hop and gained ground in the American cultural imagination.

These early substyles and social dances were brought about through a combination of events, the most notable being when DJ Kool Herc (Clive Campbell), inspired by James Brown's in-the-pocket beats, created the breakbeat (a repeated sample of a drumbeat). In response to Herc's DJing style, a new form of dance would emerge, different from the disco dancing that was predominant during that era (Ewoodzie 2017). It was Afrika Bambaataa's ambitious prophecy that formed one of the earliest dance crews, the Zulu Kings, which garnered a reputation as a force to be reckoned with in breakdancing circles. The Zulu Kings won many battles and talent shows and performed in various nightclubs in New York City. The young men were involved in breakdancing's evolution, creating moves such as Wiggles, Crazy Leggs, Frosty Freeze, Joe Joe, Rubber Band, and Charlie Rock, and their all-male breaking crews were touted as pioneers in hip-hop dance.

The most influential groups—The Electric Boogaloo, The Lockers, and Rock Steady Crew—would battle against each other; perform live at venues such as Carnegie Hall, Radio City Music Hall, and Disneyland; and frequently appeared on television and in films. The Electric Boogaloo, founded in 1970 in Fresno, California, danced a form of boogaloo from Oakland and innovated popping. The Lockers were formed by Toni Basil and Don "Campbellock" Campbell, who created the locking dance style in 1971. Basil, a former cheerleader and the group's only female and White member, also helped choreograph their moves. Together, Basil and Campbell are considered pioneers in bringing street dance to the stage and mainstream creative spaces. Simultaneously, the Rock Steady Crew, initially founded in the Bronx by Jimmy Dee and Jimmy Lee in 1977, became a franchise for multiple groups at other locations. Members of the crew were featured in the films *Flashdance* (1983) and *Breakin' 2: Electric Boogaloo* (1984), which helped ignite international interest in the b-boy subculture.

Though Black women's involvement in early breakdancing culture has been scantily highlighted at best in the hip-hop archives, crews such as the Dynamic Rockers, the Lady Rockers, and the Female Break Force were some of the early all-female crews of the 1970s and 1980s that participated in improvisation and competition. However, it was the creation of *Soul Train,* the first African American music-dance show and the longest-running show of its kind in television history, that helped make inroads in breakdancing and hip-hop. This happened despite producer and host Don Cornelius' misgivings about the advent of hip-hop and rap, which he found degrading to African Americans (Lehman 2008). *Soul Train's* origins were on a local Chicago television station, but the show relocated to Los Angeles and ran in syndication nationwide from 1971 to 2006. Coined the "hippest trip in America," thanks to *Soul Train,* we began to see Black female dancers in all their Afro Sheen glory, grooving down the line and taking turns pulling out their best moves to dazzle the crowd and the audiences eagerly watching from home.

One standout was the then fourteen-year-old Jody Watley, who would later become a member of the hit R&B group Shalamar. She was spotlighted on the show for her style and captivating dance moves, crafting new dance trends like the Robot—her signature move—and incorporating other urban moves like popping and locking. Dancers like Watley were the center of the *Soul Train* brand. By eventually evolving into a singer and performer, Watley blazed trails for future artists like Aaliyah and Ciara in the late 1990s and early 2000s, who incorporated those classic hip-hop dance moves into their own performances.

Hip-hop dance as an art form works in tandem with the creation of the sound of hip-hop and the origins of rap music. Rap music, which is the core of hip-hop and its development, has long been a lightning rod for discussions of Black womanhood and sexuality. Yet Black women were not deterred from the true strength of their womanness, and in time, they infiltrated hip-hop's hard edges. Female rappers declared affirmations of Black femininity, self-respect, and self-love by spitting rhymes in unladylike spaces. It was this same fiery energy bubbling under the surface that sounded the alarm for sidelined female street dancers. In *TRAILBLAZERS* Volume 5, I will explore how hip-hop music's deep-seated, hyper-masculine foundation evolved from the happy, ebullient, and political to "gangsta" and misogynistic. But for now, the focus here is how Black women affirmed their rightful place in hip-hop by taking on the male-dominated world of hip-hop dance.

Uniquely speaking, hip-hop dance did not develop in a straight line like tap or jazz dance. While jazz dance and jazz music naturally cohabitate, hip-hop music and dance came together to create a new art form and are inextricably bound. The roots of hip-hop come from Africa and stretch deep into America's cultural soil. The music found its origins in classic songs with heavy percussive breaks—the instrumental part of a song—that people could dance to. MCs would speak words over those breaks with catchy phrases like "and you don't stop" or "to the break of dawn." Soon, DJs isolated those breaks and repeated them while people showcased elaborate dance moves. MCs, reminiscent of West African griots, began to recite lengthy rhyming poems, recounting outlandish deeds and misdeeds, in the breaks. DJ Kool Herc has been widely credited as the father of modern rap for his spoken interjections over the breaks.

By the 1980s, hip-hop gained steam. Rappers hired their friends or popular dance crews in their communities to dance in their videos and on their concert tours. On the East coast, artists like Big Daddy Kane, a skilled hip-hop dancer, hired Scoob and Scrap. Kid 'n Play became just as popular for their feel-good rap flow as they did for their dazzling kicks and spins. Heavy D and The Boyz, sporting kente cloth-inspired hip-hop gear, featured male dancers. Meanwhile, on the West coast, the dance team The Soul Brothers performed with rapper Def Jeff, but female dancers were still largely shut out. However, it was the girl group the Gucci Girls, and their breakthrough appearance in the 1988 music video *Groove Me* by Uptown Records' supergroup Guy, that showed that Black women had the moves to go head-to-head with any male hip-hop dance group. The arrival of female dancers on the hip-hop scene in the late 1980s and early 1990s made a mark on Black culture, setting trends in hairstyling and fashion. In turn, they influenced the entire international community of hip-hop dance, which was already transitioning from the streets to concert halls and produc-tion studios. It also created a demand for music video producers, directors, choreographers, and dancers within the genre.

MTV premiered in 1981, and within a few short years, the popularity of music videos presented by video jockeys (VJs) twenty-four hours a day changed the way we consumed music forever. This led to some of the most significant moments in pop culture. However, in its early years, MTV refused to feature Black artists, alleging that White viewers would not embrace them. A combination of public and financial pressures, including Black Entertainment Television's (BET) success in airing videos from an untapped market, could no longer be ignored. MTV finally relented. When Michael Jackson moonwalked in front of a national audience on NBC's *Motown 25: Yesterday, Today, Forever* in 1983, it was reminiscent of a popping move traced back to Cab Calloway in the 1930s and James Brown's interpretation of the boogaloo in the 1960s. Shortly thereafter, MTV reluctantly began airing Black artists (Denisoff 2017). In 1983, Jackson's video *Billie Jean,* which prominently featured the step that became his signature move, aired on MTV. Later that year, there was a groundswell of Black pop and R&B performers on the network, including the premiere of Prince's "Little Red Corvette."

Films like *Beat Street* (1984) and *Krush Groove* (1985) that paid homage to the hip-hop dance style of breakdancing also led to a cultural breakthrough.

By the late 1980s, MTV had taken notice of this cultural shift. It debuted its hip-hop-centered program *Yo! MTV Raps* in 1988, the first national show ever to exclusively focus on hip-hop. (BET's *Rap City* premiered the following year.) *Yo! MTV Raps* aired on MTV for seven years and opened the door for *MTV Jams,* another program with an urban music focus that premiered in 1996.

As hip-hop music evolved through the platform of music videos, rap artists, and R&B singers, other groups began to infuse hip-hop beats into their music and add backup dancers to their performances. By the mid-1980s, Black women were making inroads in the hip-hop community. While female rapper MC Lyte stormed the scene and became the first female MC to sell millions of singles and albums, her progressive lyrics helped hip-hop evolve from a mere party vibe to a socially conscious form of expression. Her music touched on topics such as racism, sexism, and the drug epidemic that took over her hometown of Brooklyn.

MC Lyte helped make a path for other like-minded women to shake up the rap game, such as Queen Latifah, whose artistry encouraged women to embrace their heritage, their curves, and their mind; and Salt-N-Pepa, who became the first hip-hop group to go multi-platinum with music that addressed social issues like the dangers of drunk driving and the importance of safe sex. In fact, Salt-N-Pepa encouraged the "fly girl" persona of the party girl and independent woman, which they integrated into their dance moves. They spread womanist messages about self-esteem and encouraged Black women to take back the power.

Perhaps the first Black woman artist to incorporate contemporary dance with precision and polished choreography was Janet Jackson. When Jackson released her third studio album, *Control,* in 1986, her collaboration with songwriters and record producers Jimmy Jam and Terry Lewis resulted in an unconventional sound: a fusion of R&B, rap vocals, funk, disco, and synthesized percussion, which created the style and genre that came to be known as new jack swing. The birth of Janet Jackson as a music video star is credited in no small part by a then unknown choreographer, Paula Abdul. *Control* is both evolutionary and revolutionary. It was the first album to bridge the gap between R&B and rap music, and its continued influence in dance is evident in the careers of Beyoncé and Ciara, who have taken cues from Jackson's blueprint.

It is worth noting that Abdul, Rosie Perez, Fatima Robinson, and Jossie Harris are just some of the women who figured prominently during this era and have become synonymous with the flowering of hip-hop dance. While they are not all Black (Abdul is a Syrian Jew and Perez is Puerto Rican), this should not discount their contributions to hip-hop dance. Abdul began her professional dance career as a cheerleader for the Los Angeles Laker Girls at eighteen and later became their head choreographer. She was discovered by the Jacksons, and besides choreographing for Michael Jackson, Janet Jackson, and the Jackson family, Abdul choreographed for Duran Duran, ZZ Top, George Michael, Luther Vandross, INXS, Heart, and Prince at the height of the music video era.

Abdul became an award-winning choreographer before transitioning into a career as a recording artist and eventually a television host.

In 1990, hip-hop was ushered into mainstream media. When *In Living Color,* a sketch variety show, made its debut, it was a platform for hip-hop that challenged social taboos and showed what fearless television could be. Soon after, rapper Will Smith premiered in the comedy series *The Fresh Prince of Bel-Air,* proving hip-hop culture had landed front row center in mainstream America. *In Living Color* featured the Fly Girls (including up-and-comer Jennifer Lopez and Jossie Harris Thacker), an energetic dance squad that opened each episode and performed between sketches. Perez, a choreographer from Brooklyn, injected Salt-N-Pepa's fly girl persona into the Fly Girls, which meant teaching professionally-trained dancers street dance skills (Peisner 2018). They were exciting, sexy, tough, athletic, energetic, regimental, and you could not take your eyes off them when they danced.

Much like how Jody Watley got her break, Perez was a student at Los Angeles City College hanging out at nightclubs when a talent scout from *Soul Train* asked her to appear on the show in 1988. She was noticed at a dance club by Spike Lee, who then hired her for her first major acting role in *Do The Right Thing* (1989). Besides choreographing the Fly Girls, she later choreographed music videos for Janet Jackson, Bobby Brown, Diana Ross, LL Cool J, and The Boys. Perez is a three-time Emmy-nominated choreographer and actress.

Both Fatima Robinson and Jossie Harris are self-taught dancers who have danced and choreographed for some of the biggest names in the music industry, as well as in theater and film. Robinson was a hairdresser when scouts at the nightclubs recruited her to dance in music videos, which led to her first major choreography job for Michael Jackson's "Remember the Time" video in 1992 (Heinonen, Shaw, and Mitoma 2002). That triumph led to gigs choreographing music videos for Fergie, Andre 3000 of Outkast, the Black Eyed Peas, Aaliyah, and Will Smith. She garnered seven MTV Video Music Awards nominations for choreography. In 2006, she won Best Hip Hop video direction for the Black Eyed Peas' "My Humps." She has since choreographed for television, film, and theater. Harris is best known in the industry as a legendary backup dancer from the hip-hop golden era. She too began her career as a dancer in Jackson's video, "Remember the Time," appeared in numerous music videos of the era, and toured the world with artists such as Janet Jackson, Heavy D and The Boyz, and Mary J. Blige. Harris transitioned into an acting career that landed her roles on top television series, such as *Martin, Chicago P.D., NCIS* and *Empire.* She is currently a producer and director, as well as an acting coach.

The fly girls' aesthetic, along with Black women rappers and MCs who performed elaborate dance routines during their live performances, began to embody the true spirit of hip-hop culture, making an everlasting impact in the hip-hop community. With its aggressive, competitive spirit and street foundation, breakdancing clashed with the music industry's attempt to possess and shape Black women's sexuality for its own racialized patriarchal economic objectives. Many of these Black women resisted the male norms of hip-hop and objectification by dressing, dancing, and acting the way they wanted. Their hip-hop moves challenged their male counterpart's affinity to feature Black women twerking (a fetishized aspect of hip-hop dance) with bare butts in service of the male gaze. Instead, they featured breakdancing, which had been routinely gendered as a "masculine" form of dance. However, though hip-hop music was finally gaining legitimacy at the beginning of the 1990s, hip-hop dance was still a new specialty. Black women began to fill that void by becoming the creative talent responsible for the most crucial element of a hip-hop culture that relied on music videos to boost an artist's visibility and exposure.

Former New Edition members Michael Bivens, Ricky Bell, and Ronnie DeVoe became BBD and released their debut single, "Poison," in 1990. One day, while Bivens was judging a dance battle along with Rosie Perez, he spotted four young women: Debra Moton, Nikita Leone, Towilla "Tee" Lynn, and Marzella "Pluke" Lewis. The women, who grew up in Los Angeles, formed a female dance group called Str8 Ahead and often battled male dance groups. Bivens subsequently hired them to dance and choreograph the *Poison* video, and the rest is history (Neal 2004). These women quietly changed the course of hip-hop with their powerful and highly-energized dance moves. Str8 Ahead helped usher in the infamous golden era of hip-hop music videos, and their clothes and sexy moves were copied by girls all over the world.

The commercialization of hip-hop directly impacted and dictated the creative direction audiences were fed visually. Hip-hop and R&B videos were produced with high-impact choreography, gloss, and hard body pumping energy. When Queen Latifah released her debut album in 1989, she was well on her way to becoming a multi-talented artist who could rap, act, and build out celebrity during the 1990s Black cultural renaissance. Her portrayal of Khadija James on the television series *Living Single,* which debuted in 1993, represented a sense of personal and professional freedom for Black women. It was exemplified in the show's opening credits by the energetic dancing silhouette of Leslie "Big Lez" Segar, with her gravity-defying kicks, flips, and curvalicious gyrating to Queen Latifah's infectious theme song. It was not only liberating; it was seen as a call to arms by many Black women in the hip-hop community, reiterating that they were here to stay.

Conversely, towards the mid-1990s, women began to take a sexual turn in their rap persona, thanks to the rise of artists like Lil' Kim. Discovered by Biggie Smalls, Lil' Kim became a part of his rap collective, Junior M.A.F.I.A., where her engaging personality helped her stand out as the group's star. Her debut album, *Hard Core,* rife with raunchy lyrics that explored her femininity and sexuality, earned the distinction of being the highest-selling debut for a female rap album.

This ultimately made her an icon, a sex symbol, and the face of X-rated feminism. Lil' Kim's unapologetic and dominatrix-style image, combined with her lyrical prowess, has earned her honorific titles such as Queen Bee, the Queen of Hip-hop, the First Lady of X-Rated Wordplay, and the Rap Goddess. Artists like Foxy Brown and Trina followed in Lil' Kim's explicit footsteps and reclaimed their sexuality in the same manner as their male counterparts.

In 1997, a string of Hollywood blockbuster-worthy music videos with million-dollar budgets were produced and cinematically went toe-to-toe with full-length studio flicks. For example, the rapper Busta Rhymes came hard with "Put Your Hands Where My Eyes Could See," an ode to Eddie Murphy's film, *Coming To America* (1988), that featured scores of Black female dancers wearing elaborate costumes. During this era, many record companies provided huge production budgets, which also included generous costume allowances and glam stylists for both the superstar talent and the backup dancers. Black female hip-hop dancers were taking center stage with polished choreography.

Around this time, Missy Elliott had stepped onto the scene with a unique and innovative approach to rapping, and she produced a number of hip-hop hits and music videos. By 1997, her experimental concepts in music videos would dominate the charts and creatively take hip-hop dance to new heights. When Elliot's *The Rain (Supa Dupa Fly)* video hit airwaves, you saw her making pop lock moves in a giant black plastic jumpsuit fashioned much like a blown-up hefty bag, wearing vibrant colors, and her hair sculpted with close-cropped finger waves. Female dancers wearing white boy shorts and cropped tank tops, yellow raincoats, and Timberland boots were drenched, dancing in the pouring rain.

Elliot's dancers were part of an innovative shift of hip-hop into a pop-infused style of music that would propel artists like Aaliyah—one of the early hip-hop triple threats—into the spotlight. With the help of choreographer Fatima Robinson, Aaliyah developed her own R&B and hip-hop dance style that was smooth, agile, sultry, and sexy without being sexually exploitative. She was a triple threat who could sing, dance, and act. Unfortunately, Aaliyah died in a plane crash in 2001, and her potential was never fully reached.

Hip-hop dance transformed the world of dance, and many of its distinctive moves that were being performed on the street slowly became integrated into the choreography of more traditional dance styles. The dance industry itself eventually responded with a commercial, studio-based version of hip-hop—sometimes called "new style"—and a hip-hop-influenced style of jazz dance called "jazz-funk." Since more and more people were attempting to perform hip-hop movement, it began to lose the athleticism integral to original breakdancing. It has been pretty interesting to witness White bodies moving with a directed unpredictability to Juba (DeFrantz 2004).

None of the rap and hip-hop women of this era were perceived as visually hypersexual by audiences, and their lyrics communicated stories of finding female empowerment while encouraging women to take control of their bodies. Unfortunately, Black women were increasingly pressured to participate in highly visual and sexual exploitative strategies to sell mainstream, popular music. With the core hip-hop audience primarily male, the record labels were hesitant to take women in hip-hop seriously.

Whether Black women were professionally trained or self-taught, they worked hard to create moves that grooved to hip-hop in new ways, while doing the seemingly impossible by breaking down barriers within several dance styles. Camille A. Brown, a professionally-trained concert dancer, teacher, and award-winning and Tony-nominated choreographer, has become part of an elite coterie. However, Brown is most known for, and has built her reputation on, creating dialogues about race, culture, and identity through socially conscious choreography. Since 2000, she has been blending modern, African, ballet, and tap dance elements, including a great deal of hip-hop, into her choreography to tell stories that connect with contemporary culture. Following in the footsteps of dancers and choreographers such as Katherine Dunham, Pearl Primus, and Jawole Willa Jo Zollar, Brown reclaims African Americans' cultural narrative through popular and social dance.

Robin Dunn began her career at the Charlotte Pollak Dance Studio in Queens, New York. She eventually studied under Frank Hatchett at Broadway Dance Center and studied ballet under Horton and Dunham at The Ailey School. In the early 1990s, Dunn was introduced to the world of hip-hop dance and culture by Buddha Stretch and Mr. Wiggles. She has appeared in and choreographed several Off-Broadway productions and, in 1993, served as the director of *Amateur Night at The Apollo Theater.* She has worked on *Saturday Night Live,* and Nickelodeon, and for recording artists like Missy Elliott, Chris Brown, Heather Headley, The Braxtons featuring Jay Z, Wynonna Judd, Brian McKnight, and Raven Symone. Dunn has taught hip-hop dance at The Ailey School, The Ailey Extension, Steps on Broadway, New York University, Syracuse University, East Stroudsburg University/PA Dance, and Connecticut Ballet in Stamford.

Beyoncé's transition from Destiny's Child to her critically acclaimed work, *Lemonade* (2016)—a revolutionary visual album that has been credited with reinventing the album and transforming how people consume music—is remarkable. Beyoncé, who performed in various singing and dancing competitions as a child, has created a distinct, signature dance style that is a mash-up of hip-hop, crumping, ballet, and jazz. The choreography is pure, heart-pumping hip-hop with attitude, with moves from twerking, to head tossing, to a thigh-defying deep full squat and hop backward. During the 2010s, Beyoncé was the decade's defining pop star. Her songs, album rollouts, stage presence, social justice initiatives, and disruptive public relations strategy have influenced how we see and hear music.

Ciara receives high marks for her stage presence and dance routines, leading a squad of hip-hop dancers in some of the best dance breaks in the business.

The Black women choreographers behind some of Ciara's most memorable one-two steps include self-taught dancer and world-renowned choreographer Jamaica Craft who has also worked with Usher, Ne-Yo, and Nicki Minaj. Galen Hooks, an MTV VMA-nominated choreographer and dancer who has worked with over sixty artists, such as Janet Jackson, Justin Bieber, Ne-Yo, Britney Spears, Miley Cyrus, and John Legend; and Parris Goebel, a New Zealander who has choreographed routines for Jennifer Lopez, Ariana Grande, Rihanna, Janet Jackson, and Nicki Minaj.

A younger generation of Black women dancers and choreographers are breaking boundaries in hip-hop nowadays. Kaelynn "KK" Harris is a mostly self-taught elite performer who garnered traction after advancing to the finals with her dance crew, 8 Flavahz, on MTV's *America's Best Dance Crew.* Since then, she has performed with artists such as Usher, Missy Elliott, Fergie, Gwen Stefani, Ciara, and Britney Spears, and is a highly sought-out industry choreographer and instructor, selling out master classes all around the world. Khadija Shari Nicholas, the face of Pharrell Williams' "Marilyn Monroe" single, and Ashly Everett, a captain of Beyoncé's backup dancers, both studied at The Ailey School. Nicholas has danced alongside Grammy Award winners like Beyoncé and Rihanna. Everett has worked with Usher, Jennifer Lopez, Ne-Yo, Tina Turner, Ciara, Sean Paul, and Anitta. She is frequently featured in high-profile music videos, television commercials, and concert tours.

The b-girls and b-boys of the 1970s, who provided the seeds for what is now known as hip-hop dance, have grown into a worldwide, multicultural, multi-sexual industry of performances and competitions. With its aggressive competitive spirit and street foundation, breakdancing directly clashed with the music industry's attempt to possess and shape women's sexuality. The b-girls fought back and are now no longer relegated to feminine moves; they can exhibit the same level of physical exertion as their male counterparts. The identities of early female pioneers might be obscured in hip-hop history, but the future generation of b-girls and gender-nonconforming b-folks are evolving the cisheteropatriarchal tint of breakdancing culture. While breakdancing is no longer connected to a movement of social change, these women—many of them African American—have helped shape hip-hop dance into a legitimate art form.

In 2021, Cardi B and Megan Thee Stallion performed their mega hit, "WAP" at the Grammy Awards. The audience was both intrigued and outraged by their explosive, provocative, and hypersexual performance. They gloriously twerked, strutted, and owned the stage in Barbarella-esque outfits, referencing female empowerment and sexual pride, and delivering undoubtedly one of the most memorable Grammy performances of all time. Cardi B twerked on a stripper pole fashioned as the heel of a giant stiletto shoe. Later, scantily clad dancers, mostly Black women, performed provocative hip-hop moves while Cardi B and Megan crawled on a massive bed, gyrating with their legs intertwined. Some people have argued that Cardi B and Megan were expressing their sexuality in their lyrics, videos, and performances to expose misogynoir: the intersection of racism and sexism that Black women often face in the workplace.

Given the marginalization of women's contributions to the genre, it is easy to see how hip-hop has been nothing more than a man's game. Rambunctious and braggadocious lyrics about violence, sex, swagger, and masculinity reign in a space where, in most cases, women are cast as either conquests or part of a faceless chorus whose stories are largely ignored. However, Black women still managed to push through these early hip-hop barriers on the music front, refusing to be silenced or stopped. Their distinct variations in style, flow, lyrics, and presentation demanded respect right from the beginning, and created a space for female hip-hop artists to take center stage and grab the mic. What Black female rappers and dancers had in common was that they were both fiercely independent, using their power to remain consistently and resoundingly true to one's self. Criticizing female artists of color for expressing their sexuality through their lyrics, videos, and live performances strips them of their agency—as if music and art have not always been an outlet for artists and, in turn, their fans to express themselves freely. Whether you agree with Cardi B and Megan's performance or not, there is no denying that Black women artists are often held to a different standard than their male and White counterparts when it comes to their craft.

Just as video killed the radio star, the Internet has quickly overshadowed television. MTV stopped airing music videos. So did BET. All of those fresh faces we were once introduced to on television are now found on YouTube. You can interact with hip-hop dancers on social media through Facebook and Twitter, get swept into their Instagram stories, and stream videos on your cell phones. Today, young Black female dancers continue to innovate and elevate hip-hop dance by utilizing these social media and online platforms.

In 2020, we saw this in action. A Black fourteen-year-old teen—Jalaiah Harmon of Atlanta—created a dance move called the Renegade and posted it online onto a small network of young Black creatives. Her dance moves were then appropriated by a White sixteen-year-old, Charli D'Amelio, TikTok's biggest homegrown star, who has nearly 26 million followers on the platform. D'Amelio has been affectionately deemed the dance's "CEO" for popularizing it.[16] TikTok, one of the biggest video apps in the world, has taken over where MTV and BET left off and has become synonymous with dance culture. Yet many of its most popular dances, including the Renegade, Holy Moly Donut Shop, the Mmmxneil, and Cookie Shop, have come from young Black creators on a myriad of smaller apps and are then appropriated by White influencers, who make a generous amount of money off of the hits. For example, on TikTok, you need a minimum of 10,000 subscribers and over 270 million views a year to generate $100,000.

---

16. Taylor Lorenz, "The Original Renegade" February 13, 2020, *The New York Times,* https://www.nytimes.com/2020/02/13/style/the-original-renegade.html.

According to *Forbes,* D'Amelio is the second highest-earning TikTok star, earning $4 million from 2019 to 2020.[17] Although D'Amelio never claimed credit for inventing the dance, she became known mainly for the dance and was invited to award shows and red carpets to give tutorials, while Harmon was left in the dust. The backlash was brutal across social media. Perhaps the irony here is that D'Amelio had to be bullied into finally crediting Harmon for her own creation.

Soon after, twenty-year-old Morgan Bullock, a Black dancer from Richmond, Virginia, was called out for performing Irish dance to hip-hop music, something White Irish dancers have been doing for years.[18] Bullock has been a marvel of grace and patience as she bore criticism on social media and in the end, she was rewarded and vindicated with an invitation to Ireland from the Taoiseach (the prime minister and head of government of Ireland). For Bullock, fusing Irish dance to modern music is an homage to, rather than a desecration, of the genre.

To many dancers, dance is a universal human pursuit, an eons-old unending series of cultural appreciation and fluid interactions. This particular battle of America's culture war can be confusing and explosive, especially when it comes to the cultural appropriation of Black dance, which has historically been stolen and renamed without any recognition or credit given to its origins. In this regard, blackface and minstrel shows first come to mind. There is perhaps one significant difference between Bullock and Harmon's stories: Bullock never deviated from traditional Irish dance, nor did she claim it as her own. She fell in love with Irish dancing and began studying it as a young girl. Her only sin was that she was a Black woman performing Irish dance to hip-hop music.

On the other hand, D'Amelio capitalized on the notoriety of Harmon's dance by innocuously claiming it as her own, making a boatload of money in the process. This begs the nagging questions about Black vernacular dance and its continuing appropriation. Hip-hop is attractive because it has allowed Black people the agency to recreate narratives and reclaim their individuality and position in American society in a unique and compelling way. It has become the most popular dance form on the planet and has significantly strayed from its early beginnings. Hip-hop has shifted from a sociocultural statement from the streets of New York City during the 1970s to a commercialized success. However, instead of outside communities viewing the genre for its artistic and cultural significance, most White people are drawn to imitating the imagery they experience through the music because of its "outlawed" notion. As White people

---

17. Abram Brown, "TikTok's 7 Highest-Earning Stars: New Forbes List Led By Teen Queens Addison Rae And Charli D'Amelio" August 6, 2020, *Forbes,* https://www.forbes.com/sites/abrambrown/2020/08/06/tiktoks-highest-earning-stars-teen-queens-addison-rae-and-charli-damelio-rule/?sh=67a2f60c5087.

18. Petula Dvorak, "Is it cultural appropriation when a Black woman does Irish dance?" August 3, 2020, *The Washington Post,* https://www.washingtonpost.com/local/is-it-cultural-appropriation-when-a-black-woman-does-irish-dance/2020/08/03/974b16f6-d517-11ea-930e-d88518c57dcc_story.html.

appropriate the work, now more than ever, the Black people creating the work are not benefiting from its success.

There are no easy answers to this. While I am unable to fully explore this issue here, we should keep in mind how American society's general illusion of color blind ideology perpetuates an environment of justified cultural appropriation that, more often than not, is tied to economic exploitation, which leaves Black creators out in the cold. In the process, the vernacular meaning behind Black dance becomes disregarded and erased (Gottschild 2005). These issues are glaringly prominent in the hip-hop dance community, especially as more young Black women come forward to create new forms. Cultural appropriation reduces the depth and hardships of Black culture to an aesthetic trend, reversing the original intent and authenticity of hip-hop music. This is a serious repercussion of hip-hop's popularity.

Contrary to what many said would be a short-lived fad, hip-hop music, accompanied by a powerful dance style, set the world on fire. Like its forerunners, hip-hop is the product of a specific sociohistoric backdrop and time-bound cultural experience. Some believe that hip-hop dance will go the way of jazz dance, its vernacular elements will wash away and become indistinguishable, blending into other dance genres. However, nearly forty years later, hip-hop culture has evolved and reinvented itself to become a global sensation. Hip-hop dance remains a powerful movement that has gone from the streets, to the big screen, to top-rated network television shows like *So You Think You Can Dance* and *America's Next Best Dance Crew*. In the process and against all odds, Black women have taken over stages and airwaves with moves that have cemented their place in dance history—like Fatima Robinson—who helped revolutionize this dance genre. So, when people point to the history of hip-hop and the ingenuity of Blacks and Latinos in the South Bronx during the mid-1970s, it is clear that Black women and their role in hip-hop dance's development cannot be denied, and will forever be ingrained in the fabric of America and the dance world at large.

◆ ◆ ◆

DANCE, LIKE ALL FORMS of cultural expression, reflects the society in which it exists. Just as the history of the U.S. encompasses a broad array of complex influences, so does dance. American dance has embraced and incorporated individual, cultural, and stylistic elements in an ever-changing kaleidoscope that draws from and contributes to artistic, social, religious, cultural, and even political realms.

I recently recalled seeing Agnes de Mille's "Conversations About Dance" program at City Center in 1979. She sat onstage wearing a long, billowy, regal dress, with her legs in second position. As she began narrating the history of dance, from the Jacobean dances to disco, illustrated by the dancers behind her, I became pissed. Why? *No Black people.* When she introduced Irish clog dancing and explained the evolution of tap, a set of handsome Black men strutted across the stage, and de Mille credited Black culture for instituting "the beginning of our native dance."[19] While a few people were incensed by de Mille's proclamation and hurried out of the theater, I jumped out of my seat and applauded.

As de Mille indicated, African Americans have contributed to the genesis of American dance, but so too have Native Americans, Asians, Latinos, and immigrants from other countries. When I jumped out of my seat while others left the theater, it was clear to me then, as it is now, that a lot of people have very different ideas of what American culture is and is not. America is a pluralistic society, not a single monolithic culture. We are an amalgam of many different cultures that have come together as we evolve and grow. American dance is a project of this diversity.

Though African Americans artistically contributed to tap, modern, jazz, ballet, and hip-hop in big ways, Black women have still faced insurmountable challenges in the field. Yet, with persistence and love for the craft, Black women dancers, teachers, anthropologists, and choreographers have played a vital role in the development of American dance and triggered trends across the world stage.

Of course, the issue of Black female bodies remains ever-present, particularly in ballet. Copeland, who inhabits her body with peace and dignity, has openly challenged the perception of a fragile, lily-white figure with her impeccably sculpted, brown-skinned dancer's physique. Black women tap dancers are achieving recognition with rhythm-driven piston and acrobatic steps that can match any man. In modern dance, women continue to experiment, investigate, and research African-based cultures to create new styles, while others remain committed to teaching and training the next generation.

These Black women have physicalized their authentic selves into remarkable dance. While we have witnessed the pain in their struggle, we have also witnessed their joy when they dance. It is a Black story. *It is a human story.* It is a celebration of the perseverance of Black women dancers who dream with their feet. ❖

---

19. Anna Kisselgoff, "Agnes de Mille Offers a Repeat Of 'Conversations About Dance'," *The New York Times,* April 29, 1978. https://www.nytimes.com/1978/04/29/archives/agnes-de-mille-offers-a-repeat-of-conversations-about-dance.html.

Josephine Baker
(1906-1975)
Jazz dancer, singer, performer, civil rights activist, vedette

Josephine Baker was the first African American female jazz performer who garnered international acclaim that helped define the Jazz Age, and the first African American woman to star in a major motion picture who laid the foundation for future African American women entertainers to follow.

FREDA JOSEPHINE MCDONALD BAKER was born in St. Louis, Missouri to Carrie McDonald, an ex-vaudeville girl, washerwoman and domestic. Her mother married drummer Eddie Carson and led people to believe he was Baker's father, but evidence suggests her biological father was White, a secret Baker's mother took to her grave (Chase and Baker 2001). Baker's mother and Carson had done some stage shows together (reputedly bringing a young Baker on stage) but he left the marriage early on. Baker's mother would remarry and have several more children.

Baker and her family were poor and Black in St. Louis, a city shaped by rigid inequality. Since her childhood neighborhood was home to many vaudeville theaters that doubled as movie houses, as a young girl, Baker was exposed to show business. She had little formal education, attending Lincoln Elementary School only through the fifth grade, often playing hooky from school to spend time with a family of traveling musicians, or went to the movies. To help her family make ends meet, she occasionally performed on street corners, cleaned houses, and babysat for wealthy White families (Jules-Rosette and Simon 2007).

At thirteen, Baker's mother kicked her out of the family home, and she sought room and board from her employer, a man only known as "Mr. Dad," who ran an ice cream parlor where Baker worked. When rumors came to light that Mr. Dad was getting more in exchange from Baker than just waitressing, Baker's mother dragged her out of the ice cream shop, and at the advice of Baker's godmother, she married her off to a steelworker named Willie Wells (Chase and Baker 2001). The marriage did not last, but Baker finally made it onto the stage at the Booker Theatre. Though she lacked training, her enthusiasm and spark made up for it, and she was hired.

Baker worked briefly at the Old Chauffeurs Club as a waitress, but before long, she joined Bob Russell's troupe of performers and abandoned St. Louis

for Memphis. She got the job through the influence of Clara Smith, a blues singer who became Baker's protégé and one of her first bisexual relationships (Chase and Baker 2001). Baker's role in the troupe was as the last girl on a chorus line—traditionally the comic relief. There she would show her true skill, and the experience grounded her with a physical comedy that would become a trademark of Baker's style.

In 1921, when Baker was in Philadelphia, she married William Howard Baker, a Pullman porter. That same year destiny came calling by way of Sissle and Blake's *Shuffle Along* (1921), which was then struggling around the New Jersey and Philadelphia circuits. After multiple auditions, and by the time *Shuffle Along* debuted on Broadway, Baker was hired at age sixteen as the comic relief—and she nailed it. The show stayed on Broadway until 1922, then went on tour until 1924. (Chase and Baker 2001)

Her role in *Shuffle Along* and her starring role in Sissle and Blake's *The Chocolate Dandies* (1924) made her the highest-paid chorus girl in vaudeville. This experience culminated in Baker's performance at the Plantation Club, which set the stage for her departure to Paris. By this time, Baker parted ways with her husband but continued to use his last name professionally for the rest of her life (Jules-Rosette and Simon 2007).

Having spent some time in Paris, Caroline Dudley Reagan, a diplomat's wife, decided she wanted to take a company of genuine African American entertainers on tour to Europe and coaxed Baker to come along. In 1925, at nineteen, Baker sailed to Paris, opened in *La Revue nègre* at the Théâtre des Champs-Élysées, and became an instant success. The final number, the erotically charged "La Danse Sauvage," featured a topless Baker wearing feathers around her waist and ankles (Chase and Baker 2001). Paris fell in love with Baker, and she fell in love with Paris. After a successful tour of Europe, Baker broke her contract with Reagan and returned to France to star at the Folies-Bergère.

Her success coincided with the 1925 International Exhibition of Modern Decorative and Industrial Arts (Exposition internationale des arts décoratifs et industriels modernes), which gave birth to the term "Art Deco," and also a renewed interest in non-Western forms of art, including African. A year later, it was in her debut performance at the Folies-Bergére's civility/primitivism-themed *La Folie du Jour* that Baker wore what became her most famous outfit—her banana skirt. The costume consisted of sixteen rubber bananas hung from a low-slung belt around her waist. With it, she wore pearls around her neck and little else.

Baker's performance spoke to White men's infatuation and sexualized erotic obsession of Black women, and Baker played along. She possessed a unique understanding of the racial and power dynamics underlying Paris' obsession with Black women's bodies, and she obliged her audience's most lurid fantasies. After a while, Baker was the most successful American entertainer working in France.

Ernest Hemingway once said that Josephine Baker was the most exciting woman he had ever seen in his life (Chase and Baker 2001).

At the start of her career in France, Baker met Giuseppe Pepito Abatino, a Sicilian former stonemason who passed himself off as a count. He persuaded her to let him manage her, and in time he became her lover as well. Abatino was a shrewd businessman, and together they opened a nightclub, Chez Josephine, in 1926 while Baker was still performing at the Folies-Bergère. She collaborated with the French journalist Marcel Sauvage and in 1927 published *Les mémoires de Josephine Baker (The Memoirs of Josephine Baker)*. Although she was only twenty-one years old, Baker's memoirs portrayed her personality and shared opinions on various subjects. She also created and marketed a series of beauty products, such as skin creams, pomades and foundations, which helped sustain her popularity (Caravantes 2015).

By 1928, sensing the French had grown tired of Baker's antics, Abatino arranged for an extended tour of Europe and South America and used this period to transform Baker's stage and public persona, as well as her singing voice. Under his tutelage, she took singing lessons, learned to discipline her dancing, and learned to speak fluent French. Abatino succeeded in turning a great clown into a great lady (Chase and Baker 2001). Unfortunately, her reception in South America was not entirely what they expected. Baker faced charges of moral indecency and racism and was met with vigorous protests and censorship. However, despite this setback, her performances were well-attended. The public received her as a jazz dancer closely associated with the Charleston, and therefore seen as a vehicle of soul liberation (Borge 2018). When she returned to Paris, Baker gave up the Charleston and bananas, and vowed to focus on becoming an artist on her own terms (Caravantes 2015).

However, upon Baker's return, she faced other challenges. The theaters were in crisis because the new talking movies had captured audiences. Abatino, always thinking on his feet, reintroduced Baker to Paris through social events and secured a contract for Baker to star in the revue, *Paris qui renue* at the Casino de Paris, the most respectable music hall in Paris. The manager, theater producer and songwriter Henri Varna gave Baker a male cheetah to celebrate the opening. Baker adorned the cheetah with a diamond collar, named him "Chiquita," and brought him on stage. He frequently escaped into the orchestra pit and terrorized the musicians, adding another element of excitement to the show (Jules-Rosette and Simon 2007).

Baker starred in three films which found success only in Europe: the silent film *Siren of the Tropics* (1927), *Zouzou* (1934), which catapulted her to stardom as the first person of color to become a worldwide entertainer, and she starred in the major motion picture, *Princesse Tam-Tam* (1935). In 1931, she scored her most successful song, "J'ai deux amours." Due to World War II, her 1930 film, *Fausse Alerte,* would not be released until 1945.

In 1934, she took the lead in a revival of Jacques Offenbach's *La Créole,* an opéra comique in three acts for a six-month run at the Théâtre Marigny on the Champs-Élysées of Paris, which critics unanimously praised. However, despite her popularity in France, Baker never attained an equivalent reputation in America. Her star turn in a 1936 revival of *Ziegfeld Follies on Broadway* generated less than impressive box office numbers and was met by a racially hostile media. Early in the run, she was replaced by Gypsy Rose Lee, and she was heartbroken. Baker was the first and last Black woman to appear with the Ziegfeld Follies (Caravantes 2015).

While she was largely idolized in France, when Baker came to the U.S., she was expected to use the servants' entrance in hotels and was insulted by the other guests. She quickly realized that little had changed since leaving her home country, including poverty, segregation and bigotry. Abatino, who was ill, returned to Paris after the Ziegfeld run while Baker remained in the U.S., eventually traveling to St. Louis to visit her family. While there, after sixteen years she finalized her divorce from William Howard Baker. From there she went to New York to open the nightclub, Chez Josephine, on East 54th Street. Neither Baker or Abatino knew he was dying from kidney cancer, so it was with great sadness when Baker learned Abatino died suddenly in Paris. In his will, he left everything to Baker (Caravantes 2015).

Baker returned to Paris in 1937 and starred in the revue, *En Super Folies* at the Folies-Bergère. After being pursued with an intense courtship by French industrialist Jean Lion, Baker quietly married Lion that same year and became a French citizen. She also rented Les Milandes, a fifteenth-century château in the South of France. The marriage was short-lived due to competing careers, and they separated in 1942. Baker hired French composer and conductor Jo Bouillon to conduct her orchestra, and in time he would devote himself to her.

In September 1939, France declared war on Germany in response to its invasion of Poland. When the Germans occupied France, Baker worked with the Red Cross and the Résistance. She was recruited by the Deuxième Bureau, French military intelligence, as an "honorable correspondent" to collect and carry information for transmission to England about airfields, harbors, and German troop concentrations in the West of France. Notes were written in invisible ink on Baker's sheet music. Amid this activity, Baker became pregnant with Bouillon, though doctors had told her years earlier after suffering multiple failed pregnancies, she could not have children. They were proved right in 1941 when the baby was stillborn, and Baker developed an infection so severe that she needed a complete hysterectomy. After the operation, she contracted sepsis and peritonitis, and wound up being hospitalized for nearly eighteen months. After her recovery, she began touring to entertain Allied soldiers who had landed in North Africa by then. Later in the war, she joined the French Women's Auxiliary Air Force, in which she was commissioned as a lieutenant, and kept putting on shows for Allied troops. After the war, Baker received the Croix de guerre and the Rosette de la Résistance, and was made a Chevalier de la Légion d'Honneur by the French government, the highest order of France.

Following the war, Baker's activism and engagement in the civil rights movement back in America gathered momentum. Although based in France, she became involved in international public media battles. Baker married Bouillon in 1947, and they purchased Les Milandes. In 1949, a reinvented Baker returned in triumph to the Folies-Bergère.

Bolstered from the recognition of her wartime heroics, Baker assumed a new gravitas, unafraid to take on serious music or subject matters. In 1951, Baker was invited back to the U.S. for a nightclub engagement in Miami. Due to her repudiation of segregated venues, Baker became the first Black performer to take to the stage in front of an integrated audience. The engagement, a rousing success, reestablished Baker as one of Paris' preeminent entertainers.

But when Baker arrived in New York with her husband Bouillon, they were refused reservations at multiple hotels because of racial discrimination. She was so upset by this treatment that she wrote a series of articles about segregation in the U.S. She also gave a talk at Fisk University in Nashville, Tennessee, entitled "France, North Africa and The Equality of the Races In France" (Jules-Rosette and Simon 2007). Later, in front of 100,000 people in Harlem, the NAACP' named Baker "Woman of the Year," and she was presented with a lifetime membership by Nobel Peace Prize winner Ralph Bunche. In the meantime, her future looked bright. Baker followed up her sold-out engagement in Miami with six months of bookings in the U.S. and the promise of many more to come. Rave reviews and enthusiastic audiences accompanied her everywhere she went.

However, an incident at the Stork Club interrupted and overturned her plans. Baker made charges of racism at the Stork Club, where she alleged she was refused service. She criticized the club's unwritten policy of discouraging Black patrons, then scolded columnist Walter Winchell for not rising to her defense. Actor Grace Kelly, who was at the club at the time, rushed over to Baker, took her by the arm and stormed out with her entire party, vowing never to return (she did return in 1956 with Prince Rainier of Monaco). The two women became close friends after the incident.

On the other hand, Winchell responded swiftly with a series of harsh public rebukes, including accusations of Communist sympathies, a serious charge at the time, and he sent information directly to J. Edgar Hoover of the FBI. The ensuing publicity resulted in the termination of Baker's work visa, forcing her to cancel all her engagements and return to France. Winchell's attack had triggered FBI surveillance of Baker's activities for over seventeen years (Jules-Rosette and Simon 2007). It was almost a decade before U.S. officials allowed her back into the country.

Beginning in 1953, Baker and Bouillon adopted twelve children from different countries, ranging from Finland to Venezuela. They installed what she called her "Rainbow Tribe" at Les Milandes. Baker wanted to prove that children of different ethnicities and religious backgrounds could still be sisters and brothers. All of the children bore the Bouillon name, and she hired an army of nannies and tutors to care for them. She often took the children with her cross-country, and when they were at the château, she charged admission to tourists who came to hear them sing and watch them play games in their garden, so they could see for themselves how natural and happy the children were.

Baker's finances were in disarray, partly owing to her impulsive generosity, uneven management of the château and its farm, and her wild spending habits, which she and Bouillon often quarreled over. Although Baker retired in 1956 to maintain Les Milandes, she was later obliged to return to the stage. Baker and Bouillon separated in 1957, divorced in 1961, and Bouillon retired to Argentina, where he opened a French restaurant.

In 1963, Baker appeared at the March on Washington but only spoke before the start of the official program. Wearing her Free French uniform emblazoned with her medals, she introduced the "Negro Women for Civil Rights." Daisy Bates was the only woman allowed to speak at the March during the official program. In 1966, Fidel Castro invited Baker to perform at the Teatro Musical de La Habana in Havana, Cuba, at the seventh-anniversary celebration of his revolution. Her spectacular show in April broke attendance records.

Despite this momentum, Baker was in trouble. It began in 1964 when Les Milandes was first put up for auction. It had been rescued from bankruptcy proceedings by the intervention of Jean-Claude Brialy and Brigitte Bardot, who launched an appeal to the people of France. Despite all efforts, however, the situation worsened. By 1968, the château was again put into administration to be sold to the highest bidder. Baker was on tour when she learned that the new owner had put the property up for investment, so she decided to lay siege to the château and barricaded herself in the kitchen. Unfortunately, the new owner's henchmen had no scruples and booted her out of the property. Weakened and in shock, she was taken to Périgord hospital. After the bananas, Baker's second most famous image is her sitting in the rain, locked out of her home by the new owner.

As Baker's finances crumbled, her friend and patron Princess Grace moved her and the children to Monaco. Baker needed help to make ends meet, but advancing years and exhaustion began to take their toll. She sometimes had trouble remembering lyrics, and her speeches between songs tended to ramble, but Baker continued to captivate audiences. In 1968, Baker performed in Yugoslavia and Skopje and at the Olympia in Paris.

In the meantime, the children, who were now teenagers, began to chafe at their public lives and resisted Baker's authority. Short on cash, Baker sought ways to farm the children out to others. Some of them went to live with their father, Bouillon, in Buenos Aires, while others were sent to boarding schools. Baker sent a small group—including Marianne (adopted from France), whose teenage love affairs drove Baker to distraction—to live with a longtime Baker fan in the U.K. Perhaps the most puzzling outcome is when Baker found out Jarry (adopted from Finland) was gay, she chastised him in front of his siblings before sending him to live with Bouillon.

Baker made appearances in Belgrade and Carnegie Hall in 1973, the Royal Variety Performance at the London Palladium in 1974, and the Gala du Cirque in Paris in 1974. Baker starred in a retrospective revue at the Bobino in Paris, *Joséphine à Bobino 1975*, celebrating her fifty years in show business. The revue, financed notably by Prince Rainier, Princess Grace, and Jacqueline Kennedy Onassis, opened to rave reviews. Fold-out chairs had to be added to accommodate additional spectators. On opening night, audience members included Mick Jagger, Sophia Loren, Diana Ross, Liza Minnelli, and Shirley Bassey.

Four days later, Baker was found lying peacefully in her bed surrounded by newspapers with glowing reviews of her performance. She was in a coma after suffering a cerebral hemorrhage. Josephine Baker was taken to Pitié-Salpêtrière Hospital, where she died, age sixty-eight, on April 12, 1975.

She received a full Roman Catholic funeral that was held at L'Église de la Madeleine. She was the only American-born woman to receive full French military honors at her funeral. After a family service at Saint-Charles Church in Monte Carlo, Baker was interred at Monaco's Cimetière de Monaco.❖

The Legacy of Josephine Baker

WHILE IT IS OFTEN SAID THAT JOSEPHINE BAKER was at one point one of the highest-paid performer in Europe, and the highest paid Black woman performer in the world, it would be too easy to miss what a feat this was. Baker was born a poor, Black woman during the Jim Crow era, and grew up in the St. Louis slums.

But Baker was a woman of her own invention. Her story is as complicated as she was. She was largely responsible for creating myths about her upbringing, often leaving out pertinent details about her childhood. In fact, she was not interested in becoming the heroine of any tawdry old rags-to-riches story. She was, however, in many respects an activist at heart, and though she may have attained certain comforts that under different circumstances would have been denied, she remained deeply concerned by the depressing reality of race relations in America. Although Baker made Paris her home and found acceptance and a degree of liberty there, she remained mindful that these comforts were not widely available to all women of color.

Even today, Baker's cultural legacy largely exists in today's art, photography, fashion, film, literature, and social activism. How much control did Baker have over her image-making process, and what was her role in making her dream come true? While music hall impresarios, managers, fashion designers, artists, photographers, and biographers all contributed to the construction of Josephine Baker, she cleverly took advantage of these forces to mold her public persona and the narrative of her life.

Baker continues to influence women artists more than a century after her birth. Diana Ross, a fan of Baker, performed in Bob Mackie-designed outfits similar to Baker's and reenacted similar poses of the latter in many photo sessions. In 1977, she portrayed Baker in her Tony Award-winning Broadway and television show *An Evening with Diana Ross.* When the show was made into an NBC television special entitled *The Big Event: An Evening with Diana Ross,* Ross again portrayed Baker. In 1991, Baker's life story, *The Josephine Baker Story,* was broadcast on HBO. Lynn Whitfield portrayed Baker and won an Emmy Award for Outstanding Lead Actor in a Miniseries or a Special—becoming the first Black actor to win the award in this category.

Baker's performance style has also been influential. Whitney Houston paid tribute to Baker in her "I'm Your Baby Tonight" music video to represent the Harlem Renaissance. The easy contemporary parallel to Baker's "Rainbow Tribe" would be Angelina Jolie—except that when Baker's children became an attraction for tourists, she fully embraced the gawking. Beyoncé wore Baker's banana skirt and performed at the Fashion Rocks concert at Radio City Music Hall in 2006. Jean-Claude Baker, an unofficial addition to Baker's twelve adopted children, opened Chez Josephine in New York City in 1986, which celebrates Baker's life and work. In 1993, Jean-Claude published the biography *Josephine: The Hungry Heart,* co-authored with Chris Chase. In 2012, Cheryl Howard opened in *The Sensational Josephine Baker,* written and performed by Howard and directed by Ian Streicher at the Beckett Theatre in New York City, just a few doors down from Chez Josephine. Jean-Claude Baker, who suffered from severe depression, committed suicide in 2015.

"Place Joséphine Baker" in the Montparnasse Quarter of Paris was named in her honor. She was inducted into the Hall of Famous Missourians, the St. Louis Walk of Fame, and the Legacy Walk in Chicago. A swimming pool along the banks of the Seine in Paris, the Piscine Joséphine Baker, is named after her.

Ironically, Les Milandes, now known as the Château des Milandes, has been listed as a monument historique since 1986 and pays homage to Baker by the French Ministry of Culture. After Baker's death, the château passed through several owners' hands, falling into decline before it was bought in 2001 by Henry and Claude de Labarre (an architect and a viticulturist, respectively), who owned a house outside the property's gates since the early seventies. The family restored the grounds in the spirit of Baker's exotic themes and turned part of the home into a modest museum that tells Baker's extraordinary story through photographs, recordings, film clips, and artifacts such as stage costumes and posters, including the famous banana belt from her show at the Folies-Bergère. The de Labarre's daughter, Angélique de Saint-Exupéry, manages its day-to-day operations.

Today, some of Baker's children are successful entrepreneurs, teachers, civil servants and authors in France, the U.S., Italy and Argentina. Several of them gathered at the château in 2006 to mark the 100th anniversary of their adoptive mother's birth. Having made her way from desperate poverty to international acclaim, one could suspect that Baker would have loved every moment.

Baker's narrative has always been complex. She is one of the most para-doxical figures of the twentieth century, a victim of her luck and talent who ultimately victimized everyone who loved her, an embodiment of untethered will and autonomy which could not free herself from within. She was complicated. The various permutations of primal, glamour, political, and everyday images propelled Baker's master performances and narratives. However, while her legend has been dismantled with a vengeance time and again, her humanity has always been affirmed, and her talent has always remained intact. From exotic to activist, perhaps Josephine Baker's most enduring legacy is how she brilliantly managed to manipulate the White male imagination. She radically redefined notions of race and gender through style and performance in a way that continues to echo throughout the fashion and music industries, from Prada to Beyoncé, and beyond.❖

Katherine Dunham
(1909-2006)
Dancer, anthropologist, choreographer, author, activist

Katherine Dunham was a pioneer of the anthropological dance movement, bringing Caribbean and African influences into a European-dominated dance world. She was the first African American woman to lead a successful dance troupe, one of the first African American women to choreograph a major film, the first African American woman to choreograph for the Metropolitan Opera, and one of the first African Americans to earn a degree in anthropology.

KATHERINE DUNHAM was born in Glen Ellyn, Illinois to Fanny June Williams Taylor Dunham, who possessed Indian, French Canadian, English and African ancestry, was a teacher and school principal, and Albert Millard Dunham, a tailor and dry cleaner. Her mother was twenty years older than her father and had five children from a previous marriage. Together they had two children, Dunham and an older brother, Albert Jr. When Dunham was three and a half years old, her mother died from stomach cancer, and Dunham and her brother were sent to live with their father's sister on the South Side of Chicago. Dunham remembered this period as an immersion of Black vaudevillian culture, which profoundly affected her. After Dunham's father married Annette Poindexter, a schoolteacher from Iowa, the family moved to the predominantly White neighborhood of Joliet, where he ran a dry-cleaning business (Das 2017). From this experience, she not only found herself dealing with racial codes and segregation, Dunham had to navigate the light- and dark-skinned color dynamic that existed among her family members (Foulkes 2002).

Dunham had a difficult childhood; her father's volatile rage and fluctuating finances tore the family apart, and she went back and forth between her father's and her stepmother's homes. Around age twelve, Dunham's stepmother took her to St. Louis, a trip that raised her awareness of blues and jazz that had a lasting impact on her choreographic style throughout her career (Das 2017).

At a young age, Dunham became interested in both writing and dance. When she was twelve years old, she published a short story in a magazine edited by

W. E. B. Du Bois. She attended Joliet Junior Central High School, where she played baseball, tennis, basketball, and track, served as vice president of the French club and was on the yearbook staff. Around this time, Dunham joined the Terpsichorean Club, a dance group that emphasized the Dalcroze Eurhythmics method, an approach to experiencing dance through movement, and the Laban method, which adopted a scientific approach to dance. She had an opportunity to put her choreographer's imagination to the test when she organized and starred in a "cabaret party" to help raise money for her church. Dunham's liberated secular performance, however, scandalized the church (Das 2017).

Interestingly enough, as much as Dunham loved dancing, she never thought about pursuing a dance career. Instead, she ceded to her family's wishes to become a teacher. She attended Joliet Junior College and took a job at the Chicago Library (Foulkes 2002). At her brother's suggestion, Dunham joined the Cube Theater, an interracial artistic venture that welcomed White artists sympathetic to the New Negro cause. She performed in plays and met artistic luminaries such as Alain Locke, Langston Hughes, Studs Terkel and W. C. Handy (Das 2017). She also met Mary Hunter, a White director and producer who would prove influential to Dunham's career. During this period, she found herself moving out of her repressive upbringing and diving into a bohemian theater world, that added a new dimension to her personality.

In 1928, Dunham followed her brother to the University of Chicago and soon after she discovered anthropology. She attended a lecture by Robert Redfield, whose anthropological research in Mexico focused on acculturation which caught her attention. Redfield was the pioneer and, for a number of years, the principal ethnologist to focus on the processes of cultural and social change characterizing the relationship between folk and urban societies. He suggested that African Americans had preserved African traditions through vernacular dance that made its way into popular dances such as the Lindy Hop and the Cakewalk. Dunham was prompted to switch her major to anthropology and study dances of the African diaspora while simultaneously dancing and choreographing throughout her college career. She would later use Redfield's folk-urban continuum to interpret her ethnographic research in the Caribbean. Dunham attended classes taught by Redfield, A. R. Radcliffe-Browne, Edward Sapir, Lloyd Warner, and others.

Although Redfield was Dunham's advisor, Melville J. Herskovits, head of the anthropology department at Northwestern University, was her greatest influence. One of the foremost scholars of West Africa, Herskovits also argued that African Americans retained African cultural practices. Dunham's mentors represented the most progressive wing in the field of anthropology. While they challenged notions of the primitive as inferior, they still operated under the assumption that a distinction existed between the primitive and the civilized, a concept that invoked clichéd ideas of the era (Das 2017). Nevertheless, their views certainly impacted Dunham, and she soon realized that in order to develop a true Black dance aesthetic, library books, dance teachers, and professors would only take her but so far.

In 1929, Dunham married Jordis McCoo, a postal worker and dancer. Although he performed in some of her productions, they gradually drifted apart.

At age eighteen, Dunham began studying ballet with Ludmilla Speranzeva, formerly of the Moscow Theater and one of the first ballet teachers to accept Black dancers as students. Speranzeva introduced Dunham to the Spanish dancers La Argentina, Quill Monroe, and Vicente Escudero. Dunham also studied ballet with Mark Turbyfill, a choreographer, poet and painter; Ruth Page, a prominent Chicago choreographer; Bentley Stone a ballet dancer; modern dancer Siana Huebert; and Vera Mirova, who exposed her to East Indian, Javanese, and Balinese dance forms. Dunham decided to confront existing racial hierarchies through dance, an audacious move at a time when the Black female body was considered to have little capacity for intellectual expression. She also wanted to start a dance company that challenged stereotypes and establish Black dance as a serious art form (Das 2017).

In 1930, while an undergraduate, Dunham established with Turbyfill the short-lived Ballet Nègre, one of the first Black ballet companies in the U.S. In 1931, Ballet Nègre gave its debut performance at the annual Beaux Arts Ball in Chicago with "Negro Rhapsody," which was well-received. Unfortunately, the company faced resistance from the dance community and was ignored by the Black press (Das 2017). Choreographers, critics, and audience members believed that African Americans could not dance ballet. Agnes De Mille went so far as to tell Turbyfill that a Negro Ballet was not possible (Foulkes 2002). They also offered dance classes, but lost students when they were forced to move from the Loop to the South Side when the landlord found out that the school was catering to a Black clientele. Although Dunham and Turbyfill took their case to the community, no engagements followed, and the group disbanded.

In 1931, Dunham choreographed Hall Johnson's musical, *Run, Little Children,* the first Black show in Chicago's Loop district. With Speranzeva's help, Dunham opened her first dance school, the Negro Dance Group, which borrowed and reworked compositional devices of modern dance of the period (Manning 2004). It survived a rocky start and Dunham's absences when she was engaged in anthropological fieldwork. Dunham and the Negro Dance Group performed together and separately, primarily in Chicago and New York. In 1932, the company performed *Fantasie Négre* at the Chicago Artists Ball. It was accompanied by two Black pianists: the woman who composed *Fantasie Négre,* Florence B. Price, and composer Margaret Bonds, and were well-received by critics and audiences alike.

Page, the ballet director of the Chicago Opera, cast Dunham in *La Guiablesse (The Devil Woman),* a ballet based on Martinique folklore performed at the Chicago Civic Opera House in 1934. Dunham continued to appear as a guest artist with the Chicago Opera, where on occasion she also served as Page's assistant.

Erich Fromm, a psychoanalyst who was a friend and mentor at the University of Chicago, played an important role in Dunham's life. He extended an invitation to Mrs. Alfred Rosenwald of the Julius Rosenwald Fund to attend one of Dunham's dance concerts. She became fascinated with the young dancer's ideas about dance and its potential for understanding other cultures. As a result, Dunham was invited to apply for and was subsequently awarded a Julius Rosenwald Fund Fellowship to study the dance forms of the Caribbean under the aegis of the University of Chicago's anthropology department and Herskovits at Northwestern University. Armed with foundation money, Dunham sailed for the Caribbean in 1935 and began her historic journey in American dance.

Dunham spent the next two years studying traditional dances in Jamaica, Martinique, Trinidad and Haiti, an experience that changed her life. Besides finding the dance materials she sought, she developed a novel approach to ethnographic fieldwork by directly connecting with the African diaspora. Rather than merely observing, as her mentors implored her to do, Dunham participated with the people, even undergoing initiation into the Haitian religion of Vodun (she would later become a priestess in 1992). Her dancing won her the acceptance and admiration of the people she met, and she felt a new sense of kinship.

Interestingly, Dunham found a personal and artistic connection to Haiti. She purchased a seventeen acre property[1] that she used as a retreat for herself and her company. She established a clinic and leased part of the property as a hotel that became a resort and playground for the rich while she lived in a separate house alongside it. This bizarre bubble of luxury in a developing country flourished until 1985 when the fall of the Duvalier dictatorship claimed the hotel.

Dunham returned to the U.S. informed by new methods of movement and expression. Her presentation included photos, films, writings and demonstrations that would eventually transform the dance world. She submitted her thesis, "Dances of Haiti: Their Social Organization, Classification, Form, and Function," to the Department of Anthropology at the University of Chicago in partial fulfillment of her degree. During this period, Dunham choreographed and performed in many works, including the suite *Primitive Rhythms,* and "Barrelhouse," a duet, which is one of her earliest Americana works.

In 1936, Dunham received her PhB (Bachelor of Philosophy), becoming one of the first African Americans to earn a degree in anthropology. After returning to Chicago, Dunham revived her dance group as the Katherine Dunham Dance Group (later renamed the Katherine Dunham Company) and taught her dancers

---

1.   The amount of land Dunham purchased is not clear. Some reports indicate seventeen acres, thirty acres and according to *The New York Times,* forty-five acres (https://www.nytimes.com/2002/08/06/world/port-au-prince-journal-in-katherine-dunham-s-eden-invaders-from-hell.html). Dunham, who last visited Haiti in 1996, envisioned the property as a botanical garden, but then it was overrun by squatters and gangs. Eventually a portion of the land was designated as public land and in 2006, was transformed into the Katherine Dunham Cultural Center. It features a library and botanical garden in her honor (https://visithaiti.com/things-to-do/katherine-dunham-cultural-center).

the complex, polyrhythmic movements of the Caribbean. Throughout the years, the Dunham Company helped launch the careers of many African American performers. Dunham alumni include Talley Beatty, Alvin Ailey, Rosalie King, Frances Davis, Eartha Kitt, Janet Collins, Walter Nicks and Josephine Premice.

Dunham and her company made a one-time appearance at the 92nd Street YM-YWHA in New York in 1937, joining African and African American modern dancers Edna Guy, Alison Burroughs, Clarence Yates, and Asadata Dafora for *A Negro Dance Evening*. They were eager to establish Negro Dance as a serious artistic genre (Kraut 2003). In the first half of the program, Dunham presented a suite of West Indian dances. In the program's second half, "Modern Trends," Dunham presented *Tropic Death*, casting Talley Beatty as the fugitive from a lynch mob. That same year, as part of the suite called *Primitive Rhythms*, Dunham premiered "Rara Tonga" at the Goodman Theater in Chicago, which was subsequently performed as an independent work. Dunham and her dancers premiered *Tropics* at the Abraham Lincoln Center in Chicago. The suite of dances also included the infamous, "Woman with a Cigar."

Dunham was named director of the Negro Unit of the Chicago branch of the Federal Theater Project and in 1938 staged dances for several Chicago productions, including *Run Li'l Chil'lun* and *The Emperor Jones.* Her first breakthrough was with her first full-length ballet, *L'Ag'Ya,* which premiered in 1938 as part of Chicago's Federal Theatre Project. Combined with elements of Afro-Caribbean, ballet, and modern dance, *L'Ag'Ya* was based on a fable of love, jealousy, and revenge, culminating in a staged version of the *ag'ya,* the fighting dance of Martinique. Dunham's ballet became part of the repertory of Ballet Fedré, a component of the Federal Theater Project, at the Great Northern Theater. Louis Schaeffer of the Labor Stage invited Dunham to New York to create numbers for *Pins and Needles,* a satirical revue produced by the International Ladies Garment Workers Union (ILGWU) that ran on Broadway in 1939.

Shortly after Dunham's divorce in 1938, she began to work with Canadian John Thomas Pratt, a costume and theatrical set designer. Pratt, who was White, shared Dunham's interests in African-Caribbean cultures and was happy to put his talents in her service. They eventually went to Mexico in 1941 and engaged in a commitment ceremony, and they legally married in the U.S. in 1949. Soon after, they adopted their four-year-old daughter from a Catholic convent in Paris. From the beginning of their association, Pratt designed the sets and every Dunham costume for the remainder of his career. He also created designs for Agnes de Mille and Miriam Winslow.

Dunham's big breakthrough occurred after moving to New York in 1939 when she opened *Tropics* and *Le Jazz Hot* at the Windsor Theater. It was supposed to be a one-night event, but demand was so high that Dunham's company ended up doing thirteen weeks. The success of *Tropics* and *Le Jazz*

Hot catapulted Dunham into the spotlight. *Tropical Revue* soon followed, which was a hit not only in the U.S. but also in Canada.

In 1939, Dunham choreographed *Bahiana,* which premiered at the University of Cincinnati. It is about a woman from Bahia, Brazil, who dances and sings as she becomes entwined in the ropes of a group of dockside rope weavers at work. *Bahiana* would become one of Dunham's most celebrated characterizations and remained in her repertory throughout the 1940s.

In 1940, George Balanchine cast Dunham in *Cabin in the Sky*, a Broadway musical starring Ethel Waters, and later for the 1943 film. What the published credits do not reveal is that Balanchine and Dunham were, in effect, co-choreographers of the dances in the show, at least for those in which she and her dancers appeared. Dunham found their collaboration quite agreeable, and she and Balanchine enjoyed a particularly amicable working relationship. She then went to Hollywood and danced in and choreographed the movies: *Carnival of Rhythm* (1941), *Star-Spangled Rhythm* (1942), *Stormy Weather* (1943), and *Casbah* (1948). These dance performances consisted of brief, vivid numbers by African Americans that could be easily edited out for Southern distribution.

But it was the fast-paced live shows for which Dunham was celebrated. *Tropical Revue,* which was successfully produced on Broadway in 1943, toured the nation to much acclaim. Unfortunately, its sensuality also drew complaints, and it eventually closed in Boston. She codirected and danced in *Carib Song* at the Adelphi Theater in New York in 1945, and in 1946 she was producer, director, and the star of *Bal Nègre* at the Belasco Theater in New York. She also choreographed (without appearing in) *Pardon my Sarong* (1942).

Dunham is credited for developing one of the most important pedagogues for teaching dance that is still used throughout the world. She was a pioneer in folk and ethnic choreography and one of the founders of the anthropological dance movements from the Caribbean and African influences that was introduced to a European-dominated dance world. The world-famous Katherine Dunham Technique, a modern dance style that combines Caribbean folk movement with ballet in the inimitable Dunham modernist approach, was born during this period.

In 1944, she rented Caravan Hall, Isadora Duncan's studio in New York, and opened the Dunham School in New York, where artists like Marlon Brando and James Dean took classes. Until it closed a decade later, it offered courses in dance, acting, psychology, philosophy, music, design and foreign languages, later expanding to the Katherine Dunham School of Cultural Arts in 1952.

Dunham's company made its first appearance in London in *Caribbean Rhapsody,* a music and dance revue performed at the Prince of Wales Theatre in 1948, which was already a success in the U.S. It was the first time Europeans witnessed Black dance as an art form and the first time cultural elements of American modern dance appeared outside of America. It was more than an enthusiastic reaction to a brilliant theatrical experience; audiences were enthralled.

In 1949, Dunham returned from touring for a brief stay in the U.S., where she suffered a temporary nervous breakdown after the sudden death of her beloved brother, Albert Jr., a promising philosophy professor at Howard University and a protégé of Alfred North Whitehead. He became mentally ill and was institutionalized. He had a lobotomy and, after several failed suicide attempts, he removed his left eye by his own hand and died (Clark, Johnson, and Dunham 2005). Dunham, who was incredibly close to her brother, was heartbroken.

With extensive runs on Broadway and national tours during the 1940s and 1950s, Dunham's company reached a truly broad audience that was primarily White, and had an undeniable impact on theatergoers and their perceptions of Black dance (Kraut 2003). By 1955, Dunham and her company had toured Europe, Greece, North Africa, Mexico, Australia, East Asia, New Zealand and parts of the U.S. The company appeared in festivals and foreign films produced in Italy, Mexico, Germany and Vienna.

In the late 1950s, Dunham experienced a fallow period. In 1957, Dunham temporarily disbanded her company. Financial travails were part of the cause, but she grew tired of the tensions within, and considered a new career. While in Paris and Buenos Aires in 1949, she had tried painting. After returning her dancers from their last Asian tour to America, Dunham stayed in Japan in 1957 and 1958 to dabble in painting and write her autobiography, *A Touch of Innocence: Memoirs of Childhood,* which was published in 1959 (Connors 2014).

After her break, Dunham choreographed the U.S. film, the *Green Mansion* (1959), and then reunited her company to embark on their third and what would become their final European tour, which ended abruptly in Vienna. Because of bad management by their impresario, the company was stranded without money. To raise funds, Dunham quickly negotiated contracts for television shows and a club date in order to send her company home. Dunham would reassemble dancers for special events, but 1960 effectively marked the end of the continuous history of dancers trained in the Dunham Technique and coached to perform Dunham choreography.

The Katherine Dunham Dance Company had become the nation's first self-supporting Black modern-dance troupe that helped revolutionize American dance. The company toured for nearly three decades, stirring audiences around the globe in fifty-seven countries with their dynamic and highly theatrical performances. Dunham's choreography was neither an exact rendering of the ethnic dance as she had seen them, instead, she designed a sense of a place, where gesture, sound and color existed in a variety of ways, and dance was a sensory experience among many. Dunham relied on ethnography and her personal experience as Black participant-observer to validate her conception of the Black people she surveyed. She transferred her knowledge and experience of African diasporan culture into an African American setting and, in the process helped form an African American aesthetic in dance (Foulkes 2002).

In 1962, Dunham, a few former Dunham dancers, and the Royal Troupe of Morocco appeared in a new revue, *Bamboche!* at New York's 54th Street Theater. It was a three-act revue that introduced to America the dancers of Morocco, who appeared with the consent of King Hassan II. After eight performances, the show closed. It was Dunham's last Broadway performance (Das 2017).

Dunham choreographed Giuseppe Verdi's *Aida*, starring Leontyne Price at the Metropolitan Opera in 1963, and continued to secure her place in dance history by becoming its first African American woman choreographer. In 1966, President Leopold Sedar Senghor invited Dunham to Dakar for the famous Festival des Arts Nègres, and she served as the year's Ballet National director and consultant.

After Dunham disbanded her company, she turned most of her attention to teaching and social activism, which began in earnest with her long association with Southern Illinois University (SIU). In 1964, she was invited to become an artist-in-residence and choreographed Charles Gounod's *Faust* at the Carbondale campus. She then accepted a position at SIU Edwardsville and became a member of the Anthropology faculty, where she established an advanced anthropology program. Dunham settled in East St. Louis, Illinois in 1967 and founded the Performing Arts Training Center (PATC), which was co-funded by SIU. She did more than offer courses, she counseled disadvantaged young people to dance and perform. Within a few years. Dunham had turned the troubled city of East St. Louis into an important hub of the Black Arts Movement, and during this period enrolled over 1,000 students into her programs. Her African and Haitian art collection became the basis for the community's Katherine Dunham Dynamic Museum, which she opened in the late-1970s. Even as she pushed for Black empowerment, she never abandoned her commitment to integrationist liberalism (Das 2017).

Dunham served as a board member of the Institute of the Black World in Atlanta and was a co-organizer of the First International Congress of Black Dancers and Choreographers. She served on the board of the Kennedy Center for the Performing Arts, helped advanced the National Council of the Arts in Education, and reviewed applications for the National Endowment for the Arts (NEA). In 1972, she choreographed and directed Scott Joplin's opera *Treemonisha* at Wolf Trap in Washington, D.C., which also appeared in Atlanta and St. Louis.

Dunham published her ethnographic observations, articles and short stories in publications such as *Esquire, Bandwagon, Ellery Queen Magazine*, and *Educational Dance*. She also wrote several books, including *Journey to Accompong* (1946), which describes her experiences with the Maroons, *Las Danzas de Haiti* (1947) published in Mexico, *Les Danses d'Haiti* (1957) published in France, *Island Possessed* (1969), *Kasamance*, an African fable (1974), and the coffee table book *Dances of Haiti* (1983).

Dunham's husband, John Thomas Pratt, died in 1986.

The Alvin Ailey American Dance Theater (AAADT) produced *The Magic of Katherine Dunham,* which opened the company's 1987-1988 season. Among the works reconstructed under the supervision of Dunham were *Choros, L'Ag'Ya, Shango, Flaming Youth, 1927,* and *Cakewalk.* In 1990, Dunham and her colleagues began comprehensive documentation of the Dunham Technique, which has been formally preserved at the Library of Congress, including a repository of documents from her career including artifacts from her dance productions and travels.

Throughout her distinguished career, Dunham earned numerous honorary doctorates, awards and honors. Among them is the Presidential Medal of Arts, The Kennedy Center Honors, the plaque d'Honneur Haitian-American Chamber of Commerce Award, French Legion of Honor, Southern Cross of Brazil, Grand Cross of Haiti, NAACP Lifetime Achievement Award, The Albert Schweitzer Music Award at Carnegie Hall, Lincoln Academy Laureate, and the Urban Leagues' Lifetime Achievement Award. Dunham's recognitions include a star on the St. Louis Walk of Fame, inclusion in the book *I Have a Dream* (1963), and the Women's International Center's Living Legacy Award. In her final years, Jacob's Pillow gave a special Tribute to Katherine Dunham for her ninety-third birthday. In 2000, Dunham was named America's Irreplaceable Dance Treasure by the Dance Heritage Coalition.

Dunham made headlines staging a forty-seven day hunger strike in 1993 at eighty-two to protest the U.S. government's repatriation policy for Haitian immigrants and raise concerns about issues in Haiti. The Institute for Intercultural Commitments, one of the last organizations she founded before her passing, was dedicated to cultural exchange that promotes a globally connected society.

Long widowed and unable to manage her finances, Dunham lived in near destitution by the late 1990s. Friends moved her from East St. Louis to New York for adequate care. In the last few years of her life, she was the subject of retrospectives from Alvin Ailey's dance company and feted by universities and arts groups. She continued to make public appearances, grant interviews and speak of dance as a way of communicating across cultures.

Dunham appeared at the Morgan Library and Museum in New York to screen Oprah Winfrey's *Legends Ball,* an ABC special celebrating Winfrey's sheroes. She also appeared at La Boule Blanche (the White Ball) at Riverside Church in New York, organized to celebrate *Kaiso!: Writings by and about Katherine Dunham,* edited by VèVè A. Clark and Sara E. Johnson, published by University of Wisconsin Press.

Katherine Dunham, the dancer, choreographer, teacher and anthropologist whose pioneering work introduced much of the Black heritage in dance to the stage, died on May 21, 2006 at ninety-six in an assisted living facility in New York City. Her daughter survives her.❖

Margot Webb
(1910-2005)
Ballroom dancer, teacher

Margot Webb, who performed with Harold Norton and was professionally known as "Norton and Margot," was a member of one of the first African American ballroom teams in history.

MARJORIE SMITH WEBB was born in New York City to Gertrude Violet Fay Bush, a pianist who worked in nightclubs, and George Mitchell Smith, a classically-trained violinist who also taught the saxophone and clarinet. Her father traveled with the James Reese European Fifteenth Regiment Band during World War I. One of Webb's earliest memories is when her father took her to see the ballroom dancers Vernon and Irene Castle perform, which profoundly affected her (Gottschild 2011). Webb's father ended up staying in England and France and eventually abandoned his family. Many years later, Webb learned that her father was alive and still performing in Europe.

Webb's family were mulattoes, which gave them certain advantages in the color-conscious world of African American society, the segregated world of White America, and entry into the entertainment industry (Gottschild 2011). Besides her mother, her three maternal aunts were also in show business. Webb spent her formative years in Lower Manhattan before her family migrated to Harlem.

Her primary education was in Catholic schools. With the help of Catholic Charities, Webb attended St. Francis-Charles Hale High School (now known as St. Francis Academy) in Baltimore, a boarding school run by the Oblate Sisters of Providence, an order of African descent and the first of its kind in the U.S. In the sixth grade, Webb returned to Harlem to attend St. Mark the Evangelist.

She studied dance with Vivian Roberts and enrolled in the drama program at the New York Public Library on 135th Street (now known as the Schomburg Library). She studied ballet with Louis Chalif, a Russian emigre, and later taught at his studio on 57th Street. She also danced professionally, part-time, while in high school. Webb attended Hunter College until she dropped out to pursue dancing full-time, and she became a headline dancer in the Cotton Club from 1933 to 1939. She began touring in the African American vaudeville circuit in the East and Midwest, and in New York, Philadelphia, Washington D.C., and Baltimore. Webb's solo work included jazz toe-dance (*en pointe*), yet her favorite couple dance had always been the waltz. In 1933, while at one of her dance performances, she met

Harold Norton. Soon after their meeting, they became ballroom dance partners and were professionally known as Norton and Margot.

Webb modified her name from Marjorie to Margot, adding the "t" for a more "Latin" effect. In many cases, Webb and Norton had to masquerade their true identities, often presenting themselves as Hispanic in order to be hired.

Webb and Norton opened a dance studio in Harlem in 1936. Besides teaching classes for children and adults, they also choreographed routines, often for White nightclub performers. While the team was on tour, their duties were shared by other performers and teachers associated with the studio.

In 1937, Norton and Margot toured in London, Paris, and Germany, first as part of the Cotton Club Revue with the Teddy Hill Band, then as an independent act on Continental variety shows. They performed at the London Palladium, the Moulin Rouge, and Théâtre des Ambassadeurs in Paris. During this time, they received regular coverage in African American magazines and newspapers such as the *Amsterdam News, Norfolk Journal and Guide, Pittsburgh Courier,* and the *Chicago Defender.* Because of their busy schedules, they had difficulty making money from their Harlem studio, so they closed it in 1938.

Norton and Margot continued to perform at Dave's Cafe in Chicago and tour nightclubs in the Midwest in 1940. However, by this time, the Midwest White vaudeville theater circuit began to decline. The theaters became film houses, showing two-feature films, newsreels, and cartoons. When they returned from the Midwest, the team toured the Northeast African American vaudeville circuit.

With fewer bookings, Norton and Margot dissolved their partnership, but Webb continued to dance professionally. In 1941, Webb and a colleague, Al Vigal, passed as French to perform as exotic dancers in a Montreal revue, *South Sea Magic.* Webb turned to solo work, performing specialty dances and jazz toe-dance at the Apollo Theater and occasionally dancing with Al Moore.

Webb returned to Hunter College and completed her bachelor's degree in French. In 1940, she married William P. Webb Jr., an athletic director for the Children's Aid Society and a semiprofessional basketball and football player in the Black leagues. She and her husband would have two daughters.

Norton and Margot staged a comeback in 1946 and opened at Harlem's Club Baron, but received few bookings afterward. As a result, the team permanently disbanded in early 1947 (Gottschild 2011). With fewer bookings and the winding down of the Swing Era, Webb retired from show business.

Webb taught dance in after-school recreation centers while taking night courses at Columbia University's Teachers College, and graduated with a master's degree in education in 1948. When she started her family with her husband during the 1950s, they moved to the suburbs, and she became a junior high schoolteacher in Harlem, and also taught at Catholic colleges (Goittschild 2011). Her whereabouts were unknown until she was found in Miami in the 2000s. Margot Webb died on April 5, 2005. She was ninety-five years old.❖

The Legacy of Margot Webb

JUST LIKE BALLET, BALLROOM DANCING is not exactly revered for its racial diversity—and pop culture portrayals have leaned heavily on the mythology of Vernon and Irene Castle and Fred Astaire and Ginger Rogers as the standard-bearers of ballroom dancing. But the dance style's lily-white reputation hides something unexpected, that is, its innovation is based on European, African, South America and West Indian cultures, including the Waltz and the Minuet, the Lindy Hop and the Black Bottom, the Rhumba, Mambo and Tango, East Coast and West Coast Swing, and countless other dances. While these dances laid the groundwork for ballroom dancing, they bear little resemblance with their historical beginnings. One should consider that ballroom dancing is inseparable from Western imperialism and the colonialism from which it evolved. In fact, today's ballroom dancing encompasses both a fascination with Black culture and the simultaneous derision of it (McMains 2001).

By the first half of the twentieth century, modern ballroom dancing in the U.S. was one of the most popular venues of social life for middle- and upper-class urbanites. Norton and Margot was perhaps the first African American ballroom team in history who dared to challenge the status quo. They were blindsided by segregation and Jim Crow, to be sure, but because they did not perform the typical dances audiences expected from Black dancers, they held little appeal to both Black and White audiences. However, fair-minded folks and critics loved their soulfully graceful and polished dancing, regarding it as the highest standard of ballroom dancing on the same level as the Castles and Astaire and Rogers.

Even today, as ballroom dancing has become a multibillion-dollar business and is vying to become an Olympic medaled event under the auspices of DanceSport, most people see ballroom dancing as a White art form that is not culturally suitable for people of color (Picart 2012).[1] Moreover, while DanceSport has created a USA Dance team, it is breakdancing that actually made its Olympic debut in 2018 and is scheduled to return in 2024.

While Norton and Margot belonged to the Swing Era of the 1930s and 1940s, they appeared on the scene too early to enjoy success due to the nature of their performance style and the racial tenor of their time. They preceded the civil rights era when more opportunities became available to African Americans in White show business by two decades. Stuck between two eras, Norton and Margot would have certainly gained more show business opportunities if they had complied to a stereotyped "Black dance" routine. In the end, Webb's legacy amounts to her staying true to her artistic endeavors, knowing she may not fully succeed given the social circumstances, but having the fortitude to give it a try.❖

---

1.   On Quora, there is an interesting exchange about why Black people are not involved in ballroom dancing, which speaks for itself. ("Why aren't there many African Americans who dance ballroom?" https://www.quora.com/Why-arent-there-many-African-Americans-who-dance-ballroom).

Jeni LeGon
(1916-2012)
Tap dancer, actor, teacher

Jeni LeGon was the first African American woman to establish a solo tap dance career, the first African American woman to sign to a major Hollywood studio, and the only African American woman to dance with Bill "Bojangles" Robinson.

JENI LEGON was born as Jennie Bell Ligon in Chicago, Illinois to Harriet Bell Ligon, a housewife, and Hector Ligon, a Geechie from the Georgia Sea Islands who was a chef and railway porter. The youngest of four children, LeGon began dancing at a young age. Not one to be a high-heeled dancer in pretty skirts, she was a low-heeled dancer who performed toe-stand in pants, doing rigorous combinations of flash, acrobatics, and rhythm dancing. She developed her talent on the streets, in neighborhood bands and musical groups.

LeGon received her first formal training from Mary Bruce's School of Dance. By the age of thirteen, buoyed by her brother who had a job touring as a singer and exhibition ballroom dancer, she landed her first job in musical theater, dancing as a soubrette in pants. Although LeGon often skipped school to learn new dance routines from the movies, she graduated from Sexton Elementary School in 1928. In 1930, at age thirteen, she successfully auditioned for the Count Basie Orchestra's chorus line. Leaving Englewood High School a year later, LeGon was already a cutting edge professional dancer with a repertoire of knee drops, flips, slides, mule kicks, and flying splits, which she performed wearing pants.

In 1931, LeGon became a member of the Whitman Sisters, the highest paid act on the Theatre Owners Booking Association (TOBA) circuit for African American performers. This all Black, woman-managed company was successful in booking themselves continually in leading southern houses, and had the reputation for giving hundreds of dancers their first performing break. In 1933, LeGon and her half-sister, Willa Mae Lane, formed a song-and-dance team. They were given the opportunity to go to Detroit and work with nightclub owner Leonard Reed. While there, they received an offer to travel to Hollywood and perform with composer Shelton Brooks. But when they got there, they discovered there was, in fact, no job. LeGon heard about auditions being held by Ethel Waters' former manager, Earl Dancer, for a film that Fox Studios was producing. She won the part and subsequently appeared in dance numbers in several musicals. When Louella Parsons mangled her name in her Hollywood gossip column, the spelling "Jeni LeGon" stuck.

LeGon was offered a featured role and made her film debut in RKO's musical, *Hooray for Love* (1935), performing the gleeful number "Living in a Great Big Way" with Fats Waller and Bill "Bojangles" Robinson. Waller was of great help to her career by employing her as a vocalist and dancer with his band. She would be the only African American woman to dance with Robinson in a film, whose most famous duet partner was Shirley Temple.

After that triumph, MGM gave her a contract, making LeGon the first Black woman to sign with a major Hollywood studio. She was a pioneer, but also a pariah on the lot. MGM paid her handsomely, but she was still forbidden to eat with her fellow White actors. She was supposed to perform in *Broadway Melody of 1936* (1935), but when it appeared she might outshine the star of the film, Eleanor Powell, she was quickly dropped (Trenka 2021). Her enormous talent was kept behind-the-scenes at MGM, where she worked as a dance consultant and dance director, staging numbers such as "Sping" for Lena Horne in her first movie, *Panama Hattie* (1942), but receiving no onscreen credit. With no roles to offer her, MGM bought out LeGon's contract.

The cachet of LeGon's worthless contract at least led to her getting some stage work, and she travelled to Britain to work in the West End, where she found a small but significant degree of respect, unlike in Hollywood. She appeared in C.B. Cochran's revue, *Follow the Sun* (1936), and presented an uncharacteristically slow shimmy in a cabaret scene in the British film, *Dishonour Bright* (1936).

When she returned to the U.S., LeGon starred in independent Black-led feature films like *Double Deal* (1939) and turned in a number of specialty dance appearances in Hollywood films, the kind that could be edited out from Southern showings. During her career, she did get a chance to work with performers such as Ethel Waters, Al Jolson, Fred Astaire, Cab Calloway, Marlena Dietrich, Lena Horne, Ann Miller, and Josephine Baker. She toured widely with U.S. Army shows, and did club and theater performances nationally and internationally. She also starred in Fats Waller's Broadway musical, *Early to Bed,* which opened in 1943, and took dance lessons from Katherine Dunham that same year.

Her twenty-four film credits include *Broadway Melody of 1936, This Was Paris,* (1937), *Start Cheering, Fools for Scandal* (1938), *I Can't Give You Anything But Love* (1940), *Birth of the Blues, Sundown, Arabian Nights* (1941), *While Thousands Cheered, Stormy Weather* (1943), *Hi De Ho* (1945), *I Shot Jesse James* (1949), and *Somebody Loves Me* (1952). Many of her appearances were uncredited, and as the years wore on she appeared less as a dancer and more as just another maid, like in *Easter Parade* (1948). When she tired of maid roles, LeGon joined a group of Black actors and called upon Ronald Reagan, the then-president of the Screen Actors Guild, regarding their concerns about the stereotyping of Black actors, but Reagan showed no interest. In the end, LeGon was a homeless tap dancer, and was unable to sustain a film career for very long (Trenka 2021).

During the 1950s, LeGon had a recurring role on CBS's *Amos 'n' Andy*, and played the role of Daphne Jackson, the Kingfish's secretary. In 1953, she founded the Jeni LeGon Dance Studio in Los Angeles and taught jazz and tap, hiring teachers to conduct classes in ballet, African, and Caribbean dance. Former students include the playwright Mickey Grant, and the choreographer Victor Upshaw. When she created a performance group of students from the school, she quickly ran into financial problems, and had to shut the school down soon after. That same year, LeGon appeared with Dorothy Dandridge and Harry Belafonte as a teacher in *Bright Road.* Her next and final film role would not come until *Bones* (2001), which featured Snoop Dogg.

During the 1960s, LeGon toured with her multicultural revue, *Jazz Caribe*, which toured nationally and internationally into the early 1970s. By 1969, she had relocated to Vancouver, British Columbia, and taught tap, point, and the Dunham technique. In the 1970s, LeGon worked with Troupe One, a youth theater group, and traveled to London with the Pelican Players in the 1980s. It was not until the 1980s, when tap festivals got off the ground, that LeGon began receiving some of the recognition she was denied during much of her career. Rusty Frank, a dancer and preservationist, interviewed LeGon for his book, *TAP! The Greatest Tap Dance Stars and Their Stories 1900-1955* (1995), which has become a standard reference for tap history. She was also a featured performer in Frank's all-star *Jazz Tap* revues of the late 1980s and 1990s.

In 1987, LeGon was inducted into the Black Filmmakers Hall of Fame, and in 1993, she was selected for the Los Angeles Tap Dance Hall of Fame. In 1999, the National Film Board of Canada released Grant Greshuk's prize-winning documentary, *Jeni LeGon: Living in a Great Big Way,* produced by Selwyn Jacob and narrated by Fayard Nicholas of the Nicholas Brothers. In 2002, she was one of nine African American tap dancers and the only woman to receive an honorary degree of Doctor of Performing Arts from Oklahoma City University, and in 2011, she was the recipient of the Flo-Bert Award.

By 2004, LeGon was teaching dance and voice privately, as well as at the Kits Neighbourhood House in Vancover. An accomplished percussionist, she was performing every Sunday night with a five-piece band at the La Botte nightclub.

LeGon's brief marriage to composer and arranger Phil Moore ended in divorce. She met Frank Clavin, a jazz drummer, in 1977, who became her long-time companion. Jeni LeGon died on December 7, 2012 in Vancouver, British Columbia. She was ninety-six years old. The nonconformity of LeGon's appearance and dance style helped to establish women tap dancers as competent, creative performers as opposed to conventional objectified passive showgirls.❖

Janet Collins
(1917-2003)
Ballet dancer, choreographer, teacher

Janet Collins was a pioneer in concert dance and broke boundaries by becoming the first African American to grace the stage with the Metropolitan Opera Ballet.

JANET COLLINS was born in New Orleans, Louisiana, one of six children to Alma de Lavallade Collins, a seamstress, and Ernest Lee Collins, a tailor. They were both of Creole descent. Her parents' pursuit of culture and academics were utmost on their minds. Her mother attended Fisk University, and her father was an avid reader who taught his children to memorize a new word every day. At the age of four, Collins moved with her family to Los Angeles, where she received her first dance training at the Catholic community center in Los Angeles. By the time Collins attended Hooper Avenue Elementary School, she also discovered she was an artist.

Collins spent her life nurturing her talent in both dance and art. She studied ballet, modern, and ethnic dances, in addition to drawing and painting. Ironically, her parents urged her to study painting rather than dance because, at the time, art seemed to offer more opportunities to gifted African Americans than classical dance (Lewin and Collins 2011).

Like so many aspiring African American dancers during the Jim Crow era, Collins was turned away from dance schools when they became aware of her race. Her first encounter with formal training was when her mother discovered Louise Beverly had a dance studio in her home. Her mother sent her daughters to study with her in exchange for sewing dance costumes for Beverly's recitals. Beverly introduced Collins to classical ballerinas Anna Pavilova and Marie Taglioni, and she studied with her for several years. From this experience, ballet quickly became Collins' first love.

During the 1930s, while still a teen, Collins performed as an adagio dancer[1] in vaudeville shows with Al Dixon and Graham Fain. They called themselves the "Three Shades of Brown." When Dixon decided to relocate to New York, the group dissolved and Collins managed to arrange for private lessons from Charlotte

---

1. The widely accepted definition of adagio is acrobatic balance with counterbalance. It is an action, or series of actions, where one partner is hoisted up in the air and the other partner acts as the base.

Tamon, affiliated with the Tamon School of Ballet. She provided Collins with training in all aspects of ballet. In order to pay for her classes, Collins taught dance classes for the children in her neighborhood. She also attended all the major dance performances at the Los Angeles Philharmonic Auditorium and saw artists such as Mary Wigman, Harald Kreutzberg, Martha Graham, and the Ballet Russe de Monte Carlo. Her aunt, who owned a bookstore in Los Angeles, would send Collins books on African American history, poetry, and many other topics. Although Collins had been shut out from the White ballet world, she found ways to expand her knowledge and cultivate her training on her terms.

When Collins was sixteen, her aunt suggested she audition for Ballet Russe de Monte Carlo, which was conducted by its leading dancer and choreographer, Léonide Massine. Although impressed by her talent, Massine told Collins that she would have to dance in whiteface in order for her to become a member of the company. Collins declined.

As Collins tackled the dance world, she also took art classes at Jefferson High School, and was employed by President Franklin D. Roosevelt's National Youth Administration to design and paint murals. She also received a scholarship to attend the Art Center School, where she was introduced to anatomy. Collins carried quite a load, juggling dance and art. After graduating from high school, Collins attended Los Angeles Junior College (now known as Los Angeles City College) as an art major from 1935 to 1936. She studied art history and continued to paint and sketch. Up until this point, Collins undertook both gifts side-by-side, but then decided that dancing would be the major key in her life (Lewin and Collins 2011).

She was approached by Lester Horton in 1937 to perform in Igor Stravinsky's *Le Sacre du Printemps (The Rite of Spring)*. Although Collins had no experience in modern dance, Horton promised to teach her, and he did. Her performance was a success and she received great reviews.

Collins danced in a revival of Hall Johnson's *Run Little Children* with an all-Black cast in 1938, and went on to study with Dorothy Lyndall. In 1939 at twenty-two, Collins unexpectedly eloped with Charles Holland, a widowed performer who sang tenor with Johnson's choir. That same year, she performed a solo in *Swing Mikado*, an interpretation of the popular Gilbert and Sullivan operetta that featured an all-Black cast and her husband. After the revival, she toured with Eddie Anderson, who played Rochester in *The Jack Benny Program*, in a cross-country vaudevillian tour (Lewin and Collins 2011).

Her marriage collapsed after nine months, undermined by Holland's adulterous behavior, and she returned home to live with her parents. In time, Collins became distraught and deeply depressed, enough to seek psychiatric care in an institution. Without her consent and with the permission of her parents, Collins underwent a tubal ligation in 1940. The doctors convinced her family that since Collins had a mental illness, she could not fully assume responsibility for herself or any children she may bear in the future, and that the procedure would ensure Collins' health and happiness.[2] It would take Collins years before she forgave her parents, especially her mother, who insisted on the procedure.

Overwrought and withdrawn from this experience, Collins took a year off to recuperate, and found her solace in painting. She eventually met Katherine Dunham and Talley Beatty at a get-together at her aunt's house in Los Angeles and danced with her for a time. She performed with the Dunham company in the 1943 film musical *Stormy Weather,* and toured with Beatty as part of a nightclub act, appearing in a few soundies. They were often billed as "Ria and Rico de Guerra" to prevent speculation about the two light-skinned dancers' race. Their partnership ended after a year because they found themselves temperamentally incompatible.

Collins realized early on that she was not company material. She saw herself as an independent individual: a producer, choreographer, and soloist. In 1945, Collins was the recipient of the Julius Rosenwald Fund Fellowship to create a solo concert. She spent a considerable amount of time working on this project, studying with Carmelita Maracci, a Spanish dancer that used ballet technique, Mia Slavenska and Adolph Bolm. She was intrigued by liturgical dance and studied with composer Ernest Bloch, a Hebrew music expert, and began to produce a diverse repertory that explored her French and Black heritage. Unlike her peers Katherine Dunham and Pearl Primus who studied dance overseas, Collins used her fellowship to develop her repertoire in the U.S.

Her much-awaited solo concert took place in 1947 at the Las Palmas Theater in Los Angeles. The concert, which covered a wide range of dance styles, were all staged and choreographed by Collins, and received high acclaim. She presented several solo presentations in the Los Angeles area for a time, but in order to forward her career, she relocated to New York later in the year. Collins made her New York debut at the 92nd Street YM-YWHA in a joint concert of emerging artists. Her performance garnered glowing reviews from leading dance critics like John Martin and Walter Terry, which earned her a *Dance Magazine* "Debutante of the Year" award. She held her first New York solo recital at the Kaufmann Auditorium in 1949, presenting the repertory from her solo concert in Los Angeles, to great reviews. Collins also made her television debut on *The Admiral Broadway Revue* hosted by Sid Caesar. Her artistic destiny as the choreographer and performer of her own work was beginning to yield the results she desired.

During her brief time in New York, Collins' stunning achievements brought her to the attention of Ted Shawn, who was always looking for exciting new talent to present at his festival. She appeared at Jacob's Pillow's eighth season,

---

2.   The Eugenics movement, which emerged in the late nineteenth century in the U.S., was based on the belief that American society would be greatly improved by increased breeding of Anglo Saxons and Nordics, whom they assumed had the highest IQs. Most immigrants, Blacks, Indigenous people, poor Whites, and people with disabilities became targets of eugenics programs. Black women were targeted with involuntary sterilization and were susceptible if they were judged to have aggressive behavior or deemed sexually promiscuous. This practice continued as late as the 1970s.

performing works that she had developed in her repertoire since her first solo concert in California. Collins' approach was ahead of her time since the mixed-technique abilities of today's dancers were much less common during the 1930s and 1940s.

During this period, Collins was featured in *Vogue* and *Ebony*. She briefly taught at the School of American Ballet (SAB), while continuing to develop a formidable concert dance repertory. Collins relied on her creative instincts to design costumes and commission music for her concert dances.

In 1950, Collins caught the eye of Agnes de Mille for the minor role, "Night," in Cole Porter's Broadway musical, *Out of This World*. The show was a flop, but the critics could not praise Collins enough, and she earned more reviews than the stars. She won a Donaldson Award in 1951 for Best Danseuse in the Musical Division for her performance in *Out of This World,* was named Young Woman of the Year and given a Merit Award from *Mademoiselle,* and was featured in *Glamour.* The Committee for the Negro in the Arts lauded Collins for her outstanding contributions. She also appeared in television variety shows, such as *This is Show Business, The Jack Haley Show,* and *Luncheon at Sardi's.*

Around this time, Collins came to the attention of Zachary Solov, the Metropolitan Opera's choreographer and ballet master, and general manager Rudolf Bing, who hired her under contract as a prima ballerina, a first for the company. While the Metropolitan Opera had engaged Black dancers and singers previously in occasional specialty roles, Collins' hiring marked the first time a Black artist joined the company.

At thirty-four years old, Collins broke the color barrier at the Metropolitan Opera in New York City on November 13, 1951, when she performed in *Aida.* Over the next few years, she had lead roles in productions of *Carmen, La Gioconda,* and *Samson and Delilah.* But despite her success and status in New York, when the company went on tour, Collins faced racism on the road. In some Southern cities, race laws kept her off the stage, and understudies played her parts. Solov and Bing threatened not to return unless African Americans were permitted to perform and allow Collins a room in the hotel with the rest of the company. By 1954, Collins announced her retirement, mostly because as a deeply spiritual woman, she felt her dance career no longer gave her the satisfaction she once needed (Lewin and Collins 2011). It also did not help that the constraints on Black classical dancers limited the vibrant performing career she rightly deserved.

Collins remained active in the 1950s touring with her dance troupe throughout the U.S. and Canada, but the stress of touring during the Jim Crow era led her to teaching. Collins taught at the SAB, Harkness House, and the San Francisco Ballet School. She even voluntarily taught at Saint Joseph School for the Deaf, using dance as a form of rehabilitation.

She was a demanding teacher who required her students to study human anatomy and undergo extensive physical training. Collins held concurrent positions at Manhattanville College of the Sacred Heart at Purchase, New York, Mother Butler Memorial High School, and Marymount Manhattan College. Collins' last-known concert dance appearance took place in 1965 at Marymount in a lecture-demonstration. In 1970, Collins relocated back to California and returned to the opera world one last time as the choreographer of *Nabucco* for the San Francisco Opera. She also taught at Scripps College and the Mafundi Institute.

Collins's repertoire included a wide range of styles, which was unusual for Black dancers of that era. She mixed modern and classical dance, used Black and White musical themes, and performed as several racialized genders, from the blackamoor to the Mozart hero to the Creole quadroon, that were both humorous and serious. For example, *Blackamoor*, set to music by J. S. Bach, is a neatly stylized seventeenth century court dance whose character was a little black boy dressed in an elaborate and colorful costume from the French courts of Louis XIV. Collins danced *Eine Kleine Nachtmusik* to the music of Mozart, which took full advantage of her polished ballet technique (Lewin and Collins 2011). What would become her signature work, *Spirituals,* consisting of "Nobody Knows the Trouble I've Seen," and "Didn't the Lord Deliver Daniel," were stark and powerful.

On the other hand, her folk music suite, which drew on her Creole heritage, dealt exclusively with representations of African American womanhood. "The Young Fishwife" represents the haggling market woman, while "La Creole" is about a young girl dreaming of her first dance. "Apre le Mardi Gras" represents joy that features leaping and spinning movements. These pieces, all choreographed to Louisiana Creole music, represented Creole women characters dressed in vibrant costumes. It is why many credit Collins as the first transitional Black choreographer in the concert dance world (Tinsley 2018). Unfortunately, few records survive of Collins' original choreography.

In later years, Collins choreographed for the Alvin Ailey American Dance Theater and the San Francisco Opera, but she focused mainly on painting and, having turned to religion, found comfort as an oblate in the Benedictine order. Her last work to premiere in New York City was *Canticle of the Elements,* performed by the Alvin Ailey American Dance Theater in 1974 during a joint tribute to Collins and Pearl Primus as pioneering Black women in dance.

In 1974, Collins retired from choreography and teaching altogether, and donated her professional archives to the New York Public Library for the Performing Arts at Lincoln Center. Her depression ambushed her far too often, driving her to eccentric behavior and she often went in retreat (Lewin and Collins 2011). It took more than twenty years for the elusive Collins to resurface when she appeared in Philadelphia as the keynote speaker at the Eighth International Conference of Blacks in Dance in 1995, and revealed she was painting religious subjects exclusively. In failing health, she moved to Fort Worth from Seattle in 2000 to be closer to her brother, Ernest Patrick Collins. Janet Collins died on May 28, 2003, in Fort Worth, Texas. She was eighty-six years old.❖

Pearl Primus
(1919-1994)
Dancer, choreographer, anthropologist, teacher

Pearl Primus was an ambassador of African dance and the African experience in the Caribbean and U.S. She played a significant role in presenting African dance to American audiences, choreographed dances that contained messages about racism and discrimination, and developed cross-cultural teaching methods through lectures and dance courses.

PEARL EILEEN PRIMUS was born in Port of Spain, Trinidad to Albertha Emily Jackson Primus and Onwin Edward Primus, a merchant seaman. Her family immigrated to the U.S. in 1924 and eventually settled in Hell's Kitchen in New York City, where her mother gave birth to a third child. Shortly after that, they relocated to Brooklyn. Her relatives kept the memories of their West Indian roots and African lineage alive by distilling them into stories that transmitted a sense of cultural and historical heritage. Primus' familial ties would have a profound effect on the art she would later create.

Raised in a tight-knit West Indian community that did not feel limited by racism, Primus believed education and hard work would outweigh the disadvantages of segregation and bring her closer to upward economic mobility. It was in this environment that Primus excelled in school, both intellectually and athletically. After attending public schools, she became one of the few Black students enrolled in Hunter College High School and Hunter College, both selective institutions (Schwartz and Schwartz 2011). Primus was a winning athlete, setting records in the high jump and broad jump, and was a star sprinter. She was also an avid reader, wrote poetry, and started an after school dance club at Hunter College. Aspiring to become a physician, Primus graduated in 1940 from Hunter College with a BA in biology and premedical sciences. But when she applied for jobs as a laboratory technician to earn money for medical school, she could not land a job because few scientific jobs were available to African Americans.

Primus enrolled in health education courses at New York University and transferred into the graduate psychology program at Hunter College in 1941. In the meantime, she made a living doing various odd jobs, including vegetable picker, welder, burner, riveter, and health teacher.

Two things happened that changed the trajectory of Primus' life. First, she took dance classes at Dance on the Moon and the University Settlement House. She quickly discovered that the dancing body was at the center of her expressive life and that teaching would become her medium for storytelling. She also became radicalized by affiliating with cross-cultural and left-leaning organizations that would inspire her choreographic works (Schwartz and Schwartz 2011).

By the early 1940s, Primus worked for the National Youth Administration (part of the Works Progress Administration (WPA), which gave her a job in the wardrobe department in 1941, working backstage for "America Dances." When a spot opened up for a dancer, Primus filled in and quickly discovered a natural gift for movement and connecting with the audience. She also became a dance counselor at Camp Wo-Chi-Ca (a contraction of Workers Children's Camp), an interracial co-educational summer vacation camp founded by the Communist Party in 1934. The camp was supported by left-wing artists such as Charles White, Jacob Lawrence, Gwendolyn Knight, Langston Hughes, Vinnette Carroll and Paul Robeson. The camp also had a point of intersection with New Dance Group, a modern dance collective founded by Jane Dudley, Sophie Maslow, and William Bales, which Primus would become associated with as their first Black student and performer. Her early years with the dance collective grounded her in contemporary dance practices and exposed her to a unique brand of artistic activism that the organization had embraced when it was established in 1932 (Schwartz and Schwartz 2011).

Determined to explore the available resources of formal dance fully, Primus also trained with Martha Graham, Charles Weidman, Doris Humphrey, and Louis Horst, from whom she gained an eclectic foundation in modern dance. She worked closely with Asadata Dafora, a Sierra Leonean multidisciplinary musician who was one of the first Africans to introduce African drumming music to the U.S. Working as a dancer caused Primus to doubt her long-term goal of becoming a medical doctor. Encouraged to look at dancing as a healing medium, she focused more exclusively on dance while continuing her studies by taking graduate-level courses.

Through the years, Primus invited an eclectic group of people into her inner circle. Hadassah Spira Epstein, a Jerusalem-born American dancer, choreographer, and instructor specializing in Indian, Javanese, Balinese, and Jewish dance, helped infuse Jewish mysticism into Primus' choreography. Haitian-born dancer Jean-Léon Destiné introduced her to Haitian voodoo dance rituals, while former dancer turned historian Joe Nash would serve as a supporter and mentor (Schwartz and Schwartz 2011).

Even though Primus' body type was considered atypical and challenged notions of beauty in the dance world, she used this to her advantage by incorporating her athletic abilities into her work and focused on developing African-based choreography to differentiate herself from other dancers. Primus began to research African dance by consulting books, articles, pictures, and museums to develop her unique brand of choreography. She made her professional debut in 1943 at the 92nd Street YM-YWHA, where she appeared in a joint concert, *Five Dancers,* along with four other emerging young artists. Primus presented her first composition, "African Ceremonial," along with "Strange Fruit," based on the poem by Lewis Allan (Abel Meeropol) about a lynching, "Hard Time Blues," based on a song about sharecroppers by folksinger Josh White, and "Rock Daniel." Her performance was so outstanding that critics viewed her protest dancing electrifying.

A few months later, Barney Josephson, owner of New York City's Café Society Downtown, a racially integrated nightclub, invited Primus to perform there for ten months. Beginning in April 1943, she filled the club's small stage with power, emotion, and her famous five-foot-high jumps. That June, Primus performed at the Negro Freedom Rally at Madison Square Garden before an audience of 20,000 people. In December 1943, Primus appeared in Dafora's African Dance Festival at Carnegie Hall before Eleanor Roosevelt and Mary McLeod Bethune. She also choreographed a work to Langston Hughes' famous poem "The Negro Speaks of Rivers," performed at her Broadway debut in 1944. During this time, Primus also performed with her new dance group, the Primus Company, at the Belasco and Roxy Theatres. In 1943, Primus re-choreographed "African Ceremonial" for a group performance in concerts at the Roxy Theatre.

In 1944, Primus began devoting time to performing sociological fieldwork. She undertook her first fieldwork in the Deep South to research the culture and dances of Southern Blacks. Posing as a migrant worker, she visited over seventy churches and picked cotton with the sharecroppers. In 1946, Primus formed a small dance company that toured exclusively at HBCUs and other venues, often sponsored by organizations, college arts presenters and dance programs.

In 1946, Primus was invited to appear in the revival of the Broadway production *Show Boat*, choreographed by Helen Tamiris. Primus choreographed the Broadway production *Caribbean Carnival*, a show that was very much influenced by the success of Katherine Dunham's work. From 1946 through 1947, Primus toured with her company, mostly in the South. She performed in Massachusetts at the University of Dance at Jacob's Pillow. She also appeared at the Chicago Theatre in the 1947 revival of *The Emperor Jones* in the "Witch Doctor" role that Hemsley Winfield made famous.

The Julius Rosenwald Fund Fellowship awarded Primus a grant to travel to Africa in April 1948. She spent a year visiting and living with the natives of Nigeria, Liberia, Ghana, Angola, Cameroon, Senegal and Zaire, observing and recording their traditional dances. In Nigeria, she was renamed "Omowale," meaning "child returned home." When she returned to the U.S., she continued studying and enrolled in graduate classes at Columbia University and published articles and essays. In 1950, Primus married film and television director

Yael Woll, who was White and Jewish, helped her manage her studio, but they separated after three years. In 1951, Primus embarked on a nineteen-week tour of England and Israel. While the reviews from England critics reflected the ingrained racist attitudes toward African dance, she was hailed by Israeli audiences for her authentic African works.

In 1952, Primus led a group of female students on a research trip to her home island of Trinidad, where she met dancer and drummer Percival Borde, who was performing with Beryl McBurnie's Little Caribe Theatre. That same year, Primus' passport was confiscated due to her association with the Communist Party and other left-leaning organizations. She would not fully resume international travel again until 1953 (Schwartz and Schwartz 2011). Primus and Borde would eventually welcome the birth of their son in 1955, and they married in 1961. While pregnant, Primus worked at Newark Museum in New Jersey, cataloging African objects and working on exhibitions. She used this opportunity to develop her choreography even further. She withdrew from the Columbia University program and transferred to New York University, receiving her MA in educational sociology in 1958.

Often compared to Katherine Dunham, Primus was a blazing star in her own right who did not share Dunham's show business acumen. Instead, Primus spent the better part of the 1950s and 1960s honing her intellectual accomplishments through teaching, lectures, and presentations while dealing with the complexities of her marriage and raising her son.

In 1963, Primus and her husband opened the Primus-Borde School of Primal Dance in New York City, where she developed cross-cultural teaching methods. Three years later, she initiated an experimental learning project funded by the U.S. Department of Education and placed it in New York City schools to further test her methods. Primus and Borde conducted research with the Konama Kende Performing Arts Center in Liberia to establish a performing arts center, and with the help of a Rebekah Harkness Foundation grant, organized and directed dance performances in several countries from 1959 to 1962. Primus and Borde taught African dance artists how to make their indigenous dances theatrically entertaining for the western world, and worked with the U.S. government to bring touring companies from African countries such as Senegal, Gambia, Guinea to perform in the U.S. These African exchange programs helped Primus mature as an educator and an artist.

Still eager to further her academic knowledge, Primus received her PhD in anthropology from New York University in 1978, becoming the university's first student to fulfill a language requirement with dance. Her groundbreaking doctoral thesis—a dance-oriented anthropology that was the first of its kind—drew from her notebooks, and choreography, as her main source of inspiration. In 1979, she and Borde founded the Pearl Primus Dance Language Institute in

New Rochelle, New York, where they offered classes that blended African and Caribbean dance forms with modern and ballet techniques. Their performance group was called Earth Theatre. Borde suddenly died of a heart attack during a performance at the Perry Street Theater, where he was appearing with Primus. He was fifty-six years old.

After his death, Primus rarely performed. From 1984 to 1990, she became director of Cora P. Maloney College, a Black studies school at the State University of New York at Buffalo, and was a Five-College Professor of Ethnic Studies at schools in Massachusetts during the 1980s.

In 1988 the dances "Strange Fruit," "Hard Times Blues," and "The Negro Speaks of Rivers" were revived and performed at the American Dance Festival in a program called *The Black Tradition in American Modern Dance* at Duke University in Durham, North Carolina. In 1990, her piece "Impinyuza" was presented at the City Center in New York by the Alvin Ailey American Dance Theater under the direction of Judith Jamison.

In 1989, Primus worked on a project sponsored by the arts divisions of Howard and American universities, which culminated in a presentation of dances performed by students and professionals at Howard University and the Kennedy Center's Terrace Theater. They included revivals of "The Negro Speaks of Rivers" and "The Wedding," as well as the new "Dance to Save Lives," based on a war dance from Zaire. She also taught at New York University, Hunter College, and New Rochelle High School. As an anthropologist, she continued to conduct cultural projects in Europe, Africa and America for such organizations as the Ford Foundation, U.S. Office of Education, New York University, Universalist Unitarian Service Committee, New York State Office of Education, and the Council for the Arts in Westchester.

Primus received many honors, including an honorary doctorate from Spelman College and the Distinguished Service Award from the Association of American Anthropologists. In 1991, President George H. W. Bush honored Primus with the National Medal of Arts, and in that same year, was named the first recipient of the Balasaraswati / Joy Ann Dewey Beinecke Chair for Distinguished Teaching. She was the recipient of the cherished Liberian Government Decoration "Star of Africa," The Scroll of Honor from the National Council of Negro Women, Membership in Phi Beta Kappa, The National Culture Award from the New York State Federation of Foreign Language Teachers, and Commendation from the White House Conference on Children and Youth.

Pearl Primus remained active in the dance community until succumbing to diabetes at her New Rochelle home on October 29, 1994, aged seventy-four. She was survived by her son, Onwin Borde, a percussionist known for his work in dance and theater. He died in 2006 and was fifty-one years old. He had no survivors.❖

Mable Lee
(1921-2019)
Jazz tap dancer, singer, entertainer

Mable Lee, revered for her "million-dollar legs," appeared in more than one-hundred soundies (three-minute musical films), earning the title "Queen of the Soundies."

MABLE LEE was born in Atlanta, Georgia to Rosella Moore and Alton Lee. Neither of her parents were in show business, but they sang and danced around the house, which made an impression on her. Lee began singing along with her grandmother's Victrola, and soon after, sang and danced at her aunt's job at the inn (Lee 2017). Lee was producing, directing, choreographing, and staring in school shows, charging an admission fee of a quarter. When she was nine years old, she was performing with big bands in popular nightclubs around town; and at the age of twelve, she performed in the first black-owned nightclub in Georgia, the Top Hat. The Whitman Sisters noticed Lee at the Top Hat, but her mother encouraged her to finish high school first before fully realizing her career.

Lee also performed with her high school music teacher, Graham Jackson, a celebrated African American theater organist, which included a performance at President Franklin D. Roosevelt's vacation house in White Plains, Georgia.

In 1940, Lee and her mother moved to New York, and she joined the chorus line at the West End Theater in Harlem. She also did acrobatics with a chair, which she has referred to as her novelty act (Lee 2017). Lee subsequently worked at various nightclubs, which led to the Apollo Theater, doing six shows a day. While it was rare for any woman to break out of the chorus, Lee did. She often appeared as a soubrette,[1] singing and dancing as a soloist, with a line of women behind her. She appeared in comedy skits playing a straight woman to such comics as Pigmeat Markham and Spider Bruce. Wearing short dresses and baring her midriff, Lee would always feature pronounced hip motion and other moves with sexual connotations such as shimmies in her dance. These sexy moves also revealed her versatility as a jazz dancer who mastered Black vernacular dance movements (Trenka 2021).

---

1. A soubrette is an actress or other female performer playing a lively, flirtatious role in a play or opera.

After the Apollo Theater, Lee worked at various Harlem nightclubs such as Small's, the Ubangie Club, and Club Sudan. During her early career, Lee danced with the male legends of the era, from Harold Nicholas and Honi Coles to the team of Cook and Brown.

Soon theater producer and director Dick Campbell sent Lee to London, where she spent eighteen months performing at the London Palladium (Lee 2017). There she met choreographer Clarence "Buddy" Bradley in London and taught dance classes alongside him when she was not performing.

During World War II, Lee performed in the first all-black USO unit conducted by Eubie Blake and his sixteen-piece orchestra. With over forty-five performers, including Butterbeans and Susie, Cook and Brown, Lee did five shows a day, and the troupe performed at Army, Navy, and Marine camps throughout the U.S.

The soundies (which featured song hits of the era equivalent to today's music videos), short films and race films were produced for Black audiences and were prevalent during the 1940s and 1950s. More often than not, they were the only media that freely represented Black images on the screen. Lee was approached by a number of producers, namely William Forest Crouch, an Australian immigrant who produced race films and soundies. From 1940 to 1946, Lee made over one-hundred soundies, such as *Half Past Jump Time* (c. 1945), *Baby, Don't Go Way From Me* (1946), and *Everybody's Jumpin' Now* (c. 1946) with Noble Sissle and his orchestra. In *Chicken Shack Shuffle* (1943), a virtual dance instruction song, Lee performed her own interpretations of the dance with truckin', boogie shuffles, cross-back steps, and legomania.[2] In *The Cat Can't Dance* (c. 1945), she sang about the guys who sent her diamond rings and took her to the swankiest nightclubs, bemoaning, "but these cats just can't dance." She choreographed and trained dancers throughout her career, even though she never received credit (Lee 2017). She also appeared in shorts and race films such as *Swanee Showboat* (1940), *Reet, Petite and Gone* (1947), and *Ebony Parade* (1947) with the Cab Calloway and Count Basie bands (McCann 2009). Although Lee never made it to Hollywood, she was adored by Black audiences around the country, and became the first color cover subject for the March 1947 cover of *Ebony*.

During the 1950s, Lee performed overseas in the USO with her own routine, consisting of two comedians and an all-woman chorus and band (Hill 2014). After touring France, Belgium, Ireland, and Scotland, she returned to Atlanta and married a saxophone player she had known since childhood. She created a solo act and performed at the Peacock, formerly known as the Top Hat. The marriage did not last long (Lee 2017).

Lee relocated to New York to book auditions and to help raise money to star in the Broadway revival of Noble Sissle and Eubie Blake's all-black jazz-age

---

2. Legomania is a specialty dance done as a limited eccentric type of dancing. It involves leg shaking or snaking, which may also include leaps and kicks in the air. It is often known as "rubberlegs" or "rubberlegging."

musical, *Shuffle Along* (1952), featuring choreography by Henry Le Tang. Lee sang "Craving for That Kind of Love" and "You Ain't Been Vamped 'til You've Been Vamped by a Brownskin." The revival was met with bad reviews and closed after four performances. She went on to sing on the album *Eubie Blake and His Girls* (1960), making popular again the hit song "You Got to Git the Gittin,' While the Gettin's Good."

In 1969, she was one of only three women to dance in *The Hoofers,* with Chuck Green, Lon Chaney, and James Buster Brown. It was a hit Off-Broadway show that opened at the Mercury Theater to rave reviews and brought renewed attention to Black tap dancers. From 1976 to 1978, Lee performed in the leading role of Irene in the national touring production of the Broadway musical revue, *Bubbling Brown Sugar,* which looked back at the heyday of Harlem nightclubs. After receiving standing ovations for her soft shoe dancing in the AMAS Repertory Theater's 1979 production of *Suddenly the Music Starts,* Lee was nominated for an Audelco Award for Outstanding Musical Performance. In 1985, she received a grant from the National Endowment for the Arts to create master dance videos on vintage chorus line routines and other fundamentals of chorus line work.

While tap dancing was only one of Lee's many talents, it was the concerts and festivals that grew out of the revival of tap in the 1980s and 1990s that she found a late career. When Lee appeared at the annual Tap Extravaganza honoring National Tap Dance Day, it was usually with the Dancing Ladies, her chorus line of young women. Tony Waag, the artistic director of the New York City Tap Festival, performed regularly with Lee in her last two decades. Since 1999, Lee also performed in the National Tap Dance Day's Tap Extravaganza, where she was honored with a Flo-Bert Award for her lifetime contribution to tap dance. Beginning with the first New York City Tap Festival in 2001, Lee was a star attraction. Waag presented her with the Toe-Knee Award in 2004, and she was inducted into the American Tap Dance Foundation (ATDF) International Hall of Fame in 2008.

Lee continued to dance, teach, and exemplify, among other things, the sheer plain flat-out fun of tap dancing. During her performances in her later life, she behaved as she had in the 1940s, and her sexy moves made no concession to age. Her range of motion may have been diminished, but her indomitable spirit was not. Lee was secured in her ability to charm any audience, even when she forgot the lyrics and improvised instead. Her last performance was in July 2018 at Symphony Space in Manhattan as part of the New York City Tap Festival.

In fact, in the days leading up to her death, Lee was still discussing plans for a new one-woman show. On February 7, 2019, Mable Lee died at ninety-seven at a nursing home in Manhattan and is survived by her son, two grandsons and a great-grandson. ❖

Mary Hinkson
(1925-2014)
Dancer, choreographer, teacher

Mary Hinkson broke racial boundaries of the almost exclusively white world of modern dance by becoming one of the first African American members of the Martha Graham Dance Company. She was also one of the first African American women to dance for George Balanchine.

MARY DE HAVEN HINKSON was born in Philadelphia, Pennsylvania to Cordelia Chew Hinkson, a public schoolteacher, and De Haven Hinkson, a physician and the first African American to head a U.S. Army hospital. Hinkson's aunt, Mary Saunders Patterson, was famed contralto Marian Anderson's first music teacher. She grew up with her sister in a comfortable middle class environment that allowed her to become culturally aware of the arts. Her mother realized early on, before Hinkson did, that her daughter was born to dance.

Hinkson attended Philadelphia High School for Girls, where she learned formalized gymnastics and participated in competitions. Her first dance training was in a high school Eurhythmics class, which used techniques devised by Emile Jacques-Dalcroze that taught musical concepts through rhythmical body movements. She also took dance classes by Doris Haywood at summer dance camp. Even though she did not know what a plié was, Haywood pushed Hinkson to begin pointe work. While Hinkson fell in love with dance, she remained focused on becoming a physical education teacher. She decided to attend the University of Wisconsin, Madison (UWM) because they offered an extensive curriculum in physical education. But when Hinkson arrived in 1943, it was far different from Philadelphia, and her transition to campus life was not an easy one.

Although African Americans had matriculated at the UWM since the mid-nineteenth century, they faced ardent racism. An unwritten but widely acknowledged policy excluded African Americans from dormitories, and they were often excluded from social events. Hinkson had to make arrangements to live off-campus. Securing campus housing was nearly impossible—discriminatory housing policies coupled with the wartime economy made campus housing nearly impossible. However, Hinkson managed to find and share a room with Matt Turney, a Black woman who was also an upcoming dancer. This unforeseen coupling was the beginning of a personal and professional relationship that lasted their lifetime.

Despite these setbacks, Hinkson thrived in this multicultural environment, especially with the teachers in the physical education department. After taking a course with Margaret H'Doubler, the dance department director, she decided to switch her major to dance. When she told her father she changed majors; he was reluctant but supportive. Hinkson reveled in Madison's robust dance scene. She joined the university's modern dance group, Orchesis and appeared in their production of *Orpheus and Eurydice*.

While at UWM, a number of prestigious Black guests, such as Paul Robeson and Pearl Primus, appeared in and around the campus. Hinkson saw Katherine Dunham and her dancers performed *Tropical Revue* at the Parkway Theater in 1944, and Alain Locke was appointed visiting professor of philosophy in 1946 (Nuchtern 1976-1977). Hinkson was introduced to the Martha Graham Company, which performed at the Union Theatre in 1946. H'Doubler had required her students to attend the show, which changed Hinkson's life.

In 1946, Hinkson completed her bachelor's degree but continued with graduate courses. After a year of study and writing a thesis, Hinkson earned her master's degree and, in 1947, became an instructor in the Department of Physical Education for Women at UWM—one of the first Black women to teach physical education at any majority-white university. In the meantime, Hinkson and an interracial group of students, Turney, Miriam Cole, and Sage Fuller Cowles, formed the Wisconsin Dance Group and toured Toronto and the Midwest in a 1933 Buick.

In 1951, Hinkson and Turney left for New York University and were invited to attend an eight-week course with Graham that led them to become the first Black dancers to join her company. At the height of the civil rights movement, while Hinkson broke boundaries in the dance world, she resisted being defined solely by her race. Hinkson was connected to the way Graham moved her dancers. Graham discarded traditional ballet and substituted its graceful gestures and soaring leaps with blunt, forceful gestures and stark, angular movements. Graham sought to expose the bare fundamentals of the human experience—the raw imagery of joy and despair—and evoke a visceral response from the audience, which perfectly matched Hinkson's sensibilities.

Early in her career, Hinkson struggled financially. While pursuing her dance career with Graham, she made money by giving private lessons and demonstrating in Graham's classes. This experience eventually led to a teaching position at the Juilliard School of Music's dance faculty when it included Alfredo Corvino, Margaret Craske, Louis Horst, Doris Humphrey, José Limón, and Antony Tudor.

Hinkson first came to prominence in Graham's *Diversion of Angels* (1948) as the Woman in White, an abstract work that depicts the purity of love. In this production, Hinkson was partnered with Bertram Ross, who was White and Jewish and became her longtime iconic dance partner. Graham took her modernist dance to the global Cold War stage with messages about freedom, democracy, race, gender, and religion and presented it with a multiracial company. With straightforward serenity and elegance, Hinkson made the Woman in White a signature role. By 1953, Hinkson was elevated to principal dancer, a position she held for nearly twenty years. Her performances from the 1950s through the early 1970s were filled with unbridled dramatic power. During her tenure with the company, Hinkson worked alongside some of Graham's most legendary dancers: Ross, Turney, John Butler, Donald McKayle, Ethel Winter, Paul Taylor, Glen Tetley and so many others.

In 1956, Hinkson married Julien Jackson Jr., and in 1958 they had their only child, a daughter.

Other notable roles Hinkson performed included *Warrior in Seraphic Dialogue* (1954), adapted from Graham's earlier solo *Triumph of St. Joan,* a lead role in *Ardent Song* (1955), and the *Awakener in Samson Agonistes* (1962). While Graham was still dancing, she created new and custom-made roles for Hinkson, such as the *Canticle for Innocent Comedians* (1952), a poem-like suite. Another Graham-created and highly acclaimed role was *Circe* (1963), a work that was otherworldly and full of mystery. Hinkson exuded a mix of ferocity and subtlety as the sorceress who casts a spell on Ulysses. Coaching her in the role, Graham told her that she must look at him obliquely as if she were an animal sensing his presence.

When the Graham troupe was not performing, Hinkson accepted invitations from other choreographers and performed as a guest artist with other companies. She had a periodic association with Butler and Tetley, both Graham alumni. In the 1950s, when he was ballet director of the New York City Opera, Butler created several roles for Hinkson, including his staging of *Carmina Burana,* which she performed alongside Carmen de Lavallade in 1959, *Bluebeard's Castle,* and Menotti's *Amahl and the Night Visitors,* which was televised. She worked with Anna Sokolow, and in 1956 she partnered with Alvin Ailey in Harry Belafonte's touring revue *Sing Man Sing.* In 1959, choreographer McKayle, who also danced with the Graham troupe, featured Hinkson, who created the female role in the premiere of *Rainbow' Round My Shoulder,* which became his signature piece. In 1960, Hinkson became one of the first African American women to perform in a George Balanchine role he created for her at New York City Ballet, including *Figure in the Carpet,* which she performed with Arthur Mitchell. Appearing in an imagined eighteenth-century court divertissement, she and Mitchell portrayed an African prince and his consort. She appeared with Tetley's modern dance troupe and in *Ricercare,* a duet he choreographed for her and Scott Douglas at American Ballet Theatre (ABT) in 1966.

Hinkson made several film and television appearances throughout her career. She appeared in the film, *A Dancer's World* (1956), which presented

Graham offering insight into her theories about dance and a glimpse into her methodology, and the documentary *Martha Graham: An American Original in Performance* (1957). She was also featured in the documentary short, *Night Journey* (1960), which featured Graham's dramatic retelling of the climactic scene from "Oedipus Rex," and the 1962 short jazz/dance film *On the Sound* with Turney and McKayle. She also performed on the television film *Arias and Arabesques* (1962) and several television series, such as *Omnibus, NBC Television Opera Theatre, Lamp Unto My Feet, The Revlon Revue, Tonight with Belafonte,* and *Camera Three.*

But Hinkson's heart belonged to the Graham repertoire, which increasingly provided her with great roles. When Graham retired from the stage in 1969, Hinkson took on some of Graham's leading roles. She appeared in a revival of Graham's *Deaths and Entrances* as Emily Brontë, a role Graham herself had danced. Hinkson stunned audiences with the sharp-angled savagery of her dance of madness in a widely hailed performance. She also took over Graham's starring role in *Clytemnestra,* a modern retelling of the Greek myth, Aeschylus's *Oresteia.* A dazzling and complex psychological study in evil and madness, Graham debuted it in 1958 and last performed it in 1967. *Clytemnestra* was hailed as a landmark in American theater. In her willingness to revive *Clytemnestra,* Graham reworked the title role for Hinkson, and it was later danced by Pearl Lang for the season. Ross repeated his original double role as Agamemnon and Orestes.

When Graham became ill in 1970, Hinkson and Ross directed the company, but when Graham returned, Hinkson and Graham clashed, and tensions ensued. Hinkson resigned from the company in 1973 and retired as a dancer at age forty-eight. It was not an ideal way to end a rather extraordinary relationship, although Hinkson publicly stated she had no regrets years later.

Hinkson continued to teach dance around the world. She taught at the High School of Performing Arts, the Alvin Ailey American Dance Theater (AAADT), and PHILADANCO. She also periodically taught contemporary techniques to companies such as the Stuttgart Ballet, Royal Danish Ballet, Dance Theatre of Harlem (DTH), and the Joffrey Ballet. With her perfect execution of the Graham dance technique, Hinkson made her reputation as a Graham dancer and was not defined as a dancer who usually explored African American heritage. She resisted being seen through a racial prism, though she acknowledged she would be.

Hinkson's husband had bought the D&G Bakery in Manhattan's Little Italy in 1979. After he died in 1983, the bakery was managed by Hinkson's daughter and niece before they sold it in 1997.

Matt Turney retired from the Graham troupe in 1972 and died in 2009.

Mary Hinkson died of pulmonary fibrosis in Manhattan in 2014 at age eighty-nine and is survived by her daughter, grandchildren, and sister. She received the Martha Hill Award days before her death.❖

Joan Myers Brown
(1931)
Ballet dancer, dance instructor, artistic director, administrator

Joan Myers Brown has been breaking barriers in dance since her founding of the Philadelphia School of Dance Arts in 1960, and the dance company PHILADANCO in 1970, which celebrated its 50th anniversary in 2020.

JOAN MYERS BROWN was born in Philadelphia, Pennsylvania to Nellie Lewis Myers, a research and chemical engineer, and Julius Thomas Myers, a chef and restaurateur. An only child, Brown grew up in Southwest Philadelphia. She fell in love with the ethereal art of ballet and as a youngster, studied briefly with Essie Marie Dorsey, whose school was the only one in the city to accept Black children in the 1940s. However, Brown stopped dancing because she lost her dance shoes, and her mother could not afford to buy more.

Brown would not have returned to dance if it were not for her gym teacher, Virginia Lingenfelder, a former ballerina of the Littlefield Ballet Company, who noticed her natural ability when she performed ballet steps during gym class. Her teacher encouraged her to join her after school ballet club at West Philadelphia High School, but she did not know anything about ballet. Brown required additional training, but she was unable to attend any of the major dance schools in the city because they were segregated. She had a white friend teach her in the morning, so when Brown went to the ballet club in the afternoon, she could keep up with the class. She was thinking about becoming an artist because she liked watercolors and painting, but once Brown started dancing again, she resumed her studies with Sydney Gibson King and Marion Cuyjet. Eventually, her dance instructors and role models would become Dorsey, King, and Cuyjet, who represented the key figures of Black women teachers in Philadelphia (Gottschild 2012).

When Brown dreamed of becoming a ballerina, it was during the height of segregation in America during the 1940s. When she went to see *Swan Lake* at the Academy of Music, it had little impact on her because the dancers were all White. However, when Brown saw Katherine Dunham perform at the Locust Street Theater, it made a huge impression on her and her desire to become a ballet dancer. Nonetheless, Brown would be confronted by the harsh truth that the White world of ballet would never accept a young Black ballerina, no

matter how talented or determined she was. This point was driven home when Brown tried to enroll in local ballet schools and was repeatedly turned down because she was Black. She also had to deal with the fact that light-skinned children received the leading roles in Black dance performances, while children like Brown were relegated to the chorus. Undeterred, she would go home and make up her own programs, and play the lead (Hine 1996).

Brown performed at Philadelphia Cotillions, Black debutante balls that staged elaborate numbers, and she learned a great deal about production. She also took classes with the renowned English dancer and choreographer Anthony Tudor, who came to Philadelphia from New York to teach integrated classes on Sundays. As the first Black student in Tudor's class, things were not always easy for Brown, especially when none of the men would partner with her. Instead, Tudor partnered with Brown, and she learned directly from the master.

Tudor quickly recognized Brown's talent, and she performed in the corps de ballet in *Les Sylphides,* which caused quite a stir. Although he warned Brown that there was little hope for her future in ballet (Hine 1996), Tudor encouraged her to study in New York City. Brown earned a scholarship to the Katherine Dunham School and studied under Syvilla Fort and Karel Shook, attending classes in New York once a week during the summer.

Brown had dreams of becoming like Janet Collins, who broke ground as the first Black ballerina with the Metropolitan Opera. But by the time she was eighteen, she was being pressured by her father to give up dance and continue her education. However, Brown forwent college and married Frederick Johnson in 1951. When he was drafted in the Korean War, she turned elsewhere to continue dancing. Soon after, she and her husband would divorce.

One of Brown's girlfriends, Kathy Sledge (later of Sister Sledge fame), had a job with a nightclub revue. When she left, Brown took her place. In time, she worked her way up onto better shows. She toured as a jazz dancer with Cab Calloway, Sammy Davis Jr., and Pearl Bailey, then for six years was the lead dancer and choreographer with Smart Affairs, Larry Steele's Atlantic City revue. She performed with celebrated Black entertainers such as Dick Gregory, Dinah Washington, Slappy White, Damita Jo, Billy Daniels, and Gladys Knight.

She toured the U.S. and Canada for nine years, but this was not the type of dancing she wanted to do. Brown studied ballet whenever she got the chance. During that time, she started teaching, too, but was dismayed by what the schools typically offered. Soon, Brown grew weary of dancing in nightclubs and shows, and began to dream about a school where African Americans could learn and develop through methods tailored specifically to their individual needs. Brown decided to return to Philadelphia and start her own school.

In 1960, Brown opened the Philadelphia School of Dance Arts in West Philadelphia and stopped dancing professionally in 1962. Her teachers included Katherine Dunham, William Amour, Ziggy Johnson, Marie Bryant, Stanley Brown,

Thomas Madras, and Lois Smith. She married Max Brown in 1967, and they had two daughters. They would eventually divorce.

The school, which began with thirty students and grew quickly, attracting primarily African American students, most from low-income families. As her dance school grew and the students progressed, its impact on the community increased. Brown realized that the dancers would eventually face the same limited performance opportunities that she endured. In fact, many of her exceptional students quit dance altogether or moved to New York because Philadelphia lacked dance opportunities. So, in 1970, Brown, Mary Sherrill, and Sarah Conway founded the Philadelphia Dance Company (PHILADANCO), a vehicle for professional minority dancers. PHILADANCO was created as a modern dance company, but ballet, tap, jazz and African dance were incorporated into many of their performances. At the outset, the troupe consisted of seventeen star pupils from Brown's dance school, and while the company has always been racially integrated, most of the dancers have been African American.

PHILADANCO's success is due, in no small part, to Brown's persistence. As artistic director and chief administrator, she was responsible for selecting and guiding the dancers and choreographers, raising funds, controlling expenses, and securing venues for performances. Over the years, she has proven to be an exceptional administrator, managing one of the finest Black repertoire dance companies in the nation and one of the few financially-solvent (Hine 1996). Her company was one of the first to offer its dancers a paid 52-week contract, a rarity in the dance world (Gottschild 2012). She has worked with Drexel's Dornsife Center, sent dancers to local schools to teach, partnered with the African American Museum, served on the board of University City District, and has given out seventy-five scholarships to local dancers every year. Wearing multiple hats, Brown has created a supportive and familial atmosphere where the dancers often call her "mom," "JB," or "Aunt Joan." At the same time, she pushed her dancers hard to achieve even more.

Brown set the artistic tone, daring, diverse in style, technically challenging, and entertaining, with much of the work related to the Black experience. Even the music is as eclectic as the dance styles. A typical evening performance may consist of three or four dances, which might include classical music by Bach, Berlioz and Tchaikovsky; classic jazz by Duke Ellington and Charles Mingus; rock by Santana and Prince; soul music by Aretha Franklin and The Supremes; and African music and rhythms.

In 1982, Brown moved the company from its small, confining quarters in West Philadelphia to its own building in Universal City, with four spacious studios, dressing rooms, offices, and a small performance center. Although Brown has had opportunities to leave West Philadelphia behind, she has chosen to stay in the neighborhood she loves, and continues to give back in large and small ways. When PHILADANCO occupied its old location in the 1980s, there were twenty-eight empty houses nearby, so Brown decided to purchase a few with money from the U.S. Department of Housing and Urban Development (HUD) and turned them into affordable artist-housing. As always, Brown continues to use her space for community events and to service the community's needs (Gottschild 2012).

In 2000, PHILADANCO, which had already become an internationally acclaimed company that sells out venues worldwide, was selected as a resident dance company at the Kimmel Center for Performing Arts.

The growing number of Black dance companies in America led Brown to convene the International Conference of Black Dance Companies in 1988. It laid the groundwork for the founding of the International Association of Blacks in Dance (IABD) in 1991, which showcases dance companies founded and directed by African Americans across the country. Brown believed a gathering of the Black dance community would serve not only her needs but also the needs of other Black dance professionals. IABD events function almost like family reunions, where dancers and students come together to participate in dance classes, scholarly panels, workshops, a wide range of performance showcases, and an awards dinner honoring individual contributions to the field. The conference convenes in a different host city each year. IABD celebrated its thirtieth anniversary in 2021, and Brown serves as its honorary chairperson.

Regionally and nationally, Brown has served with a broad range of organizations, including the New England Foundation for the Arts' National Dance Project; the U.S. Information Agency; Arts America; the National Endowment for the Arts; the state arts councils of Pennsylvania, New Jersey, Michigan, Nevada, and Ohio; and the National Forum for Female Executives. Locally, she has been a part of the Greater Philadelphia Cultural Alliance; the Minority Arts Resource Council, Inc.; the Philadelphia Mayor's Cultural Advisory Council; the Philadelphia Dance Alliance; the Women's Heritage Society; and Dance/USA. Brown was appointed to the choreographer's panel of the Rockefeller Foundation Arts & Humanities Program and served as vice president (and cofounder) of the Coalition of African American Cultural Organizations founded in 1989.

Brown's amazing career has not gone unnoticed. She is a Distinguished Visiting Professor at the University of the Arts in Philadelphia, which bestowed upon her an Honorary Doctorate of Fine Arts. She was awarded an Honorary Doctorate in Humane Letters by Ursinus College in Collegeville, Pennsylvania, and an Honorary Doctorate of Arts from the University of Pennsylvania. Brown is a Distinguished Visiting Professor at Howard University in Washington, D.C., and is also listed in *Who's Who in America.*

In 1997, Brown was honored as one of the "Dance Women: Living Legends" during a four-day series sponsored by New York-area presenters, in tribute to five African American pioneer women who founded distinguished modern dance companies with deep roots in Black communities around the country. In 2005, the Kennedy Center honored her as a Master of African American Choreography. In 2009, she received the prestigious Philadelphia Award, and on November 7, 2010 was declared Joan Myers Brown Living Legacy Day. She was honored by the *Philadelphia Tribune* and the African American Museum in Philadelphia, and awarded membership to the Distinguished Daughters of Pennsylvania in 2012. She was designated as one of The Ten Best Philadelphians by *Philadelphia* magazine in 2012, in addition to recognition as an Outstanding Alumni of West Philadelphia High School, her alma mater. President Obama presented Brown with the 2012 National Medal of the Arts, the nation's highest civic honor for excellence in the arts, in 2013 at the White House. Brown was also named a 2013 Dance/USA honoree. She is a recipient of the *Philadelphia Inquirer's* 2017 Industry Icon Award, and received the Philadelphia Cultural Funds David Cohen Award in 2019. Brown also received the distinguished 2019 Bessie Award for Lifetime Achievement in Dance for her choreographic influence on Black dance in America.

In 2020, at eighty-eight years old, Brown celebrated two landmark achievements: PHILADANCO's fiftieth year and the Philadelphia School of Dance Arts' 60th year. Her legacy has been documented in *Joan Myers Brown & the Audacious Hope of the Black Ballerina: A Biohistory of American Performance* (2011), written by dance scholar and critic Brenda Dixon Gottschild. WHYY PBS affiliate's documentary *PHILADANCO Turns 50!* featured Brown as part of their *Movers and Makers* series in 2020.

In the fifty years since its formation, PHILADANCO has turned out a high number of successful alumni. Some went on to join the prestigious Dance Theatre of Harlem (DTH) or Alvin Ailey American Dance Theater (AAADT), one started an Aboriginal dance group called Bangarra, others joined companies in Europe, and many have gone on to choreograph for PHILADANCO or perform on Broadway.

Having developed a succession plan when the company hit the half-century mark, Brown stepped down as artistic director and announced that Kim Bears-Bailey, the company's longtime assistant artistic director, would replace her. She is now artistic adviser and retains her title of founder.

Brown is a true Philadelphia legend. She has been the visionary leader in African American dance for over sixty years, and has faced and triumphed over much adversity in her life and career. She did not get to be the ballerina she wanted to be, but she was able to help other Black girls achieve that goal. Brown has battled systemic racism, nurtured her dancers, and has provided inestimable guidance and leadership in arts education. She has thrown everything—time, labor, brains, savings, love—into her two creations and is still going strong. She continues to push hard for recognition of her arduous, underfunded art form, cajoling and criticizing, and, above all else, strives for the highest level of excellence. With everything that Brown has achieved, as she nears ninety years old, all she can think about is getting ready for "the new next."❖

Carmen de Lavallade
(1931)
Dancer, choreographer, teacher, actress

Carmen de Lavallade is a multifaceted dancer, choreographer, actor, and teacher who left a lasting mark on the stages she's worked on and the artists she's worked with.

CARMEN DE LAVALLADE was born in East Los Angeles to French Creole/African mixed-parents mother Grace Grenot de Lavallade, and father Leo Paul de Lavallade, a postman and bricklayer from New Orleans. Her mother was in ill health during most of her childhood, and after she died, de Lavallade and her two sisters were raised by their aunt, Adele de Lavallade Young, in Los Angeles. Young owned the Hugh Gordon Book Shop, one of the first African American bookshops in Los Angeles.

De Lavallade was inspired by her cousin, ballet dancer Janet Collins, and discovered her talent for dance at an early age. In 1945, she began studying ballet with Melissa Blake. When she graduated from Thomas Jefferson High School in Los Angeles at the age of sixteen, she was awarded a scholarship to study dance with the renowned Lester Horton.

In 1949, de Lavallade became a member of the Lester Horton Dance Theater until 1954. A protégé of Horton, de Lavallade enjoyed the status of lead dancer in his group. During this time, she became proficient in ballet, theatrical dancing, and other forms of modern and ethnic dance. Horton insisted that she study other art forms as well, including painting, acting, music, set design, and costuming. De Lavallade studied ballet privately with Italian ballerina Carmelita Maracci and, later, acting with Stella Adler. Possessing physical beauty, elegance, and technical polish, de Lavallade developed a reputation as a well-rounded performer who entranced audiences with a sensual quality (Hine 1997).

The first of many roles Horton created for de Lavallade was Salome in "The Face of Violence," a production that began her long association with Alvin Ailey, her classmate from high school. In pursuit of an acting career, Lena Horne introduced de Lavallade to the executives at Twentieth Century Fox, and she danced in the films *Lydia Bailey* (1952), *Demetrius and the Gladiators* (1954), and *Carmen Jones* (1954).

After Horton died in 1953, and during the filming of *Carmen Jones,* de Lavallade was invited to dance in the Broadway musical *House of Flowers* by choreographer Herbert Ross. She set off for New York with Ailey, who was her partner in that production. Her relationship with him would become one of the most significant artistic collaborations of her career.

During that engagement in 1955, de Lavallade met and married dancer and actor Geoffrey Holder. With Holder, she completed her signature solo, "Come Sunday," which he suggested choreographing to a Black spiritual, sung by Odetta Gordon. Working with Holder, she was able to develop a West Indian-influenced style of modern dance.

In 1956, de Lavallade succeeded her cousin Janet Collins as a principal dancer at the Metropolitan Opera and performed in *Samson and Delilah* and *Aida.* She also made her television debut in John Butler's ballet *Flight.* Two months after de Lavallade's son was born in 1957, she returned to work and danced in a television musical allegory by Duke Ellington, *A Drum Is a Woman.* In 1958, de Lavallade danced in Alvin Ailey's evocative *Blues Suite,* an ode to African American life in the South. In 1959, she starred in Robert Wise's film noir, *Odds Against Tomorrow,* with Harry Belafonte, and appeared in several off-Broadway productions, including *Othello* and *Death of a Salesman.*

By the early 1960s, she became a principal dancer in John Butler's company and partnered with Ailey in the iconic ballet, *Portrait of Billie,* which Butler created for de Lavallade. It has been said that de Lavallade brought Louis Armstrong and Duke Ellington to tears with her embodiment of Billie Holiday. She was a principal guest performer with Alvin Ailey's company on its first European tour in 1962, which was billed the "de Lavallade-Ailey American Dance Company." In 1964, she danced with Donald McKayle, and in 1965 appeared in Agnes de Mille's American Ballet Theatre (ABT) productions of *The Four Marys* and *The Frail Quarry.*

In 1970, de Lavallade joined the prestigious Yale School of Drama as a choreographer and performer-in-residence. She staged musicals, plays, and operas, and later became a professor and member of the Yale Repertory Theater. Her students during this time included Meryl Streep, Sigourney Weaver, Christopher Durang, and Wendy Wasserman. De Lavallade did not expect her students to become dancers. However, she helped them discover how to use their bodies to tell stories.

Between 1990 and 1993, de Lavallade returned to the Metropolitan Opera as the choreographer for *Porgy and Bess,* and *Die Meistersinger.* She was a guest artist with ABT and choreographed for Dance Theatre of Harlem, PHILADANCO, and Alvin Ailey American Dance Theater. In 1993, she appeared with Bill T. Jones/Arnie Zane Dance Company at the Joyce Theater in New York City, still commanding admiration with her unique stage presence. That same year, she choreographed the dance for a new production of Antonín Dvořák's opera, *Rusalka,* at the Metropolitan Opera.

In 2003, de Lavallade appeared in a rotating cast in the Off-Broadway staged reading of *Wit and Wisdom*. De Lavallade and her husband were the subjects of the film *Carmen & Geoffrey* (2005), which chronicled their sixty-year partnership and artistic legacy. Additional works include *651 ARTS' FLY: Five First Ladies of Dance* (2009), *Step-Mother* by Ruby Dee (2009), *Post Black* by Regina Taylor (2011), and the Broadway production of *A Streetcar Named Desire* (2012). In 2010, she appeared in a one-night-only semi-staged reading of *Evening Primrose* by Stephen Sondheim. Geoffrey Holder passed away on October 5, 2014.

In 2014, de Lavallade performed a dance/theater work about her life. *As I Remember It* was an intimate portrait about her six-decade career, mixed with dance, film, and storytelling, weaved into a memoir about her venerable life on stage. She first performed at Jacob's Pillow in 1953, and holds the record for the longest performing career at the festival until 2014 with *As I Remember It.*

De Lavallade's ability to express psychological meaning through her body, to disappear inside the choreography and mold herself to wildly different artistic styles, has been her life's work. Her career has been a tapestry of star turns in ballet, modern dance, West Indian works created by her husband, films, Broadway musicals, and Shakespearean theater. De Lavallade's most obvious gift has always been an unearthly ease of moving, in a corporeal legato. Her subtler skill is how she has used that ease to etch out a character, binding her body to the music to serve a dramatic purpose.

Awards bestowed upon de Lavallade have included an Actors' Equity's St. Clair Bayfield Award in 1978, the Black History Month Lifetime Achievement Award in 2004, the Rosie Award and the Bessie Award in 2006, the Capezio Dance Award in 2007, and the Dance USA Award in 2010. She also received an honorary Doctor of Fine Arts degree from the State University of New York through Purchase College in 2006 and the Juilliard School in 2008.

In 2016, de Lavallade received the Lifetime Achievement Award at the Obie Awards, presented by the American Theatre Wing, and *The Village Voice* for her excellence in off-Broadway theater. In December 2017, she received the Kennedy Center Honors Award in recognition of her wide-ranging career as an artist in dance, theater, film, and television.

From Broadway to the Metropolitan Opera, de Lavallade has performed on the world's greatest stages, working with luminaries such as Josephine Baker, Lena Horne, and Harry Belafonte. De Lavallade has made her mark time and time again as a mesmerizing performer. In over six plus decades, she has inspired generations of artists and audiences, gliding onto the stage with a silky poise imbued with purposeful radiance. As de Lavallade nears ninety years old, it becomes clear that another descriptor must also be added to the already lengthy chain, legend.❖

Raven Wilkinson
(1935-2018)
Ballet dancer

Raven Wilkinson was the first African American woman to receive a contract to dance full-time with a major classical ballet company, the Ballet Russe de Monte Carlo of New York City.

ANNE RAVEN WILKINSON was born in New York City to Anne James Wilkinson, a homemaker, and Frost Bernie Wilkinson, a dentist. Both of her parents were born and raised in South Carolina but moved north to pursue their education. The family, which also included a younger brother, eventually settled in Harlem and her father opened a dental practice. His office was directly across the street from what would become the Dance Theatre of Harlem, foreshadowing Wilkinson's future in dance.

Wilkinson became a ballet fan at the age of five after seeing Ballet Russe de Monte Carlo perform *Coppélia.* Her mother, who had studied ballet in Chicago, took Wilkinson to the School of American Ballet (SAB) for lessons, but it would not accept her until she was nine, so she trained in the Dalcroze school.[1] For her ninth birthday, an uncle gave her a gift of ballet lessons at the Swoboda School. Wilkinson's first teachers included dancers Maria and Vecheslav Swoboda from Russia's Bolshoi Theatre, and the Chicago Civic Opera Ballet.

Léonide Massine, artistic director of the Ballet Russe, bought the Swoboda School in 1951, which gave Wilkinson an opportunity to audition for the troupe. Although she was light-skinned, acceptance into a ballet company was unlikely because of her race. Fellow ballet students urged her not to seek a position. In 1954, Wilkinson auditioned and was rejected. On a second attempt, she was rejected once again. Frustrated, Wilkinson enrolled at Columbia University to consider an alternative career. Undeterred, she auditioned again for the Ballet Russe and, on her third try in 1955, she was accepted on a six-week trial basis. She was twenty years old.

Just before dancer and choreographer Frederic Franklin, who held the audition class, passed away in 2013, he told Wilkinson that on the day of her third audition, he went to the company staff and insisted they accept her into the

---

1. The Dalcroze method, also known as Dalcroze Eurhythmics, incorporated basic elements of music—rhythms, melody, and harmony—with body movement, to provide a multidimensional approach to music learning.

troupe. Wilkinson's acceptance into the company in 1955 marked the first time the Ballet Russe hired a Black dancer—during the height of the Jim Crow era.

Her years with Ballet Russe were filled with both happiness and hardship. Wilkinson advanced to the position of soloist in her second season and remained with the company for six years. She performed a varied repertoire that included the waltz solo in Michel Fokine's *Les Sylphides,* the Chinese tea dance in *The Nutcracker,* a featured role in *Raymonda,* and ensemble roles in numerous one-act ballets. She also performed roles in *Ballet Imperial, Le Beau Danube, Capriccio Espagnol, Gaite Parisienne, Giselle, Graduation Ball, Harlequinade, Swan Lake,* and *Variations Classiques.*

As an African American, she faced many difficulties while on tour, particularly in the segregated South, and throughout the years, Wilkinson's colleagues supported and protected her. When Ballet Russe stayed in "Whites only" hotels, Wilkinson kept her race a secret. For two years, things went well. Because there were many foreign dancers in the company, including a number of South Americans, her skin color was not an issue. In 1957, however, she was barred from staying with the company when a hotel owner in Atlanta asked her outright if she was Black. Wilkinson refused to lie and was sent away in a "colored" taxi to a "colored" motel. During the same tour, members of the Ku Klux Klan interrupted a Montgomery, Alabama performance, asking, "Where's the nigra?" When none of the Company members responded to them, the men left.

As word of Wilkinson's racial identity spread, discrimination became increasingly problematic in both her personal and professional life. The company director, Sergei J. Denham, forbade her from dancing in certain locations and sent her ahead to safer cities on the tour. Ultimately, one of the company's ballet mistresses told her she would not go any further in her ballet career, and that she should leave to start a school of African dance.

After a while it became too much. Exhausted by years of discrimination, as well as the belief that the financially stressed company had become old-fashioned, Wilkinson resigned in 1961, much to the chagrin of Denham. She searched for work in other companies, but was never offered a contract by another American ballet company again. New York City Ballet's George Balanchine told her she was not his type of dancer, American Ballet Theatre's Lucia Chase would not consider her, and the Metropolitan Opera Ballet's Alicia Markova ignored her during her audition. Despite her classical training and professional experience she was told at auditions that she should try African dance or jazz instead. After one brutal rejection after another, Wilkinson retired her pointe shoes and stopped dancing for two years.

She worked briefly in customer service for a New York department store. Then, because she had always been attracted to the spiritual life, she joined an Anglican convent in Fond du Lac, Wisconsin. She stayed for only six months when she realized she had been given a great gift she had not used to its fullest. She returned to ballet classes, and not long after, began performing wherever she could.

By the mid-1960s, Sylvester Campbell, an African American principal dancer with the Dutch National Ballet, suggested Wilkinson approach the company, and she was invited to join as second soloist. She moved to the Netherlands in 1967 and stayed with the National Ballet for seven years. Her career included the Balanchine repertoire and the *Swan Lake* pas de trois. She also performed in *Les Sylphides, The Firebird, Symphony in C, La Valse, The Snow Maiden,* and *Graduation Ball.* Wilkinson found the culture of the Netherlands much more accepting than in the U.S. In 1974, due to a mandatory retirement age, she retired at thirty-eight years old and returned to the U.S.

Wilkinson did not stay in retirement long. When she returned to New York, the New York City Opera invited her to become a member of the company. She performed with them from 1974 until 1985. She stopped dancing at fifty years old, but continued with the Opera as a character dancer and actor until 2011, when the company disbanded, at the age of seventy-six. Her acting credits include playing Bloody Mary's assistant in a Broadway revival of *South Pacific* in 1987, and the role of Malla in Stephen Sondheim's *A Little Night Music* (1990-1991).

The hurdles Wilkinson experienced opened doors for today's Black and Brown ballerinas. Misty Copeland's breakout success helped bring Wilkinson's story back into the spotlight. Wilkinson became a mentor and friend to Copeland, the first African American ballerina to be named principal dancer at American Ballet Theatre (ABT). She first discovered the then-teenage dancer while watching a television program highlighting her in a variation from *Don Quixote,* and recognized the promise of a great dancer. When Copeland learned of Wilkinson's story in a documentary on the Ballet Russe, she spoke so often of her that her publicist tracked Wilkinson down so the two could meet. When Copeland made her debut as Odette/Odile with ABT in 2015, Wilkinson, along with former Houston Ballet principal Lauren Anderson, joined her on stage, arms overflowing with flowers. Copeland's children's book, *The Firebird,* was inspired by her relationship with Wilkinson.

Wilkinson presented the 2014 *Dance Magazine* Award to Copeland in December of that year. In June 2015, Wilkinson received the 2015 Dance/USA Trustee Award from presenter Copeland. Wilkinson was featured in the 2016 documentary *Black Ballerina* with Copeland, and the publication of a children's book based on her life, *Trailblazer: The Story of Ballerina Raven Wilkinson.* The beautiful picture book is by Leda Schubert, with illustrations by Theodore Taylor III, and a foreword by Copeland.

Wilkinson managed to have a dance career that lasted much longer than her detractors of the 1950s and 1960s could have ever imagined. Raven Wilkinson died in New York City on December 17, 2018. She was eighty-three years old.❖

Judith Jamison
(1943)
Dancer, choreographer, artistic director

Judith Jamison was the first African American woman to appear on the cover of "Dance" magazine, and the first African American woman to direct a major modern dance company in the U.S. just as the post-civil rights movement was hitting its stride.

JUDITH JAMISON was born and raised in Philadelphia, Pennsylvania to Tessie Belle Brown, a teacher, and John Henry Jamison, an engineer and sheet metal worker. Her father was a part-time opera singer and concert pianist, and her mother sang and did calligraphy (Jamison and Kaplan 1993). Jamison and her older brother grew up surrounded by a family that lived in close proximity of each other (her maternal grandparents lived next door), and they were encouraged to artistically express themselves singing, dancing and playing instruments. Jamison's father taught her to play piano, and she grew up listening to Eugene Ormandy and the Philadelphia Orchestra. Her parents also exposed Jamison and her brother to the cultural institutions of Philadelphia. They often went to the theater, movies, and concerts, and attended church, which provided social and civic activities. These life experiences would later impact her career in a way that Alvin Ailey often referred to years later as "blood memory."

Jamison studied violin and piano, and began taking lessons with the Judimar School of Dance in Philadelphia at six. She studied with Marion Cuyjet, who became Jamison's early mentor, learning classical ballet and modern dance. She performed in her first dance recital at age six. When she heard the applause, something clicked and she was hooked.

By age eight, Jamison began dancing *en pointe*, and started taking classes in tap dancing and acrobatics. When she was ten, she began taking adult-level classes. Jamison attended a lecture demonstration in Philadelphia by Pearl Primus, who discussed the history of movement, and she saw the Ballet Russe de Monte Carlo perform at the Academy of Music (Jamison and Kaplan 1993).

In time, Cuyjet began sending Jamison to other teachers to advance her dance education. She studied with Delores Brown Abelson, a graduate of Judimar, who pursued a performance career in New York before returning to Philadelphia to teach; the English choreographer Antony Tudor, who introduced

Jamison to the Cecchetti method,[1] and Maria Swoboda, who taught classes at the local YWCA. By the time she was fourteen, Jamison started teaching dance to nine-year-olds, remaining true to her family's credo to always give back to the community. She made her formal ballet debut at fifteen in the role of Myrtha, the Queen of the Wilis, in *Giselle*.

While attending Germantown High School, Jamison played sports, performed in the Glee Club, and played violin in the Philadelphia String Ensemble and the All-Philadelphia String Ensemble (Jamison and Kaplan 1993). She also studied Dalcroze Eurhythmics, a system that teaches rhythm through movement, and later, the techniques of Katherine Dunham.

When Jamison graduated from high school in 1958, she attended Fisk University at the suggestion of Cuyjet, who helped her get a scholarship. Jamison pursued a degree in psychology, but continued dancing, studying under Mabel Love. It was not until her third semester that Jamison decided to devote herself to dance. In 1964, she transferred to the Philadelphia Dance Academy (now part of the University of the Arts), and studied with Nadia Chilkovsky, James Jamieson, and Yuri Gottschalk. She also took kinesiology, the history of dance, and Labanotation (structured dance notation). In addition to her studies at the Academy, she also studied under Joan Kerr, who taught her the Horton[2] technique, which required great strength, balance, and concentration. When Jamison was at Fisk, she wanted to dance more, but once she was at the Academy, it was still not clear to her whether she wanted to perform for the rest of her life (Jamison and Kaplan 1993).

Jamison saw her first performance of the Alvin Ailey American Dance Theater (AAADT) with classmates from the Academy in Philadelphia. She saw Ailey perform in his classic work, "Wade in the Water," from *Revelations*, which made a tremendous impression. When Agnes de Mille saw Jamison in a master class, she invited her to perform in her new work for American Ballet Theatre (ABT), *The Four Marys*. Jamison accepted the offer and spent the next few months working with the company and alongside Carmen de Lavallade, who took her under her wing. She made her professional debut in *The Four Marys* in New York City. After the company ended its run, Jamison found herself unemployed and took a job at the World's Fair.

It was a failed audition for choreographer, Donald McKayle, for a Harry Belafonte television special that serendipitously began Jamison's relationship

1.   The Cecchetti method is a Russian technique named after the Italian and ballet master Enrico Cecchetti (1850–1928), who was the ballet master of the Imperial School of St. Petersburg during the early twentieth century. Some of his students included notable dancers of the Imperial Ballet, such as Anna Pavlova, Léonide Massine, and Vaslav Nijinsky.

2.   The Horton technique was devised by Lester Horton (1906–1953), a dancer, choreographer, and teacher beginning in the 1920s, based on Native American dances, anatomical studies, and other movement influences. Alvin Ailey briefly ran Horton's dance company following his death, but eventually moved to New York City and launched his company in 1958. By 1969, the Horton Technique became standard training at the AAADT.

with Alvin Ailey. Struck by the five foot ten beauty, Ailey called her three days later to ask her to join his company.

Jamison made her premiere with AAADT at Chicago's Harper Theater Dance Festival in 1965, in Talley Beatty's *Congo Tango Palace.* Her height, elegance and striking presence helped make her an immediate success with the company. In 1966, Jamison toured Europe and Africa, providing her with her first opportunity to observe other cultures first-hand. Soon after, when Ailey was forced to put the company on hiatus due to financial complications, Jamison danced with the Harkness Ballet and served as an assistant to the artistic director. However, when the company reformed in 1967, she returned to AAADT and spent the next thirteen years collaborating with Ailey on many projects. She danced in some of his renowned works, including "Masekela Language," *Blues Suite* and *Revelations.* But it was "Cry," Ailey's solo dance, that would define her.

In 1971, Ailey choreographed "Cry," a sixteen-minute dance, as a birthday present for his mother, Lula Cooper, and later dedicated it to "all Black women everywhere, especially our mothers." "Cry" celebrates the journey of a woman coming out of a troubled and painful world and finding the strength to overcome and conquer. No ordinary dancer, Jamison danced the solo, an intensely emotional and physically draining dance. She looked like an African goddess, and her long body moved like a magical entity, a force of nature personified. Her performance received standing ovations and overwhelming critical acclaim. "Cry" has become a mainstay in the company.

By 1972, Jamison was appointed to the National Council on the Arts by President Nixon. That same year, Jamison married Miguel Godreau, a former member of AAADT. The marriage was annulled in 1974.

Besides dancing with Ailey's company, Jamison appeared as a guest artist in several companies, including the Cullberg Ballet, Swedish Royal Ballet, and San Francisco Ballet. She danced alongside many renowned dancers, including the ballet legend Mikhail Baryshnikov, in a duet entitled "Pas de Duke," choreographed by Ailey in 1976. In 1977, Jamison created the role of Potiphar's Wife in John Neumeier's *Josephslegende* for the Vienna State Opera, and in 1978, she appeared in Maurice Béjart's updated version of his short ballet, *Le Spectre de la rose,* with the Ballet of the Twentieth Century. Several choreographers sought to work with Jamison as a solo artist, and important collaborations included John Parks' "Nubian Lady" (1972), John Butler's "Facets" (1976), and Ulysses Dove's "Inside" (1980).

In 1980, Jamison left Ailey's company to perform in the Broadway musical, *Sophisticated Ladies,* with Gregory Hines. It was her first stage experience outside the realm of concert dance and required a new set of skills. She taught master classes at Jacob's Pillow in 1981 and began choreographing her works. She premiered her first ballet, *Divining* with AAADT in 1984. She later formed The Jamison Project, a twelve-member dance troupe to explore her talent as a choreographer as well as test her leadership skills. The Project premiered in 1988 at the Joyce Theater in New York City and performed works such as *Divining, Time Out,* and *Tease.* Jamison invited guest choreographers, including Garth Fagan, to set work for the company. That same year, a PBS special depicting her creative process, *Judith Jamison: The Dancemaker,* aired nationally.

In 1988, Ailey was dying from AIDS/HIV and asked Jamison to return to AAADT as artistic associate. Upon Ailey's death in 1989, Jamison assumed the role of artistic director and dedicated the next twenty-one years of her life building on Ailey's success. In doing so, she became the first African American woman to direct a major modern dance company in the U.S. .

When AAADT started out, it was a resident company of the YWCA's Clark Center for the Performing Arts in Manhattan. By 1962, Ailey changed his all-Black dance company into a multiracial group. In 1969, he established a school in Brooklyn, and in 1974, Ailey created the Alvin Ailey Repertory Ensemble (renamed Alvin Ailey II) as a bridge between the school and the professional dance world. By 1980, Ailey relocated both the school and company under one roof on Broadway in Manhattan, and by 1982, the school received accreditation from the National Association of Schools of Dance. Despite discrimination the company faced from the outside world, within the company, Ailey created a welcoming space for dancers of all ethnicities.

Under Jamison's direction and choreography, the company produced such major works as *Echo, Far from Home,* and *Sweet Release.* She produced thirty-eight world premieres, thirty-two new productions, twenty company premieres, and choreographed ten world premieres. She continued to rehearse and restage classics from the company's repertoire and commissioned distinguished choreographers to create new works. Jamison also choreographed and created dances such as "Forgotten Time," "Hymn," "Love Stories," and "Among Us" for the company.

In 1993, Jamison published her autobiography, *Dancing Spirit,* written with Howard Kaplan, edited by Jacqueline Kennedy Onassis, and published by Doubleday.

Jamison created the Women's Choreography Initiative and a cooperative between AAADT and Fordham University's BFA program. She also introduced a multicultural curriculum to The Ailey School, which includes instruction of West African and South Indian dances. She propelled the organization in new directions with performances at the Atlanta 1996 Summer Olympics and the 2002 Cultural Olympiad in Salt Lake City. She carried the Olympic torch during the relay before the opening ceremonies and performed in historic engagements in South Africa. Jamison was critical in establishing the company's permanent home in 2004 to construct the 77,000 square foot Joan Weill Center for Dance in New York City.

In 2008, Jamison brought the company to unprecedented heights when she led it on a fifty-city global tour, celebrating Alvin Ailey American Dance Theater's fiftieth anniversary. The celebration was a year-long series of special performances, collaborations, events, and commemorative merchandise, including an Ailey Barbie® Doll by Mattel, designed by Jamison. She retired from AAADT in 2011 but remains associated with the company as artistic director emerita.

Jamison has received many accolades throughout her career. In 1992, she was inducted into Delta Sigma Theta Sorority as an honorary member. In 1999, she received the Kennedy Center Honor, which recognizes lifetime contributions to American culture, and an Emmy for Outstanding Choreography for *Dance in America: A Hymn for Alvin Ailey* (PBS). In 2001, she was awarded the National Medal of Arts, the highest award given to an artist in the U.S. Other awards she has received include the Paul Robeson Award from Actors' Equity Association in recognition of her outstanding contribution to the performing arts and commitment to the right of all people to live in dignity and peace; a Bessie Award for her lifetime commitment to the preservation and development of dance and the arts; the Phoenix Award; the Handel Medallion Algur H Meadows Award from Southern Methodist University; The Making a Difference Award from the National Association for the Advancement of Colored People (NAACP) ACT-SO; and an honorary doctorate from Howard University.

In 2009, Jamison was honored at *The BET Honors,* an event that recognizes the lives and achievements of leading African American luminaries, was listed in the *Time* 100: The World's Most Influential People, and received the highest rank in The Order of Arts and Letters, a group recognized for contributing to the arts in France and the rest of the world.

Then, in 2010, she was honored by First Lady Michelle Obama with the first White House *Dance Series: A Tribute to Judith Jamison.* That same year, Jamison's costume from Ailey's 1975 ballet, *The Mooche,* was added to the permanent collection of the Smithsonian National Museum of American History. She also received the Montblanc de la Culture Arts Patronage Award, presented annually to an individual who has given exceptional time and energy to artists and the arts, and was named the 2010 recipient of the Congressional Black Caucus Foundation's prestigious Phoenix Award. In 2015, she became the fiftieth inductee into the Hall of Fame at the National Museum of Dance.

Jamison has found joy as a dancer, and later, as part of AAADT leadership. Although she is retired, Jamison remains committed to promoting the significance of the Ailey legacy, and continues to dedicate herself to asserting the prominence of dance in our culture. She firmly believes it is a medium that honors the past, celebrates the present, and fearlessly reaches into the future.❖

Blondell Cummings
(1944-2015)
Modern dancer, choreographer, photographer, video artist

Blondell Cummings defied expectations in the dance world by becoming one of the first African American postmodern dance artists whose work, "Chicken Soup," was designated by The National Endowment for the Arts as an American masterpiece.

BLONDELL CUMMINGS was born in Effingham, South Carolina to Oralee Williams Cummings and Roscoe Cummings, who picked cotton and tobacco, and was the oldest of three sisters. When her family relocated to Harlem, her mother worked as a domestic and a nurse's aide, and her father worked as a cab driver. When Cummings was in her teens, her family moved to Queens, New York, where she began studying dance in New York City public schools. In 1985, her father was killed by a passenger while driving his cab.

Cummings received a bachelor's degree in dance and education from New York University, did graduate work in film and photography, and received a master's in fine arts from Lehman College (CUNY). Cummings was the first in her family to graduate from college, and she made sure that her sisters did as well.

As a performer and choreographer, Cummings dance background has been rather eclectic. She studied with most of the major figures in African American modern dance, such as Alvin Ailey, Katherine Dunham, Mary Hinkson and Eleo Pomare, among others; as well as many of the seminal figures of postmodern dance, including Yvonne Rainer, and Steve Paxton. She also danced with Richard Bull, Kai Takei, the New York Chamber Dance Company, the New Jersey Repertory Company, and Rod Rodgers.

But it was her work with multidisciplinary artist Meredith Monk that helped put Cummings on the map. Monk is a composer, director, choreographer, and filmmaker who emerged from the fertile New York arts scene in the 1960s as a multi-faceted artist. Cummings already began developing her multidisciplinary yearnings and by 1969, she cofounded with Monk, The House, a company dedicated to an interdisciplinary approach to performance.

Cummings made a vivid impression in Monk's 1973 seminal work, *Education of the Girlchild* (1973), and most notably as the Dictator in "QUARRY" (1976). Critics identified her virtuosic abilities to project character through gestures and sounds. She also appeared in Yvonne Rainer's 1976 film, *Kristina Talking Pictures*.

Cummings was an artist who crossed over from modern to postmodern, and the Black to avant-garde communities. As a woman, an African American, and a choreographer, her solo dances framed those identities differently (Friedler 2014), but she also used African American historical reference points in her work. A riveting presence on stage, Cummings created dozens of solo and group works, and later oversaw her own ensemble, Blondell Cummings and Performers. Her cross-cultural activism led her to host workshops for dancers and non-dancers alike.

In 1978, Cummings began a collaboration with writer Madeleine Keller that exploded into the multidimensional piece "Cycle" (Desmond 1997). The work refers not only to the menstrual cycle, but also to the way in which ideas and images are recycled throughout the piece. "Cycle" proved to be the catalyst in Cummings's choreographic career because it lent inspiration to the development of her arts collective, Cycle Arts Foundation, which promoted interdisciplinary collaboration, and the bonding and sharing of rituals of lifestyle and art-making that affirmed her artistic process (Desmond 1977). Throughout her career, Cummings relied on collaborations with multidisciplinary artists and created pieces for student groups at Hunter College, The New School, and PHILADANCO.

Based in New York, Cummings performed her work at local venues such as P.S. 1 in Queens, the Brooklyn Academy of Music, the Joyce Theater, The Kitchen, New York Live Arts, Danspace Project, and the 92nd Street YM-YWHA. She also toured widely in Africa and Asia, as well as across the country in venues that included the Jacob's Pillow Dance Festival, where she was an artist-in-residence.

Cumming's values stayed true to her cross-cultural arts mission. She created several experimental dances that featured her remarkably concentrated solo abilities, such as "The Ladies and Me" (1979), a visual diary set to the music of Ma Rainey, Billie Holiday, Sister Rosetta Tharpe, Mary Lou Williams, Ella Fitzgerald, and others. It was first performed at the Hong Kong Arts Center at the invitation of the artistic director of the Modern Dance Theatre of Hong Kong. While there, Cummings performed excerpts of it on Hong Kong television and at the Shanghai Ballet Academy. This is just one example of how Cummings' works raised international attention. Her reputation as an innovative choreographer crosses boundaries and merges dance with other art forms taking her around the world (Dixon-Stowell 1980).

It was "Chicken Soup" (1981), a portrait of lifetime domesticity, that would become her signature work. The work reflected her ability to capture the universality of personal movements and gestures, erasing blurred lines between genres such as postmodern and Black dance. In "Chicken Soup," Cummings proved that, at its heart, dance is a universal language that can speak to everyone. For example, the dance was interpreted by some as depicting a Black domestic working for a White household, but for Cummings, it was about her childhood recollections of her grandmother in her kitchen. It is this universality that she became best known for in her work. She went on to develop *Food for Thought* in 1985, a suite of dances that includes "Chicken Soup," "Meat and Potatoes," "Tossed Salad," and "Chocolate." In 2006, "Chicken Soup" was designated an American masterpiece by the National Endowment for the Arts.

"The Art Of War/Nine Situations" (1984) is a meditation on connections between military strategy and daily life, created with Jessica Hagedorn. In 1988, Cummings choreographed the series "3B49," a piece about a taxi driver and his passenger, and the hermetic world of the taxicab. Dedicated to her father's life and work, "3B49" received critical acclaim for its urban commentary. Cummings created "For J.B." (1990), dedicated to Josephine Baker. She choreographed "Omadele and Giuseppe" (1991), a contemplation of interracial living, created with Tom Thayer. Cummings' workshop/performance practice often invited audience participation, confirming her belief that choreography is always the act of sharing. Her arresting multimedia collaborations that centered on social rituals also include "Women in the Dunes" (1995), a collaboration with Junko Kikuchi, inspired by Kobo Abe's 1962 novel *The Woman in the Dunes,* and "100% Cotton Nature Fiber"(1998), which was set to the music of Malian singer Oumov Sangaré.

Cummings has taught at numerous institutions, including Lincoln Center Institute, City College of New York, New York University, Cornell University, and elsewhere. Her wisdom and insights have been a highly valued addition to dance panels, including the Selection Committee of the prestigious New York Dance and Performance Awards (the Bessies). A testament to her reputation in the dance scene and performance community, Cummings was on the Bessie Award Selection Committee for many years.

Cummings was also an inaugural NYFA fellow in choreography and went on to receive a second fellowship in 1989, and a third in 1996. She also served on NYFA's Artist Advisory Committee from 1999 to 2003. She was profiled, along with eight other choreographers, in the Michael Blackwood documentary, *Retracting Steps: American Dance Since Postmodernism* (1988), and the PBS series *Free to Dance: The African American Presence in Modern Dance* (2001) about Black choreographers within the modern dance field.

Cummings's work, which fused dance, theater, mime, spoken word, and video into small quasi-narrative worlds was unlike anyone else's. It is because Cummings successfully straddled different choreographic approaches—one anchored by the iconoclastic concerns of the avant garde and the other rooted in the more familiar landscape of human relationships. More importantly, she was one of the first African American women dancers who delved into experimental work rooted in the Black experience and identity.

Blondell Cummings died from pancreatic cancer on August 30, 2015 in New York City. She was seventy years old.❖

Dianne McIntyre
(1946)
Dancer, choreographer, curator, teacher

Dianne McIntyre is a cultural investigator who creates work in dance, theater, film, and opera. She has won numerous honors for her work, including an Emmy nomination, three Bessie Awards, a Guggenheim Fellowship, and a Helen Hayes Award.

DIANNE MCINTYRE was born in Cleveland, Ohio to Dorothy Layne McIntyre, the first woman and first Black woman to receive a pilot's license by the Civil Aeronautics Authority, and Francis Benjamin McIntyre, a motorist and postal worker. After seeing Janet Collins in the Metropolitan Opera Company's Cleveland production of *Aida* at age five, McIntyre wanted to become a dancer. After attending Cleveland Public Schools and graduating from John Adams High School in 1964, she studied ballet with Elaine Gibbs and modern dance with Virginia Dryansky.

McIntyre attended The Ohio State University (OSU). Although she was taking dance classes, she first studied French to become a linguist for the United Nations. During her third year, after taking a dance history course with Shirley Wynne, McIntyre became a dance major. In that course she discovered that in many cultures dance is vital to the stability of the community. During her time at OSU, the university commissioned McIntyre to choreograph a piece for an evening with works by esteemed choreographers Lucas Hoving and Doris Humphrey. In 1966, McIntyre attended the American Dance Festival as a student, where she would later return as a faculty member in the early 1990s and 2008.

After receiving her BFA in dance, she was taking graduate courses at OSU when Helen P. Alkire, head of the dance department, put McIntyre's name up for a position at the University of Wisconsin-Milwaukee. McIntyre was hired, and she taught and choreographed for a year. She also developed dances for the productions of professor, director and activist Chestyn Everett, who emphasized the urgency of Black expression in the arts. She then moved to New York in 1970, where she studied under Viola Farber and Gus Solomons Jr., among others. She took workshops with Anna Sokolow, the Nikolais Dance Theater and when studying with dancer Judith Dunn and musician Bill Dixon, McIntyre found herself drawn to the connection between dance composition, avant-garde jazz, and free jazz. She attended the rehearsals and performances of musicians, specifically the Master Brotherhood, where she taught herself how to move to jazz. Her frequent attendance at the Master Brotherhood rehearsals earned her the nickname the "Cancer Dancer" because she was born in July.

While in New York, McIntyre performed with Solomons Company/Dance for two years, and around this time, she did a solo performance in a concert at the Clark Center for the Performing Arts. In 1972, she founded and directed the Sounds in Motion Company in Harlem and infused so-called jazz and poetry into her work. She held concerts at the Cubiculo Theatre and Washington Square Church, while supporting her endeavors by working part-time at the New York Public Library for the Performing Arts in the Dance Collection.

Upon advice from others, McIntyre began applying for grants to fund her projects, and Sounds in Motion was accepted into the National Endowment for the Arts Dance Touring Program. The company performed around the country and at well-known venues such as the Joyce Theater, Brooklyn Academy of Music, and the John F. Kennedy Center for the Performing Arts. It also toured in Europe. The company's repertoire included *Life's Force* (1979), created in collaboration with Ahmed Abdullah, *Take-Off from a Forced Landing* (1984), which was based on her mother's experiences as an aviator, and a performance in 1986 based on Zora Neale Hurston's novel, *Their Eyes Were Watching God* (1937). During the 1970s and 1980s, Sounds in Motion was the only modern dance studio in Harlem that became a gathering place for dancers, musicians, scholars, activists, and artists to engage in furthering Black consciousness.

The company toured and performed in concert with Olu Dara, Lester Bowie, Cecil Taylor, Amina Claudine Myers, Max Roach, Butch Morris, Hamiet Bluiett, Ahmed Abdullah, Don Pullen, Abbey Lincoln, Sweet Honey in the Rock, Hannibal Lokumbe, Oliver Lake, and countless other musicians. Sixteen years after its founding, McIntyre closed Sounds in Motion to pursue independent work. She is credited with renewing interest in the work of modern dance pioneer Helen Tamiris through a recreation of her 1937 masterpiece, *How Long, Brethren?* in 1991. As a freelancer, McIntyre choreographed the Broadway productions of *Mule Bone* (1991), the original and revival of *Paul Robeson* (1988 and 1995 respectively), *King Hedley II* (2001), and Joe Turner's *Come and Gone* (2009).

McIntyre also choreographed Obie Award winner Ntozake Shange's *Spell #7* at The Public Theater, and *King, the Musical* for London's West End. She has choreographed over forty plays and musicals in New York and regional theaters. Her choreography has also been featured in HBO's *Miss Evers' Boys* (1997), for which she was nominated an Emmy Award for Outstanding Choreography, and in the film *Beloved* (1998), based on the novel of the same name by Toni Morrison.

In 2005, McIntyre directed the world premiere of *Daughter of a Buffalo Soldier* at Cleveland's *Karamu House,* a dance-theater piece honoring ninety-six-year-old Cleveland choreographer Marjorie Witt Johnson, founder of the Karamu Dancers. McIntyre has also reached into her own history, creating *I Could Stop on a Dime and Get Ten Cents Change,* which features dances and narratives from her father's life in Cleveland. She also developed another narrative-dance play, *Open the Door, Virginia!,* about teenager Barbara Rose Johns' bold actions against the segregated school system and the school closings in Farmville, Virginia during the 1950s.

McIntyre would later reunite and collaborate with Shange in the 2007 New Federal Theatre's festival "Ntozake Shange: A Retrospective" with Shange's one-act play, *It Hasn't Always Been This Way,* and her choreopoem, *and why i had to dance* in 2012. Besides Shange, McIntyre has worked with distinguished directors and playwrights, including Marion McClinton, Regina Taylor, Des McAnuff, Jonathan Demme, Douglas Turner Ward, August Wilson, OyamO, Avery Brooks, Rita Dove, Bartlett Sher, Joe Sargent, Rick Davis, Woodie King Jr., Irene Lewis, Oz Scott, and Rick Khan.

As one of the most important Black women dance artists to emerge during the 1970s, McIntyre has developed a distinct body of work. It features an idiosyncratic use of music with a dynamic movement style which choreographically explores the lives of African Americans. McIntyre has received numerous awards including three Bessie Awards (1989, 1997, 2006), two Helen Hayes Awards, Resident Design awards (1993, 1996), a 2015 Doris Duke Impact Award, a 2016 Doris Duke Artist Award, and a 2019 Dance/USA Honor Award. She has also been honored with the Cleveland Arts Prize Lifetime Achievement Award for Dance (2006), two AUDELCO (NY Black Theatre) awards, a Helen Hayes Award (D.C. Theatre), a Master of African American Choreography Medal from the John F. Kennedy Center for the Performing Arts, and the International Association of Blacks in Dance Legendary Artist Award.

She has received grant support from The Pew Charitable Trust, the New York State Council on the Arts, the New England Foundation for the Arts, and several fellowships, including a John S. Guggenheim Fellowship, and a United States Artists (USA) Fellowship. McIntyre is also the recipient of the American Dance Festival Balasaraswati/Joy Ann Dewey Beineke Endowed Chair for Distinguished Teaching, Alumni Distinguished Achievement Award from the College of Arts and Science of The Ohio State University, and Honorary Doctor of Fine Arts degrees from SUNY Purchase and Cleveland State University.

McIntyre has been a guest artist at several arts institutions, including the American Dance Festival, Baryshnikov Arts Center, Jacob's Pillow, and the Bates Summer Dance Festival. In 2011, McIntyre acted as choreographer for the film *Fun Size.* In 2012, Sounds in Motion reunited at the American Dance Guild Festival, where they performed *Life's Force* with Ahmed Abdullah. That same year, she choreographed *Crowns* at the Goodman Theatre in Chicago. She has served on the Stage Directors and Choreographers Society board of directors and is a member of the Dramatists Guild and ASCAP.

McIntyre has sustained a dance career over many decades, and continues to choreograph with the artistic intention to "express dance as music moving," telling stories and moving the audience to see unlimited possibilities.❖

Virginia Johnson
(1950)
Prima ballerina, choreographer, artistic director, editor, author

Virginia Johnson, an acclaimed prima ballerina and a founding company member of Dance Theatre of Harlem, responded to a greater calling, which was to rescue the company and lead it into the next century.

VIRGINIA ALMA FAIRFAX JOHNSON was born in Washington, D.C. to Madeline Johnson, a physical education instructor at Howard University, and James Lee Johnson, a physicist who designed submarines for the Department of the Navy. Her father was the first African American to attend the U.S. Naval Academy in Annapolis, but he was hazed out.

When a childhood friend of her mother, Therrell C. Smith, returned to Washington, D.C. after studying dance abroad and opened her own dance studio, Madeline sent her two daughters to study with her. Johnson, who began classes when she was just three years old, was inspired by Smith's love of the art form and fell in love with ballet. While studying with Smith, Johnson performed with the Children's Theatre in Washington, D.C. in their annual recitals. When she was thirteen, she auditioned for and won a scholarship with Mary Day's Washington School of Ballet. In the past, Day had not welcomed African Americans into the school, but she accepted Johnson as one of her first Black students.

Johnson initially attended classes for several hours a day after school. As a teenager, she performed in musical theater productions put on by the American Light Opera Company, acted in Children's Theater performances, and appeared in the Washington Ballet's annual performance of *The Nutcracker*. Johnson was inspired when her class at Jefferson Junior High attended a performance of the Martha Graham Dance Company, in which Mary Hinkson, one of the first African Americans in Graham's troupe, appeared on stage. She received a full scholarship to attend Day's academy, completing high school in the ballet school's academic division and graduating at the top of her class in 1968. Ironically, Day did not encourage Johnson's professional ballet career; instead, she warned her that, while she was very talented, there was no place for her in ballet. Although Johnson knew that Black ballerinas were rare, she continued her pursuit.

Johnson's parents were extraordinary in that they believed in the importance of the arts. However, while they gave their children plenty of exposure to the arts, they never expected them to become artists. Instead, they expected them to go to college and enter some kind of profession. To make her parents happy, Johnson accepted a scholarship to New York University and majored in dance at the School of the Arts (now known as Tisch).

Around this time, she began taking classes in a ballet school in Harlem being run out of a church basement by New York City Ballet star Arthur Mitchell. Johnson lobbied Mitchell to hire her, and she became a founding member of the Dance Theatre of Harlem (DTH) in 1969. After a long discussion with her parents, Johnson promised them that she would only take a leave of absence from New York University, but in reality, she ditched a full scholarship to join Mitchell's company, which premiered in 1971.

When Mitchell and cofounder Karel Shook began DTH, George Balanchine gave them the rights to several ballets. This afforded Mitchell a repertoire of recognizable modern classics for his programs, invaluable for a fledgling company. Mitchell started the company with a strong base, and by 1979 was touring internationally with a repertoire of forty-six ballets. In the 1980s, DTH reached the forefront of the American ballet scene by carving out a niche for itself and infusing new life into works like *Firebird, Giselle, Scheherazade, Bugaku,* and *Agon.*

In 1974, Johnson danced her first solo role for DTH and gradually became one of the company's soloists and principal dancers, garnering international acclaim by illustrating to modern viewers the emotional meaning of Romanticism during the nineteenth century. She was also a natural for Balanchine's neoclassical *Serenade* and *Allegro Brilliante,* which she performed clearly and smoothly. Johnson would draw upon her broad training to develop a wide spectrum of dance roles from historical classical to contemporary experimental ballets.

Over the years, she has performed in various ballets, including Glen Tetley's modern *Voluntaries,* Louis Johnson's *Forces of Rhythm,* and John Taras' *Designs With Strings.* She was the Girl in Blue in Bronislava Nijinska's *Les Biches,* and starred in Frederic Franklin's staging of *Swan Lake,* Lester Horton's *The Beloved,* and Walter Raines' *After Corinth.* Additional principal roles include *Don Quixote, Holberg Suite, Rhythmetron, Fête Noire,* and *Haiku.* Johnson has often been praised as a lyrical dancer, noted for the dramatic effect of her superb extensions as a dancer standing at five feet and eight inches tall.

Mitchell invited Fredrick Franklin to restage the traditional European *Giselle* and reset it in Louisiana's bayou country, giving it an Afro-Creole focus. Johnson starred as the Louisiana Giselle in *Creole Giselle,* which premiered in 1984. She paired crisp, solid footwork, full of sailing turns and effortless balances, with soft arms and careful transitions throughout the program. While many purists and balletomanes felt the restaging as inappropriate, many others saw it as a groundbreaking achievement. In fact, Mitchell won a Laurence Olivier Award in 1984 for *Creole Giselle.*

In the early 1990s, Johnson traveled to the politically charged post-apartheid country of South Africa with DTH to perform at the Johannesburg Civic Theatre (now known as the Joburg Theatre), where she received critical praise for her performances. She then danced in Agnes de Mille's *Fall River Legend* as a guest artist for the Cleveland Ballet in 1991. Johnson danced the role of Blanche in *A Streetcar Named Desire* at DTH's 25th anniversary season at Lincoln Center in New York City in 1994.

Three DTH productions in which she danced leading roles were recorded for broadcast: *A Streetcar Named Desire* for *Dance in America* (PBS) (1986); *Creole Giselle (1987),* which was the first full-length ballet broadcast on NBC; and *Fall River Legend* (1991) broadcast on the Bravo network, which won a CableACE Award from the National Cable Television Association (NCTA). She was also included in two acclaimed television dance series: Margot Fonteyn's *The Magic of Dance* (1979), and Natalia Makarova's *Ballerina* (1987). She also choreographed and performed in the television film *Ancient Voices of Children* (1975).

Aside from her work with DTH, Johnson has had guest engagements with several companies, including the Washington Ballet in *The Nutcracker;* Alicia Alonso's Ballet de Cuba in *Giselle;* the Chicago Opera Ballet, 1975; the Stars of the World Ballet Australian tour, 1979; the Ballet Nacional de Cuba, 1988; the Baltimore Civic Youth Ballet, Detroit Symphony, and Cleveland Ballet, all in 1991; the Royal Ballet, *Giselle,* 1992; and Festival of Dance in Havana, Cuba. She also performed in a one-woman show at Marymount Manhattan College in 1978.

Johnson has performed before Presidents Carter and Reagan. During the late 1980s, Johnson was one of the first American ballerinas to visit what was then known as the Soviet Union, where she performed at the Kirov State Academic Theater of Opera and Ballet (now known as the State Academic Mariinsky Theatre) in Leningrad. She served as a Community Outreach Instructor during DTH's South African tour in 1992 and toured Australia, Israel, and Japan.

Johnson has choreographed ballets for Goucher College, Dancers Respond to AIDS, the Second Annual Harlem Festival of the Arts, Thelma Hill Performing Arts Center, and Marymount Manhattan College, where she was also an adjunct professor. The latter two projects were an outgrowth of Dancers Making Dances, a collaborative choreographic project with former DTH colleagues Judy Tyrus and Melanie Person.

For more than two decades, Johnson has served as a role model for young Black dancers and has exemplified American classical dancing. Not only has she exploded the myth that Black women cannot be classical ballerinas, but she also has one of the broadest repertoires in dance. While she has excelled as a romantic ballerina and has been described as a lyrical performer, Johnson has been noted for her ability to dance both dramatic and contemporary roles.

While still performing, Johnson's interest in journalism led her to Fordham University, where she pursued a degree in communications. After she retired from performing in 1997, Johnson founded *POINTE* magazine for Lifestyle Ventures, the publisher of *Dance Spirit* and other magazines. *POINTE's* first issue was published in February 2000, and Johnson served as editor-in-chief until 2009. She successfully developed *POINTE* as a mainstay in the dance world for professional dancers and ballet lovers alike.

In the first thirty-five years of its existence, DTH traveled the world with its message that ballet was wide open—that it was not exclusively an elite White art form. Yet, outside DTH's predominantly African American forty-four-member troupe, the racial makeup throughout the ballet world changed little. When a debt of more than $2 million forced DTH to disband, it seemed that Mitchell's model of inclusion would amount to a historical curiosity.

In 2010, Mitchell stepped down and asked Johnson to take over as the organization's artistic director, with Mitchell becoming Artistic Director Emeritus. Since she was a founding member and former principal dancer of the company, Johnson's appointment signaled confidence on the part of the board that there was a future for DTH. She worked closely with Executive Director Laveen Naidu to bring the debt down and make a DTH rebirth possible. Unfortunately, when the company folded, some forty ballet dancers of color were suddenly unemployed, and few found jobs in other ballet companies. For years, DTH was more than a thriving, internationally touring troupe; it showed that ballet no longer existed in a White vacuum. But when the company folded it made its reopening even more important than ever. After thirty-five years, there was still no place for young ballet dancers of color. Although the school and the Dance Theatre of Harlem Ensemble remained open, the organization was no longer what it once was. Losing the main company had become disheartening for the fans and, even worse, thwarted many young Black ballet dancers' ambitions.

Bringing the company back took much longer than anyone expected, and Johnson developed a distinctly new approach to their challenges. From 2009 to 2012, the youthful Ensemble, which was initially developed from the professional training program of the DTH school, became the physical face of DTH. They appeared at colleges and other venues and toured nationally and internationally.

In 2010, she created the series Harlem Dance Works 2.0, a choreographic laboratory and audience engagement initiative to develop new work. In 2012, Johnson returned DTH to full company status, but there were some distinct differences. First, Johnson decided to streamline the company from forty-four members to eighteen members, which meant that the company would no longer produce the traditional ballets like *Swan Lake* and *Giselle.* She also wanted to bring back as many of the dancers from 2004 as possible, but too much time had passed. When the touring company went on hiatus in 2004, it left a gaping hole in the Black dance community. When a small number of African Americans auditioned for the company's relaunch in 2012, it reconfirmed that there are few opportunities for Black dancers in the ballet world, *still,* and that DTH's lengthy hiatus might have thwarted the ambitions of young Black ballet dancers. Instead of taking top-level dancers and making them into a company, Johnson did what Mitchell originally had done over forty years ago: train and mold dancers *into* a new company. DTH made its New York debut at the Rose Theater at Jazz at Lincoln Center in 2013. Like Judith Jamison of Alvin Ailey American Dance Theater, Johnson did not plan a career as an artistic director of a major company, but became one to save and secure DTH, succeeding beyond anyone's expectations.

Under Johnson's leadership, DTH has performed a wide range of classical, neoclassical, and contemporary ballets, from the Black Swan pas de deux from *Swan Lake* to George Balanchine's *Agon,* and has commissioned world premieres from Helen Pickett, John Alleyne, Tanya Wideman-Davis and Thaddeus Davis, Darrell Grand Moultrie, and Robert Garland. The company has also performed *The Lark Ascending,* choreographed by Alvin Ailey for his dance company in 1972. DTH is the first U.S. company to perform this classic work *en pointe.* DTH has also presented ballets by Nacho Duato, Donald Byrd, Ulysses Dove, and Christopher Huggins. It has held its subsequent seasons at the Rose Theater at Jazz at Lincoln Center and New York City Center.

With so many small to midsize repertory companies today, DTH remains a stand out due in part to its commitment to outreach, which, along with the company and school, is integral to the organization and the community it serves. DTH's performances also make people see the world differently than what they saw before the curtain went up, *the unexpected.* As for Johnson, she is continuing what Mitchell set out to do, which is not only to teach dance, but also to teach her dancers how to become vital members of their communities.

Johnson's honors include a Young Achiever Award from the National Council of Women, the Outstanding Young Woman of America and the *Dance Magazine* Award, a Pen and Brush Achievement Award, the Washington Performing Arts Society's 2008-2009 Pola Nirenska Lifetime Achievement Award, and the 2009 Martha Hill Fund Mid-Career Award. Her commitment to community service is maintained through volunteer assignments with New York Cares.

When DTH turned fifty in 2019, Arthur Mitchell's company proved to be just as tenacious and resilient as he was. At times it looked like it would not make it, but with the spirit of the phoenix, it has risen again. However, as the company moved forward after Mitchell's passing in 2018, it battled the expectations of what DTH should look like and what stories it should tell. In effect, what does today's DTH belong to, and who does it serve? If ballet companies are setting out to truly improve diversity, what is DTH's relevance? It is an incredible responsibility for Black classical artists to forge a new identity through this company, but with Virginia Johnson at the helm, the possibilities remain endless.❖

Jawole Willa Jo Zollar
(1950)
Modern dancer, teacher, choreographer

Jawole Willa Jo Zollar established the Urban Bush Women, which became the first major dance company consisting of all-female African American dancers.

JAWOLE WILLA JO ZOLLAR was born in Kansas City, Missouri to Dorothy Delores Zollar, a singer in the blues tradition, and Alfred Zollar Jr. The third of six children, Zollar grew up in an inner city environment, listening to jazz music while imagining movement in her head. She briefly studied ballet with her sister in a school run by a Russian teacher, but she was very strict and it did not suit her and her sister's creative inclinations. They soon left the school.

Zollar continued her dance education with Joseph Stevenson, a former student of American dance pioneer Katherine Dunham. The Dunham technique laid a foundation for her continuing exploration of the African diaspora, and she found herself exposed to different performance experiences, including appearances at nightclubs and burlesque shows. She also had early training in Afro-Cuban and other native dance forms, which later helped shape her teaching aesthetic.

During her high school years, Zollar danced in talent shows. When she went to college, Zollar was amazed that she could major in dance and earn a degree in something she truly loved. She received a BA in dance in 1975 from the University of Missouri at Kansas City and an MFA in dance from Florida State University in 1979.

In 1980, Zollar moved to New York City and studied under Dianne McIntyre of Sounds in Motion Dance Company. The two women were both interested in using aspects of African American culture as key components of their choreography, and this was especially true when it came to jazz music. Zollar also realized that powerful dance could emanate from the history and culture of her own people, and in 1984, she founded Urban Bush Women (UBW), the first major dance company of all-female African American dancers. Zollar broke every rule she was taught about composition. In the process, she created a choreographic style that synthesizes modern dance influences (a combination of Katherine Dunham, Martha Graham, Merce Cunningham, and José Limón techniques) with Afro-Cuban, Haitian, and Congolese dance. Her work emphasizes the use of weight and fluidity as opposed to creating clean shapes. She uses her Afro-Cuban dance training to employ a strong sense of dynamic timing, rhythmic patterns, and a continuous flow of movement derived from African American culture. Zollar had fearlessly discarded the softness and lyricism that characterized balletic movement aesthetics in favor of a more informed movement like pioneering artist Ruth St. Denis.

Often characterized as a dance company, Zollar's work for UBW is more complex than that: she incorporates layers of visual imagery, props, and human-made sounds with dance steps that seamlessly merge into an avant-garde dance-theater production that speaks from a Black female perspective. She creates collaborative performances between dancers, vocalists, artists, actors, composers, and musicians, including vocalizations, a cappella singing, story-telling, and social commentary. Through these mediums, Zollar pushes toward social awareness and change by tackling controversial topics such as abortion, racism, sexism, and homelessness in a hard-edged and straightforward way. Some dance critics have observed that Zollar's choreography also reveals how African Americans express themselves when not in the presence of White people.

In 1988, four years after establishing her company, Zollar made the first of what would be many appearances at Jacob's Pillow. Her company's very first performance was on the Inside/Out stage, and it featured the three repertory works they brought to the festival. The performance was well-received, proving that UBW brings to audiences bold, innovative, demanding, and exciting works that bring under-told stories to life through the art and vision of its founder. Her choreography is distinctive in its physically poetic, almost ritualistic exploration of African American heritage and racial and sexual stereotypes. UBW manages to weave contemporary dance, music, and text with the history, culture, and spiritual traditions of the African Diaspora. More importantly, the company's repertory asks audiences to reimagine the Black body in space and motion, the power of story and drama, histories of oppression, the place of spirituality, and the community's role in affecting social change.

Her company has toured five continents and has performed at venues including Brooklyn Academy of Music, Lincoln Center, and the Kennedy Center for the Performing Arts. UBW has won praise for one of Zollar's popular dances, "Batty Moves," a funky tribute about the "batty" (Jamaican for butt), which is proudly suggestive with swivels and bumps. Her work, "Shelter," is a wrenching dance about the homeless. "Walking with Pearl . . . Africa Diaries" was inspired by the choreography and writing of Pearl Primus, one of the earliest American modern-dance artists to draw on African and West Indian dance forms. "Visible," which Zollar co-choreographed with Nora Chipaumire—a Brooklyn-based choreographer and performer born in Zimbabwe—explores immigration and migration. "Hair & Other Stories" was created by UBW artistic director

Samantha Speis and Chanon Judson. It was inspired by Zollar's "HairStories," created in 2011.

Zollar has also collaborated with artists from other disciplines. Moved by Jewel Gomez's novel, *The Gilda Stories* (1991), Zollar conceived, directed, and choreographed "Bones and Ash: A Gilda Story" in collaboration with the novelist. With *The Gilda Stories'* sprawling tale of two centuries, and its uncertain wavering between the comical and the deadly serious, "Bones and Ash: A Gilda Story" should not work, but somehow, it does. Zollar collaborated with co-choreographer Pat Hall-Smith, composer Carl Riley, writer Angelyn DeBord, and visual artist Leni Schwendinger on "Praise House" in 1989. For 1988's "Song of Lawino," based on the poem by exiled Ugandan writer Okot p'Bitek, Zollar worked with director Valeria Vasilevski and composer Edwina Lee Tyler. She has often collaborated with folklorist and vocalist Tiye Giraud and percussionist David Pleasant.

UBW has earned five grants from the National Endowment for the Arts and a fellowship from the New York Foundation for the Arts and, in 2010, was selected as one of three U.S. dance companies to inaugurate a cultural diplomacy program for the Department of State. In addition to creating works for UBW, Zollar has choreographed works for Alvin Ailey American Dance Theater (AAADT), the American Dance Theater, Ballet Arizona, PHILADANCO, and Dayton Contemporary Dance Company, and has collaborated with artists such as Compagnie Jant-Bi from Senegal and others. In 2009, Zollar was invited to participate in a meeting at the White House to discuss using creative and collaborative approaches to community-building and civic engagement.

Since 1997, Zollar has garnered accolades as a teacher and speaker and has engaged in artistic and social activism through extended residencies aimed at community empowerment. She was the Nancy Smith Fichter Professor of Dance at Florida State University and has been a Worlds of Thought Resident Scholar at Mankato State University (1993-94), Regents Lecturer in the Departments of Dance and World Arts and Culture at UCLA (1995-96), Visiting Artist at Ohio State University (1996), and the Abramowitz Memorial Lecturer at Massachusetts Institute of Technology (1998), with university commissions at Florida A&M University and the University of Maryland, College Park. Zollar was named Alumna of the Year by the University of Missouri (1993) and Florida State University (1997). In 1999, Zollar received the Martin Luther King Distinguished Service Award and was awarded honorary doctorates from Columbia University, Columbia College, Tufts University, and Rutgers University. She also directs the UBW Summer Leadership, an intensive training program in dance and community engagement for artists with leadership potential interested in developing a community focus in their art-making. Zollar is also a former board member of Dance/USA.

Zollar is the recipient of the Alumni Achievement Award from the University of Missouri, the Doris Duke Performing Artist Award, and was designated a Master of African American Choreography by the John F. Kennedy Center for the Performing Arts in 2005. She has also received a 2006 NY Dance and Performance Award for her work as choreographer and creator of *Walking With Pearl . . . Southern Diaries,* a 2008 United States Artists Wynn Fellowship, and a 2009 Guggenheim Fellowship. In 2013, she received the Arthur L. Johnson Memorial Award from Sphinx Music at its inaugural conference on diversity in the arts, and was awarded the Meadows Prize from Southern Methodist University's Meadows School of the Arts in 2014.

In 2015, Zollar was the recipient of the *Dance Magazine* Award and the 2016 Dance/USA Honor Award. She has been honored with three Bessie Awards and two Doris Duke Awards. In 2020, she was recognized by the Ford Foundation as part of the series, "The Future is Hers," which recognizes women who challenge how art is defined.

UBW was featured in the PBS documentary, *Free to Dance: The African American Presence in Modern Dance* (2001). The three-hour documentary chronicled African American dancers and choreographers' crucial role in modern dance development as an American art form. In 2012, Zollar was a featured artist in the film, *Restaging Shelter,* produced and directed by Bruce Berryhill and Martha Curtis, which chronicles the artistic process of UBW and its founder.

Over the past thirty years, Urban Bush Women has changed perceptions about body types, redefined what performance can be in terms of both form and content, and most importantly, shown how choreographers can address sociopolitical issues and involve whole communities in making art. Zollar, who occasionally performs, toured with UBW in 2019 to a sold-out national tour, presented by 651 Arts as a leading influential dancer and choreographer on a program that included her early mentor Dianne McIntyre, her collaborator Germaine Acogny, Carmen de Lavallade, and Bebe Miller. Zollar continues to do what she does best, creating work that moves people and makes them think.❖

Dianne Walker
(1951)
Tap dancer, choreographer, lecturer, mentor

Dianne Walker, known as "Lady Di," is the ultimate "tap mastress" and "professor of tapology." She is the link between the classic age of tap and its modern revival and development.

DIANNE TAYLOR WALKER was born in Boston, Massachusetts to Helen M. Johnson, a housewife, and Arthur Taylor, and was the younger of two children. At two years old, Walker was stricken by polio, which can cause temporary and sometimes permanent paralysis. To rebuild her daughter's strength, Walker's mother enrolled her in dance classes, which uncovered her passion for dance. Her first instructor was Ethel Covan, whose forte was ballet, but Walker's interest was tap. At age seven, she was referred to Mildred Kennedy-Bradic, who ran the Kennedy Dancing School in Boston. Kennedy-Bradic was a professional tap dancer nicknamed the "Brown Bomber," who had a successful career on the New England vaudeville circuit. Shortly thereafter, Walker became her star student.

Her mother remarried when she was eight years old to Luther L. Johnson, who served in the U.S. Air Force. At age ten, her family left Boston for Edwards Air Force Base in Southern California. Living there for five years, Walker taught dance classes to young children. When she was fourteen, her stepfather transferred to the Pacific island of Okinawa, where there were no tap classes to be found. Walker returned to Boston in 1968 and completed high school. After graduation, she married Rodney Walker, and the couple had two children. Walker earned an associate's degree in education in 1974 from Boston University, and was accepted into the master's program at Antioch University in Ohio. She completed both degrees while raising her family and working at Boston University's Department of Child Psychiatry. She graduated with a M.Ed. in 1976.

By 1978, Walker was working full-time as a staff psychologist at Boston University Hospital when she experienced a major life change. She attended an event and met Willy "Prince" Spencer, an eccentric vaudevillian who reminded her of the kind of men who came by Kennedy-Bradic's studio. Spencer suggested she take lessons from Leon Collins, a veteran tap dancer who taught at a Brookline studio. Walker began studying with Collins in 1977. She also studied with Jimmy Slyde, and through them she met tap dancers like Jeni LeGon, Marion Coles, Mable Lee,

and Harriet Brown. She reveled in this community, which had an impact on her life. In 1981, Walker embarked on a full-time career performing and teaching dance.

By 1982, Collins founded Collins & Company, which consisted of Collins, Walker, fellow students Pam Raff and C.B. Hetherington, and pianist Joan Hill. Walker was the only Black woman in the group. That same year, Walker attended Jane Goldberger's By Word of Foot Festival in New York City, and was disappointed to witness the paucity of Black dancers. She returned to Boston to teach and help revive tap through children, particularly Black children.

In 1985, Walker made her solo debut at a tap festival in Rome, Italy. When Collins fell ill, he urged her to attend in his place and perform his classic work, "Flight of the Bumblebee." Collins passed away suddenly, and Walker made a triumphant debut in Italy. When she returned to Boston, Walker and another Collins student took over his Brookline studio, and Walker eventually became its director.

Walker came onto the tap scene at a propitious time. Tap was in sharp decline due to a number of causes, among them the demise of vaudeville and the variety act. Having spent considerable time with the tap elders, Walker realized that tap did not die but was just neglected, so she decided to help a new generation rediscover tap. This is why Walker is credited for the resurgence of tap and is considered by many tap dance artists to be a transitional figure in the tap community.

At age thirty-six, Walker's first audition landed her a role in both the Paris and Broadway productions of *Black and Blue* (1989), a revue celebrating the artistic achievements of African American expatriates in Paris in the 1920s. She was featured as a shim-sham dancer in *Tap!*, the 1989 film that helped reintroduce tap to mainstream audiences. In the Broadway version of *Black and Blue,* Walker served as assistant choreographer and dance captain.

She made her Jacob's Pillow debut in 1996 performing the jazz waltz "Emily," her trademark tune. A woman of regal ease, Walker's taps have a crystalline tone that is nearly pearlescent, augmented by her conversationally active hands, head, and shoulders. Walker and Slyde headed a Jazz Tap Residency Project, performing and teaching in the Berkshires. Even after the funding ran out, Walker kept returning, giving workshops, and giving of herself.

When Walker met Savion Glover, she quickly became his mentor. Glover often refers to Walker affectionately as "Aunt Dianne," but a more frequent nickname from her colleagues is "Lady Di," due to her elegant, seemingly effortless routines. Keeping up a busy schedule of appearances as a dancer, Walker left the Collins studio in 1997 and became a full-time teacher on her own.

Beginning in the 1990s, Walker began touring jazz nightclubs and festivals around the U.S. A memorable appearance was at the Rainbow Room in New York with Ruth Brown, Grady Tate, Al McKibbon, and Sir Roland Hanna in 1990. Walker's festival appearances include North Sea (The Hague), Pouri (throughout Europe), Chicago Jazz Festival, and Montreal Jazz Festival with Gregory Hines. She was featured in "Fascinating Rhythms," a thirteen-city Dance Umbrella tour with Slyde, Glover, and bucket drummers Drummin Too Deep, from 1993 to 1994. Walker appeared at the Smithsonian on several occasions, honoring distinguished artists such as Cholly Atkins and Jeni LeGon, and as a special lecturer and performer in "Women in Tap" in the late 1990s. In 2000, she did a year-long engagement of Glover's Concert Tour, "Footnotes," with Slyde, Buster Brown, and Cartier Williams. Walker also appeared in the documentaries *JUBA: Masters of Tap & Percussive Dance* (1998), *Songs Unwritten: A Tap Dancer Remembered* (1998), *Honi Coles: The Class Act of Tap* (1994), the PBS production of *Black and Blue* (1993), and *Tap Dance in America* (1989). In 2010, she became director of the first Tap Program for the School at Jacob's Pillow.

Walker has held guest teaching positions at numerous colleges and universities, including Harvard University; Williams College in Williamstown, Massachusetts; the University of Michigan; University of California in Los Angeles; Bates College in Lewiston, Maine; and Wesleyan University in Middletown, Connecticut. She was appointed by the governor of Massachusetts to serve on the board of the Massachusetts Cultural Council. She has also served on the boards of several tap dance organizations, participated in the Dance USA Task Force on Dance Education, and, in 1997, represented the U.S. as an adjudicator for the Tap Dance Championships held in Dresden, Germany. She currently serves on the boards of Heartbeat Studios in Minneapolis, the Artn Tap Studio in Tokyo, and the Deborah Mason School of Dance in Sommerville, Massachusetts.

A tireless promoter of tap, Walker's venerated status has been richly honored. In 1997, she received the Tapestry Award for Excellence in Teaching from Thelma Goldberg of the Dance Inn in Lexington, Massachusetts. In 1998, Walker became the youngest dancer and first woman to be awarded the Living Treasure in American Dance Award from Oklahoma City University. She received the Savion Glover Award in 2000 for "Keeping the Beat Alive." In 2003, she was presented with the Flo-Bert Award from the New York Committee to Celebrate National Tap Dance Day. In 2004, Walker received the Hoofers Award from Tap City in New York City, and the Humanitarian Award from Jason Samuels Smith of the Debbie Allen Dance Academy. In 2005, Walker received lifetime achievement recognition from director Sas Selford of the Vancouver Tap Dance Society. She was honored in 2006 at a luncheon sponsored by Tapology in Flint, Michigan and presented by Artistic and Executive Director Alfred Bruce Bradley, and the Mott Foundation. In 2008, Walker received the highly distinguished honor of United States Artist, and was awarded as a USA Fellow of the Ernest and Irma Rose Foundation. She received the *Dance Magazine* Award in 2012 for lifetime achievement in dance.

While Walker never became famous beyond the field of tap, she is a pillar of the tap community: a teacher, role model, and, always, a mighty fine dancer. She is the artistic director of TapDancin' Inc. of Boston and continues to facilitate collaborations and work opportunities for tap dancers.❖

Debra Austin
(1955)
Ballet dancer, ballet master, teacher

Debra Austin was the first African American woman to join the corps de ballet of the New York City Ballet, first African American woman to dance a major role with the New York City Ballet, and the first African American female principal dancer of a major American ballet company to attain this rank outside of Dance Theatre of Harlem.

DEBRA KING AUSTIN BOIERU was born in Brooklyn, New York to Joyce Howard and Joseph King. An only child, her mother worked as a sales clerk at Lord & Taylor and later on worked at Banker's Trust, while her father was a printer. When her parents divorced, Austin and her mother lived with her grandmother for a while and later lived in Harlem. When her mother married Lionel Austin, the family moved to the Riverdale section of the Bronx.

Austin began dancing when she was eight years old, when a neighbor friend taking ballet classes referred her to the local ballet school. While she instantly knew that she wanted to pursue a ballet career, her teacher, a former Rockette from Radio City Music Hall, told Austin that she had no talent. Her mother felt otherwise and arranged for her to take classes at the Christine Neubert Children's Ballet Theatre affiliated with the Children's Ballet Theatre at Carnegie Hall. Austin studied under Barbara Walczak, a former soloist of the New York City Ballet and an original cast member of *Agon* (1957).

When she was eleven years old, Austin auditioned for and appeared as a mouse in Rudolf Nureyev's *The Nutcracker* for The Royal Ballet at the Metropolitan Opera House. Nureyev was featured as the Prince with Merle Park as Clara. As the only Black girl in the production, the chances of Austin being cast in the first act were slim to none, but it would not be the last time she would appear on the same stage as Nureyev. Austin received her first review in 1968 from Anna Kisselgoff of *The New York Times* for her performance in *Little Women* at the Fashion Institute of Technology in New York.

Walczak felt that she had done all she could for Austin's development, so she introduced her to Diana Adams, the director of the School of American Ballet (SAB) in New York City. Adams offered Austin a slot at SAB when she turned twelve. She received a full Ford Foundation scholarship to SAB and a half scholarship to Professional Children's School for academics, which she attended while studying and performing ballet.

Austin was handpicked by George Balanchine at age sixteen to join the corps de ballet of the New York City Ballet, and at age nineteen, became the company's first African American woman to dance principal roles. At Balanchine's direction, there was very little publicity surrounding her appointment, because he felt her talent should speak for itself. However, she was featured in the New York Daily News[1] for being the first Black ballerina to dance a major role in the company.

While Austin never became a principal dancer, she danced soloist and principal parts during her tenure at New York City Ballet. Some of her Balanchine roles include the third movement principal in Symphony in C, and she appeared as one of the five soloists in Divertimento No. 15. Austin also performed as Hippolyta in A Midsummer Night's Dream, was featured in Raymonda Variations, and notably, Ballo Della Regina, her signature solo created by Balanchine, which The New York Times[2] cited for her extraordinary performance.

She also danced featured roles for other choreographers. John Clifford gave Austin her first principal role when she was eighteen in his Bartok No. 3 in 1974, which received a great mention in The New York Times.[3] Austin appeared as Fall in Jerome Robbins' Four Seasons, and performed the pas de deux in his "Interplay." For the 1975 Ravel Festival, Robbins choreographed a ballet for Austin, Patricia McBride, Helgi Tomasson, and Hermes Conde called Chansons Medecasses, which is now lost.

In 1979, Austin appeared in performances that were televised for the PBS series Live from Lincoln Center, performing Ballo Della Regina, and the NBC television special Live From Studio H. After dancing with New York City Ballet for nine years, at age twenty-four, Austin decided to leave the company to dance for the Zurich Ballet in Switzerland, a sister company to New York City Ballet. Balanchine, who was the artistic adviser, made frequent trips to Switzerland. Austin was promoted to soloist and spent two years with the Zurich Ballet. She worked with European choreographers such as Heinz Spoerli and appeared in his Giselle as Myrtha. She also appeared in some of Hans Van Manen's works, giving her another taste of what dancing outside her comfort zone was like.

Nureyev had sought to bring to the U.S. Manfred, a ballet he choreographed in 1979 about Lord Byron's life and poetry, set to Tchaikovsky's "Manfred Symphony." He brought the work to the Zurich Ballet, and once again, Austin found

1. Michael Iachetta, "First Black Ballerina Stars With City Ballet," New York Daily News, May 30, 1974: 261.

2. Anna Kisselgoff, "City Ballet Presents the Premiere of Balanchine 'Ballo della Regina'," The New York Times, January 14, 1978, https://www.nytimes.com/1978/01/14/archives/city-ballet-presents-the-premiere-of-balanchine-ballo-della-regina.html.

3. Clive Barnes, "The Ballet: 'Bartok.No.3'," The New York Times, May 25, 1974, https://www.nytimes.com/1974/05/25/archives/the-ballet-bartok-no-3.html.

herself performing on stage with Nureyev, who had become a friend at this point in her career. Although she liked Switzerland, Austin became homesick. While she was treated fairly, the company did not have nearly as many performances as the companies in the states. She decided to go home.

When Austin returned to the U.S. in 1982, Balanchine became ill and passed away the following year. Peter Martins, who was then co-ballet master-in-chief alongside Jerome Robbins, offered her the opportunity to rejoin New York City Ballet, but Austin wanted to do something different. Martins suggested she contact former fellow dancer Robert "Ricky" Weiss, then the Pennsylvania Ballet's artistic director. Austin did and became the first African American woman to reach the rank of principal dancer in a major American ballet company.

At the Pennsylvania Ballet, Austin danced in many Balanchine ballets like *Rubies,* as Titania in *A Midsummer Night's Dream, Symphony in C, Donizetti Variations,* and *Concerto Barocco.* She also performed as Odette/Odile in *Swan Lake,* as Swanhilda in *Coppélia,* as Myrtha and Giselle in *Giselle,* as the Sylph in *La Sylphide,* and as the Sugar Plum Fairy and the Dewdrop in *The Nutcracker.* In some cases, she was the first African American woman to perform these roles and perform a pas de deux with a White partner. She danced with Nureyev in *Apollo* as Calliope, and with Suzanne Farrell as Terpsichore in a Gala Performance at the Academy of Music, hosted by Bill Cosby. In that same program, she danced and was accompanied by Grover Washington on the saxophone. She also performed in Richard Tanner and Lynne Taylor-Corbett ballets.

After running Pennsylvania Ballet for eight years, Weiss departed in 1990. When he left, Austin also decided to leave. She and fellow ballet dancer Marin Boieru were invited by Roy Tobias to appear as guest artists in the Universal Ballet. Tobias, a former member and teacher of the New York City Ballet, had settled in South Korea in the 1980s, where he worked with companies like the Universal Ballet. Austin, however, was not interested in permanently relocating to South Korea, and at the end of her contract, decided to return home.

She officially retired from dancing that same year. Austin and Boieru, a dancer from Romania whom she met in 1982 while they were both performing with Pennsylvania Ballet, married in 1992, and they would have two daughters. Austin ended up training dancers. She has taught ballet at the American Cultural Center, Palm Beach Dance Center, the Miami City Ballet School, and Cary Ballet Conservatory. In 1995, Austin assisted Taylor-Corbett in her ballet *The Dancing Princesses* for Miami City Ballet, which premiered at the John F. Kennedy Center for the Performing Arts in Washington, D.C. She also served as a preliminary judge for the National Foundation for the Advancement of the Arts.

In 1997, when Weiss was hired as artistic director of a new company—Carolina Ballet in North Carolina—he asked Austin and her husband to train and develop the dancers, so they relocated to Raleigh in 1998. Since its founding, Carolina Ballet has become one of America's preeminent ballet companies. Austin and her husband continue to serve as ballet masters of the company. In 2018, Carolina Ballet launched the School of Carolina Ballet. In addition to working with the company dancers, Austin teaches ballet to ten year olds up to pre-professional teens. The school's mission is to make ballet training available to the community and develop some of those students into professional dancers and potential members of Carolina Ballet. Austin thoroughly enjoys the prospect of discovering and mentoring little girls who have the potential to dance professionally in the same way that Barbara Walczak did for her those many years ago.

She also conducts workshops, residencies and teaches dance at Duke University, Carolina Dance Center, and several dance companies, notably Dance Theatre of Harlem. Austin recently served as the Cecil H. and Ida Green Honors Chair for an unprecedented five-day intensive residency at Texas Christian University's School of Classical and Contemporary Dance in Fort Worth.

Unlike the Black women who paved the way before her, Austin had a great career with few obstacles in her path. She worked from sixteen years old until her retirement at thirty-five. Except for a brief six-month break, she enjoyed nineteen years of continuous work. She got along and worked closely with collaborators and choreographers like Balanchine, Robbins, and Weiss, among others. When this little girl with "no talent" jumped, she soared. This is evident in the handful of videos available online of some of Austin's performances. Her technical strength is executed effortlessly, and the joy is apparent in her performances. She is both buoyant and radiant. Every now and then, Austin would be reminded that she was a Black ballerina in the middle of a flock of white swans. However, despite those challenges, she persevered and managed racism with grace, sometimes even with a naivety that often steered her towards focusing on the work.

Austin is the recipient of the Raleigh Chapter of the Links Emerald Award of Excellence, honoring North Carolina Women, was honored by North Carolina Governor Cooper for her work in dance during Black History Month; and was honored by the North Carolina History Museum, hosted by the Triangle Friends of African American Arts. She was featured in 50 for 50: Artists Celebrate North Carolina by The North Carolina Arts Council.

Austin also participated in the Chevrolet and National Newspaper Publishers Association (NNPA) Second 2017 Discover the Unexpected (DTU) Journalism Fellowship whereby HBCUs students interviewed Austin. The Museum at the Fashion Institute of Technology in New York City presented "Ballerina: Fashion's Modern Muse," the first large-scale exhibition of classical ballerinas, and unveiled Austin's costume next to Margot Fonteyn's (Nureyev's former partner) in 2020.

In 2016, Austin set the record straight after learning the media had inaccurately labeled Lauren Anderson as the first Black principal ballerina of a major American ballet company. Anderson, who danced with the Houston Ballet, was promoted to principal dancer eight years after Austin achieved the title. It may not be Debra Austin's style to tout her achievements, but her accomplishments are as real as they are historical.❖

Cynthia Oliver
(1961)
Dancer, choreographer, scholar, author

Cynthia Oliver, an award-winning choreographer and performance artist whose research intersects contemporary dance, feminism, Black popular culture and the expressive performances of African Americans and the Anglophone Caribbean, is making waves in the dance world.

CYNTHIA OLIVER was born in the Bronx, New York to Mary Oliver, who was born and raised in Harlem, and Everett Oliver from St. Croix in the U.S. Virgin Islands. Both worked as civil servants, and their union represented an extended family of six children from previous relationships. Oliver was the seventh and last child. She attended a Montessori school in Mount Vernon, New York, and acquired an interest in drawing and painting. She was also taking, albeit sporadically, dance classes because of her older sisters' interest in dance. When Oliver was eight years old, she, her parents, and two other siblings moved to St. Croix. She attended St. Dunstan's Episcopal school and the experimental Tamarind School. She returned to St. Dunstan for high school, where she focused on visual art while taking AP courses in physics, calculus, and drafting.

Oliver wanted to use her artistic skills to pursue a career in architecture or engineering, but dancing eclipsed that goal. She studied at Theatre Dance Inc. under the direction of Atti van den Berg Bermudez, a ballet dancer and former member of Kurt Jooss' German Dance Theatre who taught ballet, modern dance, and improvisation. One of Bermudez's guest artists was Trinidadian dancer Montgomery Thompson, who introduced Oliver to her first "official" theatrical Afro-Caribbean dance experience, which she would revisit when she returned to New York. Thompson eventually relocated to St. Croix and founded the Caribbean Dance Company.

Oliver's association with Bermudez and Thompson shifted her life trajectory. Taking classes, performing with Theatre Dance Inc., the Caribbean Dance Company, and the theater company Courtyard Players in Frederiksted; teaching young children to dance; and working for the Virgin Islands Council on the Arts helped reshape her career objective. While Oliver's father was nervous about her artistic pursuits, her mother encouraged her because she believed in the power of art. Mary was an illustrator and seamstress who could not practice her craft due to racism, so

she understood the importance of pursuing one's dreams. When college recruiters convinced Oliver to study and major in dance, she never looked back.

Oliver returned to New York at age seventeen to attend Adelphi University. She accepted an offer to join their dance department as a freshman on probation, earned a merit scholarship for her BFA in Dance, and graduated cum laude in 1982. After graduating from Adelphi, Oliver studied with renowned teachers Nadine Revene, Benjamin Harkavy, and Janet Panetta in ballet, Milton Myers and Debbie Lukitch in modern, and, later in her career, with Baba Richard González, who reignited her Afro-Caribbean sensibility in her dancing.

Her first professional engagement was with Rush Dance Company, directed by Patrice M. Regnier. She danced with several choreographers and companies, including the David Gordon Pick Up Co., Ronald Kevin Brown/Evidence, Prowess Dance Arts Collective, and the Nanette Bearden Contemporary Dance Theatre. As an actor, she performed in works by Greg Tate, Ione, Laurie Carlos, and Ntozake Shange. In 1991, Oliver founded Cynthia Oliver Co. Dance Theatre as an umbrella organization in order to operate as an independent artist. In 1996, she completed her masters from the Gallatin School at New York University, specializing in Caribbean literature, performance studies, and museum studies.

As a woman of Caribbean descent, Oliver creates work that is a mélange of dance theater and spoken word, which she incorporates into textures of Caribbean performance with African and American sensibilities. Her first choreographic piece, "At A Loss" in 1991, premiered at the Joseph Papp Public Theater as part of the "Haphazard Cabaret" showcase curated by rocker Vernon Reid. It was the only work that was pure movement. Oliver admits she named it "At a Loss" because it was how she felt at the time. Her follow-up solo work "Elisa," performed at Performance Space 122, successfully launched her career as a choreographer. She later created her first evening-length work, "Death's Door," at P.S. 122, for which she won a New York Dance and Performance (Bessie) Award for choreography in 1996. She followed this success with evening-length works "Unremoveable Jacket" (1997) and "SHEMAD" (2000). Both works were also performed at Performance Space 122, a venue Oliver credits as having offered her support at a crucial time and contributed to her success.

Moving forward, she found that using her fears and insecurities to address cultural, social, environmental, gender, class, and racial conditions in society was an asset, making her work viscerally enticing, and, at times, extremely personal. More importantly, Oliver sets out to intertwine different disciplines such as music, art, history, and text into her work, which is why she sees herself as an interdisciplinary artist. After having spent eighteen years as a fixture in the New York performance world, Oliver joined the Dance faculty at the University of Illinois, Urbana-Champaign in 2000. She earned her PhD in Performance Studies from Tisch School of the Arts at New York University in 2003. She has steadily produced more than twenty-two works while focusing on her research on African American and Caribbean women.

Oliver's recent works represent a wide range of her talent. She choreographed "BOOM!" in 2012 in collaboration with Leslie Cuyjet, a former student from the University of Illinois. It began as a short duet, featured in Ishmael Houston-Jones' "Parallels in Black Platform Series" at Danspace at St. Mark's Church in New York City and was subsequently commissioned for an extended presentation in its evening-length entirety at the 2014 New York Live Arts season. "BOOM!" builds on Oliver's signature investigation of slippages in everyday life, wherein truest the selves and real-life conditions are revealed.

Rigidigidim De Bamba De: Ruptured Calypso premiered at the Painted Bride Art Center in Philadelphia in 2009 as an evening-length multidisciplinary dance theater project which presents Afro-Caribbean identity across geographical, national, and aesthetic borders. The international cast of "Rigidigidim" layered myth, herstory, the spoken word, and dance to deliver subversive truth-telling with a rawness of downright unrespectable levels.

As Oliver garnered greater national and international acclaim as a "woman's artist," she produced *Virago-Man Dem,* her first evening-length piece that featured men. Having spent the majority of her career looking at and offering insights into women's worlds, she wanted to examine the nuances and complexities of contemporary Black masculinities, which ultimately served as a love letter to her then fourteen-year-old son. In 2015, Oliver accepted a fellowship at New Waves Institute in Trinidad, which collaborated with Dancing While Black, an organization in New York. Working with local dancers and community members, she initiated conversations about race and gender issues, which led to the creation of *Virago-Man Dem.*

In support of Oliver's research, later that year, Vermont Performance Lab (VPL) created a discussion series through individual conversations and workshops with Black men living in southeastern Vermont. Oliver worked with community members along with performer Niall Jones, also a University of Illinois alum, to investigate how they embodied and "performed" masculinity. Oliver held workshops in Urbana, Illinois with Black men who watched sections of the work and discussed its issues with her. Ultimately, *Virago-Man Dem* included a spectrum of male and male-identifying gender performances.

Without resorting to stereotypes, *Virago-Man Dem* strived to present the certainties and uncertainties of masculinity and ask questions of race in a variety of communities. During her residency in 2016, Oliver dug further into the complexities of masculine representation in performance and presented a work-in-progress to VPL audiences. The work premiered at the Brooklyn Academy of Music's Next Wave Festival in 2017 and toured the country.

Oliver has performed around the globe, and her work has been reviewed and praised by a number of print and online publications, including *The New York Times, Pittsburgh City Paper, Chicago Tribune, The New Yorker, Amsterdam News, The Philadelphia Inquirer, The Washington Post, The Village Voice, Dance*

Magazine, Culturebot, thINKingDANCE, and *Smile Politely.* In addition to performing and choreographing, Oliver has published work that focuses on performance in the Anglophone Caribbean, particularly in the U.S. Virgin Islands. Her work has appeared in anthologies, exhibition booklets, and journals such as *Caribbean Dance, Movement Research Journal,* and *Women & Performance: A Journal of Feminist Theory.* Her book, *Queen of the Virgins: Pageantry and Womanhood in the Caribbean* (2009), examines the cultural phenomena of beauty pageants in the U.S. Virgin Islands and how mechanisms of pageantry move toward defining Black womanhood in the region.

Early in her career, Oliver was named Outstanding Young Choreographer by the German magazine *Ballet Tanz,* and featured in *Dance Magazine* in 2002. She has received numerous awards from national arts foundations in support of her work, including Creative Capital (2002), Illinois Arts Council Choreography Fellowships (2004, 2014, 2017), the Rockefeller Foundation's MAP Fund (2007, 2016), the New England Foundation's National Dance Project (2009, 2017), awards from the National Performance Network's Creation Fund (2009, 2014, 2017), and a prestigious nomination for the Alpert Award in the Arts for dance (2009). In 2011, Oliver was selected for a University Scholar Award from the University of Illinois, Urbana-Champaign for her research and performance work. In 2020, she was the first Black female faculty member to be inducted into the Center for Advanced Study at the university. She was nominated for a Doris Duke Impact Award in 2015 and is a 2021 United States Artist Doris Duke Fellow, which is a nomination-only honor. *Virago-Man-Dem* was nominated for two Bessie categories in 2018.

Oliver continues to perform with others like the Bebe Miller Company, Tere O'Connor Dance, and Deke Weaver. She has taught at Bates Dance Festival, New York University's Department of Drama, Tisch School of the Arts, The Newcomb Summer Dance Festival at Tulane University, Florida State University, the University of Utah, and the University of Maryland, College Park.

She is currently a Professor of Dance at the University of Illinois, Urbana-Champaign, where she teaches technique, composition, performance, post-colonial and feminist theory, and courses emphasizing the African American and African-Caribbean influences in American performance. In 2017, Oliver was appointed to the Office of the Vice Chancellor for Research and Innovation as an Associate Vice Chancellor for Research and Innovation in the Humanities, Arts, and Related Fields.

Oliver is married to her creative partner, Jason Finkelman, a musician she met in Philadelphia in 1991 when she briefly managed the Urban Bush Women. He has composed the music for all of her works which feature music. They have a son, Elias, born in 2004. As Oliver continues to push boundaries using research, works of literature, and movement, it will be interesting to see what fresh ideas she comes up with next to share with her growing audience.❖

Fatima Robinson
(1971)
Dancer, choreographer, producer, director

Fatima Robinson, an award-winning choreographer, is one of the most sought-after hip-hop and popular music choreographers in the world. Her choreography has been featured in music videos, movies, and television shows.

FATIMA ROBINSON was born in Little Rock, Arkansas to Kadijah Lewis and Nasid Rasol. When she was four years old, she, her mother, and her two younger sisters moved to Los Angeles. Dancing was a hobby, but Robinson had no idea at the time that she could make a career out of it. Nevertheless, she taught herself various moves by watching films like *Flashdance* (1983) and a lot of music videos. Robinson would then create dance routines for her sisters to entertain family and friends. Since her mother enrolled her in school when she was four years old, Robinson graduated from high school at age sixteen. She became a certified cosmetologist and started working at her mother's hair salon, but her heart remained in dance.

Robinson started going to dance clubs and hung out with the likes of Dr. Dre and Easy E, helping them to sell mix-tapes out of their cars. She competed in dance contests, and began to appear in music videos, namely a Rich Nice video. Toni Basil gave Robinson her first audition for Busta Rhymes' Young Me Tour. Later she met Lionel C. Martin, a music video producer and director who was instrumental in her career. She appeared as an extra in movies, on tours, and found herself rubbing shoulders with Puff Daddy (Sean Combs), Big Daddy Kane, Jay Z, and Brandy. She hung out with Rosie Perez, who gave her sound advice, and as she became entrenched in this nascent hip-hop scene, she discovered the connection between African dance and hip-hop. Even without formal training, Robinson quickly rose up the ranks by learning dance steps and then adding her own flavor to popular dance moves. Over the years, Robinson would occasionally take dance classes to aide her in her choreographic pursuits.

Robinson happened to be in the right place at the right time when she met director John Singleton, who made her an extra in *Boyz n the Hood* (1991). While she was dancing in music videos, she was also putting together stage shows for artists she had danced for. It was her work with The Backstreet Boys, however, that introduced her to the pop world. She helped give them authentic street moves, and the experience helped refine her stage show strategy. She also enrolled in acting and directing classes to further improve her choreography.

Robinson was quickly making the transition to choreography, becoming known for her ability to blend modern hip-hop styles with more classical dance moves. In 1992, after Singleton's success with *Boyz n the Hood* the previous year, he recruited a then twenty-one-year-old Robinson to choreograph the Michael Jackson music video he was filming: the hit 1991 single, "Remember the Time." The video, which is nine minutes long, featured not only Jackson but also Eddie Murphy, Iman, and Magic Johnson, among other noteworthy personalities. Working with Jackson was, in fact, the break that Robinson needed. Jackson was the measuring stick in the music video industry, and artists in all genres tried to achieve his greatness by hiring his choreographers.

She saturated the video market in the 1990s working with artists like Sade, Notorious B.I.G., and Aaliyah. Robinson also choreographed the Mary J. Blige Summer Jam tour. In 1995, she received her first MTV Video Music Award nomination for Best Choreography for Brandy's "Baby." The nomination started a trend: Robinson would go on to be nominated each year between 1997 and 2001 for an MTV Video Music Award. She won her first Best Choreography Award in 1997 for the video short "Been There, Done That" by Dr. Dre.

By the early 2000s, with her star rising, Robinson experienced some joy and pain in her personal life. Robinson had met poet Saul Williams, and they celebrated the birth of their son in 2000, but a year later, she suffered the loss of her close friend and colleague, Aaliyah, who died in a plane crash in 2001.

Robinson also began transitioning into directing and producing. She directed videos for the Black Eyed Peas, Meghan Trainor, Hillary Duff, and Fergie. She won the MTV Video Music Award for Best Choreography in a Music Video in 2004 for the Black Eyed Peas video, *Hey Mama.* Working on such high-level projects launched Robinson into the upper echelons of the entertainment industry, which landed her substantial television and film work. Known for her work in music videos, Robinson began choreographing for hit films such as *Save the Last Dance* (2001). She worked with director Michael Mann on four of his films: *Ali* (2001), *Collateral* (2004), *Dreamgirls* (2006), and *Miami Vice* (2006).

Robinson took a chance when she auditioned as choreographer for *Dreamgirls.* Asked to come up with a version of the show-stopping number "Steppin' to the Bad Side," Robinson brought an entirely different perspective to the piece. She forwent the explicitly theatrical and jazz-based stage choreography by Michael Bennett and Michael Peters, and presented an amalgam of styles: gospel, jazz, blues, soul and rock. Instead of dancing horn players, Robinson featured tambourines and chairs, providing a more church-like feel to the piece. When director Bill Condon selected Robinson to choreograph *Dreamgirls,* she kept that influence palpable throughout the film. She would go on to choreograph other films such as *Norbit* (2007), *American Gangster* (2007), *The Cheetah Girls: One World* (2008), and *Sparkle* (2012), working with Academy Award-winning directors like Mike Nichols, and Ridley Scott, and celebrated actors such as Will Smith, Uma Thurman, and John Travolta. She recently choreographed the Eddie Murphy film, *Coming 2 America* (2021).

Her work behind-the-scenes in film and television productions led her to enroll at the New York Film Academy, where she expanded her creative skill set, learning the technical aspects and intricacies behind directing. Robinson found that her role as choreographer had also expanded to hair, makeup, wardrobe, lighting and staging, which all helps to set the overall tone of a performance.

She has worked on a variety of major television events and series such as the Super Bowl Halftime Show with the Black Eyed Peas, and performances by The Weeknd and Pharrell Williams. Robinson was the second African American woman in history to choreograph the Academy Awards in 2006 and 2007 (Debbie Allen was the first from 1991 to 1994). She served as coproducer of the television specials *Fashion Rocks* (2008), *Movies Rock* (2007), and the Soul Train Awards (2009, 2010, 2012), and choreographed for the BET Awards, The American Music Awards, and the Grammy Awards.

Robinson made her theatrical debut in *Radiant Baby,* a musical based on the life of artist Keith Haring, produced and directed by George C. Wolfe at the New York Public Theater in 2003. For Robinson, her experience with Wolfe's genius-like artistic vision was like going back to school. She choreographed the television movies *Their Eyes Were Watching God* (ABC 2005), *Lackawanna Blues* (HBO 2005), *Whitney* (Lifetime 2015), and NBC's live television production of *The Wiz Live!* in 2015. Her choreography has been featured on popular television shows such as *American Soul, Black-ish, The Voice, Dancing with the Stars, So You Think You Can Dance,* and *American Idol.* Robinson has also choreographed for notable commercial spots including Pepsi, Apple, Target, Chanel, H&M, Burberry, Pepsi, Gap, iPod, Nissan, Verizon, Motorola and Heineken. She produced "Taking the Stage: Changing America," the concert honoring the opening of the Smithsonian National Museum of African American History and Culture. She was also invited to teach a Master Class at the Obama White House, celebrating "African American Women and Dance" in 2016.

Robinson received multiple nominations for American Choreography Awards, Choreography Media Honors, and a Lucille Lortel Award nomination for Outstanding Choreographer Off-Broadway for *Radiant Baby.* She was named by *Entertainment Weekly* as one of the 100 most creative people in the world of entertainment, and inducted into the Arkansas Black Hall of Fame in 2004.

From her humble roots on the dance floors of local clubs to concert stages and the silver screen, Robinson has been strategic with every syncopated step. Unlike many choreographers who work in oversized black sweat clothes, Robinson wears four-inch jeweled heels, skinny jeans, a white wrap-around sweater and a red bandanna that perfectly matches her shade of lipstick. With nearly 100 credits to her name, she is as creative as she is fastidious and demanding. ❖

Dormeshia
(1976)
Tap dancer, choreographer, teacher

Dormeshia is recognized and revered as one of the most dynamic performers in the industry today and the "tap mastress" of her generation.

DORMESHIA SUMBRY was born in Inglewood, California to Emily Sumbry and Albert Sumbry. The youngest of three sisters, she grew up in Los Angeles. Dormeshia's interest in dance began at age three when she began watching her teenage sister dance. Her mother enrolled her at Universal Dance Theatre in Los Angeles under the instruction of siblings Paul and Arlene Kennedy whose mother, Mildred, had performed as "The Brown Bomber" on the New England vaudeville circuit.

Kennedy's students performed at events attended by tap legends such as John Bubbles and the Nicholas Brothers. Dormeshia gained a wider sense of the tradition when, at nine years old, she, along with Cyd Glover, were chosen to perform at the Tip Tap Festival in Rome. Also on the bill were The Copasetics and The Hoofers, swing-era performers who had been coaxed out of retirement by a new generation interested in the art. While extremely shy, Dormeshia picked up on every step and repeated it exactly as shown. She rarely made a mistake.

When she was twelve, Dormeshia made a brief appearance in the film *Tap!* (1989), starring Gregory Hines and Sammy Davis Jr., as one of the young dancers in the studio taking a class with Savion Glover. Dianne Walker, one of tap's foremost matriarchs, was a featured dancer in *Black and Blue* during its Paris run, with Glover, the only child in the cast. When the production transferred to Broadway, Walker, who had moved up from featured dancer to assistant choreographer, lobbied for more kids to get exposure. During the run of her Broadway debut in *Black and Blue* in 1989, Dormeshia realized tap dancing was what she wanted to do professionally for the rest of her life.

While working in *Black and Blue,* Dormeshia had the opportunity to watch and listen to tap masters Jimmy Slyde, Bunny Briggs, Lon Chaney, Ralph Brown, and Chuck Green. She would later tour with *Black and Blue* in Europe, rising to the adult women's dance captain and even singing in the production. At the

end of the show's run and after graduating from high school, Dormeshia joined Lynn Dally's Jazz Tap Ensemble, based in Los Angeles, made appearances in Hong Kong, New York, Ohio, and Alaska, and eventually became a soloist. In the Ensemble, she learned how to choreograph and improvise to live music by creating visually engaging works, such as "All Blues" and "Oracle," choreographed by Dally, in which she and Derick K. Grant skated effortlessly across the stage and danced both as one and in counterpoint to each other.

In 1997, Dormeshia joined the Tony Award-winning *Bring In 'Da Noise, Bring In 'Da Funk* (1995) as the first and only female tap dancer in the show. The show initially featured an all-male cast consisting of Savion Glover's buddies, and the style was aggressive and hard-hitting. A year into the run, when cast replacements were needed, Glover asked Dormeshia to join the cast. He knew she could do it. She was forced to take on a male character except in one number, in which she dressed as a businesswoman and did the same steps as the men but in high heels. In the 2003 world tour of the show, she was allowed to take on a female character and wear female attire, except in the industrial scene. During this period, Dormeshia began hearing comments about her ability to maintain her strong sound in heels, which motivated her to share her techniques for tap dancing in heels.

When she joined the *Bring In 'Da Noise,* Dormeshia reunited with Omar Edwards, a dancer and cast member with whom she had first been acquainted when performing in *Black and Blue.* They married in 1998 during the closing weeks of *Bring In 'Da Noise.* Soon they had children: a son, a daughter, and —nearly a decade later—another daughter, and they opened a dance studio in Harlem. Although the couple rarely performed together, they both considered themselves rhythm tap dancers or tap dance artists.

Dormeshia's career has developed largely under the radar of the wider culture, in venues such as tap festivals, little known independent films, and bit parts in projects involving more famous colleagues like Glover, or Michael Jackson, for whom she served as a personal tap coach for eleven years. Yet, despite this slight, Dormeshia has managed to bring to light some stellar performances.

In 1999, Ayodele Casel and Dormeshia appeared in the tap number "You Musn't Kick It Around" from *Pal Joey* in the television documentary, *The Rodgers and Hart Story: Thou Swell, Thou Witty.* In 2000, she performed the role of Pickaninny Topsy in the Spike Lee film *Bamboozled,* starring Glover and Tommy Davidson, in which she served as assistant choreographer to Glover. Choreography credits also include Michael Jackson's music video "Rock My World" in 2001.

In a 2005 performance of "Turned On Tap" at London's Queen Elizabeth Hall, Dormeshia and Jason Samuels Smith blew the audience away with their style, technique, and raw energy. In 2006, Dormeshia announced a new course in her Harlem Tap Studio: "Mastering Femininity in Tap (MFIT)," a four-week tap class that countered the downward-driving, piston-driven attack of traditional (male) rhythm-tapping styles with steps that are structured along more circuitous paths of attack—steps in ronde de jambs shapes, pullbacks that use the momentum of a traditional straight-back pullback but that are circular and aerial, and preparations for shuffles made by twisting and spiraling the torso. MFIT might have been developed to master femininity in tap, but the class was really about regaining it through a revolutionary new approach to technique.

Dormeshia was a featured soloist of *Imagine Tap!* (2006), a musical revue directed and choreographed by Grant. She starred in the Stacie Hawkins independent film, *The Rise and Fall of Miss Thang* (2007), as a tap dancer on a journey of rediscovery, and was nominated "Best Actress" for her performance. On stage, she was Smith's muse in his jazz tap tribute to Charlie "Bird" Parker in "Charlie's Angels," alongside Michelle Dorrance and Chloe Arnold in 2009. Dormeshia was also a featured performer in Broadway's *After Midnight* in 2013.

Other stage performances include the national tour of *Wild Woman Blues* (2000), an appearance as a special guest performer with Fantasia Barrino on tour, and in Debbie Allen's *SAMMY (The Life and Times of Sammy Davis Jr.)* (2008). Dormeshia was also featured at the Freedom Sounds Festival in 2016 as part of the launch of the Smithsonian African American Museum. That same year, she performed at International Jazz Day at The Kennedy Center with Al Jarreau and Dee Dee Bridgewater. Dormeshia has toured extensively in the U.S. and abroad, and continues to be in demand as a teacher and choreographer.

Dormeshia was all of seventeen in 1993 when she made her first appearance at Jacob's Pillow. In 2013, she returned to Jacob's Pillow—after a gap of two decades—as a co-star and co-choreographer (along with Dorrance and Grant) for Dorrance's *The Blues Project.* The choreography cleverly crossed the Lindy Hop with poses, up rocking, and top rocking borrowed from hip-hop, illuminating an under-recognized lineage. Dormeshia's big moment came in her improvisational solo to "Dream Variations," drawn from a Langston Hughes poem, which was the show's climax and resonated with her spirit.

Sometime during *The Blues Project,* Ella Baff, then artistic director of Jacob's Pillow, invited Dormeshia to put together her own show. Roping in her old friends Grant and Smith, along with a jazz trio and contemporary dancer and award-winning choreographer Camille A. Brown, Dormeshia created a production called *And Still You Must Swing,* which premiered in 2016.

The work demonstrates the missing element found in tap these days, and the phrase comes from the 1985 documentary *About Tap,* in which Jimmy Slyde says, "There's balance involved. There's movement involved...And still you must swing." What Slyde meant is that, in order to achieve balance, the upper body and footwork must work together to tell a story. It is what Dormeshia noted over ten years ago, when she created her master class to teach young dancers who had extraordinary technique but stumbled over simple steps because they lacked musicality. *And Still You Must Swing* demonstrates basics, deep roots, strong foundations, and what glorious structures of intricacy and feeling can be built from tap. Excerpts from the project have since been performed in Los Angeles, Texas, and Vancouver, with an engagement at The Joyce Theatre in New York City in 2019. Dormeshia was the official Tap Spokesperson for Capezio, and she and her family were featured in their international advertising campaign. She currently serves on *Dance Magazine's* board as a Tap Advisor.

Dormeshia has appeared as herself on the television series, *Superstars of Dance* (2009), and in the documentaries *Tap or Die* (2014), *Tap World* (2015), and *American Tap* (2018). As an instructor, she has taught on the International Tap Festival circuit, including the St. Louis Tap Festival, New York City Tap Festival, the Los Angeles Tap Festival, the Campinas Tap Festival (Brazil), Stockholm Tap Festival, Rhythm World (Chicago), Tapology (Flint, Michigan), Seoul Tap Festival (Korea), Taptastic (Germany), and Monterrey Tap Festival (Mexico), to name a few.

Dormeshia helped keep tap dance thriving in New York City by becoming a mainstay at the Broadway Dance Center. After a year with no tap classes due to the COVID-19 pandemic, Dormeshia joined Barnard College's dance department to teach tap classes, beginning the summer of 2021.

Her accolades include a Princess Grace Scholarship in Dance (1994), the Hoofer Award from The American Tap Dance Foundation (2010); a Bessie Award for Outstanding Performer in Jason Samuels Smith's work "Chasing The Bird, " performed at The Joyce Theater (2012); an Astaire Award for Best Performance (2013) for *After Midnight* on Broadway; The Princess Grace Statue Award (2017); and a Bessie Award for her role as co-creator and choreographer for *The Blues Project.* Her work, *And Still You Must Swing,* was also selected in both 2016 and 2019 as *The New York Times'* "Best of Dance." She also appeared on the cover of *Dance Magazine* twice.

While Dormeshia has been long considered a master by her peers, her career did not take off in the same way as her male counterparts. After taking time off to focus on raising her family, Dormeshia is finally receiving critical acclaim. Most ballerinas her age would be thinking of retiring, but it is not unusual for tap dancers to perform well into their eighties or nineties. In the prime of her career, it looks like Dormeshia is finally getting her due.❖

Camille A. Brown
(1979)
Dancer, choreographer, director, dance educator

Camille A. Brown, the founder and artistic director of Camille A. Brown & Dancers, is an award-winning choreographer and the third African American woman nominated for a Tony for Best Choreography.

CAMILLE A. BROWN was born in Jamaica, New York to Lorraine Brown, a social worker, and Stanley Brown, a parole officer. As an only child, Brown always loved dancing and moving in space, which her parents encouraged her to do. From the time she was three, Brown watched Michael Jackson and Janet Jackson videos and became preternaturally good at recreating the Jacksons' complex choreography. When she was four, Brown's mother enrolled her in tap and ballet classes at The Bernice Johnson Dance Center.

By the time Brown was eleven, she began studying under Carolyn DeVore. Brown's mother wanted her to learn how to play an instrument, so she picked the clarinet. Playing the clarinet was something she enjoyed doing, but not as much as dance. In fact, when Brown auditioned for Fiorello H. LaGuardia High School of Music & Art and Performing Arts in New York, she decided to audition for dance only. While attending LaGuardia, Brown simultaneously attended The Ailey School on scholarship. She was a standout and won several awards in 1997 during her senior year: a Young Artist's Award, Presidential Scholar of the Arts Award, and the Helen Tamiris Award. After graduation, Brown enrolled in the University of North Carolina School of the Arts, a top-ranked creative and performing arts conservatory in Winston-Salem.

Unfortunately, and as is typical in the dance community among Black women dancers, Brown struggled with body image. Brown had been repeatedly told over the years that she had a less than ideal body for dance, and began dieting as early as sixteen years old. Once she began studying dance at North Carolina, she was being sent to the school nutritionist and not being called for auditions due to her body type. Brown found this so disheartening that she considered a transfer, but her mother encouraged her to find something she loved about dance, at least until the end of the semester. Soon after, Brown found herself gravitating towards composition and improv, and placed all of her anxiety and energy into creating her own dances. Eventually she discovered that she had a love for choreography.

After Brown earned her BFA from North Carolina, unlike most dance students, she never really had any strong opinions about which company and choreographer she wanted to dance with. An amazing string of coincidences in New York City led her to become a member of Ronald K. Brown's Evidence Dance Company. She danced with him for five seasons. She also was a guest artist with Rennie Harris Puremovement, and the Alvin Ailey American Dance Theater. A colleague sent Brown a letter about the Hubbard Street 2 Competition for emerging choreographers, and she decided to submit to the competition. She won at age twenty-two, which snowballed into a choreographing career.

Having received numerous commissions, in 2006 Brown decided to form her own company, Camille A. Brown & Dancers. Initially, she did not want to dive into creating and managing a company, wearing multiple hats as a dancer, choreographer and administrator. However, once she began developing larger works, Brown realized that she needed a longer and more intimate process, which prompted her desire to start a company. She quickly realized she could use the company to instill cultural curiosity, introspection, and reflection in its audiences through performances, dialogue, and outreach activities to students and young adults in local communities across the country. While Brown also choreographs theater projects and is involved in numerous community and social engagement initiatives, she has managed to create an award-winning repertoire as artistic director of her own company.

This quest for Black people's voices and identities weaves itself through Brown's choreographic works. She created a trilogy of work on race, culture and identity that began with *Mr. TOL E. RAncE,* for which she won a Bessie Award for Outstanding Production in 2014. In *Mr. TOL E. RAncE,* Brown took on racial stereotypes portrayed in the entertainment industry, inspired by Spike Lee's *Bamboozled* (2000), and the Langston Hughes poem "Minstrel Man." It Is as comedic as it is serious—and perhaps even startling—when Brown indirectly poses the uncomfortable question: "Has anything changed?"

Black GIRL: Linguistic Play, which premiered in 2015, explores Black female identity by transporting her dancers and audiences to the playground and using childhood games as a source of empowerment and conscious joy. Brown provides study guides in her programs, and at the end of her shows, she offers post-show conversations. *Black GIRL: Linguistic Play* was nominated for a 2016 Bessie Award for Outstanding Production. Brown premiered the final part of her trilogy, *Ink,* in late 2017. Building on *Mr. TOL E. RAncE* (2012), *Black GIRL: Linguistic Play,* and *Ink* celebrates the rituals, gestures, and traditions of the African diaspora. Highlighting themes of brotherhood, Black love, community, and resilience, the work seeks to reclaim African American narratives. Following *Ink's* premiere in 2019, Brown and her company were invited to partner with Google Arts & Culture to film a site-specific performance of *Ink* at the Brooklyn Historical Society for Black History

Month. Separately, the three works look like completely different pieces, but together, they comment on race and perception from different lenses. Brown's choreography focuses on unmasking small, intimate, and familiar everyday movements, using modern, hip hop, tap, African and social dance, and brings them to the fore, connecting the dancers to the audience with energy and urgency. Her focus on social and vernacular dance instead of classical dance has also challenged the "ideal" body type that Brown endured and what continues to loom large in the dance community. She uses culture, music, and the celebration of the Black body to create stories that connect to the audience. In this case, familiarity breeds comfort.

Brown created the EVERY BODY MOVE (EBM) platform in 2015, which inspires and incites ambitious collective action fueled by the art of social dance. Under this platform are several initiatives, notably the Black GIRL SPECTRUM (BGS), a multi-faceted community engagement initiative created in 2014 that seeks to spur the creative capacity and cultural empowerment of Black girls and women through social dance, dialogue, using the creative tools and the rich history of movement and music from the African diaspora. In 2018, Brown launched Black Men Moving (BMM), a similar initiative for boys and men.

In 2017, Brown choreographed both the revivals of *Once On This Island* and NBC's live performance of *Jesus Christ Superstar* featuring John Legend on Easter Sunday. By 2019, Brown had been propelled to the forefront of the Broadway and concert dance with her unique way of using dance in modern and contemporary storytelling. She choreographed Tarell Alvin McCrawly's play, *Choir Boy,* which had a limited run at the Samuel J. Friedman Theater in 2019. She also choreographed Shakespeare in the Park's *Much Ado About Nothing,* the revivals of Pittsburgh Civic Light Opera's *Once,* The Metropolitan Opera's *Porgy and Bess* and The Public Theater's *for colored girls who have considered suicide/when the rainbow is enuf.* She also choreographed Lydia R. Diamond's play *Toni Stone,* which premiered Off-Broadway. Additional theater credits include the revivals of *A Streetcar Named Desire* (2012) on Broadway, *Cabin in the Sky* (2015) at New York City Center Encores!; and Jonathan Larson's *tick, tick...BOOM!* (2014). Brown performed as a guest artist in the 2016 world premiere of *And Still You Must Swing* with tap artists Dormeshia, Derick K. Grant, and Jason Samuels Smith at Jacob's Pillow, which was reprised at the Joyce Theater in 2019. Brown made her feature film debut choreographing the award-winning *Ma Rainey's Black Bottom,* directed by George C. Wolfe, and released by Netflix in 2020.

· Her work has been commissioned by Alvin Ailey American Dance Theater, PHILADANCO, Complexions, Ballet Memphis, and Urban Bush Women. She was nominated in 2018 for a Drama Desk Award for Outstanding Choreography for *Once on This Island* (2017), and nominated in 2019 for a Tony Award for Best Choreography for *Choir Boy,* becoming the third Black woman nominated for choreography, alongside Marlies Yearby (1996) and Hope Clarke (1993).

During the COVID-19 pandemic, Brown initiated Social Dance for Social Change, a free virtual dance school, and in-person socially distant outdoor workshops in Jamaica, where she grew up. When live performances return to New York, Brown is slated to codirect The Metropolitan Opera's *Fire Shut Up In My Bones,* direct and choreograph the Broadway revival of for *colored girls who have considered suicide/when the rainbow is enuf,* and direct and choreograph *Ain't Misbehavin'.*

Brown has been nominated and won numerous awards. Some of her honors include being the four-time winner of the Princess Grace Award (2006, 2013, 2016, 2016), and the Princess Grace Choreography Mentorship Co-Commission (CMCC) Award (2019). She is a two-time Bessie Award winner (2014, 2016); recipient of the The Founder's Award by the International Association of Blacks in Dance (IABD) (2013); winner of the Doris Duke Artist Award (2015), Jacob's Pillow Dance Award (2016); Audelco Award (2017, 2019); Obie Award for Sustained Excellence in Choreography (2020); Antonyo Award Winner for Best Choreography (2020); *Dance Magazine* Award Honoree (2020); and an ISPA Distinguished Artist Award (2021). She is a recipient of several grants and fellowships, including a USA Jay Franke & David Herro Fellow (2015), a three-time recipient of NEFA's National Dance Project: Production Grant, 2015 MAP Fund Grantee, 2015 Engaging Dance Audiences Grantee, a Jerome Foundation 50th Anniversary Grantee, a Guggenheim Fellow (2016), Ford Foundation Art of Change Fellow (2017), and an Emerson Collective Fellow (2020).

A 2015 TED Fellow, Brown's TED talk on the influence of African and African American social dance in the U.S. was chosen as one of the most notable talks of 2016 by TED Curator Chris Anderson. She has been featured on the covers of *Dance Magazine* and *Dance Teacher Magazine.* She codirected the Social Dances: Jazz to Hip-Hop program with Moncell Durden at The Jacob's Pillow School.

Brown's journey was not one of overnight success but one of perseverance. A visionary artist working at the fertile crossroads of music, theater, and politics, Brown rejects one-dimensional cultural narratives of Black identity. Instead, she mines a complex mix of ancestral stories and dance styles to examine aspects of Black existence that have been revised, appropriated, or silenced altogether. Her versatility is demonstrated in works that range from the light-hearted to spiritually based, politically charged with comedic flair to personal. She leads her dancers through excavations of ancestral stories both timeless and traditional, connecting history with contemporary culture. While her work is tagged with cultural identifiers, her strong technical modern dance foundation makes her repertoire sing. She embraces the beauty of Black bodies that have been excluded and presents them in a safe space that is both compelling and original. *Thinking outside the box.* This is Brown's mantra, and it works.❖

Misty Copeland
(1982)
Ballet dancer, author, activist

Misty Copeland is the fourth African American soloist (and third female), and the first African American woman to be promoted to principal dancer in American Ballet Theatre's seventy-five year history.

MISTY DANIELLE COPELAND was born in Kansas City, Missouri. Her mother, Sylvia DelaCerna, is of Italian and African American descent and was adopted by African American parents. Her father, Doug Copeland, is of German and African American descent. Her mother, a former Kansas City Chief's cheerleader, became a medical assistant but worked mostly in sales. Copeland was their fourth child.

Copeland's mother had several successive marriages and two more children, one each from her third and fourth marriages. Copeland would not see her father between the ages of two and twenty-two. At times, the family packed up and moved under harried conditions, eventually settling in the coastal community of San Pedro in California. Her mother's relationship and eventual marriage to her fourth husband was tumultuous (Copeland 2018).

Copeland found solace in school and the world of performance. She connected to Romanian gymnast Nadia Comăneci, and performed dance routines at home to the songs of Mariah Carey. When chosen as captain of her drill team at her middle school, her teacher believed Copeland should take ballet. She eventually took classes at the Boys and Girls Club under the tutelage of Elizabeth Cantine, who referred her to Cynthia Bradley, who had her own school. She quickly recognized that the youngster was a prodigy. Copeland was able to see and perform choreographed movements after a very short period of ballet training. Bradley invited Copeland to attend class at her ballet school, the San Pedro Dance Center. After three months of study, Copeland was *en pointe* (Copeland 2018.)

While her dancing life blossomed, Copeland's home life was in distress. Her mother left her fourth husband, and the family moved into a motel. With her mother's permission, the thirteen-year-old Copeland moved in with Bradley and her family to continue training as she entered the public spotlight. Copeland would spend nearly three years with the Bradleys. Around this time, Copeland had a lead role in the Debbie Allen production, *The Chocolate Nutcracker.*

After attending a summer intensive program on scholarship at San Francisco Ballet, a battle ensued between Bradley and Copeland's mother, heightened further by media coverage of fifteen-year-old Copeland seeking legal emancipation from her biological parent. Eventually, Copeland dropped the case and returned to live with her mother.

Copeland continued to pursue her career. After taking classes at Lauridsen Ballet Centre, Copeland auditioned for and was accepted in American Ballet Theatre's (ABT) 1999 Summer Intensive program. By the end of the summer, Copeland was invited to join the ABT Studio Company, but her mother insisted she finish high school, so she returned to California. When Copeland attended ABT's 2000 Summer Intensive Program, she danced the role of Kitri in *Don Quixote*. She also performed in Twyla Tharp's "Push Comes to Shove." Of the 150 dancers in the program, she was one of six selected to join the junior dance troupe.

After studying at ABT on a full scholarship, she was declared ABT's National Coca-Cola Scholar in 2000. That year, she was invited to join the ABT Studio Company, became a member of ABT's corps de ballet in 2001, and performed the "Pas de Deux" in Tchaikovsky's *The Sleeping Beauty*. Unfortunately, eight months after joining the company, she was sidelined for nearly a year by a lumbar stress fracture. When Copeland joined the company, at five feet and two inches, she weighed 108 pounds. As with most ballet dancers, at age nineteen, Copeland's puberty had been delayed. Her doctor prescribed birth control pills to induce puberty to help strengthen her bones, and Copeland gained ten pounds.

Grappling with professional pressure to conform to conventional ballet aesthetics resulted in Copeland struggling with body image and a binge eating disorder. Also, as the only Black woman in the company, Copeland felt the burden of her ethnicity, and struggled to gain perspective by connecting with Black women arts figures like Victoria Rowell and Susan Fales-Hill.

When she returned to the stage, Copeland received favorable reviews for her roles as a member of the corps in *La Bayadère* and William Forsythe's *workwithinwork*. In 2003, *Dance* magazine named Copeland on their "25 to Watch." The year 2004 is regarded as Copeland's breakthrough season. She performed roles in *Raymonda, Amazed in Burning Dreams, Sechs Tänze, Pillar of Fire*, and in "Pretty Good Year," "VIII," and "Sinfonietta." Copeland also danced as the Hungarian Princess in Tchaikovsky's *Swan Lake*. She was featured in the 2004 picture book by former ABT dancer Rosalie O'Connor, *Getting Closer: A Dancer's Perspective*. Copeland also met her biological father for the first time and regretted that she had not done so sooner.

In 2005, Copeland's most notable performance was in George Balanchine's *Tarantella,* and she danced in *Prince Igor* as the Lead Polovtsian Girl in "Polovtsian Dances." In 2006, she was acknowledged for her meticulous classical performance style in *Giselle* and performed in Jorma Elo's *Glow-Stop*. She returned to Southern California to perform at Orange County Performing Arts

Center, danced in *Swan Lake* as one of the cygnets, and, in New York, reprised her role as the Hungarian Princess. In both 2006 and 2007, Copeland danced the role of Blossom in James Kudelka's *Cinderella.*

In 2007, Copeland was appointed as soloist at ABT, one of the youngest dancers to be promoted, and was described by the press as the "Jackie Robinson" of classical ballet. Although she was being touted as the second African American woman promoted to soloist in ABT, Anne Benna Sims and Nora Kimball had previously performed as soloists. During the first decade of her career at ABT, Copeland was the only African American woman in the company. Danny Tidwell, the only African American man in the company at that time, left in 2005. The obvious lack of African American soloists and principal dancers in the ballet world, coupled with public outcry calling for diversity, forced ballet companies to reconsider their hiring practices.

As an ABT soloist, Copeland has performed with an artistic forcefulness that has been seen in productions like Marius Petipa's *La Bayadère,* Alexei Ratmansky's *Firebird* and *The Nutcracker,* and Twyla Tharp's *Sinatra Suite* and *Bach Partita,* which critics have lauded. During the 2008-2009 season, Copeland was praised for performances in Twyla Tharp's *Baker's Dozen* and Paul Taylor's *Company B.* In 2010, after recovering from another stress fracture, Copeland performed in *Birthday Offering* at the Metropolitan Opera and danced to David Lang's music at the Guggenheim Museum. In early 2011, she performed as the Milkmaid in Ratmansky's *The Bright Stream,* a remake of a banned comic ballet, which was well received at the Kennedy Center.

In 2012, Copeland began performing solo roles in full-length standard repertory ballets rather than relatively modern works. She starred in *The Firebird,* with choreography by Ratmansky, at the Segerstrom Center for the Arts in Costa Mesa, California, and performed it again later that spring at the Met, set to alternate in the lead. It was Copeland's first leading role at ABT and her most prestigious part to date. Unfortunately, after one New York performance, Copeland was forced to withdraw from the entire ABT season due to six stress fractures in her tibia. Doctors told her she would never dance again. To her good fortune, she found a physician at the Hospital for Special Surgery in New York willing to undergo a new procedure that involved screwing a plate into her tibia and she was sidelined for seven months.

When Copeland returned to the stage in 2013, she was the Queen of the Dryads in *Don Quixote.* She also reprised her role as Gulnare in the pirate-themed *Le Corsaire* and played an Odalisque in the same ballet. Later in the year, she danced in Twyla Tharp's *Bach Partita* for Violin No. 2 in D minor for solo violin, and as Columbine in ABT's revival of Ratmansky's *The Nutcracker* at the Brooklyn Academy of Music.

In 2014, Copeland ascended to more prominent roles as three ABT principal dancers—Paloma Herrera, Julie Kent and Xiomara Reyes—entered their final seasons before retirement. She had the lead role of Swanilda in *Coppélia* and the Fairy Autumn in the Frederick Ashton *Cinderella* at the Met. Copeland performed the double role, Odette/Odile, in *Swan Lake* when the company toured Brisbane, Australia. In 2015, Copeland made her American debut as Odette/Odile in *Swan Lake* with The Washington Ballet at the Eisenhower Theater in the Kennedy Center. The performance was the company's first presentation of *Swan Lake* in its seventy-year history.

On June 30, 2015, Copeland became the first African American woman to be promoted to principal ballerina in ABT's seventy-five-year history, a groundbreaking achievement since there have been few African American principal ballerinas at major companies. That same month, she made her debut in the role of Odette/Odile with ABT at the Metropolitan Opera in New York. In 2016, Copeland reprised her role as Princess Florine in Ratmansky's *The Sleeping Beauty* at the Kennedy Center. She also performed leads in the ABT productions of *The Firebird, La Fille Mal Gardee, Le Corsaire, The Golden Cockerel, Swan Lake,* and *Romeo and Juliet.* In 2016, Copeland appeared as a guest artist with La Scala Theatre Ballet where she performed *Romeo and Juliet* with Roberto Bolle.

Ballet careers tend to be short, dangerous, and not particularly well-paid compared with other fields of entertainment. When Copeland blazed the trail as ABT's first Black female principal dancer, she became a pioneer, earning the kind of endorsement contracts that have defied ballet's notoriously homogeneous conventions. Beginning in 2010, Copeland has been a celebrity spokesperson for companies such as T-Mobile, Diet Dr. Pepper, Coach, Inc., Dannon Company for its Oikos brand, Naked Juice, Seiko, and Estée Lauder fragrance. In 2014, Copeland became a sponsored athlete for Under Armour, and in 2017, she debuted her collection of activewear, Misty Copeland Signature Collection, with the company.

Like other well-known ballet dancers, Copeland has performed outside ballet's realm. In 2009, Copeland filmed a music video with Prince for a cover of "Crimson and Clover," his first single from his 2009 album *Lotusflower.* She also made appearances in Prince's *Welcome 2 America* tour, performing a pas de deux *en pointe* to his song "The Beautiful Ones," which she also performed alongside Prince on *The Lopez Tonight Show.* Copeland was featured in Season 1, episode five of the Hulu web series, *A Day in the Life,* and has appeared as a guest judge for the eleventh season of FOX's *So You Think You Can Dance.*

In 2008, Copeland won the Leonore Annenberg Fellowship in the Arts. In 2011, she was selected by *Essence* as one of its thirty-seven boundary-breaking Black women in entertainment. In 2012, Copeland won a Breakthrough Leadership Award from The Council of Urban Professionals. In 2013, she was named National Youth of the Year Ambassador by the Boys & Girls Clubs of America. In 2014, Copeland was named to the President's Council on Fitness,

Sports, and Nutrition; received an honorary doctorate from the University of Hartford for her contributions to classical ballet and for helping to diversify the art form; and was a *Dance Magazine* Awards honoree. In 2015, Copeland was named one of *Glamour's* Women of the Year, included in *Vanity Fair's* 2015 International Best Dressed List and ESPN's 2015 Impact 25 athletes and influencers for women in sports, and named one of Barbara Walters' "10 most fascinating" people of 2015. In 2016, Copeland won a Shorty Award for Best in Dance in Social Media.

Copeland was featured in Nelson George's documentary, *A Ballerina's Tale,* which debuted at the Tribeca Film Festival and was released through video on demand and in limited release in theaters in 2015. That same year, she was featured on a *60 Minutes* segment with correspondent Bill Whitaker, and served as a presenter at the 69th Tony Awards. The photography book, *Misty Copeland: Power and Grace* (2015), was released by photographer Richard Corman, with an introduction by Cindy Bradley. Copeland joined the cast of the Broadway revival of Leonard Bernstein's *On the Town* for two weeks in late summer, succeeding Megan Fairchild in the role of Ivy Smith. Her debut on Broadway was favorably reviewed in *The New York Times, The Washington Post,* and other media outlets. In October, she performed on *The Late Show with Stephen Colbert,* accompanied by cellist Yo-Yo Ma, who played "Courante" from Bach's Cello Suite No. 2.

In 2016, Copeland was interviewed with President Obama in the first of a three-part video series, by *Time* and *Essence* magazines to discuss race, gender, achievement and creating opportunity for young people. That same month, she walked the runway at New York Fashion Week to support the American Heart Association's "Go Red for Women" campaign to increase awareness of the dangers of heart disease for women. She appeared in *Harper's Bazaar,* recreating Edgar Degas ballerina poses in a photospread ahead of a Museum of Modern Art exhibition: "Edgar Degas: A Strange New Beauty." She authorized the photographic tribute, *Misty Copeland* (2016), by photographer Gregg Delman.

As part of Barbie's Sheroes program, which honors sheroes who break boundaries, Mattel created the Copeland-inspired Barbie doll wearing a costume reminiscent of the one she wore in *Firebird.* She voiced herself on a 2016 episode of the animated TV series *Peg + Cat,* and in 2017, appeared as a guest judge on the *World of Dance.* In 2018, Copeland made her film debut as the Ballerina Princess in the Disney film, *The Nutcracker and the Four Realms,* based on the 1816 story *The Nutcracker and the Mouse King.*

Copeland has published several books, becoming a *New York Times* Best Seller. In 2014, Copeland released her memoir, *Life in Motion: An Unlikely Ballerina,* and her children's picture book, *Firebird,* with illustrator Christopher Myers, which has a message of empowerment for young people of color. In 2017, Copeland released a third book, *Ballerina Body: Dancing and Eating Your Way to a Leaner, Stronger, and More Graceful You.* In 2018, she published *Your*

Life in Motion: A Guided Journal for Discovering the Fire in You, and wrote the introduction to *The Dance of the Realms.*

She is also known for her outspoken activism in and out of the studio and continues to help pave the way for other girls and women of color. Copeland is a spokesperson for Project Plié, an ABT national initiative to help increase racial and ethnic representation in ballet and diversify America's ballet companies. She has also supported organizations such as the 92nd Street YM-YWHA, American Cancer Society, American Foundation for AIDS Research (amFAR), MindLeaps, and Black Girls Rock!. She continues her work to diversify and broaden ballet's reach with her new children's book, *Bunheads* (2020), illustrated by Setor Fiadzigbey, the first in a series of picture books inspired by Copeland's own early experiences in ballet. *Black Ballerinas: My Journey to Our Legacy,* illustrated by Salena Barnes, educates the public by paying homage to Black women ballet dancers. It will be published in 2021.

While Copeland has never shied away from controversial issues, especially when it applies to diversity and inclusion, she has always carefully considered what political issues to speak out on and the potential for her to bring about change. In 2017, Copeland spoke out against Under Armour CEO Kevin Plank, who stated that a pro-business president like Donald Trump was a real asset for the country, right after Trump issued an executive order banning people from Muslim-majority countries from entering the U.S.[1] She was joined by Under Armour-sponsored athletes, Stephen Curry and Dwayne "the Rock" Johnson, in opposition to Plank's comments. Plank apologized for his statement and, soon after, quit Trump's manufacturing council. He stepped down as CEO in 2019.

During the pandemic, Copeland and Joseph Phillips, created Swans For Relief. Featuring a video of thirty-two ballerinas from around the world portraying The Dying Swan, they fundraised almost $300,000 to help dancers and companies impacted by the pandemic. Copeland continues to explore her personal mission through other mediums and professional endeavors. She is currently working on a short dance film project, *Flower,* which addresses homelessness. It is produced by Life in Motion Productions, her television and film company.

Copeland and her husband, attorney Olu Evans, reside in Manhattan. They disclosed their engagement in a 2015 cover story in *Essence* magazine and married in 2016.

Ballet's relationship with race has always been strained at best, hostile at worst. Nevertheless, Copeland's high visibility, persistent message, and star quality have finally forced the ballet industry to start talking about racial diversity, inclusivity, and representation. To ABT's credit, the company has become more diversified than it has ever been. Having accomplished so much thus far, it will be interesting to see what Copeland achieves during the next phase of her career.❖

---

1.   Holden Wilen, "Kevin Plank dares to dabble in politics again following Biden election victory," *Baltimore Business Journal,* November 9, 2020, https://www.bizjournals.com/baltimore/news/2020/11/09/kevin-plank-under-armour-biden.html.

Michaela Mabinty DePrince
(1995)
Ballet dancer, author

Michaela Mabinty DePrince, a second soloist for the Boston Ballet, is a former member of the Dutch National Ballet. She formerly danced with the Dance Theatre of Harlem as its youngest member in the history of the company.

MICHAELA MABINTY DEPRINCE was born Mabinty Bangura in Sierra Leone, during the country's decade-long civil war. Her father was killed by the Revolutionary United Front when she was three years old, and her mother starved to death soon after. DePrince has vitiligo, a medical disorder of skin pigmentation that causes the appearance of white patches on her neck and chest. She was shunned in her native land and considered cursed because of it. For that and perhaps other reasons, DePrince's uncle abandoned her at an orphanage (DePrince 2016).

The women at the orphanage ranked the children according to their favorites, and DePrince was last at number twenty-seven, which meant she got last dibs for food and clothes and was less likely to be adopted. She was malnourished, mistreated, and derided as the "devil's child" because of vitiligo. After witnessing the butchering of a pregnant teacher by rebels, when the orphanage was bombed, she fled to a refugee camp in Guinea. Amid these bleak conditions, she found a glossy magazine cover that featured a ballerina. Though she had no knowledge of ballet, she treasured the photo and aspired to become just like her (DePrince 2016).

In 1999, at the age of four, she and another girl, also named Mabinty (later given the name Mia), were adopted by Elaine and Charles DePrince, a Jewish couple from Cherry Hill, New Jersey. The DePrinces have had eleven children, nine of whom were adopted, including Michaela and Mia. DePrince showed her new mother the magazine cover of the ballerina and told her she wanted to be just like her, and her mother obliged her childhood dream to become a ballet dancer. She enrolled DePrince in the Rock School for Dance Education (RSDE) in Philadelphia at age five. After she studied classical ballet there for six years, the family moved to Vermont. The following year, DePrince resumed her training at RSDE as a boarder, commuting between Philadelphia and Vermont. She also began performing at the Youth America Grand Prix, among other competitions.

As it has been for most Black ballet dancers, it was not easy for DePrince when she came up against the ethereal, White classical ballerina prototype. In 2010, when she competed in the Youth America Grand Prix (YAGP) for the fourth time, her performance earned her a full scholarship from the Jacqueline Kennedy Onassis School at American Ballet Theatre (ABT). She was also one of six young women profiled in filmmaker Bess Kargman's *First Position* (2011) when she participated at YAGP and vied for a place in an elite ballet company or school. While at ABT, DePrince studied under Franco De Vita, performed with the ABT Studio Company, and toured with the Albany Berkshire Ballet. In 2012, she performed on *Dancing with the Stars*. Concurrent with intense ballet training and performance, DePrince took online classes through Keystone National High School and earned her high school diploma.

In 2012 and 2013, DePrince was a guest artist with Johannesburg's South African Mzansi Ballet. At age seventeen, she joined the Dance Theatre of Harlem (DTH) as the youngest member in its history. In 2013, DePrince left DTH because she wanted to perform in the "white ballets," which DTH could no longer perform as a smaller company. DePrince could not find her fairy tale in an American company because she did not have the right skin color or body type, so she did what Raven Wilkinson did: she left the U.S. and joined the Dutch National Ballet (DNB), based in Amsterdam.

When DePrince joined DNB, she first became a junior company member as an élève (student) and was the only dancer of African origin among DNB's thirty nationalities. In 2015, she was promoted to the rank of coryphée (a ranking above the corps de ballet and below a soloist) in DNB's main company. In 2016, she was promoted to the rank of grand sujet (soloist). That same year, she performed in the "Hope" sequence of Beyoncé's *Lemonade* video.

Throughout her tenure at DNB, DePrince has performed in a wide range of roles. In 2014, she performed as an élève in Christopher Wheeldon's *Cinderella*, Krzysztof Pastor's *The Tempest,* Alexei Ratmansky's *Don Quixote,* and Sir Peter Wright's *The Sleeping Beauty.* In 2015, she played Clara in Wayne Eagling's *Notenkraker en Muizenkoning (The Nutcracker)* and as coryphée in Bustamante's *Giselle.* She also appeared in Hans van Manen's *Live,* John Neumeiers' *La Dame Aux Carmélias,* and George Balanchine's *Jewels.* In 2016, DePrince performed the principal role in Ted Brandsen's *Coppélia*, and in his *Mata Hari* as grand sujet. She has also performed as second soloist in George Balanchine's *Tarantella* in the pas de deux.

DePrince worked hard to develop her skills and to overcome the stereotypes of conventional beauty and racial barriers in the world of ballet. She pursued a professional career despite encountering instances of racial discrimination. At the age of eight, she was told that she could not perform as Marie in *The Nutcracker* because America was not ready for a Black ballerina. A year later, a teacher told her mother that Black dancers were not a worthy investment.

DePrince always had to ward off classmates and teachers who made her feel different and tried to steer her away from ballet toward modern dance. She had to fight for years to wear tights that matched her skin color instead of the pink tights that White dancers traditionally wear. Obviously, she did not listen to her detractors. DePrince has cited Lauren Anderson, one of the first African American principal ballerinas, as her role model. She never gave up (DePrince 2016).

DePrince's public profile grew following the publication of her memoir, *Taking Flight: From War Orphan to Star Ballerina* (2016), which she wrote with her mother, Elaine DePrince. Since its initial publication, her memoir has been published under different titles and languages throughout the world. In 2015, MGM acquired the film rights to DePrince's book. She also published another book with her mother in 2014, *Ballerina Dreams,* targeted at young readers between six and eight years old.

Besides dancing, DePrince loves reaching out to disadvantaged young people, with whom she shares her message of hard work, perseverance, and hope to encourage them to strive for their dreams. DePrince was honored with the 2016 Great Immigrants Award from the Carnegie Corporation of New York. That same year, she was named an ambassador for War Child Netherlands, an organization that provides education, psychosocial support, and protection for children forced to live with the effects of armed conflict. One of her larger contributions to the organization was her "Dare to Dream" gala, held in 2019 at the ASFS Live concert hall in Amsterdam. The event brought together benefactors from around the globe to participate in an auction, followed by performances by herself, Sam Smith, and Brandi Carlile. As a whole, the gala raised enough money to help more than 5,000 children. In 2020, she partnered with Tommy Hilfiger's Tommy Icons Campaign, which celebrated the brand's 35th anniversary.

That same year, DePrince lost her father during the COVID-19 pandemic and was unable to see him before he passed away. He is the second father she has lost in her short twenty-five years. To deal with the grief and loss, DePrince decided to prioritize her mental health and took a leave of absence from DNB.

When DePrince returns to the stage as a second soloist for the Boston Ballet, she will return to a world changed, and completely foreign to the one she had experienced before this lost season of dance. Given the uncertainty that the pandemic has presented to dancers and their companies, DePrince is trying to figure out, as with most African American dancers, how she will fit in a post-George Floyd world, since diversity and inclusion have become a top priority in the dance world.

Two decades since her entry in to the ballet world, DePrince is still very much an outsider, but one who has shattered conventions and remolded them. She has become an example of what can be accomplished when dance moves outside of the constraints of its tradition. While DePrince remains committed to artistic excellence, she continues to fight for and support, in her words, "all my Black and Brown beauties."❖

SPORTS

Black Women Breaking Barriers

"I've always believed that I could do whatever I set my mind to do."

— Alice Coachman

SPORTS HAVE BECOME A NATIONAL PAST-TIME for Americans because they emphasize talent, perseverance, responsibility, hard work, and other excellent character attributes. They also provide an emotional outlet that indulges one's competitive instincts while enlivening a spirit of civic or national camaraderie. Parents overwhelmingly cite personal and social values when asked why they want their children to participate in sports. *It builds character. It develops honesty and a cooperative attitude. It develops mental and physical toughness. It makes them better human beings.* Some would even argue that sports have become an essential tool that help develop human interaction, self-discovery, and self-control. While there is no denying that sports provide an insatiable desire for victory, there is an even deeper reason that makes all the other reasons possible: *to see justice done.* In sports, justice translates into fairness. We expect that the rules of the game will be strictly enforced. If not, the spirit of sports would become a sham and render winning meaningless.

The three major team sports—baseball, football, and basketball that have defined us as a nation—were developed from the games European settlers brought to America beginning in the seventeenth century. These different cultural games have melded and grown into the sports we enjoy today. In the process, various social rituals have developed around these athletic contests, which have greatly impacted our communities and helped mold the identities of towns and cities across the country.

Native Americans played a variety of ball games, including some that have been viewed as early forms of lacrosse. Even traditions from African cultures, such as ancient forms of boxing, wrestling, and stick fighting, can be found in American sports (Guttmann 2002). To the extent that slaves participated in sports, their involvement reflected the prevailing attitudes regarding race. For entertainment, plantation owners selected and entered the enslaved into boxing matches. They also served as jockeys and trainers under their owner's supervision. Not only did their participation in sports serve as a source of entertainment

PHOTO: Alice Coachman, the first African American woman to win an Olympic gold medal. Photo by Reginald H. Christian for Albany State University, 2012.

for slaveholders, but it was believed to have an anti-rebellion effect as a safe activity where the enslaved could vent their anger, aggression, and hostility.

The experience of Northern Blacks was markedly different. The North failed to develop the large-scale agrarian slavery that later arose in the Deep South. This had little to do with morality and much to do with climate and economy (Ross 2018). The enslaved worked chiefly as household servants, and, coupled with a Puritan influence that evolved into abolitionist reform, lent a peculiar character to slavery that sometimes eased its severity in comparison to the South. Despite enduring racial discrimination, and limited access to public recreational facilities, Northern Blacks, both freed and enslaved, participated in a broad range of sports and recreational activities by creating their own clubs, and amateur and professional leagues and teams (Davis 2008). Even though White America went to extraordinary lengths to discourage Black participation, sports managed to play a meaningful role in unifying different social and ethnic backgrounds that would later develop into a less-than-conventional platform for change.

While Black athletes struggled for acceptance in sports, a small yet growing number of Black women made significant contributions and set standards of excellence in every aspect of their respective fields. During segregation, pioneers such as Ora Washington, Alice Coachman, Althea Gibson, and Wilma Rudolph helped pave the way for later generations of greats like Cheryl Miller, Jackie Joyner-Kersee, Debi Thomas, Venus and Serena Williams, and Simone Biles. For African Americans and especially Black women like me, we see ourselves when we root for these women who dare to compete in the public sphere.

Growing up in a female-oriented household with my father as the only male, sports did not play a pivotal role in my life. Certainly, we biked and occasionally played outside, but it was only during the summer, when I was shipped off to camp, that I participated in group sports like softball, volleyball, and dodgeball (which has its roots from Africa). I also swam, learned how to rowboat and canoe, and went hiking and horseback riding. I detested handball, and even tried to learn tennis, golf, and racquetball, but they did not hold my interest.

I never really cared to participate in team sports, but since I am six feet and two inches tall, by the time I arrived in high school, I was wooed by all the teams. The basketball team wanted me to play center, the volleyball team wanted me to spike the ball, and I was encouraged to join the swimming team because I have long limbs. I played briefly on the basketball and volleyball teams, and lasted, I believe, an entire season on the swim team, until I got fed up with being bullied by the coach. Suffice it to say, my personal sports experience compared to others is pretty pathetic.

However, my lack of participation or interest in sports does not mean I did not have an appreciation of it. I grew up with fabled tales about Alice Coachman, Althea Gibson, and Wilma Rudolph, and witnessed Arthur Ashe's success as well as Serena and Venus Williams' groundbreaking entry into the tennis world.

While not an avid follower of women's basketball and the emergent Women's National Basketball Association (WNBA), players like Lynette Woodard, Cheryl Miller, and Sheryl Swoopes caught my attention. When the Olympics rolled around every four years, I would watch most of it, especially to look for Black and Brown faces representing the U.S. and, in particular, women. The success of Olympians Jackie Joyner-Kersee, Florence Griffith Joyner, and Debi Thomas was amazing to witness. And in recent years, the ascension of Dominique Dawes, Maritza Correia McClendon, Simone Biles, Ibtihaj Muhammad, and Allyson Felix has been absolutely mesmerizing. It is women like them that have ushered in a new era of sports.

Despite my sports shortcoming, I did not dread writing this section: I am always open to a challenge, and I love doing research, but I was apprehensive. Then, along the way I discovered that even the most astute sports fanatics know little about the history of Black women athletes. I enjoyed discovering Ora Washington—a woman that was the "Serena Williams" of her day—digging into the genesis of Black women in track and field from HBCUs, learning about the shifting parameters of women in baseball and basketball, and finding so many other women that are not known in the public eye. I soon realized that this is more than a sports story: *it is a story about Black women achievement.*

It is also important to note that even in sports, Black women have been culturally coded and misunderstood through the lens of a White-dominated society that cites Black women's bodies as either mannish or overtly sexualized. A recent study in 2018 examined Black women's participation in basketball, track and field, tennis, golf, and swimming, the cultural factors that get in the way of their success, and how they adapt as a response to those barriers. The study illuminated that there has almost always been an emphasis on Black women athletes' skills and femininity just for participating in what is perceived as a traditionally White field.[1]

This study also reconfirmed what Black women have known all along. One would imagine that training, competing, dealing with heated rivalries or fearsome opponents, breaking world records, and excelling in championship games would be enough to handle. Unfortunately, Black women are still forced to deal with other defining aspects of competition: always having to be an ambassador for the race; dealing with assumptions about how fast, strong, or aggressive they performed; and, most importantly, how their hair looked while they were doing it. Instead of getting caught up in a whirlwind of commentary that would throw her off her game, *the Black woman prevails.* But no matter how phenomenal her game, *it is never enough.*

---

1. *The Undefeated*, a sports and pop culture website owned and operated by ESPN, commissioned a study from Morgan State University, School of Global Journalism and Communications entitled "Beating Opponents, Battling Belittlement: How African American Female Athletes Use Community to Navigate Negative Images." https://theundefeated.com/features/morgan-state-university-study-examines-history-of-Black-women-fighting-to-be-respected-as-athletes.

Navigating the obstacles of race and gender is a constant burden to these Black women trying to get their body and soul across a finish line. It is this game within a game that Black women athletes have played for more than a century, and it continues to this day. These women deal with all of this even before they suit up. *The pressure is constant.*

◆ ◆ ◆

FROM THE DAWN OF OUR CIVILIZATION to the present, women have always been denied access to sports. But even when the public deemed it inappropriate, they played anyhow (Guttmann 2002). For over 150 years, women had to challenge sexist barriers and restrictive notions about women's physical appearance, athletic abilities, and participation in sports,

This story begins as a gender-biased story that becomes racialized when Black women start participating in sports on a national and international level. Until the mid-1800s, women in sports—that is, White women—partook in activities that were acceptable to the wealth and leisure class of the Gilded Age such as horseback riding, showboating, croquet, bowling, archery, and swimming at racially restricted lakes or beaches. These sports were deemed acceptable because it was believed that excessive physical activity would put women's reproductive health at risk. Ironically, American women had to be tough to survive in this era as mothers, child brides, farm wives, sharecroppers, factory girls, millhands, pioneers, and even the enslaved. But where physical endurance was a highly sought after quality in women, strength on the home front had nothing to do with an athletic identity. No one has ever denied the muscular effort involved in carrying a child and giving birth; it was the public athletic performance by girls and women that was condemned as immodest, selfish, and attention-seeking. People believed that sports would lead to women's masculinization and that it was a foolhardy endeavor, especially in prime childbearing years (Cahn 2015). Essentially, women were denied access to the philosophical empowerment and camaraderie sports could provide because they were considered nothing more than sex objects and babymakers.

But with the dawning of the twentieth century, an interest in sports began to foment and capture the public's attention. More Americans were participating as spectators and competitors in a variety of sports. At the same time, a woman's place in society was evolving; they were becoming educated, entering the workforce, and participating in political reform movements in unprecedented numbers. In fact, popular interest in sports and concern over women's changing status had tossed aside some of the Victorian constraints, and the "athletic girl" was becoming a striking symbol of modern womanhood (Cahn 2015).

By the early 1900s, White women began creating informal athletic clubs, and some men's clubs allowed them to join and participate in different activities. Things began to loosen up, in part because suffrage activists began to demand it. If boys had sport programs in public schools and colleges, then girls should have them too. In response, a cottage industry of quack science developed to promote the idea that sports would cause women to become infertile, masculine, or sexually active. But for many women, access to sports came to symbolize liberation. When they narrowly won the right to attend gym classes, the first generation of physical education teachers argued that classes had to be segregated by sex. They also profoundly objected to women's competitive sports because competition, they argued, was counterproductive to one's femininity.

When the modern Olympics returned in 1896, while women were not specifically included, they were not explicitly excluded. Women made their first appearance in the Paris 1900 Summer Olympics when twenty-two women competed at the games in sailing, tennis, golf, and croquet. Tennis and golf were the only sports where women could compete in individual disciplines. Margaret Abbott, the first American woman to win an Olympic event, won a gold medal in the women's golf tournament (Guttmann 2002).

Their participation was more accidental than planned and did not represent any significant advancement for women. The seven American women who participated represented nineteenth-century scions of wealth, and it was through their country club affiliations that they were allowed to compete. At the St. Louis 1904 Summer Olympics, six American women competed in archery, the only event open to women. Women also stepped into the ring as part of the Olympic boxing card, but their bouts were considered showcases, and no medals were awarded. Due to the tensions caused by the Russo-Japanese War, only sixty-two athletes from outside North America participated in St. Louis. At the London 1908 Summer Olympics, thirty-seven female athletes competed in archery, tennis, and figure skating. The Stockholm 1912 Summer Olympics featured forty-seven women and saw the addition of swimming and diving, as well as the removal of figure skating and archery (Cahn 2015). Needless to say, all of the American women who participated were White.

When African American women were brought to this country enslaved, they had little or no time for games. When they did participate in some kind of play activity, it was merely recreational at best. As middle class free Blacks emerged from the ashes of the Civil War, they began to partake in some of the leisure class sports that White women engaged in, but to a far lesser degree due to restrictions dictated by racism and Jim Crow (Hine 1997). As the Olympics and other competitions began to develop during the early twentieth century, the growth of popular sports in the 1920s expanded opportunities beyond the rarefied atmosphere of amateur collegiate and club athletics. The playground movement also created additional spaces for potential athletes to play and compete in schoolyards and local teams (Cahn 2015). Black communities began to see sports as a vehicle for individual and collective achievement in the face of a dominant White society (Lansbury 2014).

What is particularly striking is the Black community's interest and early acceptance of women's athletics. In fact, the Black community saw sports as a way for athletically talented Black women, many from poor backgrounds, to attend college, travel, and experience life in a way that would otherwise be unknown to them. With the help of teachers, coaches, mentors, entrepreneurs, and patrons, they supported programs in high schools, historically Black colleges and universities (HBCUs), and established leagues and clubs—safe spaces—for the women to compete in (Lansbury 2014). When the women traveled, they not only dealt with sexism like their White counterparts, but they also had to deal with racism as well.

In the meantime, the International Olympic Committee (IOC), with great hesitation, considered tennis, golf, swimming, and archery compatible with women's femininity and fragility (Guttmann 2002). They also decided not to allow women's athletics—which included physically intensive sports like track and field—to be part of the Olympics. Baron Pierre de Coubertin, credited for the Olympics' revival in 1896, had a gendered vision of the games and viewed sports solely as a male venture. His committee strongly opposed women's full participation in the Olympics. In response to their refusal, Alice Milliat, a French amateur athlete, founded the Women's Olympiad, held in Monte Carlo in 1921. Finding absolutely no support from the governing sports bodies, which all agreed to maintain male hegemony, Milliat would go on to form the Fédération Sportive Féminine Internationale (FSFI) (also known in English as the International Women's Sports Federation (IWSF)) and created the Women's Olympic Games, which were held in Paris in 1922 (Vertinsky and Park 2013).

Its success bred contempt from the athletic establishment, including the IOC and the International Association of Athletics Federations (IAAF),[2] who chafed at the independence under which Milliat's organization flourished. When the IOC refused to include women's athletics at the Paris 1924 Summer Olympics and objected to Milliat's use of the term "Olympics," the FSFI changed the event's name to the Women's World Games (WWG), and the enterprise reconvened in Gothenburg, Sweden in 1926. There would be two more editions of the WWG: 1930 in Prague and 1934 in London. Each game had over 20,000 spectators, which finally convinced the IOC to sanction women's track and field in the Olympics. The WWG was forced to fold after the government of France pulled funding in 1936. It did, however, succeed in getting the IOC to recognize the legitimacy of women's participation in sports (Cahn 2015).

There were other competitions. James E. Sullivan founded the Amateur Athletic Union (AAU) in 1888 to create common standards in amateur sports.

2. Established in 1912, the IAAF, also known as the International Amateur Athletic Federation, and International Association of Athletics Federations, is the international governing body for the sport of athletics, covering track and field, cross country running, road running, racewalking, mountain running and ultrarunning. Included in its charge are the standardization of rules and regulations for the sports, recognition and management of world records, and the organization and sanctioning of athletic competitions. In 2019, the organization chose to rebrand as World Athletics.

In 1916, the AAU held its first national championship for women in swimming and also sponsored the first American track and field championships for women. This arrangement fluctuated over the years, as the AAU would prohibit both Black and White women from competing in certain sports. Finally, beginning in 1924, the AAU began offering a women's national track and field championship. Overseas in England, the Women's Amateur Athletic Association (WAAA) held their first championships in 1923. It was the first domestic athletic event for women until it merged into an all-gender Amateur Athletic Association (AAA) Championship in 1988.

My intention here is to explore the history of Black women athletes, many of whom were game-changers in tennis, track and field, basketball, baseball, golf, boxing, gymnastics, soccer, and swimming, and helped integrate and transform sports. I also include the "sports we can't do," such as bobsledding, volleyball, and fencing, and go into some detail about sexism, homophobia, body shaming, and the future of Black women athletes in American sports.

♦ ♦ ♦

THE UNITED STATES TENNIS ASSOCIATION (USTA) (formerly known as the United States National Lawn Tennis Association) banned Black players from their tournaments as tennis began to take hold among athletes at HBCUs like Tuskegee Institute (now known as Tuskegee University), which held tournaments as early as the 1890s. The USTA had historically used persiflage on the issue of discrimination, with tournament committees following club rules and practices in order to exclude African Americans (Kimball and Haggerty 2017). In addition to the expense of owning a racquet and purchasing white uniforms and regulation tennis shoes, tennis was developed in private clubs, which meant that it was largely inaccessible to working class families and, in particular, people of color. This created a class prejudice that became inherent in tennis culture (Lansbury 2014).

In response, a group of African American businessmen, college professors, and physicians founded the American Tennis Association (ATA) in 1916, the oldest Black sports organization in the U.S. They also created tennis clubs such as Baltimore's Monumental Tennis Club and Washington, D.C.'s Association Tennis Club. This ensured that tournaments could provide court time and housing for players and officials during the Jim Crow era. The facilities also allowed the players to meet and organize, and host high-profile events to cultivate donors (Harris 2020).

In 1917, Lucy Diggs Slowe became the first Black woman to win a major sports title from the ATA. That same year, Slowe played in mixed-doubles and became the champion in 1921 and 1922. In 1924, she hung up her tennis racquet for good, and there is no record of her returning to competition (Miller and Pruitt-Logan 2012). Ora Washington won her first ATA singles title in 1929. She held the title for the next seven years, until 1936, then regained it in 1937.

Washington's record of seven consecutive ATA titles would stand until 1947 when it was broken by Althea Gibson, who won ten straight titles (Lansbury 2014).

In 1950, Gibson became the first Black player to compete in a USTA event at Forest Hills, New York. A year later, she repeated a historic first at Wimbledon. She won her first Grand Slam singles title at the French Open in 1956 and then won back-to-back titles at Wimbledon and the U.S. Open in 1957 and 1958 (Lansbury 2014). Despite Gibson's outstanding accomplishments during the 1950s, women's professional tennis remained primarily a White sport.

Bonnie Logan made history by becoming the first African American woman to play in a Virginia Slims circuit. She dominated the ATA during the 1960s and was a legend in the Black community. Zina Garrison was a women's doubles gold medalist and singles bronze medalist at the South Korea 1988 Summer Olympics, a women's singles runner-up at Wimbledon in 1990, and a three-time Grand Slam mixed doubles champion. Partnering with Garrison, Katrina Adams won seven of her twenty Women's Tennis Association (WTA) (founded by Billie Jean King in 1973) doubles titles between 1987 and 1996, including the 1988 World Doubles Championships. She became the first African American and the youngest person to serve as President and CEO of the USTA in 2015.

Washington and Gibson's legacies gained new life in the twenty-first century with Venus and Serena Williams' extraordinary careers. Although Serena was the first Williams to win a Grand Slam singles title in the 1999 U.S. Open, Venus emerged at the top of her game in 2000, winning her first Grand Slam at Wimbledon, as well as the U.S. Open and an Olympic gold medal. During the next decade, the power and athleticism of the Williams sisters would be credited with bringing women's tennis to a new level, and final-round match-ups between the two sisters became legendary at Grand Slam events. The Williams sisters' legacy planted seeds in a garden that bore fruit when we witnessed breakthrough players like Madison Keys, Taylor Townsend, and Sloane Stephens.

Keys competed at the 2016 WTA Finals, and was a semi-finalist at the Rio de Janeiro 2016 Summer Olympics. Keys played in one major final at the 2017 U.S. Open, and won five WTA tournaments, all at the Premier level. Her biggest title came at the 2019 Cincinnati Open, a Premier 5 event. Townsend was named the International Tennis Federation (ITF) Junior World Champion in 2012 for finishing the year No. 1 in the girls' junior rankings, making her the first American to do so since 1982. But even with this achievement, the USTA questioned Townsend's fitness due to her weight and would suffer body-shaming the early part of her career. She reached a career-best WTA ranking of No. 61 in the world in 2018. That same year, she was ranked No. 4 by the WTA and achieved a career-best ranking of No. 3 in the world. Townsend has now played six seasons with World TeamTennis (WTT), earning the 2018 WTT Female MVP honor by having the top winning percentage in Women's Singles and Women's Doubles for the season.

Stephens has won a total of six WTA single titles. Despite being hindered by a left foot injury for most of 2016, she is a 2017 U.S. Open champion. Although she had foot surgery in 2017, Stephens rebounded that same year, winning her first Grand Slam singles tournament and awarded WTA Comeback Player of the Year. In 2018, she continued her success by winning her first Premiere Mandatory Title at the Miami Open, won a second Grand Slam singles final at the French Open, and finished runner-up at the WTA finals. However, beginning in 2019, Stephens has struggled with a diminished ranking. If she is able to pull out of this slump, she is still widely regarded as a potential successor to Serena Williams to become America's next top female tennis player.

And then there is Naomi Osaka, born in Japan to a Haitian father and a Japanese mother, who has lived in the U.S. since she was three years old. Holding dual citizenship in the U.S. and Japan, Osaka decided to represent Japan. She won the U.S. Open in 2018, defeating 23-time major champion Serena Williams in the final to become the first Japanese player to win a Grand Slam singles tournament. In 2019, Osaka became a U.S. Open and Australian Open champion in women's singles and No. 1 in the WTA rankings. By 2020, Osaka had won her second U.S. Open title, becoming the first player in twenty-six years to win a U.S. Open women's singles final after losing the first set. Osaka was seeded third at the 2021 Australian Open. She went on to defeat Hsieh Su-wei in the quarterfinals, Serena Williams in the semifinals, and 22nd seed Jennifer Brady in the final to claim her second Australian Open title. Osaka became one of only three players in the Open Era to win her first four Grand Slam finals, alongside Roger Federer and Monica Seles.

Osaka's achievement is historically significant because her dual cultural background has increased the possibilities for people of color to excel at a sport that was once considered solely a White person's playground. It is not hyperbolic to state that American tennis' vibrant state is attributed to Black women creating another era of promise. Yet tangible signs of progress by White tennis players, private tennis clubs, and the USTA to become more inclusive and diverse, remain at a stalemate (Harris 2020). Nevertheless, these women are setting the stage for the next generation of Black and Brown women from all over the world, which has helped increase the popularity and accessibility of the sport.

◆ ◆ ◆

BLACK WOMEN WERE RESPONSIBLE for creating the demand for track and field, which had followed an up-and-down trajectory. At first, it was sanctioned as a healthy sport for women and grew internationally, but it fell out of favor during the early twentieth century. The issue at hand was whether women should be involved in the sport. Given the success of the WWG, the IOC and the AAU initially facilitated its growth. Once it gained institutional support from the HBCUs, African American women overwhelmingly populated track and field.

However, Black and White physical education instructors began targeting track and field because it did not live up to the middle- and upper middle class vision of White femininity. They created enough attention around the issue that the public concept of femininity and sports ended up changing dramatically. As a result of such concerted opposition, by the late 1930s, the sport was living at the margins of women's sports. However, even in this depressed state of track and field, Coach Cleveland "Cleve" Abbott would become directly responsible for developing women's track and field into a national powerhouse (Lansbury 2014).

Abbott, a Midwestern star athlete and war veteran, and his wife Jessie Abbott arrived in Alabama at Tuskegee Institute in 1923. Officially, Abbott was brought in to serve as the director of both physical education and athletics, and his wife worked as an administrator. Together, they helped build up the school's athletic department and created multiple sports programs.

Though the women's track and field team existed since 1916, it had little impact on the regional black collegiate athletic organization, the Southeastern Intercollegiate Athletic Conference (SIAC). However, Abbott took aggressive steps to strengthen student participation. His effort, along with growing female student interest and a shifting context for understanding women in sport at the school, saw Tuskegee's women's track and field team become a viable entity by 1929.

In order to counter the dearth of available rivals and other negative effects of Jim Crow on student athletes, Abbott created a large-scale meet for Black schools, breathing new energy into SIAC's sluggish attitude. He created a massive regional track and field event, the Tuskegee Relays, for his male athletes in 1927 and eagerly sought to establish its legitimacy in American sport. In light of the men's success in the Tuskegee Relays, the women students clamored for him to reactivate the women's track and field team. Abbott was ambitious. Within one year of including women in the Tuskegee Relay Carnival, he announced plans to mold his young runners into Olympians. Beginning in 1937, the Tigerettes, as they would become known, won fourteen AAU national senior outdoor championships and four AAU national indoor championships.

Tidye Pickett and Louise Stokes were the first Black women to participate in the Olympics' selection process. While neither ran for Tuskegee, they were athletes in their own right. Pickett was a hurdler and sprinter from the Chicago Park District team, and Stokes was a member of the Onteora Club in Boston. They both were selected to become members of the U.S. Olympic team in the 4×100-meter relay, but at the last minute, neither were allowed to compete in the Los Angeles 1932 Summer Olympics. Both would go on to earn reserve spots on the Berlin 1936 Summer Olympics team. Stokes was part of the 4×100-meter relay pool but did not compete. Pickett competed in the 80-meter hurdles but went out in the semi-finals when she hit a hurdle and injured herself. Nevertheless, she secured her place in history by becoming the first African American woman to represent the U.S. at the Olympics.

Alice Coachman, a Tigerette, dominated the AAU outdoor high jump championship from 1939 through 1948. Winning a total of twenty-five national championships titles, she became the first Black woman to win Olympic gold, and set records with her high jump at the London 1948 Summer Olympics. By then, a significant number of Black women represented the U.S., and virtually all the women on the Olympic track and field team came from Tuskegee.

While White women worked toward overcoming the odds of participating in sports, Black women had to overcome gender and race's double jeopardy. During these separate and unequal times, African Americans formed sports clubs to safely cultivate and celebrate sports excellence away from the harsh gaze of White people. Black men, who were banned from major sports teams, created their own leagues after the Civil War. For example, a Black baseball scene formed in the East and Mid-Atlantic states, and Negro leagues[3] proliferated.

The term "Black Fives"[4] referred to the all-Black basketball teams that thrived from 1904 until 1950 when the National Basketball Association (NBA) became racially integrated. Since African American culture generally accepted female athleticism, Black women were able to participate in sports freely. For example, the Smart Set Club, organized in 1905 in Brooklyn was one of the earliest known club teams, whose athletic programs were built around basketball and track. The Alpha Big Five basketball team was formed in 1907 under the sponsorship of the Alpha Physical Culture Club, which was America's first all-Black athletic club. Both clubs also had girls' teams.

Other clubs that produced champions of national stature at the time were the New York Mercury Club and the Illinois Women's Athletic Club, which afforded Black women an opportunity to showcase their talent (Hine 1996). But it was the HBCUs' track and field programs that really flourished. Perhaps this is because track and field did not require expensive equipment to train and play. While White schools concentrated on expensive male-dominated sports such as football, track and field proved to be the sport in which all African Americans could participate and excel in. Even as the Tuskegee track and field program was growing, other schools worldwide were canceling competitive athletics for women due to sociopolitical pushback. And since White women refused to participate in such a masculine, competitive sport, African American women's success in track and field only reinforced racial and sexual stereotypes long-held by White society.

Racism was a defining element among Black and White women in sports. While they came together to combat common gender stereotypes, White women did not necessarily believe in integration. Besides racism, Black women also had to contend with and push back against hypersexual and racial stereotypes, something that White women did not have to deal with and in some cases, perpetuated.

---

3. The term "Negro leagues" is being used narrowly for the seven relatively successful leagues, and used broadly to include professional Black teams outside the leagues, unless specified.

4. Early basketball teams were often called "fives" in reference to the five starting players.

But Abbott kept pushing forward. He brought discipline and motivation to Tuskegee's athletics. He successfully inculcated Booker T. Washington's Tuskegee model,[5] a winning formula that would eventually become internationally acclaimed and adopted by several track and field teams. The Tigerettes would dominate track and field until the early 1950s.

Abbott suddenly died in 1955 after a brief illness. Later that summer, the Tigerettes lost the national AAU championship to a regional neighbor, Tennessee Agricultural & Industrial State College (Tennessee State University), another HBCU. With Abbott's passing went much of the drive and inspiration that made the school preeminent in women's track for so many years (Davis 1992).

In 1943, when Tennessee entered the field of women's track, its first coach, ironically, was Abbott's daughter and former Tigerette, Jessie Ellen. Although she coached at Tennessee for only a short period of time, she managed to introduce her father's Tuskegee model to the women's track team, which became known as the Tigerbelles. After graduating from Tennessee in 1950, Ed Temple was asked to help coach the school's track team, including a handful of women. He worked for three years as an assistant coach before becoming the women's track team's head coach.

Tuskegee and Tennessee were not the only HBCUs that encouraged women's track and field. Prairie View Agricultural and Mechanical of Texas added women's events to its annual relays, followed by Alabama State University, Florida Agriculture and Mechanical University (FAMU), Acorn College in Mississippi, and Fort Valley State College of Georgia (Cahn 2015). By the mid-1950s, Tennessee surpassed Tuskegee and dominated women's track and field until the 1970s. In all, Temple coached forty Olympians at Tennessee, and combined, they won twenty-three medals, thirteen of them gold. Some of the Tigerbelles' best-known stars include Mae Faggs, Wilma Rudolph, and Wyomia Tyus. Temple would retire in 1994 and pass away in 2016.

The HBCUs used their athletic programs to challenge racial discrimination and demonstrate feminine ideals to counter sexist stereotypes. The women's travels, which were a combination of painful and wondrous awakenings, offered experiences that nurtured the hope that racial justice might soon prevail.

Mae Faggs was the first in a long line of female track stars to run for Tennessee and obtain international acclaim at the Olympics. She was the first American woman to participate in three Olympics in 1948, 1952, and 1956, and the AAU 200-meter relay from 1954 to 1956. She also won the silver medal in the 200-meter and the gold medal in the 4×100-meter relay at the Pan American Games in 1955, won the gold medal in the 4×100-meter relay at the Helsinki

---

5   Abbott melded Booker T. Washington's model of industrial education with his experience growing up in South Dakota, and as an athlete at South Dakota State College to create a model for Tuskegee's athletic programs. The idea was to combine integrity, scholarship and athleticism to transform the stature and place of Tuskegee's student athletes in American society. This model would soon be adopted by a number of HBCUs, including Tennessee University.

1952 Summer Olympics, and the bronze medal in the 4×100-meter relay at the Melbourne 1956 Summer Olympics. Faggs retired after Melbourne, but she left a powerful legacy. She arrived at Tennessee as their sole track star in a woefully underfunded program, but by the time she left, she had laid down the foundation for one of the most successful women's track teams in collegiate history (Smith 1992c).

If Gibson was an inspiration in the tennis world, Wilma Rudolph proved herself equally in the realm of track and field. Stricken by polio as a young girl, Rudolph won three gold medals each in the 100- and 200-meter races and the 4×100-meter relay at the Rome 1960 Summer Olympics. She was the first American woman to accomplish that feat, and in 1961, she became the first Black woman to win the James E. Sullivan Award, America's highest honor in amateur athletics. Wyomia Tyus won consecutive Olympic gold medals for the 100-meter race during the Black Power controversy at the Mexico City 1968 Summer Olympics. She chose to compete rather than boycott or give the Black Power salute as some of the other athletes did upon winning their medals (Lansbury 2014).

Earlene Brown competed at the 1956, 1960, and 1964 Olympics in the shot put and discus throw. She won two gold medals at the Pan American Games in 1959. The antithesis of an Olympic star, Brown was a tall, heavy-set woman who was married, had a child, was a beautician, and had less than an ideal training regime when she joined the AAU at twenty-one years old. From 1959 on, Brown was associated with Tennessee and won a bronze medal at the Rome 1960 Summer Olympics. She was the only American woman to win a medal in the shot put until Michelle Carter, another Black woman, won a gold medal at the Rio de Janeiro 2016 Summer Olympics. To this day, Brown is considered "the most unheralded U.S. athlete of all time" (Aaseng 2003).

The 1980s marked a golden era in track and field. Evelyn Ashford was the Olympic gold-medal champion in the 100-meter race and won gold medals in the 4×100-meter relay at the 1984, 1988, and 1992 Olympics. She also won a silver medal in the 100-meter race at the Seoul 1988 Summer Olympics. Ashford, one of six women to have won four gold medals in track and field Olympic history, was inducted into the National Track and Field Hall of Fame in 1997.

Valerie Brisco-Hooks entered the Los Angeles 1984 Summer Olympics as a virtual unknown and left with three gold medals for the 200-meter, 400-meter, and 1600-meter sprint relays. She ran nine races in seven days and became the first American athlete, female or male, to capture the 200-meter and 400-meter titles at the same Olympics, which she won two years after giving birth to her son.

However, it was Jackie Joyner-Kersee and Florence Griffith Joyner who dominated track and field during this era. Joyner-Kersee, often described as the best all-around female athlete in the world,[6] competed in the long jump and the

---

6.   Rhiannon Walker, "The day Jackie Joyner-Kersee was called 'the greatest athlete who ever lived'," *The Undefeated*, August 1, 2018, https://theundefeated.com/features/the-day-jackie-joyner-kersee-was-called-the-greatest-athlete-who-ever-lived.

grueling two-day-long heptathlon, winning two gold medals at the Seoul 1988 Summer Olympics. She earned her second gold medal in the heptathlon at the Barcelona 1992 Summer Olympics. Griffith Joyner, dubbed "Flo-Jo," earned a reputation as "the fastest woman in the world" by smashing world records at the Seoul 1988 Summer Olympics, winning gold medals in the 100- and 200-meter runs, and anchoring the gold-medal-winning 4×100-meter relay team. Both Joyner-Kersee and Griffith Joyner were winners of the Associated Press Female Athlete of the Year, and the Sullivan Award.

Gail Devers is a two-time Olympic champion in the 100-meter race. Her win at the Atlanta 1996 Summer Olympics made her the second woman after Wyomia Tyus to successfully defend an Olympic 100-meter title. She also won a third gold medal in the 4×100-meter relay. Additionally, Devers is the 1993 World champion in the 100-meter and a three-time World champion in the 100-meter hurdles. In 2011, she was inducted into the National Track and Field Hall of Fame (Edelson 2014). Joetta Clark Diggs is a four-time Olympian specializing in middle distance running in the 800- and 1500-meters. She participated in the 1988, 1992, 1996, and 2000 Olympics, and ran for more than twenty-eight consecutive years, never missing an indoor or outdoor season. Sanya Richards-Ross was the best 400-meter runner in the world, ranking no. 1 from 2005 to 2009, and again in 2012. She has medaled at three Olympics, is a seven-time medalist at the World Championships in Athletics, and in 2009, she was the World Champion in the 400-meter race.

Marion Jones, a sprinter and a long jumper, became a dominant force in women's sprinting during the late-1990s. By the time she captured the public's attention with her beauty, skills, and hypnotic smile, she was on her way to winning three gold and two bronze medals at the Sydney 2000 Summer Olympics (Edelson 2014). When she was accused and finally admitted to taking steroids, she was stripped of her medals, ordered to pay a hefty fine, and was sent to prison. Her accomplishments were struck from the records and washed away by a deluge of recrimination, anger, and public humiliation. Jones would never be forgiven because, when it comes to sports, people believe in fairness and justice for all.

At the pinnacle of her career, Jones was one of track's first female sports millionaires, but that quickly changed after her cheating confession. She retired from athletics in 2007, played briefly for the WNBA's Tulsa Shock in 2010, and eventually filed for bankruptcy. Her fall from grace will be remembered as one of the most shocking doping scandals in track and field history.

Of course, the sports establishment was shocked at Jones' steroid-fueled Olympic wins. But should they really be shocked and surprised? Certainly, the sports institutions and the media's misplaced fixation on fame, fortune, and winning at all costs have unintentionally created a growing market for doping substances and anxious athletes, a somewhat lethal combination. I am not suggesting that an athlete should not be held accountable for their actions; I just believe the viable solution may be to widen the search for those who are culpable—not to absolve the athlete from guilt, but to recognize that those who control the "payoff matrix" bear as much responsibility for the corruption of sports as the athletes themselves. Because, in the end, it is nothing more than people hitching their wagon to greed and graft in pursuit of gold.

Black women athletes were aided by an extended community of dedicated coaches and mentors who made it possible for them to train and compete in track and field. Alice Coachman, the first Black woman to win an Olympic gold medal, was nurtured at Tuskegee. By the time Jackie Joyner-Kersee approached her fourth Olympics in 1996, Black women had been competing in track and field for nearly sixty years, and used other means to get to the Olympics, such as personal coaches. Twenty years later, Allyson Felix, whose career began in 2003, is the most decorated track athlete, female or male, of all time, with nine Olympic medals and eighteen World Championships, including thirteen gold-medals. These women who jumped, threw, and ran with blistering speed have shown the world their tenacity and athleticism as they pushed the boundaries of acceptable femininity and redefined their place as Black women athletes.

◆ ◆ ◆

THE HISTORY OF WOMEN'S BASKETBALL is a long one and includes local, amateur, collegiate, and professional teams, intercollegiate competitions, and the Olympics, as well as the failed attempts of professional leagues. While James Naismith is credited with the invention of basketball in 1891, Senda Berenson Abbott, a Lithuanian Jewish immigrant and a physical educator at Smith College, is considered the "mother" of women's basketball. She modified the existing men's rules and adapted them to women's basketball. Beginning in 1892, Abbott used the game in her gym classes, and organized the first women's basketball game at Smith College in 1893 (Kirsch, Harris, and Nolte 2000). Black women were not allowed to participate. Abbott formalized her rules in her book *Line Basketball or Basket Ball for Women,* often referred to as *Basket Ball for Women,* which was published by the Spalding Library 1901. The rules would remain in use with only minor modification until the 1960s. In 1985, Abbott became one of the first women (and Jewish female) to be enshrined in the Naithsmith Hall of Fame.

Thirteen years after the invention of basketball, Coach Edwin Henderson introduced basketball to a physical education class at Howard University in Washington, D.C. Other HBCUs followed suit. By 1910, basketball had become the most popular sport among young African Americans and was mainly promoted by the Young Men's Christian Association (YMCA) in Black neighbor-hoods. Many HBCUs had women's and men's basketball teams. Bennett College in Greensboro, North Carolina, had early success playing college, high school, and community teams, amassing an amazing record.

One of the first independently all-Black female basketball teams was the New York Girls, founded in 1910. Other early African American women's teams included the Jersey Girls, the Spartan Girls, and the Chocolate Coeds. The era's dominant barnstorming squads during the 1920s and 1930s were the Germantown Hornets and the Quick Steppers, which became the Tribune Girls of Philadelphia and the Chicago Roamers, also known as the "Roamer Girls."

Edward "Sol" Butler, an editor and former basketball and track star, formed the Roamer Girls in 1921. They played both Black and White teams in Chicago. The Roamer Girls, who were mostly schoolteachers, played women's and boy's teams before joining the women's division of Chicago's City League in 1924. They were national basketball champions throughout the 1920s, captivating sports fans across race and gender lines. By 1928, the heart of the Roamer Girls' lineup left to join the newly formed sister team of the Savoy Big Five men's basketball team, the Savoy Colts. By the early 1930s, the Roamer Girls had faded away, and Philadelphia's Tribune Girls would become one of the greatest female basketball teams of all time.

The Tribune Girls, sponsored by the Black newspaper, *The Philadelphia Tribune,* dominated women's basketball for over a decade. Inez Patterson, the team captain of the Quick Steppers—established in 1931—persuaded *The Philadelphia Tribune* to sponsor and promote her team. In return, Patterson renamed the team for the paper. Teams like the Tribune Girls received coverage from Black newspapers, although less than their male counterparts, and were mostly ignored by the White press.

Meanwhile, tennis player Ora Washington played for the Germantown Hornets, a championship basketball team formed in 1929 and affiliated with the first Black branch of the Young Women's Christian Association (YWCA). She was the team's captain and had previously played with the Savoy Colts in Chicago. Patterson managed to woo Washington and several other players to join the Tribune Girls. For the Germantown Hornets, it was a devastating blow. Although they played until the mid-1930s, the team would never rise to its former greatness.

By 1938, the Tribune Girls had achieved a string of victories. They traveled over 5,000 miles to fill their schedule, including a tour of Southern states. However, in addition to a change in the newspaper's management, America's entry into World War II stalled the momentum of all major sports, particularly women's basketball. Following the war, support of women's participation in sports never quite reestablished itself. Neither did the Tribune Girls.

Over time, a backlash developed against women's participation in basketball. Organizations such as the National Association of College Women, founded in 1923 to improve higher education opportunities for Black women, issued a position paper opposing intercollegiate athletics for women, deeming it "too strenuous" (Lansbury 2014). For years, they campaigned vigorously by holding seminars and meetings with HBCUs to drop basketball and other competitive sports for women, and encouraged them to focus their energy on more appropriate physical activities, like intramural and play-day activities. Bennett College was one of the last schools to hold out before discontinuing its women's basketball team in 1942 (Witherspoon and Rider 2018).

It was not until the passage of the federal law, Title IX, in 1972 that women's sports teams and leagues made a comeback. The Association for Intercollegiate Athletics for Women (AIAW) was formed in 1971 to govern women's athletics in the U.S. and administer national championships. Organizations like the National Collegiate Athletic Association (NCAA) did not administer women's athletics. However, in 1982 after the AIAW disbanded, the NCAA began offering national championship events for women in Division I, which is considered to be the highest level of collegiate competition that declares its winner the "national champion."

By the late 1970s, women's college basketball was beginning to regain its popularity. In fact, basketball became a rival to track and field for the participation of Black women. After the NCAA, other college athletic associations followed suit in offering championships for women: the National Junior College Athletic Association (NJCAA), the National Association of Intercollegiate (NAIA), the National Christian College Athletic Association (NCCAA), the California Collegiate Athletic Association (CCAA), and the Central Iowa Sports (CIS). While basketball has been a sport at the Summer Olympics since 1936, it took until 1976 for women's basketball to make its debut.

The history of American basketball tells a compelling story about athletic competition in a nation struggling to live up to its ideals of gender equity. It is a sport that was transformed by the presence of African Americans, with Black women becoming a signifier of the cultural, sexual, and social changes in the sport. But it is only within the last couple of decades that women's basketball has begun to gain the recognition and national backing we are witnessing today.

By the mid-1970s, after years of successful women's collegiate teams, entrepreneurs attempted to create and sustain a professional women's basketball league. Founded in 1978 by sports entrepreneur Bill Byrne, the Women's Professional Basketball League (WBL), was the first such iteration. One of its first stars was Lusia "Lucy" Harris-Stewart (center), considered a pioneer of modern women's basketball. She began playing when she was eleven years old with her siblings in their backyard and then joined her junior high school team. By the time she attended Delta State University, she had won three consecutive NCAA Championships in 1975, 1976 and 1977. Harris-Stewart set an unprecedented Olympic record when she scored the first basket ever recorded with the women's team at the Montreal 1976 Summer Olympics, and, in the process, won a silver medal. Harris-Stewart later played professional basketball with the Houston Angels of the WBL. Additionally, she was the first and only woman ever officially drafted by the National Basketball Association (NBA), the men's professional basketball league. She was pregnant at the time though, which prevented her from attending the training camp. Harris-Stewart was inducted into the Naismith Memorial Basketball Hall of Fame in 1972, and was among the first women inducted into the Women's Basketball Hall of Fame in 1999 (Dwight and Sewell 1984).

The WBL disbanded in 1981 due to financial problems, but it had some exceptional Black players in its league during its run. Pearl Moore (forward) began playing basketball while attending high school and continued throughout college. She started her WBL career in 1979 with the New York Stars, and joined the St. Louis Streak the following season. When the WBL folded, Moore played the final season of her professional career with Venezuela's Foreign Pro League. Althea Gwyn (center) attended Queens College, where she was a member of the first women's basketball team to play at Madison Square Garden before playing professionally. Debra Waddy-Rossow (forward), who played for the Chicago Hustle, perfected a nearly unstoppable turnaround jump shot in high school by practicing against a coach wielding a tennis racket (Porter 2005).

Lynette Woodard (forward) did a lot to popularize the sport. In 1985, Woodard became the first woman to play for the Harlem Globetrotters (Porter 2005). During her career, she eventually played overseas, was the women's team captain at the Los Angeles 1984 Summer Olympics, won a gold medal, and played for the WNBA for two years before retiring in 1999. Cheryl Miller (center/forward) became one of the most decorated high school and collegiate women's basketball players in history and helped lead the U.S. team to a gold medal in the Los Angeles 1984 Summer Olympics.

The second women's professional league, the Women's American Basketball Association (WABA) (also known as the WWBA), was founded by former WBL owner Bill Byrne, who wanted to cash in on the 1984 U.S. Olympic team's success in Los Angeles.[7] Most of the teams folded before the league championship, but before it did, Janice Lawrence Braxton (forward) played briefly for the league. She had played college basketball for Louisiana Tech University, where she helped lead the Lady Techsters to national championships in 1981 and 1982. In addition to being named a Kodak All-American, Women's Basketball Coaches Association (WBCA) Player of the Year, and a 1984 Wade Trophy winner, Braxton also won a gold medal with the women's team at the Los Angeles 1984 Summer Olympics. After playing for the WABA, she played overseas before joining the WNBA's Cleveland Rockers in 1997 and becoming their assistant coach in 2003. Braxton was inducted into the Louisiana Tech University Athletic Hall of Fame in 1987 and elected to the Women's Basketball Hall of Fame in 2006.

---

7.   The Women's American Basketball Association (WABA/WBA/ABA) has existed as different incarnations over the past thirty-six years. After the WBA folded the year of its founding in 1984, Lightning N. Mitchell formed the WBA in 1992 as the first women's professional basketball summer league, which played three full seasons from 1993 to 1995. The league reappeared in 2001 and played one season in 2002. The WABA returned in 2017 as the sister league of the American Basketball Association (ABA) (a semiprofessional men's basketball minor league founded in 1999 that bears no relation to the original American Basketball Association, 1967-1976). This newly-formed WABA is under the leadership of Marsha Blount, ABA team owner of the Jersey Express.

The American Basketball League (ABL)[8] was founded in 1996, around the same time the NBA was creating the WNBA. The ABL, which was founded by Steve Hams, Anne Cribbs and Gary Cavalli, consisted of eight teams and began playing in 1997. That same year, the Columbus Quest defeated the Richmond Rage in a five-game series to win the inaugural league's first championship. Yolanda Griffith (center) played basketball in high school and college. After playing professional basketball overseas, she joined the ABL in 1997. She played one season for the Long Beach Stingrays, leading the team to the brink of an ABL title, only to be defeated by the defending champions, the Columbus Quest. When the Stingrays team folded, Griffith briefly played with the Chicago Condors before the league dissolved, and then played with the WNBA for ten years before retiring in 2009. Nikki McCray-Penson (guard) made a name for herself as a world class defender. She won gold medals at the 1996 and 2000 Olympics and participated in America's 1998 Fédération Internationale de Basketball (The International Basketball Federation (FIBA)) World Championships team. She was an ABL star and played with the Columbus Quest and several other teams. When the ABL declared bankruptcy and folded in 1998, Nikki McCray-Penson joined the WNBA, beginning with the Washington Mystics, and retired from the Chicago Sky in 2018.

Early on, the ABL signed players from the 1996 USA women's national team, acquiring a high-quality roster of players, and offered higher salaries than the other leagues. But the ABL found itself in trouble: it was already under-financed and this was exacerbated by the WNBA's entry to the game with financial resources and marketing muscle from the NBA. This became too much for ABL to overcome. Players and coaches mourned the passing of a league that put women's basketball front and center and tried to blaze its own trail (Grundy and Shackelfiord 2017). When the dust settled, the WNBA became the sole survivor of women's basketball leagues.

The WNBA premiered with eight teams located in cities that were also home to an NBA team, often with nicknames and uniform labels evocative of their male counterparts. Initially framed as a summer league, the WNBA operated with a short 28-game season to avoid competing with the men's league, thereby allowing players to augment their season by playing abroad.

In 1996, former Texas Tech University basketball star Sheryl Swoopes (shooting guard/small forward) became the first player to sign with the WNBA, which made its debut the following year. An Olympic gold-medalist in 1996, 2000, and 2004, Swoopes played for the WNBA's Houston Comets for eleven years and was named the league's MVP three times. She was one of the top shot blockers and rebounders in the league and the first woman to have a sneaker named after her: the Air Swoopes. Other top African American WNBA players during this era include Cynthia Cooper-Dyke (point guard/shooting guard), Lisa

8. American Basketball League is a name that has been used by three defunct basketball leagues and a recently active league in the U.S.

Leslie (center), Tamika Catchings (small forward), and Tina Thompson (small forward/power forward).

When the WNBA first opened its doors, fans enthusiastically responded, fueling enough optimism that the league doubled in size to sixteen teams by 2000. But while the league drew a diverse demographic of fans, not every WNBA team was a success, nor was every team owner or organization committed to supporting their sister teams. By 2002, the NBA allowed the sale of its teams to third parties in cities that were not affiliated with its organization. Teams relocated, numerous teams folded, and the league seemed to flounder. In fact, in 2007, it was estimated that the league was losing up to $10 million a year.[9] Even with financial support from the NBA, it did not look promising. Its saving grace was the players' dedication to the sport. By 2010, the WNBA began to rebound and stabilize with new rising stars. They brought a new level of excitement to the game with higher scoring, better defense, and higher shooting percentages. News outlets began covering the league more frequently on a dozen networks, including NBA-TV and ESPN2, with increased viewership, merchandise sales, and league-wide sponsors. Moreover, the Connecticut Sun became the first team in the league to have positive cash flow as of the 2010 season. Hopefully, the WNBA's financial stability will continue to grow.

As the older players retired, new players like Tina Charles, Sylvia Fowles, Angel McCoughtry, and Candace Parker injected a much-needed vitality into the league. When Charles (center) played with the Connecticut Sun, she set a league record for 23 double-doubles in a season. In 2016, when she played for New York Liberty, Charles had the best season of her career, averaging a career-high 21.5 points per game while shooting 43.9 percent from the field and 81.2 percent from the free-throw line. Fowles (center) of the Chicago Sky became the second player in WNBA history to finish a season averaging at least 20 points and 10 rebounds per game. She was the MVP of the 2015 WNBA Finals, was named the WNBA Defensive Player of the Year for the third time in 2016, and won the 2017 WNBA MVP Award. In 2020, Fowles, who plays for the Minnesota Lynx, overtook Jalen Brunson to become the reigning WNBA career rebound leader.

McCoughtry (forward) of the Atlanta Dream was the first player in league history to average over 20 points per game while playing under 30 minutes in 2010. She led her team to the Finals for the second straight year in 2011, but despite breaking her own Finals scoring record, the Atlanta Dream was swept for the second time, this time by the Minnesota Lynx, which won its first title behind a healthy Seimone Augustus (small forward/shooting guard), who had recently recovered from surgery. McCoughtry now plays for the Las Vegas Aces.

The San Antonio Silver Stars experienced a boost from their young players as well. Rookies Danielle Adams (power forward/center) scored 32 points off

9. Doug Feinberg, "WNBA crossroads: league looks to cut losses, hire president" *Associated Press*, December 28, 2018, https://apnews.com/75e117e82df7470c94784438048171d1.

the bench in 2011, and Danielle Robinson (point guard) had a 36-point game in 2010. In 2016, Candace Parker (power forward/center) and other stars, such as Alana Beard and Nneka Ogwumike, helped the Los Angeles Sparks win their first WNBA Finals title since 2002. In 2020, Atlanta Dream rookie Chennedy Carter (shooting guard) scored 35 points just six games into her professional career, becoming the youngest player in league history to score 30 points or more.

Today, there is a whole new generation of players in the WNBA, including stars like Brittney Griner, Elena Delle Donne, Maya Moore, DeWanna Bonner, and Australian Liz Cambage. The level of play continues to improve through-out the league. The earlier generations of players have returned to coach in the NCAA, WNBA, and NBA. They have become the face of the game through broadcasting, joining the league as administrators, publishing books, and build-ing businesses in their communities. By the time the WNBA approached its twenty-fifth anniversary, it was only getting better and better.

The key to the WNBA's success is that it opened doors for young women and empowered women athletes worldwide. The NBA's Milwaukee Bucks walkout in 2020 after the shooting of Jacob Blake in Kenosha, Wisconsin during the play-offs was historic,[10] but the WNBA has spoken out on racial injustice as a unified voice for years. They were among the first athletes to wear warm-up shirts with social justice messaging affirming Black Lives Matter, #SayHerName, and Bre-onna Taylor; hold media blackouts and even kneel during the national anthem. The WNBA players have always made a point to be socially conscientious and relevant in their communities.[11]

It is also worth noting that the WNBA has more players with college degrees than any other league to date. They are the only league that requires four years of education post-high school to be eligible for the draft. More importantly, the WNBA, along with the defunct leagues such as the ABL and WABA, were formed as fully integrated organizations that were open to Black female talent from the start, a rarity in the sports world.

◆ ◆ ◆

THE REAL HISTORY OF BASEBALL is a little more complicated than the Abner Doubleday legend in Cooperstown, New York—a claim that has been thoroughly debunked by baseball historians. References to games resembling baseball in the U.S. date as far back as the eighteenth century. Baseball evolved from older bat-and-ball games already being played in England. Its most direct ancestors appear to be rounders (a children's game brought to New England by the earliest

---

10. James Herbert, "'Enough is enough': By walking out, Bucks show what it looks like for NBA players to use their platform," August 27, 2020, CBS/NBA, https://www.cbssports.com/nba/news/enough-is-enough-by-walking-out-bucks-show-what-it-looks-like-for-nba-players-to-use-their-platform.

11. Leah Asmelash, "WNBA dedicates season to Breonna Taylor and Say Her Name campaign"July 25, 2020, *CNN* https://www.cnn.com/2020/07/25/us/wnba-season-start-breonna-taylor-cnn/in-dex.html.

colonists) and cricket. By the mid-nineteenth century, different versions of base-ball, which were being played on schoolyards and college campuses across the country, had become even more popular in newly industrialized cities. In 1845, the New York Knickerbocker Baseball Club would codify a set of rules that would form the basis of modern baseball (Shattuck 2017).

Baseball flourished during the Reconstruction period and quickly became a game played by both Black and White people. The first two organized women's baseball teams were formed at Vassar College in 1866 in Poughkeepsie, New York. Other colleges followed suit over the next several years, and eventually, there were a few dozen collegiate women's teams across the country. While there is no way to confirm whether Black women were allowed to participate, it would not be far-fetched to conclude they were not. However, a backlash from the public forced them to mostly shut down by the mid-1870s because it was considered "unladylike." In 1875, women gained a foothold in professional baseball when two teams competed in Springfield, Illinois. Dubbed the Blondes and Brunettes, the players became the first known women paid to play baseball (Shattuck 2017).

There has also been some evidence of Black women playing baseball in barnstorming teams during the mid-1800s. While there were a number of baseball teams throughout the U.S. named the Dolly Vardens[12] in the early decades of baseball, they were mostly White, male squads. There was, however, an all-Black women's team assembled in 1883 in Chester, Pennsylvania by barber-turned-sports entrepreneur John Lang, who created the team expressly as an entertainment venture. It has also been noted that it was the first team at any level to be paid to play baseball, though this has been difficult to confirm.[13] Newspapers largely ignored their existence or found them too amateur to bother reporting on them, and the accounts that do exist focus on their appearance (the team played in corsets, long skirts, and high button shoes), rather than how they played. Moreover, they were often riddled with racist and sexist remarks. Lang disbanded the Dolly Vardens several months later because no matter how good they were, Black women playing baseball was unprofitable, and the team could not overcome the racism and sexism of the era (Shattuck 2017). But in the three months of their existence as semiprofessional baseball players, these Black women made history.

At the turn of the twentieth century, as the U.S. emerged as a power on the global scene, baseball was becoming associated with America's national identity.

---

12. The name "Dolly Varden" first appeared as a minor character in Charles Dickens' *Barnaby Rudge*, (1841) and was something of a phenomenon because of the bright colored dresses she wore. The dress quickly became popular in England and America and soon Dolly Varden was named for everything, from fish to slang terms to ships, and became particularly attached to baseball.

13. News stories about the Dolly Vardens have been limited in number and coverage. This is one of the few articles that verify their existence, "Miss Harris' Base-Ball Nine; Dusky Dolly Vardens Of Chester Give An Exhibitions," *The New York Times,* May 18, 1883. https://www.nytimes.com/1883/05/18/archives/miss-harriss-baseball-nine-dusky-dolly-vardens-of-chester-give-an.html.

During the 1910s and the 1920s, Black girl teams played for various YMCAs and YWCAs, as evidenced by surviving photographs with no real identification of the players. Some of them earned their living playing ball. They toured internationally, and signed minor league contracts. A Black female first baseman named Pearl Barrett (also recorded as Pearl Barnett) played first base for the semiprofessional Havana Stars in 1917. At the time, she was the only Black woman playing baseball on a men's team.[14] However, public opinion reflected an entrenched belief that baseball was far too dangerous and strenuous for the "delicate" female constitution, and many female teams ceased to exist. Although a handful of White women—like Elizabeth "Lizzie" Stroud Arlington, Lizzie Murphy, and Jackie Mitchell tried to make a living in the sport and appeared in a few games, the White major and minor leagues were off-limits to all women.

Despite this setback, there were a few Black women who managed to play baseball. In 1933, Isabelle Baxter played second base for three innings of one game for the Cleveland Giants of the Cleveland Colored Baseball League: an all-male, semiprofessional team that eventually joined the Negro National League (Cohen 2009). She later became manager of the Harlem Queens of Chicago, a Black bowling team. (It seemed bowling, one of the biggest participatory sports in the world, would remain rigidly segregated until the mid-twentieth century.) Sarah "Mutt" Roberts pitched 23 innings for the Philadelphia Stars of the Negro National League during the 1930s and 1940s. If this record is accurate, Baxter and Roberts were the first Black women to play in an all-Black league before Toni Stone did. These Black women were not there to wear shorts or skirts as their White sisters did. They wore men's uniforms and played like men.

In the meantime, the All-American Girls Professional Baseball League (AAGPBL) entered the scene. It was more than a novelty; it was an innovative, entrepreneurial, leisure-time enterprise that took advantage of peculiar wartime conditions (Fidler 2015). AAGPBL was founded by Philip K. Wrigley, Branch Rickey, and Paul V. Harper in 1943 after the U.S. entered World War II and gender codes changed, if only temporarily. They surmised that Major League Baseball (MLB) might temporarily cease due to the loss of talent from the war and travel restrictions due to gasoline rationing. In the meantime, women were permitted to work in factories and join the Women's Army Corps (WAC), allowing "Rosie the Riveter" to serve. For that reason, wartime America was ready to embrace the AAGPBL as an unlikely symbol of victory with players that demonstrated they were up to the task. Black women, however, were not allowed to participate.

The self-esteem and self-confidence gained by women during World War II propelled the movement for women's equal rights in sports. Many women believed that if they could compete successfully in the workforce, they could compete on the athletic field. But when the war ended, women's baseball fell out of popularity, and the country set about getting "Rosie the Riveter" out of

---

14. "Woman to Play First Base for the Havana Stars," *Chicago Defender,* May 12, 1917:. 5.

the factory and back into the kitchen. The efforts to sustain the AAGPBL failed, and it shut down in 1954.

The AAGPBL's efforts did not affect Black women one way or the other since they were banned from participating. While Black women have been involved with baseball since its creation and have a long history of playing semiprofessionally, they were shunned by White-only leagues. Since there were few, if any, Black all-female baseball teams for the women to join, they played with the men in the Negro leagues. This certainly did not stop the unstoppable Toni Stone, who has been recognized as the first Black woman to play professional baseball. She played for the American Legion Junior League during the 1940s, and in the 1950s, was the first woman to play professionally in the Negro leagues. After a short stint with the Black Pelicans, Stone joined the New Orleans Creoles from 1949 to 1952. She signed with the Indianapolis Clowns in 1953 to play second base, but her contract was sold to the Kansas City Monarchs before the 1954 season, and she retired the following season due to lack of playing time (Ackerman 2010). Her statistics with the Negro league included an incredible .243 batting average. Some have credited Stone with delaying the death of the Negro leagues by a season and a half (Cohen 2009).

Connie Morgan played second base with the Indianapolis Clowns in 1954, replacing Stone. Before signing with the Clowns at age nineteen, she played five years with the North Philadelphia Honey Drippers, an all-girl baseball team, and finished with a .368 batting average to demonstrate her tenure with the team. Morgan later batted .178 for the Clowns (Cohen 2009).

Mamie "Peanut" Johnson was a right-handed pitcher with a deceptively hard fastball. She also threw a slider, circle changeup, curveball, screwball, and knuckleball. Johnson attended a try-out for one of AAGPBL's teams in 1952, but because of her dark skin, was told she was in the wrong place. Interestingly though, the AAGPBL signed several light-skinned Cuban women to the league (Cohen 2009). This failed experience turned Johnson toward the Negro league and what would eventually be her unique place in history (May and Heaphy 2016). Johnson was signed by the Indianapolis Clowns in 1953 and played with them until her retirement in 1955.

When these Black women played baseball with the men, it was not to make a political statement—*it was the only choice.* In the process, these women unwittingly did something quite remarkable: they challenged male supremacy at a time when gender roles were strictly enforced. The women did receive some benefits under these challenging circumstances, like getting paid to play, traveling to different places and meeting different people, which greatly changed the trajectory of their lives.

It should be noted that not only have Black women broken barriers on the field, but in the front office as well as a manager. The first known Black woman to own a Negro league team was Olivia Taylor. Taylor became the owner of the

Indianapolis ABC's from the Negro National League following the death of her husband in 1922. She ran the team for three years before it folded in 1926. Taylor faced a number of obstacles: players were hesitant to play for a woman, she was accused of underpaying her players, and she faced public humiliation when a team member and Taylor exchanged scathing op-eds in the national Black press. As soon as she took over the team, other league owners demanded she sell, claiming that she was ruining her husband's legacy. The deck had been stacked against her from the start, and her accomplishments have since been diminished. Taylor died in 1935 and lay in an unmarked grave until 2013, when the Negro League Grave Marker Project finally gave her a headstone (Heaphy 2015).

Taylor was not the only Black woman who owned and managed teams in the Negro leagues. In 1935, local papers on the East Coast listed Clara Jones as the president of the Boston ABCs, which played major Negro league teams. By all accounts, she ran a well-organized and talented ball club. Unfortunately, little else is known about Jones and her off-the-field accomplishments (Heaphy 2015). As the 1940s came to a close, Henryene Green took over the Baltimore Elites after the death of her husband Vernon in early 1949. The team won the 1949 Negro American League pennant, and Green sold the team in 1950. The Elites played for one more season before they folded. In the early 1950s, Hilda Bolden-Shorter took over the Philadelphia Stars from her father Ed Bolden. She ran the operation from 1950 to 1952 before she sold her interest. Bolden-Shorter then went on to complete her degree at Meharry Medical school and became a pediatrician. Minnie Forbes was the last female owner in the Negro league who owned the Detroit Stars from 1956 to 1958. Since league rules prevented her uncle from owning two teams, Forbes bought out his interest. She sold the team after the 1958 season when it became apparent the Negro leagues were fading away. Shorty thereafter, Forbes played third base for the Kansas City Monarchs. She was honored for her contributions to baseball when President Obama invited a number of Negro league veterans to the White House in 2013 (Heaphy 2015).

Effa Manley is perhaps the most well-known of the female league owners. She managed and co-owned the Newark Eagles with her husband, Abe Manley, from 1935 to 1948. The Eagles were one of the league's best teams, and under the Manley's leadership, the Eagles posted a .539 winning percentage going 480-411-16. In 1946, the Eagles won the Negro League World Series, defeating the Kansas City Monarchs in a seven-game series. The team featured seven future Hall of Famers, including Monte Irvin, Leon Day and Larry Doby. Don Newcombe pitched for them in 1944-1945 and went on to become a four-time All-Star with the Dodgers (Heaphy 2015). Manley lobbied for black causes on and off the field, and co-authored the book, *Negro Baseball* (1976). Born into an interracial family, Manley was raised by her mother and her mother's husband, an African American man. When her true parentage was revealed to her as a teenager, she continued living as a Black woman and married a Black man. Manley was the first woman inducted into the National Baseball Hall of Fame in 2006 (May and Heaphy 2016).

When the Brooklyn Dodgers signed Jackie Robinson in 1945, it signaled the end of segregation in baseball and the demise of the Negro leagues. It is impossible to categorize the league as a failure because it failed for the right reasons—but there was an unintended consequence. One of America's most remarkable pre-civil rights Black-owned business enterprises ceased to exist and was lost to history.

This erasure included the presence of Stone, Johnson, Morgan and so many other Black women who played baseball, including the team managers and owners. They were ignored by contemporary sports writers in the mainstream press. They were ignored in the 1988 "Women in Baseball" exhibit at the National Baseball Hall of Fame at Cooperstown, which revived the public memory of the AAGPBL and enshrined them. Even the award-winning documentary producer, Ken Burns, slighted women in baseball with hardly a mention of Black women in his celebratory PBS series, *Baseball,* in 1994 (Ring 2015). While the Hall of Fame eventually honored Stone along with seventy-three Negro league players in 1991, it would take another decade before a series of awards, articles, books, films, and scholarship would surface (Cohen 2009). Even so, much of the recognition focused on the self-determination and persistence of these women instead of dealing with the root of institutionalized racism, which got them there in the first place.

After the demise of the AAGPBL, women's baseball did not reappear until Title IX in 1972. From the 1950s through the 1970s, young women played on organized Little League teams across the country. Although a special clause in Little League regulations made it technically illegal for girls to participate, it was the decision of each individual manager as to whether they would break the rules and let girls onto the team, or turn them away. After the passage of Title IX, twelve-year-old Maria Pepe tried out for her local Little League team in Hoboken, New Jersey. While she was initially accepted by her teammates and coaches, Little League headquarters intervened and threatened to disband Hoboken's local charter if Pepe was not cut. Backed by the National Organization for Women (NOW), Pepe sued on the grounds of gender discrimination. The courts ruled in her favor in 1974, making it possible for girls to play in Little Leagues and eventually helping to reignite women's baseball (Cohen 2009).

Other amateur leagues and organizations continued to materialize. In 1988, the American Women's Baseball Association (AWBA) was founded in Chicago by freelance editor and publicist Darlene Mehrer, the first organized women's league since AAGPBL. By 1992, the AWBA floundered. The Washington Metropolitan Women's Baseball League (WMWBL) is an amateur league that was founded in 1990 by Lydia Moon, who modeled the organization after the AWBA. During the first year of the WMWBL, players showed up for informal pick-up games. In 1991, three teams were playing in formal games. By 1992, the film *A League of their Own* prompted the press to increase its coverage of women's baseball, and as a result, the WMWBL expanded to four teams. In 1998, several other teams joined the WMWBL, and it reorganized as the Eastern Women's Baseball Conference (EWBC). Over the years, some teams left the league, others folded, and new teams emerged. Today, EWBC is one of the oldest self-sustaining women's amateur baseball league. Currently based in the D.C. and Baltimore metro areas, the players come from all walks of life—students, teachers, doctors, lawyers, scientists, and more. They span all ages and all levels of experience, including current and former U.S. National players and semiprofessional softball players (Kovach 2005).

There were quite a few women's baseball leagues that came and went with the wind, but this was not an anomaly: creating and sustaining a league is no easy feat. Some start on shaky ground, and most are underfunded. Some leagues folded quickly while others saw some success. Yet, the fact they had the gumption to undertake such an unyielding enterprise is not only admirable, but also paved the way for others to follow. The American Women's Baseball League (AWBL) (also known as American Women's Baseball (AWB)) was founded in the 1990s by Jim Glennie to provide support and unite women's baseball teams and leagues around the country, but it eventually failed. The Women's National Adult Baseball Association (WNABA), formed in 1994, had sixteen women's teams and played in a world series in Phoenix that same year. The Ladies League Baseball (LLB), founded in 1997 by San Diego businessman Mike Ribant, was forced to cancel its second season in 1998 due to low fan turnout.

Finally, by 2003, the AAU became the first U.S. national organization to sanction and support women's baseball as an official sport. In 2004, the Olympics followed when USA Baseball sanctioned the first official national women's baseball team. They competed in the 2004 Women's World Cup of Baseball and won the gold medal. These sanctions were lifted in no small part due to women players, teams, and leagues lobbying for women's baseball to be officially recognized in the U.S.

Women baseball players are far less known to the general public than basketball or soccer players. There is no existing infrastructure for women to play baseball at the collegiate level, so women baseball players eligible for an athletic scholarship have to switch to softball. Softball was invented in 1887 initially as an indoor game for men who did not want to play outdoors. In time, it came to be known as an easier and more suitable game for women. As softball rose to prominence during the 1930s, high schools, colleges, and recreation centers began offering it to girls instead of baseball. However, women continued to play baseball informally in neighborhood games, with sandlot ball being especially common in rural Black communities. But social and institutional restrictions on who could play baseball funneled many women athletes into softball instead. This shift intensified under Title IX legislation. To satisfy their requirements, many schools classified softball and baseball as equivalent sports, but they are not. Frankly, there is no rational basis to claim that girls cannot throw overhand, run 90-feet between bases, or handle a hardball. The cultural imperative that girls play softball and boys play baseball has created an awkward status that is unmistakably unfair. Simply put, *baseball has been stolen from girls* (Ring 2009).

Moreover, there are few Black players on either women's or men's baseball teams. For years, baseball was perceived as a White man's sport with sacred unwritten rules that sent an implicit and coded message about its whiteness. There are also socioeconomic reasons why there are hardly any Black players, including lack of access to the Little Leagues, which are almost non-existent in the poorer communities. The crux of the issue comes down to money and where the MLB chooses to invest. In this case, it is no secret that the MLB prefers to invest in sports academies in the Caribbean and South America rather than low-income Black and White communities in the U.S. As a result, there are fewer Black players in high school, never mind on the collegiate level.[15]

Although the MLB has shown a marked increase in their racial hiring practices, the amount of Black players has decreased from 13 percent during the start of the twenty-first century to 7.7 percent today.[16] But as the sport has lost its popularity among Black and White millennial audiences in recent years, immigrants have become key participants in the MLB. This recent development has buoyed baseball's profits from a growing Latino fan base both here and abroad.

Even though baseball these days is not as popular or profitable as other sports, it remains integral to America's identity in a way no other sport is. Yet, women are still actively kept from participating in baseball and discouraged from pursuing it. Only a handful of notable Black women have played in semiprofessional and independent leagues. Tamara Holmes is a power hitter that played with the Colorado Silver Bullets, an all-female professional baseball team that played in the U.S. from 1994 to 1997. In 1996, she hit the first and only home run in Silver Bullets history. The Silver Bullets were the first all-female team since the folding of the AAGPBL in 1954, but after four seasons, it folded in 1997 when Coors Brewing Company decided not to continue with their sponsorship. Since then, Holmes has become a decade-long staple on the USA Baseball Women's National Team, winning first place in the 2006 International Baseball

---

15. Earl Smith and Marissa Kiss, "Why are there so few Black American players in MLB 74 years after Jackie Robinson took the field?" April 1, 2021, *The Philadelphia Inquirer,* https://www.inquirer.com/opinion/commentary/baseball-black-african-american-players-jackie-robinson-20210401.html.

16. Nikole Tower, "In an ethnic breakdown of sports, NBA takes lead for most diverse," Global Sports Matter, December 12, 2018, https://globalsportmatters.com/culture/2018/12/12/in-an-ethnic-breakdown-of-sports-nba-takes-lead-for-most-diverse/

Federation (IBAF) Women's Baseball World Cup. She would win third place in 2008 and 2010, and second place in 2012 and 2014. In 2012, she was aptly named USA Baseball's Sportswoman of the Year, and three years later, helped lead the team to win gold at the 2015 Pan American Games. Holmes is the starting left fielder and cleanup hitter for the No. 2-ranked U.S. women's national baseball team (Ring 2015).

Malaika Underwood, an infielder, is the longest-tenured player ever, female or male, serving on eleven USA Baseball National Teams. Underwood played baseball, volleyball, and basketball at La Jolla High School. She attended the University of North Carolina on a full volleyball scholarship and was a four-year starter and ACC tournament MVP. Once Underwood headed off to college, she figured her baseball days were done. She graduated in 2003 and spent a few years coaching Little League. But in 2004, USA Baseball decided to establish a women's national team, and Underwood joined in 2006. She has five IBAF Women's Baseball World Cup medals to her name, earned a Women's Baseball World Cup All-Tournament Team in 2008 and 2014, and a Pan American Games title in 2015 (Ring 2015).

When pitcher Mo'ne Davis became the first African American girl to play in the Little League World Series in 2014, and the first girl to pitch a shutout in the tournament, there was speculation that women players would eventually take the field for an MLB team. This idea was popularized by the Fox network television drama *Pitch* (2016). A victory on the screen could finally get America's nonfictional women baseball players some mainstream airtime. Unfortunately, after one season, *Pitch* was prematurely canceled, and it seemed women in baseball would receive more screen time via Hollywood than on ESPN. It also seems remarkable that MLB appears not to scout women at all—imagine excluding an entire population from consideration solely on the basis of their gender. However, in recent years, there has been some hope. The 2018 Women's Baseball World Cup, which was played at Space Coast Stadium in Viera, Florida, provided American fans with an opportunity to see the world's top female talent in action.

When the MLB made Mélissa Mayeux, a French shortstop, the first female player to be eligible to sign with a major league team in 2015, they made history. But by 2017, with no word from the MLB, Mayeux switched to softball in order to attend the University of Louisiana and play for the Ragin' Cajuns, a softball team in the NCAA. Clearly, the MLB is dragging its feet. A woman can, and should, make the seminal play of a game, or score the winning run in the World Series, *but it is still not happening*.

Only a handful of women, like Stacy Piagno, a pitcher, and Kelsie Whitmore, an outfielder, have played for Minor League Baseball (MiLB), a hierarchy of professional baseball minor leagues that compete below the level of the MLB. The Minor League also includes teams affiliated with MLB that have been created specifically to help prepare players to join their major league teams. As of this writing, though, there are not any Black women playing in the Minor League. However, in 2020, Bianca Smith made history when the MLB named her a Minor League coach for the Red Sox, becoming the first Black woman to coach for a professional baseball organization. She has already received sponsorships from Nike, Oakley, and Topps, and is even getting a baseball card.[17] Make no mistake, her ascension was years in the making. With an eye on pursuing a career as a baseball general manager, Smith played on both the varsity softball team and the club baseball team at Dartmouth, and graduated with a BA in sociology. She obtained both a JD degree and MBA degree in sports management from Case Western Reserve University in 2017. At the same time, from 2013 to 2017, Smith worked as director of baseball operations for the Case Western Reserve Spartans. Perhaps her success will help open the doors for both Black and White women players on the field.

Though the MLB continues to drag its feet, change is in the air. While there have been a few Black minority owners of MLB teams, there have been even fewer Black majority owners. Tom Lewis was the first: he owned the South Atlantic League's Savannah Cardinals from 1986 to 1987. Brandon Bellamy, who has owned the Gastonia Honey Hunters since 2020, is currently the only Black majority owner in professional baseball. There have never been any majority Black women owners, but now there is hope. Award-winning singer and songwriter Ciara and her husband, Seattle Seahawks quarterback Russell Wilson, are part of an initiative aimed toward bringing an MLB team to Portland, Oregon. They are just two of a handful of African American women and men looking to open the doors to Black ownership in the MLB, which has been long overdue. If they succeed, it will be history in the making. But for the time being, efforts continue to be made to kick down doors for girls and women to play baseball. Is there a future for Black women in the national pastime? *I certainly hope so.*

◆ ◆ ◆

AFRICAN AMERICANS HAVE BEEN PLAYING golf since it was introduced to America in 1888 (Johnson 2008). Free and enslaved African Americans both designed and manicured courses in the eighteenth and nineteenth centuries, but they were almost universally outlawed from playing. By the 1980s, most African Americans involved at the highest levels of the sport were caddies who earned a living by working for elite professional athletes and country clubs.

The first known African American golfer was John Shippen, who competed in the second U.S. Open in 1896. A few notable African American golfers, mostly men like Lee Elder and Charlie Sifford, found success in golf and demonstrated their mastery of the sport before Tiger Woods' emergence. But even today, African American access to professional and elite country clubs remains limited,

---

17. Juliet Macur, "The First Black Woman to Coach in Pro Baseball Thanks Her Mom for the Job" *The New York Times,* March 3, 2021. https://www.nytimes.com/2021/03/03/sports/baseball/bianca-smith-red.html.

and the number of successful African American golfers continues to be small, with the number of Black women even smaller.

The first major golf organization to be created, the United States Golf Association (USGA), is the national association of golf courses, clubs and facilities and the governing body of golf for the U.S. and Mexico, which produces and interprets the rules of golf. Founded in 1894 as the Amateur Golf Association of the United States, the USGA tournaments frequently barred Black golfers, and remained fully segregated until the mid-1950s.

Since the Professional Golf Association of America's (PGA) founding in 1916, it has fought long and hard to maintain its all-White status. In 1921, a group of African American investors bought property for the Shady Rest Golf and Country Club in Scotch Plains, New Jersey, becoming the first Black-owned club in the U.S. By 1925, a group of African American golfers had founded the United Golfers Association (UGA). They operated a separate series of professional golf tournaments for African Americans during the era of racial segregation. Black golfers created their own clubs and organizations of touring professionals, and while women were allowed to participate from the group's inception, Black women struggled for acceptance, though were not deterred from joining.

Anna Mae Robinson founded the Chicago Women's Golf Club in 1930, which became the first women's golf association to be affiliated with the UGA. In 1937, Helen Webb Harris helped create the first club for Black women golfers, the Wake-Robin Golf Club in Washington, D.C., and joined the UGA under her leadership. In 1973, Harris was inducted into the National Afro-American Golfers Hall of Fame. A loosely knit circuit of tournaments were available to Black golfers, but the UGA was far and away the most important tournament and drew the best golfers (Kennedy 2005).

Women flocked to the links when golf made its first appearance in the U.S. in the late nineteenth century, in part because it was socially accepted as an appropriate sport for women. The Americanization of golf included men's disapproval of female golfers, to the extent that they restricted women from courses, clubs and organizations, regardless of whether they were beginners or tournament-celebrity players (Kirsch 2009). The Ladies Professional Golf Association (LPGA), founded in 1950, is one of the longest-running women's professional sports associations, created to help women golfers. But it historically struggled with a lack of diversity in the game, including its restriction against Black women. It took just over a decade until retired tennis professional Althea Gibson launched another pioneering sports career and joined the tour in 1964, becoming its first Black member. After all these years, the LPGA has yet to see the total number of Black participants in its history reach double digits.

During the civil rights movement, Maggie Hathaway, an avid golfer, became a major activist in the Los Angeles-Hollywood region, especially when it came to golf. She agitated against local golf courses that restricted Black patrons and players by leading picket lines, wrote newspaper columns about golf, and made White golf stars like Arnold Palmer and Jack Nicklaus squirm when she openly challenged them about racism in golf (Kennedy 2005). In 1994, Hathaway was inducted into the National Black Golf Hall of Fame. The Jack Thompson Golf Course in Los Angeles was renamed the Maggie Hathaway Golf Course in 1997.

Ann Gregory, the best amateur African American female golfer of the twentieth century, broke the USGA color line by becoming the first African American to play in a national championship in 1956. Throughout her career, she won nearly 300 tournaments and was given the title "Queen of Negro Golf" by the press because of her domination of the woman's playing field. She was the brightest star in any field of competition (Johnson 2008). Renee Powell and LaRee Pearl Sugg followed soon after Gibson and Gregory, with notable success on the professional golf tour.

Renee Powell began playing at age eight and was coached by her father, Bill Powell, owner of the Clearview Golf Club. By age twelve, she began competing against adults in the UGA. By fifteen, and with the encouragement and support of her parents, Powell competed in the U.S. Women's Amateur Championship in 1956, becoming the first African American woman to play in a national championship conducted by the USGA. At twenty-one, she made the LPGA Tour—the second Black woman ever to do so after Althea Gibson. Powell was the first woman of color to captain the women's golf team at The Ohio State University. She joined the LPGA in 1967 and moved to the U.K. in the 1970s to further her career and joined the British PGA. At age twenty-seven, she got her first and only LPGA win at the 1973 Kelly Springfield Open in Brisbane, Australia. In 1977, Powell became the first woman to compete in a men's golf tournament. She then returned to her roots and became the director at the Clearview Golf Club (Johnson 2008). When she retired from the LPGA, Powell had competed in more than 250 professional golf tournaments. Among her many honors and awards, Powell is a member of the Ohio Golf Hall of Fame, and was inducted into the United Golf Association Hall of Fame in 1966, the African American Golfers Hall of Fame in 2006, the National African American Golfers Hall of Fame in 2011, the National Black Golf Hall of Fame in 2012, and the PGA of America Hall of Fame in 2017.

LaRee Pearl Sugg became the third African American woman to play on the LPGA tour playing from 1995 to 1996 and 2000 to 2001, and made multiple appearances at the U.S. Women's Open Championship and the Women's British Open. Apart from the LPGA, Sugg played for the LPGA Futures Tour and won the 1998 Aurora Health Care Futures Classic. She ended her LPGA career in 2001 when she lost her tour card for a second time. Sugg became the inaugural head coach of the University of Richmond women's golf team in 2002, and briefly coached the men's golf team in 2005 before working as an assistant athletic director for the university from 2005 to 2008. From 2008 she continued her athletic director career with Richmond as an associate director and deputy director.

The so-called "Tiger Effect" was supposed to boost minority participation in the sport, but Tiger Woods' presence as a global phenomenon has had a negligible impact. Even in those fleeting moments when golf has appeared on the precipice of change, it always has been just a step away from tumbling back to the depths from which it came. Growing the game is a fine goal, but golf associations continue to absolve themselves of the sins of their past without forthrightly addressing the need for institutional change. This is why Black golfers continue to tackle discrimination in the golf industry, and why golf associations for African Americans like the African American Golf Association (AAGA), United Black Golfers Association (UBGA), Western States Golf Association, and the Black Jewels Ladies Golf Association continue to flourish. Currently, the LPGA tour can count among its ranks Black women like Mariah Stackhouse, Shasta Averyhardt, Sadena Parks, Cheyenne Woods, and Ginger Howard, who at age seventeen became the youngest Black female golfer to turn pro. While this sounds impressive, it barely makes a dent in LPGA's roster.

African American participation accounts for just three percent of recreational golfers, one percent higher than in 1990. Junior golf has become more diverse than any other category, as 36 percent of players are girls and nearly one-quarter are girls of color.[18] Programs like First Tee and the World Golf Foundation's Diversity Task Force, which were created to help spur play among African Americans and other people of color, have not been effective because high costs make golf inaccessible. Though there remain remnants of exclusionary attitudes in the game, Black women golfers have persisted in their efforts to acquire access and equity on the green.

◆ ◆ ◆

THE FIRST RECORDED WOMEN'S BOXING MATCH in the U.S. occurred in New York in 1888, when Hattie Leslie beat Alice Leary in a brutal fight. Although women have participated in boxing for almost as long as the sport has existed, albeit under the radar, female matches were effectively outlawed for most of boxing's history. Athletic commissioners refused to sanction or issue licenses to women boxers, and most nations officially banned women from the sport. Women's boxing officially appeared at the St. Louis 1904 Summer Olympics in a demonstration bout. It fueled a huge boom in the number of women joining gyms to box, with some setting their sights on entering amateur tournaments, hoping to become Olympians or professionals boxers (Smith 2014).

After the 1904 Olympics demonstration, women's boxing was relegated to amateur boxing clubs that followed rules promulgated by the AAU and other

---

18. Steve Keating, "Diversity remains golf's biggest challenge, says PGA of America CEO," *Reuters*, August 8, 2018, https://www.reuters.com/article/us-golf-pgachamp-diversity/diversity-remains-golfs-biggest-challenge-says-pga-of-america-ceo-idUSKBN1KT2OE; Erik Matuszewski, "The Changing Face of Junior Golf," National Golf Foundation, May 2016, https://www.ngf.org/news/2016/05/the-changing-face-of-junior-golf.

national bodies (Smith 2014). It would not be until 1999 that the International Boxing Association (IBA) would approve the first European Cup for women, and in 2001, the first World Championship for women. The IOC would authorize the inclusion of women's boxing beginning with the London 2012 Summer Olympics.

Women's boxing in the U.S. was rarely acknowledged publicly until the 1970s when several pioneers made some inroads. Not surprisingly, Black women boxers paved the way for others. In the mid-1970s, when Maine, Connecticut, and several other states licensed professional female boxers, New York remained firmly opposed to granting women boxing licenses. One of the first women to challenge the New York State Boxing Commission were African American boxers Marian "Lady Tyger" Trimiar and Jackie Tonawanda. Finally, in 1978, after numerous lawsuits, New York State finally agreed to license professional female boxers.

Trimiar began boxing when she was ten years old. She fought in exhibition bouts, and won the women's Lightweight Championship of the World in 1979. Having engaged in over twenty-five professional bouts, Trimiar retired in 1987 (Callis 2009). Tonawanda, dubbed "the Female Ali," was a heavyweight boxer during the 1970s and 1980s who won all thirty-six bouts as an amateur. She was the first woman to box in Madison Square Garden, and knocked out her opponent, Larry Rodania, in the second round. She was well past her prime when she lost her only professional bout. Tonawanda later became a member of Ring 8, a nonprofit organization to help former boxers in need (Schiot 2016). She was inducted into the Veterans Boxing Association and Madison Square Garden's Hall of Fame.

However, professional fights for women remained rare, since not all states issued licenses to women. It took Gail Grandchamp eight years to win her battle in Massachusetts to become an amateur boxer, but by the time she won the right to do so, she was past the maximum age of thirty-six, so she instead boxed professionally for a time. After women won the legal right to box, the pay was so low that many of the best women also had to work full-time jobs. During the 1980s, women's boxing was somewhat stagnant, but it experienced a boom in the 1990s, coinciding with the emergence of professional women's sports leagues such as the Women's National Basketball Association (WNBA). This helped push the sport, albeit temporarily, to the forefront.

Black women boxers met the challenges of being Black and female when Laila Ali and Jacqui Frazier-Lyde—the daughters of heavyweight boxing champions Muhammad Ali and Joe Frazier—entered into the fray. Ali began competing in 1999. During her career, she held the World Boxing Council (WBC), World Boxing Association (WBA), International Women's Boxing Federation (IWBF) and the International Boxing Association (IBA) female Super Middleweight titles, including IWBF Lightweight and Heavyweight titles. In 2000, Frazier-Lyde announced at age thirty-eight (sixteen years older than Ali) that she would become a boxer, with the express purpose to fight Ali. While boxing fans questioned Frazier-Lyde's abilities and motives, the two squared off in 2001 before a pay-per-view audience in the first boxing card headlined by women. Although Ali won by a majority decision after eight rounds, Frazier-Lyde won the boxing community's respect (Smith 2014). She also won the WBA Light Heavyweight title in 2001 and the IWBF Intercontinental Super Middleweight title in 2002. Frazier-Lyde would retire in 2004 with a record of thirteen wins, nine by knockout, and one loss. Ali retired in 2007 with a record of twenty-four wins, twenty-one by knockout, and no losses.

Another Black female boxer from this era worth noting is Ann Wolfe, who is regarded by many within the sport as the greatest fighter and the hardest puncher in women's boxing history. Wolfe was on record repeatedly requesting a fight with Ali, but it never came to fruition. She was one of two fighters (the other being Henry Armstrong) to hold titles in four weight divisions simultaneously before retiring in 2006. She was inducted into the Women's International Boxing Hall of Fame in 2015, and in 2021 into the International Boxing Hall of Fame and Museum.

Mary Jo Sanders, daughter of National Football League (NFL) Hall of Famer, Charlie Sanders, developed a reputation as a classic boxer with a fluid style and a powerful punch. Sanders was named Top Rookie of the Year by Women Boxing Archive Network (WBAN) in 2003. She retired in 2008 after her second fight with Holly Holm and fought to a draw, with a record of twenty-five wins, eight by knockout, and one loss (Heiskanen 2012).

Some believed what the whole enterprise of boxing rested on famous last names because by the mid-2000s, women's boxing had declined, falling back to relative obscurity due to lack of promotion, television exposure, and poor matchmaking. Even at the London 2012 Summer Olympics, the women's bouts were fought in the afternoon while men fought in prime time; the women fought on consecutive days with only one rest day, while the men fought every other day to include rest. Despite this setback, the women's boxing was well-received and became more legitimized (Finkel 2014).

While women continue to fill amateur ranks in the U.S. and overseas, the professional ranks are especially thin in quality opponents. Even with women boxers getting some of the recognition they deserved, one of the main issues was that they were not allowed to compete in the Olympics as professional boxers. This left women boxers in a conundrum: turning professional allowed them to earn some income but disqualified them from competing in the Olympics, one of the few major competitions where they could win a globally-recognized award and gain a financial bargaining chip when they turned pro. Even when women boxers held out to compete in the Olympics, the sport lacked professional boxers and bouts. The other problem was that the wage ceiling for women boxers was far less than their male counterparts, who earned prize money between $100,000 and $1 million.[19] Coupled with the lack of interest in women's boxing from most television networks, women boxers could not earn enough money to cover their expenses, let alone make a living. It was not until 2016, when the IBA finally voted to allow professionals box in the Olympics, that the wage ceiling opened up so women boxers could advance the sport they loved to an international level.

Without the ability to sell women's bouts on televised cards, the signing and development of women boxers had been rendered an unprofitable business. Some have finally begun to grasp the fact that women's boxing is a fertile area of growth, worthy of an investment. Some have even suggested that boxing needs its own Ronda Rousey, someone who captures the casual fight fan's imagination while also garnering attention from hardcore fans who are unfairly dismissive of women's boxing. Suffice it to say, women's boxing still has a long way to go before it reaches the status of its male counterpart.

At least now we are witnessing a new era. Claressa Shields is currently a unified World champion in three weight classes and became the first American woman to win Olympic gold medals in boxing in 2012 and 2016. Perhaps Shields has what it takes to help usher in a new era of women's boxing in the U.S. In the meantime, Black women are continuing to find their place in the rosters. They are world champions, and they are an inspiration to all.

◆ ◆ ◆

FOR THOSE WHO FOLLOW THE SPORT every four years, the story of Black woman gymnast probably begins with Dominique Dawes. When she first stepped onto the Olympic stage during the Barcelona 1992 Summer Olympics and helped the U.S. women's gymnastics team win bronze medals, she and Betty Okino, a 1991 World team silver medalist, became the first African Americans to win Olympic gymnastics medal.

A member of the gold-medal-winning team, the "Magnificent Seven," at the Atlanta 1996 Summer Olympics, Dawes was also the first African American of any nationality or gender to win an individual Olympic medal (in this case, bronze) in the floor routine. She is one of three female American gymnasts to compete in three Olympics, and the first to be a member of three Olympic-medal-winning teams (1992/bronze, 1996/gold, 2000/bronze) since Russian gymnast Ludmilla Tourischeva in the early 1970s. Dawes has garnered twenty-seven medals throughout her career, including fifteen gold medals at National Championships.

It is easy to assume that gymnastics is almost entirely bereft of Black representation. While this may be true in the higher ranks, as a whole, you will find that Black women, and other women of color, have participated in the sport from elementary school through college, winning national and World Championships

19. Mark Lelinwalla, "Amanda Serrano and Heather Hardy are tired of the wage gap between women and men boxers," *Sporting News,* September 7, 2018, https://www.sportingnews.com/us/boxing/news/amanda-serrano-and-heather-hardy-are-tired-of-the-wage-gap-between-women-and-men-boxers/i9y4kap6xjdp16a39wmhdpli7.

for years (Smith 2013). Gymnastics was just beginning to be televised thanks largely to the superstardom of Romanian gymnast Nadia Comăneci, in the Montreal 1976 Summer Olympics (Braddock 2017). The gymnast superstars that followed hailed from the Soviet Union and Eastern European countries, and set the "perfect gymnast" standards we have come to know: thin, flexible, and White. This standard, however, did not stop Black women from participating in gymnastics. YMCAs, YWCAs, and public schools have played a significant role in encouraging Black gymnasts. Team fees were also nominal, which made it accessible to everyone, even lower-income youth. Wendy Hilliard became the first African American woman to represent the U.S. gymnastics team in 1978.

In 1980, Luci Collins was the first African American woman to be named to the U.S. Olympic Team. However, she never got to compete due to the U.S. boycott of the Moscow 1980 Summer Olympics. Dianne Durham became the first African American woman all-around champion at the National Championships in Chicago in 1983. Then, after Mary Lou Retton became the first American woman to win the Olympic gold medal in the Los Angeles 1984 Summer Olympics, her popularity triggered costlier training that impacted the participation of people of color in the sport. Yet, Black female gymnasts continued to make inroads on state, national, and international levels.

Dionne Foster joined the USA national team while still in high school in 1988 and is the only NCAA gymnast to finish in the top three in all-around for four straight years. Tasha Schwikert won a bronze medal as a member of the U.S. team at the Sydney 2000 Summer Olympics, became a World team gold medalist, and was a two-time all-around NCAA gold medalist. Andreé Pickens is a two-time NCAA champion and the only gymnast in NCAA history to earn five All-American honors in two different seasons (1999 and 2002). Ashley Miles is a World team bronze-medalist in 2001 and captured the NCAA national vault titles in 2003, 2004, and 2005. Sophina DeJesus was a member of the UCLA Bruins gymnastic team from 2012 to 2016. Other Black women gymnasts have come and gone from the Olympic spotlight, such as Jair Lynch and Donovan Bailey. They all helped pave the way for the superstars that would follow.

However, it would be Gabrielle "Gabby" Douglas and Simone Biles that exposed an entirely new level of influence than those who came before them through social media, socioeconomics and timing. They would set the stage for a new generation of elite Black gymnasts to emerge in what has been known as a predominantly White sport (Braddock 2017).

After Dawes' retirement in 2000, most people skip ahead to Douglas, the first African American to become the Olympic individual all-around champion at the London 2012 Summer Olympics. She was also the first American gymnast to win gold in both the individual all-around and team competition. Douglas achieved all of this at the same Olympics where she competed alongside African American team member, Kyla Ross. After becoming the 2015 World all-around silver medalist, she returned to the Rio de Janeiro 2016 Summer Olympics and won gold alongside team member Simone Biles, who would become the most decorated American gymnast in history.

Biles would go on to win three individual gold medals in all-around, vault, and floor; and bronze in balance beam, setting an American record for most gold medals in women's gymnastics at a single Olympics. As of 2019, Biles has won thirty-five medals, including nineteen gold medals at the World Championships. With the postponement of the Tokyo 2020 Summer Olympics due to the COVID-19 pandemic, as with most athletes, Biles is trying to figure out a way forward to regain the spark that has made her one of the most celebrated athletes of the Olympic movement. Since Biles, some new faces have emerged on the scene, like Konnor McClain, Margzetta Frazier, Shilese Jones, Trinity Thomas, and Stasya Generalova.

Even though the sport has changed significantly over the last fifteen years, the ideal gymnast image has not shifted much—lithe, young, and White. But Black little girls and women have managed to prevail. You cannot ignore their sweat and sacrifice, physical labor, sore muscles, steely drive, and determination that it takes to win, which is why Biles' accomplishment as the most decorated American gymnast in history is of such symbolic importance. Biles' legacy cannot be measured in titles or medals; her impact on little Black girls will last long after her illustrious career ends.

◆ ◆ ◆

SOCCER—KNOWN AS FOOTBALL most everywhere else—has been played on American soil since at least the mid-1800s and became an organized college sport in the years following the Civil War. The sport had its first wave of popularity in the 1920s due to the influx of immigrant workers who grew up playing soccer in gym class and informal pickup games. Women's soccer, however, developed quietly. The first recorded women's soccer competitions were at Smith College, which began offering soccer competitions in 1924 (Williams 2007). These contests were not only held in physical education classes, but also via intramural competitions.

While women have been playing soccer in organized women's leagues in Europe as early as the late nineteenth century, it was not until the mid-twentieth century that the first organized women's league in the U.S. was established: the Craig Club Girls Soccer League. Consisting of four teams in St. Louis, Missouri, the league completed two seasons in 1950 and 1951 (Williams 2007). Although their history was short, it was a milestone in the history of women's soccer, although it would be over a decade before the sport began to make its appearance in colleges. The first college women's varsity soccer team was established at Castleton State College (now known as Castleton University), in Vermont in the mid-1960s (Williams 2007). There are no records that Black women were allowed to participate.

However, organized women's soccer did not take root in the U.S. until Title IX's passage in 1972, which mandated equal access and spending on college institutions' athletic programs (Markovits and Hellerman 2014; Reck and Dick 2015). The growth of women's college soccer did not start out primarily in one region of the country. With the seeds planted by men's soccer, the women's program was able to take root all over the country at once. The University of North Carolina (UNC) immediately took a commanding position in women's soccer, one they would maintain well into the twenty-first century. Of the first twenty NCAA championships, sixteen were won by UNC, including nine in a row from 1986-1994.[20]

It was not until 1985, though, that the first women's national squad was formed, the U.S. Women's National Soccer Team (USWNT), which was also created for international competition, and eventually the Olympics. The USWNT made history in 1986 when it invited Kim Crabbe, the first Black woman to join the team. Crabbe, who played until 1988, did not earn a cap. The first Black woman to earn a cap with the USWNT was Sandi Gordon, who played from 1987 to 1988.[21]

Momentum for the USWNT would not begin to build until 1991 when the Fédération Internationale de Football Association (FIFA), the international league, established the Women's World Championship. In 1996, women's soccer was added to the Olympics, and when the U.S. took the gold, it grabbed the nation's attention. The final penalty shot gave the U.S. a victory over China after a hard-fought scoreless tie at the 1999 Women's World Cup, catapulting women's soccer to the international stage.

While collegiate soccer created more popularity for the game during the 1980s, there were few professional opportunities for women in the U.S. The U.S. Interregional Women's League (later known as the USL W-League), was a semi-professional league that launched in 1995. When it folded in 2015, the United Women's Soccer (UWS), a second-division professional-amateur women's soccer league, was founded that same year to provide high level competition for college players, aspiring and former professionals, and international stars.

But it was not until 2001 when the first professional women's league, the Women's United Soccer Association (WUSA) made its debut. The league, which had eight teams, disbanded at the conclusion of its third season in 2003 due to financial problems and lack of public interest in the sport. Its successor, Women's Professional Soccer (WPS), began to play in 2007, and became the highest level in the U.S. soccer pyramid for the women's game. When the WPS folded in 2013 due to financial issues, the National Women's Soccer League

20. Mikyla Williams. "UNC women's soccer looks to end streak of NCAA title game defeats," The Daily Tar Heel, April 20, 2021, https://www.dailytarheel.com/article/2021/04/unc-womens-soccer-look-ahead-ncaa-tournament-national-championship-hopes-brianna-pinto.

21. In soccer, a cap is a term used to describe how many international matches a player has played. In order to receive a cap, a player has to actually make an appearance on the soccer field during a game.]

(NWSL) was formed, becoming America's top professional women's league. It currently has ten teams across the U.S.

Since soccer is viewed by many as primarily a White sport, there are few women of color in coaching and the player pool, with team ownership almost exclusively White and male. But when it comes to the history of Black women soccer players and the women's national team, most signs point to one player: former national team goalkeeper Briana Scurry. Besides being a founding player for the Atlanta Beat (WUSA), she is known for her save during penalty kicks that helped the U.S. defeat China in the 1999 World Cup final, Scurry totaled 173 caps for the USWNT. Considered one of the best goalkeepers in women's soccer history, Scurry is featured at the recently erected Smithsonian National Museum of African American History and Culture in Washington, D.C., sandwiched between greats Eddie Robinson and Michael Jordan, as a representative of the impact of Title IX.

Other Black women who were stand outs during this era include Danielle Slaton, Angela Hucles, and Danesha Adams. Slaton (defender) played for Santa Clara University, where she was a four-year starter, three-time first-team All-American defender, and team captain for the Santa Clara Broncos from 1998 to 2001. She was a member of USWNT and won a silver medal at the Sydney 2000 Summer Olympics. Slaton also played for the Carolina Courage (WUSA) and was named the league's defender of the year. She briefly played for Olympique Lyonnais before retiring in 2005, and became a high school and later a university coach. Hucles (midfielder), is a four-time Atlantic Coast Conference (ACC) Player of the Year at the University of Virginia and a two-time Olympic gold medalist who played in both the WUSA and WPS leagues. In 2020, she joined a majority-female investor group, led by actress Natalie Portman, to become a copartner of the recently awarded NWSL California team, Angel City FC, which will premiere in 2022. Adams (forward and midfielder), led UCLA to four NCAA Final Four College Cups. She was also a three-time Pac-10 Conference First Team selection and two-time Hermann Trophy finalist. Adams played professionally with the Chicago Red Stars, Philadelphia Independence, and Sky Blue FC before retiring in 2014. She transitioned into a coaching career and went on to earn a Bachelor's in sociology from UCLA.

A new crop of players is climbing up the ranks and busting stereotypes. The Black Women's Player Collective (BWPC) comprised of soccer players was founded in 2020, to promote diversity, equity and inclusion (DEI). The group, which includes non-Black allies, has collaborated on initiatives to help promote soccer in underprivileged communities. According to BWPC, as of 2020 there were forty-three Black women on the NWSL's team rosters. Out of the twenty-one women in the USWNT, eight are Black. On and off the field, Crystal Dunn, Christen Press, Adrianna Franch, Mallory Pugh, Catarina Macário, Casey Krueger, Lynn Williams, and Sophia Smith are inspiring Black girls all over the world.

Dunn (defender) was the first overall pick in the 2014 NWSL College Draft by the Washington Spirit, and was the 2015 NWSL's MVP. She would play for the Chelsea Football Club Women in England from 2017 to 2018, and currently plays with the North Carolina Courage. Dunn was also a member of the gold-winning team of the 2019 World Cup. Press (forward), broke every offensive record in Stanford University history as the all-time leader in shots, goals, assists, and points after making her World Cup debut in 2015. She played for the Chicago Red Stars from 2014 to 2017, and has played for the Utah Royals FC from 2018 to 2020. She recently signed a two-year contract with Angel City FC, becoming the highest-paid player in NWSL history. Franch (goalkeeper) who played for the Portland Thorns from 2016 to 2021, won the NWSL Goalkeeper of the Year award in 2017 and 2018, and was the first player to ever win the award twice. Franch currently plays for Kansas City. And at age seventeen, Pugh (forward), joined the Rio de Janeiro 2016 Summer Olympics team, making her the second-youngest player to ever travel to the Olympics, and then played in the 2016 World Cup. Pugh enrolled at UCLA and played in three spring games, but decided to skip college to go straight to the pros. After playing for the Washington Spirits and Sky Blue FC, Pugh currently plays for the Chicago Red Stars.

Brazilian-born Macário (midfielder) plays for Lyon of the French Division 1 Féminine, and represents the U.S. internationally. Until her arrival in the U.S. in 2011, Macário had always played for men's teams. A decorated collegiate player for Stanford University, she was named ESPNW Player of the Year for multiple years, won the TopDrawerSoccer.com National Player of the Year Award, the Honda Sports Award and has twice won the Hermann Trophy. Krueger (defender) played collegiate soccer for the Florida State Seminoles, and was the fifth overall pick in the 2013 NWSL College Draft. Krueger, who plays for the Chicago Red Stars, has accumulated over thirty caps for the USWNT. She previously played for Avaldsnes IL in Norway's top-division league, Toppserien, and was named a Top XI player in the league.

Williams (forward) played for Pepperdine University and was named the National Player of the Week by the NSCAA and CollegeSoccer360.com, and WCC Player of the Week. She plays for the North Carolina Courage and previously played for Western New York Flash and Western Sydney Wanderers in the Australian W-League. Williams received her first call-up to the USWNT in 2016. Smith (forward) played for Stanford University, helping her team win the national title in 2019. Smith's long history with the national team started when she was thirteen playing for junior leagues, and she worked her way up to joining the USWNT in 2020. That same year, Smith was selected by the Portland Thorns as the top overall pick in the 2020 NWSL College Draft. Players Dunn, Press, Krueger and Williams were included on the roster for the Tokyo 2020 Summer Olympics, and helped the U.S. team win a bronze medal behind Canada and Sweden.

Soccer has always suffered from a diversity problem. Although its popularity has skyrocketed worldwide, diversity on the field has been slow to follow in the U.S. Part of the problem is that soccer has become the White suburban kid's sport. Black and Brown children do not have easy access to the sport, and their parents are less likely to have the disposable income required to invest in soccer camp and pay-to-play soccer leagues, which are costly and require a long-term commitment.

On top of that, there are also cultural barriers—many women of color receive the signal that they do not belong in soccer. Crystal Dunn, one of the world's best soccer players, feels as though she receives less publicity compared with her contemporaries, and fewer endorsement deals and sponsorships, which make up a significant portion of an athlete's income.[22] Whether it was the incident with a stadium security guard threatening to call the police on Jessica McDonald's seven-year-old son who wanted to see his mother after the game,[23] or when Adrianna Franch was subjected to racial slurs from Portland Thorns fans,[24] these microaggressions add up, solidifying the whiteness of the sport.

There also seems to be a disconnect between management and the women of color who play on the field. This was certainly reflected when in 2016, U.S. Soccer announced its policy requiring national team members to stand during the anthem when player Megan Kapinoe (who is White) followed suit in the aftermath of Colin Kaepernick kneeling during the anthem. Under heavy pressure from players and especially fans, who signed petitions, donated to different organizations, and were vocally disappointed by White players who did not make strong statements in support of the Black Lives Matter movement,[25] U.S. Soccer finally repealed its policy in 2020 and apologized to the Black community.

The lack of women coaches in the NWSL remains an ongoing issue, especially among women of color. As of 2021, there are only three female coaches, and they are all White. Retired goalkeeper, Briana Scurry, became the first Black woman coach when she was first assistant coach at Washington Spirit in 2018. In 2020, when Nikki Washington, a retired forward and right midfielder, was named as an interim assistant coach for Utah Royals FC, becoming the second Black woman to coach for a NWSL team, her position was short-lived when the

22. Mariah Lee, "Crystal Dunn, one of the world's best soccer players, feels 'like someone has dimmed my light'," The Undefeated, July 21, 2021, https://theundefeated.com/features/crystal-dunn-one-of-the-worlds-best-soccer-players-feels-like-someone-has-dimmed-my-light.

23. McDonald, Jessica. Twitter, July 28, 2019. https://twitter.com/j_mac1422/status/115550674 1133451271?lang=en..

24 Stephanie Yang, "We all have a responsibility to kick racism out of NWSL," SBNation, September 9, 2019, https://www.allforxi.com/2019/9/9/20855809/kick-racism-out-nwsl-royals-franch-thorns.

25. Nicole Wetsman, "NWSL fans are online, organized, and refuse to be ignored," The Verge, July 17, 2020, https://www.theverge.com/21325419/nwsl-womens-soccer-fandom-twitter-uswnt.

team abruptly ceased operations. Whether it is the lack of applicants for coaching positions or male head coaches and English footballers having a better and longer track record, the NWSL can definitely use a few more women in charge.

As this is an obvious issue in the NWSL, two teams will be joining the professional league, expanding the league to twelve teams that will hopefully bring much-needed diverse female talent in all of these areas. Angel City FC, out of Los Angeles, will make its debut in 2022. The team's ownership group consists of a multicultural group of athletes (former and current) and female celebrity investors who encourage women's inclusivity in leadership positions. Additionally, there will be a Sacramento expansion team making their debut in 2022 with their club out of San Diego. Former U.S. Women's National Team coach Jill Ellis, was named president, and Casey Stoney was made head coach. They are both former English players. While this is all good news, with the mounting popularity of soccer in the U.S. comes the need to form a positive and inclusive culture surrounding the sport.

So the progress continues. Several youth soccer teams have emerged in the past decade that catered to inner city youth. The Anderson Monarchs were a standout as the only all-girl African American soccer club in the U.S. Founded in 1998 by Coach Walter Stewart and based in Philadelphia, the program was initially part of the Anderson Monarchs' Girls Soccer Club, but later branched off to form Soccer Sisters United (SSU), which competed on a national level. The team was nominated in 2008 by *Sports Illustrated* as "Sports Team" of the year. In 2011, First Lady Michelle Obama invited the team to the White House and hosted a soccer clinic on the south lawn, which was featured in the documentary, *The Anderson Monarchs* (2012), produced and directed by Eugene Martin.

The Black Soccer Membership Association (BSMA) was founded in 2018 to help develop and promote inclusiveness at all levels, including management and coaching. The welcome presence of Black women in soccer highlights a potential turn of the page for U.S. women's soccer, but even with input from the leagues, teams and outside organizations, there is still a long way to go.

◆ ◆ ◆

IN THE U.S., SWIMMING POOLS have long been a contested space where African Americans have had little to no access. Swimming had become a popular activity among many working class boys and young men throughout the nineteenth century in the U.S. They swam nude, swore, fought, played, and avoided authority in the lakes, rivers, and bays that surrounded most American cities, creating a patriarchal swimming culture that violated Victorian norms. The authorities attempted to transplant this unacceptable swimming culture into a controlled space by creating public pools.

The earliest pools were built in large northern cities during the late-nineteenth and early-twentieth centuries and served mostly poor and working class boys who eagerly waited on long lines to use the facilities (Wiltse 2009). Advances in pool sanitation and the widespread use of chlorine relieved many Americans' fears of germs and disease, and the popularity of swimming increased. As a result, the social composition of swimmers changed when cities across the country built large, resort-like swimming pools, allowing women and men of different ethnicities to swim together. Institutionalized segregation quickly brought that to an end when public officials and White swimmers objected to Black men interacting with White women in such visually and physically intimate spaces. And so, throughout the U.S., public pools became racially segregated.

Even after the landmark U.S. Supreme Court decision of *Brown v. Board of Education* (1954), many communities fought to retain their segregated pools. As it became clear that segregation would become a thing of the past, some communities simply closed their pools rather than see them become integrated. The final nail in the coffin occurred with the passage of the Civil Rights Act of 1964. Pools that remained open saw a significant decline in attendance because of real or perceived racial tensions. It was more than just discrimination; it was a change in the quality of community life and civic engagement in modern America (Wiltse 2009).

Public pools fostered a community life that was sustained and interactive, but also raised issues about what kind of activities and clothing were appropriate, including who should be allowed to use the facilities. Millions soon sought recreational activities within smaller and more socially selective communities, fencing themselves into their own backyards. The increase of gated communities and homeowners associations led to the privatization of recreation. By losing the support of taxpayers who no longer wanted them, most public pools fell into disrepair and were forced to close. Over time, cities defunded their recreational facilities, leaving many urban dwellers with little access to pools. This history of exclusion is the reason why 64 percent of African American children have little to no swimming ability.[26] Even today, African Americans continue to experience racism at both public and private pools, which would explain why it took over 120 years for Black women to compete and win medals in swimming.

Girls and women did not experience the freedom that boys and men had when it came to swimming. Due to the social norms of the time, women were required to be covered from head to toe, as it was frowned upon for women to show any skin. It would take years before women were free to wear the type of swim wear we see today. As they fought for appropriate swim apparel, they also fought to have equal access in the pool, either for competitions or leisure activity. The first two known women's swimming groups were the National Women's Life-Saving League and the Women's Swimming Association. They held small swim competitions and fought to compete in swimming events that did not

26. Steven Roberts, "Most Black kids can't swim, and segregation is to blame," *Vice*, August 30 2018, https://www.vice.com/en_us/article/8xbyax/most-Black-kids-cant-swim-its-not-just-a-stereotype-its-history.

entirely revolve around the physical aspects of the sport. Women were first allowed to participate in the Olympics in 1912, but American women were not eligible to swim until the Antwerp 1920 Summer Olympics, due to the long skirt rule in the 1910s, which required women to wear full length skirts and show no leg. Apparently, what women wore was more important than their swimming abilities. The only events swum by women at the time were the 100-meter free, 300-meter free, and 4x100-meter free relays (Bier 2011).

A few women, like Charlotte "Eppy" Epstein, Gertrude Ederle, and Dara Torres, participated in swimming competitions, but none of them were African American. It was not until the 1980s that we began to see a handful of Black women in national and international swim meets. In 1988, Sybil Smith from Boston University, was the first Black woman to score in an NCAA final in the 100-yard backstroke. In 1999, Alison Terry was the first Black woman to make a U.S. national team for the Pan American Games. But it was Enith Brigitha from the Netherlands who would become the first Black woman swimmer to medal at the Olympics.

Brigitha set the stage for Black swimmers' success for decades to come. She was a four-time finalist at the 1972 Munich Games and earned two bronze medals at the Montreal 1976 Summer Olympics. Alongside her Olympic accomplishments, Brigitha raced to five world records and earned silver and bronze medals between the 1973 and 1975 World Championships, and a silver medal at the 1977 European Championships. She was inducted into the International Swimming Hall of Fame in 2015, and will always be credited with creating a path for future Black women Olympian swimmers such as Americans Maritza Correia McClendon, Lia Neal, and Simone Manuel.

Maritza Correia McClendon, specializing in freestyle, became the first of African American and Puerto Rican descent to become a member of the U.S. Olympic swimming team at the Athens 2004 Summer Olympics, winning a silver medal with the 400-meter freestyle relay team. McClendon also won gold medals in 2001 and 2004 at the World Championships as a member of the U.S. team. She became the U.S. Open record holder in the 50-yard freestyle and as a member of the 200- and 400-yard freestyle relay teams in 2002. A member of the University of George's Lady Bulldogs, McClendon is an eleven-time NCAA Champion and a twenty-seven-time NCAA All American, and is the only swimmer to ever win an SEC title in every freestyle event. She is the first to break two American and NCAA records, the first to win a NCAA Division I Championship.

Lia Neal, specializing in freestyle, competed in the 2008 Olympic Trials when she was thirteen. She made her Olympic debut when she was seventeen at the London 2012 Summer Olympics and won a bronze medal in the 4×100-meter freestyle relay, becoming the second African American woman to compete and medal at the Olympics. She won a silver medal in the same event at the Rio de Janeiro 2016 Summer Olympics, and announced her retirement from competition in 2021 with plans to work full time for Swimmers for Change, an organization she cofounded in 2016 to provide water safety programs for children of color.

Simone Manuel completed her collegiate career at Stanford University, where she helped lead the Stanford Cardinal to two Pac-12 Championships as well as two NCAA championships. She was a 13-time Pac-12 champion as well as a 14-time NCAA champion. Finishing her career, Manuel held six American records and seven NCAA records, most notably being the first woman to swim under 46 seconds in the 200-yard freestyle. At the Rio de Janeiro 2016 Summer Olympics, Manuel became the third African American woman to compete and medal at the Olympics, winning four medals: a gold medal in the 100-meter freestyle, a gold medal in the 4x100-meter medley, a silver medal in the 50-meter freestyle, and a silver medal in the 4×100-meter freestyle relay. By winning the 100-meter freestyle in a tie with Penny Oleksiak of Canada, Manuel became the first Black woman to win an individual Olympic gold in swimming and set an Olympic and American record. In the Tokyo 2020 Summer Olympics, Manuel won a bronze medal in the 4x100-meter freestyle relay. For the time being, Manuel plans to remain in competitive swimming.

Natalie Hinds swam for the University of Florida's Florida Gators during her collegiate career, becoming the SEC Freshman of the Year in 2013. She was a twenty-time All-American and a member of the trio of African American women that swept the top three spots at the 2015 NCAA Championships in the 100-freestyle, alongside Manuel and Neal, part of a historic finish as the first ever top three spots for Black swimmers. When Hinds did not qualify for the Rio de Janeiro 2016 Summer Olympics Trials, she decided to take a break from swimming and did app development as part of her job at Turner Broadcasting based in Atlanta, Georgia. She returned to competitive swimming after being inspired by the 2018 USA National Championships and qualified for the Tokyo 2020 Summer Olympics. She swam third leg in the 4x100-meter freestyle and won the bronze medal, becoming the fourth African American woman to compete and medal at the Olympics. After the Olympics, Hinds joined the Cali Condors, a professional swimming club based in San Francisco, and one of the original eight clubs of the International Swimming League.

The significance is not lost that these Black women champions experienced the same poolside confrontations during their training years that African Americans have dealt with for over fifty years and continue to deal with today. Their performance was the refutation of years of racist ideology—including studies on the buoyancy of Black folks. Although these and other issues weighed them down, when they earned medals and recognition in the sport, they succeeded in turning a liberating page for Black swimmers, worldwide.

◆ ◆ ◆

AS MORE BLACK WOMEN BEGAN TO PARTICIPATE IN SPORTS, organizations for women athletes increased and sports became more competitive, while intercollegiate and interscholastic competition spread. The White women who worked for the AAU and United States Olympic Committee (USOC) began to call for more investment in women's track and field. Although their demands were inspired by Black sports culture, their developmental plans did not necessarily include Black women. Even when the national AAU had desegregated, district associations determined their own racial policies, especially in the South where most Black women athletes were located. But the fact that White women recognized Black athletic womanhood, embodied by Alice Coachman and other Black women athletes as imitation-worthy, was significant.

After World War II, as African Americans took matters into their own hands and pressed for redress in practically every major sport, the nation had become more receptive to Blacks participating in professional sports leagues. The result was an unprecedented five-year period between 1946 and 1950 when the American sports establishments finally opened their doors to Blacks. While the South initially resisted, it too eventually integrated.

Another problem that both Black and White women athletes continue to face is virulent homophobia. Sports have always functioned as a male preserve that affirmed manhood, which labeled aggression, physicality, competitive spirit, and athletic skill as masculine attributes necessary to achieve true sportsmanship. On the other hand, the athletic woman has always sparked controversy over her femininity and sexual identity in sports. By the turn of the twentieth century, as women began breaking barriers in sports, homophobia was used to relegate women athletes as outliers who were "rough" and "mannish," a coded reference to lesbianism. As a result, women were pressured to overtly display their femininity with hair, makeup, and pretty clothes, while lesbians stayed hidden and remained silent (Hargreaves 2001). By the 1950s, during the height of McCarthyism, women athletes operated under a cloud of sexual suspicion. Even the passage of Title IX in 1972 did little to diminish the orientation of the feminine heterosexual ideal and the lesbian stigma of women in sports.

Homophobia has remained a controlling force over the sporting lives of women in the U.S. While knowledge about and visibility of lesbian women in sports is much greater today, many LGBTQ athletes have chosen to stay in the closet because they fear rejection from teammates and fans. There is also the unspoken fear among many teams, leagues, and sports organizations about alienating sponsors and angering fans when players announce their sexual orientation. In fact, in 2015, the largest ever study of LGBTQ athletes confirmed this attitude when it found evidence of rampant homophobia in sports.[27] Yet,

---

27. Erik Denison and Alistair Kitchen. *Out on the Fields, The first international study on homophobia in sport. Nielsen,* Bingham Cup Sydney 2014, Australian Sports Commission, Federation of Gay Games. www.outonthefields.com.

there is hope that LGBTQ athletes will be able to live openly and flourish in professional sports in the foreseeable future.

To further complicate matters, the IAAF and IOC have spent more than half a century vigorously policing women's gender. Their rationale for decades was to catch male athletes masquerading as women, though they never once discovered an impostor. In reality, they set their sights on trying to prevent women with an allegedly unfair, male-like physical advantage from competing in female-only events. Throughout the years, they relied on quack science. When that was not effective, they developed the humiliating practice of gender verification using a number of tactics, such as requiring women to provide a "femininity certificate," or, even worse, physical examinations of their genitalia. Soon, chromosome and testosterone tests were being administered to address growing concerns about women who might have reproductive organs or secondary sex characteristics that did not align in a typical manner, or higher than normal testosterone levels. It only takes a few people to question the validity of a woman's win, and once she is accused, her future in sports is destroyed (Erikainen 2019). It is amazing that despite the many advances of female athletes in the last half-century, powerful male athletes are celebrated while powerful female athletes are suspect. *She won because she is strong and muscular—she must be a guy.*

This long and sordid treatment of women athletes has developed into a cultural issue. While the IAAF and its allies have worked to avoid the perception of cultural bias, the ongoing targeting of athletes like South African track star Caster Semenya, a middle-distance runner, has made race a contributing factor as well. Although many people have levels of estrogen and testosterone that diverge from statistical norms, when sports governing bodies decide on how to determine sexual identity, they are making a social determination (Cahn 2015). In the case of Semenya, she is an intersex woman, assigned female at birth, with XY chromosomes and naturally elevated testosterone levels.

It is worth pointing out that when Semenya first began competing, her sex was not initially questioned. But then she started winning, *a lot.* Beginning in 2009, Semenya won two Olympic gold medals and three World Championships in the women's 800-meter. She also earned a bronze medal in the 1500-meter at the World Championships in 2017. But her breathtaking wins were spoiled by accusations from White women athletes who ate dust. They cried that she was a "man" competing against women, and the grapes were soured. In an effort to appease the IAAF, Semenya took medication to suppress her testosterone levels, which made her ill. When the IAAF insisted she take the medication or else, Semenya fought back and took her case to court. In 2018, the IAAF announced new rules that required athletes with specific differences of sexual development to take medication to suppress their testosterone levels.

By 2019, after numerous court filings and appeals, Semenya publicly stated that the ongoing issue had destroyed her mentally and physically. That same year she joined the South African soccer club, SAFA Sasol Women's League JVW F.C. In 2021, she filed an appeal with the European Court of Human Rights.[28]

Besides dealing with invasive and humiliating exams that were wholly unwarranted, Semenya was suspended from competition. In an effort to clear her name, she was subjected to multiple court hearings, which progressed to a series of ultimatums. It is a case of misogynoir: an ugly, dangerous combination of sexism and racism that specifically targets Black women. For every Black woman who has reached the pinnacle of excellence, their athletic superiority threatens White women's spaces, and, in the process, their femininity is questioned.

Frankly, Title IX was really about gender equality between White women and men. It was never about racial equity. It certainly did not cover LGBTQ rights or sex testing in sports. Perhaps the most glaring outcome of the legislation is that White women have been its overwhelming beneficiaries. Socially constructed notions of race, class, and sexuality have always compounded how sports have developed in this country. Race is by far the most debilitating limitation of Title IX, yet you barely hear discussion of it (Cahn 2015).

Class has also played a role because it prevented Black women from engaging in sports that traditionally and financially excluded them. For example, Black women in track and field might seem less of an anomaly, and the Williams sisters' success in tennis is more out of the ordinary. Race, class, and sexuality are the operative notions in which certain sports became less "traditional" for certain groups. With sports remaining one of the bastions of male supremacy in which Black men easily excel due to their stereotyped athletic and masculine prowess—where do Black women athletes fit within this spectrum?

◆ ◆ ◆

A GROUP OF BLACK WOMEN shattered the myth of "sports we can't do" because of sex or race. One could say that all Black athletes have challenged racial barriers in sports at one time or another, but some of these women have excelled in sports where few African Americans have followed or the public knows little about. They are the game-changers who have broken into hockey, skiing, rowing, refereeing, volleyball, ice skating, bobsledding, speedskating, and fencing with distinction. Shining a light on them also highlights the under-representation and misconstrued perceptions of blackness within each sport.

Tina Sloan Green was the first African American to play for the U.S. women's national field hockey team (USWNT) from 1969 to 1973. She went on to become the first African American to become head coach of a women's college lacrosse team, the Temple Owls, from 1975 to 1992, becoming. Sloan Green was inducted into the U.S. National Lacrosse Hall of Fame in 1997, the Philadelphia Sports Hall of Fame in 2013, and the IWLCA Hall of Fame in 2017.

---

28. Susie Rushton, "Caster Semenya, The exceptional South African runner," Spring & Summer 2020, *The Gentlewoman,* http://thegentlewoman.co.uk/library/caster-semenya.

Flora "Flo" Jean Hyman is inarguably one of the first and most prolific Black women to play volleyball. Considered by many as "The Goddess of Volleyball," Hyman was over six feet tall. She played at the University of Houston as the school's first female scholarship athlete and was the first winner of the Broderick Award (now known as the Honda Sports Award) as the nation's best female collegiate volleyball player in 1977. She spent three years there and led the Houston Cougars to two top-five national finishes. Instead of completing her final year, she focused on her volleyball career, playing for Colorado. Hyman played in the World Championships and was a silver medalist at the Los Angeles 1984 Summer Olympics. Her specialty was the "Flying Clutchman," a fast and hard volleyball spike that traveled 110 miles per hour. Hyman died suddenly in 1986 at the age of thirty-one. She suffered from undiagnosed Marfan syndrome, which caused a fatal aortic dissection—a dime-sized weak spot in her aorta. Hyman was posthumously inducted into the Volleyball Hall of Fame in 1988 (Edelson 2014).

Racial diversity at the Winter Olympics remains relatively dismal. It should be no surprise that the U.S. has produced few successful Black Winter Olympians. Besides racism, little access to winter sports such as skating and skiing, and the high costs of training, traveling, and equipment have made it nearly impossible for Black and Brown children to participate in winter sports, let alone compete. In fact, since 1924, of the twenty-two Winter Olympics and over 1,000 medals awarded, only twelve recipients have been Black, and they represent both women and men from several countries. When Debi Thomas took home bronze in figure skating at the Calgary 1988 Winter Olympics, she became the first Black athlete to medal as an individual at a Winter Olympics. She also became the first Black woman to win the U.S. figure skating singles championship in 1986, and achieved all of this while studying as a pre-med student. There have been a few Black women who may not have medaled in the Olympics, but still participated in national and international competitions, though we hardly hear of them (Weisbord 2017).

While Thomas was the first Black woman skater to win an Olympic medal, she was not the first in skating. Few people know of Mabel Fairbanks, the first notable Black figure skater and coach. During the 1930s, Fairbanks was not allowed to compete in the national qualifying event for the Olympics or any competition due to her race. She performed in shows instead, including the Ice Capades in Mexico and later with the Ice Follies. She also paved the way for others, especially people of color, to compete in figure skating by coaching singles and pairs, including Thomas, Scott Hamilton, Kristi Yamaguchi, Rudy Galindo, Tai Babilonia, and Randy Gardner. In 1997, Fairbanks became the first African American inducted into the U.S. Figure Skating Hall of Fame and was inducted into the International Women's Sports Hall of Fame in October 2001 (Aaseng 2003).

It has been thirty-four years since Thomas medaled at the Winter Olympics, remaining the only Black woman to do so. This may change in the immediate future with upcoming ice skaters like Starr Andrews from Los Angeles. Andrews, who has been skating since she was three years old, has been moving up the junior level in recent years. She made her international debut in 2016 and wowed the American figure skating community at the 2018 U.S. National Championships. She skated a flawless free skate program, landing sixth place overall in her senior nationals debut with a performance that brought the audience to their feet. As one of only a handful of Black women to ever reach the upper echelons of figure skating, Andrews hopes to be the first to capture a gold medal at a Winter Olympics.

Anita DeFrantz captained the U.S. women's rowing team and rowed in the women's eight and won a bronze medal at the Montreal 1976 Summer Olympics. In 1977, she started her career as a staff attorney at the Juvenile Law Center of Philadelphia and was admitted to the Pennsylvania Bar. The U.S. led a boycott of the Moscow 1980 Summer Olympics to protest the late 1979 Soviet invasion of Afghanistan. In total, sixty-five nations refused to participate in the games, whereas eighty countries sent athletes to compete. DeFrantz led the U.S. athletes' fight for the right to compete, which included suing the USOC. Although she lost the suit, the IOC honored her with the Olympic Order's bronze medal and appointed her to lifetime membership in the organization. DeFrantz became the first female vice president of the IOC executive committee in 1997 and served until 2001 (Edelson 2014).

Bonnie St. John, a ski racer, was the first African American to medal in the Winter Paralympics. She won a bronze medal in the slalom, a bronze medal in the giant slalom, and a silver medal for overall performance at the Austria 1984 Winter Paralympics. Seba Johnson competed in the Calgary 1988 Winter Olympics. She was the first African American woman to ski in the Olympics and, at age fourteen, the youngest alpine ski racer in Olympic history. Her skis are on display at the Smithsonian National Museum of African American History and Culture.

Vonetta Flowers was a star sprinter and long jumper who initially aspired to make the Summer Olympics team. After several failed attempts, Flowers turned to bobsledding and found success as a brake-woman. At the Salt Lake City 2002 Winter Olympics, she and driver Jill Bakken won the gold medal in the two-woman event, becoming the first Black person to win a gold medal in a Winter Olympics. Elana Meyers Taylor, also a brake-woman, has competed in bobsledding since 2007. She won a bronze medal at the Vancouver 2010 Winter Olympics in the two-woman event with Erin Pac, and won the silver medal at the Sochi 2014 Winter Olympics in the two-woman event with Lauryn Williams (Edelson 2014).

In 2016, Blake Bolden became the first African American woman to play in the National Women's Hockey League (NWHL), a subsidiary of the National Hockey League (NHL). Bolden played collegiate hockey for Boston College as a defender before being drafted fifth overall by the Boston Blades in the Canadian Women's Hockey League (CWHL), helping the team win the 2015 Clarkson Cup. Later that year, she joined the NWHL, and in 2019 was named NWHL Defensive Player of the Year.

Erin Jackson is an inline skater, and roller derby player. She qualified as an inline speedskater for the World Games in 2017 to compete in the 500-meter long track speedskating event at the Pyeongchang 2018 Winter Olympics. There is a stunning caveat that is worth mentioning: Jackson had only four short months to learn to cross-train into a speedskater, and make it onto the Olympic team. Despite Jackson's incredibly brief training period, she became the first African American woman to join the U.S. Olympic ranks of long track speedskating.

Beyond winter sports, women referees and coaches have begun to make waves in the sports community. For decades, the idea of female referees in the National Basketball Association (NBA) or, in any professional sport for that matter, was unheard of, but it did not stop women refereeing on the local level in schools, public gyms, sports clubs, and semiprofessional teams. Sandra Ortiz-Del Valle pursued her dream of officiating in the NBA and, along the way, became the first woman to referee a men's professional basketball game in 1992 for the United States Basketball League (USBL).[29] Ortiz-De Valle sued the NBA in 1998 because, despite her qualifications, she was denied entry into the NBA's training program as a woman. Although she won a $7.85 million verdict, it was reduced to under $400,000.[30] By most accounts, the NBA then set out to prove it was not a discriminatory business by hiring Dee Kantner and Violet Palmer in 1997. They were the first women to officiate NBA regular season games. Kantner was fired after five seasons, but Palmer became a standout until she retired from the league.

In 1997, Palmer broke barriers by becoming the first African American woman referee of the NBA. Palmer officiated 919 NBA games and became the first woman to helm an NBA playoff game in 2006, before retiring at fifty-two in 2016. She crossed over into the overtly masculine world of NBA basketball as the first openly lesbian referee, paving the way for more women to follow. Danielle Scott and Angelica Suffren, two African American basketball referees in the NBA's G League (minor league), made sports history by becoming the first two Black women to referee an NBA game together in 2018, making it an intersectional feminist victory. But if the NBA wanted to show that hiring two women was an earnest move toward gender quality, it has not exactly followed

---

29. The United States Basketball League (USBL) was a professional men's spring basketball league. The league was formed in 1985 and ceased operations in 2008.

30. Stefan Bondy, "20 years ago Sandhi Ortiz-Del Valle sued the NBA charging she was blocked from becoming a referee because she's a woman; the jury agreed, though today it still hurts," *The Daily News*, September 16, 2018. https://www.nydailynews.com/sports/basketball/ny-sports-endzone-sandhi-nba-ref-20180914-story.html#skip-to-content.

through. From 1997 to 2018, the number of NBA female officials dropped from two to one.

In 2020, Jennifer King made football history by becoming the NFL's first Black female assistant coach when the Washington Football Team elevated her to a running back coach. She attended Guilford College, where she played college basketball and softball before graduating with a degree in sports management in 2006. Following graduation, she played in the Women's Football Alliance (WFA) as a quarterback and wide receiver for the Carolina Phoenix from 2006 to 2017, a defensive back and wide receiver for the New York Sharks in 2018, and safety for the D.C. Divas in 2019. She was a part of the Sharks team that won the 2018 WFA Division II Championship. After spending three years as an intern, first with the Carolina Panthers and then in Washington, getting an assistant job was the logical next step for King.

Maia Chaka became the first Black woman to work as an NFL referee in 2021. Chaka, a health and physical education teacher, began her officiating career in 2006 at high school games. She moved into the collegiate ranks with Conference USA, and in 2014, entered the NFL Officiating Development Program after scouts observed her officiating college football games. She first made history in 2014 when she became the first Black woman to officiate a Football Bowl Subdivision (FBS) collegiate bowl game. Chaka recently worked at Pac-12 games, and also worked the sidelines for the short-lived XFL in 2020.

Fencing is one of the first sports played in the Olympics. Its roots can be traced back to swordsmanship and dueling that is believed to have originated in Spain. There are three forms of modern fencing, each of which uses a different weapon and has different rules; the sable, the épée, and the foil. In America, dueling metamorphosed into a sport, and took place in private clubs where only White men were allowed to join. In time, fencing lost its snob appeal and gained enough democratic vigor to become egalitarian enough in some quarters to promote women's fencing. In 1936, the New York Fencers Club allowed women to become active members, and in 1949, it contributed to the official breaking of the color line.

During the 1930s, Violet Barker, who learned to fence at the Harlem YWCA from fencing coach Alec Hern, won a recreational league championship sponsored by the Works Programs Administration (WPA), earning a membership card to the Amateur Fencers League of America (AFLA).[31] But when she arrived at the New York Fencers Club to participate in an AFLA open foil meet, she was barred from competition and her membership card was torn up. Barker never fenced again.

During the 1950s, African Americans were gaining acceptance from the AFLA and were winning fencing titles in intercollegiate meets. Sophronia Pierce Stent was captain of the New York University Fencing team in 1951 and became

---

31. The Amateur Fencers League of America (AFLA) changed its name to the United States Fencing Association in 1981, and moved its headquarters in New York to Colorado Springs.

the first Black woman to gain admission to the AFLA. In 1969, Ruth White became the first Black woman to win a national fencing title when she won the under-nineteen crown in foil in high school. After winning her second Senior national championship, she became the first African American female fencer to represent the U.S. at the Munich 1972 Summer Olympics. She was inducted into the USA Fencing Hall of Fame in 2001.

Nikki Franke competed in the women's individual and team foil events at the Montreal 1976 Summer Olympics. She competed at the 1975 and 1979 Pan American Games, earning a silver medal in the individual competition in 1975 and a bronze medal in the team event both years. She qualified for the U.S. Olympic team but did not compete due to the Moscow 1980 Summer Olympics boycott. Franke has served as head coach of the Temple University women's fencing team in Philadelphia since 1972, and is the cofounder, along with Tina Sloan Green, of the Black Women in Sport Foundation.

Sharon Monplaisir, a foil fencer, was a member of the U.S. Olympic fencing team in 1984, 1988, and 1992; a member of the U.S. World Team from 1985 to 1992 and a U.S. national champion in 1988; and a member of the Pan American teams that won the gold medal in 1987 and 1991. Erinn Smart was a member of the U.S. Fencing team at the Beijing 2008 Summer Olympics and won a silver medal in her team event. She was the U.S. national champion in 1988, 2002, 2004, and 2008, and was ranked 11 at the 2003 World Championships (Kirsch, Harris, and Nolte 2000).

Ibtihaj Muhammad, a sabre fencer, earned the bronze medal as part of Team USA at the Rio de Janeiro 2016 Summer Olympics, becoming the first Black woman and Muslim American athlete to do so. She retired from competition in 2019. Nzingha Prescod, a foil fencer, was a bronze medalist at the 2015 World Fencing Championships, and took part in the individual event at the London 2012 Summer Olympics. In 2020, facing the necessity of hip replacement surgery, Prescod announced her retirement from competition.

With the introduction of professional women's leagues, increased sponsorship for women's athletic endeavors, and new young stars on the horizon, Black women's participation in nontraditional sports continues to grow exponentially.

◆ ◆ ◆

BODY SHAMING: EXPRESSING MOCKERY or criticism about a person's body shape or size. *Her butt and thighs are too big. Her arms and legs are too muscular. She is an "ape" and a "gorilla." She looks like a man. She is a freak.* Body shaming is a unique brand of discrimination African American women are subjected to that is highly prevalent in the sports world. Make no mistake; it is racist, sexist, anti-Black misogyny (also known as *misogynoir*), as much as it is disturbing and hurtful. Instead of admiring the physique of Black women athletes who take their sport seriously with a trophy case to prove it, they often find themselves body shamed in a hurtful way that is reminiscent of the Hottentot Venus.[32]

When I selected photographs for this book's sports section, I wanted to illuminate these women's power and beauty. I deeply admired their physique as well as their expressions of drive and determination, knowing they would never be fully accepted in the sports community because of the shape of their bodies and the color of their skin.

This association between beauty and whiteness has been hard to shake. There is a reason so many people still think of an "all-American beauty" as a thin, blonde, blue-eyed White woman. In time, Americans, both consciously and unconsciously, have accepted this narrow definition of beauty even though few White women can live up to it. For a while, the success of Black women athletes was ignored by the White media and the athletic establishment due to segregation, but the underlying racial assumptions also played a role (Cahn 2015). Black women still had to deal with how they dressed, how they wore their hair, and if their bodies could come close to meeting a European standard. Anything less was often met with subtle racist attacks. But by the 1960s, the genie was out of the bottle, and Black women athletes were no longer being fully ignored.

The Black is Beautiful movement in the 1960s and 1970s that came about during the Black Power Movement was about affirming the beauty of blackness, which still resonates to this day. The continued prominence of Black women in sports and the impact of the civil rights movement forced some change in how athletes were being depicted, especially when they found themselves under the international glare of the U.S.-Soviet Union's Cold War athletic rivalry.

It should then come as no surprise that the sports industry perpetuated racist notions that Black women are hypermasculine and unattractive because it had been instilled in all aspects of American society. Of all the Black women athletes, it is the body shaming of Serena Williams that is the most prevalent. Since she is the world's most successful African American female athlete and the most visible, Williams has endured more abuse than any other athlete in recent memory. Her body has been scrutinized and lampooned, and she has been called a "gorilla" and likened to being a man. Williams' integrity has also been questioned, and rumors about her taking steroids have circulated repeatedly. Ironically, as Black women, we see Williams as curvy, sensual and attractive, and we see ourselves in her.

Williams has earned more prize money than any female player in tennis history, but when it comes to endorsements, for years, she has been continually

---

32. Sara Baartman aka Saartjie Bartman (1789-1815) was best known as a South African Khoikhoi woman who, due to the European objectification of her buttocks, was exhibited as a freak show attraction in nineteenth century Europe under the name "Hottentot Venus." After her death, she was autopsied and her body parts were displayed at the Musée de l'Homme for 150 years. When Nelson Mandela became president of South Africa in 1994, he formally requested that France return the remains. After much legal wrangling, Baartman's remains were repatriated to her homeland and buried in 2002. Today she is seen by many as the epitome of colonial exploitation and racism, and of the ridicule and commodification of Black women throughout the world.

overshadowed by Maria Sharapova. How is it possible that Sharapova, whom Williams has beaten nearly twenty times, earned more endorsements than Williams? Because endorsements do not necessarily reward the best athlete, but rather, reward the most marketable to Western culture. For the Black woman athlete, beauty is in the eye of its beholder, which, in this case, is White America.[33]

After Williams became injured in 2003 and underwent a surgical procedure and temporarily gained weight, she was fat-shamed by the international media and tennis community. When the seventeen-year-old Sharapova defeated Williams and won the 2004 Wimbledon crown, the tennis community and the public breathed a collective sigh of relief. This was the winner they could get behind: a young, thin, blonde, green-eyed beauty. She was not muscular or powerful, nor exciting or interesting. She was non-threatening. *She fits in.* But her winner status did not last long, and in time, Williams would beat Sharapova in nineteen straight matches, though it did not matter. Sharapova, who was more likable and marketable, was justly awarded, quickly becoming the highest-paid endorsed female athlete before injuries and a suspension for taking a banned substance dented her earnings and her reputation, forcing her to retire. To be clear, Sharapova's talent was not a fluke, but she was nowhere near the tennis player Williams is. Still, it was not until 2016 that Williams broke Sharapova's eleven-year reign as tennis' highest paid endorsed female athlete.

Williams would be attacked over her hairstyles and tennis attire throughout the years while also being ridiculed for her drive and determination. Anytime she stood up for herself, she would get swatted down. It illustrates how women of color—particularly Black women—cannot stand up for themselves without being perceived as abusive. *The New York Times* even published an article in 2015 during the Wimbledon tournament that consisted of firsthand commentary from several of Williams' top competitors in which they expressed the desire to "not look manly like Serena."[34] Besides the fact that many people found the article absurd because Williams' body does not conform to some tiny little White girl paradigm, it was outrageously narrow-minded and insulting.

The beauty standard in sports seemingly translates to women being more concerned with a marketable image than athletic ability, with White women athletes being particularly self-conscious about being judged by their physicality. *Does she want to be the highest-paid female athlete or the best one?* Williams always wanted to be both, even if it meant rejection in certain spaces. And this is what countless Black women athletes have always had to deal with: racist, sexist, and transphobic scrutiny because of their beautiful, muscular Black bodies. This subtle interplay of racial and gender stereotypes have certainly done great

33. Kareem Abdul-Jabbar, "Body Shaming Black Female Athletes Is Not Just About Race," *Time* magazine, July 20, 2015, https://time.com/3964758/body shaming-Black-female-athletes.

34. Ben Rothenberg, "Tennis' Top Women Balance Body Image With Ambition," *The New York Times,* July 10, 2015, https://www.nytimes.com/2015/07/11/sports/tennis/tenniss-top-women-balance-body image-with-quest-for-success.html.

damage to Black women athletes, but it may have indirectly constricted the athletic possibilities of other women as well, helping to make sports a somewhat illegitimate activity for all women.

It is hard to separate Williams' race and gender from how she has been treated during her tremendous career in the predominantly White sport of tennis. Even as Williams is nearing the end of a career that has changed the face of tennis forever, she continues to be slighted by corporate elites, the media, and the sports community because she does not meet their ideal of what a tennis player should look like. For decades, Black women athletes have faced similar criticism, compounded by inequality, lack of support, and unrealistic societal expectations. Although there has been progress, it has not been enough. As for Williams, her mindset is unbreakable, and throughout her career she has done her best to ignore this narrative simply by virtue of being her authentic self.

If Americans are to acknowledge their authenticity, we must question our ideals of physical beauty and overcome preconceived notions based on one set of standards. There is beauty in all cultures and all races, and there is a whole new narrative breaking through—that women athletes come in all shapes, sizes, and colors. If body shaming is to be eradicated from our culture, we must do so in an intersectional way that empowers all aspects of our daily lives.

◆ ◆ ◆

AFTER SPENDING CONSIDERABLE TIME researching women in sports and the Black athlete, it led me to ask: Why do women's sports leagues and teams struggle to gain traction, even as hundreds of thousands of girls and young women are developing an interest in sports? My initial take came from a feminist viewpoint that women were simply being betrayed due to sexism. I also questioned whether women and men should play together and compete against each other to have true equality in sports. But when I further investigated this issue by talking to male colleagues who are not only sports enthusiasts, but feminists and former athletes, *I learned some things.*

I thought spectators looked at sports for the purity of the game. Nothing could be further from the truth. Although the attraction of sports was once owed entirely to its unpredictability and uncertainty, the nature of sports has evolved into an entertaining spectacle because it is the fans that create and shape the experience of sports. They are not just passive receptors, but active participants of the game itself. As they influence action on the field of play, the players oblige with winning moves that entertain. This is one reason why men's sports are seen as more exciting and entertaining than women's.

Take basketball, for example. I have named some women basketball players who are phenomenal in their own right, but they will never play like their male counterparts. The men play differently. They do dunks and play above the rim, shoot better from the field, and dazzle audiences with leaps and fancy footwork.

The men are bigger, stronger, and more powerful than women. The average height of an NBA player is nearly a foot taller than the average man. And if this is not convincing, imagine this: Have you ever tried shaking the hand of an NBA player? LeBron James, who is six feet and eight inches tall, has a hand length of nine inches and a hand span of nine and a quarter inches. When you shake his hand, your hand is engulfed and seemingly disappears. He can catch and pass a basketball with the palm of that hand—something few women, if any, can do.

For this reason, women basketball players cannot deliver the showmanship that fans expect from the men. Sports fans will tell you they think women's basketball is less compelling than men's basketball because there is not enough scoring or dunking, and they do not run as fast. The reasoning for this is cultural; a woman's version of "something" is always portrayed as slower and dumbed down. This has been the primary reason why the women's leagues have not been as popular or sustainable as the men's leagues.

Am I suggesting that women are inferior to men? *Absolutely not.* Nor do I hold the belief that "boys are better at sports than girls" or that women on average are smaller and weaker than men. What I am suggesting is that the public has been conditioned to expect certain things from certain sports through the lens of how men play, which is often translated as "better" than women.

This also hinges on the fact that the NBA, MLB, NHL, and NFL are part of a multibillion-dollar industry that develops entertainment-driven strategies around its major sporting events on a global scale that is far superior than it was merely a decade or two ago. It is no longer enough to win on the court, or on the field; there is an even greater need to entertain as well. The 60,000 people filling an arena for a sporting event expect entertainment as much as the 60,000 filling an arena for a rock concert. Women's showmanship is not seen as being on par with the men's, and because they lack resources, they have been unable to draw an equal following. The same goes for the millions who watch the games on television, where advertising dollars have become the men's leagues' bread and butter.

Some believe that due to gender inequity, men's sports have higher production values, higher-media coverage, and higher-quality commentary. Others have chastised feminist and women-based media for not promoting and covering women's sports. I suspect that all of these things play a part, but a major contributing factor is women's role within American society. While women have gained relative equality, they have not fully squashed gendered stereotypes, especially in sports. Plainly stated, some female and male spectators have no interest in watching women play sports simply because they see most team sports as a man's game. But in recent years, the opinion of sports fans seem to be shifting. There is a growing consensus that female athletes are just as skillful as their male counterparts, and that women's sports are just as exciting to watch.

And then, some success stories have been undercut due to gender discrimination. For example, the USWNT, the most successful team in international women's soccer, sued the U.S. Soccer Federation (USSF) in 2019, claiming discrimination in pay and working conditions. The U.S. women's soccer games have generated more revenue than U.S. men's games over the past three years. For example, from 2016 to 2018, women's games generated approximately $50.8 million in revenue, compared with $49.9 million for men's games.[35] Unfortunately, in May 2019, a U.S. district court judge rejected the USWNT's allegations of pay inequity and ruled in favor of the USSF, declaring that the team has not been underpaid, but will allow their allegation of discriminatory working conditions to go to trial. As of 2021, the pay decision is under review by the 9th U.S. Circuit Court of Appeals, but there is a chance that the USSF will settle. This stunning decision has buoyed the USWNT and made them more captivating than ever before, while, for the USSF, it has been a public relations nightmare. Their most hard-line argument has been that women's and men's national team players do not perform equal work requiring equal skill, effort, and responsibility under similar working conditions. The USSF, which has a track record of not doing the right thing until called out publicly, is on notice.

On the flip side, some sports teams have created successful financial formulas. In Oregon, the women's soccer team, the Portland Thorns, has seen its attendance continuously rise and improve. Their average regular-season attendance in 2019 was 20,098 fans and has become more popular than their affiliated male counterpart, the Portland Timber of Major League Soccer (MLS), the first men's soccer team willing to partner with a women's team. In fact, the Portland Thorns are considered the most successful professional women's sports team in the world. Women's soccer teams like the Orlando Pride, Houston Dash, and the North Carolina Courage are gaining success after using a similar formula forged in Portland.[36] It appears that women's sports teams are beginning to gain recognition as they build fan bases on their own terms.

Losing money had become commonplace for women's leagues for years. When we look at the oldest surviving women's league, the Women's National Basketball Association (WNBA), founded in 1996 and subsidized by the NBA, it just managed to survive relative to other women's professional sports leagues, but it did not achieve immediate financial success. Nowadays, it looks like the WNBA has finally turned the corner with better teams, a stronger union, and better venues.

In fact, women's sports leagues and organizations are focused on devising better practices that could increase profitability and draw more spectators to their events. We know this is possible because on a collegiate level, for example,

---

35. Abigail Hess, "US women's soccer games now generate more revenue than men's—but the players still earn less," *CNBC-Make It,* July 10, 2019, https://www.cnbc.com/2019/06/19/uswomens-soccer-games-now-generate-more-revenue-than-mens.html.

36. Caitlin Murray, "A Blueprint for Women's Sports Success. But Can It Be Copied?", *The New York Times,* October 13, 2017, https://www.nytimes.com/2017/10/13/sports/soccer/portland-thorns-nwsl.html.

basketball teams—such as Tennessee's Lady Volunteers—regularly sell out and often draw bigger crowds than the men's team. Connecticut's Lady Huskies also draw sell-out crowds, just like the men. Throughout the years, as quickly as one league folds, another pops up to take its place. Women, if nothing else, are persistent and hard-pressed not to give up.

This is attributed to Title IX's passage forty-four years ago, which paved the way for girls and women to participate in sports in unprecedented numbers. Forty percent of all sports participants are female, and roughly a third of major sports fans are women.[37] There has also been a generational shift since the 1970s, with many father-daughter relationships evolving to include sports, whether it is on a spectator or participatory level. The evolution of women's sports has been spectacular. Women's participation in the Olympics, competitions, and tournaments, particularly in gymnastics, track and field, and tennis, is flourishing, especially with the help of superstar Black women athletes.

Some have immediately concluded that if there was more sponsorship and media coverage, women's sports would become more popular. Media outlets and sponsors retort that if women's sports attracted more interest in the first place, then they would invest more time and money into it. But all sides agree that for a sport to be successful, it requires a balance of consumer, media, and commercial appeal. In the end, regardless of what anyone thinks, women's sports leagues and teams are not going away.

As someone who firmly believes in and supports gender equality—and in this day and age, everyone should—I have come to accept the fact that the physical differences between women and men have played a role in the development of some of the women's sports leagues. This is compounded by the lack of television rights and sponsorship agreements, the corresponding lack of funding for salaries, training and development facilities, and the lack of affiliation with profitable men's professional clubs, all of which have hampered the growth of women's leagues in the U.S. Moreover, men's sports leagues and teams receive other benefits, like billions in taxpayer subsidies and far more free coverage from a sports media dominated by men. It is the classic chicken-and-egg question—should the media create audiences for new subjects, or do they exist to reflect what audiences already want? Or is it all an excuse for gender discrimination?

We also cannot discount race when we talk about the lack of coverage of women athletes, especially when the number of people of color competing vastly outnumbers the people of color reporting on them. While more women sportswriters should lead to more coverage, that is not the overall solution. Just as we need more women, we also need more LGBTQ and people of color to counteract how homogeneous sports reporting has always been.

---

37. Amanda Ottaway, "Why Don't People Watch Women's Sports? Ask sports journalists." *The Nation,* July 20, 2016. https://www.thenation.com/article/archive/why-dont-people-watch-womens-sports.

There is also something else to consider: men's sports leagues did not start out as an overnight success, but it was years in the making. We have witnessed an organic process that includes the purity of sports during the 1950s and 1960s when it was rougher, tougher, smaller, and less visible; the creativity and growth of sports during the 1970s; the rise of sports television programming in the 1980s; the ascension of professional football and basketball, and the substantial increase of advertising revenue during the 1990s; the raw athleticism of the 2000s; and the huge multimedia deals of the 2010s. One should take note that for a long time, it was not uncommon for athletes to hold off-season jobs, and it was not until the early 1970s that we first saw million-dollar contracts, followed by multimillion-dollar deals in the 1990s. When player salaries and endorsement deals exploded in the millennium, it had taken nearly sixty years to reach these unprecedented levels. So it can be said that men's sports, as we know them today, benefit from a far greater track record than women's sports. Because the history of women's sports is relatively shorter, one could argue that women's leagues today are much like the men's leagues of the past.

Two of the oldest professional organizations—the Ladies Professional Golf Association (LPGA), founded in 1950, and the Women's Tennis Association (WTA) founded in 1973—have garnered great success. Perhaps not surprisingly, it is in these two sports that women earn the most money, even as they struggle to attain prize earnings comparable to men. It is highly likely that as women's sports leagues and teams continue to develop, they will find their own following and niche and become economically sustainable and successful in their own right.

The gender pay gap spans almost every industry, and the sports industry is no exception. Most women athletes are paid like mailroom scrubs in a major corporation compared to their male counterparts, but discrepancies vary between particular sports. In tennis, pay is comparable, but in basketball, players are in entirely different zip codes. For example, in 2020, DeWanna Bonner (forward) of the Phoenix Mercury was one of the WNBA's top earners at $215,000 per year, while Stephen Curry (point guard) of the Golden State Warriors was the top paid NBA player with an annual income of $40.2 million, including endorsements.[38] Unfortunately, the pay disparities come down almost entirely to their teams and leagues' revenue, with women players earning less than 25 percent of their team's total revenue.[39] Bearing this in mind, women players focus on changes

---

38. Angela Bucalo, "Who is the Highest Paid WNBA Player?," *ONE37PM*, September 9, 2020, https://www.one37pm.com/strength/sports/highest-paid-wnba-player; Jill Painter Lopez, "Here Are The Five NBA Players Whose 2019-2020 Salaries Top LeBron James'," *Sports Illustrated,* April 30, 2020, https://www.si.com/nba/lakers/news/here-are-the-five-nba-players-whose-2019-2020-salaries-top-lebron-james.

39. David Berri, "Basketball's Growing Gender Wage Gap: The Evidence The WNBA Is Underpaying Players," *Forbes,* September 20, 2017, https://www.forbes.com/sites/davidberri/2017/09/20/there-is-a-growing-gender-wage-gap-in-professional-basketball/#29afe39536e0.

that will directly impact them, like where and how often they play, how they train and travel, their medical treatment, and the coaching they receive.

For some players, their WNBA salary is not their highest source of income. After a tough WNBA season, some players hop on a plane overseas to tend to their more lucrative six-figure league contracts. I think it is clear: the ballers of the WNBA work harder for less pay. Endorsement deals in the WNBA have been scarce since Sheryl Swoopes' history-making sneaker deal with Nike in 1995. In 2020, the Washington Mystics' Natasha Cloud became the first women's basketball player to ink a shoe deal with Converse, but she is not earning the big bucks. This, of course, begs the larger question: Should women athletes be paid the same as their male counterparts? It is a question that produces an emotional and heated debate, but in the end, we need to do better to recognize the value and power of all women athletes. The sports industry needs to acknowledge and highlight the talent of women in sports who deserve the same campaign and endorsement deals as their male counterparts.

Finally, do I still believe women and men should play together and compete with each other? Certainly, physical differences remain a significant factor, but in all honesty, I really do not know if it is feasible in all sports, nor do I think it is absolutely necessary to achieve true equality. As a woman, I like that there are differences between women and men, and sometimes I enjoy the "separateness" from men in not only sports, but in other aspects of our lives—a somewhat sentimental notion that will no doubt exasperate some readers. But what I do believe is that it should be for the good of the sport when it happens.

Sports carries a great deal of responsibility for diversity and inclusion. In recent years, it has been very encouraging to witness most of the major professional and amateur sports leagues take this concept to heart. I believe that the most important aspect of sports is that, as it coincides with community values and political agencies, it will continuously attempt to define the morals and ethics attributed not only to athletes but also to society as a whole. If we continue to ignore and diminish the importance of women athletes, and Black and Brown athletes in particular, we are subconsciously sending a message that women of every stripe are unimportant and ultimately unequal. This attitude is wholly unacceptable in the world we live in today.

◆ ◆ ◆

THE SPORTS ARENA OPERATES as an important symbolic space in the struggle for freedom and liberty, cultural recognition, and civic rights against the ideologies and practices of White supremacy. Because sports were among the first and most high-profile spaces to accept African Americans on relative terms of equality, they have had a unique role in American culture. From the refusal to allow African Americans an opportunity to compete, to the formation of segregated sporting teams and leagues, to integration and the dismantling of those leagues, as well as the hard-won battles to compete at the highest levels of the game, the African American presence in sports has always had social and political implications on American society.

As a result, the Black athlete has been more successful than any other group in any other endeavor in American life. Despite the odds, Black women athletes' achievements have been nothing less than spectacular. These women have broken barriers, raised the bar, shifted perspectives, and achieved parity with Black male athletes and their White female counterparts in college sports, the Olympics, and professionally. Although there are hardly any people of color, including Black women, in major positions in each of the major sports leagues, including discrepancies in the number of Black owners, coaches, officials, and administrators, the sports world continues to grow toward equality. It may not be as fast as we would like, but we have witnessed some progress.

It is clear that women's involvement in sports was slow to develop due to sexism, racism, and classism. The advent of the civil rights and women's liberation movements and Title IX has been monumental in women's and girls' sports participation. While it helped close the gap between women and men's participation, a disparity still looms large, in that White women have become the overwhelming beneficiaries.[40] This underrepresentation of athletes of color is not just an issue for female athletes: male athletes of color have yet to achieve parity in all areas of sports as well.

One should appreciate that these athletes do not labor under radically different stereotypes than any other Black women in society. The difference is that they do it on a field of play, court, or in a pool under intense scrutiny and under the gaze of fans who often feel entitled to take everything they do personally. Unfortunately, Black women athletes are forced to deal with a whole other layer of athleticism, including hypervisibility, sexuality, body shaming, media influences, and athletic status. But despite these hurdles, each athlete in her own way has made history, won a race, shattered a record, and endured a loss. Collectively, they have created ripples that have become waves. Their experience is uniquely American. They are champions. *They are us.*❖

---

40. William C. Rhoden, "Black and White Women Far From Equal Under Title IX," *The New York Times,* June 10, 2012, https://www.nytimes.com/2012/06/11/sports/title-ix-has-not-given-Black-female-athletes-equal-opportunity.html.

Ora Washington
(1898-1971)
Tennis player, basketball player

Ora Washington was the first African American female sports celebrity during the height of the Great Depression and Jim Crow era who dominated tennis and basketball.

ORA WASHINGTON was born in Caroline County, Virginia to Laura O. Young-Washington and James "Tommy" Washington. Her family owned a farm and grew corn, wheat, rye, and tobacco, their biggest crop. They also raised hogs and some occasional cows and sold meat (Lansbury 2014). The fifth of nine children, Washington worked on the farm from an early age, doing household tasks since her father did not want his daughters working in the fields. In the summertime, the small Black community would play sports like baseball and croquet, which is where Washington began to show her athletic skills and competitive edge. After her mother died in 1908, Washington's father sent her to live with an aunt in Philadelphia, and she found work as a maid. Her family eventually moved North around 1912, and they settled in Germantown, a racially diverse community in northern Philadelphia.

Washington did not begin to play organized sports seriously until she was nearly twenty-five. After one of her sisters died from tuberculosis, an instructor at the Young Women's Christian Association (YWCA) in Germantown suggested she might soothe her grief by engaging in physical activity. When organized tennis in the Black community was still in its infancy, the Germantown YMCA was deservedly proud of its courts (Lansbury 2014). Also, with workweeks reduced to eight-hour days, an increasing number of leisure activities became available—amusement parks, dance halls, movie theaters and sports. Sports were capturing the imagination of the American public, and Washington chose to play tennis. Within a year, she won her first national tournament championship.

Since sports were racially segregated, Washington only competed against other African Americans. In response to the United States Tennis Association (USTA) ban on Black players, a group of African American businessmen, college professors, and physicians founded the American Tennis Association (ATA) in 1916, which would become the oldest Black sports organization in the U.S. Washington's unorthodox stroke—she held the racket above the grip and stabbed at the ball with a short poke—powerful serve and overhead, combined with her agility and quickness, enabled Washington to reign as the undisputed "Queen of Tennis." In her first five seasons for singles, she won titles up and down the East Coast and held the ATA's national crown from 1929 to 1936.

Helen Willis Moody, who conquered the prestigious White world of Wimbledon and Forest Hills with much of the same thoroughness as Washington in the Black community, and was considered by many to be the best White tennis player during that era, refused to play her. Segregation had its grip on America, and the color line in tennis would remain undisturbed until 1951, when Althea Gibson made history by becoming the first African American to be invited to play at Wimbledon.

Washington lived for a short period in Chicago, where she worked as a hotel maid and attended the Chicago Presbyterian Training School. She also began playing basketball with the Savoy Colts, the sister team of the city's Savoy Big Five, one of the era's leading professional Black basketball teams. She enjoyed basketball and found that it kept her in shape for the tennis court. While tennis was a sport for the upper classes, working class Black women embraced basketball. It was an accessible sport that required no equipment and was inexpensive to play. These Black women on barnstorming teams from public schools and community teams played like their male counterparts, and Washington played just as hard, competing to win (Lansbury 2014).

When she returned to Philadelphia, she joined the Germantown Hornets basketball team in 1930, sponsored by the YWCA. As the starting center, Washington helped the team post a 22-1 record and win the female national title that same year. She played tennis and basketball simultaneously for almost twenty years.

At the end of the basketball season in 1931, the Hornets had the best record in the country, 21-1, and were declared the National Champion. The team broke away from the YWCA the following year to become a semiprofessional team, providing much-needed income for Washington and her teammates. The Hornets' success caught the attention of the Tribune Girls, who were sponsored by the *Philadelphia Tribune,* the city's oldest Black newspaper. They signed Washington away from the Hornets the very next season.

Washington never married, and it was alleged that she lived with a series of female companions. As a result, her questionable lifestyle and her plain-looking demeanor made her a less than ideal female sports star of the ATA, and some even felt her dominance in the sport was bad for the game. An injury on the basketball court forced Washington to retire from tennis single competitions. Then unexpectedly, she came out of retirement in 1939 to compete against up-and-coming star Flora Lomax, a doctor's daughter who epitomized the ATA's ideal woman athlete. Washington was determined to put to rest rumors that she retired to avoid defeat to the new Black woman star. So she enrolled in a tournament in Buffalo specifically to play Lomax. She beat her, and after proving her point, retired from singles for good.

Nevertheless, she continued to play doubles until the late 1940s and earned twelve doubles titles and three mixed doubles championships to add to her already impressive trophy case. Still, Washington's achievement did not go unnoticed and would have long-reaching effects. As part of Depression-era work and recovery programs, her success encouraged the Franklin D. Roosevelt administration to build public tennis courts in urban areas where the game was unfamiliar. Future champions like Gibson and Arthur Ashe, the first Black woman and man to win Wimbledon and the U.S. Open, would learn the game on those courts.

The Tribune Girls was considered Black America's first premier female sports team. Although the team's opponents were mostly Black teams, they occasionally played against White teams. Washington led the Tribune Girls in scoring and had a brief stint as the head coach. Not all games were played by women's rules, though; the team often played by men's rules, without any noticeable strain. The Tribune Girls barnstormed throughout the East Coast and the South and the Midwest. They had no rivals, and Washington was their star. They only lost six games during the 1930s and won ten straight Women's Colored Basketball World Championships. Washington played with the Tribune Girls until 1943. The team disbanded due to a shake-up at the newspaper coupled with America's entry into World War II, which also stalled the momentum of all major sports. Washington retired from sports altogether after she and tennis partner George Stewart defeated Gibson and Walter Johnson to win the 1947 ATA mixed doubles title, defending their doubles crown. And then, she disappeared from the public eye.

Off the courts, Washington was described as a kind, caring person, who was always looking out for others. Had Washington been born White and fifty years later, she undoubtedly would have been crowned by acclamation the greatest woman athlete of the twentieth century, much in the same way that Babe Didrikson is celebrated. But her competitive zeal remained fierce. During her sports career, Washington had supplemented her income by working as a domestic and eventually bought a house with her younger sister, securing a place to live for the remainder of her life. Over the years, nobody paid attention to her. Everyone was paying attention to Gibson, Jackie Robinson, and Wilma Rudolph, who had come along at a time when a broader spotlight shined on Black athletes. Washington never left sports completely; she regularly coached tennis and gave free clinics on the public courts near her home in Germantown.

After a long illness, Ora Washington died on May 28, 1971, in Philadelphia. She was seventy-three years old and had been largely forgotten. Five years later, she was inducted into the Black Athletes Hall of Fame along with Paul Robeson in 1976, and then she was inducted into Temple University's Sports Hall of Fame in 1986, elected to the Women's Basketball Hall of Fame in 2009, and inducted in the Naismith Memorial Basketball Hall of Fame in 2018.❖

Toni Stone
(1921-1996)
Baseball player

Toni Stone made history when she signed with the Indianapolis Clowns, becoming the first African American woman to play professionally for the Negro League.

MARCENIA LYLE STONE ALBERGA was born in Bluefield, West Virginia to Willa Stone and Boykin Stone. A decade later her family joined the Great Migration to the North, and moved to St. Paul's Rondo neighborhood in Minneapolis, where Stone's parents opened a beauty shop. When she was barely a teenager, people began to notice that Stone was far from ordinary. She was an astonishing athlete who seemed to excel at everything she attempted: swimming, golf, track, basketball, hockey, tennis and ice skating. She was even the most feared kid in the neighborhood when it came to playing red rover, but baseball won her heart and she devoted hours toward reading books to improve her game (Ackmann 2017).

Stone did not share the same talent in the classroom as her siblings. By the time she was ten years old, Stone's parents asked a local Catholic priest to talk her out of playing baseball, but instead the priest invited her to play with his team, the St. Peter Clavers in the Catholic Midget League. She moved on to play for the Girls' Highlex Softball Club in St. Paul. As a student at Roosevelt High School in Minneapolis, she lettered in track and field, high jump and softball.

At age fifteen, Stone was quietly earning a reputation as something of a phenom. She attended a baseball camp at Lexington Park, home of the St. Paul Saints of the American Baseball Association. When former Major Leaguer Charles Evard "Gabby" Street, who ran the camp, told Stone that the camp was only for boys, she was persistent and was allowed to play. He even bought Stone her first pair of cleats (Ackmann 2017). During the 1936-1937 season, Stone worked out with the St. Paul Saints, and eventually dropped out of high school to earn money playing for the Twin City Colored Giants, a men's semiprofessional barnstorming team that took her throughout the Midwest and Canada.

Since baseball was no longer a national priority during World War II, Stone moved to San Francisco to help her sick sister, who moved there with her husband when he joined the military. She eventually met her future husband, Aurelious P. Alberga, who was forty years older than her, and one of the first Black officers in the U.S. Army after the Civil War. They married in 1950.

Living in California, Stone scraped together a living working at a cafeteria, and as a forklift operator in a shipyard. She also began what can only be described as a personal reinvention: she changed her name to "Toni Stone" and dropped ten years off her age to increase her appeal to baseball teams. She played for the Wall Post American Legion team, before joining the barnstorming semiprofessional team, the San Francisco Sea Lions, of the West Coast Negro League. Stone left the team when she did not receive the salary she had been promised.

By 1949, Stone joined the Black Pelicans of New Orleans. After a short stint with them, she played for the New Orleans Creoles from 1949 to 1952. Yet during the spring and summer, she traveled the country playing baseball before returning home to Oakland in the off-season. When Jackie Robinson made his first appearance in the majors in 1947, Black baseball players made their departures, including the Indianapolis Clowns' prized second baseman, Hank Aaron, who left to play for the Milwaukee Braves. In the wake of this upheaval, team owner Syd Pollack figured Stone might draw some fans because she was a woman.

In 1953, Stone signed to play with the Indianapolis Clowns in the Negro American League, replacing Aaron. The team, which had developed a reputation as a showy kind of team, not unlike what basketball's Harlem Globetrotters would become, needed a boost. While most sports fans believed the Clowns signed Stone merely as a box-office attraction, she surprised everyone by turning in a business-like job at both second base and at the plate. In her first game against a semiprofessional team in Elizabeth, North Carolina, she walked and then drove in two runs with a sharp single, but it was not an easy life.

Since Stone was one of the first women to play in the Negro Leagues, she drew a great deal of attention. Some of it had to do with her baseball skills, but most of it focused on her being a woman. Although she was subject to a barrage of insults from fans and even teammates who objected to seeing a woman compete in a man's game, she prevailed. The complicated rules surrounding Jim Crow only amplified the pressure, as she and other Black players had to be careful not to patronize White-only establishments.

Even though she was part of the team, Stone was not allowed in the locker room. If she was lucky, she would be allowed to change in the umpire's locker room and would come out by the middle of the game so she could shower and change before the rest of the team returned.

On the playing field she would wear an oversized shirt to accommodate her bustline, and would think, talk, and play like a man. Once, Stone was asked to wear a skirt while playing for sex appeal, but she refused. Even though she felt like she was "one of the guys," the men felt otherwise. Her opponents showed little deference, sometimes coming hard at her on a slide with their spikes pointed up. She often brandished her wounds as battle scars.

Despite facing discrimination on all fronts, Stone maintained her impact on the field (Ackmann 2017), Stone played hard and did not back down from any challenges that came her way. Backed by some pretty good publicity to showcase their new female player, she managed to play in fifty games that year. She also got a chance to play with some excellent talent, including Willie Mays, Ernie Banks, and actually notched a hit off Satchel Paige, who was perhaps the best pitcher to ever live.

After the 1953 season, Stone's contract was sold to the Kansas City Monarchs. Her spot in the Indianapolis infield was taken by another woman, Connie Morgan, and the Clowns added pitcher Mamie "Peanut" Johnson. The trade proved to be a difficult adjustment, and Stone spent most of the game on the bench sitting next to the men who hated her. During the 1954 season, Stone discovered something she never thought would happen, she lost her joy for the game, and she retired from professional baseball. Her two-year batting average in the Negro Leagues estimated at .243 (Ackmann 2017). After the Negro Leagues dissolved, the achievements of Stone and countless others, were quickly forgotten. Stone moved to Oakland to work as a nurse, but continued to play semiprofessional baseball and coached local teams, well into her sixties. She cared for her husband until his death in 1987 at the age of 103.

Stone did live to witness public acknowledgment of her sports career later in life, and was thankful for the recognition. She was featured in local and national media, and in 1990, Stone was included in two exhibits at the Baseball Hall of Fame: "Women in Baseball" and "Negro League Baseball." That same year her hometown of St. Paul, Minnesota declared March 6 "Toni Stone Day." In 1991, she was invited to attend the first official recognition of the Negro League in the Hall of Fame's history in Cooperstown. In 1993, Stone was inducted into the Women's Sports Foundation's International Women's Sports Hall of Fame, and the Sudafed International Women's Sports Hall of Fame. In 1996, the Dunning Baseball Complex in St. Paul dedicated The Toni Stone Field.

No other woman ever matched Stone's accomplishments in baseball during her nearly two decades of play. She was the first woman to play professional baseball on men's teams in the Negro Leagues of the 1950s. Known as a tenacious athlete with quick hands, a competitive bat, and a ferocious spirit, Stone was a professional (Ackmann 2017). Toni Stone died on November 2, 1996 at a nursing home in Alameda, California. She was seventy-five years old.

The Great American History Theater presented *Tomboy Stone,* a play about Stone, in 1997. Martha Ackmann published *Curveball: The remarkable story of Toni Stone, the first woman to play professional baseball in the Negro League* (2010); and in 2019 it was adapted into the play, *Toni Stone,* by award-winning playwright Lydia R. Diamond.❖

Alice Coachman
(1923-2014)
Track and field athlete, educator, trainer, activist

Alice Coachman was the first African American woman to win an Olympic gold medal at the London 1948 Summer Olympics in the high jump, and the first African American athlete to receive an endorsement deal.

ALICE COACHMAN DAVIS was born in Albany, Georgia to Evelyn Jackson Coachman, of half-Cherokee descent, and Fred Coachman, a U.S. veteran, as the fifth of ten children. Coachman's family was poor, and as a youngster, she had to pick cotton and other crops to help her family meet their financial needs.

At a young age, Coachman attended baseball games with her father, and she loved playing games and competing with the boys on the school playground because the girls were too "ladylike" and not competitive. She began her track career running barefoot on dirt roads and soon developed an interest in high jumping after watching an event at a boys track meet. As a child of the segregated South, she was denied access to training facilities and sports programs, but this did not deter her ambitions. Instead, Coachman devised all sorts of improvised jumping equipment and makeshift setups to jump over—from strings and ropes to sticks and tied rags. This unorthodox training led her to adopt an unusual jumping style that was neither the traditional western roll nor straight-ahead jumping, but rather a blend of both. Since Coachman vaulted much higher than most girls her age, she sought out boys to compete against, and typically beat them as well.

She saw little prospect of an athletic career. In fact, she thought of becoming a musician or a dancer, having been enthralled by saxophonist Coleman Hawkins and child star Shirley Temple. But while she attended Monroe Street Elementary School, Coachman was encouraged by her fifth-grade teacher and her aunt to continue in sports, despite her parents' reservations and restricted access to training facilities.

She caught the attention of Harry E. Lash, the boys' track coach at Madison High School, and competed with the high school team at Tuskegee Institute, breaking high school and college records in the high jump. She then went on to set a new American record in Waterbury, Connecticut at the national AAU. The next summer, after Coachman competed at Tuskegee, she asked her parents if she could attend Tuskegee on a scholarship. They did not want her to go, but she insisted, and they eventually relented. With Lash's encouragement, she attended Tuskegee in 1939. By the time she enrolled in Tuskegee Institute, Coachman had won up to four national track and field championships in the 50-meter dash, 100-meter dash, 400-meter relay, and high jump.

Coachman's scholarship required her to clean and maintain the sports facilities, and mend uniforms. She also sang with the school choir and played in several other sports just for fun, including soccer, field hockey, volleyball, tennis, swimming and basketball. Soon after, Coachman decided she preferred jumping to running track and focused all of her energy on jumping hurdles.

While at Tuskegee, Coachman's skills were honed by women's track coach, Christine Evans Petty, and the school's famous head coach, Cleveland Abbott. Coachman dominated the AAU outdoor high jump championship from 1939 through 1948. Her athletic career culminated in 1943, her graduation year, when she won the AAU Nationals in both the high jump and the 50-yard dash. She was also a standout performer in basketball and played as an All-American guard on the Tuskegee women's basketball team. She led her team to three straight Southern Intercollegiate Athletic Conference (SIAC) women's basketball championships. But her biggest ambition was to compete in the Olympics.

Despite being in her prime, Coachman could not compete in the 1940 and 1944 Olympics as World War II led to their cancellation. She went on to graduate with a degree in dressmaking from Tuskegee in 1946. In a few short years after her graduation, Coachman had won ten straight championships in the high jump between 1939 and 1948, as well as twenty-five indoor and outdoor 50- and 100-meter championships.

She continued her studies and high jumping at Albany State College (now known as Albany State University). After nearly ten years of active competing, Coachman finally got her opportunity to compete at the London 1948 Summer Olympics. While she had not seriously considered participating in the Olympics at this point of her athletic career, Coachman quickly jumped at the chance when Olympic officials invited her to be part of the team. She qualified with a high jump of five feet and four inches, breaking her previous sixteen-year-old record by three-quarters of an inch. In the high jump finals, Coachman leaped five feet and six and one eighth inches—a feat that stood as the record for eight years. Her nearest rival, Great Britain's Dorothy Tyler, matched Coachman's jump, but only on her second try. She was the only American woman at the Olympics to win a gold medal and the first Black woman to finish first. King George VI presented her medal.

Coachman was stunned by the accolades bestowed upon her for her achievement. She quickly understood that her performance at the Olympics had made her an important symbol for Black America and that her victory encouraged other Black women to follow. More recognition greeted Coachman when she returned to the U.S., and she instantly became a celebrity. Soon after meeting President Truman and former First Lady Eleanor Roosevelt, she was honored with parades from Atlanta to Albany, acknowledging her historic achievement. But racism's status quo did not take a break from Coachman's hometown celebration: Blacks and Whites were not allowed to commingle, and while the mayor sat on the same stage with Coachman, he refused to shake her hand. She had to exit through a side door after the event. Coachman and many others believed she would have become a repeating champion, if she had the chance, but at twenty-four years old, she retired from competition. Coachman left behind a phenomenal legacy. Besides becoming the first African American woman to win an Olympic gold medal, she won twenty-five AAU national athletics championships from 1939-1948, including ten high jump titles.

She finished her degree and received a BA in home economics with a minor in science in 1949. After graduation, Coachman forged a distinguishable career as a teacher and a promoter of track and field. She taught high school physical education in Georgia and coached young athletes. She would later teach at South Carolina State College, Albany State University, and the Job Corps.

Although she formally retired from athletic competition, Coachman's star power remained: In 1952, the Coca-Cola Company tapped her to become a spokesperson, making Coachman the first Black woman to earn an endorsement deal. She was prominently featured on billboards alongside 1936 Olympic winner, Jesse Owens. And in her hometown, Alice Avenue and Alice Coachman Elementary School were named in her honor. Coachman married Frank A. Davis and was the mother of two children. Though she had faded from public view, the Black community's pride in her achievements remained undiminished.

As the Atlanta 1996 Summer Olympics approached, Coachman, along with Olympians Anita DeFrantz, Joan Benoit Samuelson, and Aileen Riggin Soule, came to New York to initiate The Olympic Woman, an exhibit sponsored by Avon that honored a century of memorable achievements. At the Olympics, she was honored as one of the 100 greatest Olympians of all time. She later created the Alice Coachman Track and Field Foundation to aid young athletes and former competitors in financial need.

During her career, Coachman won thirty-four national titles, ten for the high jump in consecutive years. She was inducted into nine halls of fame, including the National Track-and-Field Hall of Fame (1975), the U.S. Olympic Hall of Fame (2004), the Georgia Sports Hall of Fame, and the Albany Sports Hall of Fame in Georgia. She was also inducted as an honorary member of Alpha Kappa Alpha Sorority in 1998. In 2002, Coachman was designated as a Women's History Month Honoree by the National Women's History Project, and received recognition for opening the door for future African American track stars such as Evelyn Ashford, Florence Griffith Joyner and Jackie Joyner-Kersee.

Alice Coachman suffered a stroke and died a few months later, on July 14, 2014. She was ninety years old. ❖

Althea Gibson
(1927-2003)
Tennis player, golfer

Althea Gibson was a woman of many firsts. She was the first African American to win the French Open, the first to win a Wimbledon singles title, and the first to play at the U.S. Open. Her remarkable career yielded nearly 100 professional titles, including five Grand Slam crowns. She was also the first African American player to compete on the women's professional golf tour and the first African American woman to appear on the covers of "Sports Illustrated" and "Time."

ALTHEA NEALE GIBSON was born in the town of Silver, in Clarendon County, South Carolina to Annie Bell Gibson and Daniel Gibson, who worked as share-croppers on a corn and cotton farm. The Great Depression hit rural southern farmers sooner than much of the rest of the country, so in 1930 the family moved to New York and settled in Harlem when Gibson was three. Her father secured work as a handyman in a garage and struggled to make ends meet.

The oldest of five children, Gibson grappled in the classroom, often skipping school altogether, but she loved to play sports. Her father taught Gibson how to box, which ironically toughened her up from the corporeal punishment she received from him (Lansbury 2014). The block she lived on had been designated a Police Athletic League (PAL) play area so neighborhood children could play orga-nized sports. Gibson quickly became proficient in paddle tennis, and by 1939 at the age of twelve, she was the New York City women's paddle tennis champion. Her skills were eventually noticed by musician Buddy Walker, who invited her to play tennis at the Harlem River Tennis courts, where she excelled in the game.

At age thirteen, Gibson dropped out of school to devote herself to a bas-ketball team called The Mysterious Girls, and spent her days watching movies. Fearful of her father's beatings because she had become a truant, she lived for a while at the Society for The Prevention of Cruelty to Children (Schoenfeld 2004).

After winning several tournaments hosted by the local recreation depart-ment, in 1941, an African American schoolteacher, Juan Serrell, arranged for Gibson to receive lessons from Frederick Johnson, a one-armed coach. He worked at the Cosmopolitan Tennis Club in the Sugar Hill section of Harlem,

one of the leading Black tennis clubs in the nation (Lansbury 2014). A year later, Johnson entered Gibson in her first tournament: the girls' singles division of the New York State Open, an American Tennis Association (ATA) tournament. Since Black tennis players were denied access to tennis competitions due to Jim Crow laws and segregation, the ATA was founded and financed by a circuit of upwardly mobile, Black professionals and businesspeople to develop the sport among African Americans. After losing in the women's final in 1946, Gibson won her first of ten straight national ATA women's titles from 1947 to 1956, breaking Ora Washington's record.

Gibson's ATA success drew the attention of Robert Walter Johnson, a physician from Lynchburg, Virginia who was active in the African American tennis community. Under the patronage of Johnson, who was soon joined by physician Hubert A. Eaton—they would later mentor Arthur Ashe—Gibson gained access to advanced instruction, important competitions, and later, to the United States National Lawn Tennis Association (USNLTA) (later known as the USTA). In 1949, she became the first Black woman and the second Black athlete (after Reginald Weir) to play in the USNLTA's National Indoor Championships, where she reached the quarter-finals.

Her patrons and supporters helped Gibson in innumerable ways. They taught her good manners and social graces, including how to be a gracious winner, and how to properly dress. When they convinced Gibson to continue her education, she moved to Wilmington, North Carolina in 1946 under Eaton's sponsorship, and enrolled in Williston High School. She studied hard, was on the basketball team, and played the saxophone in the school band. Later that year, Gibson entered Florida Agriculture and Mechanical University (FAMU) on a full athletic scholarship. Her transition to FAMU was swift. In addition to playing the ATA circuit, she participated on the intercollegiate circuit with the FAMU team. In three years, Gibson was transformed into a member of the tennis elite. Gibsons's experience was a classic example of Black patronage by members of the Black elite, writ large (Djata 2008). In the case of Gibson, the Johnson and Eaton families became her surrogate family.

Despite her growing reputation as an elite-level player, Gibson contemplated leaving sports. A good deal of her frustration had to do with the sport being White-dominated, White-managed, and segregated in the U.S.—as was the world around it. Gibson was effectively barred from entering the premier American tournament: the U.S. National Championships (now known as the U.S. Open) at Forest Hills. While USNLTA rules officially prohibited racial or ethnic discrimination, players could only qualify for the Nationals by accumulating points at sanctioned tournaments held at White-only clubs but Gibson was undeterred.

In 1950, in response to intense lobbying by ATA officials and retired White tennis champion Alice Marble—who published a scathing open letter in *American Lawn Tennis Magazine*—Gibson became the first Black player to receive an invitation to the Nationals, where she made her Forest Hills debut on her twenty-third birthday. Although she lost narrowly in the second round during a rain-delayed, three-set match to Louise Brough, the reigning Wimbledon champion and former U.S. National winner, her participation received extensive national and international coverage, tantamount to Jackie Robinson when he first stepped out of the Brooklyn Dodgers dugout.

In 1951, Gibson won her first international title in the Caribbean Championships in Jamaica, and later that year became the first Black competitor at Wimbledon, where she was defeated in the third round by Beverly Baker. In 1952, she was ranked seventh nationally by the USNLTA.

By this time, Gibson struggled between the worlds of the ATA and the USNLTA. While the ATA sought integration, they feared that Black tennis would suffer a similar fate of the Negro leagues and with it, a loss of identity and community (Lansbury 2014). In the meantime, the USNLTA never took integration seriously. While every mixed-race match won a small battle for equality and open-mindedness, as long as tournaments were being held at private clubs that excluded Blacks, Jews, and immigrants, these players would never be able to test their talents against the finest White players of the day under championship conditions (Schoenfeld 2004). Gibson also suffered attitudes from the Black elites regarding her working class background, vis-à-vis race heroism, and latent class prejudices, topped off with 1950s womanhood. Unlike Jackie Robinson, Gibson rarely used her celebrity platform to talk about civil rights issues, which also drew criticism. Gibson preferred to let her racquet do the talking. Despite all of this, Gibson managed to be her authentic and independent self (Lansbury 2014).

In the spring of 1953, Gibson graduated from FAMU and took a job teaching physical education at Lincoln University in Jefferson City, Missouri. During her two years at Lincoln, she became romantically involved with an Army officer whom she never named publicly. She considered enlisting in the Women's Army Corps, but decided against it when the State Department sent her on a goodwill tour of Asia in 1955 to play exhibition matches with Ham Richardson, Bob Perry, and Karol Fageros. Many Asians felt an affinity to Gibson as a woman of color, and were delighted to see her as part of an official U.S. delegation. Gibson, for her part, strengthened her confidence immeasurably during the six-week tour. When it was over, she remained abroad, winning sixteen of eighteen tournaments in Europe and Asia against many of the world's best players.

In 1956, Gibson became the first African American athlete to win a Grand Slam event, the French Open singles championship. She also won the doubles title, partnered with Briton Angela Buxton. Later in the season, she won the Wimbledon doubles championship again with Buxton, the Italian Championships in Rome, the Indian Championships in New Delhi, and the Asian championship in Ceylon. She also reached the quarter-finals in singles at Wimbledon and the finals at the U.S. Nationals, losing both to Shirley Fry.

In 1957, Gibson won Wimbledon. She was the first Black champion in the tournament's eighty-year history, and the first champion to receive the trophy personally from Queen Elizabeth II. She won the doubles championship as well, for a second year. When she returned to New York, she was the second Black American, after Jesse Owens, to be honored with a ticker tape parade, and Mayor Wagner presented her with the Bronze Medallion, the city's highest civilian award. A month later, she defeated Brough in straight sets to win her first U.S. National championship. In all, she reached the finals of eight Grand Slam events in 1957, winning the Wimbledon and U.S. National singles titles, the Wimbledon and Australian doubles championships, and the U.S. mixed doubles crown; and finishing second in Australian singles, U.S. doubles, and Wimbledon mixed doubles. At season's end, she broke yet another barrier as the first Black player on the U.S. Wightman Cup team, which defeated Great Britain 6-1.

In 1958, Gibson successfully defended her Wimbledon and U.S. National singles titles, and won her third straight Wimbledon doubles championship, with her third different partner. She was the number-one-ranked woman in the world and in the U.S. in both 1957 and 1958, and was named Female Athlete of the Year by the Associated Press in both years, garnering over 80 percent of the votes in 1958. She also became the first Black woman to appear on the covers of *Sports Illustrated* and *Time.*

In late 1958, having won fifty-six national and international singles and doubles titles, Gibson retired from amateur tennis. Prior to the Open Era,[1] there was no prize money at major tournaments, and direct endorsement deals were prohibited. Players were limited to meager expense allowances, strictly regulated by the USNLTA. Professional tours for women were still fifteen years away, so Gibson's opportunities were largely limited to promotional events. In 1959, she signed to play a series of exhibition matches against Karol Fageros before Harlem Globetrotter basketball games. When the tour ended, she won the singles and doubles titles at the Pepsi Cola World Pro Tennis Championships in Cleveland, but received only $500 in prize money.

During this period, Gibson also pursued her long-held aspirations in the entertainment industry. A talented vocalist and saxophonist, she made her professional singing debut at W. C. Handy's eighty-fourth birthday tribute at the Waldorf-Astoria Hotel in 1957. She recorded an album of popular standards. *Althea Gibson Sings,* released in 1959, and performed two of its songs on *The Ed Sullivan Show* that same year, but sales were disappointing. She appeared as a celebrity guest on the television panel show, *What's My Line?* and was cast as a slave woman in the John Ford motion picture *The Horse Soldiers* (1959), which was notable for her refusal to speak in the stereotypic "Negro" dialect mandated

---

1.   The "Open Era" began in 1968 when major tournaments agreed to allow professional players to compete with amateurs. Before 1968, only amateurs were allowed to compete in Grand Slam tournaments and other events organized or sanctioned by the ILTF, including the Davis Cup.

by the script. She also worked as a sports commentator, appeared in print and television advertisements for various products, and increased her involvement in social issues and community activities. In 1960, her first memoir, *I Always Wanted to Be Somebody,* written with sportswriter Ed Fitzgerald, was published.

Her professional tennis career, however, was going nowhere. So in 1964, at the age of thirty-seven, Gibson became the first African American woman to join the Ladies Professional Golf Association (LPGA) tour. Racial discrimination continued to be a problem: many hotels still excluded people of color, and country club officials routinely refused to allow her to compete. When she did compete, she was often forced to dress for tournaments in her car because she was banned from the clubhouse. Although she was one of the LPGA's top fifty money winners for five years, and won a car at a Dinah Shore tournament, her lifetime golf earnings never exceeded $25,000.

Gibson renewed her twelve-year on-again, off-again relationship with William Darben. In 1965, they married in a quiet ceremony in Las Vegas.

She made financial ends meet with various sponsorship deals and the support of her husband. In a second memoir, *So Much to Live For* (1968) she articulated her disappointments, including unfulfilled aspirations, the paucity of endorsements and other professional opportunities, and the many obstacles that were thrown in her path over the years.

While she broke course records during individual rounds in several tournaments, Gibson's highest ranking was 27th in 1966, and her best tournament finish was a tie for second after a three-way playoff at the 1970 Len Immke Buick Open. She retired from professional golf at the end of the 1978 season.

In the early 1970s, Gibson began directing women's sports and recreation for the Essex County Parks Commission in New Jersey. In 1972, she began running Pepsi Cola's national mobile tennis project, which brought portable nets and other equipment to underprivileged areas in major cities. She ran multiple clinics and tennis outreach programs over the next three decades, and coached numerous rising competitors, including Leslie Allen and Zina Garrison. In 1976, she was appointed as New Jersey's athletic commissioner, becoming the first woman in the country to hold such a role, but resigned after one year due to lack of autonomy, budgetary oversight, and adequate funding.

Living apart much of the year due to her continued attempts to become successful in golf, Gibson and her husband divorced in 1976.

With the advent of the Open Era, Gibson began entering major tennis tournaments again; but by then, in her forties, she was unable to compete effectively against the younger players. In 1977, Gibson challenged incumbent Essex County State Senator Frank J. Dodd in the Democratic primary for his seat, and lost. Gibson went on to manage the Department of Recreation in East Orange, New Jersey. She also served on the State Athletic Control Board and became the supervisor of the Governor's Council on Physical Fitness and Sports.

In 1983 she married Sydney Llewellyn, her coach during her peak tennis years. After three years, the marriage ended in divorce. She also attempted a golf comeback in 1987 at age sixty, with the goal of becoming the oldest active tour player, but she was unable to regain her tour card. Gibson became reclusive in her later years.

Gibson became one of the first six inductees into the International Women's Sports Hall of Fame in 1980. Other inductions included the National Lawn Tennis Hall of Fame, the International Tennis Hall of Fame, the Florida Sports Hall of Fame, the Black Athletes Hall of Fame, the Sports Hall of Fame of New Jersey, the New Jersey Hall of Fame, the International Scholar-Athlete Hall of Fame, and the International Women's Hall of Fame. She received a Candace Award from the National Coalition of 100 Black Women in 1988.

In the late 1980s, Gibson suffered two cerebral hemorrhages and in 1992, a stroke. Ongoing medical expenses depleted her financial resources, leaving her unable to afford her rent or medication. Though she reached out to multiple tennis organizations requesting help, none responded. Former doubles partner Angela Buxton made Gibson's plight known to the tennis community, and raised nearly $1 million in donations from around the world.

In 1991, Gibson became the first woman to receive the Theodore Roosevelt Award, the highest honor from the National Collegiate Athletic Association. *Sports Illustrated for Women* named her in its list of the "100 Greatest Female Athletes." On opening night of the 2007 U.S. Open, the fiftieth anniversary of her first victory in 1957, Gibson was inducted into the U.S. Open Court of Champions.

In early 2003, Althea Gibson survived a heart attack, but died on September 28, 2003, at the age of seventy-six from complications following respiratory and bladder infections. She was interred in the Rosedale Cemetery in Orange near her first husband, Will Darben.❖

The Legacy of Althea Gibson

IT WOULD BE FIFTEEN YEARS before another woman of color—Evonne Goolagong,of Australia in 1971—won a Grand Slam championship; and forty-three years before another African American woman, Serena Williams, won her first of six U.S. Opens in 1999. Venus Williams would win back-to-back titles at Wimbledon and the U.S. Open in 2000 and 2001, repeating Gibson's accomplishment in 1957 and 1958. For this and other reasons, Gibson's accolades would continue long after her death. It is worth reiterating that besides tennis, Gibson was one of the few women who returned to high school, received a diploma, and earned her degree while competing, which is perhaps her biggest achievement.

Later in life, Gibson fell from the pinnacle of amateur tennis to a poverty she had not even known as a toddler in a sharecropping family. She was not allowed to earn prize money because only amateurs were allowed to compete in established tournaments. She held out as long as she could but in the end, Gibson could no longer afford to play tennis. An inability to earn income playing tennis was only part of the equation: Gibson simply did not fit the mold. She was a tall, overpowering Black woman who could serve and volley everybody off the court. And as a woman, she would never earn income proportionate to her talent. For Gibson, the woman who opened the door for so many, her years after tennis were marked by sadness. Fame proved fleeting, and the tennis star later felt somewhat abandoned and forgotten.

Now, some African American women with long-ignored contributions are at last getting their due. More than sixty years later, Gibson's legacy is finally being pushed to center stage on multiple fronts.

Gibson's five Wimbledon trophies are displayed at the Smithsonian Institution's National Museum of American History. The Althea Gibson Cup seniors tournament is held annually in Croatia, under the auspices of the International Tennis Federation (ITF). The Althea Gibson Foundation identifies and supports gifted golf and tennis players who live in urban environments. In 2005, Bill and Camille Cosby endowed the Althea Gibson Scholarship at her alma mater, FAMU.

In September 2009, Wilmington, North Carolina named its new community tennis court facility the Althea Gibson Tennis Complex at Empire Park. Other tennis facilities named in her honor include those at Manning High School (near her birthplace in Silver, South Carolina), and the Family Circle Tennis Center in Charleston, South Carolina.

In 2012, a bronze statue, created by sculptor Thomas Jay Warren, was dedicated in her memory in Branch Brook Park in Newark, New Jersey. In 2013, the U.S. Postal Service issued a postage stamp honoring Gibson, the 36th in its Black Heritage series. A documentary titled *Althea*, produced for the American Masters Series on PBS, premiered in September 2015.

In 2017, the Council of Paris named a public multisport gymnasium after her in the 12th arrondissement of Paris: the Gymnase Althea Gibson. In 2018, the USTA unanimously voted to erect a statue honoring Gibson at the Billie Jean King National Tennis Center, the home of the U.S. Open in Flushing, New York, which was revealed in 2019. That same year, the FAMU Board of Trustees approved the naming of the University's tennis complex in Gibson's honor, where a memorial plaque already adorns the complex.

Two proposed films about Gibson are in the works, and Gibson's family is seeking to have a portion of West 143rd Street between Lenox and Seventh Avenue, where she grew up, to be renamed Althea Gibson Way.

Althea Gibson will never be forgotten. She did not just break the color barrier; she became the best in the world, and in the process, forever disrupted the tennis world. It has never been the same, and it never will be again. Just ask the Williams sisters.❖

Wilma Rudolph
(1940-1994)
Track and field, coach, teacher

Wilma Rudolph became the first African American and woman to win three gold medals in track and field at a single Olympics.

WILMA GLODEAN RUDOLPH was born in Saint Bethlehem, Tennessee (now part of Clarksville) to Blanche Rudolph, a maid, and Ed Rudolph, a railroad porter who picked up odd jobs to supplement the family income. Born in the racially segregated South, Rudolph was the twentieth of twenty-two brothers and sisters from her father's two marriages. Shortly after Rudolph's birth, her family moved to Clarksville, Tennessee, where she grew up and attended elementary and high school. Her mother was a patient woman of strong faith, and her father was a strict disciplinarian who enjoyed family togetherness (Lansbury 2014).

During Rudolph's childhood, it seemed unlikely that she would live, much less reach such great athletic heights. Having been born weighing just 4.5 pounds, Rudolph was a sickly child. She suffered from several childhood illnesses, including whooping cough, pneumonia, and scarlet fever, and contracted infantile paralysis (caused by the poliovirus) at four. Since healthcare was not readily available, Rudolph rebounded from these illnesses with only her mother's aid. When her parents discovered weakness and deformity in her left leg after her bout with polio, they were forced to relent to a doctor's care.

There was little medical care available to African American residents of Clarksville in the 1940s. When they were told that Rudolph would never walk again, Rudolph's parents sought treatment at the historically Black Meharry Medical College (now known as Nashville General Hospital at Meharry) in Nashville, about fifty miles from Clarksville. Due to the treatments she received at Meharry and the daily massages from her family members, Rudolph overcame the debilitating effects of polio and learned to walk without a leg brace or an orthopedic shoe for support by the time she was twelve years old.

Initially homeschooled due to her frequent illnesses, Rudolph returned to school in seventh grade, where she began to play basketball at Burt High School, the center of Clarksville's African American community. Basketball worked well for Rudolph, who was still trying to strengthen her weakened leg. As a seventh-grader, she spent her first year training and found herself on the bench. But by the eighth grade, when her coach, Clinton Gray, would only give her limited playing time, she became frustrated. As it turned out, when Gray later announced he was resurrecting the girls' track team, Rudolph would be invited to join. While her love was still basketball, it quickly became clear that she had found her athletic calling. Her awakening came during her sophomore year when she played first string for an entire season with a team that won their conference title to advance to the state championship (Lansbury 2014).

When the team went to Alabama to participate in the Tuskegee Relay Carnival, she lost every race—a humbling experience. She understood that to further her natural talent, she required essential training in order to run competitively and win. Unbeknownst to her, Rudolph had already caught the attention of Ed Temple, the track coach at Tennessee State University (TSU), when he saw her play basketball. Temple served as a referee at area high schools, which allowed him to scout for talent in the rural areas around Nashville (Lansbury 2014). When Temple saw her at Tuskegee, he invited fourteen-year-old Rudolph to join his summer training program at TSU. After attending the track camp, Rudolph won all nine events. In 1956, she entered an Amateur Athletic Union (AAU) track meet in Philadelphia. Under Temple's guidance, she would continue to train regularly at TSU while still a high school student and raced at amateur athletic events with TSU's women's track team, the Tigerbelles.

Rudolph had a memorable junior year in high school. The basketball team went undefeated. She continued her unbeaten track record at high school meets, returned to TSU's summer track program, and competed with the Tigerbelles, who won the national championship. More astonishing is that she participated in the 1956 U.S. Olympic track and field team trials in Washington, D.C. and qualified to compete in the 200-meter individual event at the Melbourne 1956 Summer Olympics. Rudolph, the youngest member of the U.S. Olympic team, was defeated in a preliminary heat of the 200-meter race, but ran the third leg of the 4×100-meter relay. The American team won the bronze medal, matching the world-record time of 44.9 seconds. At sixteen years old, Rudolph returned to Tennessee as an Olympic medalist. She had already set her sights on winning a gold medal at the Rome 1960 Summer Olympics.

During her senior year of high school, Rudolph became pregnant by her high school sweetheart, Robert Eldridge, whom she had been dating since seventh grade. This presented a real threat to her track career since Temple refused to let mothers join his team. She gave birth to their daughter in 1958, a few weeks before her enrollment at TSU. After the birth, Temple allowed her to attend the track program. More importantly, her parents were willing to provide their support as long as Rudolph and Eldridge were no longer a couple. It was the price that Rudolph had to pay to move forward with her burgeoning career. When she left home, she became a freshman at TSU and a full-fledged Tigerbelle.

Despite the strain of being separated from her daughter and boyfriend, Rudolph trained relentlessly. At the Pan American Games in Chicago in 1959,

Rudolph won a silver medal in the 100-meter individual event and a gold medal in the 4×100-meter relay. She also won the AAU 100-meter title in 1959 and defended it for four consecutive years. During her collegiate career, Rudolph also won three AAU indoor titles. When she became a sophomore, Rudolph competed in the U.S. Olympic track and field trials, where she qualified for the 100-meter dash, and set a world record in the 200-meter dash (which stood for eight years), as well as the 4×100-meter relay. Temple was named the U.S. Olympic team's women's track and field coach as an added plus.

Rudolph became the first American woman to win a gold medal in the 100-meter dash since Helen Stephens' win in 1936. She won another gold medal in the finals of the 200-meter dash with a time of 24.0 seconds, after setting a new Olympic record of 23.2 seconds in the opening heat. After these wins, she was hailed throughout the world as "the fastest woman in history." Rudolph combined efforts with her teammates from TSU—Martha Hudson, Lucinda Williams, and Barbara Jones—to win the 4×100-meter relay at 44.5 seconds, after setting a world record of 44.4 seconds in the semifinals. She ran the anchor leg for the American team in the finals and nearly dropped the baton after a pass from Williams, but she overtook Germany's anchor leg to win the relay in a close finish. When it was all over, Rudolph became the first American woman to win three gold medals in a single Olympics.

She immediately became one of the most popular athletes of the Olympics and emerged as "The Tornado, the fastest woman on earth." The Italians nicknamed her *La Gazzella Nera* (The Black Gazelle), and the French called her *La Perle Noire* (The Black Pearl). Along with other Black Olympic athletes, Cassius Clay (later known as Muhammad Ali), Oscar Robertson, and Rafer Johnson, Rudolph became an international star due to the first worldwide television coverage of the Olympics. The Rome 1960 Summer Olympics launched Rudolph into the public spotlight, and the media, for the most part, cast her as America's athletic "leading lady" and "queen," with praises of her athletic accomplishments and her feminine beauty and poise. Rudolph rubbed shoulders with Black celebrities and civil rights activists, even gaining a private meeting with President Kennedy in the Oval Office.

However, it is important to note that this Cold War environment presented a double-edged sword. On the one hand, women's sports began to blossom, and the altering perception of Black women, particularly track and field athletes, had begun to take root in a positive light. Unfortunately, the general atmosphere remained virulently sexist and misogynistic, prompted by comments from the media (primarily by White male sportswriters) who had an overall contempt for women in sports, especially track and field, because they felt their presence debased the sport. They constantly questioned Black women's athletic abilities by equating them to a 1950s white middle class standard of femininity. In order to gain acceptance in the public sphere, the Black women athletes used this standard to their advantage. No one did it better than Rudolph (Lansbury 2014).

Rudolph returned to Clarksville after completing a post-games European tour, where she and her Olympic teammates competed in meets in London, West Germany, the Netherlands, and other venues in Europe. Rudolph's hometown of Clarksville celebrated "Welcome Wilma Day" with a full day of festivities. Rudolph adamantly insisted that her homecoming parade and banquet become the first fully integrated municipal event in the city's history.

In the months following the Olympics, Rudolph's star status gave an enormous boost to the track and field circuit. She began receiving invitations to run at track meets around the country, which up to that point traditionally excluded women (Lansbury 2014). In 1961, Rudolph was invited to compete in the New York Athletic Club track event, the Penn Relays, and the Drake Relays. She competed in the prestigious Los Angeles Invitational indoor track meet, where thousands watched her run. She also became the first woman invited to compete at the Melrose Games, setting a precedent for future women athletes.

Rudolph's appearance in 1960 on the American television shows, *To Tell the Truth,* a game show, and later as a guest on *The Ed Sullivan Show,* promoted her status as an iconic sports star. The U.S. Information Agency made a ten-minute documentary film, *Wilma Rudolph: Olympic Champion* (1961), to highlight her accomplishments on the track.

She also began considering whether to remain in the sport long enough to return to the Olympics in 1964. Rudolph eventually decided against it because earning anything less than three gold medals would cast a shadow over her career. Following her victories in the 100-meter and 4x100-meter-relay races at a U.S.–Soviet meet at Stanford University in 1962, At the age of twenty-two, Rudolph elected to retire at the peak of her career. When she retired, Rudolph was still the world record holder in the 100-meter, the 200-meter, and the 4x100-meter-relay events. She also won seven national AAU sprint titles and set the women's indoor track record at 6.9 seconds in the 60-yard dash.

Rudolph made a month-long trip to West Africa as a goodwill ambassador for the U.S. State Department, and served as the U.S. representative to the 1963 Friendship Games in Dakar, Senegal. She also visited Ghana, Guinea, Mali, and Upper Volta, where she attended sporting events, visited schools, and made guest appearances on television and radio broadcasts. When she returned after her month-long tour in Africa, she participated in a multi-day sit-in protest at a restaurant in her hometown, Clarksville, that denied service to African Americans. Many local White people responded violently. They jeered and threw things at the protesters and fired gunshots into an organizer's home, narrowly missing one of his children. Nonetheless, within a week, the city desegregated Clarksville's restaurants (Siber 2018).

In 1963, Rudolph graduated from TSU with a BA in education. Her college education was paid for by her participation in a work-study scholarship program that required her to work on the TSU campus two hours a day. She married

William Ward, a track team member from North Carolina College at Durham. They divorced that same year.

Shortly after her divorce, she married her high school sweetheart, Robert Eldridge, with whom she already had a daughter. Rudolph and Eldridge would settle down in their hometown of Clarksville, have four children together, and eventually divorce after seventeen years of marriage.

Rudolph, who did not earn significant money as an amateur athlete, shifted to teaching and coaching after retiring from competition. She was a second-grade teacher at Cobb Elementary School and coached track at Burt High School, where she had once been a student-athlete herself. Yet, the administration was not interested in the new training methods she gleaned at TSU, so when a job offer came her way, she left Tennessee for Illinois. She would move several times over the years and live in Indianapolis, St. Louis, and Detroit. Her jobs failed to live up to her expectations, plus she often felt used and exploited. As with most Black woman athletes, she struggled with the transition from a celebrity and the lifestyle that goes with it, to trying to find her footing back in the real world (Lansbury 2014).

Her autobiography, *Wilma: The Story of Wilma Rudolph,* was published in 1977, which served as the basis for several other publications and films. Since she entered the public sphere, over twenty books on Rudolph's life have been published for children from pre-school youth to high school students.

Rudolph also worked for nonprofit organizations and government-sponsored projects that supported athletic development among children. In Boston, she became involved in the Job Corps program, and in 1967 served as a track specialist for Operation Champion. Along with other athletes, including tennis pro Billie Jean King, she spoke out about gender parity in sports and the pay gap in athletics and elsewhere (Silber 2018). In 1981, Rudolph established and led the Wilma Rudolph Foundation, a nonprofit organization based in Indianapolis that trained young athletes. In 1987, she joined DePauw University in Greencastle, Indiana, as the director of its women's track program, and served as a consultant on minority affairs for the university's president.

She hosted a local television show in Indianapolis and was a sports commentator for ABC Sports during the Los Angeles 1984 Summer Olympics. Rudolph lit the cauldron to open the Pan American Games in Indianapolis in 1987 at the Indianapolis Motor Speedway. In 1992, she became vice president of Nashville's Baptist Hospital. Moreover, in 1993, Rudolph agreed to assist Berlin in the city's bid to bring the Olympic Games to Germany in the year 2000.

Rudolph has received numerous honors. She was named United Press International Athlete of the Year (1960), and Associated Press Woman Athlete of the Year (1960 and 1961). She was the recipient of the James E. Sullivan Award (1960) for the top amateur athlete in the U.S., and the Babe Didrikson Zaharias Award (1962). In 1984, the Women's Sports Foundation selected

Rudolph as one of the five greatest women athletes in the U.S., and she was honored with the National Sports Award (1993). Rudolph was inducted into several women's and sports halls of fame, including Black Sports Hall of Fame (1973), U.S. National Track and Field Hall of Fame (1974), U.S. Olympic Hall of Fame (1983), and the National Women's Hall of Fame (1994).

In July 1994, Wilma Rudolph was diagnosed with brain and throat cancer, and she died on November 12, 1994, at the age of fifty-four. She is survived by her four children, grandchildren, and many siblings, nieces and nephews. Thousands of mourners filled TSU's Kean Hall for the memorial service in her honor. In Tennessee, the state flag flew at half-mast.❖

The Legacy of Wilma Rudolph

WILMA RUDOLPH'S LEGACY lies in her efforts to overcome childhood obstacles to become the fastest woman runner in the world in 1960. Her Olympic success greatly boosted women's track and field in the U.S. and abroad, and her celebrity broke gender barriers at previously all-male track and field events, such as the Millrose Games. She was also known as the world's fastest woman and was among the most successful and famous athlete of her era. At five feet and eleven inches tall, she was graceful and lithe; she was also thoughtful, humble, and helped gain acceptance for women athletes, partly because she met the era's beauty standards.

In addition to her athletic accomplishments, Rudolph is remembered for her contributions to youth, including founding and heading the Wilma Rudolph Foundation. While her underdog story of athletic victory has been celebrated in the media and popular culture, her lifelong struggle against racism and sexism, and her role as a champion for civil rights and gender parity, are less well-known (Siber 2018).

In 1996, the Women's Sports Foundation presented its first annual award, the Wilma Rudolph Courage Award, to Jackie Joyner-Kersee. A life-size bronze statue of Rudolph was erected in Clarksville in 1996. *Sports Illustrated* ranked Rudolph first on its list of the top fifty greatest sports figures of the twentieth-century from Tennessee in 1999. ESPN ranked Rudolph forty-first in its listing of the twentieth century's greatest athletes, and she was entered in the National Black Sports and Entertainment Hall of Fame in 2001.

Rudolph is perhaps the finest female sprinter in history, which has had a positive impact on generations of women athletes who followed. There was nothing close about any of her races, and she was absolutely dominant. In the process, Rudolph laid the foundation for all women who aspire to become great athletes. She is a testament to overcoming obstacles by making adversity an impetus for success.❖

Jackie Joyner-Kersee
(1962)
Track and field athlete, philanthropist

Jackie Joyner-Kersee was named by "Sports Illustrated" as the greatest female athlete of the twentieth century, and was the first African American woman to earn a gold medal in the long jump and in the heptathlon.

JACQUELINE "JACKIE" JOYNER-KERSEE was born in East St. Louis, Illinois to Mary Ruth Joyner, a nurse's aide, and Al Joyner, who worked as an assembly-man for airplanes and a railroad company. Named after First Lady Jacqueline Kennedy, she is one of four children born to teenaged parents who endured financial hardship. Although they grew up in a tough environment, their mother provided a religious upbringing and was their champion when they needed one. Joyner-Kersee's older brother, Al Joyner, would become an Olympic star and trainer, and marry sprinter, Florence Griffith.

Joyner-Kersee was shaped by a mother who bound her to excellence, and an older brother who greatly admired her. Energetic and active from a young age, Joyner-Kersee became interested in sports and tried any kind of activity available to her, including dance and volleyball. Joyner-Kersee spent a lot of time at the Mary E. Brown Community Center, a youth organization for after school and summer programs. When she signed-up for track and field, not enough people signed-up, so the coach at the center introduced Joyner-Kersee to the track coach, George Ward, of Franklin Elementary School. Since she attended John Robinson Elementary School, Ward helped her commute after school to attend practice. She found that she did not enjoy the 440-yard dash, but when she tried the long jump one day after practice, she liked it and focused on that instead (Lansbury 2014). She also trained with Nino Fennoy, a coach at the Freeman Elementary school, who worked with Ward to create a combined squad from all the elementary schools in the area called the East St. Louis Railers to hold track meets. Fennoy would remain a constant presence in Joyner-Kersee's life and coach her throughout high school.

Joyner-Kersee was developing into a great all-around athlete. When she attended East St. Louis Lincoln Senior High School, she competed on the school's volleyball, basketball, and track teams. Starting at age fourteen, she

won the National Junior Pentathlon championships four years in a row, and as a junior, she set the Illinois high-school girls' long jump record at 6.68 meters (20 feet seven and one-half inches). As a high school athlete, Joyner-Kersee qualified for the finals in the long jump at the 1980 Olympic Trials, finishing eighth.

Joyner-Kersee's parents were hesitant about fully supporting her athletic endeavors. Despite the inroads of the 1970s, her parents worried about the negative effect that sports might have on females, especially the common fear that she might become a lesbian. When schools began sanctioning competitive sports for girls, courtesy of the passage of Title IX, they felt better about her participation in sports and the level of the school's supervision (Lansbury 2014).

After graduating in the top 10 percent of her class, coupled with her high school sporting success, Joyner-Kersee, who was wooed by a number of college recruiters, accepted a basketball scholarship to the University of California, Los Angeles (UCLA). They had always been at the top of her list because UCLA would allow her to do both basketball and track and field. Joyner-Kersee became a starting forward for the Bruins, a position she would keep throughout her college career, but track and field was still her first love. In her sophomore year, she suddenly returned home when her mother became ill and subsequently died at thirty-seven from meningitis. Joyner-Kersee was heartbroken, but determined to work even harder to honor her mother's desire for her success (Lansbury 2014).

She was focusing on the long jump when she met Bob Kersee, an assistant track coach, who convinced her that multi-event track should be her sport. The university agreed, and Kersee trained Joyner-Kersee for the heptathlon, a track and field contest made up of seven events: running, hurdles, high jump, shot put, long jump, and javelin. The goal was to participate in the Olympics. With a track coach who understood her strengths and weaknesses, Joyner-Kersee began her climb to the top. More troubling was her asthma, which she discovered she had in 1983. Later on, she would have several full-blown asthma attacks, and would sometimes wear masks while competing. Despite this struggle, she continued to improve as a track athlete (Elliott 2020).

Joyner-Kersee red-shirted[1] during the 1983-1984 academic year to focus on training for the Los Angeles 1984 Summer Olympics, specifically for the heptathlon. While she was the favorite heading into the event, she finished five points behind Australian competitor Glynis Nunn, and won the silver medal. When they returned from the Olympics, Kersee requested and received permission to coach Joyner-Kersee full-time. Their partnership would not only change both of their lives, but also put UCLA and the West Coast on the map as the preeminent place for women track and field athletes to train (Lansbury 2014). When she graduated from UCLA in 1985, Jackie Joyner-Kersee decided to place her entire focus on track and field. During the 1986 Goodwill Games in Moscow,

---

1. An athlete who spends a year not participating in official athletic activities, but does not lose his or her eligibility to participate in the following years is red-shirted.

she scored 7,148 points in the heptathlon, the highest ever scored, and received the James E. Sullivan and Jesse Owens awards as the top amateur athlete in the U.S. In 1986, the coach and the star athlete married.

At the Seoul 1988 Summer Olympics, Joyner-Kersee was the first American woman to earn a gold medal in the long jump and the heptathlon. She set a world record of 7,291 points in the heptathlon, and leapt an astonishing Olympic record of 24-3 1/2 in the long jump.

During the Olympics, Joyner-Kersee faced a couple of obstacles. First, while she was having the Olympics of her life, capped by an incredible three-year run of world records and medals, she was constantly being compared to her sister-in-law, Florence Griffith Joyner, who competed at the same Olympics. Nicknamed "Flo-Jo," Griffith Joyner won three gold medals and set a new world record in the 100-meter sprint. Due to her flamboyant media personality, she garnered far more press coverage than Joyner-Kersee, appearing on track with her long flowy hair, stylish one-legged outfits, and elaborately painted nails. On the other hand, Joyner-Kersee was an old-fashioned athlete that had a more business-like approach to competition, and as an heptathlete, she did not mind letting people see her sweat on the track and field. Although she was considered a more formidable athlete than Griffith Joyner, she was virtually ignored when it came to endorsements. Finally, rumors of the use of performance enhanced drugs by both of the sister-in-laws surfaced at a time when the shadow of drugs in sports competition had first come to light. Suddenly, everyone was suspect, and as Joyner-Kersee and Griffith Joyner became central targets, it was clear that the issues of race, racism and sexism were not far behind (Lansbury 2014).

Although Joyner-Kersee was the favorite at the 1991 World Championships to retain her World titles, she slipped on the take-off board and strained a hamstring, which forced her to pull out of the heptathlon. In the Barcelona 1992 Summer Olympics, Joyner-Kersee earned her second Olympic gold medal in the heptathlon and won the bronze medal in the long jump at 22-11 1/4. At the Olympic Trials, Joyner-Kersee sustained an injury to her right hamstring and had not fully recovered by the time the Atlanta 1996 Summer Olympics began. After running the first event, the 100-meter hurdles, the pain was so unbearable that she was forced to withdraw. While she was able to recover well enough to compete in the long jump and qualify for the final, Joyner-Kersee ended in sixth place with one jump remaining. Miraculously, her final jump of 7-meters was long enough for her to win the bronze medal. This would be the last Olympics of Joyner-Kersee's long competitive career.

Later that year, Joyner-Kersee played basketball for the Richmond Rage of the fledgling American Basketball League (ABL). Although she was very popular with the fans, she was less successful on the court. She appeared in only seventeen games and scored no more than fifteen points in any game. Returning to track, Joyner-Kersee won the heptathlon again at the 1998 Goodwill

Games, scoring 6,502 points. After the games, Joyner-Kersee announced her retirement.

Two years after retiring, Joyner-Kersee tried to qualify to compete in the long jump at the Sydney 2000 Summer Olympics. After she failed to qualify, finishing in sixth place, she retired for good. With the end of her competitive career, Joyner-Kersee turned her attention to philanthropic work.

Joyner-Kersee has always been an active philanthropist in children's education, racial equality, and women's rights. In 1988, Joyner-Kersee established the Jackie Joyner-Kersee Foundation. In 2000, the Jackie Joyner-Kersee Foundation raised over $12 million to build the Jackie Joyner-Kersee Center, a 41,000-square-foot facility with a 1,200-seat gymnasium in her hometown, East St. Louis, Illinois. The Center provides youth, adults, and families with athletic lessons and resources to improve their quality of life.

In 2007, Jackie Joyner-Kersee, along with athletes Andre Agassi, Muhammad Ali, Cal Ripken Jr., and Lance Armstrong, founded Athletes for Hope (AFH), a nonprofit organization that helps professional athletes get involved in charitable causes and inspires millions of non-athletes to volunteer and support the community. In 2011, she partnered with Comcast to create the Internet Essentials program, which offers low costs services to low-income Americans. Since the program's inception, it has provided internet access to 4 million Americans.

Joyner-Kersee is the recipient of the James E. Sullivan Award (1986), Jack Kelly Fair Play Award (1997), NCAA Silver Anniversary Awards (2010), and the Dick Enberg Award from the College Sports Information Director of America (CoSIDA) (2011). She is also the two-time recipient of the Jesse Owens Award (1986, 1987). Since 1981, the Jesse Owens Award has been given by USA Track and Field (USATF) to the women and men track and field athletes of the year. In 1996, the award was split to be given to the top athlete of each gender. In 2013, a women's award was created and named the Jackie Joyner-Kersee Award.

Joyner-Kersee was inducted into the 2000 St. Louis Walk of Fame, and was awarded the Order of Lincoln from the Lincoln Academy of Illinois by the Governor of Illinois in the area of sports in 2005. It is the state's highest honor. She has also served on the Board of Directors for USATF's track and fields national governing body. As the author of her autobiography, *A Kind of Grace* (1997), Joyner-Kersee is also a professional speaker, widely considered to be one of the most inspiring motivational speakers in sports. Her post-athletic career has been marked by her major contributions and leadership as a philanthropist and a tireless advocate for children's education, health issues, racial equality, social reform and women's rights. During the pandemic, she opened her Center's doors to the community to distribute food and provide COVID-testing and vaccinations.

Joyner-Kersee still holds the U.S. record in the long jump at 24.7, as well as the U.S. and World records in the heptathlon at 7,291 points. It is fitting that *Sports Illustrated* named her the greatest female athlete of the twentieth century. ❖

Cheryl Miller
(1964)
Basketball player, coach, general manager, sportscaster

Cheryl Miller, an Olympic gold-medalist, was enshrined in the Naismith Memorial Basketball Hall of Fame, inducted into the inaugural class of the Women's Basketball Hall of Fame, and inducted into the FIBA Hall of Fame for her success in international play. She is credited with both popularizing the women's game and elevating it to a higher level.

CHERYL D. MILLER was born in Riverside, California to Carrie Turner Miller and Saul Miller, a jazz saxophonist turned military man, who instilled a competitive spirit in all of his children. As the middle child of five siblings, Miller played sports, and her younger brother Reggie became a shooting guard for the NBA's Indiana Pacers from 1987 to 2005.

While growing up in Southern California, Miller displayed extraordinary talent on the basketball court. In 1978, at six feet and two inches tall, Miller attended Riverside Polytechnic High School, making an immediate impact on the girls' basketball team. She dominated in high school competitions and shattered virtually every state scoring record, including the highest average in a season (37.5 points a game). Over ninety games, Miller scored 3,026 points—an average of 32.8 per game—grabbed 1,353 rebounds, and had 368 assists. She once scored 105 out of 115 total points when she was a high school senior in a game against Norte Vista High School, and she was the first female player to dunk a basketball in a competition.

She was awarded the Dial Award for the National High School Scholar-Athlete of the Year in 1981. She was the first player, female or male, to be named an All-American by *Parade* magazine four times. Miller was *Street & Smith's* national High School Player of the Year in both 1981 and 1982. She received over 250 scholarship offers, but when she graduated from high school, she chose to stay close to home and attended the University of Southern California (USC), where she quickly became a star. Miller and her USC teammates, Cynthia Cooper and twins Pam and Paula McGee, utterly dominated women's basketball and helped create a path for the WNBA.

During her first season in 1983, Miller burst onto the national scene by leading the Trojans to the National Collegiate Athletic Association (NCAA) women's basketball championship. Although she was just a freshman, Miller was selected as the Most Outstanding Player (MOP) of the NCAA tournament due to her ability to dominate games with her all-around athleticism. In addition to having a shooting touch that made her dangerous from anywhere on the court, Miller was an intimidating defender and a dominating rebounder. She also guided the U.S. to win gold at the Pan American Games.

In 1984, Miller led USC to another national title, was named MOP of the NCAA tournament for the second consecutive year, won a Wade Trophy, and shared the 1984 Honda Broderick Cup as the outstanding college athlete in any sport with swimmer Tracy Caulkins. That same year, she played for the U.S. Girls Basketball Olympic team, a team considered by many to be the finest collection of women basketball players ever assembled. Her gold medal performance at the Los Angeles 1984 Summer Olympics was so compelling that Miller may have been the most famous basketball player in the world for a short time afterward, female or male. In 1985, *Sports Illustrated* named her National Player of the Year. Miller became an international celebrity, gracing magazine covers worldwide, meeting heads of state, and making television appearances varying from interviews with newswoman Barbara Walters to guest spots on the television drama *Cagney and Lacey*.

In her 128-game career at USC, Miller established herself among the all-time NCAA leaders with 3,018 points (23.6 per game) and 1,534 rebounds (12.0 per game). She was second in her NCAA tournament career, scoring 333 points (20.8 per game) and first in career rebounding with 170 (10.6 per game). She also helped USA win gold at the 1986 Goodwill Games, won the Naismith Trophy and the Broderick Award as the Female College Basketball Player of the Year, and became the first female ever nominated for the prestigious Sullivan Award. When she left USC, Miller was widely considered the best woman basketball player in its history.

After completing her career at USC, Miller was drafted by several professional basketball leagues, including the U.S. Basketball League, a men's league. However, Miller's fabled career ended prematurely when she suffered a devastating knee injury in 1986 during a pick-up game at USC. At age twenty-two, the playing days for the woman hailed as the female counterpart to Michael Jordan, were over.

But Miller did the next best thing: she utilized her degree in communications and became a sports broadcaster. She was a field reporter for the 1987 Little League World Series and served as a correspondent for the 1988 Calgary Olympics. Miller also worked for ABC Sports/ESPN from 1987 to 1993, where she was a reporter for ABC's Wide World of Sports and a commentator for the network's college basketball telecasts. Miller briefly left her broadcasting career to return to her alma mater in 1993 as the head coach of the women's basketball team in the wake of a messy departure by the previous coach. Miller said at the outset of her tenure that she still wanted to do some broadcasting while she coached, but then decided early on that coaching required all of her time—although she did work as a basketball commentator at the 1994 Goodwill Games. During her two years at the helm, the Trojans compiled a 44-14 record and won the 1994 Pacific-10 conference title. Her best player was Lisa Leslie, who was the 1994 National Player of the Year. Miller then abruptly resigned as coach in 1995 to work full-time as a sports broadcaster.

Miller joined Turner Sports in September 1995 as an analyst and reporter for the NBA on TBS and TNT. She served as a women's basketball analyst and men's basketball reporter for NBC's coverage of the 1996 Atlanta Olympics. That same year, Miller became the first female analyst to broadcast a nationally televised men's professional basketball game.

In 1997, upon the founding of the Women's National Basketball Association (WNBA), Miller returned to the court as head coach and general manager of the Phoenix Mercury. The team featured future WNBA stars Sheryl Swoopes, Cynthia Cooper, Tina Thompson, and Janeth Arcain. In 1998, Miller coached the Mercury to a 16-12 record and to the WNBA finals, where her team lost to the Houston Comets. After four seasons, Miller resigned in 2000 citing fatigue, and returned full-time to sports broadcasting.

When Miller's mother was diagnosed with Alzheimer's in the late 1990s, she took it as hard as anyone would. Things became more difficult, and while her mother slowly deteriorated for nearly a decade, Miller was not prepared for the pain of her mother's death in 2007. She asked for a leave of absence from TNT for the rest of the season. She feared a breakdown and sought counseling, and in the process, began thinking about what she valued. Basketball still remained at the top of the list, but also near the top was teaching and helping others. Combining those interests, coaching became Miller's focus but in a different way than what she did before. Miller continued to make appearances on NBA TV during the 2008-2009 season as a reporter and analyst and she also served as the sideline reporter in 2K Sports' NBA 2K Series. She left the company after her contract expired in 2013.

Miller was ready to coach again, but when she reached out to athletic directors, friends and acquaintances all over the country, Miller got nothing: no interviews, and few calls back. Athletic directors told Miller that the game had changed, the players had changed, and that she had been out of recruiting and game planning too long. A colleague suggested that her name and her fame intimidated younger administrators. As it turned out, her friend and former athletic director at USC, Mike Garrett, who hired Miller back in 1993, was the athletic director at Langston University. When Garrett suddenly did not have a coach, the Langston athletic director knew who he had to call. In 2014, Miller was selected as the women's basketball coach by Langston University, a small HBCU in Oklahoma. Garrett resigned in 2015, ostensibly to spend more time with his wife's family. Soon after, he became the executive director of the Athletics Department at California State University, Los Angeles, in 2016.

During her first year at Langston, Miller guided the Lions to a 28-4 overall record and to the program's first Red River Conference Tournament title since 2011. Langston advanced to the second round of the NAIA National Tournament. In her second season, Miller led Langston to a 20-8 overall record that included a 14-4 mark in conference play. Langston once again appeared in the NAIA National Tournament, where the Lions fell in a first-round game. Two years later, she moved to California State University as the head coach of the Golden Eagles women's basketball program.

During her first year at California State, Miller guided a short-handed team, leading the Golden Eagles to a 15-14 overall record in the 2016-2017 season and their first winning season since 2014. The following season, Miller led the Golden Eagles to an overall record of 14-15, including a 13-9 mark in conference that left California State just one game out of third place and three games out of second in a tightly-packed CCAA race. How long Miller will stick with coaching remains to be seen, but it is clear that she believes she can help young athletes to become better people and basketball players.

A member of an elite group, Miller received two of basketball's highest honors: induction into the Naismith Memorial Basketball Hall of Fame and the USC Hall of Fame in 1995. In 1999, Miller was inducted in the Women's Basketball Hall of Fame. USC retired her No. 31 jersey in 2006, and she became the first basketball player—female or male—to have her jersey number retired by the university. To this day, Miller remains the all-time leading scorer, rebounder and steals leader at USC. She was inducted into the FIBA Hall of Fame in 2010. In 2018, she was inducted into the Pac-12 Conference's Hall of Honor in a group that included women for the first time. She was also featured in the 2020 HBO film, *Women of Troy.*

Miller is a highly sought after motivational speaker and has been a spokesperson for several organizations including the Los Angeles Literacy Campaign, the African American Council for Big Sisters of Los Angeles, the Pediatric Aids Foundation, the American Lung, Diabetes and Cancer Associations, and the Muscular Dystrophy Association. She also served as the commissioner for the 1985 Los Angeles Olympic Committee Summer Youth Games.

Miller put the spotlight for women's basketball onto the court and above the rim. With tremendous grace and athletic dexterity, she established a legacy from her brief high school and college career that remains unparalleled. Miles ahead of most female players in her generation, Miller helped make the case for the WNBA before it existed, and has greatly influenced college women's basketball that we are witnessing today. ❖

Violet Palmer
(1964)
Basketball referee

Violet Palmer, a lifelong athlete, was the first female referee to reach the highest competitive tier in any major U.S. professional sports league, and the first openly lesbian referee in NBA history.

VIOLET RENICE PALMER was born in Lynwood, California to Gussie Palmer, a homemaker, and James Palmer, a furnace operator for Lattice Pacific Division. The second oldest of four children, she grew up with a white picket fence around a strict, traditional Christian Baptist household in the hard-edged Compton section of Los Angeles. Palmer's parents had both played basketball, and while they were big supporters of sports activities, they also emphasized the importance of academia.

Palmer first developed a love of basketball as a child when she played with her brother in their backyard. In time, she became a multisport athlete; she ran track, played softball and basketball, and was the only girl on the little league team. When Palmer matriculated to middle school, her love and knack for basketball took precedence above all other sports.

In high school, Palmer played softball and participated in track, but basketball was her main sport. Palmer played point guard for Compton High School's women's basketball team and was captain for her final two years. She was named Team Most Valuable Player of the Moore League her senior year and named All League her junior and senior years. As Title IX began providing money for women's athletic programs, Palmer received a scholarship to attend California Polytechnic University, Pomona. She played point guard and served as the captain of her team for three years under Coach Darlene May, a star athlete who became the first woman to referee a women's Olympic basketball game. May became a mentor and friend to Palmer and introduced her to the art of refereeing. Palmer led the Broncos to win two NCAA (National Collegiate Athletic Association) Division II Championships in 1985 and 1986.

While attending college, Palmer held several part-time jobs as a scorekeeper for men's basketball teams. When the referees did not show up, Palmer would put on the shirt and start refereeing. From that experience, she began

filling in as a substitute referee at community recreation centers and quickly became one of the most respected referees in women's college basketball.

After a successful college basketball career and graduating with a BA in recreation administration in 1987, Palmer sought a way to remain a part of the sport and found it by becoming a referee. A man with a distinguished college athletic career like Palmer's might hope to join a professional basketball team, but in the late 1980s, a professional league for women did not exist. Women athletes who wanted to continue their careers had to take jobs on European teams, but Palmer had no desire to leave the country, so playing professionally was never an option. Many ex-athletes coached teams, but when Palmer tried coaching a high school team for two seasons, she found the experience too stressful. So, she worked for the Placentia Recreation Department and refereed high school basketball games instead.

She approached officiating basketball games with the same seriousness she had shown during her career as a competitive player. Often nicknamed "zebras" because of their black and white striped jerseys, referees are perhaps the most overlooked figures on the court until fans or players loudly disagree with a call. Officiating in basketball is an art that requires physical stamina, intense focus, and a thorough knowledge of the game. Palmer had all three.

Over the next nine years, Palmer worked as a referee in all three divisions of the NCAA, officiating in the women's final four tournaments five times and working at two NCAA championships. Palmer was surprised by how quickly she had earned acceptance at the highest level of amateur basketball. As her career progressed, her quiet confidence and thorough knowledge of basketball began to attract attention outside of college athletics. In 1994, Palmer received a call from a representative of the National Basketball Association (NBA) offering her a place in their referee training program.

Palmer took the challenge eagerly, and entered the referee development program, which included training and three years officiating for the Continental Basketball Association (CBA), the men's basketball minor league that develops players for the NBA. During much of the rigorous training program, Palmer continued her full-time job as a recreation administrator and worked as a referee for the newly launched Women's National Basketball Association (WNBA).

After years of refereeing at various levels, including NBA pre-season and exhibition games, Palmer was offered an opportunity to officiate the NCAA Division I men's tournament in 1996. She accepted, but the offer was retracted when NCAA members balked at the idea of having a woman refereeing male players. In 1997, however, Palmer and Dee Kantner were signed by the NBA to become the first top-level female officials in any major U.S. professional sport. It took seven years, three fewer than the norm, for Palmer to receive her first NBA assignment.

On October 31, 1997, Palmer made history as the first woman to referee an NBA game, after taking the floor in Vancouver, British Columbia, as the

Vancouver Grizzlies lost to the Dallas Mavericks. She also became the first woman to oversee a post-season game for the NBA in 2006 when she officiated a matchup between the Indiana Pacers and the New Jersey Nets.

Initially, Palmer was received with mixed feelings. While she never experienced blatant discriminatory language or homophobic comments throughout her career, she did face intense scrutiny for her gender. Palmer would also become the first openly lesbian referee in NBA history. While publications such as *Ebony* and *Sports Illustrated* generally celebrated her achievement, others were critical. Palmer was not being handed anything, just given a chance by the league to succeed or fail on her own merits, and she took it. Remarkably, she handled the NBA's high pressure with strict confidence and came through with flying colors.

She kept the players in line with a stern poker face and an encyclopedic knowledge of the rules. She was unwavering in her calls, and the players and coaches responded by accepting her calls and no longer making sexist remarks. Palmer's ongoing presence became less of a spectacle, less of a sideshow, and more about the game. She was, in fact, one of three NBA referees who officiated the brawl-marred December 16, 2006 game between the Denver Nuggets and New York Knicks. The officiating crew, which also consisted of Dick Bavetta and Robbie Robinson, ejected all the players on the court when the brawl broke out.

During her career, Palmer volunteered to help train young officials at the Youth Referee Clinic in Los Angeles. She established the Violet Palmer Official Camp in 2001 to train youth in the art of officiating games. From 2009 to 2010, Palmer served as the coordinator of Women's Basketball Officiating (WBBO) for the West Coast and Pac-12 Conferences. She became the first woman to officiate an All-Star Game in any major U.S. sport when she officiated the 2014 NBA All-Star Game in New Orleans. She was also named a member of the NCAA Division II 40th Anniversary Tribute Team. In 2015, Palmer became a coordinator of women's basketball officials for the Western Athletic Conference (WAC).

Palmer retired from on-court duties with the NBA due to knee issues in 2016. At the time of her retirement, she had officiated 919 NBA games. She is currently codirector of the Basics Referee School, which offers basketball officials instruction using the 3-person California Collegiate Association (CCA) Women's Basketball concept.

In 1999, Palmer was named Naismith Women's College Official of the Year. In 2013, she won the WNBA Boost Mobile Pioneer Award and in 2018, Palmer was honored with the Lifetime Achievement award from the Fourth Annual Truth Awards presented by the Better Brothers Los Angeles (BBLA) in connection with actress Sheryl Lee Ralph's nonprofit organization, the DIVA Foundation. Palmer is a former member of the Board of Directors for the National Association of Sports Officials and currently sits on the NCAA Mechanics Committee.

Palmer and her wife Tanya Stine live in Los Angeles with their three children.❖

Debi Thomas
(1967)
Figure skater, physician

Debi Thomas was the first African American to win the women's title at the U.S. Figure Skating Championships and medal in the Winter Olympics competition.

DEBRA JANINE THOMAS was born in Poughkeepsie, New York to Janice Thomas, a computer analyst, and McKinley Thomas, a computer professional. Her parents divorced when Thomas was young, and she and her brother moved to San Jose, California with their mother. Striving for excellence has always been important in the Thomas family—her grandfather, Daniel Skelton, received a doctorate in veterinary medicine at Cornell University in 1939 as the only African American in his class, and her brother would earn a bachelor's degree in physics from the University of California at Berkeley and a master's in business at Stanford University. Thomas would do no less, and her attention to education would become a hallmark of her personal trajectory (Hine 1997).

Thomas' mother introduced her to figure skating at age four, and she began skating at age five. Her first coach was Barbara Toigo Vitkovits at Eastridge Mall in San Jose. Thomas competed in her first figure skating competition at age nine, finishing in first place, and from then on was hooked on competitive skating. At age ten, Thomas was introduced to skating coach Alex McGowan of Redwood City Ice Lodge. Since coaching costs were astronomical, Thomas' grandparents and parents, with occasional grants or loans, helped defray some of the costs. The training also required her mother to shuttle Thomas between skating and school, which was some 150 miles of driving almost every day. Thomas' mother even let her complete eighth grade by correspondence. However, after a disappointing finish in the junior ladies' competition that year, Thomas and her mother vowed to never again let skating come ahead of her education.

Thomas passed the U.S. Figure Skating Associate's tests at fourteen years old, and in 1983, joined the Los Angeles Figure Skating Club, which launched her career. McGowan would remain Thomas' coach until she retired from amateur competition. After graduating from San Mateo High School with a 3.5-grade point average, Thomas was accepted at Harvard, Princeton, and Stanford. She chose Stanford and became a full-time pre-med student in 1985 as her star ascended in figure skating. It was unusual for a top U.S. skater to attend college while competing: Thomas was the first female athlete to do so since Tenley Albright in the 1950s. As a freshman, Thomas won both the 1986 U.S. National title and the 1986 World Championships, and those achievements earned her ABC's *Wide World of Sports* Athlete of the Year award. She was the first African American to hold U.S. National titles in ladies' singles figure skating. That same year she received a Candace Award for Trailblazing from the National Coalition of 100 Black Women, was named Amateur Sportswoman of the year by the Women's Sports Foundation, and was named McDonald's Amateur Sportswoman of the year.

It was clear that Thomas was gearing up for the Olympics as the first African American woman to compete in figure skating. However, there were multiple stretches of time during which Thomas would put her skating lessons on hold due to financial issues. Equally as stressful, Thomas began to encounter her share of discrimination. At one point, her family returned from a competition to find a cross burning on their lawn. But she persevered. In yet another victory in 1986, Thomas upset Olympic champion Katrina Witt of East Germany at the World Championship in Geneva, Switzerland, initiating the Thomas-Witt rivalry. It attracted enough media attention that corporate sponsors finally stepped forward to support Thomas.

In 1987, Thomas suffered from Achilles tendinitis in both ankles and struggled at the U.S. Nationals, placing second to Jill Trenary. She rebounded at the World Championships, finishing a close second to Witt. Thomas completed a triple toe combination, which was rare for a female skater during the 1980s. From 1986 to 1989, she skated in sixteen competitions, winning eight of them and placing second in three.

Thomas took a leave from Stanford and went to Boulder, Colorado in 1987 to prepare for the Olympics. In January 1988, she reclaimed the U.S. national title. At the Calgary 1988 Winter Olympics, the media dubbed the Thomas-Witt rivalry "Battle of the Carmens" since both women skated their long programs to the music of Georges Bizet's opera, *Carmen*. Thomas skated strong compulsory figures and performed well in the short program, but she made mistakes in the long program and placed fourth in that segment of the competition. Overall, she finished third and won the bronze medal, behind Witt and Canadian skater Elizabeth Manley. By winning the bronze medal, Thomas became the first Black athlete to win any medal at the Winter Olympics. A few weeks after the Olympics, she married Brian Vander Hogen in Boulder, Colorado.

The drama at the Olympics had greatly bolstered the popularity of figure skating. Thomas retired from amateur skating, won three World titles consecutively in 1988, 1989, and 1992, and performed for Stars on Ice. Some believed that Thomas defied skating logic by marrying at the height of her skating career and re-entering Stanford University to complete her degree rather than cashing in on the lucrative ice shows that toured the country. Instead, she skated professionally on the weekends. Eventually, Thomas became overwhelmed with married life, school, and skating. She switched her major to engineering and graduated from Stanford in 1991. Thomas ended her marriage and retired from skating in 1992 to pursue medicine full-time. She became engaged to her second husband, former Razorback offensive lineman and sports attorney Chris Bequette, in 1996, after they dated for one month. The couple had a son a year later, who would also become a football player.

After graduating from Northwestern University Feinberg School of Medicine in 1997, following her surgical residencies, Thomas became a practicing orthopedic surgeon specializing in hip and knee replacement. In 2005, she graduated from the Orthopedic Residency Program at Charles R. Drew University in Los Angeles. After completing her fellowship, as Thomas embarked on her medical career, she found she had difficulty working with her colleagues and moved from clinic to clinic, never staying for longer than one year. In 2010, Thomas opened a private practice in the diminishing coal-mining town of Richlands, Virginia. That same year, she briefly returned to the ice to participate in *The Caesars Tribute: A Salute to the Golden Age of American Skating*, an event that featured many of America's figure skating legends and icons. It marked the first time Thomas had skated before an audience in fourteen years.

Over the years, Thomas received many accolades for her contributions to figure skating. In February 1989, Thomas ranked 12th in the Q Score athlete standings, the only woman in the top 22. She was inducted into the U.S. Figure Skating Hall of Fame in 2000, and served as a representative for the U.S. Olympic Committee at the Salt Lake City 2002 Winter Olympics. She was also selected by President George W. Bush to be part of the U.S. Delegation for the Opening Ceremonies of the Turin 2006 Winter Olympics. Thomas also supported several charities, as well as including the Make-A-Wish Foundation and the Ara Parseghian Medical Research Foundation.

Unfortunately, Thomas' medical practice floundered, and coupled with her lack of business expertise, Thomas went out of business. Having no source of income, and depleting her savings, Thomas lost custody of her son. She eventually moved in with her boyfriend, who was struggling with anger and alcohol issues, and his two sons in southwest Virginia. After a dispute in 2012 that involved a gun, Thomas was detained and given a psychological evaluation. She was diagnosed with bipolar disorder. Despite being a medical doctor, Thomas had come to despise the medical profession and refused treatment.

It is possible that Thomas' desire to fulfill her family's expectations, her inability to focus, her obsession with not winning gold at the Olympics, and her detachment towards people were perhaps the telltale signs of something more. The relentless training, personal sacrifice, emotional extremes, intense public scrutiny, and the devastating possibility of losing is more than most people can handle. More so when that someone is a "first." ❖

Dawn Staley
(1970)
Basketball player, coach, philanthropist

Dawn Staley, a three-time Olympic gold medalist and an award-winning coach, was inducted into the Women's Basketball Hall of Fame in 2012, and elected to the Naismith Memorial Basketball Hall of Fame in 2013.

DAWN MICHELLE STALEY was born in Philadelphia, Pennsylvania to Estelle Staley, a caretaker, and Clarence Staley, a carpenter, as the youngest of three boys and two girls. She grew up in a family that emphasized the value of a good education near the Raymond Rosen projects in Northern Philadelphia, a town dominated by basketball. To stay out of trouble, Staley played basketball with her older brothers. They created hoops out of milk crates, cut out the bottoms, and nailed them to the light poles for a backboard between their buildings, Staley found she could hold her own, delivering lightening-quick passes.

Staley was a very good student, primarily because if she did not get good grades, her mother would not let her play basketball. Although she was considered small for basketball, it became increasingly clear that she was born a point guard. At five feet and six inches tall, Staley worked hard to make up what she lacked in height. She realized early on that she had to rely not only on athleticism, but also on finesse, quick thinking, and strategy. She also learned how to size up and seize the resources around her and forge them into greatness.

Staley often stayed outside and played until she could no longer see the basket. At ten years old, Staley joined the Police Athletic League, traveling neighborhood to neighborhood while playing with the boys' team. When she was in the eighth grade, Staley received her first college letter of interest from Dartmouth. It encouraged her to see that someone thought she was good enough for an Ivy League team (Parker 2021). But her storied basketball career began at Murrell Dobbins Tech High School in Philadelphia where she played for the Lady Mustangs from 1986 to 1989. Staley was named *USA Today's* National High School Player of the Year, and led Dobbins to three straight Philadelphia Public League championships. Staley decided to go to the University of Virginia in Charlottesville (UVA) because it had a sound basketball program and one of the best academic reputations in the country (Rutledge 1998). From 1989 to 1992, she played point guard for the Virginia Cavaliers and helped UVA to a

110-21 record. She led her team to four NCAA Tournaments, three Final Fours, and one National Championship game.

Women's basketball made its debut in the Montreal 1976 Summer Olympics. While the women's games were gaining popularity, it still lacked the broad appeal of the men's games. Still, the Olympics offered women the rare chance to perform before the nation and expose the talent of women's basketball players. Team USA would rise to the occasion.

Staley made her first international appearance on the USA Basketball Women's Junior National Team (now called the U19 team). The team participated in the second Junior World Championship, held in Bilbao, Spain, in 1989. Team USA lost their opening game to South Korea in overtime, then lost a two-point game to Australia. After defeating Bulgaria, Team USA lost another close game, this time to Czechoslovakia, by three points. The team followed that loss with a victory against Zaire, but dropped its final game to Spain, again by three points. Staley averaged 10.8 points per game and recorded 14 steals over the course of the event, both records the second-highest on the team. Although the U.S. finished in seventh place. Staley was named Rookie of the Year in 1989. She would play for Team USA throughout her career.

In 1991, Staley was named to the U.S. Team at the World University Games held in Sheffield, England, and won the gold-medal. She averaged 4.9 points per game in this tournament. She finished her UVA career as the school's all-time scoring leader and as the Atlantic Coast Conference (ACC) all-time leader in assists with 729. Staley finished her college career with 2,135 points and held the NCAA record for career steals with 454. Staley was a three-time Kodak All-American, was named the ACC female athlete of the year, and was the National Player of the Year in 1991 and 1992.

When she graduated from UVA with a degree in Rhetoric and Communication Studies, Staley played with a number of professional teams in France, Italy, Brazil, and Spain from 1992 to 1994. In 1994, she competed in the World Championships and was named the USA Basketball Female Athlete of the Year, and played for USA Basketball in the Goodwill Games. She led the 1996 team, bolstered by the efforts of Sheryl Swoopes, Lisa Leslie, and Nikki McCray-Penson, to an undefeated record of 60-0 and the gold-medal at the Atlanta 1996 Summer Olympics.

Staley joined the American Basketball League (ABL) in 1997, and played for the Richmond Rage. She quickly became a two-time All-Star, guiding her team to the ABL finals. A year later, the team relocated to Staley's hometown of Philadelphia, and when the ABL folded shortly thereafter, she had averaged 14 points, 7.2 assists, and 3.5 rebounds per game.

In the 1999 WNBA draft, Staley was selected with the ninth overall pick by the Charlotte Sting. In 2001, she led the Sting to the WNBA Championship playoffs. During her first season in Charlotte, she averaged 11.5 points per game and ranked third in the league in assists with 5.5 assists per game, leading the Sting to a second place finish in the WNBA's Eastern Conference.

Staley had no interest in coaching when she was initially approached by Dave O'Brien, the athletic director of Temple University. She was on the Olympic team at the time, which was attending the Final Four in Philadelphia. She was still playing for the WNBA, and her friends told her it would be impossible for her to play and coach. This challenge convinced her that she should try, so she became the head coach for Temple University Owls women's basketball team in 2000.

The Athens 2004 Summer Olympics, where Staley reunited with Swoopes and Leslie, won a third gold medal with Team USA. It was a watershed moment. When Staley was traded to the Houston Comets in 2005, she announced before the start of the WNBA season that she would be retiring when the Comets' season ended. The Comets made the playoffs and faced the Sacramento Monarchs in the first round. The Monarchs swept the Comets and won the series 2-0, ending Staley's playing career. She was the only player—female or male—in ACC history to tally more than 2000 points, 700 rebounds, 700 assists, and 400 steals, and was the second person in conference history to record a triple-double, a feat she accomplished twice.

In 2008, Staley accepted the coaching position at the University of South Carolina. She left Temple with the best overall record of 172–80, along with six NCAA tournaments, three regular season conference championships, and four conference tournament titles. Her success is attributed to developing a playbook based on Olympics coach Tara VanDerveer. Like VanDerveer, Staley ascribed to an old-school and hard-driving approach, instilling in her players the mental skills needed to scheme and outwit the opposition (Parker 2021). She just could not imagine players not giving their all, all of the time.

At South Carolina, Staley was tasked to rebuild the Gamecocks, a losing team, from scratch. At first, she suffered through two losing seasons at the start of her tenure. Starting with ten wins during the 2008-2009 season, she led the program to better finishes in each subsequent season, leading to the program's first number one ranking and Final Four appearance during the 2014-2015 season. They picked up where they left off a year later in 2016, going undefeated in SEC play; however, they were upended in the Sweet 16 by Syracuse. In 2017, she guided the Gamecocks to their first NCAA Women's Basketball National Championship, making Staley the second African American to lead a women's basketball team to a national championship (Carolyn Peck had coached Purdue to the 1999 national championship). The 2019-2020 team was arguably the most talented of Staley's career, as the Gamecocks had blended a pair of seniors who helped deliver the program's 2017 National Championship with the number one recruiting class in the country. While the pandemic ended the season prior to the NCAA Tournament, the Gamecocks dominated the SEC. Staley would go on to lead South Carolina to five SEC regular season championships, five SEC tournament championships, six Sweet Sixteens, and two Final Fours. Under Staley's watch, the Gamecocks have enjoyed the most sustained success in program history. She is the only Gamecock basketball coach—women's or men's—to amass 300 victories at South Carolina.

It is no secret that Staley has forever changed the culture of women's basketball. As one of the most decorated female athlete in basketball, she has proven herself on the court as a player and on the sideline as a coach. More importantly, Staley is a brilliant teacher, role model, and tactician. She teaches her players not only what they need to learn on the court, but also provides them life lessons off the court as well. Staley's leadership has had a positive effect on both her current and former players because she believes in teaching them professionalism in every aspect of their lives.

Staley's transition from player into the coaching ranks of USA Basketball, USA World and the USA National teams was complete. She received her first USA Basketball coaching assignment as an assistant to the 2006 USA World Championship Team, and was later asked to remain on board for the Beijing 2008 Summer Olympics. The USA National Team from 2006-2008 posted a 32-2 record, captured the Olympics and 2007 FIBA Americas Championship gold-medals, and the 2006 FIBA World Championship bronze medal. She also spent one game as acting head coach for the 2006 USA National Team during its training in Australia, and led the team to victory against China.

In 2014, Staley served as an assistant coach for the USA World Championship Team and captured gold. She was also the head coach for the gold-medal winning 2014 USA U18 National Team. The following year, Staley was head coach for the gold-medal winning 2015 USA/U19 World Championship Team, and was on hand as an assistant coach for the USA National Team, which went 4-0 in its 2015 European tour against teams from Spain, Italy, and Czech Republic.

She served as an assistant coach under Team USA head coach Geno Auriemma for the Rio de Janeiro 2016 Summer Olympics and helped the Americans win their sixth straight gold medal in women's basketball and eighth gold medal in their past nine Olympic appearances. In 2017, Staley was named head coach of the USA National Team.

Staley has won numerous awards as both an athlete and a coach. As an athlete, she has won a total of ten gold medals, including three Olympic and two FIBA World Championship gold medals, one bronze medal, and seven international invitational titles from 1989 to 2004. Her performance led to her being named the 2004 USA Basketball Female Athlete of the Year. She was selected to carry the American flag during the Parade of Nations' opening ceremony at the Athens 2004 Summer Olympics, an honor never before bestowed on a basketball player—female or male (Grundy and Shackelford 2017), and then led Team USA to a perfect 8-0 record. In 2020, Staley became the first person to win the Naismith Award as a player and as a coach. While at the helm of the Gamecocks for the past twelve seasons, Staley has twice been named National Coach of the Year (2014, 2020) making her the first former Naismith Player of the Year to earn the Naismith Coach of the Year award. She is also a four-time SEC Coach of the Year (2014, 2015, 2016, 2020), and the 2012 BCA Female Coach of the Year.

Staley has also been honored by local and national organizations as an athlete and for her community service. Staley won the WNBA Entrepreneurial Spirit Award in 1999, and twice earned the Kim Perrot Sportsmanship Award (1999, 2006). She is the 1997 and 2005 recipient of Philadelphia's prestigious Wanamaker Award. Staley was also chosen as the 2007 female recipient of the Henry P. Iba Citizenship Award. Each year, it is given by the Rotary Club of Tulsa to a female and male athlete who has excelled in both their sport and in their service to others. She was named one of Philadelphia's 75 Greatest Living Residents, one of "The 100 Most Influential Sports Educators in America" by the Institute for International Sport, and one of Pennsylvania's Distinguished Daughters, an honor bestowed by Governor Rendell and his wife. In 2020, she won the Jefferson Award for Outstanding Public Service.

Several awards have been named in Staley's honor. Beginning in 2008, the WNBA presents the Dawn Staley Community Leadership Award to the player who best exemplifies the characteristics of a leader in the community in which she works or lives in (Baker 2008). The Phoenix Club of Philadelphia established the Dawn Staley Award recognizing the nation's top guard in women's Division I basketball in 2013. She even has streets named after her in Philadelphia and Columbia, South Carolina.

Additionally, Staley heads the Dawn Staley Foundation, which sponsors an after school program at the Hank Gathers Recreation Center for middle-school children. The Center focuses on academics and athletics, and sponsors basketball leagues as well as other fundraising activities. In 2013, she cofounded the Innersole Foundation, which provides new sneakers to children who are homeless and in need, and encourages children to participate in physical fitness. She initially launched Innersole via social media, and her broad network of friends, fans and colleagues immediately leapt into action. Sneakers poured in from all around the country, and a movement was born. Both organizations are based in South Carolina.

Staley is currently working on a four-book series loosely based on her childhood.

Staley's reputation, her record of success, her coaching style, her experience as a player, and her candor has propelled her into the upper echelons of basketball fame. But she has never forgotten the basics: to be a good point guard is to be everything to every player. To intuit who needs what in any second. To be the cheerleader, the scold, the shrink, the drill sergeant, the big sister, and the boss. This encapsulates who Staley is. Whether she is player, coach or mentor, she takes all of these ingredients, stirs the pot, and creates a winning dish every single time. ❖

Briana Scurry
(1971)
Soccer goalkeeper, coach

Briana Scurry is the first African American starter for the U.S. women's soccer team. She is the first goalkeeper, female or male, Black or White to play in 173 international games. She is also the first African American woman and the first goalkeeper to be inducted into the National Soccer Hall of Fame.

BRIANA COLLETTE SCURRY was born in Minneapolis, Minnesota to Robbie Scurry and Ernest Scurry, the youngest of nine children. She has a blended family of three brothers and five sisters. The first few years of her life were spent in the inner city sprawl of Minneapolis. When the family home began to sink into the filled-in lake beneath it, they moved to Galveston, Texas. After Hurricane Donna destroyed the family home in Galveston, they returned to Minnesota and lived in the lily-White suburbs of Anoka, where soccer was as common as summertime barbecues.

Scurry's love for sports came at a young age. Her first love was football, and at eleven years old, she scored nine touchdowns in a boys' league. She also competed in softball, basketball, and track. Scurry took to just about every sport she tried but did not play soccer until she was twelve. She went out for the boys' team because there was no girls' league soccer team. The coach made Scurry a goalkeeper because he thought she would be safest there, but she hated not being able to score. So after one season as a goalkeeper, Scurry played the field for three years, but returned to goal when she realized there she could control the game. She was the goalkeeper for the Anoka High School Tornadoes for four years and was instrumental in their Minnesota State Championship win in 1989, which ended in a shoot-out victory.

In high school, Scurry ran track, and played softball, soccer and basketball, her favorite sport. She was named Anoka High School's Athena Award winner as the school's top female athlete, High School All American and Minnesota's top female athlete. When Scurry applied for scholarships, however, of the seventy universities that courted her, fifty-five wanted her for soccer, while just two pursued her for basketball. Scurry accepted a soccer scholarship from the University of Massachusetts (UMass), where she refined her game under coach Jim Rudy. She split time in the net during her junior season in 1992, starting thirteen games and earning seven shutouts. Scurry played three games in 1992 as a forward. In 1993, she helped lead the UMass Minutewomen to a 17-3-3 record and the semifinals of the NCAA Women's Soccer Championship, as well as the titles of the Atlantic 10 Conference regular season and tournament. In her senior season, she started all twenty-three games and recorded 15 shutouts and a 0.48 goals-against average, the third-best in the nation. Scurry was named the Collegiate Goalkeeper of the Year twice, and in 1993 was named the National Goalkeeper of the Year by the Missouri Athletic Club Sports Foundation. She was also a second-team All-American, All-Northeast Region, and an All-New England first-team selection.

Scurry, who was majoring in political science, caught the attention of Tony DiCicco, coach of the U.S. Women's National Soccer Team, and she left college in 1994 to join the team as a goalkeeper. The team won the CONCACAF World Cup qualifying championship in Montreal that same year. Her impenetrability prompted the team to nickname her "The Rock" and "The Wall." At the World Cup in Sweden the following year, the U.S. finished a disappointing third. After Cup play ended, Scurry was in an automobile accident and hurt her back, but it did not stop her from playing in the World Cup in 1995. Scurry returned to UMass to complete her four-year collegiate career with 37 shutouts in 65 starts and a career record of 48-13-4 with a 0.56 goals-against-average. She had wanted to play for the Olympics since she was eight, so Scurry put her plans for law school on hold and went on to help lead the team to win gold at the Atlanta 1996 Summer Olympics. Scurry remained the U.S. team's number one goalkeeper until 1999.

With more than 90,000 screaming fans watching, Scurry made history at the FIFA World Cup championship in 1999 after an astounding shoot-out save against China, which resulted in a championship win that carried the U.S. to victory. Her talent protecting the goal—she had 71 shut-outs—and her team's unprecedented success led to a huge increase of women's soccer fans and inspired millions. Scurry's fist-clenched and high-stepping celebration after her famous cross-net deflection of China's Liu Ying's spot-kick in the World Cup was not only immortalized on a Wheaties cereal box, but would later become a permanent part of the National Museum of African American History and Culture Title IX exhibit in 2017.

During her playing years, Scurry donated volunteer time to promote AIDS awareness, participated in the Make-a-Wish Foundation, and visited many U.S. cities to spark interest in soccer among inner city girls and boys. After the U.S. Team won another gold medal at the Athens 2004 Summer Olympics, Scurry seriously considered joining the Women's National Basketball Association (WNBA). Instead, she became a founding member of the Women's United Soccer Association (WUSA). In its inaugural season in 2001, Scurry was assigned to the Atlanta Beat, and as captain, she competed in two WUSA Championships and was named Goalkeeper of the Year in 2003. Unfortunately, that same year, the WUSA suspended its operations due to financial woes.

Scurry was a goalkeeper for the U.S. women's national soccer team for most of the years between 1994 and 2008, earning 173 caps for the U.S.—a record among female soccer players. When the Women's Professional Soccer (WPS) league formed in 2008, seven teams were formed, and Scurry was drafted to the Washington Freedom.

Throughout her career, Scurry would constantly get hit in the head, but would think nothing of it. It was a knee to the temple while playing for the Washington Freedom and a debilitating concussion that finally led to her retirement in 2010 as she suffered from such severe migraines that she was unable to work. To make matters worse, the insurance company refused to pay for her occipital nerve release surgery because they questioned the legitimacy of the new procedure and did not want to pay for it. Too often, one of Scurry's disability checks would be sent late, and she would have an anxiety attack as a result. She ended up pawning her Olympic gold medals to make ends meet. None of her friends knew how badly off she was financially, and Scurry, embarrassed to ask for help, even contemplated suicide. Then, in 2013, Scurry met Chryssa Zizos, the founder and president of Live Wire Strategic Communications, LLC. She helped Scurry get her medals back and was instrumental in bringing Scurry's predicament to the public. Eventually, in 2013, the insurance company agreed to approve and cover the cost of Scurry's procedure at MedStar Georgetown University Hospital in Washington, D.C.

Since her surgery and physical therapy, Scurry has repurposed her visibility. As a result of her speaking out about her experiences, including testifying before Congress, she has become one of the nation's foremost thought leaders on traumatic brain injuries. Open about being a lesbian since her playing days, Scurry is also an advocate for LGBTQ rights, particularly in sports. Through her immeasurable impact on the landscape of women's soccer and American sports culture, Scurry received the National Association of Black Journalists' Sam Lacy Award, inclusion in the United States Women's National Team's All-Time Best XI, and is a permanent feature of the Title IX exhibit in the Smithsonian National Museum of African American History and Culture.

In September 2011, Scurry was named to the Anoka High School Hall of Fame's inaugural class. In 2015, Scurry was inducted into the Minnesota State High School Hall of Fame. In 2018, Scurry briefly served as the Washington Spirit's first assistant coach on its technical staff and was an adviser for the Maryland and Virginia Development Academy programs. In her fourth year of eligibility, Scurry became the first Black woman and first female goalkeeper to be inducted into the National Soccer Hall of Fame in 2018.

Scurry has played a pivotal role in soccer history as one of the first African American professional female players and has helped to diversify the sport. She married Chryssa Zizos in 2018, and has two teenage stepchildren. ❖

Sheryl Swoopes
(1971)
Basketball player, coach

Sheryl Swoopes, a former WCAA champion, four-time WWBA champion, a three-time Olympic gold medalist, and the first player to score 47 points in an NCAA Championship, was among the first players to sign with the WNBA, and helped popularize the sport.

SHERYL DENISE SWOOPES was born in Brownfield, Texas to Louise Swoopes and Billy Ray, who abandoned the family only months after Swoopes' birth. Her early years were difficult since her mother had to work several jobs to support Swoopes and her two older brothers. Father and daughter were not reunited until 2003, when Swoopes learned that her father lived in Houston and had attended some of her professional basketball games.

At the age of seven, Swoopes began playing competitive basketball in the Little Dribblers, a children's league. By the time she was in her junior year at Brownfield High School, she was the star player and led the Lady Cubs to the Texas Class 3A state championship. With the help of her two older brothers, Swoopes developed into an All-State and All-American high school player—eager to test her skills against any opponent. As a senior, her prowess earned her a place on three All-American teams.

The six-foot Swoopes was offered athletic scholarships from colleges throughout the country. She chose the University of Texas and enrolled there in the fall of 1989. But the moment Swoopes arrived on her new campus, she began to feel the distance acutely. After four days, she relinquished her scholarship and returned to her mother. Ignoring those who suggested she had ruined her career, Swoopes enrolled in South Plains Junior College in Levelland, a school within driving distance of Brownfield. That institution was glad to have her, especially when she was named National Junior College Player of the Year after her second season.

After playing at South Plains for two years, she transferred to Texas Tech University to play with the Texas Tech Lady Raiders. Swoopes won the NCAA women's basketball championship during her senior season in 1993. She scored 1,000 points in 46 games—a shorter period than anyone else in the

school's history. During her time at Texas Tech, Swoopes set more than ten school records, including most points per game and best free-throw percentage. In 1993, she was a key player in her university's bid for the NCAA Championships, scoring 47 points in the final game, the first and only player—female or male—to help clinch Texas Tech's first championship and victory over Ohio State University. Swoopes was subsequently named MVP of the NCAA Final Four Championships (Walker 2016).

Swoopes also set additional school records while at Texas Tech. She scored 955 points in the 1992-93 season, an all-time scoring record for a single season. Swoopes' 24.9 points-per-game average for her career is the best in the school's history. She also boasts three triple-doubles and twenty-three double-doubles, fourteen of which came during her senior year. Swoopes won the 1993 Naismith College Player of the Year award, was selected as that year's WBCA Player of the Year, and was chosen to the Division I All-American squad in 1992 and 1993. She was named the 1993 Sportswoman of the Year by the Women's Sports Foundation. Her jersey was retired by the school the following year, making her one of only three Lady Raiders to be honored in this way.

After graduating from Texas Tech in 1994, Swoopes continued to play for the USA Basketball Women's National Team, helping the team earn a bronze medal at the 1994 World Championships and contributing to their undefeated record in the 1995-96 season. After a failed attempt in 1992, she made the U.S. Olympic team and helped them win the gold medal at the Atlanta 1996 Summer Olympics.

Swoopes married Eric Jackson, her high school sweetheart, in 1995, and had a son. The couple would divorce in 1999.

She was an anchor of the women's national basketball team in 1996 and the first sportswoman to get her own signature line of athletic footwear: the Nike "Air Swoopes" basketball shoes. With a game as impeccable as her name, Swoopes became the heart of women's professional basketball. Young girls did not have to be "like Mike;" they could "hoop like Swoopes" while wearing her shoes.

In 1997, Swoopes became the first player to sign with the WNBA and was assigned to play for the Houston Comets, leading to four back-to-back WNBA championships from 1997 to 2000. For her performance at the 2000 championships, Swoopes was named the WNBA's MVP. That same year, she thrived in an Olympic competition, bringing home gold as part of the U.S. women's basketball team at the Sydney 2000 Summer Olympics. Swoopes continued to shine on the court, picking up two more MVP Awards in 2002 and 2005 and winning her third gold medal with the U.S. women's basketball team at the Athens 2004 Summer Olympics.

In 2005, Swoopes became one of the highest-profile professional athletes in a team sport to publicly announce that she was in a lesbian relationship.

After a back injury limited her to appearances in just three games in 2007, Swoopes went to play for the Seattle Storm in 2008, having played eleven years with the Comets. But her time with the team proved to be short, and when she was released by the Seattle Storm at the end of the season, Swoopes played with the Greek team Esperides. She made the NCAA women's basketball record books in many categories, including single-game scoring record, single-season scoring, highest championship tournament scoring average, and best single-game championship scoring performance, which broke Bill Walton's record and scoring record for championship series. She set the record for the most field goals in the championship game with sixteen.

In 2010, Swoopes was an assistant basketball coach at Mercer Island High School in Washington. She returned to the court as a member of the Tulsa Shock in 2011, marking the start of her final stint in the WNBA. That same year, she was named as one of the top fifteen players in WNBA history. After this, the Tulsa Shock reneged on her contract, and when she became a free agent, she retired from the game.

Beginning in 2013, Swoopes spent three seasons as head coach of the Loyola University Chicago women's basketball team, which finished with a 31-62 record. In 2017, Swoopes returned to her alma mater, Texas Tech, and was hired as the women's basketball program's Director of Player Development. Following the firing of head coach Candi Whitaker in 2018, Swoopes was promoted to regular assistant coach under interim head coach Shimmy Gray-Miller. She is currently focused on her Hoop with Swoopes basketball camp and her foundation Back to Our Roots, which she cofounded in 2019 (Moore 2020).

Swoopes won the female Associated Press Athlete of the Year award in 1993. That same year, she also won the Honda Sports Award for basketball and the WBCA Player of the Year award. She was named one of the twenty female athletes of the decade for 2000 to 2010 by *Sports Illustrated* and an LGBT History Month Icon by the Equality Forum. In 2008, Swoopes made an appearance on *Shirts & Skins,* a reality series on Logo TV. In 2017, she was inducted into the Women's Basketball Hall of Fame. In 2018, Nike released the" Air Swoopes 2," a new look to the retro "Air Swoopes" in homage to Swoopes and her career.

As the first player to sign up with the WNBA, Swoopes became an inspiring role model who paved the way for young girls to join basketball leagues, camps, and high school teams. She made history as the second player in WNBA history to win the regular-season MVP award and the All-star MVP award in the same season. Swoopes' six-year relationship with former Comets assistant coach Alisa Scott ended in 2011, the same year she became engaged to Chris Unclesho, whom she married in 2017. She now sees herself as a woman of evolving sexual identity, but her decision to come out created a less arduous environment for those who came after her, which has become an important part of her legacy.❖

Ann Wolfe

(1971)

Boxer, trainer

Ann Wolfe is an eight time world champion who held world titles in four different weight classes simultaneously in boxing, and the first woman to train a male boxer with a high ranking. Wolfe is considered by many within the sport as the hardest puncher and best fighter in the history of women's boxing.

ANN WOLFE was born in Oberlin, Louisiana to Theresa Eve Walker and David Wolfe II. Her mother endured a violent ten-year marriage. When her mother divorced her father, she and her six children got on a Greyhound bus bound for Los Angeles. There, Theresa married Douglas Walker, and six years later, the family returned to Oberlin. Wolfe's family was dirt poor. There was no electricity or running water in the house, and because life was hardscrabble from day one, everyone had to work, whether it was hauling water and pinecones, clearing land, cutting wood, doing weed work, or peeling crawfish.

The eleven-year-old Wolfe towered over her sixth-grade classmates. Since she was five foot ten and weighed close to 150 pounds, the coaches would let Wolfe run in high school track meets against the high school girls. Ironically, while Wolfe ran in high school meets, she never made it to high school. She dropped out in the seventh grade because her mother was sick, and Wolfe needed to earn money to help take care of her family. Despite the aching poverty, Wolfe's mother taught her children values. A strict Methodist, she made sure they went to church every day, and four-letter words were not permitted in her home (Walters 2005).

Wolfe's mother did not have health insurance so she never saw a doctor. By the time she went to the emergency room, she was diagnosed with stage four colon cancer and died soon after (Golianopoulos 2017). In 1989, Wolfe's father was murdered, allegedly during a drug dispute. In desperate straits, Wolfe turned to the streets. While she never used drugs, she sold crack and marijuana, and got caught and landed in jail in 1990. She pleaded no contest and served nine months in a Florida prison. Since Wolfe could barely read or write (Wolfe would eventually be diagnosed with severe dyslexia), she started selling drugs again when she got out of jail. When a woman was willing to sell her baby for crack, Wolfe decided she would never sell drugs again (Golianopoulos 2017).

Around this time, Wolfe's oldest brother was shot and killed by an off-duty Austin policeman after a 1994 robbery attempt. Another brother lost an eye to a bullet and is serving a life sentence in prison. She had two daughters by different fathers, one while living in New England, the other in prison. By the time she was twenty-two, Wolfe needed a fresh start, so she left Oberlin and moved to Austin, Texas in 1996 (Walters 2005). When her living arrangement with her sister and boyfriend fell apart, Wolfe, who found a job working in construction, found herself and her daughters homeless, living in the parking lot of an apartment complex underneath a boat. Sometimes, they took refuge in the emergency room at University Medical Center Brackenridge in Austin. The waiting room was open throughout the night, and the idea was that no one would suspect a mother with two girls in a crowded waiting room was actually there for shelter and not medical care. While her children slept, Wolfe passed the time watching television. One night in 1997, she saw two women boxing and wondered if they were getting paid. If so, she felt this might be her ticket out of the streets (Brick 2014).

Wolfe made her way to see Donald "Pops" Billingsley, a retired Austin school district janitor who owned the Montopolis Gym in East Austin, and asked him to become her trainer. Initially, he was skeptical about women boxing and told her no. But when she looked him in the eye and told him she would never leave him, he relented and over the years, their relationship went from boxer-trainer to father-daughter. Billingsley witnessed how Wolfe's anger and frustration dissipated as she channeled it into the ring, and he realized that he could help her become the greatest female boxer in the world. Wolfe began her career as an amateur under Billingsley's tutelage (W. L. 2009).

Wolfe was walking on Interstate 35 and was hit by a car. She survived with little medical attention. She eventually received an injury settlement check and combined with money from her job, she was able to secure shelter and buy a truck, an amazing feat considering what she and her children had gone through. But she still needed to make more money and saw boxing as a way out.

Wolfe had four amateur fights under the nickname "Brown Sugar" in the 165-pound division of the 1998 US Nationals held in California. She won a decision over Tami Hendrickson of Seattle in the quarter-final by 50-39, then stopped Shanie Keelean of Chicago 46 seconds into the first round in the semifinal, before losing to LeKiea Coffen of Washington, D.C. by disqualification at 1:23 of the third round. Wolfe's final amateur record was 3-1. Wolfe made her professional debut on October 17, 1998 at Seven Feathers Hotel and Casino Resort in Canyonville, Oregon. She won a tough, close four-round split decision over fellow Texan Brenda Bell Drexel, who fell to 1-4. She started fighting as a professional for Brian Pardo's Waco-based RPM Boxing in 1999.

In 1999 at the Mercer Arena in Seattle, Washington, Wolfe spoiled the professional debut of 1999 USA national amateur Dakota Stone of Seattle.

She knocked Stone down with a hard right in the second round, on the way to a unanimous decision win that moved her own professional record to 2-0. The two had met before, with Wolfe handing Stone the only loss of her amateur career. Highlights of Wolfe's career in 2000 include her fight with WIBF Junior Middleweight world champion Mary Ann Almager on an IFBA card at the Treasure Chest Casino in Kenner, Louisiana, with a first-round TKO.[1] Almager fell to 10-3 with this loss. Wolfe won by TKO at 1:07 of the first round over Demetra Jones in a junior middleweight bout. Jones, who was making her own professional debut, appears not to have fought since. Women Boxing Archive Network (WBAN) named Wolfe its "Fighter of the Month" in May 2000.

Wolfe suffered her first setback as a professional boxer when she was KO'd in the third round by two-time world champion Valerie Mahfood at the Radisson Astrodome in Houston. Wolfe knocked Mahfood down fifteen seconds into the first round of this exciting slugfest, but Mahfood came back with body punches in the second. Wolfe went to the canvas twice in the second round (once from a three-punch combination, and once as a slip). They traded powerful shots in the third, but then Wolfe was decked for the full count by an overhand right and left hook combination at 1:17 in the round.

In 2001, at the Hilton in Reno, Nevada, Wolfe TKO'd Kelly Whaley of Cedar City, Utah, winning a new WBF America's Junior Middleweight belt. At the Hawaii Convention Center in Honolulu, Wolfe won the IFBA Junior Middleweight title with a ten-round unanimous decision over Vienna Williams of Philadelphia, seen live on ESPN2's Tuesday Night Fights. It was a hard-hitting tactical bout between two well-schooled boxers that was well appreciated by the crowd and the ESPN2 commentators. Wolfe came away battered but victorious, while the smaller but hard-hitting Williams had her first loss in six professional fights.

In 2002, at the Convention Center in Waco, Texas, Wolfe used a relentless body attack to wear down and TKO late substitute Marsha Valley of Los Angeles in the sixth round taking the vacant IFBA Super Middleweight title. A clearly tiring Valley was hit by a left hook on a break, and then took an eight-count on one knee in the fifth. After softening up Valley with a barrage of body shots and overhand rights, Wolfe ended the fight in the sixth round with a three-punch left-right-left combination to her head that dropped Valley to one knee with her head between the ropes. Valley looked ready to beat the count when the referee called the fight over at 1:06 of the round.

Wolfe vacated her IFBA Junior Middleweight title and announced that she was looking for a high-profile bout with Laila Ali. Later that year, Wolfe had a rematch with Valley at the War Memorial Auditorium in Fort Lauderdale. She stopped Valley at 1:12 in the tenth round for the WIBC Super Middleweight title. Wolfe had knocked Valley down in the fifth, but Valley made the mistake

---

1. The difference between a TKO and a KO is that a TKO is declared when the fighter is conscious but unable to fight, while a KO happens when a fighter is unconscious and cannot continue to fight.

of taunting her when the fight continued, only to absorb a thorough beating from the muscular and powerful Wolfe. Valley fell to 9-8-4 (4 KO) with the loss.

In 2003, at the Mississippi Coast Coliseum and Convention Center, Wolfe avenged her only defeat with a ten-round unanimous decision over Mahfood for the vacant NABA Super Middleweight title. After some early exchanges, Wolfe appeared to have the upper hand and bloodied Mahfood's nose, but Mahfood fought back hard. She fell to 13-7-0 (7 KO) with the loss. This bout was on the undercard of the showdown between Ali and Christy Martin and positioned Wolfe, who signed a contract for a long-awaited showdown with Ali. Later that year, the WBAN named Wolfe its Fighter of the Month.

In 2004, at the Mississippi Coast Coliseum in Biloxi, Mississippi, Wolfe scored a spectacular first-round knockout over the undefeated Vonda Ward to win the vacant IBA Light Heavyweight world title. Trainer Emanuel Steward had advised Wolfe to attack the much taller Ward inside. Wolfe followed a vicious left hook to the body with an overhand right that caught her nine-inch taller opponent squarely on the chin and snapped her head back midway through the opening round. Ward fell to the canvas unconscious, lay there motionless for several minutes, and was sent to the hospital. She was diagnosed with a slight concussion and then kept overnight for observation. Ward, a star NCAA basketball center in Pat Summitt's prestigious University of Tennessee program, did not land a single punch before being felled by Wolfe's right hand for the KO at 1:08 into the fight. Ward fell to 18-1 (15 KOs) with the loss.

Wolfe, who moved her professional record to 17-1 (12 KO) with the win and added the IBA Light Heavyweight title to her previous IFBA/WIBA Junior Middleweight and IFBA/NABA Super Middleweight belts, called on Ali (16-0, 13 KO), the IWBF/IBA/WIBA Super Middleweight champion, to face her at Super Middleweight or Light Heavyweight, or get out of boxing, but Ali declined.

Ali had a good boxing career, but it became a widely accepted fact that her last name meant PPV buys, and she never fought top tier opponents. Wolfe had one-punch KO power, which is rare in boxing, and having achieved the status of world champion and "legend,' Ali avoided Wolfe.

In 2005, at Isle of Capri in Biloxi, Mississippi, Wolfe won by a first-round TKO in a rematch with Buckhalter in a scheduled six-rounder. She was now 19-1-0 (13 KOs) while Buckhalter fell to 2-12-1 (2 KO) with the loss. Buckhalter, who was knocked down once during the fight, had not fought since losing to Wolfe in 2002. Wolfe had a rematch with Valley at the FedEx Forum in Memphis, Tennessee, where she TKO'd Valley at 1:17 in the sixth round of a scheduled ten-rounder for Wolfe's IBA Light Heavyweight title. Valley fell to 10-11-4 (4 KOs) with the loss. In another rematch, Wolfe soundly defeated Mahfood at the Isle of Capri Casino in Biloxi, Mississippi, with a 10-round unanimous decision in the main event. Wolfe was defending her IBA Light Heavyweight title. She improved her record to 22-1-0 (15 KOs) while Mahfood fell to 19-10-1 (9 KO).

In 2006, at the FedEx Forum in Memphis, Wolfe won a six-round unanimous decision over Lisa Ested Smith of Richmond, Virginia, in a bout carried on ESPN2's Friday Night Fights. Wolfe improved to 24-1-0 (16 KOs) with the win, while Ested, a former IWBF Welterweight Champion who retired from boxing in 2000 but returned to the ring in late 2005, fell to 10-5-0 (6 KOs). Wolfe then announced she was finished with boxing and preferred to work as a trainer.

When Wolfe retired in 2006, she simultaneously held four weight class titles, and established a 24-1 (with 16 knockouts) record. Boxing became her salvation, and she became, arguably, the greatest female fighter of all time. Along the way, Wolfe invited everyone from 106 to 200-plus pounds to have a go at her. She did not have Anna Kournikova's sex appeal, Michelle Wie's child-prodigy status, or Ali's famous last name. She made some magazine covers, but not as many as Christy Martin. Unfortunately, these characteristics—rather than victories—are still the easiest ways to strike fame and fortune as a female athlete. Wolfe showed how female fighters can be as explosive, exciting, and devastating as male fighters. In fact, sports commentators become awestruck when Wolfe talks about her old school blood, sweat, and tears approach to training. But her power was not her greatest attribute in the ring. During her career she manifested a code that she still follows: to become great, you must sacrifice and suffer. And Billingsley instilled this punishment on Wolfe to set her on that track.

Wolfe has a knack for helping others. Perhaps it is because there was a time in her life when she needed help. She opened a gym in 2003 and became a mentor to young amateur boxers. In 2004, the Ann Wolfe Boxing Team challenged opponents at the Golden Gloves in San Antonio, Texas. Wolfe took ten of her fighters to the event, wining gold and silver medals in the Open Division. The team also won Best Sportsmanship of the tournament, while Wolfe's trainer, Billingsley, took home the Best Novice Coach award. Wolfe trained many amateur and professional boxers, including her oldest daughter Jennifer Fenn and light middleweight contender James Kirkland, making her the first woman to train a male boxer with a high ranking.

In 2009, Wolfe's girlfriend gave birth to their son Zion. By 2015, Wolfe closed the latest incarnation of her gym to give herself a break. That same year, she was inducted into the Women's International Boxing Hall of Fame in Fort Lauderdale. In 2017, Wolfe was cast fittingly in the supporting role of the Amazon warrior Artemis in *Wonder Woman*. Other projects include working on her memoir, film and television projects, dabbling in real estate and keeping a keen eye on world events. In 2021, Wolfe was inducted into the International Boxing Hall of Fame and Museum in Canastota, New York.

Wolfe is a self-made woman. She started at the bottom, born into poverty, tossed into lawlessness, beaten down by homelessness and despair, only to rise above her circumstances to make a life for herself. Long before she portrayed the rugged Amazonian warrior Artemis, she played one in real life, and became our Black warrior.❖

Lisa Leslie
(1972)
Basketball player, team owner, author, actress, sportscaster

Lisa Leslie was the number-seven pick in the 1997 inaugural WNBA draft, a three-time WNBA MVP, a four-time Olympic gold-medal winner, and the first player to dunk in a WNBA game. She was inducted into both the Naismith Memorial Basketball Hall of Fame and the Women's Basketball Hall of Fame.

LISA DESHAUN LESLIE was born in Gardena, California as the youngest daughter of Christine Lauren Leslie and Walter Leslie, a former professional basketball player. When her father left the family, her mother, who was four months pregnant with her, started a trucking business to support her son and three daughters.

By the seventh grade, Leslie was six feet tall (she would become six feet and five inches), and she hated it when people asked her if she played basketball or why she did not join the team. It was only after she reluctantly picked up the sport in middle school that she became hooked. When she transferred to a junior high school without a girls' basketball team, she joined the boys' basketball team, which contributed to her confidence in her playing abilities.

Remarkably, by the age of fourteen, Leslie received more than a hundred college recruiting letters, including some from top Division I programs such as those at the University of Tennessee and Stanford University. In 1986, Leslie attended Morningside High School in Inglewood, California, making an immediate impact on the basketball program. In her sophomore year, she could dunk the ball in open court, even though she could not palm the ball. She was the team's leading scorer and rebounder and led them to the 1989 California state championship.

Leslie was invited to participate in the USA's Junior World Championship team. She was also named to the USA Basketball Women's Junior National Team (now called the U19 team) when she was seventeen years old, the youngest player. The team went to Bilbao, Spain in 1989 to participate in the second Junior World Championship, and finished in seventh place. She also joined the volleyball team and competed in track and field, becoming a state qualifier in the 400-meter run and the high jump. Leslie decided to stay close to home

for college and enrolled in the women's basketball powerhouse, University of Southern California (USC), from 1990 to 1994.

While at USC, Leslie compiled an impressive 89-31 record. They won one Pac-10 conference championship and earned four NCAA tournament appearances. Leslie was honored with All-Pac-10 recognition all four years and became the first player in Pac-10 history to obtain first team all four years, earning the Pac-10 Rookie of the Year award in 1991. She played a total of 120 college games, averaged 20.1 points, hit 53.4 percent of her shots, and sank 69.8 percent of her free throws. Leslie set the Pac-10 Conference records for scoring, rebounding, and blocked shots, accumulating 2,414 points, 1,214 rebounds, and 321 blocked shots. She also holds the USC single-season record at 95 for blocked shots.

Leslie earned the Freshman of the Year award in 1991, which catapulted her to the national platform. In 1994, she won multiple national player awards—the Naismith College Player of the Year award, the USBWA Women's National Player of the Year award, the Honda Sports Award for basketball, and the WBCA Player of the Year award. She earned All-American Honors in 1992, 1993, and 1994. Then, at age twenty, Leslie was the youngest player to participate in the USA Olympic Trials in 1992.

Leslie competed with USA Basketball as a member of the 1992 Jones Cup Team, which won the gold in Taipei for the first time since 1987. She was a USA team member competing at the 1991 World University Games held in Sheffield, England. Leslie was the second-leading scorer on the USA squad, averaging 13 points per game, and helped lead the team to a 7-0 record and the gold medal. She graduated in 1997 with a BA in communications.

She is one of seven USA Basketball three-time Olympians and one of two players with four gold medals that she won in 1996, 2000, 2004, and 2008. Leslie scored 35 points against Japan in the Atlanta 1996 Summer Olympics semifinals and set an American record. She led the U.S. team in scoring during the Athens 2004 Summer Olympics, becoming the USA's all-time leading scorer, rebounder, and shot blocker. Every time Leslie competed in a major international event, she compiled double-digit scoring averages.

When the WNBA began in 1997, Leslie was drafted by the Los Angeles Sparks, becoming one of the new league's first players. Although she helped the Sparks make the playoffs five consecutive times, the team did not win a WNBA title until 2001. That same year, Leslie was named the 2001 Sportswoman of the Year by the Women's Sports Foundation.

In 2001, Leslie was the first WNBA player to win the regular-season MVP, the All-Star Game MVP, and the playoff MVP in the same season. In 2002, Leslie became the first woman to dunk the ball in a WNBA game and was named MVP of the WNBA Championship. Besides becoming the first WNBA player to score over 3,000-career points, she contributed to the Sparks winning their second straight WNBA championship that season.

Two seasons later, Leslie became the first player to reach the 4,000-career point milestone and picked up two more WNBA MVP honors in 2004 and 2006. She also became the third player in WNBA history to record a triple-double when she had 29 points, 15 rebounds and 10 blocks. In the 2005 WNBA All-Star Game, Leslie became the first WNBA player to dunk in an all-star game.

In 2005, Leslie married Michael Lockwood, who played basketball for the Air Force Academy and was a UPS pilot. In 2007, she took a year's leave for her pregnancy. After having her daughter, she returned for the 2008 season.

Upon Leslie's return, she earned her fourth and final gold medal in women's basketball at the Beijing 2008 Summer Olympics. In 2009, she announced her retirement. Leslie scored more than 6,263 points, 3,307 rebounds, and 10,444 PRA during her twelve years with the WNBA. The Sparks held a farewell ceremony during their final home game of the season. In 2011, she was voted by fans as one of the top fifteen players in the fifteen-year history of the WNBA. In 2016, she was voted into the WNBA Top 20@20 to celebrate the league's twentieth anniversary.

Apart from basketball, earlier in her career, Leslie signed a modeling contract with Wilhelmina modeling agency and has worked as an actress. She has appeared on several television shows such as *Sister Sister, The Game, One on One, The Simpsons,* and various commercials. Leslie played herself in *The Superstars* and *The Jersey,* and appeared in the reality television shows *Celebrity Wife Swap, All in with Cam,* and *The New Celebrity Apprentice.* Leslie was also a playable character in the original *Backyard Basketball* computer game and appeared in the movies *Think Like a Man* (2012) and *Uncle Drew* (2018). She has been featured in *Vogue* and *Newsweek,* as well as many sports publications.

Leslie released her autobiography, *Don't Let the Lipstick Fool You* in 2008. Since her retirement, she earned a Master's of Business Administration degree from the University of Phoenix in 2009. She had her second child, a son, in 2010. She has worked as a sports commentator and analyst for several sports networks, such as NBC, ABC, and Fox Sports Net. Leslie is a guest commentator for *Sports Zone* on KABC-TV/Los Angeles and has often appeared on ESPN.

Leslie returned to her beloved Sparks in 2011, but as one of the team's owners, becoming the first WNBA player to invest in a team. She also shares her knowledge and skills with others through the Lisa Leslie Basketball & Leadership Academy. In 2015, she was admitted to the Women's Basketball Hall of Fame and the Naismith Basketball Hall of Fame. Leslie released her second book, *From the Court to the Boardroom: The Path to Empowerment* in 2017. In 2018, she joined Fox Sports Florida as a studio analyst on Orlando Magic broadcasts, and was also a coach of Ice Cube's BIG3 expansion team in 2019.❖

Dominique Dawes
(1976)
Gymnast, business owner

Dominique Dawes is a four-time Olympic medalist, a three-time Olympian, the first African American woman to win an Olympic gold medal in gymnastics, and the first African American woman to win an individual Olympic medal in artistic gymnastics.

DOMINIQUE MARGAUX DAWES THOMPSON was born in Silver Spring, Maryland to Loretta Dawes and Don Dawes. She has two siblings who would eventually participate in the Olympics as well. Dawes was introduced to gymnastics at age six when she signed up for a tumbling class. When the class was canceled, someone suggested to her mother that she try a local gymnastics club called Marva Teens. Dawes signed up and began working with Kelli Hill, who would coach her during her entire career.

With her amazing tumbling moves, Dawes was a force to be reckoned with. She began competing as a junior elite by the age of ten. In 1988, she placed seventeenth in the all-around junior division at her first U.S. National Championships, becoming the first African American to make the national women's team. In 1989, she went to Australia at the age of twelve and competed in her first international meet, the Konica Grand Prix. By the early 1990s, Dawes achieved success both nationally and internationally. She placed third in the all-around in the junior division at the 1990 U.S. National Championships.

After an energetic floor routine at the 1992 USA versus Japan dual meet, she revived the back-to-back tumbling revolutionized by Soviet star Oksana Omelianchik, and the fifteen-year-old Dawes received a standing ovation. The judges gave her a perfect ten. Although she was not part of the 1991 World Championship team, Dawes moved up in the national and international scene throughout 1991 and 1992.

The crowd-pleasing athlete placed fourth at the Barcelona 1992 Summer Olympic trials and was awarded a place on the Olympic team. Despite battling painful tendinitis in both ankles and Osgood-Schlatter disease (knee pain) during pre-Olympic training, Dawes performed well throughout the competition and even tried out a new move in her balance beam routine—a back handspring to three layout step-outs. She won over the crowd with a solid optional floor exercise routine and tied with Kim Zmeskal with a mark of 9.925, the highest score for the American team. When the team won bronze, Dawes and teammate Betty Okino became the first African American women to win Olympic gymnastics medals.

Dawes only competed in the team competition in 1992 and would not break through as an all-around gymnast until 1993. She is perhaps best known for her performances at the 1993 and 1994 World Championships. In 1993, Dawes led the competition after three events, even beating her more famous teammate, Shannon Miller. Unfortunately, while she made the first vault, Dawes slipped and fell on the second. With the new rule that both vaults were averaged in the all-around competition, her fall dropped her to fourth place. She rebounded in the event finals, winning two silver medals on bars and beam. The same fate befell her at the 1994 Worlds and continued throughout the event finals. She left the championships without winning a single medal.

However, Dawes finished her year on a positive note. At the National Championships in 1994, she won all-around gold and all four individual events: vault, uneven bars, balance beams, and floor exercises. Dawes was the first gymnast to win all five gold medals since 1969. She would go on to lead the American team to a silver medal at the World Team Championships in Dortmund, Germany, posting the third-highest all-around score in the process. In the midst of this, Dawes attended Montgomery Blair High School in Silver Spring and graduated from Gaithersburg High School, where she was the 1994 prom queen.

In 1995, Dawes struggled with wrist and ankle injuries. She finished fourth at nationals and was forced to sit out of the World Championships that year. At the 1996 World Championships, she missed out on a medal on the uneven bars but tied Liu Xuan for a bronze medal on the balance beam. At the 1996 U.S. National Championships, Dawes swept all four event finals for the second time in her career, making her the only gymnast ever to accomplish this feat twice. She also finished first at the Olympic trials, earning a spot on the Atlanta 1996 Summer Olympics team at nineteen. Dawes planned to attend Stanford University in the fall of 1995 but did not receive an athletic scholarship because she turned professional to train for the Olympics.

The team, later nicknamed the "Magnificent Seven," dominated team competition. Dawes, a key member of the team, performed without serious error and was the only team member to have all eight of her scores count towards the total. She claimed her gold medal as part of the first American team to take the Olympic title. In another first, she became the first African American woman to win an Olympic gold medal in gymnastics.

Dawes had hoped to win an individual gold medal as well, but was devastated when a step out of bounds and a fall during her floor routine placed her out of medal contention during the all-around competition. She did win an individual bronze medal for her floor performance, making her the first African American to win an individual medal in women's gymnastics.

From 1996 to 1998, Dawes competed in various professional meets but retreated from elite competition. She returned briefly in 1998 to participate in the Goodwill Games, where she placed nineteenth in the Mixed Pairs event with Chainey Umphrey. She also made the USA Gymnastics team, placing seventh at the Sydney 2000 Summer Olympics trials, earning her a spot on her third Olympic team. At the team preliminaries, Dawes posted the second-highest score of the American team on uneven bars but the lowest on beam. In the team finals, she performed well on three events and contributed to the team's bronze medal when the International Olympic Committee stripped China of its 2000 team medal for an underage competitor. This made Dawes the first U.S. gymnast to be a member of three separate medal-winning gymnastic teams.

After the Olympics, Dawes retired from competition. She returned to school and graduated with a bachelor's degree from the University of Maryland, College Park in 2002, and pursued acting, modeling, and television production. She appeared in several music videos and the Broadway revival of *Grease,* playing cheerleader Patty Simcox. Dawes then turned her attention to speaking engagements and promoting sports for women, concentrating on youth issues.

She served as president of the Women's Sports Federation from 2005 to 2006, the youngest president in the foundation's history. Dawes, whose younger brother has autism, has supported events for autism awareness, such as the 2001 Power of One rally in Washington D.C. She has supported Girl Scouts of the USA, the Women's Sports Foundation, Boys & Girls Clubs of America, and many other organizations. Dawes served on the Advisory Board of Sesame Workshop's "Healthy Habits for Life" program, and in 2010, President Obama appointed Dawes as co-chair of the newly renamed President's Council on Fitness, Sports and Nutrition. She has provided sports commentary for Yahoo! Sports, TNT, CBS, Fox Sports Net, CNN and Comcast SportsNet.

Dawes became engaged in 2012 to Catholic schoolteacher Jeff Thompson. She converted to Catholicism, and they married in 2013. They have four children.

In 2020, Dawes opened the Dominique Dawes Gymnastics and Ninja Academy to provide a healthy and positive training environment for young gymnasts.

Out of the millions of girls who practice gymnastics, Dawes was one of only seven to make it to the Olympics in 1996. But despite having accomplished the near impossibility of this achievement, Dawes still faced a set of predetermined challenges from the moment she entered the gym, simply because she is Black. As she leaped through the air, stretching and contorting her body, the extraordinarily talented Dawes took the world by storm in the World Championships and the Olympics, leaving a lasting impression that paved the way for Black gymnasts like Gabby Douglas and Simone Biles, who followed the trail she blazed.❖

Maritza Correia McClendon
(1981)
Swimmer, marketing executive

Maritza Correia McClendon is the first African American woman to set an American and World swimming record, the first African American woman to make the U.S. Olympic swim team, the first African American woman to win a NCAA Division I Championship, and the first African American woman to win an Olympic medal in swimming.

MARITZA CORREIA MCCLENDON was born and raised in San Juan, Puerto Rico. Her parents, Anne Correia, a former tennis player and a nurse, and Vincent Correia, a former crew member and a mechanical engineer, had moved there from Guyana. McClendon is the youngest of four children in a blended family. Her youngest brother passed away from leukemia when he was eleven years old.

At the age of six, McClendon was diagnosed with scoliosis, an abnormal curvature of the spine. Her doctor suggested she take up either swimming or gymnastics to help mitigate the effects of the disorder. Living in Puerto Rico, her mother thought it made sense for her to take swimming lessons.

Eventually, McClendon asked if she could participate in a year-round program. She later joined a local swim club in San Juan and started to swim competitively. In 1990, when she was nine years old, the family moved and settled in Brandon, Florida. There, she and her brother became members of the Brandon Blue Wave Swim Team and were often the only Black athletes competing in events.

McClendon attended Tampa Bay Technical High School and joined the school's swim team. In 1999, she became the U.S. National Champion in the 50-meter freestyle in the eighteen and under category. She was also a six-time Florida High School State Champion in five different events, four of them in the 100-meter freestyle. McClendon was a member of the 1997 USA National Junior Team that competed in Sweden, and the 1999 USA Short Course World Championship Team, which competed in Hong Kong.

McClendon was accepted at the University of Georgia with a full scholarship, and she swam for Olympic Coach Jack Bauerle. When she arrived there in the fall of 1999, she became the first African American woman to swim for the Lady Bulldogs swimming and diving team, nearly twenty years after Randy

Grimes was the first African American on the men's team. She also hoped to participate in the Sydney 2000 Summer Olympics, but she missed making the team when she went to the Olympic Trials.

McClendon had always experienced pressure, which only grew when she began competing at the college level. But at the Olympic Trials, she had the most disappointing moment of her life. She was expected to make the Olympic team, but finished in 32nd place in the 200-yard freestyle. Although she had two more races to compete in at the trials, her father told her to pack her bags as he did not want to risk any more embarrassment. Not living up to one's expectations, combined with the racialization of the sport, McClendon considered quitting, but the Olympic Trials would not kill the fight in her.

After the trials, McClendon spiraled into six months of depression. She began therapy to talk about her adolescence, a childhood dominated by traveling and training for swim meets. She reevaluated her relationship with her father, which was eventually rectified, and talked about her fears. Getting help solidified her resolve to stick with swimming.

McClendon returned to the Lady Bulldogs and performed well at the National Collegiate Athletic Association (NCAA) Championships in 2001, 2002, and 2003. In 2002, she became the U.S. Open record holder for the World Championship in both the 50-yard and 100-yard freestyle, and was a member of two winning relay teams at the NCAA Championships. She earned seven All-American certificates and was awarded the Commissioner's Cup as the high point scorer in the SEC (Southeastern Conference) Championships. McClendon finished her college swimming career in 2003, having barely spoken to her father during those years.

When McClendon finished fourth in the 100-meter freestyle at the 2004 Olympic trials in Long Beach, California, she earned a spot in the 400-meter freestyle relay at the Athens 2004 Summer Olympics and won a silver medal. When McClendon reached that milestone as the first African American to compete and win a medal in swimming, her father was there, cheering her on from the sidelines. Before his death four years later, he told McClendon's mother he was proud of her. This would be her only Olympics.

After the Olympics, McClendon continued her studies at the University of Georgia. She received her degree in 2005 in sociology and became a member of Sigma Gamma Rho Sorority. That same year, she won three gold medals at the 2005 Summer Universiade (World University Games) in Izmir, Turkey.

In 2006, McClendon won a silver medal at the World Championships in the 400-meter medley and a bronze medal in the 400-meter freestyle. She competed in her last meet at the 2007 Pan American Games, winning gold medals in the 400-meter medley and the 400-meter freestyle. After receiving a double shoulder injury, McClendon's dream of gold at the Beijing 2008 Summer Olympics was cut short. She hung up her cap and goggles, unwilling to be that athlete who strained her body past her prime.

A career of firsts, McClendon was the first African American female swimmer to make the U.S. Olympic team, the first African American to break a World record in swimming, and the first African American and African American woman to break an individual American record. She served as Team USA's team captain in 2003, 2005, and 2007; and ended her competitive career as a 27-time All American with eleven NCAA titles and an Olympic silver medal. Though forced into an early retirement, McClendon remains a strong and visible personality in the world of competitive swimming and women's sports.

When she transitioned out of swimming, McClendon worked for Perry Ellis International as the senior marketing manager for Nike Swim. She held a senior marketing position at the children's clothing company, Carter's, and worked on both OshKosh B'gosh and other Carter's brands. She is currently the senior manager for Talent and Development, with an emphasis on developing a strategy for diversity and inclusion at Carter's.

In 2014, McClendon received the USA Swimming Diversity and Inclusion Award. She was inducted into the University of Georgia's Circle of Honor in 2015, which pays tribute to extraordinary student-athletes and coaches who have contributed to the Georgia Bulldogs' tradition.

McClendon serves as the ambassador for USA Swimming's Swim 1922 Program. In partnership with Sigma Gamma Rho Sorority, the program strives to lower drowning rates in the African American community, reminding us that swimming is the only sport that is also a life-saving skill. She is also on the Advisory Board for Diversity in Aquatics, is a board member for the Kensley Grace Foundation, and is the chairperson of USA Swimming Black Leadership in Aquatics Coalition (BLAC). Founded in 2020, BLAC provides strategic guidance to USA Swimming staff and other sport leaders concerning, diversity, equity, and inclusion (DEI).

Though her records in the 50-yard and 100-yard events have since been broken, McClendon remains a groundbreaking force in the world of competitive swimming. Ever since McClendon became the first Black woman to make a U.S. Olympic swim team and win a medal, she has taken that responsibility very seriously, even though it has been well over a decade since her last competition. While she continues to promote the sport as a spokesperson for USA Swimming, mentors athletes, promotes water safety, and travels the country as a motivational speaker, she has also become an advocate for, and gives voice to, a new generation of Black athletes. McClendon remains committed to creating safe spaces for all members of the sports community. More importantly, she brings to light misconceptions about DEI and the importance of integrating those efforts throughout all sports organizations.

McClendon married Chad McClendon in 2010, and they have two children. They reside in Atlanta, Georgia. As a trailblazer in her sport, McClendon's mission is to educate Black communities about the importance of learning to swim, while inspiring a new generation of Black swimmers.❖

Serena Williams
(1981)
Tennis player, entrepreneur, philanthropist

Serena Williams, who has revolutionized women's tennis, has won four Olympic medals and twenty-three Grand Slam single titles, more than any other person in the Open Era.

SERENA JAMEKA WILLIAMS was born in Saginaw, Michigan to Oracene Price Williams and Richard Williams, a former sharecropper from Louisiana. For both, this was their second marriage. Williams is the youngest of her mother's five daughters, including her older sister Venus, and has at least seven paternal half-siblings. Richard Williams envisioned Venus and Serena as tennis champions even before they were born. He bought books and instructional videotapes and taught himself and his wife how to play tennis in order to teach their daughters. The family moved to Compton, California, where Williams started playing tennis at age three. Coached by their father, the sisters practiced on city courts, cutting their teeth under less than ideal circumstances as they withstood the rigors of daily two-hour practices.

Williams entered her first tennis tournament at age four and a half, and over the next five years, she won forty-six of the forty-nine matches she entered. She and her sister excelled in the highly competitive preteen circuit in Southern California, both attaining a number-one ranking in their respective age groups. By the time they reached their teens, they had begun attracting attention far beyond the borders of their home state, receiving offers for endorsement deals from sporting goods companies and invitations to prestigious tennis camps. In 1991, Richard Williams withdrew the girls from junior tournaments, which was widely criticized because it was the conventional path to tennis stardom. Still, he wanted to protect his daughters from the intense competition and what he perceived as racial hostility from other players. He invited tennis pro Rick Macci—who had earlier coached such tennis stars as Mary Pierce and Jennifer Capriati—to come to Compton. Macci came, and he was impressed by the sisters' skill and athleticism. He invited them to study with him at his Florida academy, and soon after, when Williams was nine, the family relocated to Florida. But when Williams was in the ninth grade, her father pulled his daughters out of Macci's academy and took over their coaching.

By 1993, the girls left school and continued their education at home to spend more time honing their tennis skills. They later enrolled in a small, private school, and in 1995, at age fourteen, Williams turned pro, arousing controversy among many who felt she was too young. The Women's Tennis Association (WTA), the governing body of women's professional tennis, barred competitors from WTA events at that age. Williams' first professional event was a non-WTA tournament in Quebec, Canada, and she lost, badly. Her father pulled her from competition for the remainder of that year and the following year for additional training.

Her first year as a WTA competitor began in 1997 in the shadow of her sister Venus, who had already shown herself to be a promising player. However, by the Ameritech Cup in Chicago, Williams proved to be a budding star in her own right. She stunned the tennis world when she defeated Mary Pierce, then ranked seventh in the world among women players, in the second round. Williams defied expectations by defeating fourth-ranked Monica Seles in the quarterfinals before losing to Lindsay Davenport in the semifinals. When she finished the season, Williams ranked ninety-nine, an impressive debut year for a sixteen-year-old player.

Williams continued to build her skills and confidence in 1998, beating several players ranked far above her. She beat ninth-ranked Irina Spirlea in the first round of the Australian Open, which led to a matchup against her sister in the next round. Both sisters felt an intense drive to win, even when they faced each other as opponents.

Williams also played with Venus as a doubles team, marking the first time they won a professional match together. Williams also won two Grand Slam[1] mixed doubles titles that year—at Wimbledon and the U.S. Open—with partner Max Mirnyi. While she had yet to win a Grand Slam singles title, Williams earned more than $2 million during 1998. The following year, Williams defeated three of the top four tennis players in the world to win the singles title at the U.S. Open. It was her first victory at a Grand Slam event and the first time since Althea Gibson's win in 1958 that an African American woman won a Grand Slam singles title. Another milestone was Williams' first professional victory over her sister, beating Venus in the Grand Slam Cup in 1999. The two paired up to win two Grand Slam doubles events that year at the French Open and the U.S. Open. Williams finished the 1999 season as the fourth-ranked women's player in the world and graduated from high school that same year.

The next two years proved difficult for Williams. A series of injuries forced her to withdraw from several tournaments. The high points of the season

---

1.   The term "Grand Slam" refers to the accomplishment of winning all four major championships: the Australian Open in mid January, the French Open from late May to early June, Wimbledon in late June to early July, and the U.S. Open in August–September. Each tournament is played over a two-week period. To date, this feat has been achieved six times (by five different players). Grand Slam is commonly misused to describe any one of the four major tournaments, for example, "Grand Slam singles (or doubles) titles or events."

included doubles victories with Venus as her partner at Wimbledon and the Sydney 2000 Summer Olympics, the first of her four appearances at the Olympics. The sisters won the Australian Open's doubles title in 2001, marking their dominance in doubles at all four Grand Slam events.

Having recovered spectacularly from her various injuries, Williams seemed unstoppable in 2002. She was victorious in eight out of the eleven tournaments she entered, earning nearly $4 million in prize money. At the NASDAQ-100 Open in Miami, Williams defeated the top three players in the world, including her sister, to win the singles title. This achievement marked one of many history-making wins: she joined tennis great Steffi Graf as the only two to defeat the world's three best players in one tournament. Three times that year—at the French Open, Wimbledon, and the U.S. Open—Williams met Venus in the finals of a Grand Slam event, and three times she defeated her sister. After her victory at Wimbledon, Williams became the top-ranked women's tennis player in the world. She was also one of seven women in the game's history to win three consecutive Grand Slam titles in a single year.

In 2003, Williams completed her sweep of Grand Slam events, beating her sister to win the Australian Open's singles title. She won several other significant singles titles that year, including a second consecutive win at Wimbledon. She held on to her number-one ranking for over a year and won the ESPY for best female tennis player and best female athlete.

That year proved difficult due to injuries, but such problems would seem insignificant compared to the tragedy Williams and her family would endure. Her sister, Yetunde Price, was killed in Los Angeles in a random act of violence. Williams credited her faith as a Jehovah's Witness, as well as a life-changing journey she made to West Africa, to helping her heal and renew her competitive fire.

For much of 2004, Williams dealt with a recurring knee injury. She won the NASDAQ-100 Open in Miami for the third year in a row, but was either defeated or had to withdraw due to injury from other tournaments. Her pursuits outside of tennis also began taking up more of her time, particularly her efforts to become an actress. Starting in 2002, Williams had guest roles on various television shows, including *The Bernie Mac Show, ER, My Wife and Kids, Showtime's Street Time, Law & Order,* and *Law & Order: Special Victims Unit.* She also received a small part in the film, *Hair Show* (2004).

In 2005, Williams won the Australian Open again, but by 2006, after a series of injuries and a world ranking of 139, she was ready to quit. Nevertheless, she rebounded in 2007 to win her third Australian Open. Williams and Venus won their second doubles tennis gold medal at the Beijing 2008 Summer Olympics and won the U.S. Open for the third time. In 2009, she captured her tenth Grand Slam singles title by winning the Australian Open. Later that year, she won her third Wimbledon singles title, once again defeating her sister.

By early 2010, Williams had won the Australian Open singles and doubles matches and her fourth Wimbledon singles championship. Subsequently, she battled health issues that kept her off the court for almost a year. In 2012, a month after capturing her fifth Wimbledon singles title, Williams won a gold medal in the singles at the London 2012 Summer Olympics, becoming the second woman (behind Steffi Graf) to win a career Golden Slam.[2] She also teamed up with Venus to win the doubles event. Later that year, Williams claimed her fifteenth Grand Slam singles title with a victory at the U.S. Open. In 2013, she won her second French Open singles championship and fifth U.S. Open singles title. Williams successfully defended her U.S. Open championship in 2014, which gave her eighteen career Grand Slam titles, tying her with Chris Evert and Martina Navratilova for the second-highest women's singles total of the Open Era.[3]

In 2015, she captured her sixth Australian Open and won the French Open, her twentieth Grand Slam singles championship. This torrid streak continued at Wimbledon when she won a straight-set final to capture her sixth career Wimbledon singles title. Williams again won Wimbledon in 2016, giving her twenty-two career Grand Slam singles titles, which tied her with Graf for the most Slams in the Open Era for both women and men. Williams broke Graf's record at the 2017 Australian Open, where she defeated her sister Venus in the final.

Williams became engaged to Alexis Ohanian, cofounder of the website Reddit, in 2016. Soon after, Williams announced that she was pregnant and would miss the remainder of the 2017 season. After undergoing an emergency cesarean section, she gave birth to a daughter but experienced sudden shortness of breath, leading to the discovery of blood clots in her lungs. Additionally, doctors discovered a large hematoma in her abdomen caused by hemorrhaging at the site of her cesarean. Following multiple surgeries, Williams went home, and two months later, she married Ohanian.

Williams returned to tennis in 2018. She failed to win a tournament that year, although she reached the finals at Wimbledon and the U.S. Open. The latter, which she lost to Naomi Osaka, ended in controversy when she was fined for a coaching violation, and racket and verbal abuse toward the umpire. Williams believed she had been treated harshly by the umpire because she is Black and a woman.

In 2018, she wore a black, skin-tight catsuit at the French Open that was likened to a superhero outfit to help promote her new clothing line "Serena." The outfit was subsequently banned by the French Tennis Federation president, even though the suit's purpose was to help control blood clots in Williams' legs. The accusation that she, as one of the few Black women to dominate tennis,

---

2.   A Golden Slam is when an individual wins all four major championships and an Olympic gold-medal.

3.   The Open Era began in 1968 when the Grand Slam tournaments allowed professional players to compete with amateurs.

does not respect the game is yet another microaggression Williams has faced throughout her career. The body shaming and public scrutiny of her hairstyles and fashion choices have been part of an undercurrent of racial, sexual, class bias and discrimination.

Williams' aggressive play, a "high risk" style, is balanced in part by her powerful and consistent serve, return of serve, and forceful groundstrokes from both her forehand and backhand swings. Williams' forehand is considered to be one of the most powerful shots in the women's game, including her double-handed backhand. Williams strikes her backhand groundstroke using an open stance and uses the same open stance for her forehand. She also possesses a substantial and powerful overhead. Although many think of Williams as only an offensive player, she plays a strong defensive game as well.

Williams has had some of the biggest endorsement deals with Puma, Nike Gatorade, Delta Air Lines, Aston Martin, Pepsi, Beats by Dre headphones, IBM, and Chase Bank. She has posed for the 2003 and 2004 editions of the *Sports Illustrated* Swimsuit issue. In 2004, she developed a line of designer apparel "Aneres" (her first name spelled backward), and in 2009, launched a signature collection of handbags and jewelry. She was the first active female professional athlete to appear in a feminine hygiene product advertising campaign for Tampax Pearl tampons. She also became the first Black female athlete to have a picture by herself on the cover of *Vogue* in 2015. Williams is co-author of the book *Venus & Serena: Serving From The Hip: 10 Rules For Living, Loving and Winning* (2005), with author Hilary Beard. Williams released her first autobiography, *On the Line* (2009), followed by *My Life: Queen of the Court: An Autobiography* (2010).

Williams has established herself as a successful entrepreneur and philanthropist. In addition to her partnerships and businesses, she and Venus have been minority owners of the Miami Dolphins since 2009, the first African American women to hold an ownership stake in an NFL franchise. Williams serves on several boards, notably at SurveyMonkey, and the online fashion marketplace Poshmark. The Serena Williams Fund, established in 2014, has supported charities, foundations and several other causes. She has also collaborated on the Williams Sisters Fund for additional philanthropic projects. Williams has served as an International Goodwill Ambassador with UNICEF since 2011 and helped launch UNICEF's Schools for Asia campaign. In 2017, she became Ambassador for the Allstate Foundation's Purple Purse project that provides financial empowerment to domestic abuse victims.

From being a dominant force in tennis over the last three decades to dominating activism, business, and entertainment, Williams has been a true inspiration to Black women and girls worldwide. She has pushed through the limitations she faced as a Black woman, and in the process revolutionized women's tennis with her powerful style of play. She will leave behind a legacy as America's most iconic athlete and the greatest female tennis player of all time.❖

Allyson Felix
(1985)
Track and field sprinter, activist, entrepreneur

Allyson Felix is the only female track and field athlete to ever win six Olympic gold medals, and is tied as the most decorated female Olympian in track and field history, with a total of eleven Olympic medals. Felix is also the most decorated athlete, female or male, in World Championships history with eighteen career medals.

ALLYSON MICHELLE FELIX was born in Los Angeles to Marlean Felix, an elementary schoolteacher, and Paul Felix, an ordained minister and professor of New Testament at The Master's Seminary in Santa Clarita Valley. Her older brother is also a sprinter, and her business manager.

Felix showed a gift for athletics at a very early age. Before she discovered her talent for track, Felix's first passion was basketball. She dribbled her way onto her ninth grade varsity basketball team. During her freshman year at Los Angeles Baptist High School in North Hills, Felix tried out for the track team. A few weeks later, she finished seventh in the 200-meter dash at the CIF California State Meet, and in the coming seasons, she would become a five-time winner at the meet. Felix's teammates nicknamed her "Chicken Legs" because of her five feet and six inches tall, 125-pound sprinter's body (Calbay 2012). Her slightness was seemingly at odds with her speed on the track and her strength in the gym, where, while still in high school, she deadlifted at least 270 pounds. Felix credits much of her early success to her high school sprint coach, Jonathan Patton.

By 2003, *Track and Field News* named Felix its national girl's High School Athlete of the Year for earning gold in the 200-meter at the U.S Indoor Track and Field Championships. She also set the national high school record with a 23.14 finish. At seventeen she made history in the Banamex Grand Prix in Mexico City, finishing the 200-meter race in 22.11 seconds, smashing the U.S. high school record of Marion Jones, and setting a new world record. Unfortunately, it was not ratified as a World Junior record because there was no drug testing at the meet.

At eighteen, Felix won a silver medal in the 200-meter at the Athens 2004 Summer Olympics, finishing behind Veronica Campbell-Brown of Jamaica with

a World Junior record time of 22.98. After the Olympics, Felix was looking for a new coach, in part because hers planned to leave the state. Someone suggested Bob Kersee, whose resume ranks among the best in track and field. Felix always respected Kersee and admired his wife, Jackie Joyner-Kersee, as a trailblazing athlete. When Felix graduated from high school, she decided to forego college eligibility to sign a professional contract with Adidas. Later, the shoe manufacturer paid her college tuition at the University of Southern California. She eventually graduated with a degree in elementary education.

In 2005, Felix, at age twenty, became the youngest gold medal sprinter in the 200-meter dash at the World Championships in Helsinki, Finland. Two years later, she became the second female (Marita Kosch in 1983 was the first) to win three gold medals at the 2007 World Championships in Osaka, Japan. Felix qualified for the Beijing 2008 Summer Olympics in the 200-meter, but just missed qualifying for the 100-meter. However, at the Olympics, despite running her season's best time in the 200-meter at 21.93, Felix again finished second to Campbell-Brown (who ran 21.74, the best time in the decade to clinch the gold medal). Felix won gold with the woman's 4×400-meter relay. In 2009, Felix made history at the World Outdoor Championship in Germany by becoming the first woman ever to win three 200-meter titles. She finished in 22.02 seconds, beating rival Campbell-Brown.

In 2010, Felix focused on running the 400-meter race. She became the first person ever to win two IAAF Diamond League trophies for the 200-meter and 400-meter races. She continued her dominance by winning 21 races out of 22 starts, only losing to Campbell-Brown, who set the world leading time of 21.98. In 2011, Felix attended the "Great City Games" held in the streets of Manchester, where she set the world leading time in the 200-meter, at 22.12. She also ran at a time of 10.89 in the second 100-meters of the race.

At the 2011 World Championships, Felix participated in the 200-meter and 400-meter events, as well as the 4×100 and 4×400-meter relays. First up was the 400-meter event, where Felix was placed in lane three in the final and finished second with a time of 49.59, 0.03 behind winner Amantle Montsho, whom Felix had beaten throughout the rest of the season. In the 200-meter final, running again in lane three, Felix finished third in an under-par time of 22.42 due to fatigue. Campbell-Brown won the gold and Carmelita Jeter won silver. In the relay events, Felix ran the second leg in both the 4×100-meter and 4×400-meter relays. Team USA won both events and attained world-leading times in both finals as Felix added two World Championship gold medals to her collection.

At the London 2012 Summer Olympics, Felix won her first individual gold medal. In the 200-meter final—a race she lost at the 2004 and 2008 Olympics to Jamaican rival, Campbell-Brown—Felix won, proving that the third time was the charm. She also won two gold medals in the 4x100-meter relay with teammates Carmelita Jeter, Bianca Knight, and Sanya Richard-Ross. When Felix took first place, she became the first American woman to win three gold medals at the Olympics since Florence Griffin Joyner at the Seoul 1988 Summer Olympics.

In the 2013 World Championships in Moscow, Felix entered the 200-meter and was expected to also appear in the relay finals, but pulled up in the 200-meter final with a hamstring injury and was subsequently carried from the track. After a nine-month layoff, Felix resumed competition in the 400-meter at the Shanghai Diamond League meet in 2014, in which she finished fifth with a time of 50.81. She later competed in the Eugene Diamond League meet in the 200-meter and finished third with a season's best of 22.44. She got back into form shortly after, and in the Oslo Diamond League meet, she finished first in the 200-meter for her first win of the season with a time of 22.73. Later, she took part in the Paris and Glasgow Diamond League meetings.

In Paris, she ran her season's best again (22.34) behind only Blessing Okagbare from Nigeria, who ran a time of 22.32. In Glasgow, she lost to Dafne Schippers from the Netherlands, a heptathlon athlete, and set a national record of 22.34. Felix later took part in the Stockholm Diamond league, where she won the race with a time of 22.85, her second win of the season, and took the lead in the Diamond Race standings for the 200-meter. In the last Diamond League meeting of the season in Brussels, Belgium, she won the race with a world leading time of 22.02, and also won the Diamond Race.

Felix got off to an uncharacteristically slow start in 2016. During a gym workout in April, she dropped from a pull-up bar and landed awkwardly, twisting her right ankle and tearing multiple ligaments. As a result, she could barely even walk, and she had to switch up her training plan. In the Rio de Janeiro 2016 Summer Olympics, Felix earned a silver medal in the 400-meter race. She also won two gold medals in the 4×100-meter and 4×400-meter relays along with her U.S teammates. With nine medals—six gold and three silver—Felix became the most decorated Olympian woman in U.S. track and field history.

The following year, during the World Championships in London, Felix, earned three more medals, making her the most decorated athlete in World Championships' history. Felix tied Merlene Ottey's and Usain Bolt's fourteen medal tally by winning a bronze medal in the 400-meter final. She openly admitted, though, that the result was a bit disappointing, as she was hoping to retain her title in the discipline. Just a month prior to the championships, Felix had won the London's Diamond League meet held at the same track with a world leading time of 49.65. Felix added two gold medals by being part of the 4×100-meter and 4×400-meter winning relays, bringing her tally up to sixteen World medals. She is the only athlete in world championship history to finish on the podium in every individual and relay sprint event. She is also the most successful female track athlete in the history of the IAAF World Championships and the Olympics. Felix has won a mind-blowing twenty-five global medals combined from the Olympics and World Championships.

By 2018, Felix had reduced her schedule. In the nineteen years she has been running track, she had never taken a break. However, she also wanted to take a different approach for her sixth Olympics in 2020. Later, it was revealed that Felix, who had recently married her husband, Kenneth Ferguson, was pregnant for most of the year. After battling pre-eclampsia, she gave birth to her daughter by emergency C-section in 2018. She spent a month in the neonatal intensive care unit with her daughter and another two recovering from the surgery.

After years of being the quiet, noncontroversial champion—revered for her class and accomplishments but often ignored because of those same attributes—Felix had finally started earning more recognition when she began to speak out on issues related to Black maternal morbidity and Nike's maternity leave policies. Felix, who has had a contract with Nike since 2010, accused them of being unsupportive during her pregnancy. Nike wanted her competing again as soon as possible, offering her a 70 percent pay cut. Felix asked for guarantees that if her performance dropped due to her just having given birth, she would not be financially punished, but Nike declined. In May 2019, she penned an op-ed for *The New York Times*[1] regarding her poor maternity treatment from Nike, a company represented entirely by men. Olympic runners Alysia Montaño and Kara Goucher echoed those complaints. Felix also testified at the House of Representatives Ways & Means Committee hearing on overcoming racial disparities and social determinants in the maternal mortality crisis.

Under public pressure, Nike conceded and amended its maternity leave policies to ensure that performance-based clauses were not invoked for pregnant athletes for at least eighteen months, beginning eight months before the mother's due date. While dozens of current and former Nike athletes thanked Felix for the role she played in pressuring the company to change, she had little interest in reconciliation. Felix signed a multiyear apparel deal with the Gap brand Athleta, becoming their first sponsored athlete.

In July 2019, Felix competed in her first race since she gave birth, finishing sixth in a 400-meter run at the USA Track and Field Outdoor Championships in Des Moines, Iowa. In September 2019, Felix won the 150-meter run at the Great North City Games in Stockton. She competed in her eighth World Championships in 2019 in Doha, Qatar, and won her 12th and 13th World Championship gold medals, surpassing Usain Bolt for the most golds by any athlete in history.

In the first-ever mixed-gender 4x400-meter relay event at the World Championships, Felix ran with Michael Cherry, Wil London III, and Courtney Okolo with a world record time of 3:09.34. Felix ran a 50.4-second split for her leg. She won another gold as a runner in the preliminary heats for the women's 4×400-meter relay, although she was not selected to run in the finals.

Felix, who turned thirty-five in November 2019, was looking forward to participating in the Tokyo 2020 Summer Olympics, her fifth consecutive Olympics,

1.   Allyson Felix,. "My Own Nike Pregnancy Story." May 22, 2019, *The New York Times,* https://www.nytimes.com/2019/05/22/opinion/allyson-felix-pregnancy-nike.html

and her first as a mother. However, with the Olympics postponed due to the COVID-19 pandemic, Felix and Kersee, have shifted their calendar back to what would typically be a summer or fall workout schedule.

Felix was one of nine U.S. athletes who took part in the Inspiration Games, an ambitious virtual competition that replaced the Diamond League stop in Zurich, Switzerland. Athletes competed in eight events from seven venues around the world. It may have not been the race Felix intended on running in July 2020, but when she crossed the finish line, she was the first to win the women's 150-meter race. She is also a five-time recipient of the Jesse Owens Award (after 2013, renamed the Jackie Joyner-Kersee Award) from USA Track and Field (USATF), signifying the Athlete of the Year. She won the award for the first time in 2005, and then again in 2007, 2010, 2012, and 2015. She has received this award more than any other person.

At this stage of her career, Felix has found passions off the track which she believes are her true calling. Since she earned a degree in elementary education from the University of Southern California, Felix dedicates a lot of her down time to multiple local, national, and international nonprofits that help women and children. As a former member, Felix avidly supports the YMCA and participates in their programs and special competitions (Roos 2018). In 2010, she served as a member of President Obama's council for fitness, sports and nutrition, and traveled to Rio in 2014 as the U.S. State Department Sports Diplomacy Ambassador. Felix has worked with Project Believe, a voluntary drug testing program that goes beyond the normal drug testing requirements to protect clean athletes. She also partnered with her friend, former NFL player Nnamdi Asomogha and his foundation in Los Angeles, where they hosted college summits for local high school juniors and seniors.

She serves as a member of the Right To Play board, hoping to raise awareness for underserved children in developing regions. Along with speaking up for female professional athletes, Felix is also an activist for Black maternal health. In May 2020, she took part in (em)Power Hour, a free virtual event featuring inspiring women in sports, fitness, and female empowerment to engage in candid conversations, sponsored by Athleta. Her determination is now carrying over to the business sector, where she is an investor in a plant-based protein bar company and serves as an advisor to a fitness technology start-up.

Felix, who was already a record-breaking female track and field athlete when she competed in the Tokyo 2020 Summer Olympics and won her eleventh Olympic medal when she finished third in the 4x400-meter relay and won a bronze medal. As she chased history while also chasing a toddler, when she broke her tie with Ottey as the most decorated female Olympian in the sport, the thirty-five-year-old Felix effectively retired from the sport. Felix finished her Olympic career in style and in the process, set up a promising future for U.S. Women's Track.❖

Ibtihaj Muhammad
(1985)
Fencer, author, entrepreneur

Ibtihaj Muhammad became the first Muslim woman wearing a hijab to represent the U.S. at the Olympics, and the first African American woman to win an Olympic bronze medal for fencing.

IBTIHAJ MUHAMMAD was born in Maplewood, New Jersey to Denise Garner Muhammad, an elementary school special education teacher, and Eugene Muhammad, a police officer. Her parents encouraged her and her four siblings to participate in sports. Muhammad had a competitive streak and loved participating in sports, however, as a Muslim, sportswear conflicted with her religious observance to dress modestly. In accordance with their beliefs, Muhammad's parents sought a sport for her to participate in where she could be fully covered. When she was thirteen, Muhammad and her mother discovered fencing, an ideal solution that uniquely accommodated their religious beliefs. She could wear long sleeved clothing and a hijab, a traditional Muslim headscarf (Rodulfo 2016).

When Muhammad first tried fencing in middle school, she did not particularly care for it, but she soon changed her mind. From a practical and financial standpoint, she viewed fencing as an opportunity to obtain a sports scholarship to a prestigious university. She also changed her weaponry from the epée, finding the saber better suited to her personality. (Of the three fencing disciplines—the foil, the epée, and the saber—the saber is considered the fastest and most forceful.) Soon her enthusiasm grew and Muhammad began attending former U.S. champion and Olympic medalist Peter Westbrook's nonprofit organization, the Peter Westbrook Foundation, which teaches fencing and life skills to underprivileged inner city youth in the New York City area (Rodulfo 2016).

Muhammad attended Maplewood's Columbia High School, where she excelled and became captain of the fencing team for two years and helped to win two state championships. In 2004, she received a fencing scholarship to Duke University in North Carolina and in her freshman year earned All-America honors with a record of 49-8. From there, she went on to place second at the mid-Atlantic/South Regional and 21st at the Junior Olympics. The following year, she finished 11th for saber at the NCAA Championships, and earned her second consecutive All-America honors. A third would come in 2006. Despite being a world class athlete and a strong student, Muhammad was met with racism and condescension from her peers, so she left the team in her senior year. She graduated in 2007 with dual bachelor degrees in international relations and African American studies with a minor in Arabic.

After graduation, Muhammad expected to leave fencing behind and land a job in the corporate world. But despite sending out dozens of resumes, she did not receive many interviews. The months stretched on with no offers or job prospects, and Muhammad grew frustrated and depressed. She began working at a Dollar Store, her days consisting of stacking shelves with dishwashing liquid and watching television. One day, feeling lost, she paid a visit to her former high school fencing coach and asked for a lesson. Afterwards, he urged her to pursue fencing again on the international circuit, and to possibly compete in the Olympics. She trained non-stop, becoming a three-time NCAA All-American (2004, 2005, 2006). She paid her competition fees first with her meager earnings from her job, and eventually from Muhammad's substitute teaching job in Newark. Through it all, she kept moving up in the rankings, and she finally earned a spot on Team USA (Muhammad 2018).

In 2009, Muhammad elevated her training when she was coached by the 2000 U.S. Olympian, Akhi Spencer-El. That same year, she won a national title. Since then, Muhammad became a five-time Senior World Team medalist. She helped her team take home gold for the U.S. in 2014 in Kazan, Russia. Throughout her career, she earned numerous medals for both team and individual events on the World Cup circuit. In 2012, Muhammad was named Muslim Sportswoman of the year. In 2014, Muhammad and her siblings launched their clothing company, Louella, which manufacturers modest fashionable clothing.

She also became a sports ambassador. Muhammad served on the U.S. Department of State's Empowering Women and Girls Through Sport Initiative. She has traveled to various countries to engage in dialogue on the importance of sports and education. She was also nominated by President Obama to serve as a member of the President's Council on Fitness, Health & Nutrition.

At first, Muhammad was excited that she was officially considered a professional athlete, and thrilled her travel and competition costs would be covered by the team. She was eager to bond with her new teammates, but her attempts at friendship were rejected by much of the team. Instead, the she was intentionally excluded from team dinners, left with bizarre emails and other discriminating behavior. Muhammad was at the top of her sport, yet she was treated as an outcast (Muhammad 2018). Her family helped her face these difficult moments and obstacles, and in the process, Muhammad trounced her teammate's low expectations by earning a spot on the U.S. Saber Fencing Team for the Rio de Janeiro 2016 Summer Olympics. She was the first Muslim woman to represent the U.S. at the Olympics which meant a great deal not only to her and her family, but also for the Muslim community. She is seen as a symbol of promise for a community that has seen few traditional Muslim women competing in the Olympics.

At the Olympics, Muhammad won her first qualifying round in the individual saber event, but was defeated by French fencer Cécilia Berder in the second round. Muhammad went on to become the first female African American Muslim athlete to win an Olympic medal when she took home the bronze in the team sabre event. She was also the first Muslim to wear the hijab at this elite level of sports (Rodulfo 2016). Muhammad and teammates Dagmara Wozniak, Mariel Zagunis and Monica Aksamit defeated the Italian team 45-30 for the win. Muhammad's U.S. ranking was at No. 3, and she held a current World Ranking of 23.

In 2017, as part of its International Women's Day campaign, Mattel introduced a line of female role model Barbies, including a Barbie in hijab designed after Muhammad as part of their "Shero" line. Many Muslims and non-Muslims alike welcomed the doll as a sign of inclusion and diversity.

Muhammad's road to Olympic greatness was not easy. When she received death threats, according to Muhammad, the United States Fencing Association (USFA) and the Olympic committee did not take them seriously. They actually sent the threats to her directly, which played a role in her mental state, not only as an athlete, but as a human being (Muhammad 2018). As she went through moments like this and found herself battling bouts of depression, she sought help from a sports psychologist.

It is perhaps why Muhammad felt compelled to write her memoir, *Proud: My Fight for an Unlikely American Dream* (2018). Muhammad shares her experience of rampant racism and xenophobia, even among the athletes she trained with and competed against, and how it affected her. Her children's book, *The Proudest Blue: A Story of Hijab and Family* (2019), co-written by S.K. Ali and illustrated by Hatem Aly, is a story about two sisters being teased and bullied for wearing a hijab (Mosley 2019). Muhammad has plans to publish two follow-up books that continue their story, and the beauty of their faith. She has also become the face of Nike's first-ever Pro Hijab campaign.

Muhammad retired from competition in 2020 to focus on her clothing line, projects, and speaking engagements. As an inspirational role model, Muhammad, who was named in *Time Magazine's* 100 Most Influential list, works closely with organizations like Athletes for Impact, the Special Olympics, and Laureus Sport for Good.

As an African American Muslim woman who wears a hijab, Muhammad has succeeded in a historically White sport, and has become an important figure in a larger discussion on the importance of diversity, equity and inclusion (DEI). Although she has sustained moments in her career on the receiving end of discrimination, Muhammad never allowed those moments to define her. This triumphant journey and unwavering commitment to Muhammad's authentic self continues to inspire others❖

Blake Bolden
(1991)
Ice hockey player, trainer, scout

Blake Bolden is the first African American player in the Canadian Women's Hockey League (CWHL), the first African American player to compete in the National Women's Hockey League (NWHL), the first African American female professional scout, and the first woman to ever have her own signature stick. She also holds the honor of having the fastest and hardest slap shot in the game.

BLAKE ALEXIS BOLDEN was born in Euclid, Ohio to LaTanya Bolden, a single parent who worked different temporary jobs while going to school. Bolden is an only child. Bolden's mother showed her the value of hard work by working multiple jobs to make sure there was enough food on the table. Bolden was involved in sports at a young age, participating in track and field, karate, and gymnastics.

When Bolden was six, her mother started dating Leslie Dean, a police officer she met in the neighborhood who would become the man Bolden considers her father. Dean loved ice hockey and as his relationship with Bolden blossomed, hockey became their thing. Since he moonlighted as security for the hockey team, the Cleveland Lumberjacks, he always had front-row seats, backstage passes, and special access at the games. When Bolden attended her first game she quickly fell in love with hockey, the pace of the play, the physical nature of the game, and she wanted to play.

Bolden began playing hockey at age seven, and found she had a natural affinity for the sport. Her first team was the Tri-County Cyclones, a coed team part of a local house league. She also took power skating lessons and participated in other programs for ice time to develop her skills. The only Black child and the only girl, Bolden found she needed to develop another skill, one that would serve her throughout her career: fortitude.

Early on, Bolden learned how to navigate being a Black female in a mostly White-male dominated sport. When she felt the sneers and jeers from opposing teams' parents and players alike. Bolden leaned on her mother, who defended her, but also taught her to carry herself with dignity and respect.

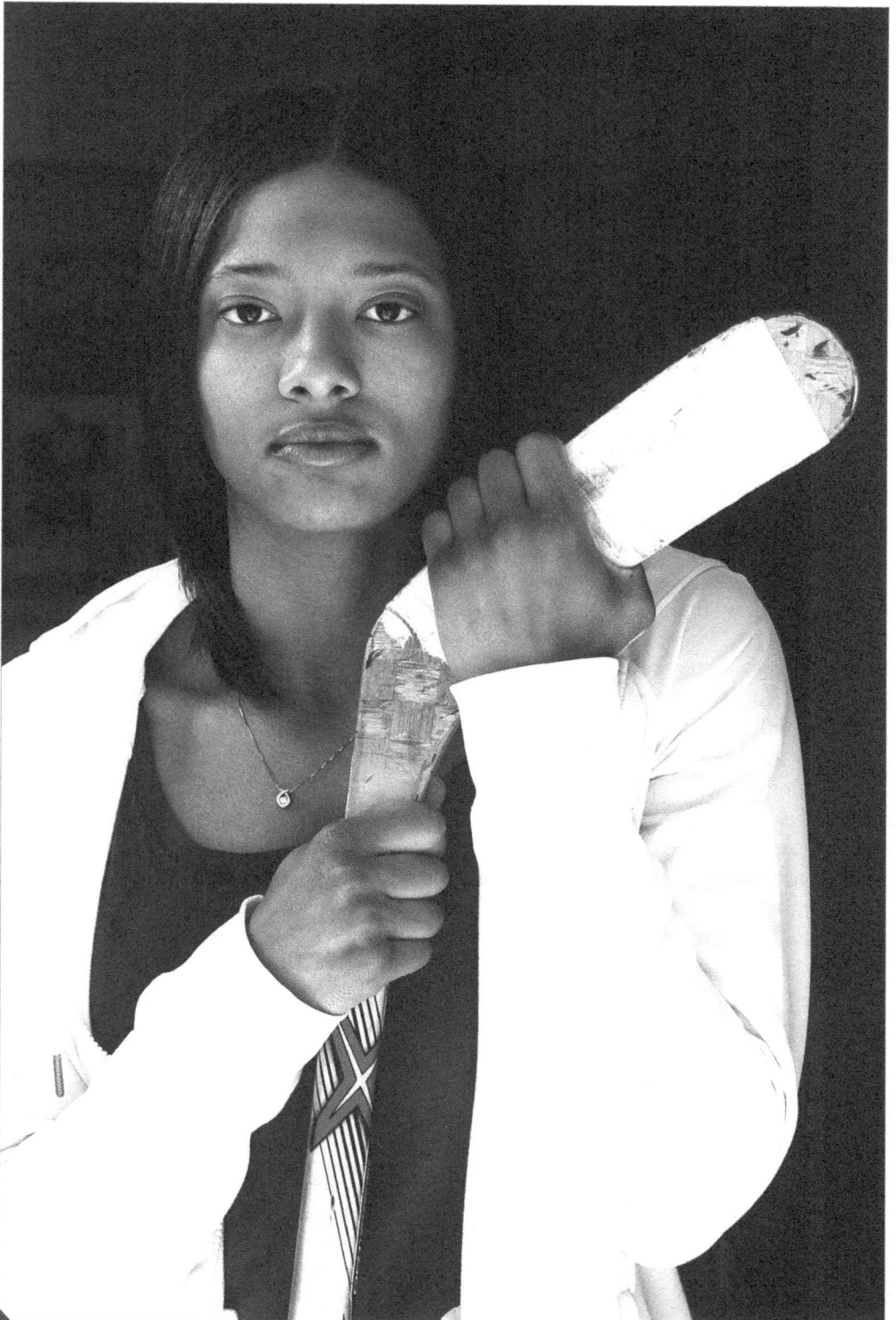

In time, Bolden tried out for a travel team and played minor youth hockey for the Cleveland Barons, the only girl and African American on the team. When she was twelve years old, Bolden was presented with her first opportunity to play on an all-girls team, the Ohio Flames. Although she joined the Flames for a tournament, she turned down an offer to stay with the Flames the following season because Bolden was headed to Northwood Prep School in Lake Placid, New York. It was known for its ice hockey programs, and home to the 1932 and 1980 Olympics. Given the fact she played mostly with boys, Bolden realized early on she had to restructure her game so it could fit within the style and rules of the league.

While at Northwood, Bolden captained the team during her senior year and played with Kelley Steadman. She participated in the first International Ice Hockey Federation Women's Under-18 World (IIHF) World Championship for Team USA, winning gold medals in both the 2008 and 2009 tournaments. Bolden attended Boston College, where she played for the Boston College Eagles women's ice hockey team from 2009 to 2013.

From 2009 to 2010, Bolden led all Hockey East freshmen defenders in scoring with four goals and nine assists for 13 points. Her first collegiate point was a goal in a 1-1 tie against Clarkson. Her first assist was also earned in a tie in a 1-1 draw with the Quinnipiac Bobcats. In 2010, in a 5-2 victory over Brown, Bolden was one of three Boston College players who scored their first goals of the 2010-11 season. Bolden also tallied two assists in the win against Brown. It was a career high for most points in one game in her college career. In 2010, she was invited to try out for the Olympics' U.S. National Women's Ice Hockey Team.

In her first three seasons at Boston College, Bolden appeared in 102 contests. Her 21 points during the 2011-12 campaign ranked second among defenders during Hockey East conference play. Statistically, she amassed 20 goals and 33 assists, which is a pretty good record. In 2012, Bolden was appointed team captain in her senior year for the 2012–13 NCAA Division I women's ice hockey season, and had 3 Frozen Four appearances, earning Hockey East Defensive Player of the Year and All-American Honors. Bolden became one of the nation's best collegiate defensemen and was nominated for the Patty Kazmaier Award, which honors the country's top female college player. She was part of the USA Hockey evaluation camp for the 2012 IIHF World Championship. Bolden graduated from Boston College with majors in human development and psychology.

After graduation, she joined the Boston Blades of the Canadian Women's Hockey League (CWHL), winning the Clarkson cup in 2015. She played for two seasons, but while the players were paid bonuses and incentives, they were not paid salaries. She left the CWHL and became one of the pioneering players of the National Women's Hockey League (NWHL), the first women's hockey league to pay a salary. The NWHL has teams in the U.S. and Canada. Bolden is the first African American player drafted in the first round of the CWHL and the first ever to compete in the NWHL.

Bolden joined the NWHL's Boston Pride in 2015. The team participated in an outdoor women's ice hockey game against the CWHL's Les Canadiennes de Montreal, known as the 2016 Outdoor Women's Classic, and was the first professional women's ice hockey outdoor game. Bolden would score Boston Pride's first and only goal of the game. In 2016, she helped the team win the inaugural Isobel Cup, and was selected as a player for the 2nd NWHL All-Star Game, in which she won the fastest shot skills game with a shot of 87 mph.

Bolden developed her outreach skills by working for Boston's InnerCity Weightlifting for several years, assisting minority students in their lives outside the gym. She also completed her first year as an assistant girls' hockey coach at Milton Academy, launched her own business as a performance coach, and led a weekly girls' elite skills clinic in Hingham.

A gifted defender who should have been the first Black skater on the U.S. women's Olympic hockey team, Bolden has yet to be given that opportunity, despite her widely acclaimed talent. In 2017, Bolden left the NWHL and signed on to play for the Swiss Women's Hockey League's (SWHL) HC Lugano team in Switzerland. During the 2017–18 season with HC Lugano, Bolden competed in twenty games. She led all defenders on the team with 27 points (16 goals, 11 assists), pacing fourth overall in team scoring with 27 points.

When she returned to the U.S., she signed a contract with the NWHL's Buffalo Beauts. Representing the Beauts, Bolden reclaimed her hardest shot title in the 2019 NWHL All-Star Skills Competition becoming a three-time winner, and was awarded Defensive Player of the Year. She played for that team until May 2019. Bolden participated in the #ForTheGame movement in connection with the Professional Women's Hockey Players Association (PWHPA), which began on May 2019. She played for Team Keller against Team Decker in PWHPA's Dream Gap Tour stop in Philadelphia.

Her love for the game has transcended some of the hardest challenges an athlete can face outside the rink. Although she holds the record of having the fastest and hardest slap shot in professional women's ice hockey at 87 mph, Bolden has been judged by people in the stands and snubbed by brands and sponsors. But in 2020, she finally earned a lightweight stick line from Verbero, which she hopes will help improve player's shots. She also connected with Willie O'Ree, the first African American to play in the National Hockey League (NHL) in 1958, and learned the history of Black players in the U.S. and Canada. In time, she herself has become known as the "Jackie Robinson" of women's ice hockey. Bolden currently is a professional scout for the Los Angeles Kings, the first African American and the second woman to ever scout in the NHL.

During the off-season, Bolden is a performance coach working with girls all over the country through her Blake Bolden Athletics platform. Her ultimate goal is to move into a front office role, and eventually run her own team so she can have a greater impact on behalf of women and women of color in hockey.❖

Bianca Smith
(1991)
Baseball coach, player, lawyer

Bianca Smith was hired by the Boston Red Sox organization, becoming the first African American woman to serve as a professional baseball coach.

BIANCA SMITH was born in Paterson, New Jersey to Dawn Patterson and Victor Smith. Her mother was a Dartmouth alumna and an attorney, and her father played football at Dartmouth College. When her parents divorced and both remarried, they created a blended family of four siblings, including stepbrother, Reggie Cannon, who became a professional soccer player. Smith lived in Edison, New Jersey, and later in Grapevine, Texas, a suburb of Dallas.

Smith was introduced to baseball by her mother, a New York Yankees fan, when she was three years old, and was propped atop her mother's lap to watch games on television. In a family of football and soccer fans, Smith and her mother shared their secret language of baseball. Smith took to the game quickly; she could watch entire games even as a toddler because she had an unusually long attention span and enjoyed watching her mother cheer for her team. Her mother also taught her about game strategy. She cheered for former Yankees shortstop Derek Jeter, one of her mother's favorite players. This was when she began to understand what baseball was all about, and she could not get enough of it. By middle school, Smith started wearing a headband with Jackie Robinson's number 42 on it.

As Smith grew up, she watched games on her own and watched classic baseball movies like *The Sandlot* (1993), *Angels in the Outfield* (1994), and *Rookie of the Year* (1994). She picked up softball late when she was about twelve years old. She was small but nimble, and base running was her specialty. Around that same time, she saved her allowance and bought her first baseball jersey: Jeter's No. 2.

Smith went to Colleyville Heritage High School in Colleyville, Texas, where she played softball and was a co-captain her senior year. The game's intricacies had always fascinated her, and during these early years, she began to study and analyze how plays unfolded and predict the manager's next move. By the time she enrolled at her parents' alma mater, Dartmouth College, a baseball career was the furthest thing from Smith's mind. Initially, she wanted to be a veterinarian, but decided it was not for her after taking a biology class. Smith realized she loved sports and really loved baseball, so she began to figure out her place in the game.

At Dartmouth, she played for the club baseball team and was the only female on the squad. The softball coach encouraged Smith to play varsity softball during her final two years at Dartmouth, which she did as an outfielder. She helped the Dartmouth softball team with video while injured, ran the scoreboard, and helped with baseball recruits. Following graduation in 2012, with a BA in sociology, Smith interned for an Arena Football League team and served as a social media director for a sporting goods store. But it still was not baseball.

Her mother died of a rare cancer called rhabdomyosarcoma at age forty-four in 2013. But her mother's legacy helped Smith, who was twenty-two at the time of her passing, with what to do next. After all, her mother ran marathons, not because she loved running—in fact, she hated it—but to conquer the distance. Her mother went to law school in her late thirties. She had confidence. So four months after her mother's death, Smith was compelled to enroll at Case Western Reserve University in Ohio for dual degrees in business and law to become a general manager for Major League Baseball (MLB). Smith collected an Ivy League education, two graduate degrees—one in sports business, the other in sports law, and certifications for multiple software programs that analyze pitching and hitting. As Smith worked through her grief, she found her strength through baseball. Determined, she would not let anything stop her from succeeding.

While attending Case Western, Smith spent four full seasons as the director of baseball operations for the Spartans. She pitched to players at batting practice, scheduled team travel and meals, helped coach circuit training, watched videos of their hitters, and sent her critiques to management. She eventually became the director of baseball operations. Her duties included managing travel, game-day operations, and social media, while working with the players on the field. Smith obtained a JD degree and an MBA in sports management from Case Western in 2017.

After graduate school, Smith was determined to make her resume so impressive that no employer could say no. But as she applied for full-time positions in baseball and reached out to more than 100 Division I college coaches, Smith only received twenty-six responses back. From those twenty-six, only one offered her a position, but it was not nearly enough to justify the move. She then applied to thirty or forty college baseball operations positions, getting only three interviews and no offers. Circling back to those jobs, she discovered that only one went to a woman, and about 95 percent of them went to White men.

In the meantime, Smith's challenge was to stay financially afloat while she went after these jobs. She held eight jobs at once to pay her student loans and her rent. She sorted packages at a UPS warehouse at night, packed online orders at Target, was a cashier at Dollar Tree, drove for Uber Eats, worked for the Texas Rangers as a tour guide and youth academy coach, and was a ticket taker for F.C. Dallas. If that was not enough, Smith volunteered as an assistant coach at the University of Dallas and interned at the MLB corporate headquarters. Sometimes, she had just thirty minutes to get from one of those jobs to another, subsisting on Lunchables and Pop-Tarts. Her internship at MLB was a turning point. Smith decided in 2018 that she wanted to coach full-time. Finally, she had figured out the thing she loved to do.

That same year, she went to her first baseball game at Yankee Stadium, on Mother's Day, in tribute to her mother. As a fan, she soaked in the atmosphere. But when the umpire shouted, "Play ball!" her mind snapped, and she realized her focus is always on the game.

In 2019, she was a baseball operations trainee with the Cincinnati Reds. During her internship, Smith helped at practices by catching throws and warming up the players. On game days, she was in the clubhouse analyzing hitters' swing decisions. Smith left the internship early because she was later hired as an assistant athletic director for compliance and administration, and as an assistant baseball coach and hitting coordinator at Carroll University in Waukesha, Wisconsin. Her coaching relied heavily on statistical metrics and data analysis.

Molly Harris, the Red Sox's senior talent acquisition specialist, first identified Smith's potential. Charged with finding talented and diverse candidates, Harris discovered that Smith's resume was everything the Red Sox had wanted and more. Rumors floated about Smith in 2020, and it became official in 2021 when the Red Sox hired Smith as part of the coaching staff. As the first African American woman to serve as a coach in a professional baseball organization, Smith begins her Red Sox career at the club's player development facility in Fort Myers, Florida, working mainly with position players. The hire is as historic as it is ironic. The Red Sox were the last Major League team to integrate when they signed Elijah Jerry "Pumpsie" Green in 1959, twelve years after the Brooklyn Dodgers broke the league's color barrier by signing Jackie Robinson. It is a footnote the Red Sox can never erase, but they have certainly made up for it by hiring Smith.

Smith's mother would have been proud of her daughter's achievement—but also furious. As a Yankees fan, her mother had particularly strong feelings about the Red Sox. It is a family joke that Smith is making history with the team her mother could not stand. She already has sponsorships from Nike, Oakley, and Topps, and is getting a baseball card.

It has been a long journey to this point for Smith. She never considered herself a role model before being hired by the Red Sox. But as a Black woman who has blazed a trail in baseball, she recognizes that women, especially women of color, are inspired by her story. By working in a White male-dominated field, women like Smith show girls—especially Black girls—that it is possible to follow their dreams, break barriers, and challenge societal norms, despite their gender and race. In that regard, Smith's role in the MLB is monumental. ❖

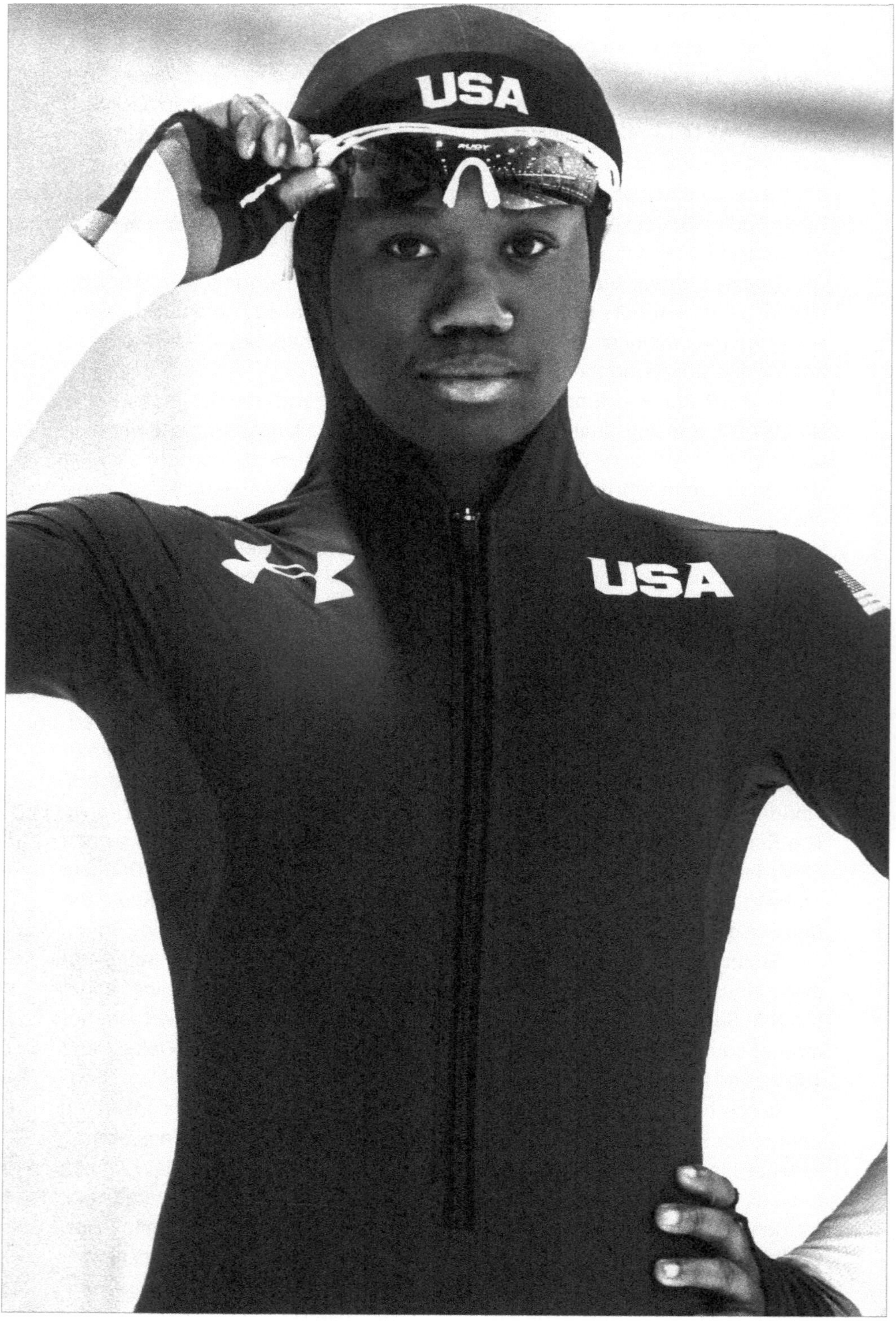
USA
USA

Erin Jackson
(1992)
Speedskater, inline skater, roller derby player

Erin Jackson is a multiple-medaled inline skater, the first African American woman to compete for the U.S. Olympic long-track speedskating team, and is a member of three national teams for three different disciplines.

ERIN JACKSON was born in Ocala, Florida to Rita Jackson, a pharmacy technician, and Tracy Jackson, a fire truck mechanic, and has one brother. Her parents were education-focused, and though she ran track in high school for two years, Jackson was more interested in math and chemistry. She wanted to be a scientist and follow in the footsteps of her grandfather, an aerospace engineer. But Jackson loved skating and, from an early age, was a rink rat.

As a child, she attended roller skating sessions at the local rink and even spent a few summers at skating summer camp. Jackson joined the figure skating team in Ocala when she was eight, but she dropped the sport after two years when her coaches left to pursue Olympic dreams for their own daughter. Her entrance into speedskating was by accident, but she received an invitation to a team party shortly after and started racing herself. When Jackson turned ten, her mother allowed her to race inline. At the rink, she was scouted by Renee Hildebrand, the storied inline coach responsible for training multiple skaters to transition to ice.

Jackson attended Shores Christian Academy, the Honors/Magnet program at Howard Middle School, and Forest High School, where she was in the EMIT (Engineering and Manufacturing Institute of Technology) program. She still loved skating, however, and would spend her weekends participating in artistic roller skating. She often jetted off to destinations like Holland, Argentina, and China for inline skating races, but never fell behind on her studies.

Jackson made the inline national team in 2008 and earned her first World medal that same year. Jackson also won gold in the 500-meter inline skating race at the 2008-2009 Junior World Championships. Then, in Jackson's senior year of high school in 2011, her mother, who suffered from diabetes, fell ill while Jackson was competing in Argentina at the Pan American Championships. When Jackson returned from Argentina, her mother had already been admitted to the emergency room and she passed away soon after. Jackson took a week off and leaned on her friends before she resumed racing and winning. That same year, Jackson received scholarships to enroll in the Materials Science and Engineering program at the University of Florida. In 2012, not long after graduating high school at the top of her class and heading to college, Jackson made a foray into roller derby when another speedskater introduced her to the sport. After a few sessions, she was hooked, and Jackson was a natural. After a rookie year playing with the Ocala Cannibals, she joined the Women's Flat Track Derby Association (WFTDA)-ranked New Jax City Rollers as a jammer in 2013.

While she attended college, she competed in inline speedskating and roller derby and excelled in both. Jackson was named the U.S. Olympic Committee's Female Athlete of the Year for roller sports in 2012, 2013, and 2015. She won a gold medal in the 500-meter race at the 2014 Pan American Championships, another gold for the 500-meter race, and a silver medal in the 200-meter at the 2014 Pan American Olympic Festival. She also competed in roller derby, earning the MVP award at the 2014 WFTDA Division 1 Playoff in Evansville, Indiana, and advanced to WFTDA Championships in 2015, 2016, and 2018.

Jackson was now a fifteen-year racing veteran with forty-seven national championships. But even at the highest levels of inline skating, Jackson found herself itching for more speed and more challenges. For inline, the highest level one can achieve are the World Championships every year and the Pan American Games every four years. Jackson was looking for more wins. It just so happened that inline became a de facto feeder school for Olympic speedskaters, producing stars such as Apolo Ohno and Brittany Bowe. Like them, Jackson craved an Olympic medal—an accolade still unavailable to inliners—but she wanted to finish college first. She was twenty-four years old when she graduated summa cum laude in 2015. By the time recruiter Chris Needham of Team USA got in touch with her in 2017, Jackson was a newbie crossover from inline, trying ice for the first time.

When Jackson traveled to the Utah Olympic Oval in Salt Lake City, it was the second time her feet hit the ice. Rubber wheels grip the surface. Blades, not so much. Placed in a fundamentals class, she struggled to not skate on the flat of the blades but instead to trust the edges. Speedskating is a daunting physical sport where skaters must cover a certain amount of distance in the shortest amount of time, racing at 30 mph. Now imagine skating at that speed while traveling 100 meters in eight anaerobic strokes, merging grace with explosiveness, ballet on a 1-millimeter-wide blade. For Jackson, it was a difficult transition, but she would not quit.

Jackson persisted, approaching the problem like an equation to be solved. In the process, she recircuited decades of inline muscle memory. She began working in the Contenders Program at Dick's Sporting Goods, which has a partnership with the U.S. Olympic Committee and provides a flexible job that works around training and competition schedules. She also took advantage of Salt

Lake Community College's scholarship offer for qualified athletes involved with the U.S. speedskating team to study computer science. After the Beijing 2022 Winter Olympics, Jackson planned on returning to school for a Master's Degree in Materials Science. It seems that Jackson aims to have as many degrees as World Championship titles, after she retires from skating. Jackson's goal is to combine all her study areas—computer engineering, computer science, and kinesiology—into one rewarding career where she can help others.

In 2017, Jackson participated in the Olympic trials in Milwaukee with no expectations. She was there solely to check her progress, with an eye on the Beijing 2022 Winter Olympics, and would have been grateful to make the top ten. Then, surprisingly, Jackson won third place and a spot on the Olympic team for the Pyeongchang 2018 Winter Olympics. This excellent showing stunned everyone, Jackson most of all. Before the qualifying races, Jackson had just gone under 40 seconds. In Milwaukee, she had two personal bests, completing the course in 39.22 seconds and 39.04 seconds, and qualified for the 500-meter distance with only four months of experience in speedskating on ice. In the blink of an eye, she went from relative obscurity into the global spotlight.

As the first Black woman to represent the U.S. in women's long-track speedskating, hers is a stunning breakthrough. It is worth noting that another Black woman qualified for speedskating: Maame Biney, who qualified for Team USA in the short track but did not make it past her qualifying heat. Jackson thus became one of two Black athletes to make the U.S. Olympic speedskating team—the other being Shani Davis of the men's team.

Jackson joined Olympic speedskaters and Ocala natives Brittany Bowe and Joey Mantia in Pyeongchang, South Korea and finished 24th out of 31 competitors. She started the evening ranked 30th among 31 skaters. While Jackson did not medal in her Olympic debut, her performance was memorable and ranked outside the medal chase. Her time, recorded after an illness that forced her out of the opening ceremony, did not quite make her training time, but she still managed to shave three-tenths of a second off of her best 2017 time of 39.51. Jackson returned to inline skating and roller derby after the Olympics. Her cross-training outside of roller derby has helped make her one of the world's quickest and hard-to-stop jammers. She is a member of Team USA/U.S. National Team for three sports: inline speedskating, roller derby, and long-track speedskating on ice. Toyota, a member of The Olympic Partners (TOP) program, which provides the highest Olympic sponsorship level, announced in 2020 that they have added Jackson to their winter roster for the Beijing 2022 Winter Olympics.

With more experience on ice under her belt, Jackson is aiming higher than ever—a top-five finish in the World Championships and medal contention at the Beijing 2022 Winter Olympics. That said, Jackson's plans for the future stretch beyond the Olympics. She recently completed an AS in Computing Science and is currently working on an AS in Exercise Science/Kinesiology. But for now, she continues to train and skate to win.❖

Simone Biles
(1997)
Gymnast

Simone Biles is the most decorated American gymnast, and the greatest woman in the history of her sport. As of 2021, Biles has won a total of thirty-two medals, including the Olympics and World Championship.

SIMONE ARIANNE BILES was born in Columbus, Ohio to Shanon Biles and Kelvin Clemons as the third of four siblings. Her birth father abandon xed the family, and her mother was unable to care for Biles and her siblings. After spending time in foster care, Biles' grandfather Ron Biles, an Air Force veteran and former air traffic controller, and his second wife Nellie Cayetano Biles, a nurse who owned and operated a string of nursing homes in the Houston area, began caring for the children. In 2003, the couple adopted the two youngest children, Simone and Adria, and her great aunt adopted the two oldest (Aguirre 2020).

Living in Spring, Texas, a suburb of Houston, Biles enjoyed a happy and secure life. From the beginning, she was an active child, running and jumping whenever she could, especially on the family trampoline. During a day care field trip at age six, she was taken to a gym and saw older girls practicing gymnastics. When the coaches saw the six-year-old successfully imitating girls in their teens, they suggested Biles should take regular gymnastic classes. She began a training program at Bannon's Gymnastix in Houston with Coach Aimee Boorman. Biles took to the training quickly, having acquired a knack for knowing where her body is in space as she flips and twists mid-flight. From that point forward, she set out on becoming a world champion gymnast.

Biles made her first appearance in the junior national competition at the 2011 American Classic in Houston, placing third in the all-around competition and first in the vault. She was now at a crossroads, as making the commitment to competitive gymnastics would require sacrifice. At age fourteen, she left public school for homeschooling, and forwent the usual round of teenage social activities to train for six to eight hours a day. She was invited to train at the USA Gymnastics' team training center at Károlyi Ranch, which at the time was run by the formidable rulers of American gymnastics, Béla and Márta Károlyi, who brought historical success to the U.S. team (Ford 2020).

At the 2012 American Classic, Biles placed third on the balance beam, tied for second in floor exercise, and took first place in both the vault and all-around competition. At the 2012 U.S. Classic, she placed second in floor exercise and again finished first in vault and all-around. She finished first on vault again at the USA Gymnastics National Championships and was named to the U.S. Junior National Team. At age fifteen, she was just a few months too young to compete for a place on the London 2012 Summer Olympics team. When she made her senior international debut at the 2013 American Cup, her strength, particularly on the vault, was apparent to all. Competing for the U.S. in Jesolo, Italy, she took gold medals in all-around, vault, balance beam, and floor exercise. Competing against teams from Germany and Romania at Chemnitz, Germany, she again won vault, balance beam, and floor exercise, but trouble lay ahead.

Biles disliked the Károlyi's training methods because she found them to be overly strict and felt that they took the "fun" out of the sport, but team members were required to go to the ranch for training. For a while, she straddled both by attending the ranch and continuing to follow her coach, Boorman, who trained her as she saw fit, and protect her from the Károlyis' overtraining (Ford 2020).

At the 2013 U.S. Classic, Biles lost control on the balance beam and fell during her floor exercise, and her coach was forced to pull her from the meet. Observers of the gymnastics circuit wondered openly whether her undeniable strength and agility were enough to overcome some of the inner turmoil she experienced at the time. After consulting with a sports psychologist, coupled with her training with Boorman and the Károlyis, Biles finally clicked with her routines (Ford 2020). She learned to put the expectations of others out of her mind and enjoy her performance in the moment. Only three weeks after her disastrous showing at the Classic, she won the USA Gymnastics National Championship, and was named to the Senior National Team. Two months after that, she won the World Championships in Antwerp, Belgium—her first international title—scoring first on floor exercise, second on the vault and first in all-around. She has not lost a meet since.

In 2014, Biles and her coach, Boorman, ended their relationship with Bannon's Gymnastix. Her grandparents opened a new facility, the World Champions Center in Spring, Texas, where Boorman and Biles trained. A shoulder injury kept Biles out of competition at the beginning of the 2014 season, but she returned in the 2014 U.S. Classic in Chicago, tying for first on the balance beam, taking first place in vault and floor exercise, and winning the all-around by a wide margin. She now routinely finished ahead of her nearest competitors by margins of whole points rather than fractions, as is more customary. At the 2014 USA Gymnastics National Championships, Biles tied for the silver on the balance beam, despite a fall during her final routine of the two-day meet. She won the gold in the vault and floor exercise to emerge as the national all-around champion after two days of competition, finishing more than four points ahead of her nearest competitor.

Later that year, at the World Artistic Gymnastics Championships in Nanning, China, Biles took a silver medal in the vault, gold in the balance beam and floor exercise, and won her second consecutive world all-around title.

Biles began 2015 with victories in the AT&T American Cup in Arlington, Texas and the City of Jesolo Trophy in Italy. At that year's U.S. Classic, she finished first in the all-around competition, with first place finishes in balance beam, vault, and floor exercise. When Biles graduated from her secondary schooling in 2015, she verbally committed to UCLA, with plans to defer enrollment until after the Rio de Janeiro 2016 Summer Olympics. Soon after, she announced that she would turn professional, forfeiting her NCAA eligibility to compete for UCLA.

Her winning streak continued with a third consecutive all-around championship at the 2015 U.S. National. She then won a third international title at the World Championships in Glasgow, Scotland. There, she took gold medals in balance beam and floor exercise again, bringing her total medal count to the highest ever won by any female in world gymnastics competition. Biles was named Team USA Athlete of the Year. She signed with Octagon in 2015, and became a Nike-sponsored athlete. She later signed with GK Elite Sportswear for an exclusive line of leotards, partnered with Core Power, and became a member of its Everyday Awesome team of athletes.

In 2016, Biles began the year winning an all-around victory at the Pacific Rim Championships with the highest scores on vault, floor, and balance beam. At the USA Gymnastics National Championships, she again won the titles in vault and floor exercise, earning the all-around title.

As expected, Biles was selected for the Olympic team. When the Károlyises lost their contract from USA Gymnastics, Boorman was selected to train the USA Gymnastics Women's Team, a coup for Biles. She went on to lead the American gymnasts to victory in the team event at the Rio de Janeiro 2016 Summer Olympics. They scored more than eight points ahead of the second-place Russian team. Two days later, Biles took the gold medal in the all-around event, with the highest scores on vault, floor, and balance beam. She won a second individual gold medal in the vault. Despite her first-place finish on the balance beam in the all-around competition a few days earlier, an unexpected error marred an otherwise impressive performance on the balance beam final, and she received a bronze medal for that event. Biles ended by winning a fourth gold medal in the floor exercise final. Besides tying a number of other world records, she set a new American record for most gold medals in gymnastics at a single Olympics game. Between her performances at the Olympics and in World Championship competition, she had won thirty medals, making her the most decorated American gymnast of all time. As Team USA's outstanding star of the Olympics, Biles was chosen by her teammates to carry her country's flag in the closing ceremonies.

In the wake of the Olympics, Russian computer hackers gained access to the medical records of Biles and other Team USA athletes. They tried to discredit Biles' performance by disclosing that she had tested positive for Ritalin. Biles freely admitted that she has long taken Ritalin for ADHD (attention-deficit/hyperactivity disorder), and the Olympics Committee confirmed that she had received a therapeutic exemption to continue her medication while competing. Her forthright discussion of her experience with ADHD encouraged people to pursue proven treatment options (Santos 2016).

Biles moved into her own house and after thirteen years of incessant practice and competition, decided to take a year off before training for the Tokyo 2020 Summer Olympics. In recent years, she has grown comfortable using her voice and platform to advocate for social causes, such as the Black Lives Matter. In 2017, she was given the ESPY Award for Best Female Athlete of the Year. She published her autobiography, co-authored by Michelle Burford, *Courage to Soar: A Body in Motion, A Life in Balance.* Biles competed on Season 24 of *Dancing with the Stars,* and was paired with dancer Sasha Farber. Despite high scores throughout the season, they were eliminated one week before the finals, finishing in fourth place.

After the Olympics, Biles received endorsements from Kellogg's, Procter & Gamble, Hershey Company, United Airlines, and Beats By Dr Dre. She was a spokesperson for Mattress Firm, and partnered with Spieth America to create a line of gymnastics equipment. When Biles coach, Boorman, relocated to Florida, she announced her new coaches, Cecile and Laurent Landi, who had guided Olympic teammate Madison Kocian.

The world of female competitive gymnastics was rocked in 2018 when over 150 former patients of Team USA doctor Larry Nassar accused him of sexual abuse. Biles released a statement confirming she was sexually assaulted, and called out USA Gymnastics for having an alleged role in allowing the abuse to happen and for covering it up. Nassar was sentenced on federal child pornography charges and for multiple counts of sexual assault. For Biles, coming forward was all at once depressing, courageous, and cathartic.

After a 711-day layoff, Biles made a triumphant return to public competition at the U.S. Classic in July 2018. She posted the highest scores on vault, floor exercise, balance beam, and all-around performance. At the USA Gymnastics National Championships the following month, Biles won gold medals in all four events—her first medal for the uneven bars, previously regarded as her weakest event—and took the all-around title. She is the second woman in history to win all five gold medals at the National after Marion Jones in track and field. Biles wore a teal-colored leotard for her historic performance, a gesture of solidarity with all victims of sexual assault.

At the 2018 World Gymnastics Championship, Biles won a medal in every event: bronze in the balance beam, silver in the uneven bars, and gold medals in the floor exercise, vault, team final, and for all-around individual performance. The first American competitor to win a medal in every event at the

World Championship, she achieved this remarkable performance while suffering from a painful kidney stone. She had delayed treatment until after the competition, declining pain medication that would have prevented her from qualifying under anti-doping regulations. To date, she has won twenty-five World medals, surpassing Vitaly Scherbo's record of twenty-three medals.

Biles was named the Team USA Female Olympic Athlete of the Year in 2015, making her the fourth gymnast to win the honor. In 2016, Biles won the *Glamour* Award for the Record Breaker, was chosen as one of BBC's 100 Women; was named one of ESPNW's Impact 25, and was chosen as the Sportswoman of the Year by the Women's Sports Foundation. In July 2017, Biles was the second gymnast to win the ESPY Award for Best Female Athlete, won the Shorty Awards for the best in sports, won the 2017 Teen Choice Award for favorite female athlete, and won Laureus World Sports Award for Sportswoman of the Year in 2017. Biles was named one of the most influential people in the world by *Time Magazine,* and was named ESPN *The Magazine's* most dominant athlete of 2018. In 2019, she was named Laureus' Sportswoman of the Year for the second time.

She has become well-known for executing performances at the highest level. Her routines on vault and floor exercise in women's artistic gymnastics, are the most difficult of all time so much so that as of 2020, there are four skills named after her. Through it all, Biles has also suffered injuries such as bone spurs, a broken rib, and cracked and shattered toes. In 2021, she split with longtime sponsor Nike to sign with Athleta, the athletic clothing arm of Gap.

Biles has always had to deal with being one of a handful of Black women participating in elite gymnastics. She has faced demeaning and repulsive attacks about her body from spectators, competitors, and relentless online trolls who talk about her hair or how big her legs are (Buckner 2021). And while most gymnasts peak as teenagers, when Biles returned to competition after the Rio de Janeiro 2016 Summer Olympics, she easily won national and international titles at age twenty-one. She could have retired on top after the Olympics, but for her, returning to the gym after a one-year break and preparing for the Tokyo 2020 Summer Olympics was part unfinished business, and part "why not."

But her carefully laid plans were thrown into limbo due to the pandemic. Her family gym was forced to shutter, and the Olympics was postponed to 2021. In the unforgiving timeline of an elite gymnastics career, a year's delay is an eternity—especially for Biles, who will be twenty-four in 2021, unusually old for an Olympian. Following her qualifications performance for the Tokyo 2020 Summer Olympics, Biles felt the weight of the world on her shoulders. Suffering with "the twisties" where you cannot tell up from down, Biles pulled out of the team and all-around finals, and withdrew from the uneven bars and vault individual finals to focus on her mental health. Although Biles performed a relatively scaled down routine with an easier double pike dismount in the beam final, she won the bronze medal. What happens next remains uncertain, but one thing is certain: Biles is the greatest gymnast of our time—or of any time in history.❖

AFTERWORD:
Ayanna Pressley Reminds Us of Who We Are

"I've been robbed of my hair, I lost my hair, and I was saying to people that's nothing new. Hardship is transcendent, hardship is universal and for the issue of alopecia, of which, there are millions of sufferers, certainly there are many Black women. So I've been robbed of my hair, but Black women have been robbed of things for a long time."

~Ayanna Pressley, remarks on stage at the 50th anniversary Martin Luther King Jr. Memorial Breakfast held at the Boston convention center, January 20, 2020

WHEN REPRESENTATIVE AYANNA PRESSLEY of Massachusetts posted a video on *The Root* on January 16, 2020, announcing to the world that she suffered from alopecia, revealing her beautiful bald head, I thought it was awesome and courageous. At that moment, you could see she was clearly in mourning over the loss of her hair. Yet she went on to say that since her election to the House of Representatives, Black women, especially young Black girls, had looked up to her for wearing her signature Senegalese twists, which became synonymous and conflated with her political brand. For that reason, Pressley felt that for her to be transparent and be her authentic self, she needed to reveal her baldness.

I also thought it was interesting that Pressley considered her hairstyle as part of her "brand," especially when it was clear, at least to me, that her very being was the thing that shone through, with or without hair. But I also understood on a far deeper level Pressley's loss. Historically, Black women have always had an obsessive and complicated relationship with our hair. Many of us were taught at an early age that something was wrong with our hair and our mother's job was to fix it, tame it, and to make it "acceptable." For that reason, generations of Black women have endured hair straighteners and the dreaded hot comb so that they could live up to a European standard of beauty. Even with the freedom to wear our hair in braids, twists, or natural hairstyles, our hair has always been culturally and politically challenged. It is why all Black

PHOTO: Official Photo of Rep. Ayanna Pressley (D-Massachusetts) during the 117th Congress.

women have personal stories and experiences to share about how they have dealt with this conundrum.

Pressley's braids were not the only thing that stood out; she entered Congress in 2019 as part of the most diverse generation of women to arrive on Capitol Hill. She quickly became incredibly visible with a powerful voice, an open desire to create change, and a willingness to throw her political weight behind what she believes is right. Ironically, Pressley's hair became an integral part of that visibility. She became one of the few politicians who wore a natural hairstyle despite being told it was "too ethnic" or it "wasn't polished enough." For Pressley, seeing an elected official proudly wear her hair in braids mattered.

Moreover, the loss of Pressley's hair drives home the varying degrees of stress that Black women live with on a daily basis. Here was a woman who dedicated herself to a career in community service, which led to politics. She did what was seemingly impossible by winning a coveted seat in the House of Representatives, thinking that once she won, she could roll up her sleeves and represent her constituents and continue to do good work on a larger scale. Instead, she stepped into a situation fraught with the stress of being constantly attacked by the president and his minions, with threats and harassment that would push any mortal being over the edge. And whether it is medically true or not, we were all thinking the same thing: that this compounded stress was a contributing factor toward her suffering from alopecia. Pressley represents what all Black women face in our daily lives: always having to be twice as good, always having to sacrifice in ways that others do not. We combat racial and gender stereotypes that in many cases threaten our livelihood, while juggling our family life and dealing with health issues and the lack of self-care, all with the expectation that we manage this with the grace that is demanded by all.

Hair. It is a Black woman's crowning glory. Our hair has always been intrinsic to our authentic self for thousands of years. The dense spiraling curls and frizzy, kinky hair was created to insulate our heads from the brutal intensity of the sun's rays on the continent (Byrd and Tharps 2014). Black women wore beautifully complicated braids, twists, and threaded styles to express their status, which clan they belonged to, or to signify whether or not they were married, or had gone through puberty. When we were captured and dragged to America's shores, our hair then became our curse. Unable to properly care for it, we resorted to covering our heads with rags and scarves, which became ubiquitous with slave culture. Some cities like New Orleans implemented laws that required Black women to wear a *tignon* (scarf or handkerchief) over their hair, regardless of whether they were free or enslaved.[1] Either way, they forced us to cover our hair because it was a powerful reminder that our culture was a threat to the status quo.

---

1.   Donald E. Everett, "Free Persons of Color in Colonial Louisiana," *Louisiana History: The Journal of the Louisiana Historical Association* 7, no. 1 (1966): 21-50, http://www.jstor.org/stable/4230881.

For hundreds of years, we have been forced to straddle two cultures and the competing beauty standards that come with it. Throughout history, Black people's hair has been mocked and scorned, often compared to wool, and described derogatorily as "nappy" or "kinky." This was further complicated when the terms "good hair" and "bad hair" became part of the African American lexicon. Good hair is considered to be hair that is wavy or straight in texture, soft to the touch, has the ability to grow long, and requires minimal intervention by way of treatments or products. More importantly, it is used metaphorically to characterize beauty that is acceptable to European standards. The idea of good hair is perpetuated by pervasive cultural messages that idealize this vision of hair and offer treatments or products to achieve it, while bad hair is the extreme opposite because it reflects African ancestry. Our hair's natural state represents a wholesale rejection of European values and norms for many White people. In other words, it makes them feel uncomfortable. As a result, Black people, especially Black women, have spent an exorbitant amount of time and money trying to meet this European standard. At some point in her life, Pressley rejected this standard when she decided to wear braids and twists.

It was in the mid-1960s when African Americans began to wear natural hairstyles that our hair was being seen less as a cultural aberration and more as a political statement. How can something so essential to our identity be so misunderstood? Over time, it seemed that White people always had something to say about how we wear our hair, whether it is permed or natural, bought or grown, straightened or fluffy, or even bald. Yes, some women intentionally shave their heads because it empowers them. This is why I think it is very telling that Pressley decided to forgo wigs and present her bald head to the public. She could have easily made the announcement and continued wearing wigs or head wraps, or she could have said nothing at all. But I am convinced she did it because she was trying to take back her power when she lost her hair.

When Black protesters demanded the signing of the Civil Rights Act of 1964, which "ended segregation in public places and banned employment discrimination," no one foresaw that Black hair would need equal protection as well. When we began rocking afros in the late sixties, the first natural hair discrimination cases did not appear until the 1976 case of *Jenkins v. Blue Cross Mutual Hospital Insurance.* The U.S. Court of Appeals for the Seventh Circuit upheld this race discrimination lawsuit against an employer for bias against afros under Title VII of the Civil Rights Act. They agreed that workers were entitled to wear afros.

But although afros were allowed in the workplace, and assimilation became more dominant in the late 1970s, more Black women sported pressed and permed hair instead, thanks to prevalent haircare ads on television and magazines, and the overwhelming desire to "fit in." However, during this period, we also witnessed the popularization of styles like braids and cornrows. While most

White people like to credit the actress Bo Derek, who appeared in the 1979 movie *10*, for popularizing cornrows, Black women had been wearing braids and cornrows since forever. In fact, in the mid-1960s, Oscar-nominated actress Cicely Tyson was the first Black woman to wear her hair in a short, natural style on television, and donned cornrows for her role in the 1972 film *Sounder*. But when we wore braids and cornrows, it came with a price and created a legal firestorm.

In 1981, Renee Rogers took American Airlines to court because the company demanded she not wear her hair in braids. In *Rogers v. American Airlines,* the court sided with the airline, stating that braids were not an immutable racial characteristic—unlike the afro—establishing a standing legal precedent. In 1988, the Hyatt Regency Crystal City, a hotel in a Virginia suburb near Washington, D.C., used this ruling to make employee Cheryl R. Tatum resign after she refused to take out the cornrows she wore to work. While the Hyatt Regency had a local policy that prohibited multibraided hairstyles, its corporate headquarters, Hyatt Hotels, publicly stated it never had a policy banning braided hair. Nevertheless, as images of Black women celebrities showcasing braids—like Janet Jackson in *Poetic Justice* (1993)—became prevalent, more Black women were encouraged to braid their tresses or grow dreadlocks.

Spurred by popular culture and the advent of social media, the 2000s welcomed the second wave of the natural hair movement that fueled a cultural shift, which caused legions of Black women to abandon their perms and pressing combs. Chris Rock would release *Good Hair* (2009), a documentary that focused on the economics of Black women buying weaves and perming their hair. Director Regina Kimbell's *My Nappy Roots: A Journey Through Black Hairitage* (2010) followed, which showcased our natural hair's history and politics. *The Natural Hair Movie* (2018), produced by Ashanti Titus and Reginald Titus Jr., shares women's stories about overcoming discrimination, suppression, and western standards of beauty in hair styling. With natural hair becoming the new normal, sales of relaxers in the Black haircare market have plummeted 36.6 percent between 2012 and 2017.[2] By 2020, relaxers became the smallest segment of the market. The fact that, at a great, painful personal price, many Black women develop lesions on their scalps or lose their hair when they chemically straighten their hair is perhaps the main reason that they have chosen to abandon straighteners altogether.

While natural hair care practices have gained increased acceptance in mainstream society, the debate about what is professional, presentable, and acceptable looms. Even today, in certain workplaces, traditional Black hairstyles, such as dreadlocks, are restricted and can be a cause for termination. Why? Because the Equal Employment Opportunity Commission (EEOC) states

---

2.   "Black haircare regimens boost shampoo sales in the U.S. to reach $473 million in 2017," Mintel Press Office, Beauty and Personal Care, September 19, 2017, https://www.mintel.com/press-centre/beauty-and-personal-care/Black-haircare-regimens-boost-shampoo-sales-in-the-us.

that employers can impose "neatness and grooming standards," but to what end? Racist hair discrimination is so subtle that it has manifested itself in the form of microaggressions with specific ideas on what is "neat" being based on a European standard. Does anyone know of any White woman fired or denied a job opportunity due to her hairstyle? If you do, *please let me know.*

In the meantime, the intolerance toward our hairstyles and the lawsuits keep coming. In 2010, Chastity Jones accepted a job offer, but it came with one caveat—she had to cut off her dreadlocks. Jones refused, and the company rescinded its job offer. The EEOC filed a suit on Jones' behalf in 2013 and lost. In 2016, the 11th Circuit Court of Appeals upheld the district court's ruling and dismissed the case. In 2012, KTBS meteorologist Rhonda A. Lee, who wears a close-cropped natural, was fired after she replied to a viewer post on the station's Facebook page chastising her hairstyle, even though hers was a thoughtful response and he apologized. After a lengthy period of unemployment, Lee worried she would never work in the news again. She filed an EEOC complaint against the station, but it is unclear if the mediation resolved her dismissal or if the complaint was dismissed. In 2017, nineteen-year-old Destiny Tompkins filed a discrimination lawsuit against Banana Republic, the Gap Inc.-owned chain, for at least $1 million. Tompkins, who was hired as a sales representative in a White Plains, New York store, started wearing braids soon after she began working. When told her hair was inappropriate, she refused to change it. Rather than outright firing her, Tompkins was removed from the work schedule. The store manager was eventually fired, and her lawsuit was settled in February 2018. Banana Republic has since publicly stated it has zero-tolerance for discrimination.

Discriminatory hair experiences can be emotionally taxing and cause people to question their worth, and even little girls who are still exploring their identity are not exempt from this harassment. For example, in 2013, seven-year-old Tiana Parker of Tulsa, Oklahoma was brought to tears after being told that her dreadlocks violated school policy and she faced being kicked out. Rather than cut her dreadlocks, she transferred to another school, and after receiving national media attention over the issue, the school reversed its policy. That same year, twelve-year-old Vanessa VanDyke in Orlando, Florida faced expulsion from her private school over her natural hair before administrators were shamed into reconsidering their position. When the young girl was being bullied by her peers about her natural hair, and her self-esteem began to decline, her mother founded her own natural hair care line called Vanessa's Essence Natural Hair Care. Together, they help inspire girls and women around the world to wear their natural hair.

In 2017, Mystic Valley Regional Charter School in Malden, Massachusetts banned black twins Deanna Cook and Maya Cook from playing after school sports and attending their prom because they wore hair extensions to school, violating school policy. When Massachusetts Attorney General Maura Healey stepped in on the twins' behalf with a strongly worded letter indicating that her office was investigating allegations, the school suspended the policy. No matter the intent, discrimination remains at the heart of these wrongful firings and expulsions.

So while the courts have reasoned that discrimination based on race is forbidden because race is immutable, they also hold the belief that hairstyles can be changed. Hairstyles indeed involve some degree of personal choice, but that should not give schools or employers free rein to discriminate against people who wear braids, dreadlocks, or other natural hairstyles.

Unfortunately, little Black girls and boys, and Black women and men, will continue to be discriminated against even though traditional Black hairstyles have no bearing in either a school or job setting. And Black women will continue to confront a choice: be excluded from the workplace entirely or be forced to conform to a European standard. Although there is no existing federal law that prohibits this kind of discrimination in the twenty-first century, multiple states and local governments have passed laws that prohibit such discrimination, California being the first state to do so in 2019 with the Crown Act. Hair discrimination might sound like a trivial issue, but it is inextricably intertwined with racism and should be legally recognized as such.

Ask any Black woman and they will tell you how they have struggled with haircare and with people who have no consideration about one's personal space, asking them stupid questions about their hair. Our hair, or lack of it, is believed to be public property, to be touched and commented on, especially by White people. It is perceived as making a statement beyond appearance: weaves emulating straight hair is seen as an exercise in White supremacist self-hatred, or letting one's hair grow naturally represents some radical political statement. Perhaps the question we should be asking is, why are White people so obsessed with our hair? The fixation and demonization of our hair is not only discomfiting, it is also downright disrespectful. *Stop policing our hair!*

It should then be no surprise that as African American women candidates and elected officials navigate through an uncertain political landscape, the way they dress and how they wear their hair determines how they are perceived by their colleagues and constituents. Certainly, Pressley considered this when she ran and won her seat in the House of Representatives. In fact, when former Representative Cynthia McKinney (D-GA) became the first black woman elected to Congress from Georgia in 2006, she got into a scuffle with a U.S. Capitol police officer who stopped her from entering the building because she changed her hairstyle and he did not recognize her. McKinney's position is that she was racially profiled because "all Black people look alike." Without the familiar braids, she maintained, the officer only paid attention to her race.

Regardless of whether this episode was an innocent mistake, as the officer insisted, or a telling example of profiling, as McKinney argued, it offers insight into how racialized and gendered assumptions have become the norm. Sadly, we also understand how our Black bodies, skin tone, hairstyle, and hair texture fall outside the dominant construct of beauty and femininity. White people use these physical markers to determine who we are and what we represent (Brown 2014).

Representatives Barbara Lee (D-CA), Gwen Moore (D-WI), Marcia Fudge (D-OH), Karen Bass (D-CA), and Lauren Underwood (D-IL) have worn their hair in seemingly natural or "ethnic" styles, and Mia Love (R-UT) occasionally wore her hair in braids. Ilhan Omar (D-MN) overcame a 181-year headwear ban to become the first to wear a hijab in Congress. But it was Pressley who captured the spotlight and the public's attention with her signature Senegalese twists.

Pressley was very aware of the visual politics of her hair and its outsized significance. She also understood that our hair is laden with messages, and for young Black girls, it has the power to dictate how others treat you, and in turn, how you feel about yourself (Thompson 2008). Of course, Pressley is no stranger to the fact that Black women are frequently policed for their hairstyle choices. As a Black woman in Congress who wore her hair in braids and twists, she made a cultural statement and challenged the status quo. Black women across the country had never seen a politician in the national spotlight go out of their way to wear their hair in braids. She did so with such dignity and grace that Pressley quickly became an inspiration to young Black girls worldwide.

It is why Pressley's announcement about the loss of her hair went to the core of Black womanhood. For Pressley, her hair helped define and establish her identity, was no longer, yet she felt obliged to make public this private moment that so many Black women could relate to. Make no mistake about it, despite the sociohistorical issues and drama tied to our hair, when Pressley lost her hair, she lost a piece of herself. But she did what Black women have done for years when faced with loss and disappointment: she rose to the occasion, never losing sight of the values and beliefs that helped establish who she is.

Less than twenty-four hours after Pressley posted her video, it spread across the internet like wildfire. It was seen by her colleagues, constituents, women of all ages, and, more importantly, young Black girls who share a complicated relationship with their hair. Not only did we applaud Pressley, we also embraced her. She reminded us that history, culture, tradition, and our social struggles may be challenged but should never be denied. When we ignore these elements' importance, we deny our authentic selves, obliterating the very makeup of who we are. No matter how hard they try to disassemble us by attacking both our bodies and our hair, we must always remember this is intrinsically tied to our personal and cultural identity. We have always known this, but Ayanna Pressley, quite daringly and eloquently, has once again reminded us of who we are.❖

REFERENCES

Aaseng, Nathan. 2003. *African-American Athletes (A to Z of African Americans).* New York: Facts on File.

Abdul-Jabbar, Kareem. 2015. "Body Shaming Black Female Athletes Is Not Just About Race." *Time,* July 20, 2015. https://time.com/3964758/body shaming-Black-female-athletes.

Acharya, Amitav, and See Seng Tan. 2008. *Bandung Revisited: The Legacy of the 1955 Asian-African Conference for International Order.* Honolulu: University of Hawaii Press.

Ackmann, Martha. 2017. *Curveball: The Remarkable Story of Toni Stone, The First Woman to Play Professional Baseball in the Negro League.* Illinois: Chicago Review Press.

African American Policy Forum, The (AAPF), "#SayHerName Campaign." N.p. https://aapf.org/sayhername.

Afrika, Nyar. "White Feminism's concept of 'unity' is a joke. Shoot me." *AFROPUNK,* January 12, 2018. https://afropunk.com/2018/01/White-feminisms-concept-unity-joke-shoot.

Aguirre, Abby. 2020. "Simone Biles on Overcoming Abuse, the Postponed Olympics, and Training During a Pandemic." *Vogue,* July 9, 2020, https://www.vogue.com/article/simone-biles-cover-august-2020.

Akinleye, Adesola. 2021. *(Re:) Claiming Ballet.* Bristol, U.K.: Intellect Books Limited.

Alexander, Michelle. 2020. "America, This, is Your Chance." *The New York Times,* June 8, 2020. https://www.nytimes.com/2020/06/08/opinion/george-floyd-protests-race.html.

Alexander, Michelle. 2010. *The New Jim Crow, Mass Incarceration in the Age of Colorblindness.* New York: New Press.

Anderson, Monica and Gustavo López. 2018. "Key facts about black immigrants in the U.S." Pew Research Center, January 24, 2018. https://www.pewresearch.org/fact-tank/2018/01/24/key-facts-about-black-immigrants-in-the-u-s.

Angyal, Chloe. 2021. *Turning Pointe: How A New Generation of Dancers Is Saving Ballet from Itself.* New York: PublicAffairs.

Asmelash, Leah. 2020. "WNBA dedicates season to Breonna Taylor and Say Her Name campaign." *CNN,* July 25, 2020. https://www.cnn.com/2020/07/25/us/wnba-season-start-breonna-taylor-cnn/index.html.

Associated Press. 2017. "Ferguson attorney: Michael Brown's family settles with city for $1.5 million." *The Los Angeles Times,* June 23, 2017. https://www.latimes.com/nation/nationnow/la-namichael-brown-ferguson-settlement-20170623-story.html.

Associated Press. 2012. "Whites to lose majority status by 2043, the census projects." *Politico,* December 12, 2012. https://www.politico.com/story/2012/12/census-whites-no-longer-a-majority-in-us-by-2043-084971.

Baker, Christine A. 2008. *Why She Plays: The World of Women's Basketball.* Lincoln, NE: Bison Books.

Barnes, Clive. 1974. "The Ballet: 'Bartok. No. 3'." *The New York Times,* May 25, 1974. https://www.nytimes.com/1974/05/25/archives/the-ballet-bartok-no-3.html.

Baumann, Jason. 2019. *The Stonewall Reader.* New York: Penguin Books.

BBC News Online. 2020. "Breonna Taylor: What Happened on the Night of Her Death?" October 8, 2020. https://www.bbc.com/news/world-us-canada-54210448.

Bell, Janet Dewart. 2018. *Lighting the Fires of Freedom: African American Women in the Civil Rights Movement.* New York: The New Press.

Belmont Report, The. 1979. Office of the Secretary. *Ethical Principles and Guidelines for the Protection of Human Subjects of Research,* by The National Commission for the Protection of Human Subjects of Biomedical and Behavioral Research, April 18, 1979. https://www.hhs.gov/ohrp/regulations-and-policy/belmont-report/read-the-belmont-report/index.html.

Bennett, Michael. 2002. *Recovering the Black Female Body: Self-Representation by African American Women.* New Jersey: Rutgers University Press.

Benzing, Rachel. 2012. "Heels and Gumption: Tap Dance Empowered by Women." *Dance Department Student Works, 6.* Loyola Marymount University. http://digitalcommons.lmu.edu/dance_students/6.

Berman, Ari. 2015. *Give Us the Ballot: The Modern Struggle for Voting Rights in America.* New York: Farrar, Straus and Giroux.

Berri, David. 2017. "Basketball's Growing Gender Wage Gap: The Evidence The WNBA Is Underpaying Players." *Forbes,* September 20, 2017. https://www.forbes.com/sites/davidberri/2017/09/20/there-is-a-growing-gender-wage-gap-in-professional-basketball/#29afe39536e0.

Berry, Mary Frances, and John Blassingame. 1982. *Long Memory: The Black Experience in America.* New York: Oxford University Press.

Bier, Lisa. 2011. *Fighting the Current: The Rise of American Women's Swimming, 1870-1926.* Jefferson, NC: McFarland & Company, Inc.

Billingsley, Andrew. 1993. *Climbing Jacob's Ladder: The Enduring Legacies of African-American Families.* New York: Touchstone Books.

Blain, Keisha, and Tiffany Gill, eds. 2019. *To Turn the Whole World Over: Black Women and Internationalism.* Champaign: University of Illinois Press.

Blyden, Nemata, and Jeannette Eileen Jones. 2020. "Between Africa and America, Recalibrating Black Americans' Relationship to the Diaspora." *Perspectives on History,* August 20, 2020. https://www.historians.org/publications-and-directories/perspectives-on-history/september-2020/between-africa-and-america-recalibrating-black-americans-relationship-to-the-diaspora.

Bondy, Stefan. 2018. "20 years ago Sandhi Ortiz-Del Valle sued the NBA charging she was blocked from becoming a referee because she's a woman; the jury agreed, though today it still hurts." *The Daily News,* September 16, 2018. https://www.nydaily-news.com/sports/basketball/ny-sports-endzone-sandhi-nba-ref-20180914-story.html#skip-to-content.

Borge, Jason. 2018. "Chapter 7: The portable jazz age, Josephine Baker's tour of South American cities (1929)."In *Urban Latin America: Images, Words, Flows and the Built Environment,* edited by Bianca Freire-Medeiros, and Julia O'Donnell. England, U.K.: Routledge.

Bouie, Jamelle. 2019. "Will America Make Trump Great Again?" *The New York Times,* June 22, 2019. https://www.nytimes.com/2019/06/22/opinion/trump-2020-win.html.

Braddock, Jomills Henry. 2017. *Women in Sports: Breaking Barriers, Facing Obstacles.* Santa Barbara, CA: ABC-CLIO.

Braukman, Stacy Lorraine, and Susan Ware. 2004. *Notable American Women: A Biographical Dictionary Completing the Twentieth Century.* Cambridge, MA: Belknap Press.

Brick, Michael. 2014. "The Lady Was a Champ, In the Corner with Boxer James Kirkland, A Woman Hangs Tough." *SBNation,* August 19, 2014. https://www.sbnation.com/long-form/2014/8/19/6031751/james-kirkland-ann-wolfe-profile-boxing-trainer.

Brown, Abram. 2020. "TikTok's 7 Highest-Earning Stars: New Forbes List Led By Teen Queens Addison Rae And Charli D'Amelio." *Forbes,* August 6, 2020. https://www.forbes.com/sites/abrambrown/2020/08/06/tiktoks-highest-earning-stars-teen-queens-addison-rae-and-charli-damelio-rule/?sh=67a2f60c5087.

Brown, Jayna. 2008. *Babylon Girls, Black Women Performers and the Shaping of the Modern.* Durham, NC: Duke University Press.

Brown, Nadia E. 2014. "It's More than Hair…And You Do Care: The Politics of Appearance for Black Women State Legislators." *Politics, Groups, and Identities* 2, no. 3: 295-312.

Brown, Pei-San. 2013. "The History of Modern Dance." Ballet Austin.

Bucalo, Angela. 2020. "Who is the Highest Paid WNBA Player?" *ONE37PM,* September 9, 2020. https://www.one37pm.com/strength/sports/highest-paid-wnba-player.

Buckner, Candace. 2021. "For exceptional Black women like Simone Biles, greatness is never enough." *The Washington Post,* July 27, 2021. https://www.washingtonpost.com/sports/olympics/2021/07/27/simone-biles-out-greatness.

Buckner, Jocelyn L. 2012. "'Spectacular Opacities': The Hyers Sisters' Performances of Respectability and Resistance." *African American Review* 45, no. 3: 309-23. http://www.jstor.org/stable/23783542.

Bucknor, Cherrie. 2016. "Black Workers, Unions, and Inequality." The Center for Economic and Policy Research (CEPR), August 2016. https://cepr.net/report/black-workers-unions-and-inequality.

Byrd, Ayana, and Lori Tharps. 2014. *Hair Story: Untangling the Roots of Black Hair in America.* New York: St. Martin's Griffin.

Cahn, Susan K. 2015. *Coming on Strong: Gender and Sexuality in Women's Sport.* Champaign: University of Illinois Press.

Calbay, Cielestia. 2012. "Portrait Of A Lady: Allyson Felix." *Outside,* June 19, 2012. https://www.podiumrunner.com/culture/portrait-of-a-lady-allyson-felix.

Callis, Tracy. 2009. *Boxing in the Los Angeles Area, 1880-2005.* Bloomington, IN: Trafford Publishing.

Caravantes, Peggy. 2015. *The Many Faces of Josephine Baker: Dancer, Singer, Activist, Spy.* Illinois: Chicago Review Press.

Carrega, Christina, and Sabina Ghebremedhin, 2020. "Timeline: Inside the Investigation of Breonna Taylor's Killing and its Aftermath." *ABC News,* November 17, 2020. https://abcnews.go.com/US/timeline-inside-investigation-breonna-taylors-killing-after-math/story?id=71217247.

Chase, Chris, and Jean-Claude Baker. 2001. *Josephine: The Hungry Heart.* Lanham, MD: Cooper Square Press.

Chateauvert, Melinda. 1998. *Marching Together: Women of the Brotherhood of Sleeping Car Porters.* Champaign: University of Illinois Press.

Chicago Defender. 1917. "Woman to Play First Base for the Havana Stars." May 12, 1917: 5.

Clark, Lara P., Dylan B. Millet, and Julian D. Marshall. 2014. "National Patterns in Environmental Injustice and Inequality: Outdoor NO2 Air Pollution in the United States." *PLOS ONE* 9(4): e94431, April 15, 2014, https://doi.org/10.1371/journal.pone.0094431.

Clark, Septima Poinsette. 1990. *Ready from Within: Septima Clark and the Civil Rights Movement, A First Person Narrative.* Lawrenceville, NJ: Africa World Press.

Clark, VèVè A., Johnson, Sarah East, and Katherine Dunham. 2005. *Kaiso! Writings by and about Katherine Dunham.* Madison: University of Wisconsin Press.

Cohen, Marilyn. 2009. *No Girls in the Clubhouse: The Exclusion of Women from Baseball.* Jefferson, NC: McFarland & Company, Inc.

Cole, Johnnetta B., and Beverly Guy-Sheftall. 2003. *Gender Talk: The Struggle For Women's Equality in African American Communities.* London: One World.

Collier-Thomas, Bettye, and V.P. Franklin, eds. 2001. *Sisters in the Struggle : African-American Women in the Civil Rights-Black Power Movement.* New York: New York University Press.

Connors, Joseph. 2014. "Berenson and Katherine Dunham: Black American Dance." In *Bernard Berenson: Formation and Heritage,* edited by Joseph Connors and Louis A. Waldman, 363-391. Florence and Cambridge MA: Villa I Tatti with Harvard University Press.

Cooke, Mervyn, and David Horn, eds. 2003. *The Cambridge Companion to Jazz.* Cambridge University Press.

Copeland, Joy M. 2015. *Clara Day, A Teamster's Life, A Biography.* New York: International Brotherhood of Teamsters.

Copeland, Misty. 2018. *Life in Motion: An Unlikely Ballerina.* New York: Aladdin.

Crawford Vicki L., Jacqueline Anne Rouse, and Barbara Woods, eds. 1993. *Women in the Civil Rights Movement: Trailblazers and Torchbearers, 1941-1965.* Bloomington: Indiana University Press.

Das, Joanna Dee. 2017. *Katherine Dunham: Dance and the African Diaspora.* New York: Oxford University Press.

Davies, Carole Boyce. 2008. *Left of Karl Marx: The Political Life of Black Communist Claudia Jones.* Durham, NC: Duke University Press.

Davis, Michael D. 1992. *Black American Women in Olympic Track and Field: A Complete Illustrated Reference.* Jefferson, NC: McFarland & Company, Inc.

Davis, Timothy. 2008. "Race and Sports in America: An Historical Overview." *Virginia Sports & Entertainment Law Journal.* Wake Forest Univ. Legal Studies Paper No. 1141868, https://ssrn.com/abstract=1141868.

DeFrantz, Thomas F. 2004. "The Black Beat Made Visible: Hip Hop Dance and Body Power." In *Of The Presence of the Body, Essays on Dance and Performance Theory*, edited by André Lepecki, 64-81. Middletown, CT: Wesleyan University Press.

———. 2002. *Dancing Many Drums: Excavations in African American Dance*. Madison: University of Wisconsin Press.

de la Cretaz, Britni. 2015. "To White Feminists Who Don't Want to Discuss Racism: Here Are 7 Things You Need to Know." *Everyday Feminism,* October 12, 2015. https://everydayfeminism.com/2015/10/White-feminists-dont-talk-race.

Denisoff, R. Serge. 2017. *Inside MTV*. Oxfordshire, U.K.: Taylor & Francis.

Denison, Erik, and Alistair Kitchen. 2014. *Out on the Fields, The first international study on homophobia in sport. Nielsen,* Bingham Cup Sydney 2014, Australian Sports Commission, Federation of Gay Games. www.outonthefields.com.

Dennis, Anita K., and Benjamin G. Dennis. 2008. *Slaves to Racism: An Unbroken Chain from America to Liberia*. New York: Algora Publishing.

Department of Labor. 1821-1928. Commissioner General of Immigration,

Department of Labor. 2021. U.S. Bureau of Labor Statistics. "Union Members, 2020." January 22, 2021. https://www.bls.gov/news.release/pdf/union2.pdf.

DePrince, Michaela, and Elaine DePrince. 2016. *Taking Flight: from War Orphan to Star Ballerina*. New York: Penguin Random House (Ember).

DeSilver, Drew. 2018. "A record number of women, will be serving in the new Congress." *FACTANK,* Pew Research Center, December 18, 2018, https://pewrsr.ch/2Lp3XMa.

Desmond, Jane. 1997. *Meaning in Motion: New Cultural Studies of Dance*. Durham, NC: Duke University Press.

Dicaire, David. 2010. *Jazz Musicians of the Early Years, to 1945*. Jefferson, NC: McFarland & Company, Inc.

Diouf, Esailama, Kariamu Welsh, and Yvonne Daniel, eds. 2019. *Hot Feet and Social Change: African Dance and Diaspora Communities*. Champaign: University of Illinois Press.

Dixon, David E., and Davis W. Houck. 2009. *Women and the Civil Rights Movement, 1954-1965*. Jackson: University Press of Mississippi.

Dixon, Melanye White. 2011. *Marion Cuyjet and Her Judimar School of Dance: Training Ballerinas in Black Philadelphia 1948-1971*. New York: Edwin Mellon Press.

Dixon-Stowell, Brenda. 1980. "Blondell Cummings: 'The Ladies and Me'." *The Drama Review: TDR* 24, no. 4 (1980): 37-44. doi:10.2307/1145322.

Djata, Sundiata. 2008. *Blacks at the Net: Black Achievement in the History of Tennis, Volume Two*. New York: Syracuse University Press.

Doak, Robin S. 2007. *The March on Washington: Uniting Against Racism*. Minneapolis, MN: Compass Point Books.

DuBois, Ellen Carol. 1978. *Feminism and Suffrage: The Emergence of an Independent Women's Movement in America, 1848 1869*. Ithaca, NY: Cornell University Press.

Dudden, Faye E. 2014. *Fighting Chance: The Struggle Over Woman Suffrage and Black Suffrage In Reconstruction America*. New York: Oxford University Press.

Durkin, Hannah. 2019. *Josephine Baker and Katherine Dunham: Dances in Literature and Cinema*. Champaign: University of Illinois Press.

Dvorak, Petula. 2020. "Is it cultural appropriation when a Black woman does Irish dance?" *The Washington Post,* August 3, 2020. https://www.washington-post.com/local/is-it-cultural-appropriation-when-a-black-woman-does-irish-dance/2020/08/03/974b16f6-d517-11ea-930e-d88518c57dcc_story.html.

Dwight, Margaret L., and George A. Sewell. 1984. *Mississippi Black History Makers.* Jackson: University Press of Mississippi.

Edelson, Paula. 2014. *A to Z of American Women in Sports.* New York: Facts On File.

Eichenwald, Kurt. 2014. "The Family Feud Over Martin Luther King Jr.'s Legacy." *Newsweek*, April 3, 2014. https://www.newsweek.com/2014/04/11/family-feud-over-martin-luther-king-jrs-legacy-248083.html.

el-Khoury, Laura J. 2012. "Being while Black: Resistance and the Management of the Self." *Social Identities* 18, no. 1(2012): 85. https://www.tandfonline.com/doi/abs/10.108 0/13504630.2012.629516.

Elliott, Helene. 2020. "How Jackie Joyner-Kersee conquered the Olympics and earned GOAT status." *The Los Angeles Times,* March 9, 2020. https://www.latimes.com/sports/story/2020-03-09/jackie-joyner-kersee-track-field-olympics.

Emery, Lynne Fauley. 1989. *Black Dance: From 1619 to Today.* New Jersey: Princeton Book Company.

Erikainen, Sonja. 2019. *Gender Verification and the Making of the Female Body in Sport: A History of the Present.* Oxfordshire, U.K.: Taylor & Francis.

Essed, Philomena. 1991. *Everyday Racism: Reports from Women of Two Cultures.* Thousand Oaks, CA: SAGE Publishing.

Everett, Donald E. 1966. "Free Persons of Color in Colonial Louisiana," *Louisiana History: The Journal of the Louisiana Historical Association* 7, no. 1 (1966): 21-50, http://www.jstor.org/stable/4230881.

Ewoodzie, Joseph C. 2017. *Break Beats in the Bronx: Rediscovering Hip-Hop's Early Years.* Chapel Hill: University of North Carolina Press.

Faderman, Lillian. 2016. *The Gay Revolution, The Story of the Struggle.* New York: Simon & Schuster.

Feinberg, Doug. 2018. "WNBA crossroads: league looks to cut losses, hire president." *Associated Press,* December 28, 2018. https://apnews.com/75e117e82df7470c9 4784438048171d1.

Felder, Deborah G. 2020. *The American Women's Almanac: 500 Years of Making History.* Canton, MI: Visible Ink Press.

Felix, Allyson. 2019. "My Own Nike Pregnancy Story." *The New York Times,* May 22, 2019. https://www.nytimes.com/2019/05/22/opinion/allyson-felix-pregnancy-nike.html.

Fidler, Merrie A. 2015. *The Origins and History of the All-American Girls Professional Baseball League.* Jefferson, NC: McFarland & Company, Inc.

Fields, Armond. 2007. *Tony Pastor, Father of Vaudeville.* Jefferson, NC: McFarland & Company, Inc.

Finkel, Rebecca. 2014. "Broadcasting from a neutral corner? An analysis of the mainstream media's representation of women's boxing in the 2012 London Olympic Games." In *Sports Events, Society and Culture,* edited by Katherine Dashper, Nicola Mccullough, and Thomas Fletcher. Oxfordshire, U.K.: Taylor & Francis.

Finney, Carolyn. 2014. *Black Faces, White Spaces: Reimagining the Relationship of African Americans to the Great Outdoors.* Chapel Hill: University of North Carolina Press.

FitzPatrick, Hayde Adams, and Carol Guensburg, 2020. "Two Decades After Diallo Killing, Mother Finds Hope in New Protests." *Voice of America,* June 25, 2020. https://www.voanews.com/usa/race-america/two-decades-after-diallo-killing-mother-finds-hope-new-protests.

Ford, Bonnie D., and Alyssa Roenigk. 2020. "The Gymnastics Factory The Rise and Fall of the Karolyi Ranch." *ESPN,* July 14, 2020. https://www.espn.com/espn/feature/story/_/id/29235446/the-karolyi-ranch-where-us-women-gymnastics-gold-was-forged-price.

Ford, Tanisha C. 2015. *Liberated Threads: Black Women, Style, and the Global Politics of Soul.* Chapel Hill: University of North Carolina Press.

Foulkes, Julia L. 2002. *Modern Bodies: Dance and American Modernism from Martha Graham to Alvin Ailey.* Chapel Hill: University of North Carolina Press.

Fradin, Dennis Brindell, and Judith Bloom Fradin. 2003. *Fight On!: Mary Church Terrell's Battle for Integration.* New York: Clarion Books.

Franklin, Vincent P. 2001. *Sisters in the Struggle: African American Women in the Civil Rights-Black Power Movement.* New York: New York University Press.

Freeman, Scott. 2020. "Atlanta Ballet called out on social media for not having black female dancers." *ArtsATL,* June 24, 2020. https://www.artsatl.org/atlanta-ballet-called-out-on-social-media-for-not-having-black-female-dancers.

Friedler, Sharon E., and Susan B. Glazer. 2014. *Dancing Female.* Oxfordshire, U.K.: Taylor & Francis.

Gaines, Kevin K. 2008. *American Africans in Ghana: Black Expatriates and the Civil Rights Era.* Chapel Hill: University of North Carolina Press.

Garcia, Sandra E. 2017. "The Woman Who Created #MeToo Long Before Hashtags." *The New York Times,* October 20, 2017. https://www.nytimes.com/2017/10/20/us/me-too-movement-tarana-burke.html.

Gardner, Bettye J., and Niani Kilkenny. 2008. "In Vogue: Josephine Baker and Black Culture and Identity in the Jazz Age." *The Journal of African American History* 93, no. 1 (2008): 88-93. http://www.jstor.org/stable/20064259.

George-Graves, Nadine. 2010. *Urban Bush Women: Twenty Years of African American Dance Theater, Community Engagement, and Working It Out.* Madison: University of Wisconsin Press.

German, Michael. 2020. "Hidden in Plain Sight: Racism, White Supremacy, and Far-Right Militancy in Law Enforcement." Brennan Center for Justice, August 27, 2020. https://www.brennancenter.org/our-work/research-reports/hidden-plain-sight-racism-white-supremacy-and-far-right-militancy-law.

Gill, Tiffany M. 2010. *Beauty Shop Politics: African American Women's Activism in the Beauty Industry.* Champaign: University of Illinois Press.

Giovanni, Nikki. 1988. *Sacred Cows—and Other Edibles.* New York: William Morrow & Co.

Glass, Barbara, S. 2012. *African American Dance: An Illustrated History.* Jefferson, NC: McFarland & Company, Inc.

Glave, Dianne D. 2010. *Rooted in the Earth: Reclaiming the African American Environmental Heritage.* Chicago, IL: Lawrence Hill Books.

Goldman, Danielle. 2010. *I Want to Be Ready: Improvised Dance as a Practice of Freedom.* Ann Arbor: University of Michigan Press.

Golianopoulos, Thomas. 2017. "The Wonder of Ann Wolfe." *The Ringer,* June 6, 2017. https://www.theringer.com/2017/6/6/16044728/ann-wolfe-wonder-woman-boxing-3f4cf786a9aa.

Goodrich, Matthew Miles. 2017. "Learning from Fannie Lou Hamer." *Dissent,* October 6, 2017. https://www.dissentmagazine.org/online_articles/learning-fannie-lou-hamer-legacy-democratic-party.

Gordon, Tamela J. 2018. "ENOUGH IS ENOUGH, Why I'm giving up on intersectional feminism." *Quartzy,* April 30, 2018, https://qz.com/quartzy/1265902/why-im-giving-up-on-intersectional-feminism.

Gottschild, Brenda Dixon. 2012. *Joan Myers Brown the Audacious Hope of the Black Ballerina: a Biohistory of American Performance.* New York: Palgrave Macmillan.

———. 2011. *Waltzing in the Dark: African American Vaudeville and Race Politics in the Swing Era.* New York: St. Martins Press.

———. 2005. *The Black Dancing Body: A Geography from Coon to Cool.* New York: Palgrave Macmillan.

Greer, Christina M. 2013. *Black Ethnics: Race, Immigration, and the Pursuit of the American Dream.* New York: Oxford University Press.

Grundy, Pamela, and Susan Shackelford. 2017. *Shattering the Glass: The Remarkable History of Women's Basketball.* Chapel Hill: University of North Carolina Press.

Guttmann, Allen. 2002. *The Olympics: A History of the Modern Games.* Champaign: University of Illinois Press.

Hamilton, Tod G. 2019. *Immigration and the Remaking of Black America.* New York: Russell Sage Foundation.

Hancock, Black Hawk. 2013. *American Allegory: Lindy Hop and the Racial Imagination.* Illinois: University of Chicago Press.

Hanson, Joyce A. 2011. *Rosa Parks: A Biography.* Westport, CT: Greenwood Publishing.

Hargreaves, Jennifer. 2001. *Heroines of Sport: The Politics of Difference and Identity.* England, U.K.: Routledge.

Harris, Cecil. 2020. *Different Strokes: Serena, Venus, and the Unfinished Black Tennis Revolution.* Lincoln: University of Nebraska Press.

Harrold, Stanley. 2014. *American Abolitionists.* Oxfordshire, U.K.: Taylor & Francis.

Hazzard-Gordon, Katrina. 1998. "Dancing Under the Lash: Sociocultural Disruption, Continuity, and Synthesis." In *Africa Dance, An Artistic Historical and Philosophical Inquiry* edited by Kariamu Welsh Asante, 101-130. Trenton, NJ: African World Press, Inc.

Heaphy, Leslie A. 2015. *The Negro Leagues, 1869-1960.* Jefferson, NC: McFarland & Company, Inc.

Heard, Marcia E., and Mansa K. Mussa. 2002. "African Dance in New York City." In *Dancing Many Drums: Excavations in African American Dance,* edited by Thomas F. DeFrantz, 143-167. Madison: University of Wisconsin Press.

Height, Dorothy I. 2005. *Open Wide the Freedom Gates: A Memoir.* New York: PublicAffairs.

Heiskanen, Benita. 2012. *The Urban Geography of Boxing: Race, Class, and Gender in the Ring.* Oxfordshire, U.K.: Taylor & Francis.

Herbert, James. 2020. "'Enough is enough': By walking out, Bucks show what it looks like for NBA players to use their platform." *CBS/NBA,* August 27, 2020. https://www.cbssports.com/nba/news/enough-is-enough-by-walking-out-bucks-show-what-it-looks-like-for-nba-players-to-use-their-platform.

Hess, Abigail. 2019. "US women's soccer games now generate more revenue than men's—but the players still earn less." *CNBC-Make It,* July 10, 2019. https://www.cnbc.

com/2019/06/19/uswomens-soccer-games-now-generate-more-revenue-than-mens.html.

Hill, Constance Valis. 2014. *Tap Dancing America A Cultural History.* New York: Oxford University Press.

Hine, Darlene Clark. 1997. *Hine Sight: Black Women and the Re-Construction of American History Blacks in the Diaspora.* Bloomington: Indiana University Press.

———. 1996. *Facts on File Encyclopedia of Black Women in America: Dance, Sports, and Visual Arts.* New York: Facts on File.

Hoffman, Lindsay H. 2015. "Black Woman, White Movement: Why Black Women are Leaving the Feminist Movement." *Huffington Post,* November 12, 2015. https://www.huffpost.com/entry/Black-woman-White-movemen_b_8569540.

Human Rights Campaign, The. 2020. *Fatal Violence Against the Transgender and Gender Non-Conforming Community in 2020.* https://www.hrc.org/resources/violence-against-the-trans-and-gender-non-conforming-community-in-2020

Iachetta, Michael. 1974. "First Black Ballerina Stars With City Ballet," *New York Daily News,* May 30, 1974: 261.

Jacobs, Michelle S. 2017. "The Violent State: Black Women's Invisible Struggle Against Police Violence." *William & Mary Journal of Race, Gender, and Social Justice William & Mary Journal of Race, Gender* 39, no. 24. https://scholarship.law.wm.edu/wmjowl/vol24/iss1/4.

Jamison, Judith, and Howard Kaplan. 1993. *Dancing Spirit: an Autobiography.* New York: Anchor Books.

Jasen, David A., and Gene Jones. 2013. *Black Bottom Stomp: Eight Masters of Ragtime and Early Jazz.* Oxfordshire, U.K.: Taylor & Francis.

Johnson, M. Mikell. 2008. *The African American Woman Golfer: Her Legacy.* Westport, CT: Praeger Publishers.

Jones, Martha S. 2020. *Vanguard: How Black Women Broke Barriers, Won the Vote, and Insisted on Equality for All.* New York: Basic Books, 2020.

Jones, William P. 2013. *The March on Washington: Jobs, Freedom, and the Forgotten History of Civil Rights.* New York: W. W. Norton.

Journal of Blacks in Higher Education, The. 2009. "Blacks Making Solid Progress in Graduate School Enrollments: Women Are in the Lead." 2009. http://www.jbhe.com/news_views/61_gradschoolenrolls.html.

Jules-Rosette, Bennetta, and Njami Simon. 2007. *Josephine Baker in Art and Life: The Icon and the Image.* Champaign: University of Illinois Press.

Keating, Steve. 2018. "Diversity remains golf's biggest challenge, says PGA of America CEO." *Reuters,* August 8, 2018. https://www.reuters.com/article/us-golf-pgachamp-diversity/diversity-remains-golfs-biggest-challenge-says-pga-of-america-ceo-idUSKBN1KT2OE.

Kelly, Deirdre. 2012. *Ballerina: Sex, Scandal, and Suffering Behind the Symbol of Perfection.* Vancouver, Canada: Greystone Books.

Kendi, Ibram X. 2019. "The Day Shithole Entered the Presidential Lexicon." *The Atlantic,* January 13, 2019. https://www.theatlantic.com/politics/archive/2019/01/shithole-countries/580054.

Kennedy, John H. 2005. *A Course of Their Own: A History of African American Golfers.* Lincoln: University of Nebraska Press.

Kennicott, Philip. 2014. "The Great Society at 50: Lyndon B. Johnson's cultural vision mirrored his domestic one." *The Washington Post,* May 20, 2014. https://www.washingtonpost.com/lifestyle/style/50-years-later-assessing-lyndon-b-johnsons-legislative-legacy-and-cultural-vision/2014/05/20/726ee3a2-dd35-11e3-8009-71de85b9c527_story.html.

Kent, Deborah. 2016. *The Seneca Falls Convention: Working to Expand Women's Rights.* New York: Enslow Publishing, LLC.

Kimball, Warren F., and Dave Haggerty. 2017. *The United States Tennis Association: Raising the Game.* Lincoln: University of Nebraska Press.

King, Coretta Scott, and Rev. Dr. Barbara. 2017. *Reynolds. My Life, My Love, My Legacy.* New York: Henry Holt and Company.

Kirsch, George B. 2009. *Golf in America.* Urbana: University of Illinois Press.

Kirsch, George B., Othello Harris, and Claire Elaine Nolte. 2000. *Encyclopedia of Ethnicity and Sports in the United States.* Westport, CT: Greenwood Publishing.

Kisselgoff, Anna. 1978. "Agnes de Mille Offers a Repeat Of 'Conversations About Dance'." *The New York Times,* April 29, 1978. https://www.nytimes.com/1978/04/29/archives/agnes-de-mille-offers-a-repeat-of-conversations-about-dance.html.

———. 1978. "City Ballet Presents the Premiere of Balanchine 'Ballo della Regina'," *The New York Times,* January 14, 1978,. https://www.nytimes.com/1978/01/14/archives/city-ballet-presents-the-premiere-of-balanchine-ballo-della-regina.html.

Kolchin, Peter. 2003. *American Slavery: 1619-1877.* New York: Farrar, Straus and Giroux.

Korstad, Robert R. 2003. *Civil Rights Unionism: Tobacco Workers and the Struggle for Democracy in the Mid-Twentieth-Century South.* Chapel Hill: University of North Carolina Press.

Kovach, John M. 2005. *Women's Baseball.* Mount Pleasant, SC: Arcadia.

Kraut, Anthea. 2003. "Between Primitivism and Diaspora: The Dance Performances of Josephine Baker, Zora Neale Hurston, and Katherine Dunham." *Theatre Journal* 55, no. 3 (2003): 433-50. http://www.jstor.org/stable/25069279.

Lacey, Kyla Jenée. 2017. "White Privilege" @WANPOETRY, *Write About Now,* YouTube Video, 3:38, August 2, 2017, https://www.youtube.com/watch?v=Qkz5UmXugzk.

Lansbury, Jennifer H. 2014. *A Spectacular Leap: Black Women Athletes in Twentieth-Century America.* Fayetsville: University of Arkansas Press.

Larson, Kate Clifford. 2004. *Bound for the Promised Land: Harriet Tubman: Portrait of an American Hero.* New York: One World.

Lee, Chana Kai. 1999. *For Freedoms Sake: The Life of Fannie Lou Hamer.* Champaign: University of Illinois Press.

Lee, Mable. 2017. "Interview with Mable Lee." By Brenda Bufalino, Jerome Robbins Dance Division, The New York Public Library. February 16, 2017, New York Public Library Digital Collections. https://digitalcollections.nypl.org/items/a93a61e7-0549-4a86-955e-0dd056125c9e.

Lee, Mariah. 2021. "Crystal Dunn, one of the world's best soccer players, feels 'like someone has dimmed my light'." *The Undefeated,* July 21, 2021. https://theundefeated.com/features/crystal-dunn-one-of-the-worlds-best-soccer-players-feels-like-someone-has-dimmed-my-light.

Lee, MJ. 2019. "Donald Trump's Accusers: The 'Forgotten Women of the #MeToo Movement." *CNN,* July 19, 2019. https://www.cnn.com/2019/07/19/politics/donald-trump-accusers-me-too-movement/index.html.

Lehman, Christopher P. 2008. *A Critical History of Soul Train on Television.* Jefferson, NC: McFarland & Company, Inc.

Lelinwalla, Mark. 2018. "Amanda Serrano and Heather Hardy are tired of the wage gap between women and men boxers." *Sporting News,* September 7, 2018. https://www.sportingnews.com/us/boxing/news/amanda-serrano-and-heather-hardy-are-tired-of-the-wage-gap-between-women-and-men-boxers/i9y4kap6xjdp16a39wmhdpli7.

Lewin Yaël, and Janet Collins. 2011. *Night's Dancer: The Life of Janet Collins.* Middletown, CT: Wesleyan University Press.

Lindhorst, Marie. 1998. "Politics in a Box: Sarah Mapps Douglass and the Female Literary Association, 1831-1833." *Pennsylvania History: A Journal of Mid-Atlantic Studies,* 65: 263-278.

Loiacano, Darryl K. 1989. "Gay Identity Issues among Black American: Racism, Homophobia, and the Need for Validation." *Journal of Counseling and Development* 68, no. 1 (September-October): 21-25.

Lopez, Jill Painter. 2020. "Here Are The Five NBA Players Whose 2019-2020 Salaries Top LeBron James'." *Sports Illustrated,* April 30, 2020. https://www.si.com/nba/lakers/news/here-are-the-five-nba-players-whose-2019-2020-salaries-top-lebron-james.

Lorenz, Taylor. 2020. "The Original Renegade." *The New York Times,* February 13, 2020. https://www.nytimes.com/2020/02/13/style/the-original-renegade.html.

Lotz, Rainer E. 1997. *Black People: Entertainers of African Descent in Europe and Germany.* Germany: Birgit Lotz.

Mabee, Carleton. 1995. *Sojourner Truth: Slave, Prophet, Legend.* New York: New York University Press.

Macur, Juliet. 2021. "The First Black Woman to Coach in Pro Baseball Thanks Her Mom for the Job." *The New York Times,* March 3, 2021. https://www.nytimes.com/2021/03/03/sports/baseball/bianca-smith-red.html.

Manning, Susan. 2004. *Modern Dance, Negro Dance: Race in Motion.* Minneapolis: University of Minnesota Press.

Markovits, Andrei S., and Steven L. Hellerman. 2014. *Offside: Soccer and American Exceptionalism.* New Jersey: Princeton University Press.

Marshall, Dawn I. 1982. "The History of West Indian Migration." *Caribbean Review* 11 (1982): 6-11.

Matuszewski, Erik. 2016. "The Changing Face of Junior Golf." National Golf Foundation, May 2016. https://www.ngf.org/news/2016/05/the-changing-face-of-junior-golf.

May, Mel Anthony, and Leslie A. Heaphy. 2016. *Encyclopedia of Women and Baseball.* Jefferson, NC: McFarland & Company, Inc.

May, Vivian M. 2012. *Anna Julia Cooper, Visionary Black Feminist: A Critical Introduction.* Oxfordshire, U.K.: Taylor & Francis.

McCann, Bob. 2009. *Encyclopedia of African American Actresses in Film and Television.* Jefferson, NC: McFarland & Company, Inc.

McClain, Dani. 2017. "Can Black Lives Matter Win in the Age of Trump?" The Nation, September 19, 2017. https://www.thenation.com/article/archive/can-black-lives-matter-win-in-the-age-of-trump.

McDonald, Jessica. Twitter, July 28, 2019. https://twitter.com/j_mac1422/status/1155506741133451271?lang=en.

McDuffie, Erik S. 2011. *Sojourning for Freedom: Black Women, American Communism, and the Making of Black Left Feminism.* Durham, NC: Duke University Press.

McKay, Nellie. 2002. *Sister Circle: Black Women and Work.* New Jersey: Rutgers University Press.

McMains, Juliet. 2001. "Brownface: Representations of Latin-Ness in Dancesport." Dance Research Journal 33, no. 2 (2001): 54–71. https://doi.org/10.2307/1477804.

McRae, Elizabeth Gillespie. 2020. *Mothers of Massive Resistance: White Women and the Politics of White Supremacy.* New York: Oxford University Press.

Melton, Marissa. 2017. "Is 'Make America Great Again' Racist?" *Voice of America,* August 31, 2017, https://www.voanews.com/usa/make-america-great-again-racist.

Mijs, Jonathan J.B. 2017. "Inequality is getting worse, but fewer people than ever are aware of it." *The Conversation,* May 2, 2017. https://theconversation.com/inequality-is-getting-worse-but-fewer-people-than-ever-are-aware-of-it-76642.

Miller, Carroll L.L., and Anne S. Pruitt-Logan. 2012. *Faithful to the Task at Hand: The Life of Lucy Diggs Slowe.* Albany: State University of New York Press.

Millman, Cynthia R., and Frankie Manning, 2007. *Frankie Manning: Ambassador of Lindy Hop.* Philadelphia: Temple University Press.

Mills, Glendola Yhema. 1997. "Is It Is or Is It Ain't: The Impact of Selective Perception on the Image Making of Traditional African Dance." *Journal of Black Studies* 28, no. 2 (1997): 139-56. http://www.jstor.org/stable/2784848.

Miranda, Marie Lynn, Sharon E. Edwards, Martha H. Keating, and Christopher J. Paul. 2011. "Making the Environmental Justice Grade: The Relative Burden of Air Pollution Exposure in the United States." *Int J Environ Res Public Health.* 2011 Jun; 8(6): 1755–1771. May 25, 2011, https://www.ncbi.nlm.nih.gov/pmc/articles/PMC3137995.

Moore, Kevin. 2020. "Sheryl Swoopes, the First Woman to Sign a WNBA Contract, Helped Pave the Way for Women in Basketball." *Sportscasting,* August 14, 2020. https://www.sportscasting.com/sheryl-swoopes-the-first-woman-to-sign-a-wnba-contract-helped-pave-the-way-for-women-in-basketball.

Moreno, Paul D. 2008. *Black Americans and Organized Labor, A New History.* Baton Rouge: Louisiana State University Press.

Morris, Gay, ed. 2005. *Moving Words: Re-Writing Dance.* Oxfordshire, U.K.: Taylor & Francis.

Morrison, Toni. 1987. *Beloved: A Novel.* New York: Alfred A. Knopf Inc.

Mosley, Tonya. 2019. "Olympic Fencer Ibtihaj Muhammad Turns Bullying Experiences Into New Children's Book." *WBUR,* September 30, 2019. https://www.wbur.org/hereandnow/2019/09/30/ibtihaj-muhammad-childrens-book-hijab.

Murray, Caitlin. 2017. "A Blueprint for Women's Sports Success. But Can It Be Copied?" *The New York Times,* October 13, 2017, https://www.nytimes.com/2017/10/13/sports/soccer/portlandthorns-nwsl.html.

Neal, Mark Anthony. 2004. *That's the Joint! The Hip-hop Studies Reader.* England, U.K.: Routledge.

New York Times, The. 1883. "Miss Harris' Base-Ball Nine; Dusky Dolly Vardens Of Chester Give An Exhibitions." May 18, 1883. https://www.nytimes.com/1883/05/18/archives/miss-harriss-baseball-nine-dusky-dolly-vardens-of-chester-give-an.html.

Nuchtern, Jean. 1976-1977. "Interview with Mary Hinkson." Jerome Robbins Dance Division, The New York Public Library Digital Collections, 1976-1977. https://digitalcollections.nypl.org/items/a35cd800-b30d-0133-ef3d-3c07547a230f.

O'Farrell, Brigid, and Joyce L. Kornbluh. 1996. *Rocking the Boat: Union Women's Voices, 1915-1975.* New Jersey: Rutgers University Press.

Olson, Lynne. 2002. *Freedom's Daughters: The Unsung Heroines of the Civil Rights Movement from 1830 to 1970.* New York: Scribner.

Oppel, Jr., Richard A., Derrick Bryson Taylor, and Nicholas Bogel-Burroughs. 2020. "What to Know about Breonna Taylor's Death." *The New York Times,* October 30, 2020. https://www.nytimes.com/article/breonna-taylor-police.html.

Ottaway, Amanda. 2016. "Why Don't People Watch Women's Sports? Ask sports journalists." *The Nation,* July 20, 2016. https://www.thenation.com/article/archive/why-dont-people-watch-womens-sports.

Painter, Nell Irvin. 2011. *The History of White People.* New York: W. W. Norton & Company.

———. 2007. *Sojourner Truth: A Life, A Symbol.* New York: W. W. Norton & Company.

Parker, Adam. 2021. "The NBA could be in her future, but for now Dawn Staley has fights to wage at home." *The Post and Courier,* July 17, 2021. https://www.postandcourier.com/news/local_state_news/the-nba-could-be-in-her-future-but-for-now-dawn-staley-has-fights-to/article_2a76d080-e027-11eb-a786-e3075637be07.html.

Parker, Alison. 2012. "Frances Watkins Harper and the Search for Women's Interracial Alliances." In *Susan B. Anthony and the Struggle for Equal Rights,* 145-171. New York: University of Rochester.

Parks, Rosa, and James Haskins. 1992. *Rosa Parks: My Story.* New York: Dial Books.

Patterson, Brandon. 2017. "How the Black Lives Matter Movement Is Mobilizing Against Trump." *Mother Jones,* February 7, 2017. https://www.motherjones.com/politics/2017/02/black-lives-matter-versus-trump.

Peisner, David. 2018. *Homey Don't Play That! The Story of In Living Color and the Black Comedy Revolution.* New York: Simon & Schuster.

Perpener III, John O. 2005. *African American Concert Dance: the Harlem Renaissance and Beyond.* Champaign: University of Illinois Press.

Picart, Caroline Joan. 2012. *From Ballroom to DanceSport: Aesthetics, Athletics, and Body Culture.* Albany: State University of New York Press.

Pitney, John. 1995. "The Tocqueville Fraud." *The Weekly Standard,* November 12, 1995. https://www.weeklystandard.com/john-j-pitney/the-tocqueville-fraud.

Porter, David L. 2005. *Basketball: A Biographical Dictionary.* Westport, CT: Greenwood Publishing.

Porter, Karra. 2006. *Mad Seasons: The Story of The First Women's Professional Basketball League, 1978-1981.* Lincoln: University of Nebraska Press.

Prison Policy Initiative. 2019. *Policing Women: Race and gender disparities in police stops, searches, and use of force.* May 14, 2019. https://www.prisonpolicy.org/blog/2019/05/14/policingwomen.

Quigley, Joan. 2016. *Just Another Southern Town: Mary Church Terrell and the Struggle for Racial Justice in the Nation's Capital.* New York: Oxford University Press.

Ransby, Barbara. 2005. *Ella Baker and the Black Freedom Movement: A Radical Democratic Vision.* Chapel Hill: University of North Carolina Press.

Reck, Gregory G., and Bruce Allen Dick. 2015. *American Soccer: History, Culture, Class.* Jefferson, NC: McFarland & Company, Inc.

Reid, Ira De Augustine. 1939. *The Negro Immigrant: His Background, Characteristics, and Social Adjustment, 1899-1937.* New York: Columbia University.

Renshaw, Patrick. 1999. *The Wobblies: The Story of the IWW and Syndicalism in The United States.* Chicago, IL: Ivan R. Dee.

Rhoden, William C. 2012. "Black and White Women Far From Equal Under Title IX." *The New York Times,* June 10, 2012. https://www.nytimes.com/2012/06/11/sports/title-ix-has-not-given-Black-female-athletes-equal-opportunity.html.

Richards, Yevette. 2000. *Maida Springer: Pan-Africanist and International Labor Leader.* Pennsylvania: University of Pittsburgh Press.

Rickford, Russell John. 2003. *Betty Shabazz: A Remarkable Story of Survival and Faith Before and After Malcolm X.* Naperville, IL: EBSCO Publishing.

Riley, Jason L. 2017. "Why Obama's Presidency Didn't Lead to Black Progress." *New York Post,* June 17, 2017. https://nypost.com/2017/06/17/why-obamas-presidency-didnt-lead-to-black-progress.

Ring, Jennifer. 2015. *A Game of Their Own: Voices of Contemporary Women in Baseball.* Lincoln: University of Nebraska Press.

———. 2009. *Stolen Bases: Why American Girls Don't Play Baseball.* Champaign: University of Illinois Press.

Roberts, Dorothy E. 1999. *Killing the Black Body: Race, Reproduction, and the Meaning of Liberty.* New York: Vintage Books.

Roberts, Rebecca Boggs. 2017. *Suffragists in Washington, D.C.: The 1913 Parade and the Fight for the Vote.* Mt. Pleasant, SC: The History Press.

Roberts, Steven. 2018. "Most Black kids can't swim, and segregation is to blame." *Vice,* August 30, 2018. https://www.vice.com/en_us/article/8xbyax/most-Black-kids-cant-swim-its-not-just-a-stereotype-its-history.

Robertson, Ashley N. 2015. *Mary Mcleod Bethune in Florida: Bringing Social Justice to the Sunshine State.* Mt. Pleasant, SC: History Press, 2015.

Robinson, Jo Ann, and David J. Garrow. 1987. *Montgomery Bus Boycott and the Women Who Started It: The Memoir of Jo Ann Gibson Robinson.* Knoxville: University of Tennessee Press.

Robnett, Belinda. 1997. *How Long? How Long?: African American Women in the Struggle for Civil Rights.* New York: Oxford University Press.

Rodulfo, Kristina. 2016. "How Fencer Ibtihaj Muhammad Is Changing the Face of Team U.S.A." *Elle,* June 1, 2016. https://www.elle.com/culture/news/a36735/ibtihaj-muhammad-2016-olympics.

Rogers, Katie. 2016. "White Women Helped Elect Donald Trump." *The New York Times,* November 9, 2016. https://www.nytimes.com/2016/12/01/us/politics/white-women-helped-elect-donald-trump.html.

Roos, Meghan. "Meet the Elite: Our Q&A with Allyson Felix." *Outside,* July 24, 2018. https://www.womensrunning.com/culture/people/meet-the-elite-allyson-felix.

Rosenberg, Rosalind. 2017. *Jane Crow: The Life of Pauli Murray.* New York: Oxford University Press.

Ross, Janell. 2015. "White Americans long for the 1950s, when they didn't face so much discrimination." *The Washington Post,* November 17, 2015. https://www.washingtonpost.com/news/the-fix/wp/2015/11/17/White-americans-long-for-the-1950s-when-they-werent-such-victims-of-reverse-discrimination.

Ross, Marc Howard. 2018. *Slavery in the North: Forgetting History and Recovering Memory.* Philadelphia: University of Pennsylvania Press.

Rothenberg, Ben. 2015. "Tennis' Top Women Balance Body Image With Ambition." *The New York Times,* July 10, 2015. https://www.nytimes.com/2015/07/11/sports/tennis/tenniss-top-women-balance-body image-with-quest-for-success.html.

Rushton, Susie. 2020. "Caster Semenya, The exceptional South African runner." *The Gentlewoman,* Spring & Summer 2020. http://thegentlewoman.co.uk/library/caster-semenya.

Russonello, Giovanni. 2018. "Read Oprah Winfrey's Golden Globes Speech." *The New York Times,* January 7, 2018. https://www.nytimes.com/2018/01/07/movies/oprah-winfrey-golden-globes-speech-transcript.html.

Rutledge, Rachel. 1998. *The Best of the Best in Basketball.* Minneapolis, MN: Millbrook Press.

Sacchetti, Maria, Abigail Hauslohner, and Danielle Paquette. 2020. "Trump expands long-standing immigration ban to include six more countries, most in Africa." *The Washington Post,* January 31, 2020. https://www.washingtonpost.com/immigration/trump-expands-long-standing-immigration-ban-to-include-six-more-countries-most-from-africa/2020/01/31/413e93ec-443e-11ea-aa6a-083d01b3ed18_story.html.

Santos, Alex Abad. 2016. "Russian hackers tried to embarrass Simone Biles. They completely failed." *Vox,* September 15, 2016. https://www.vox.com/2016/9/15/12915106/simone-biles-hack-adhd.

Schiot, Molly. 2016. *Game Changers: The Unsung Heroines of Sports History.* New York: Simon & Schuster.

Schoenfeld, Bruce. 2004. *The Match: Althea Gibson & Angela Buxton: How Two Outsiders—One Black, the Other Jewish—Forged a Friendship and Made Sports History.* New York: HarperCollins.

Schwartz, Peggy, and Murray Schwartz. 2011. *The Dance Claimed Me: a Biography of Pearl Primus.* New Haven, CT: Yale University Press.

Seibert, Brian. 2015. *What the Eye Hears: A History of Tap Dancing.* New York: Farrar, Straus and Giroux.

Shattuck, Debra A. 2017. *Bloomer Girls: Women Baseball Pioneers.* Champaign: University of Illinois Press.

Sheffield, Charles, ed. 1895. *The History of Florence, Massachusetts, Including a Complete Account of the Northampton Association of Education and Industry.* Florence, MA, 1895.

Siber, Kate. 2018. "How Wilma Rudolph Became the World's Fastest Woman." *Outside,* June 8, 2018. https://www.outsideonline.com/health/running/wilma-rudolph-worlds-fastest-woman.

Smith, Earl and Marissa Kiss. 2021. "Why are there so few Black American players in MLB 74 years after Jackie Robinson took the field?" *The Philadelphia Inquirer,* April 1, 2021. https://www.inquirer.com/opinion/commentary/baseball-black-african-american-players-jackie-robinson-20210401.html.

Smith, Jessie Carney, and Lean'tin L. Bracks, eds. 2014. *Black Women of the Harlem Renaissance Era.* New York: Rowman & Littlefield Publishers.

Smith, Jessie Carney, ed. 2013. *Handy African American History Answer Book.* Canton, MI: Visible Ink Press.

Smith, Jessie Carney, and Shirelle Phelps, eds. 1992c. Notable Black American Women: Book III. Farmington Hills, MI: Gale Research.

Smith, Malissa. 2014. *A History of Women's Boxing.* New York: Rowman & Littlefield Publishers.

Snipe, Tracy D. 1998. "African Dance: Bridges to Humanity." In *Africa Dance, An Artistic Historical and Philosophical Inquiry* edited by Kariamu Welsh Asante, 63-77. Trenton, NJ: African World Press, Inc.

Sonmez, Felicia and Ashley Parker. 2019. "As Trump stands by Charlottesville remarks, the rise of white-nationalist violence becomes an issue in 2020 presidential race." *The Washington Post,* April 28, 2019. https://www.washingtonpost.com/politics/as-trump-stands-by-charlottesville-remarks-rise-of-white-nationalist-violence-becomes-an-issue-in-2020-presidential-race/2019/04/28/83aaf1ca-69c0-11e9-a66d-a82d3f3d96d5_story.html.

Spelman College: *News and Events.* 2018. "US Senator Kamala Harris Speaks at Spelman: Remaining Undaunted by the Fight." August 26, 2018, https://www.spelman.edu/about-us/news-and-events/kamala-harris.

Spiro, Jonathan Peter. 2008. *Defending the Master Race: Conservation, Eugenics, and the Legacy of Madison Grant.* Lebanon: University of New Hampshire.

Stancliff, Michael. 2010. *Frances Ellen Watkins Harper: African American Reform Rhetoric and the Rise of a Modern Nation State.* Oxfordshire, U.K.: Taylor & Francis.

Standley, Anne. 1993. "The Role of Black Women in the Civil Rights Movement." In *Women in the Civil Rights Movement: Trailblazers and Torchbearers, 1941-1965,* edited by Vicki L. Crawford, Jacqueline Anne Rouse and Barbara Woods. Bloomington: Indiana University Press.

Starks, Glenn L. and F. Erik Brooks. 2011. *Historically Black Colleges and Universities: An Encyclopedia.* New York: ABC-CLIO.

Sterling, Dorothy, ed. 1997. *We Are Your Sisters: Black Women in The Nineteenth Century.* New York: W. W. Norton & Company.

Stevens, Erin, and Tamara Stevens. 2011. *Swing Dancing.* Westport, CT: Greenwood Publishing.

Stowe, Harriet Beecher. 1863. "Sojourner Truth, The Libyan Sibyl," *The Atlantic,* April 1863, https://www.theatlantic.com/magazine/archive/1863/04/sojourner-truth-the-libyan-sibyl/308775.

Stuckey, Sterling. 2013. *Slave Culture: Nationalist Theory and the Foundations of Black America.* New York: Oxford University Press.

Tate, Shirley Ann. 2015. *Black Women's Bodies and The Nation, Race, Gender and Culture.* New York: Palgrave Macmillan.

Taylor, Keeanga-Yamahtta. 2017. *How We Get Free: Black Feminism and the Combahee River Collective.* Chicago, IL: Haymarket Books.

Terborg-Penn, Rosalyn. 1998. *African American Women in the Struggle for the Vote, 1850–1920.* Bloomington: Indiana University Press.

Terry, Terlene Darcell. 1982. *A Survey of Black Dance In Washington, 1870-1945.* The American University, M.A.

Theoharis, Jeanne. 2018. *A More Beautiful and Terrible History, The Uses and Misuses of Civil Rights History.* Boston: Beacon Press.

Thompson, Cheryl. 2008. "Black Women and Identity: What's Hair Got to Do With It?" *Politics and Performativity* 22, no. 1, (Fall).

Tinsley, Omise'eke Natasha. 2018. *Ezili's Mirrors: Imagining Black Queer Genders.* Durham, NC: Duke University Press.

Tower, Nikole. 2018. "In an ethnic breakdown of sports, NBA takes lead for most diverse," *Global Sports Matter,* December 12, 2018. https://globalsportmatters.com/culture/2018/12/12/in-an-ethnic-breakdown-of-sports-nba-takes-lead-for-most-diverse.

Trenka, Susie. 2021. *Jumping the Color Line: Vernacular Jazz Dance in American Film, 1929-1945.* Eastleigh, UK: John Libbey Publishing.

Tucker, Rosina Corrothers, and C. Bernard Ruffin. 2011. *My Life as I Have Lived It: the Autobiography of Rosina Corrothers-Tucker (1881-1987).* Westminster, MD: Heritage Books.

Undefeated, The. N.d. "Beating Opponents, Battling Belittlement: How African American Female Athletes Use Community to Navigate Negative Images." N.d., Morgan State University, School of Global Journalism and Communications. https://theundefeated.com/features/morgan-state-university-study-examines-history-of-Black-women-fighting-to-be-respected-as-athletes.

University of Pennsylvania. 2020. *New Deal Resident Camps for Unemployed Women, A New Deal Program, c. 1933 1937,* a research initiative of PennPraxis, 2020, https://storymaps.arcgis.com/stories/02050ee5b4d543cf93821f56382367c2.

Urban Suite Jazz. N.d. "StaceyAnn Chin Performs 'Tweet This, You Small-Minded M**********r." Video, *Up Magazine* (Nairobi) https://www.urbansuitejazz.com/return-to-categories/13-poets-corner-see-all/1401-up-magazine-staceyann-chin-performs-tweet-this-you-small-minded-m-r-in-nairobi.

Vertinsky, Patricia, and Roberta J. Park, eds. 2013. *Women, Sport, Society: Further Reflections, Reaffirming Mary Wollstonecraft.* Oxfordshire, U.K.: Taylor & Francis.

Vohra, Sweta. 2017. "Documents show US monitoring of Black Lives Matter." *Al Jazeera,* November 28, 2017. https://www.aljazeera.com/news/2017/11/28/documents-show-us-monitoring-of-black-lives-matter.

Walker, Alice. 2004. *In Search of Our Mothers' Gardens: Womanist Prose.* New York: Harcourt Brace Jovanovich.

Walker, Rhiannon. 2018. "The day Jackie Joyner-Kersee was called 'the greatest athlete who ever lived'." *The Undefeated,* August 1, 2018. https://theundefeated.com/features/the-day-jackie-joyner-kersee-was-called-the-greatest-athlete-who-ever-lived.

———. 2016. "Her Airness, Sheryl Swoopes, attains Hall of Fame status." *The Undefeated,* September 9, 2016. https://theundefeated.com/features/her-airness-sheryl-swoopes-attains-hall-of-fame-status.

Walker-McWilliams, Marcia. 2016. *Reverend Addie Wyatt: Faith and the Fight for Labor, Gender, and Racial Equality.* Champaign: University of Illinois Press.

Wang, Vivian. 2017. "Erica Garner, Activist and Daughter of Eric Garner, Dies at 27." *The New York Times,* December 30, 2017. https://www.nytimes.com/2017/12/30/nyregion/erica-garner-dead.html.

Walters, Joanna. 2005. "Meet the real million dollar baby." *Observer Sport Monthly,* July 2, 2005. https://www.theguardian.com/observer/osm/story/0,,1517179,00.html.

Weisbord, Robert G. 2017. *Racism and the Olympics.* Oxfordshire, U.K.: Taylor & Francis.

Wells, Christopher J. 2019. "'You Can't Dance to It': Jazz Music and Its Choreographies of Listening." *"Why Jazz Still Matters" Daedalus* 148, no. 2 (Spring): 36-51. https://www.jstor.org/stable/10.2307/48563007.

Wetsman, Nicole. 2020. "NWSL fans are online, organized, and refuse to be ignored." *The Verge,* July 17, 2020. https://www.theverge.com/21325419/nwsl-womens-soccer-fandom-twitter-uswnt.

Wilen, Holden. 2020. "Kevin Plank dares to dabble in politics again following Biden election victory." *Baltimore Business Journal,* November 9, 2020. https://www.bizjournals.com/baltimore/news/2020/11/09/kevin-plank-under-armour-biden.html.

Williams, Jean. 2007. *A Beautiful Game: International Perspectives on Women's Football.* Oxford, England: Berg Publishers.

Williams, Mikyla. 2021. "UNC women's soccer looks to end streak of NCAA title game defeats." *The Daily Tar Heel,* April 20, 2021. https://www.dailytarheel.com/article/2021/04/unc-womens-soccer-look-ahead-ncaa-tournament-national-championship-hopes-brianna-pinto.

Willis, Cheryl M. 2016. *Tappin' at the Apollo: The African American Female Tap Dance Duo Salt and Pepper.* Jefferson, NC: McFarland & Company, Inc.

Wiltse, Jeff. 2009. *Contested Waters: A Social History of Swimming Pools in America.* Chapel Hill: University of North Carolina Press.

Wintz, Cary D., and Paul Finkelman. 2012. *Encyclopedia of the Harlem Renaissance.* Oxfordshire, U.K.: Taylor & Francis.

Witherspoon, Kevin B., and Toby C. Rider, eds. 2018. *Defending the American Way of Life, Sport, Culture, and the Cold War.* Fayetteville: University of Arkansas Press.

W. L. Stacy. 2009. " A Brief History of Pops Billingsley—Trainer of Ann Wolfe." *Bleacher Report,* January 9, 2009. https://bleacherreport.com/articles/109035-a-brief-history-of-pops-billingsley-trainer-of-ann-wolfe.

Yang, Stephanie. 2019. "We all have a responsibility to kick racism out of NWSL," *SBNation,* September 9, 2019, https://www.allforxi.com/2019/9/9/20855809/kick-racism-out-nwsl-royals-franch-thorns.

Yee, Shirley J. 1992. *Black Women Abolitionists: A Study in Activism, 1828-1860.* Knoxville: University of Tennessee Press.

Zieger, Robert H. 2000. *The CIO, 1935-1955.* Chapel Hill: University of North Carolina Press.❖

BIBLIOGRAPHY

Aaseng, Nathan. *African-American Athletes (A to Z of African Americans)*. New York: Facts on File, 2003.

Abrams, Jasmine. "Blurring the Lines of Traditional Gender Roles: Beliefs of African American Women." Master's thesis, Virginia Commonwealth University, 2012.

Abdul-Jabbar, Kareem. "Body Shaming Black Female Athletes Is Not Just About Race." *Time*, July 20, 2015. https://time.com/3964758/body shaming-Black-female-athletes.

Acharya, Amitav, and See Seng Tan. *Bandung Revisited: The Legacy of the 1955 Asian-African Conference for International Order*. Honolulu: University of Hawaii Press, 2008.

Ackmann, Martha. *Curveball: The Remarkable Story of Toni Stone, The First Woman to Play Professional Baseball in the Negro League*. Illinois: Chicago Review Press, 2017.

Acocella, Joan Ross. "Van Grona and his First American Negro Ballet." *Dance* (March 1982): 22–24, 30–32.

African American Policy Forum, The (AAPF). "#SayHerName Campaign." N.d. https://aapf.org/sayhername.

Afrika, Nyar. "White Feminism's concept of "unity" is a joke. Shoot me." *AFROPUNK*, January 12, 2018. https://afropunk.com/2018/01/White-feminisms-concept-unity-joke-shoot.

Aguirre, Abby. "Simone Biles on Overcoming Abuse, the Postponed Olympics, and Training During a Pandemic." *Vogue*, July 9, 2020. https://www.vogue.com/article/simone-biles-cover-august-2020.

Akinleye, Adesola. *(Re:) Claiming Ballet*. Bristol, U.K.: Intellect Books Limited, 2021.

Alexander, Michelle "America, This, is Your Chance." *The New York Times*, June 8, 2020, https://www.nytimes.com/2020/06/08/opinion/george-floyd-protests-race.html.

Alexander, Michelle. *The New Jim Crow, Mass Incarceration in the Age of Colorblindness*. New York: New Press, 2010.

Ailey, Alvin. *Revelations: The Autobiography of Alvin Ailey*. New York: Birch Lane Press, 1995.

Anderson, Monica and Gustavo López. "Key facts about black immigrants in the U.S." Pew Research Center, January 24, 2018. https://www.pewresearch.org/fact-tank/2018/01/24/key-facts-about-black-immigrants-in-the-u-s.

Angyal, Chloe. *Turning Pointe: How A New Generation of Dancers Is Saving Ballet from Itself.* New York: PublicAffairs, 2021.

Arthur, John A. *African Women Immigrants in the United States: Crossing Transnational Borders.* New York: Palgrave Macmillan, 2009.

Asmelash, Leah. "WNBA dedicates season to Breonna Taylor and Say Her Name campaign." *CNN,* July 25, 2020. https://www.cnn.com/2020/07/25/us/wnba-season-start-breonna-taylor-cnn/index.html.

Associated Press. "Ferguson attorney: Michael Brown's family settles with city for $1.5 million.," *The Los Angeles Times,* June 23, 2017. https://www.latimes.com/nation/nationnow/la-namichael-brown-ferguson-settlement-20170623-story.html.

———. "Whites to lose majority status by 2043, the census projects." *Politico,* December 12, 2012. https://www.politico.com/story/2012/12/census-whites-no-longer-a-majority-in-us-by-2043-084971.

Atencio, Matthew, and Jan Wright. "Ballet it's too whitey: discursive hierarchies of high school dance spaces and the constitution of embodied feminine subjectivities." *Gender and Education* 21, no. 1 (2009): 31-46.

Bagley, Edythe Scott, and Joseph H. Hilley. *Desert Rose: The Life and Legacy of Coretta Scott King.* Tuscaloosa: University of Alabama Press, 2012.

Baker, Christine A. *Why She Plays: The World of Women's Basketball.* Lincoln, NE: Bison Books, 2008.

Banister, Lindsey. "Sporting Bodies: The Rhetorics of Professional Female Athletes." PhD diss. Syracuse University, 2017. https://surface.syr.edu/etd/742.

Bandele, Ramla. "Understanding Airican Diaspora Political Activism: The Rise and Fall of the Black Star Line." *Journal of Black Studies* 40, no. 4 (2010): 745-61.

Banes, Sally. *Writing Dance in the Age of Postmodernism.* Middletown, CT: Wesleyan University, 1994.

Barnes, Clive. "Barnes on . . . the Position of the Black Classic Dancer in American Ballet." *Ballet News* 3, no. 9 (March 1982): 46.

———. "The Ballet: 'Bartok. No. 3'." *The New York Times,* May 25, 1974. https://www.nytimes.com/1974/05/25/archives/the-ballet-bartok-no-3.html.

Barnett, Bernie McNair. "Invisible Southern Black Women Leaders in the Civil Rights Movement: The Triple Constraints of Gender, Race, and Class." *Gender and Society* 7, no. 2 (June 1993): 162-182.

Bates, Daisy. *The Long Shadow of Little Rock: A Memoir.* Fayetteville: University of Arkansas Press, 2007.

Baumann, Jason. *The Stonewall Reader.* New York: Penguin Books, 2019.

Bayard, Marc. "Partnership between the Labor Movement and Black Workers: The Opportunities, Challenges, and Next Steps." *Black Worker Initiative at the Institute for Policy Studies.* January 15, 2016. https://ips-dc.org/wp-content/uploads/2015/04/MarcReport.pdf.

BBC News Online, "Breonna Taylor: What Happened on the Night of Her Death?" October 8, 2020. https://www.bbc.com/news/world-us-canada-54210448.

Bier, Lisa. Fighting the Current: The Rise of American Women's Swimming, 1870-1926. Jefferson, NC: McFarland & Company, Inc., 2011.

Bell, Janet Dewart. *Lighting the Fires of Freedom: African American Women in the Civil Rights Movement.* New York: The New Press, 2018.

Bell, Ramona J. "Competing Identities: Representations of the Black Female Sporting Body From 1960 to the Present." PhD diss. Bowling Green State University, 2008.

Belmont Report, The, Office of the Secretary. *Ethical Principles and Guidelines for the Protection of Human Subjects of Research,* by The National Commission for the Protection of Human Subjects of Biomedical and Behavioral Research, April 18, 1979. https://www.hhs.gov/ohrp/regulations-and-policy/belmont-report/read-the-belmont-report/index.html.

Bennett, Michael. *Recovering the Black Female Body: Self-Representation by African American Women.* New Jersey: Rutgers University Press, 2000.

Benzing, Rachel. "Heels and Gumption: Tap Dance Empowered by Women" (2012). *Dance Department Student Works.* 2012. http://digitalcommons.lmu.edu/dance_students/6.

Berman, Ari. *Give Us the Ballot: The Modern Struggle for Voting Rights in America.* New York: Farrar, Straus and Giroux, 2015.

Berri, David. "Basketball's Growing Gender Wage Gap: The Evidence The WNBA Is Underpaying Players." *Forbes,* September 20, 2017. https://www.forbes.com/sites/davidberri/2017/09/20/there-is-a-growing-gender-wage-gap-in-professional-basketball/#29afe39536e0.

Berry, Mary Frances, and John Blassingame. *Long Memory: The Black Experience in America.* New York: Oxford University Press, 1982.

Bier, Lisa. *Fighting the Current: The Rise of American Women's Swimming, 1870-1926.* Jefferson, NC: McFarland & Company, Inc., 2011.

Billingsley, Andrew. *Climbing Jacob's Ladder: The Enduring Legacies of African-American Families.* New York: Touchstone Books, 1993.

Blain, Keisha, and Tiffany Gill, eds. *To Turn the Whole World Over: Black Women and Internationalism.* Champaign: University of Illinois Press, 2019.

Blyden, Nemata, and Jeannette Eileen Jones. "Between Africa and America, Recalibrating Black Americans' Relationship to the Diaspora." *Perspectives on History,* August 20, 2020. https://www.historians.org/publications-and-directories/perspectives-on-history/september-2020/between-africa-and-america-recalibrating-black-americans-relationship-to-the-diaspora.

Bolling, Hans. "The Beginning of The IAAF, A Study of its Background and Foundation," Stockholm, Sweden, 2007. https://media.aws.iaaf.org/competitioninfo/9ae4cea1-f84c-44ec-852f-74bb974d0f5a.pdf

Bondy, Stefan. "20 years ago Sandhi Ortiz-Del Valle sued the NBA charging she was blocked from becoming a referee because she's a woman; the jury agreed, though today it still hurts." *The Daily News,* September 16, 2018. https://www.nydailynews.com/sports/basketball/ny-sports-endzone-sandhi-nba-ref-20180914-story.html#skip-to-content.

Borge, Jason. "Chapter 7: The portable jazz age, Josephine Baker's tour of South American cities (1929)."In *Urban Latin America : Images, Words, Flows and the Built Environment,* edited by Bianca Freire-Medeiros, and Julia O'Donnell. England, U.K.: Routledge, 2018.

Bouie, Jamelle. "Will America Make Trump Great Again?" *The New York Times,* June 22, 2019, https://www.nytimes.com/2019/06/22/opinion/trump-2020-win.html.

Braddock, Jomills Henry. *Women in Sports: Breaking Barriers, Facing Obstacles.* Santa Barbara, CA: ABC-CLIO, 2017.

Branch, Taylor. *Pillar of Fire: American in the King Years: 1963-1965.* New York: Simon & Schuster, 1999.

Brantley, Ben. "The Story of Tap as the Story of Blacks." *The New York Times,* November 16, 1995. https://www.nytimes.com/1995/11/16/theater/theater-review-story-of-tap-as-the-story-of-Blacks.

Braukman, Stacy Lorraine, and Susan Ware. *Notable American Women: A Biographical Dictionary Completing the Twentieth Century.* Cambridge, MA: Belknap Press, 2004.

Breines, Winifred. "Struggling To Connect: White and Black Feminism in The Movement Years." *Contexts* 6, no. 1 (2007): 18-24.

———. *The Trouble Between Us: An Uneasy History of White and Black Women in the Feminist Movement.* New York: Oxford University Press, 2007.

Brick, Michael. "The Lady Was a Champ, In the Corner with Boxer James Kirkland, A Woman Hangs Tough." *SBNation,* August 19, 2014. https://www.sbnation.com/long-form/2014/8/19/6031751/james-kirkland-ann-wolfe-profile-boxing-trainer.

Brinkley, Douglas. *Rosa Parks, A Life.* New York: Penguin Books, 2005.

Brown, Abram. "TikTok's 7 Highest-Earning Stars: New Forbes List Led By Teen Queens Addison Rae And Charli D'Amelio." *Forbes,* August 6, 2020. https://www.forbes.com/sites/abrambrown/2020/08/06/tiktoks-highest-earning-stars-teen-queens-addi-son-rae-and-charli-damelio-rule/?sh=67a2f60c5087.

Brown, Jayna. *Babylon Girls, Black Women Performers and the Shaping of the Modern.* Durham, NC: Duke University Press, 2008.

Brown, Nadia E. "It's More than Hair…And You Do Care: The Politics of Appearance for Black Women State Legislators." *Politics, Groups, and Identities* 2, no. 3 (2014): 295-312.

Brown, Pei-San. "The History of Modern Dance." Ballet Austin, 2013.

Bucalo, Angela. "Who is the Highest Paid WNBA Player?" *ONE37PM,* September 9, 2020. https://www.one37pm.com/strength/sports/highest-paid-wnba-player.

Buckner, Candace. "For exceptional Black women like Simone Biles, greatness is never enough." *The Washington Post,* July 27, 2021. https://www.washingtonpost.com/sports/olympics/2021/07/27/simone-biles-out-greatness.

Buckner, Jocelyn L. "'Spectacular Opacities': The Hyers Sisters' Performances of Respectability and Resistance." *African American Review* 45, no. 3 (2012): 309-23. http://www.jstor.org/stable/23783542.

Bucknor, Cherrie. "Black Workers, Unions, and Inequality." *The Center for Economic and Policy Research (CEPR),* August 2016. https://cepr.net/report/black-workers-unions-and-inequality.

Byrd, Ayana, and Lori Tharps. *Hair Story: Untangling the Roots of Black Hair in America.* New York: St. Martin's Griffin, 2014.

Cahn, Susan K. *Coming on Strong: Gender and Sexuality in Women's Sport.* Champaign: University of Illinois Press, 2015.

Calbay, Cielestia. 2012. "Portrait Of A Lady: Allyson Felix." *Outside,* June 19, 2012. https://www.podiumrunner.com/culture/portrait-of-a-lady-allyson-felix.

Callis, Tracy. *Boxing in the Los Angeles Area, 1880-2005.* Bloomington, IN: Trafford Publishing, 2009.

Caravantes, Peggy. *The Many Faces of Josephine Baker: Dancer, Singer, Activist,* Spy. Illinois: Chicago Review Press, 2015.

Carrega, Christina, and Sabina Ghebremedhin. "Timeline: Inside the Investigation of Breonna Taylor's Killing and its Aftermath." *ABC News,* November 17, 2020, https://abcnews.go.com/US/timeline-inside-investigation-breonna-taylors-killing-aftermath/story?id=71217247.

Chase, Chris, and Jean-Claude Baker. *Josephine: The Hungry Heart.* Lanham, MD: Cooper Square Press, 2001.

Chateauvert, Melinda. *Marching Together: Women of the Brotherhood of Sleeping Car Porters.* Champaign: University of Illinois Press, 1998.

Chicago Defender. "Woman to Play First Base for the Havana Stars." May 12, 1917: 5.

Clark, Lara P., Dylan B. Millet, and Julian D. Marshall. "National Patterns in Environmental Injustice and Inequality: Outdoor NO2 Air Pollution in the United States." *PLOS ONE* 9(4): e94431, April 15, 2014, https://doi.org/10.1371/journal.pone.0094431.

Clark, Septima Poinsette. *Ready from Within: Septima Clark and the Civil Rights Movement, A First Person Narrative.* Lawrenceville, NJ: Africa World Press, 1990.

Clark, VèVè A., Johnson, Sarah East, and Katherine Dunham. *Kaiso! Writings by and about Katherine Dunham.* Madison: University of Wisconsin Press, 2005.

Clements, Julie. "Participatory Democracy: The Bridge from Civil Rights to Women's Liberation." *The Public Purpose* 1, no. 1 (Spring 2003): 5-24.

Cohen, Marilyn. *No Girls in the Clubhouse: The Exclusion of Women from Baseball.* Jefferson, NC: McFarland & Company, Inc., 2009.

Cole, Johnnetta B., and Beverly Guy-Sheftall. *Gender Talk: The Struggle For Women's Equality in African American Communities.* London: One World, 2003.

Collier-Thomas, Bettye, and V.P. Franklin, eds. *Sisters in the Struggle : African-American Women in the Civil Rights-Black Power Movement.* New York: New York University Press, 2001.

Connors, Joseph. "Berenson and Katherine Dunham: Black American Dance." In *Bernard Berenson: Formation and Heritage,* edited by Joseph Connors and Louis A. Waldman, 363-391. Florence and Cambridge MA: Villa I Tatti with Harvard University Press, 2014.

Conyers, Liana D. "Shedding Skin In Art-Making: Choreographing Identity of The Black Female Self Through Explorations of Cultural Autobiographies." Master's thesis, University of Oregon, 2012.

Cooke, Mervyn, and David Horn, eds. *The Cambridge Companion to Jazz.* United Kingdom: Cambridge University Press, 2003.

Copeland, Joy M. *Clara Day, A Teamster's Life, A Biography.* International Brotherhood of Teamsters, 2015.

Copeland, Misty. *Life in Motion: An Unlikely Ballerina.* New York: Aladdin, 2018.

Crawford Vicki L., Jacqueline Anne Rouse, and Barbara Woods, eds. *Women in the Civil Rights Movement: Trailblazers and Torchbearers, 1941-1965.* Bloomington: Indiana University Press, 1993.

Crease, Robert P. "Jazz and Dance." In *The Cambridge Companion to Jazz,* edited by Mervyn Cooke and David Horn, 69-80. United Kingdom: Cambridge University Press, 2002.

Crenshaw, Kimberlé. "Demarginalizing the Intersection of Race and Sex: A Black Feminist Critique of Antidiscrimination Doctrine, Feminist Theory and Antiracist Politics." In *University of Chicago Legal Forum* no. 1, 1989, Article 8.

Dabiri, Emma. *Don't Touch My Hair.* New York: Penguin Books, 2020.

Das, Joanna Dee. *Katherine Dunham: Dance and the African Diaspora.* New York: Oxford University Press, 2017.

———. *Katherine Dunham (1909-2006).* Dance Heritage Coalition, 2012.

Davies, Carole Boyce. *Left of Karl Marx: The Political Life of Black Communist Claudia Jones.* Durham, NC: Duke University Press, 2008.

Davis, Angela Yvonne. 1988. *Angela Davis—an Autobiography.* New York: International Publishers.

Davis, Michael D. *Black American Women in Olympic Track and Field: A Complete Illustrated Reference.* Jefferson, NC: McFarland & Company, Inc., 1992.

Davis, Timothy. "Race and Sports in America: An Historical Overview." *Virginia Sports & Entertainment Law Journal,* 2008, Wake Forest Univ. Legal Studies Paper No. 1141868, https://ssrn.com/abstract=1141868.

———."Racism in Athletics: Subtle Yet Persistent," *Little Rock Law Review* 21, 881 (1999). https://lawrepository.ualr.edu/lawreview/vol21/iss4/10.

DeFrantz, Thomas F. "The Black Beat Made Visible: Hip Hop Dance and Body Power." In *Of The Presence of the Body, Essays on Dance and Performance Theory,* edited by André Lepecki, 64-81. Middletown, CT: Wesleyan University Press, 2004.

———. *Dancing Many Drums: Excavations in African American Dance.* Madison: University of Wisconsin Press, 2002.

de la Cretaz, Britni. "To White Feminists Who Don't Want to Discuss Racism: Here Are 7 Things You Need to Know." *Everyday Feminism,* October 12, 2015. https://everyday-feminism.com/2015/10/White-feminists-dont-talk-race.

Denisoff, R. Serge. *Inside MTV.* Oxfordshire, U.K.: Taylor & Francis, 2017.

Denison, Erik and Alistair Kitchen. *Out on the Fields, The first international study on homophobia in sport. Nielsen,* Bingham Cup Sydney 2014, Australian Sports Commission, Federation of Gay Games. www.outonthefields.com.

Dennis, Anita K., and Benjamin G. Dennis. *Slaves to Racism: An Unbroken Chain from America to Liberia.* New York: Algora Publishing, 2008.

Department of Labor. Commissioner General of Immigration, 1821-1928.

Department of Labor. U.S. Bureau of Labor Statistics. "Union Members, 2020." January 22, 2021. https://www.bls.gov/news.release/pdf/union2.pdf.

DePrince, Michaela, and Elaine DePrince. *Taking Flight: from War Orphan to Star Ballerina.* New York: Penguin Random House (Ember), 2016.

DeSilver, Drew. "A record number of women, will be serving in the new Congress." *FACTANK,* Pew Research Center, December 18, 2018, https://pewrsr.ch/2Lp3XMa.

Desmond, Jane. *Meaning in Motion: New Cultural Studies of Dance.* Durham, NC: Duke University Press, 1997.

Dicaire, David. *Jazz Musicians of the Early Years, to 1945.* Jefferson, NC: McFarland & Company, Inc., 2010.

Dils, Ann, and Ann Cooper Albright. *Moving History/Dancing Cultures: A Dance History Reader.* Middletown, CT: Wesleyan University Press, 2001.

Diouf Esailama, Kariamu Welsh, and Yvonne Daniel, eds. *Hot Feet and Social Change: African Dance and Diaspora Communities.* Champaign: University of Illinois Press, 2019.

Dixon, David E., and Davis W. Houck. *Women and the Civil Rights Movement, 1954-1965.* Jackson: University Press of Mississippi, 2009.

Dixon, Melanye White. *Marion Cuyjet and Her Judimar School of Dance: Training Ballerinas in Black Philadelphia 1948-1971.* New York: Edwin Mellon Press, 2011.

Dixon-Stowell, Brenda. "Between Two Eras: 'Norton and Margot' in the Afro-American Entertainment World." *Dance Research Journal* 15, no. 2 (1983): 11-20.

———. "Blondell Cummings: 'The Ladies and Me'." *The Drama Review: TDR* 24, no. 4 (1980): 37-44. doi:10.2307/1145322.

Djata, Sundiata. *Blacks at the Net: Black Achievement in the History of Tennis, Volume Two.* New York: Syracuse University Press, 2008.

Doak, Robin S. *The March on Washington: Uniting Against Racism.* Minneapolis, MN: Compass Point Books, 2007.

Drozdek-Małolepsza, Teresa. "Women's World Games (1922–1934)" *Prace Naukowe Akademii* im. Jana Długosza w Częstochowie Kultura Fizyczna 2014, t. XIII, nr 1.

DuBois, Ellen Carol. *Feminism and Suffrage: The Emergence of an Independent Women's Movement in America, 1848 1869.* Ithaca, NY: Cornell University Press, 1978.

Dudden, Faye E. *Fighting Chance: The Struggle Over Woman Suffrage and Black Suffrage In Reconstruction America.* New York: Oxford University Press, 2014.

Durkin, Hannah. *Josephine Baker and Katherine Dunham: Dances in Literature and Cinema.* Champaign: University of Illinois Press, 2019.

Dvorak, Petula. "Is it cultural appropriation when a Black woman does Irish dance?" *The Washington Post,* August 3, 2020. https://www.washingtonpost.com/local/is-it-cultural-appropriation-when-a-black-woman-does-irish-dance/2020/08/03/974b16f6-d517-11ea-930e-d88518c57dcc_story.html.

Dwight, Margaret L., and George A. Sewell. *Mississippi Black History Makers.* Jackson: University Press of Mississippi, 1984.

Edelson, Paula. *A to Z of American Women in Sports.* New York: Facts On File, 2014.

Eichenwald, Kurt. "The Family Feud Over Martin Luther King Jr.'s Legacy." *Newsweek,* April 3, 2014. https://www.newsweek.com/2014/04/11/family-feud-over-martin-luther-king-jrs-legacy-248083.html.

el-Khoury, Laura J. "Being while Black: Resistance and the Management of the Self." *Social Identities* 18, no. 1(2012): 85. https://www.tandfonline.com/doi/abs/10.1080/13504630.2012.629516.

Elliott, Helene. "How Jackie Joyner-Kersee conquered the Olympics and earned GOAT status." *The Los Angeles Times,* March 9, 2020. https://www.latimes.com/sports/story/2020-03-09/jackie-joyner-kersee-track-field-olympics.

Elsas, Louis J., Arne Ljungqvist, and Malcolm A. Ferguson-Smith, et al. "Gender verification of female athletes." *Genetics In Medicine* 2, (2000): 249–254.

Emery, Lynne Fauley. *Black Dance: From 1619 to Today.* New Jersey: Princeton Book Company, 1989.

Emmanuel, Karen D. "The Struggles Within A Society Where Black Women Suffer The Struggles Within a Society Where Black Women Suffer Racism, Sexism, and Violence." Master's thesis, City University of New York, City College, 2014. https://academicworks.cuny.edu/cc_etds_theses/224.

Erikainen, Sonja. *Gender Verification and the Making of the Female Body in Sport: A History of the Present.* Oxfordshire, U.K.: Taylor & Francis, 2019.

Essed, Philomena. *Everyday Racism: Reports from Women of Two Cultures.* Thousand Oaks, CA: SAGE Publishing, 1991.

Everett, Donald E. "Free Persons of Color in Colonial Louisiana," *Louisiana History: The Journal of the Louisiana Historical Association* 7, no. 1 (1966): 21-50, http://www.jstor.org/stable/4230881.

Evers Williams, Myrlie, and Melinda Blau. *Watch Me Fly: What I Learned on the Way to Becoming the Woman I Was Meant to Be.* Boston, MA: Little Brown & Co., 1999.

Ewoodzie, Joseph C. *Break Beats in the Bronx: Rediscovering Hip-Hop's Early Years.* Chapel Hill: University of North Carolina Press, 2017.

Faderman, Lillian. *The Gay Revolution, The Story of the Struggle.* New York: Simon & Schuster, 2016.

Farmer, Ashley D. *Remaking Black Power: How Black Women Transformed an Era.* Chapel Hill: University of North Carolina Press, 2017.

Farrington, Lisa E. *Creating Their Own Image: The History of African American Women.* New York: Oxford University Press, 2011.

Feinberg, Doug. "WNBA crossroads: league looks to cut losses, hire president." *Associated Press,* December 28, 2018. https://apnews.com/75e117e82df7470c94784438048171d1.

Felder, Deborah G. *The American Women's Almanac: 500 Years of Making History.* Canton, MI: Visible Ink Press, 2020.

Felix, Allyson. "My Own Nike Pregnancy Story." *The New York Times,* May 22, 2019. https://www.nytimes.com/2019/05/22/opinion/allyson-felix-pregnancy-nike.html.

Fidler, Merrie A. 2015. *The Origins and History of the All-American Girls Professional Baseball League.* Jefferson, NC: McFarland & Company, Inc.

Fields, Armond. *Tony Pastor, Father of Vaudeville.* Jefferson, NC: McFarland & Company, Inc., 2007.

Finkel, Rebecca. "Broadcasting from a neutral corner? An analysis of the mainstream media's representation of women's boxing in the 2012 London Olympic Games." In *Sports Events, Society and Culture,* edited by Katherine Dashper, Nicola Mccullough, and Thomas Fletcher. Oxfordshire, U.K.: Taylor & Francis, 2014.

Finney, Carolyn. *Black Faces, White Spaces: Reimagining the Relationship of African Americans to the Great Outdoors.* Chapel Hill: University of North Carolina Press, 2014.

FitzPatrick, Hayde Adams, and Carol Guensburg, "Two Decades After Diallo Killing, Mother Finds Hope in New Protests." *Voice of America,* June 25, 2020. https://www.voanews.com/usa/race-america/two-decades-after-diallo-killing-mother-finds-hope-new-protests.

Flynn, Anne, and Lisa Doolittle, eds. *Dancing Bodies, Living Histories: New Writings about Dance and Culture.* Alberta, Canada: Banff Centre Press, 2000.

Fobbs, Joyelle. "Black Ballerinas in U.S. Popular Culture." *The Arts: 3rd Place* (The Ohio State University Edward F. Hayes Graduate Research Forum) 2013.

Ford, Bonnie D., and Alyssa Roenigk. "The Gymnastics Factory The Rise and Fall of the Karolyi Ranch." *ESPN,* July 14, 2020. https://www.espn.com/espn/feature/story/_/id/29235446/the-karolyi-ranch-where-us-women-gymnastics-gold-was-forged-price.

Ford, Tanisha C. *Liberated Threads: Black Women, Style, and the Global Politics of Soul.* Chapel Hill: University of North Carolina Press, 2015.

Foulkes, Julia L. *Modern Bodies: Dance and American Modernism from Martha Graham to Alvin Ailey.* Chapel Hill: University of North Carolina Press, 2002.

Fradin, Dennis Brindell, and Judith Bloom Fradin. *Fight On!: Mary Church Terrell's Battle for Integration.* New York: Clarion Books, 2003.

Franklin, John Hope, and Evelyn Higginbotham. *From Slavery to Freedom: A History of African Americans.* New York: McGraw-Hill, 2010.

Franklin, Vincent P. *Sisters in the Struggle: African American Women in the Civil Rights-Black Power Movement.* New York: New York University Press, 2001.

Freeman, Scott. "Atlanta Ballet called out on social media for not having black female dancers." *ArtsATL,* June 24, 2020. https://www.artsatl.org/atlanta-ballet-called-out-on-social-media-for-not-having-black-female-dancers.

Friedler, Sharon E., and Susan B. Glazer. *Dancing Female.* Oxfordshire, U.K.: Taylor & Francis, 2014.

Fung, Jenny Sky. "B-Girl Like a B-Boy: Marginalization of Women in Hip-Hop Dance." Master's thesis, University of Hawaii-Manoa, 2014. http://hdl.handle.net/10125/101072.

Gaines, Kevin K. *American Africans in Ghana: Black Expatriates and the Civil Rights Era.* Chapel Hill: University of North Carolina Press, 2008.

Garcia, Sandra E. "The Woman Who Created #MeToo Long Before Hashtags." *The New York Times,* October 20, 2017. https://www.nytimes.com/2017/10/20/us/me-too-movement-tarana-burke.html.

Gardner, Bettye J., and Niani Kilkenny. "In Vogue: Josephine Baker and Black Culture and Identity in the Jazz Age." *The Journal of African American History* 93, no. 1 (2008): 88-93. http://www.jstor.org/stable/20064259.

George-Graves, Nadine. *Urban Bush Women: Twenty Years of African American Dance Theater, Community Engagement, and Working It Out.* Madison: University of Wisconsin Press, 2010.

German, Michael. "Hidden in Plain Sight: Racism, White Supremacy, and Far-Right Militancy in Law Enforcement." Brennan Center for Justice, August 27, 2020. https://www.brennancenter.org/our-work/research-reports/hidden-plain-sight-racism-white-supremacy-and-far-right-militancy-law.

Giovanni, Nikki. *Sacred Cows—and Other Edibles.* New York: William Morrow & Co, 1988.

Gill, Tiffany M. *Beauty Shop Politics: African American Women's Activism in the Beauty Industry.* Champaign: University of Illinois Press, 2010.

Gittens, Angela Fatou. "Black Dance and the Fight for Flight: Sabar and the Transformation and Cultural Significance of Dance from West Africa to Black America (1960-2010)." *Journal of Black Studies* 43, no. 1 (2012): 49-71. http://www.jstor.org/stable/23215195.

Glass, Barbara S. *African American Dance: An Illustrated History.* Jefferson, NC: McFarland & Company, Inc., 2012.

Glave, Dianne D. *Rooted in the Earth: Reclaiming the African American Environmental Heritage.* Chicago, IL: Lawrence Hill Books, 2010.

Glocke, Aimee. "Preserving Katherine Dunham's Legacy: A New Call to Action." *The Journal of Pan African Studies* 6, no. 4 (September 2013): 111-119.

Goldman, Danielle. *I Want to Be Ready: Improvised Dance as a Practice of Freedom.* Ann Arbor: University of Michigan Press, 2010.

Golianopoulos, Thomas. "The Wonder of Ann Wolfe." *The Ringer,* June 6, 2017. https://www.theringer.com/2017/6/6/16044728/ann-wolfe-wonder-woman-boxing-3f4cf786a9aa.

Goodrich, Matthew Miles. "Learning from Fannie Lou Hamer." *Dissent,* October 6, 2017. https://www.dissentmagazine.org/online_articles/learning-fannie-lou-hamer-legacy-democratic-party.

Gordon, Tamela J. "ENOUGH IS ENOUGH, Why I'm giving up on intersectional feminism." *Quartzy,* April 30, 2018, https://qz.com/quartzy/1265902/why-im-giving-up-on-intersectional-feminism.

Gottschild, Brenda Dixon. *Joan Myers Brown the Audacious Hope of the Black Ballerina: a Biohistory of American Performance.* New York: Palgrave Macmillan, 2012.

———. *Waltzing in the Dark: African American Vaudeville and Race Politics in the Swing Era.* New York: St. Martins Press, 2011.

———. *The Black Dancing Body: A Geography from Coon to Cool.* New York: Palgrave Macmillan, 2005.

Greer, Christina M. *Black Ethnics: Race, Immigration, and the Pursuit of the American Dream.* New York: Oxford University Press, 2013.

Grundy, Pamela, and Susan Shackelford. *Shattering the Glass: The Remarkable History of Women's Basketball.* Chapel Hill: University of North Carolina Press, 2017.

Guttmann, Allen. *The Olympics: A History of the Modern Games.* Champaign: University of Illinois Press, 2002.

———. *Women's Sports: A History.* New York: Columbia University Press, 1991.

Hall, Jacquelyn Dowd. "The Long Civil Rights Movement and the Political Uses of the Past." *The Journal of American History* 91, no. 4 (March 2005): 1233-1263.

Hamilton, Tod G. *Immigration and the Remaking of Black America.* New York: Russell Sage Foundation, 2019.

Hamilton, Tod G., Janeria A. Easley, and Angela R. Dixon. "Black Immigration, Occupational Niches, Earnings Disparities Between U.S.-Born and Foreign-Born Blacks in the United States." *RSF: The Russell Sage Foundation Journal of the Social Sciences* 4, no. 1 (2018): 60-77.

Hancock, Black Hawk. *American Allegory: Lindy Hop and the Racial Imagination.* Illinois: University of Chicago Press, 2013.

Hanson, Joyce A. *Rosa Parks: A Biography.* Westport, CT: Greenwood Publishing, 2011.

Hargreaves, Jennifer. *Heroines of Sport: The Politics of Difference and Identity.* England, U.K.: Routledge, 2001.

Harris, Cecil. *Different Strokes: Serena, Venus, and the Unfinished Black Tennis Revolution.* Lincoln: University of Nebraska, 2020.

Harrold, Stanley. *American Abolitionists.* Oxfordshire, U.K.: Taylor & Francis, 2014.

Hazzard-Gordon, Katrina. "Dancing Under the Lash: Sociocultural Disruption, Continuity, and Synthesis." In *Africa Dance, An Artistic Historical and Philosophical Inquiry* edited by Kariamu Welsh Asante, 101-130. Trenton, NJ: African World Press, Inc., 1998.

Heaphy, Leslie A. *The Negro Leagues, 1869-1960.* Jefferson, NC: McFarland & Company, Inc., 2015.

Heard, Marcia E., and Mansa K. Mussa. "African Dance in New York City." In *Dancing Many Drums: Excavations in African American Dance,* edited by Thomas F. DeFrantz, 143-167. Madison: University of Wisconsin Press, 2002.

Height, Dorothy I. *Open Wide the Freedom Gates: A Memoir.* New York: PublicAffairs, 2005.

Heinonen, Nelli, Norah Zuñiga Shaw, and Judith Mitoma. *Envisioning Dance on Film and Video.* England, U.K.: Routledge, 2002.

Heiskanen, Benita. *The Urban Geography of Boxing: Race, Class, and Gender in the Ring.* Oxfordshire, U.K.: Taylor & Francis, 2012.

Herbert, James. "'Enough is enough': By walking out, Bucks show what it looks like for NBA players to use their platform." *CBS/NBA,* August 27, 2020. https://www.cbssports. com/nba/news/enough-is-enough-by-walking-out-bucks-show-what-it-looks-like-for-nba-players-to-use-their-platform.

Hering, Doris. "Ballet Americana." *Dance* (August 1958): 57.

Hess, Abigail. "US women's soccer games now generate more revenue than men's—but the players still earn less." *CNBC-Make It,* July 10, 2019. https://www.cnbc. com/2019/06/19/uswomens-soccer-games-now-generate-more-revenue-than-mens.html.

Hill, Constance Valis. *Tap Dancing America A Cultural History.* New York: Oxford University Press 2014.

———. "Tap Dance in America: A Short History." Library of Congress, 2002.

———. "What's New in Tap . . . or Should I Ask?" *International Tap Association Journal* 3, no. 1 (Spring/Summer 1991): 2-8.

Hine, Darlene Clark, and Kathleen Thompson. *A Shining Thread of Hope.* Portland, Oregon: Broadway Books, 1998.

Hine, Darlene Clark. *Hine Sight: Black Women and the Re-Construction of American History Blacks in the Diaspora.* Bloomington: Indiana University Press, 1997.

———. *Facts on File Encyclopedia of Black Women in America: Dance, Sports, and Visual Arts.* New York: Facts on File, 1996.

Hitchins, Aubrey. "Creating the Negro Dance Theatre." *Dance and Dancers* (April 1956): 12-13.

Hoffman, Lindsay H. "Black Woman, White Movement: Why Black Women are Leaving the Feminist Movement." *Huffington Post,* November 12, 2015. https://www.huffpost. com/entry/Black-woman-White-movemen_b_8569540.

Holsaert, Faith S., Martha Prescod, and Norman Noonan, et. al. *Hands on the Freedom Plow: Personal Accounts by Women in SNCC.* Champaign: University of Illinois Press, 2012.

hooks, bell. *Ain't I a Woman: Black Women and Feminism.* England, U.K.: Routledge, 2015.

Human Rights Campaign, The. *Fatal Violence Against the Transgender and Gender Non-Conforming Community in 2020.* https://www.hrc.org/resources/violence-against-the-trans-and-gender-non-conforming-community-in-2020.

Iachetta, Michael. "First Black Ballerina Stars With City Ballet," *New York Daily News,* May 30, 1974: 261.

Jackson, Harriet. "American Dancer, Negro." *Dance* (September 1966): 35-42.

Jacobs, Michelle S. "The Violent State: Black Women's Invisible Struggle Against Police Violence." *William & Mary Journal of Race, Gender, and Social Justice* 24, no. 39, 2017. https://scholarship.law.wm.edu/wmjowl/vol24/iss1/4.

Jamison, Judith, and Howard Kaplan. *Dancing Spirit: an Autobiography.* New York: Anchor Books, 1994.

Jasen, David A., and Gene Jones. *Black Bottom Stomp: Eight Masters of Ragtime and Early Jazz.* Oxfordshire, U.K.: Taylor & Francis, 2013.

Johnson, M. Mikell. *The African American Woman Golfer: Her Legacy.* Westport, CT: Praeger Publishers, 2008.

Jones, Martha S. *Vanguard: How Black Women Broke Barriers, Won the Vote, and Insisted on Equality for All.* New York: Basic Books, 2020.

Jones, William P. *The March on Washington: Jobs, Freedom, and the Forgotten History of Civil Rights.* New York: W. W. Norton, 2013.

Journal of Blacks in Higher Education, The. "Blacks Making Solid Progress in Graduate School Enrollments: Women Are in the Lead." 2009, http://www.jbhe.com/news_views/61_gradschoolenrolls.html.

Jules-Rosette, Bennetta, and Njami Simon. *Josephine Baker in Art and Life: The Icon and the Image.* Champaign: University of Illinois Press, 2007.

Kealiinohomoku, Joann W. "An Anthropologist Looks at Ballet as a Form of Ethnic Dance." In *Moving History/Dancing Cultures: A Dance History Reader,* edited by Ann Dils and Ann Cooper Albright, 33-43. Middleton, CT: Wesleyan University Press, 2001.

Keating, Steve. "Diversity remains golf's biggest challenge, says PGA of America CEO." *Reuters,* August 8, 2018. https://www.reuters.com/article/us-golf-pgachamp-diversity/diversity-remains-golfs-biggest-challenge-says-pga-of-america-ceo-idUSKBN1KT2OE.

Kelly, Deirdre. *Ballerina: Sex, Scandal, and Suffering Behind the Symbol of Perfection.* Vancouver, Canada: Greystone Books, 2012.

Kendi, Ibram X. "The Day Shithole Entered the Presidential Lexicon." *The Atlantic,* January 13, 2019. https://www.theatlantic.com/politics/archive/2019/01/shithole-countries/580054.

Kennedy, John H. *A Course of Their Own: A History of African American Golfers.* Lincoln: University of Nebraska Press, 2005.

Kennicott, Philip. "The Great Society at 50: Lyndon B. Johnson's cultural vision mirrored his domestic one." *The Washington Post,* May 20, 2014. https://www.washingtonpost.com/lifestyle/style/50-years-later-assessing-lyndon-b-johnsons-legislative-legacy-and-cultural-vision/2014/05/20/726ee3a2-dd35-11e3-8009-71de85b9c527_story.html.

Kent, Deborah. *The Seneca Falls Convention: Working to Expand Women's Rights.* New York: Enslow Publishing, LLC, 2016.

Kimball, Warren F., and Dave Haggerty. *The United States Tennis Association: Raising the Game.* Lincoln: University of Nebraska Press, 2017.

King, Coretta Scott, and Rev. Dr. Barbara. Reynolds. *My Life, My Love, My Legacy.* New York: Henry Holt and Company, 2017.

Kirsch, George B. *Golf in America.* Urbana: University of Illinois Press, 2009.

Kirsch, George B., Othello Harris, and Claire Elaine Nolte. *Encyclopedia of Ethnicity and Sports in the United States.* Westport, CT: Greenwood Publishing, 2000.

Kisselgoff, Anna. "Limning the Role of the Black Dancer in America." *The New York Times,* May 16, 1982, https://www.nytimes.com/1982/05/16/arts/dance-view-limning-the-role-of-the-Black-dancer-in-america.html.

———. "City Ballet Presents the Premiere of Balanchine 'Ballo della Regina'," *The New York Times,* January 14, 1978, https://www.nytimes.com/1978/01/14/archives/city-ballet-presents-the-premiere-of-balanchine-ballo-della-regina.html.

———. "Agnes de Mille Offers a Repeat Of 'Conversations About Dance." The New York Times, April 29, 1978. https://www.nytimes.com/1978/04/29/archives/agnes-de-mille-offers-a-repeat-of-conversations-about-dance.html.

Kolchin, Peter. *American Slavery: 1619-1877.* New York: Farrar, Straus and Giroux, 2003.

Korstad, Robert R. *Civil Rights Unionism: Tobacco Workers and the Struggle for Democracy in the Mid-Twentieth-Century South.* Chapel Hill: University of North Carolina Press, 2003.

Kovach, John M. *Women's Baseball.* Mount Pleasant, SC: Arcadia, 2005.

Kraut, Anthea. "Between Primitivism and Diaspora: The Dance Performances of Josephine Baker, Zora Neale Hurston, and Katherine Dunham." *Theatre Journal* 55, no. 3 (2003): 433-50. http://www.jstor.org/stable/25069279.

Lacey, Kyla Jenée "White Privilege" @WANPOETRY, *Write About Now,* YouTube Video, 3:38, August 2, 2017, https://www.youtube.com/watch?v=Qkz5UmXugzk.

Lansbury, Jennifer H. *A Spectacular Leap: Black Women Athletes in Twentieth-Century America.* Fayetteville: University of Arkansas Press, 2014.

Larson, Kate Clifford. *Bound for the Promised Land: Harriet Tubman: Portrait of an American Hero.* New York: One World, 2004.

Lee, Chana Kai. *For Freedoms Sake: The Life of Fannie Lou Hamer.* Champaign: University of Illinois Press, 1999.

Lee, Mable, "Interview with Mable Lee," by Brenda Bufalino. Jerome Robbins Dance Division, The New York Public Library, February 16, 2017, New York Public Library Digital Collections. https://digitalcollections.nypl.org/items/a93a61e7-0549-4a86-955e-0dd056125c9e.

Lee, Mariah. "Crystal Dunn, one of the world's best soccer players, feels 'like someone has dimmed my light'." *The Undefeated,* July 21, 2021. https://theundefeated.com/features/crystal-dunn-one-of-the-worlds-best-soccer-players-feels-like-someone-has-dimmed-my-light.

Lee, MJ. "Donald Trump's Accusers: The 'Forgotten Women" of the #MeToo Movement." *CNN,* July 19, 2019, https://www.cnn.com/2019/07/19/politics/donald-trump-accusers-me-too-movement/index.html.

Lehman, Christopher P. *A Critical History of Soul Train on Television.* Jefferson, NC: McFarland & Company, Inc., 2008.

Lelinwalla, Mark. "Amanda Serrano and Heather Hardy are tired of the wage gap between women and men boxers." *Sporting News,* September 7, 2018. https://www.sportingnews.com/us/boxing/news/amanda-serrano-and-heather-hardy-are-tired-of-the-wage-gap-between-women-and-men-boxers/i9y4kap6xjdp16a39wmhdpli7.

Lewin Yaël, and Janet Collins. *Night's Dancer: The Life of Janet Collins.* Middletown, CT: Wesleyan University Press, 2011.

Lewis, Ladel. "The Portrayal of African American Women in Hip-Hop Videos." Master's theses, Western Michigan University-Kalamazoo. 2005. https://scholarworks.wmich.edu/masters_theses/4192.

Lindhorst, Marie. "Politics in a Box: Sarah Mapps Douglass and the Female Literary Association, 1831-1833." *Pennsylvania History: A Journal of Mid-Atlantic Studies,* 65 (1998), 9-39 (263-278): 267.

Loiacano, Darryl K. "Gay Identity Issues among Black American: Racism, Homophobia, and the Need for Validation." *Journal of Counseling and Development* 68, no. 1 (September-October 1989): 21-25.

Long, Richard A. *The Black Tradition in American Dance.* New York: Smithmark Publishers, 1995.

Lopez, Jill Painter. 2020. "Here Are The Five NBA Players Whose 2019-2020 Salaries Top LeBron James'." *Sports Illustrated,* April 30, 2020. https://www.si.com/nba/lakers/news/here-are-the-five-nba-players-whose-2019-2020-salaries-top-lebron-james.

Lorenz, Taylor. "The Original Renegade." *The New York Times,* February 13, 2020. https://www.nytimes.com/2020/02/13/style/the-original-renegade.html.

Lott, Eric. *Love and Theft: Blackface Minstrelsy and the American Working Class.* New York: Oxford University Press, 2013.

Lott, Martha. "The Relationship Between the 'Invisibility' of African American Women in the American Civil Rights Movement of the 1950s and 1960s and Their Portrayal in Modern Film." *Journal of Black Studies* 48, no. 4 (2017): 331–354.

Lotz, Rainer E. *Black People: Entertainers of African Descent in Europe and Germany.* Germany: Birgit Lotz, 1997.

Mabee, Carleton. *Sojourner Truth: Slave, Prophet, Legend.* New York: New York University Press, 1995.

Macur, Juliet. "The First Black Woman to Coach in Pro Baseball Thanks Her Mom for the Job." *The New York Times,* March 3, 2021. https://www.nytimes.com/2021/03/03/sports/baseball/bianca-smith-red.html.

Manning, Susan. *Modern Dance, Negro Dance: Race in Motion.* Minneapolis: University of Minnesota Press, 2004.

Markovits, Andrei S., and Steven L. Hellerman, *Offside: Soccer and American Exceptionalism.* New Jersey: Princeton University Press, 2014.

Marshall, Dawn I. "The History of West Indian Migration." *Caribbean Review* 11: (1982): 6-11.

Martin, John. "The Dance: Newcomer, Janet Collins in a Brief But Auspicious Debut." *The New York Times,* February 27, 1949, https://www.nytimes.com/1949/02/27/archives/the-dance-newcomer-janet-collins-in-a-brief-but-auspicious-debut.html.

———. "De Mille Ballet Seen as Novelty." *The New York Times,* January 23, 1940, https://www.nytimes.com/1940/01/23/archives/de-mille-ballet-seen-as-novelty-Black-ritual-has-premiere-at-the.html.

———. "The Dance: A Negro Art Group." *The New York Times,* February 14, 1932, https://www.nytimes.com/1932/02/14/archives/the-dance-a-negro-art-group-advantages-and-dangers-in-the-way-of-an.html.

Matuszewski, Erik. "The Changing Face of Junior Golf." National Golf Foundation, May 2016. https://www.ngf.org/news/2016/05/the-changing-face-of-junior-golf.

May, Mel Anthony, and Leslie A. Heaphy. *Encyclopedia of Women and Baseball.* Jefferson, NC: McFarland & Company, Inc., 2016.

May, Vivian M. *Anna Julia Cooper, Visionary Black Feminist: A Critical Introduction.* Oxfordshire, U.K.: Taylor & Francis, 2012.

McArdle, Danielle H. "Women's Professional Sports: A Case Study on Practices that Could Increase Their Profitability." Honors undergraduate theses, University of Central Florida, 2016. https://stars.library.ucf.edu/honorstheses/151.

McCann, Bob. *Encyclopedia of African American Actresses in Film and Television.* Jefferson, NC: McFarland & Company, Inc., 2009.

McClain, Dani. "Can Black Lives Matter Win in the Age of Trump?" *The Nation,* September 19, 2017. https://www.thenation.com/article/archive/can-black-lives-matter-win-in-the-age-of-trump.

McDonagh, Don. "Negroes in Ballet." *New Republic* 159 (1968): 41–44.

McDonald, Jessica. Twitter, July 28, 2019. https://twitter.com/j_mac1422/status/11555 06741133451271?lang=en.

McDuffie, Erik S. *Sojourning for Freedom: Black Women, American Communism, and the Making of Black Left Feminism.* Durham, NC: Duke University Press, 2011.

McGuire, Danielle L. *At the Dark End of the Street: Black Women, Rape, and Resistance—a New History of the Civil Rights Movement From Rosa Parks to the Rise of Black Power.* New York: Vintage, 2011.

McKay, Nellie. *Sister Circle: Black Women and Work.* New Jersey: Rutgers University Press, 2002.

McMains, Juliet. "Brownface: Representations of Latin-Ness in Dancesport." *Dance Research Journal* 33, no. 2 (2001): 54–71. https://doi.org/10.2307/1477804.

McRae, Elizabeth Gillespie. *Mothers of Massive Resistance: White Women and the Politics of White Supremacy.* New York: Oxford University Press, 2020.

McSpadden, Lezley, and Lyah Beth LeFlore. *Tell the Truth & Shame the Devil: The Life, Legacy, and Love of My Son Michael Brown.* New York: Regan Arts, 2016.

Melton, Marissa. "Is 'Make America Great Again' Racist?" *Voice of America,* August 31, 2017, https://www.voanews.com/usa/make-america-great-again-racist.

Mijs, Jonathan J.B. "Inequality is getting worse, but fewer people than ever are aware of it." *The Conversation,* May 2, 2017, https://theconversation.com/inequality-is-getting-worse-but-fewer-people-than-ever-are-aware-of-it-76642.

Milkman, Ruth, and Veronica Terriquez. "'We Are the Ones Who Are Out in Front': Women's Leadership in the Immigrant Rights Movement." *Feminist Studies* 38, no. 3 (2012): 723-52. http://www.jstor.org/stable/23720205.

Miller, Carroll L.L., and Anne S. Pruitt-Logan, *Faithful to the Task at Hand: The Life of Lucy Diggs Slowe.* Albany: State University of New York Press, 2012.

Miller, Margaret, "American Tap Dance History and Proposed Preservation." Honors College Theses. 186. Pace University, 2018. https://digitalcommons.pace.edu/honorscollege_theses/186.

Millman, Cynthia R., and Frankie Manning, *Frankie Manning: Ambassador of Lindy Hop.* Philadelphia: Temple University Press, 2007.

Mills, Glendola Yhema. "Is It Is or Is It Ain't: The Impact of Selective Perception on the Image Making of Traditional African Dance." *Journal of Black Studies* 28, no. 2 (1997): 139-56. http://www.jstor.org/stable/2784848.

Miranda, Marie Lynn. Sharon E. Edwards, and Martha H. Keating, et. al. 2011. "Making the Environmental Justice Grade: The Relative Burden of Air Pollution Exposure in the United States." *Int J Environ Res Public Health.* 2011 Jun; 8(6): 1755–1771. https://www.ncbi.nlm.nih.gov/pmc/articles/PMC3137995.

Moore, Alex. "Cross-Cultural Perspectives on the Creation of American Dance 1619-1950." Master's thesis, Hofstra University, 2010.

Moore, Kevin. "Sheryl Swoopes, the First Woman to Sign a WNBA Contract, Helped Pave the Way for Women in Basketball." *Sportscasting,* August 14, 2020. https://www.sportscasting.com/sheryl-swoopes-the-first-woman-to-sign-a-wnba-contract-helped-pave-the-way-for-women-in-basketball.

Moreno, Paul D. *Black Americans and Organized Labor, A New History.* Baton Rouge: Louisiana State University Press, 2008.

Morris, Gay, ed. *Moving Words: Re-Writing Dance.* Oxfordshire, U.K.: Taylor & Francis, 2005.

Morrison, Toni. *Beloved: A Novel.* New York: Alfred A. Knopf Inc., 1987.

Mosley, Tonya. "Olympic Fencer Ibtihaj Muhammad Turns Bullying Experiences Into New Children's Book." *WBUR,* September 30, 2019. https://www.wbur.org/hereand-now/2019/09/30/ibtihaj-muhammad-childrens-book-hijab.

Murray, Caitlin. "A Blueprint for Women's Sports Success. But Can It Be Copied?" *The New York Times,* October 13, 2017, https://www.nytimes.com/2017/10/13/sports/soc-cer/portlandthorns-nwsl.html.

Murray, Pauli. *Song in a Weary Throat: Memoir of an American Pilgrimage.* New York: Liveright, 2018.

———. *Pauli Murray: The Autobiography of a Black Activist, Feminist, Lawyer, Priest, and Poet.* Knoxville: University of Tennessee Press, 1989.

Nalett, Jacqueline. "History of Jazz Dance." In *Jump Into Jazz,* by Minda Goodman Kraines and Esther Pryor. New York: McGraw Hill-Education, 2004.

Nash, Jennifer C. *Black Feminism Reimagined: After Intersectionality.* Durham, NC: Duke University Press, 2019.

Neal, Mark Anthony. *That's the Joint! The Hip-hop Studies Reader.* England, U.K.: Routledge, 2004.

Negroes in Ballet. Dance and Dancers (October 1957): 9.

New York Times, The. "Miss Harris' Base-Ball Nine; Dusky Dolly Vardens Of Chester Give An Exhibitions." May 18, 1883. https://www.nytimes.com/1883/05/18/archives/miss-harriss-baseball-nine-dusky-dolly-vardens-of-chester-give-an.html.

Nuchtern, Jean. "Interview with Mary Hinkson." Jerome Robbins Dance Division, The New York Public Library Digital Collections, 1976-1977. https://digitalcollections.nypl.org/items/a35cd800-b30d-0133-ef3d-3c07547a230f.

Nwankwo Ifeoma C., Ifeoma Kiddoe Nwankwo, and Mamadou Diouf. *Rhythms of the Afro-Atlantic World: Rituals and Remembrances.* Ann Arbor: University of Michigan Press, 2010.

O'Farrell, Brigid, and Joyce L. Kornbluh. *Rocking the Boat: Union Women's Voices, 1915-1975.* New Jersey: Rutgers University Press, 1996.

Olson, Lynne. *Freedom's Daughters: The Unsung Heroines of the Civil Rights Movement from 1830 to 1970.* New York: Scribner, 2002.

Oppel, Jr., Richard A., Derrick Bryson Taylor, and Nicholas Bogel-Burroughs. "What to Know about Breonna Taylor's Death." *The New York Times,* October 30, 2020, https://www.nytimes.com/article/breonna-taylor-police.html.

Oray, Patrick B. "Another Layer of Blackness: Theorizing Race, Ethnicity, and Identity in the U.S. Black Public Sphere." PhD. diss. University of Iowa, 2013.

Osumare, Halifu. *Dancing in Blackness: A Memoir.* Gainesville: University Press of Florida, 2019.

Ottaway, Amanda. "Why Don't People Watch Women's Sports? Ask sports journalists." *The Nation,* July 20, 2016. https://www.thenation.com/article/archive/why-dont-people-watch-womens-sports.

Painter, Nell Irvin. *The History of White People.* New York: W. W. Norton & Company, 2011.

———. *Sojourner Truth: A Life, A Symbol.* New York: W. W. Norton & Company, 2007.

Palmer, Colin A. "Ballet." *Encyclopedia of African American Culture and History, The Black Experience In The Americas,* New York: Macmillan, 2006. 179-183.

PapersOwl.com. "Foot Soldiers of the Civil Rights Movement." December 12, 2019. https://papersowl.com/examples/foot-soldiers-of-the-civil-rights-movement.

Parker, Adam. "The NBA could be in her future, but for now Dawn Staley has fights to wage at home." *The Post and Courier,* July 17, 2021. https://www.postandcourier.com/news/local_state_news/the-nba-could-be-in-her-future-but-for-now-dawn-staley-has-fights-to/article_2a76d080-e027-11eb-a786-e3075637be07.html.

Parker, Alison. "Frances Watkins Harper and the Search for Women's Interracial Alliances." In *Susan B. Anthony and the Struggle for Equal Rights,* edited by Christine L. Ridarsky and Mary M. Huth, 145-171. New York: University of Rochester, 2012.

Parks, Rosa, and James Haskins. *Rosa Parks: My Story.* New York: Dial Books, 1992.

Parks, Rosa, and Gregory J. Reed. *Quiet Strength: the Faith, the Hope, and the Heart of a Woman Who Changed a Nation.* Grand Rapids, Michigan: Zondervan, 2000.

Patterson, Brandon. "How the Black Lives Matter Movement Is Mobilizing Against Trump." *Mother Jones,* February 7, 2017. https://www.motherjones.com/politics/2017/02/black-lives-matter-versus-trump.

Peisner, David. *Homey Don't Play That! The Story of In Living Color and the Black Comedy Revolution.* New York: Simon & Schuster, 2018.

Perpener III, John O. *African American Concert Dance: the Harlem Renaissance and Beyond.* Champaign: University of Illinois Press, 2005.

Picart, Caroline Joan S. *From Ballroom To Dancesport, Aesthetics, Athletics and Body Culture.* Albany: State University of New York Press, 2006.

Pitney, John. "The Tocqueville Fraud." *The Weekly Standard,* November 12, 1995. https://www.weeklystandard.com/john-j-pitney/the-tocqueville-fraud.

Porter, David L. *Basketball: A Biographical Dictionary.* Westport, CT: Greenwood Publishing, 2005.

Porter, Karra. *Mad Seasons: The Story of The First Women's Professional Basketball League, 1978-1981.* Lincoln: University of Nebraska Press, 2006.

Prison Policy Initiative. *Policing Women: Race and gender disparities in police stops, searches, and use of force.* May 14, 2019. https://www.prisonpolicy.org/blog/2019/05/14/policingwomen.

Quigley, Joan. *Just Another Southern Town: Mary Church Terrell and the Struggle for Racial Justice in the Nation's Capital.* New York: Oxford University Press, 2016.

Ransby, Barbara. *Ella Baker and the Black Freedom Movement: A Radical Democratic Vision.* Chapel Hill: University of North Carolina Press, 2005.

Ratna, Aarti, and Samaya F. Samie. *Race, Gender and Sport: The Politics of Ethnic 'Other' Girls and Women.* England, U.K.: Routledge, 2019.

Reck, Gregory G., and Bruce Allen Dick. *American Soccer: History, Culture, Class.* Jefferson, NC: McFarland & Company, Inc., 2015.

Reid, Ira De Augustine. *The Negro Immigrant: His Background, Characteristics, and Social Adjustment, 1899-1937.* New York: Columbia University, 1939.

Renshaw, Patrick. *The Wobblies: The Story of the IWW and Syndicalism in The United States.* Chicago, IL: Ivan R. Dee, 1999.

Revel, Layton. *Early Pioneers of the Negro Leagues: Abel Linares.* N.d.: Center for Negro League Baseball Research, 2017.

Reyburn, Susan. *Rosa Parks: in Her Own Words.* Athens: University of Georgia Press, in association with The Library of Congress, 2020.

Rhoden, William C. "Black and White Women Far From Equal Under Title IX." The New York Times, June 10, 2012. https://www.nytimes.com/2012/06/11/sports/title-ix-has-not-given-Black-female-athletes-equal-opportunity.html.

Richards, Yevette. *Maida Springer: Pan-Africanist and International Labor Leader.* Pennsylvania: University of Pittsburgh Press, 2000.

———. "Race, Gender, and Anticommunism in the International Labor Movement: The Pan-African Connections of Maida Springer." *Journal of Women's History* 11, no. 2 (Summer 1999). http://muse.jhu.edu/article/17263#info_wrap.

Rickford, Russell John. *Betty Shabazz: A Remarkable Story of Survival and Faith Before and After Malcolm X.* Naperville, IL: EBSCO Publishing, 2003.

Riley, Jason L. "Why Obama's Presidency Didn't Lead to Black Progress." *The New York Post,* June 17, 2017. https://nypost.com/2017/06/17/why-obamas-presidency-didnt-lead-to-black-progress.

Ring, Jennifer. *Stolen Bases, Why American Girls Don't Play Baseball.* Champaign: University of Illinois Press, 2015.

———. *A Game of Their Own: Voices of Contemporary Women in Baseball.* Lincoln: University of Nebraska Press, 2015.

Roberts, Dorothy E. *Killing the Black Body: Race, Reproduction, and the Meaning of Liberty.* New York: Vintage Books, 1999.

Roberts, Rebecca Boggs. *Suffragists in Washington, D.C.: The 1913 Parade and the Fight for the Vote.* Mt. Pleasant, SC: The History Press, 2017.

Roberts, Steven. "Most Black kids can't swim, and segregation is to blame." *Vice,* August 30, 2018. https://www.vice.com/en_us/article/8xbyax/most-Black-kids-cant-swim-its-not-just-a-stereotype-its-history.

Robertson, Ashley N. *Mary Mcleod Bethune in Florida: Bringing Social Justice to the Sunshine State.* Mt. Pleasant, SC: History Press, 2015.

Robinson, Jo Ann, and David J. Garrow. *Montgomery Bus Boycott and the Women Who Started It: The Memoir of Jo Ann Gibson Robinson.* Knoxville: University of Tennessee Press, 1987.

Robnett, Belinda. *How Long? How Long?: African American Women in the Struggle for Civil Rights.* New York: Oxford University Press, 1997.

Rodulfo, Kristina. "How Fencer Ibtihaj Muhammad Is Changing the Face of Team U.S.A." *Elle,* June 1, 2016. https://www.elle.com/culture/news/a36735/ibtihaj-muhammad-2016-olympics.

Rogers, Katie. "White Women Helped Elect Donald Trump." *The New York Times,* November 9, 2016. https://www.nytimes.com/2016/12/01/us/politics/white-women-helped-elect-donald-trump.html.

Roos, Meghan. "Meet the Elite: Our Q&A with Allyson Felix." *Outside,* July 24, 2018. https://www.womensrunning.com/culture/people/meet-the-elite-allyson-felix.

Rose, Tricia. *Black Noise: Rap Music and Black Culture in Contemporary America.* Middletown, CT: Wesleyan University Press, 1994.

Rosenberg, Rosalind. *Jane Crow: The Life of Pauli Murray.* New York: Oxford University Press, 2017.

Ross, Janell. "White Americans long for the 1950s, when they didn't face so much discrimination." *The Washington Post,* November 17, 2015. https://www.washingtonpost.com/news/the-fix/wp/2015/11/17/White-americans-long-for-the-1950s-when-they-werent-such-victims-of-reverse-discrimination.

Ross, Marc Howard. *Slavery in the North: Forgetting History and Recovering Memory.* Philadelphia: University of Pennsylvania Press, 2018.

Rothenberg, Ben. "Tennis' Top Women Balance Body Image With Ambition." *The New York Times,* July 10, 2015. https://www.nytimes.com/2015/07/11/sports/tennis/tenniss-top-women-balance-body image-with-quest-for-success.html.

Russonello, Giovanni. "Read Oprah Winfrey's Golden Globes Speech." *The New York Times,* January 7, 2018. https://www.nytimes.com/2018/01/07/movies/oprah-winfrey-golden-globes-speech-transcript.html.

Rushton, Susie. "Caster Semenya, The exceptional South African runner." *The Gentlewoman,* Spring & Summer 2020. http://thegentlewoman.co.uk/library/caster-semenya.

Rutledge, Rachel. *The Best of the Best in Basketball.* Minneapolis, MN: Millbrook Press, 1998.

Sacchetti, Maria, Abigail Hauslohner, and Danielle Paquette. "Trump expands long-standing immigration ban to include six more countries, most in Africa." *The Washington Post,* January 31, 2020. https://www.washingtonpost.com/immigration/trump-expands-long-standing-immigration-ban-to-include-six-more-countries-most-from-africa/2020/01/31/413e93ec-443e-11ea-aa6a-083d01b3ed18_story.html.

Sailes, Gary A. *African Americans in Sports.* Oxfordshire, U.K.: Taylor & Francis, 2017.

Santos, Alex Abad. "Russian hackers tried to embarrass Simone Biles. They completely failed." *Vox,* September 15, 2016. https://www.vox.com/2016/9/15/12915106/simone-biles-hack-adhd.

Schiot, Molly. *Game Changers: The Unsung Heroines of Sports History.* New York: Simon & Schuster, 2016.

Schoenfeld, Bruce. *The Match: Althea Gibson & Angela Buxton: How Two Outsiders--One Black, the Other Jewish—Forged a Friendship and Made Sports History.* New York: HarperCollins, 2004.

Schwartz, Peggy, and Murray Schwartz. *The Dance Claimed Me: a Biography of Pearl Primus.* New Haven, Connecticut: Yale University Press, 2011.

Seibert, Brian. *What the Eye Hears: A History of Tap Dancing.* United States: Farrar, Straus and Giroux, 2015.

Seidman, S. A. "Profile: An investigation of sex-role stereotyping in music videos." *Journal of Broadcasting & Electronic Media* 36, no. 2 (1992): 209-216.

Shattuck, Debra A. *Bloomer Girls: Women Baseball Pioneers.* Champaign: University of Illinois Press, 2017.

Shaw, Stephanie. *What a Woman Ought to Be and Do: Black Professional Women Workers During the Jim Crow Era.* Illinois: University of Chicago Press, 1996.

Sheffield, Charles, ed. *The History of Florence, Massachusetts, Including a Complete Account of the Northampton Association of Education and Industry.* Florence, MA, 1895.

Siber, Kate. "How Wilma Rudolph Became the World's Fastest Woman." *Outside,* June 8, 2018, https://www.outsideonline.com/health/running/wilma-rudolph-worlds-fastest-woman.

Silveira Karnas, Luiza, "Tap Dance Choreography: An exploration of tradition and innovation" (2018). Dance Master's Theses. 22. The College at Brockport: State University of New York. https://digitalcommons.brockport.edu/dns_theses/22.

Sloan, Leni. "Irish Mornings and African Days on the Old Minstrel Stage." *Callahan's Irish Quarterly,* no. 2 (Spring, 1982): 50-53.

Smith, Earl, and Marissa Kiss. "Why are there so few Black American players in MLB 74 years after Jackie Robinson took the field?" *The Philadelphia Inquirer,* April 1, 2021. https://www.inquirer.com/opinion/commentary/baseball-black-african-american-players-jackie-robinson-20210401.html.

Smith, Jessie Carney, and Lean'tin L. Bracks, eds. *Black Women of the Harlem Renaissance Era.* New York: Rowman & Littlefield Publishers, 2014.

Smith, Jessie Carney, and Shirelle Phelps, eds. *Notable Black American Women: Book III.* Farmington Hills, MI: Gale Research, 1992c.

Smith, Jessie Carney, ed. *Handy African American History Answer Book.* Canton, MI: Visible Ink Press, 2013.

———. ed. *Notable Black American Women: Book I.* Farmington Hills, MI: Gale Research, 1992a.

———. ed. *Notable Black American Women: Book II.* Farmington Hills, MI: Gale Research, 1992b.

Smith, Malissa. *A History of Women's Boxing.* New York: Rowman & Littlefield Publishers, 2014.

Smith, Maureen M. *Wilma Rudolph: a Biography.* Westport, CT: Greenwood Publishing, 2006.

Snipe, Tracy D. "African Dance: Bridges to Humanity." In *Africa Dance, An Artistic Historical and Philosophical Inquiry* edited by Kariamu Welsh Asante, 63-77. Trenton, NJ: African World Press, Inc., 1998.

Sonmez, Felicia and Ashley Parker. "As Trump stands by Charlottesville remarks, the rise of white-nationalist violence becomes an issue in 2020 presidential race." *The Washington Post,* April 28, 2019. https://www.washingtonpost.com/politics/as-trump-stands-by-charlottesville-remarks-rise-of-white-nationalist-violence-becomes-an-issue-in-2020-presidential-race/2019/04/28/83aaf1ca-69c0-11e9-a66d-a82d3f3d96d5_story.html.

Sorell, Walter. *The Dance through the Ages.* New York: Grosset & Dunlap, 1967.

Spelman College: *News and Events.* "US Senator Kamala Harris Speaks at Spelman: Remaining Undaunted by the Fight." August 26, 2018, https://www.spelman.edu/about-us/news-and-events/kamala-harris.

Spiro, Jonathan Peter. *Defending the Master Race: Conservation, Eugenics, and the Legacy of Madison Grant.* Lebanon: University of New Hampshire, 2008.

Stahl, Norma Gengal. "Janet Collins: The First Lady of the Metropolitan Opera Ballet." *Dance* (February 1954): 27–29.

Stancliff, Michael. *Frances Ellen Watkins Harper: African American Reform Rhetoric and the Rise of a Modern Nation State.* Oxfordshire, U.K.: Taylor & Francis, 2010.

Standley, Anne. "The Role of Black Women in the Civil Rights Movement." In *Women in the Civil Rights Movement: Trailblazers and Torchbearers, 1941-1965,* edited by Vicki L. Crawford, Jacqueline Anne Rouse and Barbara Woods. Bloomington: Indiana University Press, 1993.

Starks, Glenn L., and F. Erik Brooks. *Historically Black Colleges and Universities: An Encyclopedia.* Ukraine: ABC-CLIO, 2011.

Staurowsky, E. J., DeSousa, M. J., Miller, K. E., Sabo, D. et al. "Her Life Depends On It III: Sport, Physical Activity, and the Health and Well-Being of American Girls and Women." East Meadow, New York: Women's Sports Foundation, 2015.

Sterling, Dorothy, ed. *We Are Your Sisters: Black Women in The Nineteenth Century.* New York: W.W. Norton & Company, 1997.

Stevens, Erin, and Tamara Stevens, eds. *Swing Dancing.* Santa Barbara, CA: ABC-CLIO, 2011.

Stowe, Harriet Beecher. "Sojourner Truth, The Libyan Sibyl," *The Atlantic,* April 1863, https://www.theatlantic.com/magazine/archive/1863/04/sojourner-truth-the-libyan-sibyl/308775.

Stuckey, Sterling. *Slave Culture: Nationalist Theory and the Foundations of Black America.* New York: Oxford University Press, 2013.

Takougang, Joseph, and Bassirou Tidjani. "Settlement Patterns and Organizations Among African Immigrants in the United States." *Journal of Third World Studies* 26, no. 1 (2009): 31-40.

Tate, Shirley Ann. *Black Women's Bodies and The Nation, Race, Gender and Culture.* New York: Palgrave Macmillan, 2015.

Taylor, Debra Colleen, and Marilyn Renee McClain. "Conflict in Black Male/Female Relationships, Conflict in Black Male/Female Relationships." Theses Digitization Project, 1997. https://scholarworks.lib.csusb.edu/etd-project/1322.

Taylor, Dorceta E. "Race, Class, Gender, and American Environmentalism." Gen. Tech. Rep. PNW-GTR-534. Portland, OR: U.S. Department of Agriculture, Forest Service, Pacific Northwest Research Station, 2002: 51.

Taylor, Keeanga-Yamahtta. *How We Get Free: Black Feminism and the Combahee River Collective.* Chicago, Illinois: Haymarket Books, 2017.

Terborg-Penn, Rosalyn. *African American Women in the Struggle for the Vote, 1850–1920.* Bloomington: Indiana University Press, 1998.

Terry, Terlene Darcell. *A Survey of Black Dance In Washington, 1870-1945.* The American University. M.A. 1982.

Theoharis, Jeanne. *A More Beautiful and Terrible History, The Uses and Misuses of Civil Rights History.* Boston: Beacon Press, 2018.

———. *The Rebellious Life of Mrs. Rosa Parks.* Boston: Beacon Press, 2015.

Thomas, Sonja. "Black Soundwork, Knowledge Production, and the 'Debate' Over Tap Dance Origins." *Resonance: The Journal of Sound and Culture* 1, no. 4, (2020): 412–421.

Thompson, Cheryl. "Black Women and Identity: What's Hair Got to Do With It?" *Politics and Performativity* 22, no. 1, (Fall 2008-2009).

Tinsley, Omise'eke Natasha. *Ezili's Mirrors: Imagining Black Queer Genders.* Durham, NC: Duke University Press, 2018.

Tower, Nikole. "In an ethnic breakdown of sports, NBA takes lead for most diverse," *Global Sports Matter,* December 12, 2018. https://globalsportmatters.com/culture/2018/12/12/in-an-ethnic-breakdown-of-sports-nba-takes-lead-for-most-diverse.

Trenka, Susie. *Jumping the Color Line: Vernacular Jazz Dance in American Film, 1929–1945.* Eastleigh, UK: John Libbey Publishing, 2021.

Tuck, Stephen. *We Ain't What We Ought to Be: The Black Freedom Struggle from Emancipation to Obama.* Cambridge, MA: The Belknap Press of Harvard University Press, 2010.

Tucker, Rosina Corrothers, and C. Bernard Ruffin. *My Life as I Have Lived It: the Autobiography of Rosina Corrothers-Tucker (1881-1987).* Westminster, MD: Heritage Books, 2011.

Undefeated, The. "Beating Opponents, Battling Belittlement: How African American Female Athletes Use Community to Navigate Negative Images." N.d., Morgan State University, School of Global Journalism and Communications. https://theundefeated.com/features/morgan-state-university-study-examines-history-of-Black-women-fighting-to-be-respected-as-athletes.

University of Pennsylvania. *New Deal Resident Camps for Unemployed Women, A New Deal Program, c. 1933 1937,* a research initiative of PennPraxis, 2020. https://storymaps.arcgis.com/stories/02050ee5b4d543cf93821f56382367c2.

Urban Suite Jazz. "StaceyAnn Chin Performs 'Tweet This, You Small-Minded M***********r." Video from *Up Magazine* (Nairobi) N.d. https://www.urbansuitejazz.com/return-to-categories/13-poets-corner-see-all/1401-up-magazine-staceyann-chin-performs-tweet-this-you-small-minded-m-r-in-nairobi.

VanDyke, Erika. "Race, Body, and Sexuality in Music Videos." Honors Projects, Grand Valley State University, 2011. http://scholarworks.gvsu.edu/honorsprojects/69.

Vertinsky, Patricia, and Roberta J. Park, eds. *Women, Sport, Society: Further Reflections, Reaffirming Mary Wollstonecraft.* Oxfordshire, U.K.: Taylor & Francis, 2013.

Vohra, Sweta. "Documents show US monitoring of Black Lives Matter." *Al Jazeera,* November 28, 2017. https://www.aljazeera.com/news/2017/11/28/documents-show-us-monitoring-of-black-lives-matter.

Walker, Alice. In Search of Our Mothers' Gardens: Womanist Prose. New York: Harcourt Brace Jovanovich, 2004.

Walker, Rhiannon. "Her Airness, Sheryl Swoopes, attains Hall of Fame status." *The Undefeated,* September 9, 2016. https://theundefeated.com/features/her-airness-sheryl-swoopes-attains-hall-of-fame-status.

———. "The day Jackie Joyner-Kersee was called 'the greatest athlete who ever lived'." *The Undefeated,* August 1, 2018. https://theundefeated.com/features/the-day-jackie-joyner-kersee-was-called-the-greatest-athlete-who-ever-lived.

Walker-McWilliams, Marcia. *Reverend Addie Wyatt: Faith and the Fight for Labor, Gender, and Racial Equality.* Champaign: University of Illinois Press, 2016.

Wallace, Danielle. "Where the Ladies At? Examining the Visibility of Black Women in Hip Hop an How It Reflects a Larger Understanding of Black Womanhood." Cultural Studies Capstone Papers, 22. Columbia College, 2017. https://digitalcommons.colum.edu/cultural_studies/22.

Waller, Steven, Dawn M. Norwood, LeQuez Spearman and Fritz G. Polite. "Black American female Olympic Athletes have not reaped the same social standing and economic benefits that their counterparts have since the 1968 Olympics in Mexico City." *Sport Science Review* XXV, nos. 1-2 (2016): 53-72.

Wang, Vivian. "Erica Garner, Activist and Daughter of Eric Garner, Dies at 27." *The New York Times,* December 30, 2017. https://www.nytimes.com/2017/12/30/nyregion/erica-garner-dead.html.

Walters, Joanna. "Meet the real million dollar baby." *Observer Sport Monthly.* July 2, 2005. https://www.theguardian.com/observer/osm/story/0,,1517179,00.html.

Warner, Oswald. "Black in America Too: Afro-Caribbean Immigrants." *Social and Economic Studies* 61, no. 4 (2012): 69-103. http://www.jstor.org/stable/24384427.

Warren, Charmaine Patricia, Suzanne Youngerman, and Susan Yung. *A Brief History of American Modern Dance.* Brooklyn Academy of Music (BAM), 2013.

Waters, Mary C., Philip Kasinitz, and Asad L. Asad. "Immigrants and African Americans." *Annual Review of Sociology* 40 (2014): 369-90. http://www.jstor.org/stable/43049540.

Weisbord, Robert G. *Racism and the Olympics.* Oxfordshire, U.K.: Taylor & Francis, 2017.

Wellman, Judith. *The Road to Seneca Falls: Elizabeth Cady Stanton and the First Woman's Rights Convention.* Champaign: University of Illinois Press, 2004.

Wells, Christopher J. "'You Can't Dance to It': Jazz Music and Its Choreographies of Listening." *"Why Jazz Still Matters" Daedalus* 148, no. 2 (Spring 2019): 36-51. https://www.jstor.org/stable/10.2307/48563007.

Wetsman, Nicole. "NWSL fans are online, organized, and refuse to be ignored." *The Verge,* July 17, 2020. https://www.theverge.com/21325419/nwsl-womens-soccer-fandom-twitter-uswnt.

White, Deborah Gray. *Too Heavy a Load: Black Women in Defense of Themselves, 1894–1994.* New York: W. W. Norton & Company, 1999.

Wilham, Elise. "Tap for the Times: A Study of Contemporary Tap Dance" (2020). Honors College Capstone Experience/Thesis Projects. Western Kentucky University. https://digitalcommons.wku.edu/stu_hon_theses/859.

Wilen, Holden. "Kevin Plank dares to dabble in politics again following Biden election victory." *Baltimore Business Journal,* November 9, 2020. https://www.bizjournals.com/baltimore/news/2020/11/09/kevin-plank-under-armour-biden.html.

Williams, Jean. *A Beautiful Game: International Perspectives on Women's Football.* Oxford, England: Berg Publishers, 2007.

Williams, Mikyla. "UNC women's soccer looks to end streak of NCAA title game defeats." *The Daily Tar Heel,* April 20, 2021. https://www.dailytarheel.com/article/2021/04/unc-womens-soccer-look-ahead-ncaa-tournament-national-championship-hopes-brianna-pinto.

Willis, Cheryl M. *Tappin' at the Apollo: The African American Female Tap Dance Duo Salt and Pepper.* Jefferson, NC: McFarland & Company, Inc., 2016.

Wiltse, Jeff. *Contested Waters: A Social History of Swimming Pools in America.* Chapel Hill: University of North Carolina Press, 2009.

Winter, Maria Hannah. "Juba and American Minstrelsey," *Chronicles of the American Dance,* ed. Paul Magriel. Boston, MA: Da Capo Press, 1978.

Wintz, Cary D., and Paul Finkelman. *Encyclopedia of the Harlem Renaissance.* Oxfordshire, U.K.: Taylor & Francis, 2012.

Witherspoon, Kevin B. and Toby C. Rider, eds. *Defending the American Way of Life, Sport, Culture, and the Cold War.* Fayetteville: University of Arkansas Press, 2018.

W. L. Stacy. " A Brief History of Pops Billingsley—Trainer of Ann Wolfe." *Bleacher Report,* January 9, 2009. https://bleacherreport.com/articles/109035-a-brief-history-of-pops-billingsley-trainer-of-ann-wolfe.

Yang, Stephanie. "We all have a responsibility to kick racism out of NWSL," *SBNation,* September 9, 2019, https://www.allforxi.com/2019/9/9/20855809/kick-racism-out-nwsl-royals-franch-thorns.

Yee, Shirley J. *Black Women Abolitionists: A Study in Activism, 1828-1860.* Knoxville: University of Tennessee Press, 1992.

Zieger, Robert H. *The CIO, 1935-1955.* Chapel Hill: University of North Carolina Press, 2000. ❖

ABOUT THE AUTHOR

PHOTO: Sam Lahoz

GABRIELLE DAVID is a multidisciplinary artist who is a musician, photographer, digital designer, poet and writer. She attended LaGuardia Community College (CUNY) and New School University. She worked as a desktop publisher and word processing specialist at Fortune 500 firms, and through her former company, Chimeara Communications, Inc., designed promotional materials for a wide range of clients. David managed and performed in bands during the 1970s and early 1980s; and was a partner of hotshots unlimited photography (1982-1986). She became involved in the New York poetry scene during the 1990s, and served as literature coordinator at the Langston Hughes Community Library and Cultural Center throughout most of that decade. Her work with the library prompted the creation of *phati'tude Literary Magazine,* which eventually became a programming incentive under the Intercultural Alliance of Artists & Scholars, Inc. (IAAS) which she founded in 2000, and founded 2Leaf Press in 2012. She currently serves as executive director of 2Leaf Press Inc., the predecessor organization that manages 2Leaf Press, and continues to serve as publisher. David has participated in panel discussions and workshops, published articles and essays in numerous publications. She is the co-editor of *Hey Yo! Yo Soy!* (2012), *What Does it Mean to be White in America* (2016), and editor of *Branches of the Tree of Life* (2014), ❖

ABOUT THE EDITOR

CAROLINA FUNG FENG is a translator, copy editor, ESOL teacher and administrator, and immigrant rights activist. Born and raised in Costa Rica to Chinese
parents, Fung Feng has been living in New York City since her early teens. She
graduated from Hunter College (CUNY) with a BA in English/Spanish translation
and interpretation, and English Language Arts. She has worked with several
nonprofit organizations to empower the community to fight for dignity and justice
for all immigrants and people. Specializing in Spanish translations, her first literary translation was the publication of *¡Hey Yo! ¡Yo Soy! 40 Years of Nuyorican
Street Poetry* (2012), and has since copy edited and translated a number of
2Leaf Press titles. ❖

ABOUT THE CONTRIBUTORS

CHANDRA D. L. WARING is an Assistant Professor at the University of Massachusetts-Lowell. Her research focuses on the growing bi/multiracial population. Her interest in race stems from being raised in a multiracial family in three very different contexts: Germany, Georgia and Connecticut. Her work has been published in *Sociological Perspectives, Du Bois Review: Social Science Research on Race, Social Identities, Feminist Teacher, Race, Gender & Class* and *Sociological Imagination.* Waring earned her Ph.D. in sociology from the University of Connecticut, where she was a Multicultural Fellow.❖

PHOTO: Suzy Gorman

LYAH BETH LEFLORE is a television and film executive producer, and music supervisor. She has worked at Nickelodeon, Uptown Records/Entertainment, Wolf Films/Universal, Alan Haymon Development, and is currently a producing partner with Anthony Hemingway, where she has brokered lucrative deals on various high-profiled television and film projects. LeFlore is also the author of eight critically-acclaimed books, two of which are National Best sellers.

LeFlore is the author of the novels *Wildflowers* (2009), and *Last Night A DJ Saved My Life* (2006); and the co-author of *Tell the Truth & Shame the Devil: The Life, Legacy, and Love of My Son Michael Brown* (2020) by Lezley McSpadden, *The Strawberry Letter: Real Talk, Real Advice, Because Bitterness Isn't Sexy* (2012) by Shirley Strawberry, and *I Got Your Back: A Father and Son Keep It Real About Love, Fatherhood, Family, and Friendship* (2007) by Eddie Levert Sr. and Gerald Levert.

She is the cofounder and executive director of the literary arts-based non-profit, The Shirley Bradley LeFlore Foundation/Creative Arts and Expression Laboratory, which honors LeFlore's late mother, St. Louis Poet Laureate Emeritus, and 2Leaf Press author, Shirley Bradley Price LeFlore. ❖

PHOTOGRAPHY CREDITS

The following photographs are copyright protected and cannot be used without permission. Photographs that are in the public domain have been fully credited where applicable.

COVER

Harriet Tubman. Studio portrait by M. Seymour Squyer, ca. 1885. Courtesy of the National Portrait Gallery, Smithsonian Institution.

Hattie McDaniel. Promotional photograph, ca. 1939.

Maggie L. Walker. Studio portrait by the Photography Studio, ca. 1905. Courtesy of the National Park Service, Maggie L. Walker National Historic Site. Used with permission.

Katherine Dunham. Studio portrait by Phyllis Twachtman, the *New York World-Telegram* and the *Sun* Newspaper Photograph Collection, 1956. U.S. Library of Congress Prints and Photographs.

Anna Julia Cooper. Scurlock Studio Records, Archives Center, ca. 1923. National Museum of American History, Smithsonian Institution.

Mary Eliza Mahoney. Unknown photographer, ca. late 1800s.

Shirley Chisholm. Photo by Thomas J. O'Halloran, *U.S. News & World Reports,* 1972. U.S. Library of Congress Prints and Photographs.

Jessie Maple. Photo by Leroy Patton, N.d. Used with permission.

Lorraine Hansberry. *New York World-Telegram* and the *Sun* Newspaper Photograph Collection, 1959. U.S. Library of Congress Prints and Photographs.

Althea Gibson. Photo by Fred Palumbo, *World-Telegram* and the *Sun Newspaper,* 1956. U.S. Library of Congress Prints and Photographs.

BOOK PHOTOGRAPHS

Acknowledgements
Michelle Obama. Photo by Mark Wilson/Getty Images, 2018.

Kadiatou Diallo. Photo by Frank Franklin II/AP Photo, 2003.

Michelle Alexander. Photo by Megan Leigh Barnard, 2016. Courtesy of the Heinz Foundation. Used with permission.

Glynda C. Carr. Photo by ShaDonna Jackson, 2018. Used with permission.

Lezley McSpadden. Photo by Vanessa Charlot, 2021. Used with permission.

Leah Penniman. Photo by Jamel Mosely, 2020. Used with permission.

LaSaia Wade. Photo by Xavier Maatra, 2019. Used with permission.

Dance

Introduction
Katherine Dunham. Photo by Jack Mitchell/Getty Images, 1987.

Chapters

Josephine Baker. Photo by Lucien Walery, 1926.

Katherine Dunham. Studio portrait, ca. 1945. Courtesy of the Special Collections Research Center, Morris Library, Southern Illinois University.

Margot Webb. Studio portrait, ca. 1930s.

Jeni LeGon. Photo by Bettmann/Getty Images, 1935.

Janet Collins. Photo by Sam Falk/The New York Times Co./Getty Images, 1955.

Pearl Primus. Photo by © Hulton-Deutsch Collection/CORBIS/Corbis via Getty Images, 1951.

Mable Lee. Photo by Kurt Hutton/Picture Post/Hulton Archive/Getty Images, 1948.

Mary Hinkson. Photo by Martha Swope, 1973 © The New York Public Library for the Performing Arts. Used with permission.

Carmen de Lavallade. Photo by Julieta Cervantes, 2011. Used with permission.

Raven Wilkinson. Photo by Maurice Seymour, ca. 1950s. Used with permission by the Maurice Seymour Estate.

Joan Myers Brown. Photo courtesy of Joan Myers Brown/PHILADANCO. Used with permission.

Judith Jamison. Photo by Jack Mitchell/Getty, 1976.

Blondell Cummings. Photo by Jack Mitchell/Getty, 1991.

Dianne McIntyre. Photo by Larry Coleman, 2018. Used with permission.

Virginia Johnson. Photo by Toby McAfee, 1990. Used with permission.

Jawole Willa Jo Zollar. Photo © Lois Greenfield, 1986. Used with permission.

Dianne Walker. Photo by Everett Hayward, Hayward Photography, 2008. Used with permission.

Debra Austin. Photo by Steven Caras, ca. 1980s. Used with permission.

Cynthia Oliver. Photo by Valerie Oliveiro, 2019. Courtesy of Cynthia Oliver. Used with permission.

Fatima Robinson. Photo by Stephan Schacher, 2020. Used with permission.

Dormeshia. Photo by Eduard Patino, 2019. Used with permission.

Camille A. Brown. Photo by Whitney Brown, 2018. Used with permission.

Misty Copeland. Photo by Brad Trent, 2015. Used with permission.

Michaela Prince. Photo by Michel Schnater, 2015. Used with permission.

Sports

Introduction
Alice Coachman. Photo by Reginald H. Christian for Albany State University, 2012. Used with permission.

Chapters

Ora Washington. Photo courtesy of the John W. Mosley Photograph Collection, Charles L. Blockson Afro-American Collection, Temple University Libraries, Philadelphia, PA.

Toni Stone. Photo reproduction by Transcendental Graphics/Getty Images, 1950.

Alice Coachman. Photo by AP Photo/1948.

Althea Gibson. Photo by © Hulton-Deutsch Collection/CORBIS/Corbis via Getty Images, 1956.

Wilma Rudolph. Photo by Bettmann/Getty, 1960.

Jackie Joyner-Kersee. Photo by Stephan/ullstein bild via Getty Images, 1993.

Cheryl Miller. Photo by Tony Duffy/Getty Images, 1983.

Violet Palmer. Photo by Mark J. Terrill/AP Photo, 2010.

Debi Thomas. Photo by AP Photo/NewsBase, 1988.

Dawn Staley. Photo by Javier Soriano/AFP via Getty Images, 2018.

Briana Scurry. Photo by T. Quinn/WireImage, 2006.

Ann Wolfe. Photo by Eric Doggett, 2010. Used with permission.

Lisa Leslie. Photo by Otto Greule Jr./Allsport via Getty Images, 2001.

Sheryl Swoopes. Photo by Kellie Landis/Allsport via Getty Images, 2000.

Dominque Dawes. Photo by Matthew Stockman/Allsport via Getty Images, 2000.

Maritza Correia McClendon. Photo by Cat Harper from @catharperphotography, 2019. Courtesy of Maritza Correia McClendon. Used with permission.

Sereena Williams. Photo by Adam Pretty/Getty Images, 2016.

Allyson Felix. Photo by Maja Hitij/Getty Images, 2019.

Ibtihaj Muhammed. Photo by Sean M. Haffey/Getty Images, 2016.

Blake Bolden. Photo by Keith Bedford/The Boston Globe via Getty Images, 2017.

Bianca Smith. Photo by Sara Stathas, 2021. Used with permission.

Erin Jackson. Photo by Ramona Rosales, 2018. Used with permission.

Simone Biles. Photo by Michael Starghill Jr., 2018. Used with permission.

Afterword

Ayanna Pressley. Official Photo of Rep. Ayanna Pressley (D-Massachusetts) during the 117th Congress, 2021.❖

ABOUT THE GRANTORS AND SPONSORS

2Leaf Press Inc. would like to thank the following foundations and organizations for sponsoring this project.

Open Meadows Foundation is a grant-making organization seeking projects that promote gender/racial/economic justice. http://www.openmeadows.org.

The Women's Sports Foundation (WSF) exists to enable girls and women to reach their potential in sport and life. Founded by Billie Jean King in 1974, WSF seeks to strengthen and expand participation and leadership opportunities through its research, advocacy, community programming and partnerships. All girls. All women. All sports.® www.WomensSportsFoundation.org.

The New York Women's Foundation (NYWF) is a platform for women (cis and trans) and non-binary people, and a force for change. The Foundation's mission is to create an equitable and just future for all women and girls. It achieves this goal by uniting cross-cultural and community alliances that ignite action. The Foundation invests in women-led, innovative, and bold community-based solutions that promote the economic security, safety, and health of the most overlooked women. https://www.nywf.org/

The National Sorority of Phi Delta Kappa, Inc. (NSPDK) is a nonprofit, educational sorority founded by eight African American educators desiring to establish a sisterhood among teachers and promote the highest ideals of the teaching profession. NSPDK was the idea of Gladys Merritt Ross, who, on Good Friday, March 30, 1923, convened a group of young teachers from Jersey City Normal School in Jersey City, New Jersey to discuss the idea of forming a sorority.

Eight members of those present concurred, and Newark attorney, J. Mercer Burrell, incorporated the new organization on May 23, 1923, which is now recognized as the official Founders Day. Because the original members were all minors, their parents or guardians, Dr. G.E. Cannon, Mr. J.L. Merritt, Mrs. Lottie Cooper and Mrs. Estelle Morris became trustees. https://www.nspdk.org.

The eight founders are Gladys Merritt Ross (Mother Founder), Julia Asbury Barnes, Ella Wells Butler, Marguerite Gross, Florence Steele Hunt, Edna McConnell, Gladys Cannon Nunery and Mildred Morris Williams.

Alpha Kappa Alpha Sorority, Incorporated® had its humble beginnings as the vision of nine college students on the campus of Howard University in 1908. Since then, the sorority has flourished into a globally-impactful organization of nearly 300,000 college-trained members, bound by the bonds of sisterhood and empowered by a commitment to servant-leadership that is both domestic and international in its scope.

As Alpha Kappa Alpha has grown, it has maintained its focus in two key arenas: the lifelong personal and professional development of each of its members; and galvanizing its membership into an organization of respected power and influence, consistently at the forefront of effective advocacy and social change that results in equality and equity for all citizens of the world. Visit www.aka1908.com for more information.

Alpha Kappa Alpha Sorority, Incorporated Original Nine Founders: Anna Easter Brown, Beulah Burke, Lillie Burke, Marjorie Hill, Margaret Flagg Holmes, Ethel Hedgeman (Lyle), Lavinia Norman, Lucy Diggs Slowe and Marie Woolfolk (Taylor).

THE
INTERNATIONAL
ASSOCIATION OF
BLACKS IN DANCE

The International Association of Blacks in Dance (IABD) preserves and promotes dance by people of African ancestry or origin, and assists and increases opportunities for artists in advocacy, audience development, education, funding, networking, performance, philosophical dialogue, and touring..

Our vision is for dance, by people of African ancestry or origin, to be revered, respected, and preserved in the consciousness and cultural institutions of all people. https://www.iabdassociation.org.

INDEX

B

Baartman Sara (aka Saartjie Bartman), 465, n.32
Babilonia, Tai, 460
Baby, Don't Go Way From Me (soundie), 314
Bach, J. S., 305, 325, 397, 399
Baez, Iris, 185
Bahiana (dance), 288
Bailey, Donovan, 447
Bailey, Pearl, 252, 324
Baker, Ella, 28, 29, 56, 58, 62, 93–97, 164
Baker, Jean-Claude, 280
Baker, Josephine, 272–281, 298, 345
Baker's Dozen (ballet), 397
Balanchine, George, 226, 230, 237, 248, 254, 255, 288, 317, 319, 334, 335, 352, 355, 368–370, 396, 404
Baldwin, James, 232
Bales, William, 308
ballet, 247–258
Ballerina (dance series), 353
Ballerina's Tale, A (documentary), 399
Ballet Frankfort, 256
Ballet Imperial (ballet), 334
BalletMet, 257
Ballet Nègre, 251, 285
Ballet Russe de Monte Carlo, 253–255, 302, 332, 335, 337
Ballets Russes, 253
Ballo Della Regina, (ballet), 368
ballroom dance, 250, 294
Bal Nègre (ballet), 288
Baltimore's Monumental Tennis Club, 417
Bambaataa, Afrika, 259
Bamboche! (revue), 290
Bamboozled (film), 384, 390
Bandung Conference, The, 53
banned substance, 424, 466
Barcelona 1992 Summer Olympics, 424, 446, 505
Barker, Alice, 226
Barker, Violet, 463
Barnard College, 46, 114, 116, 386
Barocco (ballet), 369
Barrelhouse (dance), 286
Barrett, Pearl, 433
Bartok No. 3 (ballet), 368
Baseball (documentary), 436
Basil, Toni, 259, 379
basketball, 428–431, 471, 478
Bass, Charlotta, 29
Basse-Wiles, Marie, 246

Bassey, Shirley, 279
Bass, Karen, 595
Bates, Daisy, 29, 42, 115, 278
Battle, Hinton, 253
Baxter, Isabelle, 433
Bayadère, La (ballet), 249, 396, 397
b–boys, 259, 267
Beal, Francis M., 43
Beame, Abraham, 160
Beard, Alana, 431
Bears-Bailey, Kim, 327
Beat Street (film), 261
Beatty, Talley, 225, 230, 231, 287, 303, 339
Bebe Miller Company, 232, 376
Bechet, Sidney, 220
Beijing 2008 Summer Olympics, 464, 526, 545, 552, 557, 562
Beijing 2022 Winter Olympics, 581
Belafonte, Harry, 130, 151, 299, 319, 330, 331
Bennett College, 251, 425, 427
Berlin 1936 Summer Olympics, 420
Bermudez, Atti van den Berg, 372
Bernie Mac Show, The (tv show), 557
Bethel, Pepsi, 224
Bethune, Mary McLeod, 28, 42, 106, 114, 116, 117, 309
Bevel, James, 164, 165
Bey, Chief, 243, 244
Beyoncé (Knowles-Carter), 240, 262, 266, 267, 280, 281, 404
Beyond Bold and Brave's 2016 Black Lesbian Conference, 47
b–girls, 259, 267
Biches, Les (ballet), 352
Big Daddy Kane, 261, 379
Biggie Smalls, 264
Biles, Simone, 7, 412, 413, 447, 448, 549, 582–587
Billie Jean (video), 261
Biney, Maame, 581
biracial, 20, 256
Birthday Offering (ballet), 397
Birth of the Blues, Sundown, Arabian Nights (musical), 298
Birthright (film), 219
Black Alliance for Just Immigration, The (BAJI), 55
Blackamoor (concert dance), 305
Black and Blue (musical), 239, 364, 365, 382, 384
Black Arts Movement, 232, 243, 290

A BLACK/BROWN FEMALE-LED PRESS

FLORIDA ■ NEW YORK

www.2leafpress.org

DISTRIBUTED BY UNIVERSITY OF CHICAGO PRESS, USA